C++
INTERACTIVE
COURSE

ROBERT LAFORE

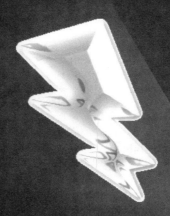

WAITE GROUP PRESS™

A Division of

Sams Publishing

Corte Madera, CA

PUBLISHER • Mitchell Waite
ASSOCIATE PUBLISHER • Charles Drucker

ACQUISITIONS MANAGER • Jill Pisoni

EDITORIAL DIRECTOR • John Crudo
PROJECT EDITOR • Andrea Rosenberg
CONTENT EDITOR • Lyn Cordell
COPY EDITOR • Deirdre Green
TECHNICAL REVIEWER • Michael Radtke

PRODUCTION DIRECTOR • Julianne Ososke
PRODUCTION MANAGER • Cecile Kaufman
DESIGN • Sestina Quarequio
PRODUCTION • Jude Levinson, Bill Romano
ILLUSTRATION • Larry Wilson
CHAPTER OPENER ILLUSTRATION • ©Steven Hunt/Image Bank
COVER ILLUSTRATION • Robert Dougherty

© 1996 by The Waite Group, Inc.®
Published by Waite Group Press™, 200 Tamal Plaza, Corte Madera, CA 94925.

Waite Group Press™ is a division of Sams Publishing.

Printed in the United States of America
97 98 99 • 10 9 8 7 6

Library of Congress Cataloging-in-Publication Data
Lafore, Robert (Robert W.)
      C++ interactive course / Robert Lafore.
        p.   cm.
      Includes index.
      ISBN 1-57169-063-8
      1. C++ (Computer program language).   2. Object oriented programming.
      I. Title.
      QA76.73.C153L3415 1996   96-6765
      005.13'3--dc20   CIP

`Requested User ID`—Type the name you'd like to use online.
`Password (5-8 Characters)`—Type the password you'd like to use online.
`Password (Verify)`—Retype your selected password, to be sure it's properly recorded.

Once you've supplied all the information, click the *Register* button to submit the form to the eZone's data banks. A confirming message lets you know that you've successfully registered. Registration is important. If you don't register, you can't take advantage of the full power of the eZone.

Entering the eZone as a Registered User

Once you've registered, you'll use your unique ID and password to enter the eZone. Next time you enter the eZone, you need only click the *Learn Zone* icon in the navigation frame or the *Learn* link in the main frame. A simple two-line form pops up, allowing you to type in the user ID and password you created when you registered.

THE LEARN ZONE

Now that you're registered, it's time to get down to business. Much of the course work is done in the *Learn Zone*, shown in Figure 4. To get here, click the *Learn* icon in the navigation frame.

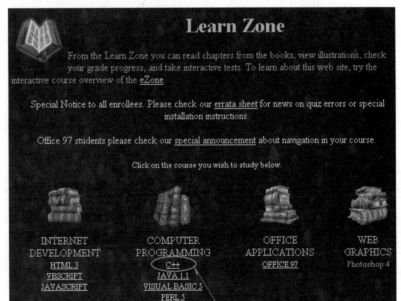

Figure 4
Use the Course Matrix in the Learn Zone to select courses

The Course Matrix

When you enter the Learn Zone, you'll see lists of courses and certification programs. This is called the Course Matrix, and it provides a way to select the various eZone courses. Under each discipline—such as Web Designer, Business, or Code Master—are a list of core courses. To select the *C++ Interactive Course* using this Course Matrix, click on the *C++* link in the column labeled "Code Master." In a moment, a three-columned table appears.

Verification

The first time you select a specific course, you must enroll. You'll need a copy of the book to do so. You will be asked to provide a specific word from the book. This verifies that you have the proper book for the selected course. The verification process uses the familiar page-line-word formula; in other words, you'll need to look and enter a word from a specified line of text on a specified page of your book. Click your mouse in the text box and type the specified word to verify that you have the course book.

Passing Percentage

You can also set a minimum passing percentage for your course. This determines what percentage of test questions you need to answer correctly in order to pass the course. The percentage is preset at 70%, but you can select 50%, 60%, 70%, 80%, 90%, or 100%.

To set a minimum passing percentage, click the text box for this option to see a list of choices, then click the option you prefer. Once you've typed in the correct word and set the desired passing percentage, click the *Verify* button to enroll in the course. The Chapters Grid appears.

The Chapters Grid

The table shown in Figure 5 displays the 12 chapters of this book, and it shows your completion status and average score for each of them.

Click here to go back to the
Course Matrix

Click on a Chapter to view the
Quizzes within

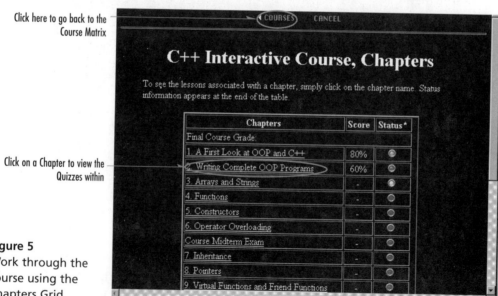

Figure 5
Work through the
course using the
Chapters Grid

The left-hand column lists the chapters of the book; clicking on a chapter lets you view the lessons within it. The middle column, Score, shows your current overall grade for the section (as a percentage). The Status column uses a colored indicator to let you know with a glance whether you've passed (green), failed (red), are still working through (yellow), or have not yet started (gray) a particular chapter.

Click a Chapter, and the Lessons Grid appears. (Remember, only the first lesson is enabled for Guests.)

The Lessons Grid

As you take the course, the Lessons Grid (Figure 6) tracks your performance within each section of the book. You can use it to read a chapter lesson or take the related lesson quiz.

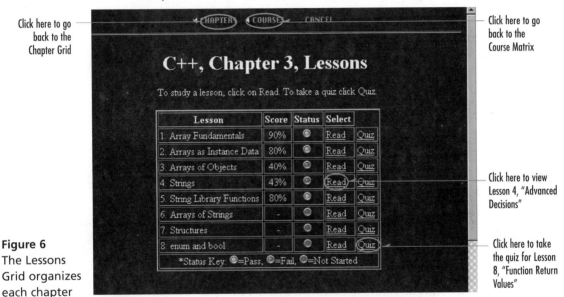

Click here to go back to the Chapter Grid

Click here to go back to the Course Matrix

Click here to view Lesson 4, "Advanced Decisions"

Click here to take the quiz for Lesson 8, "Function Return Values"

Figure 6
The Lessons Grid organizes each chapter

To read a lesson, click the *Read* link in the Select column. To take a quiz, click the *Quiz* link in the Select column. The LEDs in the status column show whether you've passed (green), failed (red), or not yet started (gray) each quiz. A percentage grade appears for each completed quiz in the Score column.

Most likely, you'll achieve the best results if you read through the lessons, then take the quiz. If you prefer, however, you can jump directly to the corresponding quiz, without reading through the lesson.

Testing

Each quiz is a multiple choice questionnaire. In some quizzes, there is only one answer to each question, but others allow more than one answer. Read the instructions for your course so you know how the quizzes work.

Taking Quizzes

To answer a quiz question, click the check box next to the answer you want to choose. When you've answered all the questions, click the *Grade My Choices* button. Your quiz is corrected and your score shown. To record your score, click either the *Lessons* or *Chapters* link at the top of the main frame.

CAUTION
Do not use your browser's Back button after taking a quiz. If you use the Back button instead of the Lessons or Chapters link, your score will not be recorded.

Midterm and Final Exams

The Interactive Course includes midterm and final examinations. The midterm covers the first half of the book, while the final is comprehensive. These exams follow the same multiple-choice format as the quizzes. Because they cover more, however, they're somewhat longer. Once you have successfully passed all the quizzes, as well as the midterm and final exams, you'll be eligible to download a certificate of completion from Waite Group Press.

MENTOR ZONE

In the *Mentor Zone*, shown in Figure 7, you can review FAQs (Frequently Asked Questions) for each chapter. You can also ask a question of a live expert, called a mentor, who is standing by to assist you. The mentor is familiar with the book, an expert in the subject, and can provide you with a specific answer to your content-related question, usually

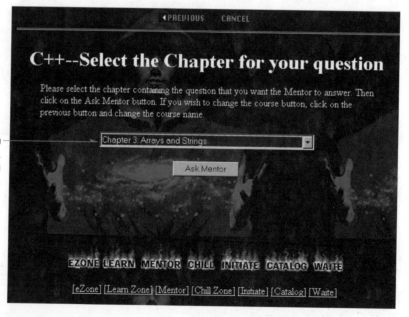

Click on this pull down menu to see a list of chapters. Click on the chapter to which your question relates.

Figure 7
Get personalized help in the Mentor Zone

within one business day. You can get to this area by clicking on the Mentor icon in the navigation frame.

Just the FAQs

Before you ask a mentor a question, you're first shown a set of FAQs. Be sure to read through the list. Since you have a limited number of questions you may ask, you'll want to use your questions carefully. Chances are that an answer to your question has already been posted, in which case you can get an answer without having to ask it yourself. In any event, you may learn about an issue you hadn't even considered.

If the FAQ list does not contain the answer you need, you'll want to submit your own question to the mentor.

Ask Your Mentor

eZone students may ask 10 questions of their course mentor. This limit ensures that mentors will have the opportunity to answer all readers' questions. Questions must be directly related to chapter material. If you ask unrelated or inappropriate questions, you won't get an answer; however, the question will still be deducted from your allotment.

If the FAQ doesn't provide you with an answer to your question, click the button labeled *Ask Mentor*. The first time you contact the mentor, the rules and conditions for the mentor questions are provided. After reading these, click the *Accept* button to continue. In a moment, a form like the one shown in Figure 8 appears.

This form specifies the course, the chapter, and other information pertinent to your question. The mentor e-mails the answer to your question directly to you, but keep in mind that Mentor Zone questions must be *directly* related to the chapter subject matter.

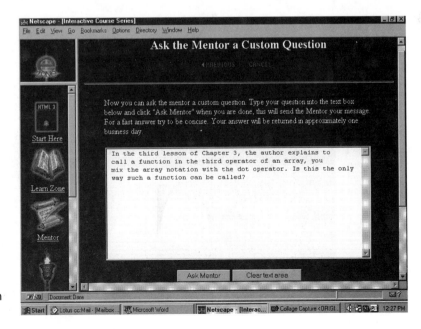

Figure 8
Use this form to send your question to your mentor

More Assistance

Keep in mind that there are other sources of assistance in the eZone, too. If you are experiencing technical problems with the book or CD, you'll want to contact the Webmaster; you'll find a link on the eZone's main page. If you want to discuss related issues, such as developments and applications, check out the newsgroups available in the Chill Zone. There are other ways to discuss issues with real people, as you'll discover, when you visit the eZone.

CHILL ZONE

Think of the Chill Zone as your student lounge, a place where students hang out and discuss their classes. But the Chill Zone does a student lounge one better—it's also a library chock full of information. It's a place where you can interact with others reading the same book and find expert resources to assist you as you develop and use your new skills. Perhaps the coolest thing about the Chill Zone is that its options are all included with the cost of your book.

To get into the Chill Zone, click the Chill Zone icon in the navigation frame. Once there, you can click three Chill Zone options:

Discussion List—You can subscribe (or unsubscribe) to a dedicated newsgroup centered on your book.

Newsletter—Select this option to subscribe (or unsubscribe) to the quarterly eZone newsletter.

Resources—These are links to Web sites, tools, and other useful materials related to the course subject.

To select a Chill Zone option, click the link and follow the on-screen instructions.

THE EZONE AWAITS

As you have seen from this tour, this Interactive Course book is a lot more than the pages before you. It's a full-blown, personalized training system—including textbook, testing, guidance, certification, and support—that you can pick up and work through at your own pace and at your own convenience.

Don't settle for just a book when you can get a whole education. Thanks to this comprehensive package, you're ready to log on and learn in the eZone.

ABOUT THE AUTHOR

Robert Lafore has been writing books about computer programming since 1982. His best-selling titles include *Assembly Language Programming for the IBM PC and XT*, *C Programming Using Turbo C++*, *Microsoft C Programming for the PC*, and *Object-Oriented Programming in C++*. Mr. Lafore holds degrees in mathematics and electrical engineering, and has been active in programming since the days of the PDP-5, when 4K of main memory was considered luxurious. His interests include hiking, windsurfing, and recreational mathematics.

Dedication

This book is dedicated to the memory of my father, who got me started with superheterodyne circuits and the 6SJ7. And everything else, for that matter.

TABLE OF CONTENTS

CONTENTS

Chapter 9
Virtual Functions and Friend Functions 495

Chapter 12   The Standard Template Library 713

ACKNOWLEDGMENTS

This book has taken so long to write that it's gone through a whole series of Waite Group managing editors. My thanks to Andrea Rosenberg, John Crudo, and—in the distant past—Scott Calamar.

Special thanks also to Mitch Waite, who—once again—is dragging me kicking and screaming into today's technology.

Lyn Cordell, in her dual role as a content editor plus copy editor, is the best. If she says change it, I change it; I know she's right. Mike Radtke, technical editor, pulled the fat out of the fire on more occasions than I care to think about. (Any remaining problems are, of course, entirely my fault.)

INTRODUCTION

If you want to know whether you should buy this book, read this introduction!

First question: Why learn C++ at all? That's easy: It's today's dominant computer language. When the going gets tough, the professionals turn to C++. There are many other languages, of course, but they lack the universality and power of C++. For example, Visual Basic is useful for quickly putting together applications that aren't too large or demanding, assembly language is good if you're writing a device driver, and Java is great for the World Wide Web. (Java is derived from C++ anyway.) But for a major stand-alone application, C++ is the most popular language that has the power and flexibility to produce the fastest, best-performing code. For these reasons, C++ is a major part of the Computer Science curriculum at almost every school and university. If you're a programmer, chances are that sooner or later you'll need to know it.

What's Different About This Book?

This book is a C++ tutorial. But there are a lot of C++ tutorials on the market. How is this one different? Three ways: It's easy to understand, it's organized in a better and unique way, and it comes with a free backup system if there's anything that's giving you trouble. Let's look at these features in detail.

Easy to Understand

This book starts off with very easy examples; we don't assume you're a rocket scientist. We try to explain everything with no assumptions about what you may already know. We use plenty of figures and analogies to clarify the text. The program examples are heavily commented to make everything as clear as possible.

As you progress further into the book, the examples become more challenging, but we try to keep the increase in difficulty gradual, so you're always ready for what comes next. Ultimately we cover all the main features of C++.

Unique Organization

Unlike most other C++ books, this one uses, from the very first example, real object-oriented programs. Most books, in an attempt to stick with the familiar, start with old-fashioned procedural examples and work up to full object-based examples halfway through. This may seem easier, but in the long run it's counter-productive, because it encourages bad thinking habits. The whole point of C++ is to write object-oriented programs. If they don't do that from the beginning, they're missing the point. And, as it turns out, object-oriented programs aren't that hard anyway.

The Waite Group Interactive Series

The third way this book differs from other C++ books is that it's a Waite Group Interactive book. This isn't just publisher's hype: By connecting you to the Waite Group via the World Wide Web, this new approach can actually play a significant role in helping you to learn C++. There are many aspects to the Interactive Series. We won't dwell on them here, since the details are presented elsewhere. We should note, however, that this book was written from the ground up to work as part of the Interactive Series.

First, each chapter is divided into short, easily digestible lessons. Each lesson is devoted to a specific topic and requires only an hour (approximately) to read and understand. This makes it easy to sit down with the book and learn something, even if your time is limited.

Each lesson is followed by a quiz to ensure that you've understood the material. You can answer the quizzes by yourself, or you can do them on the Web, which will grade them automatically. There are almost 500 quiz questions in the book, so you'll really find out how well you understand the subject.

The Waite Group Web site offers many other advantages. A principle one is mentoring, which is the ability to ask questions and get answers back, just as you would if you were taking a class at a university and could talk to the professor.

As a final plus, this book includes a full chapter on the Standard Template Library (STL), which is fast becoming an essential part of every C++ programmer's bag of tricks, but which has not yet made its way into many C++ books.

What Do You Need to Know?

This book is intended for anyone who wants to learn C++ from the ground up. That is, it does not assume any previous knowledge of C (or any other specific programming language). It's nice if you've had some exposure to another language, but even that is not essential. In fact, it may be better not to have bad old (procedural) habits to unlearn.

If you already know the C language, you'll find that perhaps a third of the material in this book is familiar to you. You'll know the basic syntax of `for` loops, `switch` statements, and pointers, for example. However, you'll be surprised by how much of the material is new. Almost all the examples, including those that explain basic syntax, use the object-oriented approach, so you'll find you're learning OOP even when you're reading about syntax you already know.

What Hardware and Software Do You Need?

You should have some kind of C++ compiler at your disposal. The example programs in this book are—for the most part—generic: That is, they will work with most compilers. Thus, you aren't constrained to use any particular system.

In a few instances we wrote compiler-specific code so we could use more sophisticated screen displays. This applies to only a half-dozen examples out of more than 200 programs in the book. For these, the code in the book is specific to Borland C++ (and Turbo C++, which is similar). These are probably the most popular compilers and among the easiest to use.

However, if you're using Microsoft Visual C++, Appendix C shows you how, by inserting a special header file (provided on the CD-ROM) into the example's source code, you can easily convert these few programs to work with your compiler.

Go For It!

Learning C++ has never been easier. With its short lessons, easy-to-understand writing style, and the support of Waite Group Press via their Web site, you should be on your way to C++ mastery in less time than you thought possible.

INSTALLATION

The companion CD-ROM contains all of the source code and the executables from the lessons in the book, as well as the NetManage Chameleon installer. Since all of the code for the lessons in this book are on the companion CD-ROM, there is no need to type the code if you want to use it for your own projects. We will illustrate how to copy the files from the companion CD-ROM to your hard drive.

This section will walk you through the steps necessary to install the source code from the CD-ROM to your hard drive for DOS/Windows 3.x and Windows 95. To install the NetManage Chameleon, please see the section *The Chameleon Sampler*.

For the following examples, we are going to assume that the CD-ROM drive you want to copy files from is the D: drive and the hard drive you want to copy files to is the C: drive. If your system is set up differently, please substitute the appropriate drive letters for your system.

DOS

These instructions for DOS assume you have no familiarity with DOS commands. If you feel uncomfortable with DOS and are using these instructions from the Windows DOS Prompt, please exit and follow the instructions for your version of Windows.

1. Move to the drive that you want to copy the files to. If you want to copy the files onto the C: drive, type

```
C:
```

and press ENTER. Ensure you are at the root directory by typing

```
CD \
```

and pressing ENTER.

2. Create the directory you would like to store your files into. If you want to store the files into the CPPIC directory, type

```
MD CPPIC
```

and press ENTER.

3. Move to that directory. If you created a directory called CPPIC, move to that directory by typing

```
CD CPPIC
```

and press ENTER.

4. To copy all of the files to your hard drive, simply type

```
XCOPY D:\*.* /V /S
```

and press ENTER. To copy individual subdirectories from the CD-ROM to the CPPIC directory on your hard drive, you must create the chapter directories before you copy the contents. For example, if you wanted to copy the code for Chapters 2, 5, and 7, you would type

```
MD CHAP_02
MD CHAP_05
MD CHAP_07
```

and press ENTER after each line. Then you would type

```
CD \CPPIC\CHAP_02
XCOPY D:\CHAP_02 /V /S

CD \CPPIC\CHAP_05
XCOPY D:\CHAP_05 /V /S

CD \CPPIC\CHAP_07
XCOPY D:\CHAP_07 /V /S
```

and press ENTER after each line. The /V is a DOS switch to verify files while copying and /S is a DOS switch to copy the subdirectories. Depending on the configuration and performance of your system, these steps may take from a few moments to a few minutes.

Windows 3.x

The following steps are for the use of Windows 3.x with short file names.

1. Open the File Manager.

2. In File Manager, locate the drive you want to copy to and click on it.

3. If you have a directory to copy the files to, skip to Step 4. Otherwise, create a new directory by selecting File, Create Directory. Type

```
CPPIC
```

or a directory name of your choice and press ENTER or click on the OK button.

4. Click on CPPIC or the directory you created.

5. Select the drive letter of your CD-ROM drive.

6. Double-click on the D: drive icon. You should see the following directory structure:

```
APP_C
CHAP_02
CHAP_03
CHAP_04
```

```
CHAP_06
CHAP_07
CHAP_08
CHAP_09
CHAP_10
CHAP_11
CHAP_12
NTMANAGE
```

Control-click on the directories that you want to copy and drag the selection to the destination drive. Depending on how fast your computer is and also depending on the options set for your computer, the copying process may take a few moments to a few minutes.

When Windows copies a CD-ROM, it does not change the Read-only attribute for the files it copies. You can view the files, but you cannot edit them until you remove this attribute. To change it on all of the files, select the top-most directory with the files in it. In File Manager, select File, Properties and click on the Read-only checkbox to deselect it and click on OK.

Windows 95

The easiest way to copy files using Windows 95 is by using the Desktop.

1. Double-click on the My Computer icon. Your drives will appear in a window on the desktop.

2. Double-click on your hard drive and create a new folder, such as C++ Interactive Course, by selecting File, New, Folder from the window menu. A folder called New Folder will be created on your hard drive with the name highlighted. Type in the name you want and press the ENTER key.

3. Go back to your drive window and double-click on the icon that represents your CD-ROM. You will see a window that has 11 chapter folders, one appendix folder, and one Program folder.

4. Select the directories you want to copy (control-click on the folders if you're not copying all of them) and drag your selection to the directory you created on your hard drive. You might need to reposition your windows to make the window for your hard drive visible. Depending on your system's performance, this may take a few moments to a few minutes.

When Windows (any version) copies a CD-ROM, it does not change the Read-only attribute for the files it copies. You can view the files, but you cannot edit them until you remove this attribute. To change it on all of the files, select the top-most directory with the files in it. In Explorer, select File, Properties and click on the Read-only checkbox to des-

INTERNET EXPLORER 3.0: A FIELD GUIDE

A new day dawned. The sun reached its fingers over the digital outback. The mighty Navigators (*Netscapus navigatorus*)—a species that reproduced like rabbits and ran nearly as fast—covered the landscape. Yonder, on a cliff that seemed to be beyond the horizon, a trembling new creature looked out over the Internet jungle. This strange new creature, calling itself the Explorer (*Microsoftus interneticus explorus*), sniffed around, considering whether it should enter the fragile ecosystem. Netscape gators gnashed their teeth, but the Explorer was not daunted. Explorer was a formidable beast. It became a part of the jungle and thrived. And even though it began as a mere pup, it evolved, and it evolved and it evolved.

Now the jungle is rife with two intelligent species.

What follows is a guide to domesticating Internet Explorer. You will learn how to care for your Explorer and even how to teach it tricks. Before long, you shall find truth behind the old axiom that the Explorer is man's (and woman's) best friend.

INTRODUCING EXPLORER

Whether you're running Windows NT or Windows 95, installing Explorer is easy. Explorer's own installation program makes setup a breeze, and you need only to select the appropriate file on the CD-ROM to launch this installer. Make sure the CD-ROM included with this book is in the CD-ROM drive; then, depending upon your system, follow the directions below for either Windows 95 or Windows NT.

Windows 95 Installation

1. Click the Start button in the lower left corner of your screen.

2. Click on the Run... option in the Start menu. The Run dialog box appears.

3. Using the Run dialog box, type in a pathname and specify the location of the Explorer installation program. IE301M95.EXE is in the CD's \Explorer directory, so if your CD-ROM drive is designated as D:, you'd type

```
d:\explorer\ie301m95.exe
```

If your CD-ROM drive has a different designation letter, type in the appropriate drive designation letter in place of `d:`.

4. After typing the proper pathname, click the OK button to start the Explorer's installation program. Depending upon your system, it may take a moment to load.

5. Once the installation program loads, follow the on-screen prompts to set up Explorer on your computer.

Windows NT 4 Installation

1. Click the Start button in the lower left corner of your screen.

2. Click on the Run... option in the Start menu. The Run dialog box appears.

3. Using the Run dialog box, type in a pathname and specify the location of the Explorer installation program. MSIE30M.EXE is in the CD's \Explorer directory, so if your CD-ROM drive is designated as D:, you'd type

```
d:\explorer\ie301mnt.exe
```

If your CD-ROM drive has a different designation letter, type in the appropriate drive designation letter in place of `d:`.

4. After typing the proper pathname, click the OK button to start the Explorer's installation program. Depending upon your system, it may take a moment to load.

5. Once the installation program loads, follow the on-screen prompts to set up Explorer on your computer.

Windows 3.1 and Windows NT 3.51 Installation

1. Click on File in the main menu bar at the top of your screen.

2. Click on Run... option in the File menu. The Run dialog box appears.

3. Using the Run dialog box, type in a pathname and specify the location of the Explorer installation program. SETUP.EXE is in the \Explorer\Win31NT3.51 directory. If your CD-ROM drive is designated D:, type:

```
d:\explorer\win31nt3.51\setup.exe
```

If your CD-ROM drive has a different designation letter, type in the appropriate drive designation letter in place of D:.

4. After typing the proper pathname, click the OK button to start Explorer's installation program. Depending on your system, it may take a moment to load.

5. Once the installation program loads, follow the on-screen prompts to set up Explorer on your computer.

Once you've run the installation, you'll need to restart your system. You can then click on the Internet icon on your desktop. If you've already selected an Internet provider with Windows dial-up networking, you'll be connected. If not, you'll be walked through the dial-in process. You'll need to enter the phone number of your Internet provider, your modem type, and other related information. Ultimately, you'll be taken to Microsoft's home page, where you can register your Explorer and find out about its latest features.

The Explorer is a constantly evolving animal. For the latest updates, plug-ins, and versions, be sure to regularly check out Microsoft's neck of the woods at `http://www.microsoft.com/ie/`.

THE NATURE OF THE BEAST

Internet Explorer features very up-to-date HTML. It supports HTML 3.2, including the following:

- *Frames*—These break up the Web page window into several areas. For example, you can keep an unchanging row of navigation controls along the top of the page while constantly updating the bottom. You can use *borderless frames*, which split up the page without making it seem split. A special type of frame known as the *floating frame* lets you view one Web page within another.

- *Cascading Style Sheets*—This allows all your Web sites to have the same general look and feel.

- *Tables*—You can create or view all sorts of fancy tables, with or without graphics, borders, and columns.

- *Embedded Objects*—Internet Explorer can handle Java applets, ActiveX controls, and even Netscape plug-ins. These objects are discussed later, in the Symbiotic Partners section of this appendix.

- *Fonts*—Explorer supports many fonts, allowing Web pages to have a variety of exciting designs.

From the get-go, Internet Explorer has included a few special bells and whistles. For example, it's easy to create and view marquees across Web pages. This lets you scroll a long, attention-drawing message, similar to a tickertape, that puts a great deal of information in a very small space.

TRAINING THE EXPLORER

By its very nature, the Explorer is a friendly beast. You can access the full range of the Explorer's talents by pushing its buttons. These buttons, which appear in the toolbar as depicted in Figure B, are as follows:

- *Back*—Use this to return to the Web page you've just come from. This will help you retrace your steps as you take Explorer through the Internet maze.

- *Forward*—Use this after you've used the Back button, to jump forward again to the page from which you began.

- *Stop*—If a Web page is taking too long to load, press this button. Any text and graphics will immediately stop downloading.

- *Refresh*—If your Web page is missing some graphics, or if you've previously stopped its loading using the Stop button, you can reload it using Refresh.

- *Home*—This takes you to your pre-set home page. By default, this is Microsoft's main Web page, but you can set your home to any you'd like. See the Taming the Beast section.

- *Search*—This takes you to a special page that allows you to search for a Web page, using a number of cool search engines. See the Hunting Skills section.

- *Favorites*—This button lets you access a list of your favorite Web sites. See the Favorite Haunts section.

- *Print*—This allows you to print out the current Web page, allowing you to keep a perfect hard copy of it.

- *Font*—Find yourself squinting at a Web page? Just click here to zoom in. The font size will grow several degrees. Too big now? Click a few more times and the size will shrink once again.

- *Mail*—This will launch the Internet Mail program, which allows you to send and receive e-mail and to access newsgroups.

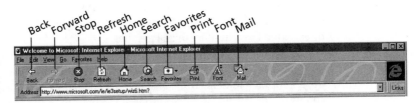

Figure B
A cosmetic look at
Explorer

PLAYING FETCH

Your Explorer is a devoted friend. It can scamper anywhere within the Internet, bringing back exactly what you desire.

If you know where you want to go, just type the URL into Explorer's Address box at the top of the screen. If you like, you can omit the `http://` prefix. The Web page will be loaded up. You can also search for a page or load up a previously saved page.

You can now click on any *hyperlink*—an underlined or colored word or picture—to zoom to that associated Web page or Internet resource. Some hyperlinked graphics may not be obvious. Explorer will tell you when you are positioned over a valid hyperlink, because the cursor will change into a pointing finger. Continue following these links as long as you like. It's not uncommon to start researching knitting needles and end up reading about porcupines.

HUNTING SKILLS

If you want to find Web pages dealing with a specific category, the Explorer makes it easy to find them. Click the Search button. You can search for more than Web pages. With Explorer, it's easy to find

● Phone numbers, ZIP codes, and addresses

● Information on a number of topics—health, home, education, consumer affairs, finance, weather, sports, travel, and so on

● References—maps, a dictionary, a thesaurus, quotations, and an encyclopedia

● On-line books, newspapers, and magazines

FAVORITE HAUNTS

It's easy to keep track of the Web pages you visit most. When you want to save a page for future reference, simply click the Favorites button or choose the Favorites menu item. Select the Add To Favorites option. The current Web page will now be added to the list of favorites, which appears each time you click on the Favorites button or menu.

After a while, your list of favorites will get long and cluttered. It's simple to keep track of huge lists of favorites—just put them into separate folders. Organize your favorites by selecting Favorites|Organize Favorites.

To create a new folder, click on the New Folder icon (the folder with the little glint on it) at the top of the window. Now drag and drop your Web page bookmarks into the appropriate folders. You can also move, rename, or delete a folder by selecting it and using the corresponding buttons at the bottom of the screen.

MEMORY

Internet Explorer keeps track of every Web page you visit. This is kept in a vast History list. You can view the entire History list, in chronological order, by clicking the View History button. Just click on any page you'd like to revisit.

The History list is cleared every 20 days—you can set this value within the Navigation properties sheets.

TAMING THE BEAST

Now that you and your Explorer are getting acquainted, why not tame it so that it acts and looks exactly like you want? Select View|Options and pick a tab at the top of the window to customize the following properties:

● *General*—Since multimedia content (such as sounds, movies, and graphics) takes longer to load in Web pages, you can choose not to load certain media types. You can also easily customize the color of the text and hyperlinks. Finally, you can decide how little or how much information appears in your toolbar.

You can change the size and position of your toolbar simply by clicking on its borders and dragging it to a desired location.

● *Connection*—You can adjust your connections settings, as shown in Figure B-8, by clicking on this tab. This lets you choose your Internet provider. If you're connecting to the Internet through a network firewall, you can also set your proxy server information here.

● *Navigation*—You can customize which page you'd like to use as your starting home page. Just enter its URL in the Address box here.

● *Programs*—This allows you to set which programs you'd like to use for e-mail and for Usenet news. By default, you can use Microsoft's Internet Mail and Internet News, which are included with Explorer. You can also tell Explorer how to handle various types of files by selecting the File

Types button. It allows you to designate which program or plug-in should be launched whenever Explorer comes across various unfamiliar file formats.

● *Security*—You are able to customize how securely documents will be handled by Explorer. If you want to keep your computer extremely safe, you may tell Explorer not to download possible security risks such as ActiveX controls, Java applets, or other plug-ins. Another nice feature is a Content Advisor. Click on Settings; the Content Advisor window will appear. You may now decide which Web pages to skip based on Adult Language, Nudity, Sex, or Violence. Many questionable Web pages are written with certain tags so that the pages can be weeded out by people who don't want to see them. This is a great option to use if your kids surf the Internet, or if your sensibilities are offended. To turn ratings on, click on the Enable Ratings button. You can also lock this window with a password.

● *Advanced*—This properties sheet lets you customize when Internet Explorer will issue warnings. This is useful if you deal with sensitive information and want to know which Web pages are secure and which are not. You can also set a number of other advanced Java and Security options here.

A FIRST LOOK AT OOP AND C++

Welcome to the exciting world of object-oriented programming! In this first chapter, I'll start by discussing why object-oriented programming (OOP) was invented and why it offers advantages to the programmer. I'll also provide a quick overview of the main features of object-oriented languages. You'll learn about the two most fundamental aspects of OOP, objects and classes. Then I'll focus on a particular kind of object—hot dog stand—and show how real hot dog stands on the street relate to hot dog stand objects in a program. You'll see how to use C++ to describe a class of hot dog stand objects and how to make these objects carry out tasks.

This approach goes to the very heart of OOP. Most books begin by skittering around the edges of C++, talking about old-fashioned procedural details. This one attacks objects and classes head-on. If you

1

think of OOP as a fierce fire-breathing dragon, then you're going to walk right up to it, look it square-ly in the eye, and tell it you want answers, now!

WHY DO WE NEED OOP?

In this session, I'll discuss, in a general way, how object-oriented programming arrived on the scene. OOP was developed because limitations were discovered in earlier approaches to programming. To appreciate what OOP does, you need to understand what these limitations are and how they arose from traditional programming languages.

Procedural Languages

Pascal, C, BASIC, Fortran, and similar traditional programming languages are *procedural* languages. That is, each statement in the language tells the computer to *do* something: Get some input, add these numbers, divide by 6, display that output. A program in a procedural language is a *list of instructions*.

For very small programs, no other organizing principle (often called a *paradigm*) is needed. The programmer creates the list of instructions and the computer carries them out.

Division into Functions

When programs become larger, a single list of instructions becomes unwieldy. Few programmers can comprehend a program of more than a few hundred statements unless it is broken down into small-er units. For this reason, the *function* was adopted as a way to make programs more comprehensible to their human creators. (The term function is used in C++ and C. In other languages, the same con-cept may be called a *subroutine*, a *subprogram*, or a *procedure*.) A program is divided into functions and—ideally, at least—each function has a clearly defined purpose and a clearly defined interface to the other functions in the program.

The idea of breaking a program into functions can be extended by grouping a number of func-tions together into a larger entity called a *module*, but the principle is similar: a grouping of instructions that carry out specific tasks.

Dividing a program into functions and modules is one of the cornerstones of *structured program-ming*, the somewhat loosely defined discipline that has influenced programming design for several decades.

Problems with Structured Programming

As programs grow ever larger and more complex, even the structured programming approach begins to show signs of strain. You may have heard about, or been involved in, horror stories of pro-gram development. The project is too complex, the schedule slips, more programmers are added, complexity increases, costs skyrocket, the schedule slips further, and disaster ensues (see *The Mythical Man-Month*, by Frederick P. Brooks, Jr., Addison-Wesley, 1982, for a vivid description of this scenario).

Analyzing the reasons for these failures reveals weaknesses in the procedural paradigm itself. No matter how well the structured programming approach is implemented, large programs become exces-sively complex.

What are the reasons for this failure of procedural languages? One of the most crucial is the role played by data.

Data Is Undervalued

In a procedural language, the emphasis is on doing things—read the keyboard, invert the vector, check for errors, and so on. The subdivision of a program into functions continues this emphasis. Functions *do things*, just as single program statements do. What they do may be more complex or abstract, but the emphasis is still on the action.

What happens to the data in this paradigm? Data is, after all, the reason for a program's existence. The important part of an inventory program isn't a function that displays the data or a function that checks for correct input; it's the inventory data itself. Yet data is given second-class status in the organization of procedural languages.

For example, in an inventory program, the data that makes up the inventory is probably read from a disk file into memory, where it is treated as a global variable. By *global,* I mean that the variables that constitute the data are declared outside of any function so they are accessible to all functions. These functions perform various operations on the data. They read it, analyze it, update it, rearrange it, display it, write it back to the disk, and so on.

I should note that most languages, such as Pascal and C, also support *local* variables, which are hidden within a single function. But local variables are not useful for important data that must be accessed by many different functions. Figure 1-1 shows the relationship between global and local variables.

Suppose a new programmer is hired to write a function to analyze this inventory data in a certain way. Unfamiliar with the subtleties of the program, the programmer creates a function that accidentally corrupts the data. This is easy to do, because every function has complete access to the data. It's

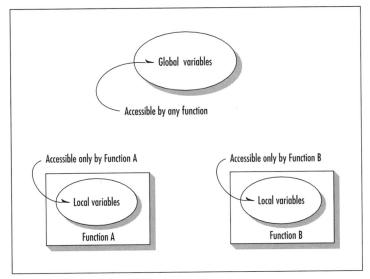

Figure 1-1 Global and local variables

like leaving your personal papers in the lobby of your apartment building: Anyone can change or destroy them. In the same way, global data can be corrupted by functions that have no business changing it.

Another problem is that, because many functions access the same data, the way the data is stored becomes critical. The arrangement of the data can't be changed without modifying all the functions that access it. If you add new data items, for example, you'll need to modify all the functions that access the data so that they can also access these new items. It will be hard to find all such functions and even harder to modify all of them correctly. It's similar to what happens when your local supermarket moves the bread from aisle 4 to aisle 12. Everyone who patronizes the supermarket must figure out where the bread has gone and adjust their shopping habits accordingly. The relationship of functions and data in procedural programs is shown in Figure 1-2.

What is needed is a way to restrict access to the data, to *hide* it from all but a few critical functions. This will protect the data, simplify maintenance, and offer other benefits, as you'll see.

Relationship to the Real World

Procedural programs are often difficult to design. The problem is that their chief components—functions and data structures—don't model the real world very well. For example, suppose you are writing code to create the elements of a graphics user interface: menus, windows, and so on. Quick now, what functions will you need? What data structures? The answers are not obvious, to say the least. It would be better if windows and menus corresponded more closely to actual program elements.

New Data Types

There are other problems with traditional languages. One is the difficulty of creating new data types. Computer languages typically have several built-in data types: integers, floating-point numbers, characters, and so on. What if you want to invent your own data type? Perhaps you want to work with complex numbers, or two-dimensional coordinates, or dates—quantities the built-in data types don't

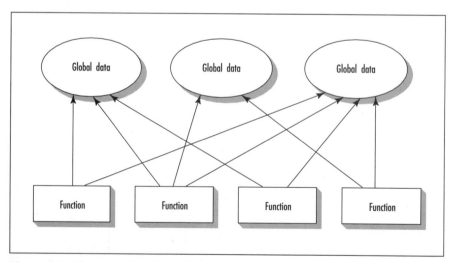

Figure 1-2 The procedural paradigm

handle easily. Being able to create your own types is called *extensibility* because you can extend the capabilities of the language. Traditional languages are not usually extensible. Without unnatural convolutions, you can't bundle both x and y coordinates into a single variable called *Point* and then add and subtract values of this type. Traditional programs are more complex to write and maintain.

The Object-Oriented Approach

The fundamental idea behind object-oriented languages is to combine into a single program entity both *data* and *the functions that operate on that data*. Such an entity is called an *object*.

An object's functions, called *member functions* in C++ (because they belong to a particular class of objects), typically provide the only way to access its data. If you want to read a data item in an object, you call a member function in the object. It will read the item and return the value to you. You can't access the data directly. The data is *hidden*, so it is safe from accidental alteration. Data and its functions are said to be *encapsulated* into a single entity. *Encapsulation* and *data hiding* are key terms in the description of object-oriented languages.

If you want to modify the data in an object, you know exactly what functions interact with it: the member functions in the object. No other functions can access the data. This simplifies writing, debugging, and maintaining the program.

A C++ program typically consists of a number of objects that communicate with each other by calling one another's member functions. Figure 1-3 shows the organization of a C++ program.

I should mention that what are called member functions in C++ are called *methods* in some other object-oriented (OO) languages such as Smalltalk, one of the first OO languages. Also, data items may be called *instance variables*. Calling an object's member function is often referred to as *sending a message* to the object. These terms are often used by C++ writers.

The Corporate Analogy

You might want to think of objects as departments—such as sales, accounting, personnel, and so on—in a company. Departments provide an important approach to corporate organization. In most companies (except very small ones), people don't work on personnel problems one day, payroll the next, and then go out in the field as salespeople the following week. Each department has its own personnel, with clearly assigned duties. It also has its own data: payroll, sales figures, personnel records, inventory, or whatever, depending on the department.

The people in each department control and operate on that department's data. Dividing the company into departments makes it easier to comprehend and control the company's activities and helps maintain the integrity of the information used by the company. The payroll department, for instance, is responsible for payroll data. If you work in the sales department and you need to know the total of all the salaries paid in the southern region in July, you don't just walk into the payroll department and start rummaging through file cabinets. You send a memo to the appropriate person in the department and then wait for that person to access the data and send you a reply with the information you want. This ensures that the data is accessed accurately and it is not corrupted by inept outsiders. This view of corporate organization is shown in Figure 1-4. In the same way, objects provide an approach to program organization while helping to maintain the integrity of the program's data.

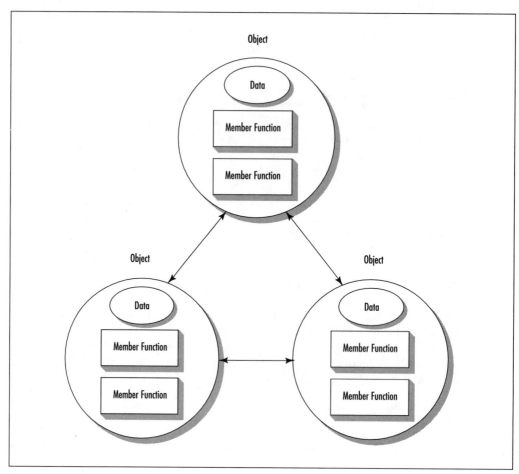

Figure 1-3 The object-oriented paradigm

The Dinner Table Analogy

Here's another analogy. Let's compare an old-fashioned procedural program with a table set for—let's say—Thanksgiving dinner. The guests seated around the table—Uncle Harry, Aunt Beatrice, and so on—represent functions and the dishes of food on the table—turkey, cranberry sauce, sweet potatoes—are the data. Let's further assume that the guests never ask their neighbors to pass any of the dishes; they just reach across the table for the food. This corresponds to a procedural program, in which functions access global data directly.

This approach works all right as long as there aren't too many guests at the table. Six or eight guests is probably the maximum. In a larger party—20 guests, say—people must reach too far, their sleeves dip into the gravy, dishes collide midtable, several guests reach for the same dish at the same time, things are spilled, fights break out—you get the picture. This sort of chaos is what happens in large

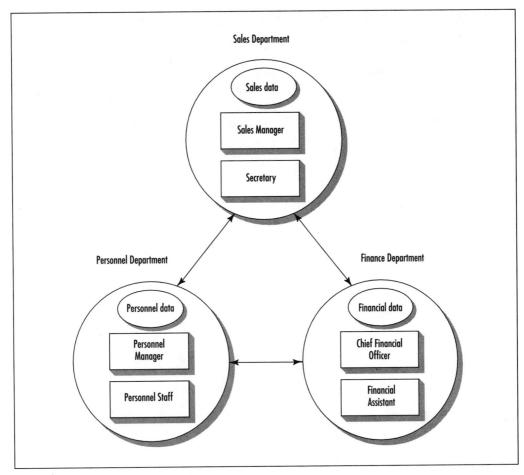

Figure 1-4   The corporate paradigm

procedural programs where the only form of organization is data and functions. The organization-al paradigm can't support the complexity.

What's needed is a more powerful organizational unit. For the dinner party, several smaller tables might be used rather than one large one. Each table has its own supply of food and guests; it's the new organization unit. The guests at these small tables can easily reach the food on their own table. If someone wants something from another table—the pepper, perhaps—she asks a guest at that table to bring it to her.

Each of the small tables corresponds to an object. Each object has its own functions and data. Most of the interaction between functions and data takes place within the objects, but it's also possible for one object to exchange data with another. By using a larger organizational unit, the object, which combines functions and data, we've restored order to a chaotic situation.

OOP: An Approach to Organization, Not Details

Keep in mind that object-oriented programming is not primarily concerned with the *details* of program operation. Instead, it deals with the *overall organization* of the program. Most individual program statements in C++ are similar to statements in procedural languages and many are identical to statements in C. Indeed, an entire member function in a C++ program may be very similar to a procedural function in C. It is only when you look at the larger context that you can determine whether a statement or a function is part of a procedural C program or an object-oriented C++ program.

(Note: In this—and all quizzes in this book—a question may have more than one correct answer.)

1. Pascal, BASIC, and C are _____ languages, whereas C++ is _____.
   a. object-oriented, traditional
   b. interpreted, compiled
   c. traditional, procedural
   d. procedural, compiled
   e. procedural, object-oriented

2. Which of the following are weaknesses of traditional languages such as C?
   a. Important data is vulnerable to accidental modification.
   b. Such languages are hard to use for small programs.
   c. Functions don't correspond neatly to real-world entities.
   d. It is difficult to extend such languages by adding new data types.
   e. The syntax is excessively complex.

3. In C++, you will typically access an object's data using
   a. member functions of other objects in that class.
   b. member functions of any class.
   c. any function with that object's password.
   d. member functions associated with that particular object.
   e. any function outside of the object's class.

4. The two major components of an object are _____ and _____.
   a. a class, its data
   b. data, functions that may act on that data
   c. messages, member functions
   d. encapsulation, polymorphism
   e. hidden data, ordinary data

5. Asking the sales manager of a company to get you data from the sales department is like
   a. calling the member function of an object to access the object's data.
   b. creating a class of objects with data hidden inside.
   c. programming a member function that can insert data in an object.

  d. creating an object with a member function that can access its own data.

  e. sending a message to a class.

SESSION 2

FEATURES OF OBJECT-ORIENTED LANGUAGES

Now that you have some idea why OOP languages were invented, let's briefly examine a few of the major elements of object-oriented languages in general and C++ in particular. This lesson serves as a quick overview of things to come. Don't worry if everything I say here isn't crystal clear; I'll be discussing these topics in more detail later.

Real-World Objects

When you approach a programming problem in an object-oriented language, you no longer ask how the problem will be divided into functions, but how it will be divided into objects. Thinking in terms of objects rather than functions has a surprisingly helpful effect on how easily you can design programs. This results from the close match between objects in the programming sense and objects in the real world.

What kinds of things become objects in object-oriented programs? The answer is limited only by your imagination, but here are some typical categories to start you thinking:

 Physical objects
Elevators in an elevator control program
Automobiles in a traffic flow simulation
Countries in an economics model
Aircraft in an air traffic control system

 Elements of the computer user environment
Windows
Menus
Graphics objects (lines, rectangles, circles)
The mouse, keyboard, disk drives, printer

 Data-storage constructs
Customized arrays
Stacks
Linked lists
Binary trees

 Human entities
Employees
Students
Customers
Salespeople

Collections of data
An inventory
A personnel file
A dictionary
A table of the latitudes and longitudes of world cities

 User-defined data types
Time
Angles
Complex numbers
Points on the plane

 Components in computer games
Ghosts in a maze game
Positions in a board game (chess, checkers)
Animals in an ecological simulation
Opponents and friends in adventure games

States and Abilities

The match between programming objects and real-world objects is the happy result of combining data and member functions. This is an important concept, so let's look at it another way. Many real-world objects, at least the interesting ones, have both a *state* (characteristics that can change) and *abilities* (things they can do).

For example, an elevator could be in the following state: It's on the 3rd floor, it contains four passengers, and the passengers have pushed buttons for the 7th, 11th, and 15th floors. The elevator might also have the following abilities: It can go down, it can go up, it can open and close its doors, it can query other elevators to see where they are, and it can calculate where it should go next.

In C++, an object's *data* records its state and its *member functions* correspond to its abilities. For an elevator object, the data might be

 Current_floor_number

 Number_of_passengers_aboard

 List_of_buttons_pushed

The member functions might be

 GoDown()

 GoUp()

 OpenDoors()

 CloseDoors()

 GetInfo()

 CalculateWhereToGo()

The underscore character (_) is often used to separate words in C++ names, as is the technique of running words together but capitalizing the first letters. Parentheses (( )) after a name indicate a function. Incidentally, most C++ compilers allow names (variable names, function names, and so on) to be as long as you want, but only the first 32 characters are meaningful to the compiler. Upper- and lowercase letters, the underscore, and the digits from 0 to 9 are permissible characters, but a name cannot start with a digit.

Object-oriented programming combines the programming equivalent of states and abilities—which are represented in a program by data and functions—into a single entity called an *object*. The result is a programming entity that corresponds neatly with many real-world objects.

Making objects the central feature of program design constitutes a revolution in programming. No such close match between programming constructs and the items being modeled exists in procedural languages.

Classes

In OOP, objects are *instances of classes*. What does this mean? Let's look at an analogy. Almost all computer languages have built-in data types. For instance, a data type `int`, meaning *integer*, is predefined in C++. You can declare as many variables of type `int` as you need in your program:

```
int day;
int count;
int divisor;
int answer;
```

In a similar way, you can define many *objects* of the same *class*, as shown in Figure 1-5. A class serves as a plan, or a template. It specifies what data and what functions will be included in objects of that class. Defining the class doesn't create any objects, just as the mere existence of a type `int` doesn't create any variables of type `int`.

A class is thus a description of a number of similar objects. This fits your nontechnical understanding of the word *class*. Sting, Madonna, and the artist formerly known as Prince, are members of the class of rock musicians. There is no one person called "rock musician," but specific people with specific names are members of this class if they possess certain characteristics.

An object can be called an *instance* or an *instantiation* of a class because the object is a "real" example or an instance of the specifications provided by the class. This leads to a name commonly used for an object's data: *instance data*. It is called this because there is separate data for each object; that is, for each instance of the class.

Inheritance

The idea of classes leads to the idea of *inheritance*. In our daily lives, we use the concept of classes being divided into subclasses. You know that the class of animals is divided into mammals, amphibians, insects, birds, and so on. The class of vehicles is divided into cars, trucks, buses, and motorcycles.

The principle in this sort of division is that each subclass shares common characteristics with the class from which it's derived. Cars, trucks, buses, and motorcycles all have wheels and a motor and are used to transport people or goods; these are the defining characteristics of vehicles. In addition

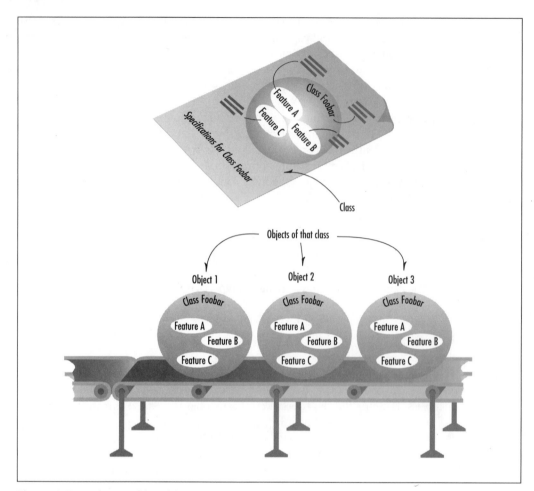

Figure 1-5 A class and its objects

to the characteristics shared with other members of the class, each subclass also has its own particular characteristics: Buses, for instance, have seats for many people, whereas trucks have space for hauling heavy loads.

This idea is shown in Figure 1-6. Notice in the figure that features A and B, which are part of the base class, are common to all the derived classes, but that each derived class also has features of its own.

In a similar way, an OOP class can be used as the basis for one or more different subclasses. In C++, the original class is called the *base class*; other classes can be defined that share its characteristics, but add their own as well. These are called *derived classes*.

Inheritance is somewhat analogous to using functions to simplify a traditional procedural program. If you find that three different sections of a procedural program do almost exactly the same thing, you can recognize an opportunity to extract the common elements of these three sections and put them into a single function. The three sections of the program can call the function to execute the common actions and they can perform their own individual processing as well. Similarly, a base class contains elements common to a group of derived classes. As functions do in a procedural program, inheritance shortens an object-oriented program and clarifies the relationship among program elements.

Reusability

Once a class has been written, created, and debugged, it can be distributed to other programmers for use in their own programs. This is called *reusability*. It is similar to the way a library of functions in a procedural language can be incorporated into different programs.

However, in OOP, the concept of inheritance provides an important extension to the idea of reusability. A programmer can take an existing class and, without modifying it, add features and capabilities to it. This is done by deriving a new class from the existing one. The new class will inherit all the capabilities of the old one, but may also include new features of its own.

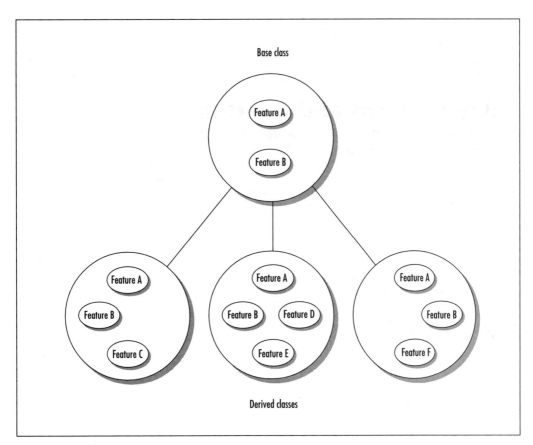

Figure 1-6 Inheritance

For example, you might have written (or purchased from someone else) a class that creates a menu system, such as that used in the Turbo C++ Integrated Development System (IDE). This class works fine and you don't want to change it, but you want to add the capability to make some menu entries flash on and off. To do this, simply create a new class that inherits all the capabilities of the existing one but adds flashing menu entries.

The ease with which existing software can be reused is a major benefit—possibly *the* major benefit—of OOP. Many companies find that reusing classes on a second project provides a major return on their original investment. I'll have more to say about this as I go along.

Creating New Data Types

One of the benefits of objects is that they give the programmer a convenient way to construct new data types. Suppose you work with two-dimensional positions (such as x and y coordinates or latitude and longitude) in your program. You would like to express operations on these positional values with normal arithmetic operations, such as

```
position1 = position2 + origin;
```

where the variables `position1`, `position2`, and `origin` each represent a *pair* of independent numerical quantities. By creating a class that incorporates these two values and declaring `position1`, `position2`, and `origin` to be objects of this class, you can, in effect, create a new data type. Many features of C++ are intended to facilitate the creation of new data types in this manner.

Polymorphism and Overloading

Note that the = (equal) and + (plus) operators, used in the position arithmetic shown above, don't act the same way they do in operations on built-in types such as `int`. The objects `position1` and so on are not predefined in C++, but are programmer-defined objects of class `Position`. How do the = and + operators know how to operate on objects? We must define new operations for these operators. These operators will be member functions of the `Position` class.

Using operators or functions in different ways, depending on what they are operating on, is called *polymorphism* (one thing with several distinct forms). When an existing operator, such as + or =, is given the capability to operate on additional data types, it is said to be *overloaded*. Functions are overloaded when multiple functions have the same name but different arguments. Overloading can make programs easier to write and to understand. It's a kind of polymorphism; it is also an important feature of OOP.

C++ and C

Although this book assumes no knowledge of the C language, you may be curious about how C and C++ are related. C++ is derived from the C language. Strictly speaking, it is a superset of C: Almost every correct statement in C is also a correct statement in C++, although the reverse is not true. The most important elements added to C to create C++ are concerned with classes, objects, and object-oriented programming. (C++ was originally called "C with classes.") However, C++ has many other features as well, including an improved approach to I/O and a new way to write comments. Figure 1-7 shows the relationship between C and C++.

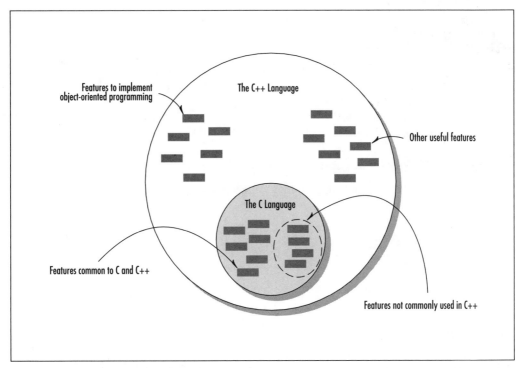

Figure 1-7 The relationship between C and C++

In fact, the practical differences between C and C++ are larger than you might think. You *can* write a program in C++ that looks like a program in C, but doing so misses the whole point of object-oriented programming.

If you already know C, you will have a head start in learning C++ (although you may also have some habits to unlearn), but much of the material will be new.

OOP in a Nutshell

In summary, OOP is a way of organizing programs. Object orientation has to do with how programs are designed, not the details of individual program statements. In particular, OOP programs are organized around objects, which contain both data and functions. These functions, which act on the data, are called member functions. A class is the specification for a number of similar objects.

C++ is a superset of C. It adds to the C language the capability to implement OOP. It also adds a variety of other features. In addition, the emphasis is changed in C++ so that some features common to C, although still available in C++, are seldom used, whereas others are used far more frequently. The result is a surprisingly different language.

The general concepts discussed in this chapter will become more concrete as you learn more about the details of C++. You may want to refer back to this chapter as you progress further into this book.

1. When you design a program for an object-oriented language, you look first for _____ in real life that will correspond to _____ in the program.
   a. organizations, data types
   b. information, data
   c. things, objects
   d. actions, functions
   e. categories, classes

2. A widget is to the blueprint for a widget as an object is to
   a. a member function.
   b. a class.
   c. an operator.
   d. a data item.
   e. a program.

3. Inheritance allows you to start with _____ and derive _____ from it, which will share common characteristics with it.
   a. a class, objects
   b. an object, classes
   c. a member function, other member functions
   d. an object, other objects
   e. a class, other classes

4. Which of the following would probably make reasonable objects in an OOP program?
   a. The 4:30 flight to Dallas.
   b. The alphabet.
   c. A document.
   d. Happiness.
   e. Bill Jones.

5. Overloading an operator in C++ involves
   a. giving an operator different meanings depending on the context.
   b. writing new member functions.
   c. allowing an operator to work on a different data type.
   d. causing the operator to carry out several operations at once.
   e. making the operator carry out an operation on user-defined objects.

SESSION 3

HOT DOG STANDS AS OBJECTS

There's no better way to get a feel for what objects and classes are all about than to look at actual examples. For the next few sessions, you'll look in detail at a particular class of objects. This class models a hot dog stand. This is the kind of hot dog stand that one sees on street corners or at ball games. It has only one item for sale: hot dogs. (I'm not talking here about some kind of effete gourmet deli.) Figure 1-8 shows such a stand.

Actually, an object in this program is not going to model an *entire* hot dog stand. It will model only the data necessary to run the stand. These objects don't cook the hot dogs or make change. Their job is to keep track of an important aspect of the stand's operation: how many hot dogs and buns are on hand at the stand. It would be more accurate to say that an object will model the hot dog stand's *inventory*.

Let's say an entrepreneur named Sally owns six hot dog stands, located in different parts of town. She has hired someone to operate each stand while she remains at the central office with her computer.

Figure 1-8   Hot dog stand

Each stand has a telephone, so she can stay in touch with the operators. The stands are numbered from 1 to 6. Sally has hired you to write a program that she can use to keep track of the supplies on hand at each stand.

At the beginning of the day, each stand's operator calls Sally and tells her the number of buns and hot dogs on hand. Also, each time a hot dog is sold, the operator calls to inform her of this fact. (This may not sound too realistic but remember, these are not high-volume locations.) With this input and the output of the hot dog stand program, Sally can keep track of how many buns and hot dogs remain in each stand. This information enables her to call the supplier to order more hot dogs and buns at appropriate times.

Interaction with the Hot Dog Stand Program

What do you want the hot dog stand program to do? Let's say three kinds of interaction are desirable. You want Sally to be able to

    1. enter the number of hot dogs and buns on hand at the beginning of the day

    2. record each hot dog sale (which decreases the number of buns and hot dogs by 1)

    3. ask the program how many hot dogs and buns remain at any given time

Figure 1-9 shows how Sally interacts with some of her hot dog stands.

For the moment, don't worry about the part of the program that asks you which of these three options you want to choose. Instead, concentrate on designing the class of hot dog stands. I'll present the overall program in the next chapter.

Inputting the Data

Here's how the first step, inputting the data, might look as Sally interacts with the program:

```
Stand number: 3                    <--user enters stand number
Number of hot dogs on hand: 347    <--user enters quantity
Number of buns on hand: 298        <--user enters quantity
```

The program prints the prompts and Sally fills in the data, starting with the stand number.

Incidentally, you might expect the number of buns and hot dogs always to be equal because the operator always sells a bun and hot dog together, but reality doesn't always conform to logic. Some operators accidentally drop hot dogs through the grill into the fire; others burn the buns. Hot dogs are stolen by cats and go bad if there's a power failure; buns, stored in a cardboard box, are likely to be nibbled by mice. Thus, over time the number of hot dogs and the number of buns differ more and more.

Recording a Sale

When an operator calls Sally and tells her a hot dog has been sold, she simply enters the stand number:

```
Enter stand number: 3              <--user enters stand number
```

The program then subtracts one hot dog and one bun from its data.

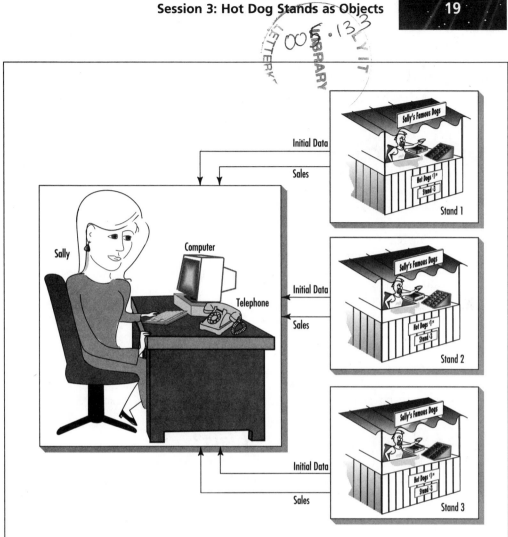

Figure 1-9   Data flow between Sally and her hot dog stands

Displaying the Data

Sally can ask the program what the situation is at any given hot dog stand.

```
Enter stand number: 2            <--user enters stand number
Hot dogs on hand = 30            <--program displays data
Buns on hand = 52
```

Here Sally enters the stand number and the program reports the buns and hot dogs remaining at that stand.

Designing the Hot Dog Stand Program

You've seen the kind of desired interaction with the hot dog stand program. How do you go about designing an object-oriented program that will allow this interaction?

What Are the Objects?

The first question an OOP programmer asks is, what are the program's objects going to be? Sometimes the answer isn't easy. However, whenever you find a number of similar items in the real world, they are candidates to be made into objects in the program.

But there are several categories of similar objects in the hot dog stand situation. There are hot dogs, there are buns, there are hot dog stands, there are operators. Which should be the objects?

The hot dogs and the buns are probably too simple. They don't do much except get sold. The hot dog stands, on the other hand, are more interesting. They contain a variable number of hot dogs, a variable number of buns, and you can imagine asking them how many buns and hot dogs they have on hand and telling them you've made a sale. The operators aren't really connected with the inventory of buns and hot dogs; if Sally fires Joe and hires Alphonse, that doesn't affect the inventory. (But if you were writing a program that dealt with employees, the operators would be an obvious candidate for objects.)

In more complex situations, you sometimes need to experiment a bit in choosing what entities to make into objects. You may guess wrong the first time and find your initial program too awkward. However, with experience you will become increasingly able to select appropriate objects on the first try.

What's in a Hot Dog Stand Object?

What kinds of things should go in each hot dog stand object? You can deduce that its data should include the number of buns and the number of hot dogs on hand:

 Hot dogs on hand

 Buns on hand

These two *kinds* of data will be the same for each object. That is, every stand must store the number of buns and the number of hot dogs. Of course the actual *quantities* of these items will vary from stand to stand. Stand 1 has 101 hot dogs and stand 2 has 30, but they both must have a variable that stores this quantity, whatever it is.

To interact with the stand, you need some member functions as well. Member functions will interact with the data in specific ways. Looking at the kinds of interaction you want with the program, you see that you need functions to

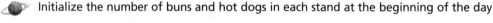 Initialize the number of buns and hot dogs in each stand at the beginning of the day

 Tell the stand that a sale has been made

 Ask the stand for the number of buns and hot dogs remaining

The two data items and the three member functions will be the same for each object.

Specifying the Class of Hot Dog Stand Objects

When many objects in a program are the same, it doesn't make sense to describe each one separately. It's more efficient to develop a single specification for *all* such objects. You could call this specification a *plan* or a *blueprint*. Once you've designed the specification, you can use it to create however many objects you actually need.

In OOP, this specification for creating objects is called a *class*. Let's see how such a class specification would look in C++. Create a `HotDogStand` class that can be used to make `HotDogStand` objects. Many aspects of this specification won't be clear yet, but you should see that it embodies two data items and three member functions. I'll get to the details soon.

```
class HotDogStand          <-- a class called HotDogStand
   {                       <-- beginning of class specification
   private:
      int HotDogsOnHand;   <-- instance data
      int BunsOnHand;
   public:
      void initData()      <-- member function to set data
         {
                           <-- (function body will go here)
         }
      void SoldOneDog()    <-- member function to adjust data
         {
                           <-- (function body will go here)
         }
      void displayData()   <-- member function to display data
         {
                           <-- (function body will go here)
         }
   };                      <-- end of class specification
```

This class specification is divided into two parts, with data in one part and functions in the other. This is a common approach, although you can mix up the data and functions if you want.

This class specification embodies many of the essential elements of C++ syntax. Besides the class specification itself, there are also variable declarations and member functions. Let's examine these program elements.

Syntax of the Class Specification

The class specification consists of the keyword `class`, the name of the class (here it's `HotDogStand`), an opening brace, a closing brace, and a semicolon:

```
class HotDogStand      <-- keyword "class" and class name
   {                   <-- opening brace
                       <-- other program lines go here
   };                  <-- closing brace and semicolon
```

The braces (sometimes called *curly brackets*) are *delimiters*. They enclose the body of the class specification so you (and your C++ compiler) can see where it begins and ends. They serve the same purpose as the `BEGIN` and `END` keywords in Pascal and BASIC. Paired braces are the standard delimiters in C++ and you'll encounter them in many other situations as well.

Notice how the opening brace is aligned vertically over the closing brace. This makes it easier to tell which brace goes where when you read a listing.

The semicolon ends the entire specification. Semicolons are used to end program statements, data declarations, and class specifications (but not functions). In the case of classes, *both* a closing brace and a semicolon are necessary.

Remember that the class specification does not create any hot dog stand objects; it merely specifies how they will look when (and if) they are created. You'll see later how to create the objects themselves.

Variable Declarations

Two variables, `HotDogsOnHand` and `BunsOnHand`, are declared and specified to be integers (type `int`). This is one of several basic data types available in C++. I'll discuss data types in detail in the next session.

```
int HotDogsOnHand;
int BunsOnHand;
```

Notice that these declarations don't give values (such as 47) to these variables, they merely give them names and specify that they will require a certain space in memory (although memory space is not actually set aside until an object is created).

Functions

There are three functions in the class specification: `initData()`, `SoldOneDog()`, and `displayData()`. Tell the C++ compiler that these names apply to functions (and not variables or something else) by appending parentheses to the name:

```
void initData()        <--parentheses designate a function
   {

   }
```

The keyword preceding the function name indicates the type of data returned by the function. None of the hot dog stand functions returns a value, so the `void` keyword is used. Later you'll see that functions may return a value of any data type. If a function returns an `int`, for example, you can write

```
int someFunc()
   {
   }
```

You could also add *parameters* to the function by placing values or variable names within the parentheses. Arguments convey values to the function, like this:

```
void anotherFunc(float temperature, float humidity)
   {
   }
```

However, I'll postpone a discussion of return types and parameters until later.

As with the class specification itself, the body of the function is delimited with braces:

```
void initData()    <-- function named initData with no return type, no arguments
   {               <-- start of function body
                   <-- other statements would go here
```

```
}              <-- end of function body (NO semicolon)
```

For simplicity, I haven't inserted any statements into the function bodies. You'll need to learn a little more before we're ready for that.

Remember that whereas a class specification is terminated by a semicolon, a function is not.

Public and Private

The idea behind public and private is to allow some parts of an object to be accessed by program statements outside the object while other parts can be accessed only from within the object itself, as shown in Figure 1-10.

The `public` and `private` keywords, followed by colons, are used to designate these parts. Here all the data is private and all the member functions are public. This is the usual situation: You want to hide the data from the outside world so it is protected from accidental alteration. However, you

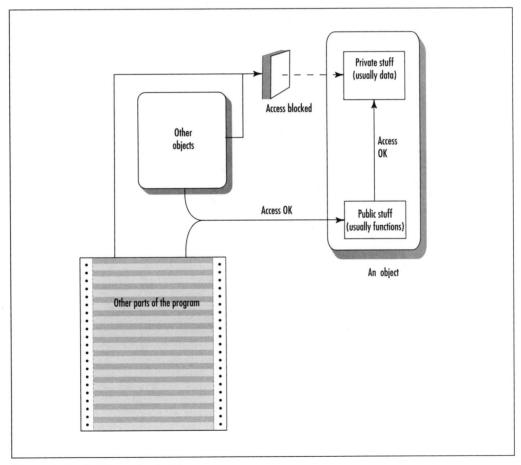

Figure 1-10 Public and private access

want the member functions to be public so other parts of the program can call them to tell the object to do something. To work with the data, don't access it directly; instead, ask a member function to access it for you.

1. An object in our hot dog stand program will correspond to what entity in the real world?
    a. An entire hot dog stand, including the operator.
    b. All relevant data for all the hot dog stands.
    c. The inventory data for a particular hot dog stand.
    d. The physical hot dogs and buns at a particular stand.
    e. A hot dog.

2. What items will be part of a **HotDogStand** object?
    a. A function to initialize the number of hot dogs and buns to zero.
    b. The number of buns.
    c. The number of hot dogs.
    d. A function to increment the number of buns and hot dogs.
    e. A function to display the number of hot dogs and buns on hand.

3. Data is often private and member functions are often public because
    a. data is not accessed as often as functions.
    b. an object's data should be hidden for safety but its member functions should be accessible so the rest of the program can interact with the object.
    c. data must be accessed only by objects of the same class, whereas member functions can be accessed by any object.
    d. data must not be changed, whereas member functions may be.
    e. data takes up less memory space than member functions do.

4. An object's member functions usually operate on
    a. data within the functions themselves.
    b. global data.
    c. data in another specified object.
    d. data in that object.
    e. data in any object of the same class.

5. Which item is *not* always part of a class specification?
    a. Braces.
    b. A semicolon.
    c. The keyword **class**.
    d. A class name.
    e. The definition of an object.

BASIC C++ DATA TYPES

As you've seen, objects are composed of two major elements: instance data and member functions. In this lesson, I'll talk about data. More specifically, I'll show the basic data types that are built into C++. Then I'll show member functions in more detail.

As you'll see later, you can use C++ to define any data type you want, but the built-in types save you from going to this trouble in most common situations.

There are seven basic types built into C++. Of these basic types, one represents characters, three represent whole numbers (integers), and three represent real (floating-point) numbers. Table 1-1 summarizes the C++ data types.

Type Name	Used to Store	Examples of Values Stored
char	Characters	'a', 'B', '$', '3', '?'
short	Small whole numbers	7, 30,000, -222
int	Normal-sized whole numbers (same as short or same as long)	
long	Large whole numbers	1,000,000,000, -123,456,789
float	Small real numbers	3.7, 199.99, -16.2, 0.000125
double	Large real numbers	7,553.393.95,47, -0.048512934
long double	Extra-large real numbers	9,123,456,789,012,345.666

Table 1-1   C++ data types

Characters

Let's look at each of these data types in turn. Characters are stored in variables of type char. The statement

```
char ch3;
```

creates space in memory for a character and names it ch3. To store a particular character in this variable, use a statement like

```
ch3 = 'a';
```

Character constants, such as 'a', 'B', '&' or '4', are surrounded by single quotes.

Assignment Operator

The equal sign (=) causes the value on its right to be assigned to (placed in) the variable on its left; that is, following this statement, the variable ch3 will have the value 'a'. The equal sign is called the *assignment operator* because it assigns the value on the right to the variable on the left.

All characters are actually stored as numbers (which, as you know, is all a computer understands). The *ASCII code* is used to translate characters into numbers. Thus '**A**' is 65, '**B**' is 66, and so on. The ASCII code is shown in Appendix E.

Escape Sequences

Various special characters are represented by letters preceded by a backslash. This is called an *escape sequence* because the backslash causes the interpretation of the next character to "escape" from the normal ASCII code and indicate something different. Table 1-2 shows the most common escape sequences.

Escape Sequence	Character Represented
'\n'	New line. Causes the cursor to move to the start of the next line. (Same as a carriage return plus a line feed.)
'\t'	Tab character.
'\b'	Backspace.
'\r'	Carriage return. Causes the cursor to move to the start of this line. Also generated by the [ENTER] key.

Table 1-2   *Common escape sequences*

Variables of type char are occasionally used to store whole numbers rather than characters. You can say

```
ch3 = 44;
```

However, the range of numerical values that can be stored in type char is from -128 to 127, so this works only for very small numbers. Whole numbers are usually stored in variables of type int, which is faster for the computer to process than type char.

A variable of type char occupies 1 byte, or 8 bits, of memory.

Integers

Integers represent whole numbers, that is, values that can be counted, such as the number of people living in Thomasville (12,348) or lines of text on a page (33). Integers cannot represent numbers with decimal points or fractional parts, such as 2.3 or 4/7. Integers can be negative: -7, -413.

There are three integer types in C++: short, int, and long. They are similar but occupy different amounts of memory and can handle numbers in different numerical ranges, as Table 1-3 shows. I also include type char in this table, even though it is mostly used for characters, because it can be used to store small whole numbers as well.

Type Name	Size	Range
char	1 byte (8 bits)	-128 to 127
short	2 bytes (16 bits)	-32,768 to 32,767

Type Name	Size	Range
int	Same as `short` on 16-bit systems, same as `long` on 32-bit systems	
long	4 bytes (32 bits)	-2,147,483,648 to 2,147,483,647

Table 1-3   *Integer types in C++*

Type `short` always occupies 2 bytes. It can store numbers in the range of -32,768 to 32,767. Type `long` always occupies 4 bytes and can store numbers in the range of -2,147,483,648 to 2,147,483,647.

In 16-bit systems, type `int` occupies 2 bytes, the same as `short`. In 32-bit systems, it occupies 4 bytes, the same as `long`, and can therefore handle a larger range of values. Older operating systems, such as DOS and Windows 3.1, are 16-bit systems. Newer systems, such as Windows 95, OS/2, and Windows NT, are 32-bit systems. Unix has always been a 32-bit system.

The `int` type is the most commonly used integer type and operates the most efficiently whatever system you use. However, if you want to guarantee a 2-byte variable even in a 32-bit system (to save space), you must use `short`; if you want to guarantee a 4-byte variable on a 16-bit system (to hold large values), you must use `long`.

Here's an example of defining some integer variables and giving them values:

```
int MilesDriven;        <-- declare variables
long population;

MilesDriven = 1024;     <-- give the values
population = 1405836L;
```

The L is used to designate a type `long` constant, one that won't fit in an integer (in a 16-bit system).

Unsigned Integers

All the integer types have *unsigned* versions. Unsigned variables can't hold negative numbers, but their range of positive values is twice as large as that of their signed brothers. Table 1-4 shows how this looks.

Type Name	Size	Range
unsigned char	1 byte (8 bits)	0 to 255
unsigned short	2 bytes (16 bits)	0 to 65,535
unsigned int or unsigned	Same as `unsigned short` on 16-bit systems	
	Same as `unsigned long` on 32-bit systems	
unsigned long	4 bytes (32 bits)	0 to 4,294,967,295

Table 1-4   *Unsigned integers*

Ordinary integers, without the `unsigned` designation, are signed by default. You can use the keyword `signed`, but it's not necessary.

Floating Point

Floating-point numbers are used to represent values that can be measured, such as the length of a room (which might be 5.32 meters) or the weight of a rock (124.65 pounds). Floating-point values are normally expressed with a whole number to the left of a decimal point and a fraction to the right.

Instead of a decimal point, you can use *exponential notation* for floating-point numbers. Thus, 124.65 in normal notation is 1.2465e2 in exponential notation, where the number following the e indicates the number of digits the decimal point must be moved to the right to restore the number to normal notation. Exponential notation is commonly used to display numbers that are inconveniently long in decimal notation. Thus, 9,876,000,000,000,000,000 in normal notation is 9.876e18 in exponential notation.

There are three kinds of floating-point numbers in popular operating systems, as shown in Table 1-5. (Some systems don't have `long double`.)

Type Name	Size	Range	Precision
`float`	4 bytes (32 bits)	10e-38 to 10e38	5 digits
`double`	8 bytes (64 bits)	10e-308 to 10e308	15 digits
`long double`	10 bytes (80 bits)	10e-4932 to 10e4932	19 digits

Table 1-5 *Floating-point numbers*

The most common floating-point type is probably type `double`, which is used for most C++ mathematical library functions. Type `float` requires less memory than `double` and may speed up your calculations. Type `long double` is used in the floating-point processor in Intel microprocessors and is useful for *very* large numbers.

Here's an example of defining and using variables of the various floating-point types:

```
float pi_float;
double pi_double;
long double pi_long_double;

pi_float = 3.1415;
pi_double = 3.14159265358979;
pi_long_double = 3.141592653589793238;
```

Here I've assigned constants representing the mathematical constant pi to variables of the three types, using as many digits of precision as each type will allow.

Figure 1-11 shows the amounts of memory required for all the data types except `long double`. You can initialize variables to specific values when they are first declared. Thus the six statements above could be condensed into

```
float pi_float = 3.1415;
double pi_double = 3.14159265358979;
long double pi_long_double = 3.141592653589793238;
```

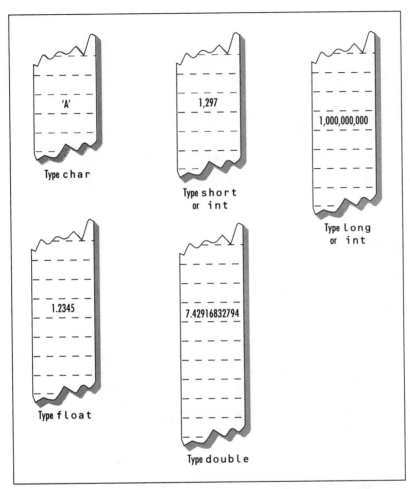

Figure 1-11 Variables of basic data types in memory initialization

Whitespace

C++ doesn't mind if you put extra spaces into a program line. You can use them to align things so they're easier to read. You could say

```
float pi_float            = 3.1415;
double pi_double          = 3.14159265358979;
long double pi_long_double = 3.1415926535897793238;
```

You can put as many spaces, tabs, and new lines as you want in your program. These characters constitute *whitespace*, and the C++ compiler ignores whitespace in almost all situations. Programmers use whitespace to make the program easier for humans to follow.

Comments

You can add comments to your program listing to help yourself—and anyone else who might need to look at your listing—understand what it does. Comments are preceded with a double slash: //.

Here's a code fragment, taken from the previous section, that uses a full-line comment and comments following each of three statements:

```
// these variables are declared and initialized at the same time
float pi_float              = 3.1415;                    //  5-digit precision
double pi_double            = 3.14159265358979;          // 15-digit precision
long double pi_long_double  = 3.141592653589793238;      // 19-digit precision
```

Any text following the // symbol until the end of the line is ignored by the compiler.

Another kind of comment allows you to write comments that span multiple lines. Here's an example:

```
/*
if you have a really long multiline
comment it is easier to
use this arrangement than to write
the double-slash symbol before
every line
*/
```

The /* symbol starts the comment and the */ ends it. The end of a line does *not* automatically end a comment that starts with /* (as it does with those starting with //), so you can write as many comment lines as you want before terminating with the */ symbol. This comment style is harder to type and requires two symbols per comment instead of one, so it is not usually used for single-line comments.

As you know, adding numerous comments to your code makes it far more comprehensible to anyone else who must understand your program. And, difficult as it may be to believe, you yourself may find comments helpful if you try to read a listing you haven't seen for some time.

1. To represent a 4-digit employee serial number, you would most likely use type
   a. unsigned int.
   b. long.
   c. char.
   d. float.
   e. double.

2. Several different integer types (and also several different floating-point types) are necessary because
   a. there is a trade-off between operating speed and memory storage space.
   b. there is a trade-off between speed and memory space, on the one hand, and the size of the numbers that can be stored, on the other.
   c. there is a trade-off between the number of significant digits that can be used and the size

of the exponent.

    d. different computer systems have different storage requirements.

    e. different computer languages have different storage requirements.

3. To represent the atomic weights of elements (e.g., iodine is 126.932) you would most likely use type

    a. `double`.

    b. `long double`.

    c. `unsigned long`.

    d. `unsigned char`.

    e. `int`.

4. The assignment operator

    a. asserts that one variable is equal to another.

    b. places the value on the right into the variable on the left.

    c. sets the constant on the right equal to the constant on the left.

    d. places the constant on the left into the variable on the right.

    e. makes an equivalence between the names of two variables.

5. The term whitespace in a source file is related to

    a. the margins of the paper.

    b. the characters `' '`, `'\t'`, `'\n'` and perhaps a few others.

    c. formatting used in a program listing to make it easier for humans to read.

    d. program statements that don't change any data.

    e. symbols that are ignored by the compiler.

Now that you know enough about C++ to write actual program statements, I'll include exercises at the end of each lesson.

EXERCISE 1

Write statements to create variables called `LetterCode`, `SalePrice`, and `Quantity` of types `char` `double`, and `long`.

EXERCISE 2

Write statements to set the three variables in Exercise 1 to `'V'`, 67.95, and 1,000,000, respectively.

MIDCHAPTER DISCUSSION

Imagine that this book is being used in a programming class and that the students get together from time to time to discuss how the course is going. The following is an example of one such discussion. I'll include two discussions per chapter: one halfway through the chapter and one at the end.

George: Oh, boy, I'm in trouble. The only thing I understood at all was about data types, because they're the same as C.

Estelle: You know C? Then this course should be a pushover for you.

George: Are you kidding? Everything but the data types was over my head. Objects? Classes? I don't have a clue.

Estelle: I know what you mean; it's not totally clear to me either. I think I have to take it on faith that all this will lead to something useful.

Don: But you get the main idea, don't you? About needing a better way to design programs because the old procedural approach just got too out of control?

Estelle: Well, I guess I understand it in theory. But I've never written such a huge program. Just what I took in my Pascal class.

Don: I was involved in a big project in C at work, and it certainly got complicated. If there's some way to make working with huge programs easier, I'm all for it.

George: Yeah, but how does this object stuff lead to anything practical? I'm not learning how to write program statements that actually do things, like adding two numbers or whatever.

Estelle: But C++ isn't a procedural language. It's based on objects, so I've got to learn to make objects before I can do anything useful.

Don: Right. In a procedural language, the programmer gives instructions to the computer to do things but in an OOP language, the programmer tells objects to do things. And you can't tell an object something if you don't have any objects.

Estelle: And to create objects you need a class to tell you what the objects will look like.

Don: But to specify the class you need to know how to declare data variables, which I just learned about, and write functions, which I bet I get to this afternoon.

George: Well, I want to display some numbers! Do some arithmetic! I want a complete program!

Estelle: Patience, George, patience.

SESSION 5

INTRODUCTION TO INPUT/OUTPUT

Before I talk about the second component of objects—member functions—let's examine one of the most important things that member functions do: performing input and output. If you can't put data into objects and get it out again, they're not going to be too useful. In this lesson, I'm going to explore some basics of performing input/output (I/O) in C++.

In this lesson, I'll show I/O statements by themselves; in the next lesson, you'll see how they look in member functions, where they would ordinarily appear.

Output to the Screen

Here's a statement that causes a line of text to be displayed on the screen:

```
cout << "This text will appear on the screen.";
```

The name `cout`, pronounced "C out," represents a C++ object that is associated with the screen display. The `<<` operator, called the *put to operator*, causes whatever is on its right to be sent to whatever is on its left. The `cout` object and the `<<` operator are part of the C++ standard stream library, so you don't need to define them yourself or even worry too much about how they work. (You will need to insert a header file into your program to declare them, as you'll see in the next chapter.) Figure 1-12 shows how `cout` works.

String Constants

The text `"This text will appear on the screen."` is called a *string constant*. A string constant is surrounded by double quotes (unlike a character constant, which is surrounded by single quotes). The entire statement, as with all C++ statements, is terminated with a semicolon.

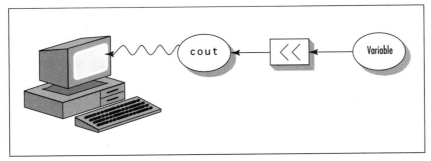

Figure 1-12 Output with `cout`

You can output numerical constants the same way. The statement

```
cout << 27;
```

causes a 27 to appear on the screen, whereas

```
cout << 123.45;
```

displays 123.45.

You can display the values of variables as well as numbers. For example, this code displays 2.7:

```
float fvar1 = 2.7;
cout << fvar1;
```

More than one value can be displayed with a single `cout` statement, using multiple put to operators:

```
float height = 2.7;
cout << "It is " << height << " meters high.";
```

This would produce the output

```
It is 2.7 meters high.
```

You can also reformat such a statement so that the put to operators line up vertically, thus making the statement easier to read:

```
cout << "It is "
     << height
     << " meters high.";
```

Or you could use three separate `cout` statements to produce the same output.

Formatting Output

It's nice to have some control over the way output is formatted. In C++ stream I/O, a variety of techniques are available for this purpose. I'll show two examples here.

New Lines Not Automatic

Some languages, such as BASIC, automatically move to a new line at the end of every output statement, but C++ does not. Nor are different variables in the same statement placed on separate lines. New lines are not created automatically by the `cout` object or the put to operator. For example, the statements

```
cout << 6.25;
cout << 30.9 << 2.5;
```

produce the output

```
6.2530.92.5
```

where all the output is run together. This is probably not what you want.

Escape Sequences

One of the easiest ways to format data is to insert a character called an *escape sequence* into a string constant. For example, you can use the `'\n'` escape sequence to start a new line:

```
cout << "\nNow I'll ask you some questions about yourself.";
cout << "\nFirst, enter your age: ";
```

produces the display

```
Now I'll ask you some questions about yourself.
First, enter your age:
```

The `'\n'` before `"First"` causes the second string constant to be displayed on a separate line from the first. (The `'\n'` before `"Now"` ensures that the first line begins on a new line as well, even if something else has already been printed by a preceding statement.)

You can use the escape sequence `'\t'` to generate tab characters. The code

```
cout << "\nJoe\tFred\tSally";
cout << "\nGeorge\tBud\tSandy";
```

lines up the names in columns.

```
Joe     Fred    Sally
George  Bud     Sandy
```

The endl *Manipulator*

There's another approach to starting new lines in C++. An object called a *manipulator* can be inserted into an output stream, just like a data item. Manipulators can be used to format output, among other purposes. Probably the most common manipulator is `endl` (a contraction of "end line"). Inserted into a `cout` statement, `endl` causes the cursor to move to the start of the next line, just as `'\n'` does. (Also, `endl` flushes any output that may be waiting in the output buffer to the display.)

Earlier, I showed two lines that used the `'\n'` escape sequence to start text on a new line. Here's how to achieve the same result using `endl`:

```
cout << endl;
cout << "Now I'll ask you some questions about yourself." << endl;
cout << "First, enter your age: ";
```

The first statement ensures you start on a new line and the `endl` at the end of the second statement causes the text beginning with `"First"` to start on a new line.

Input from the Keyboard

Here's how to input a number, entered by the user from the keyboard, and store it in a variable intvar:

```
int intvar;
cin >> intvar;
```

The `cin` object (for "C in") represents the keyboard, and the *get from* operator (`>>`) takes whatever is on the left and puts it in the variable on the right. When this statement is executed, the program waits for the user to type a number and press ENTER. Figure 1-13 shows how this looks.

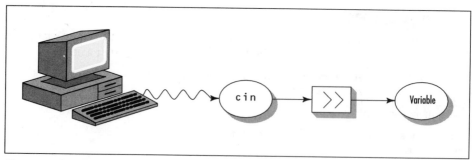

Figure 1-13 Input with cin

Usually, of course, you want to prompt the user before waiting for input:

```
int age;
cout << "Enter your age: ";
cin >> age;
```

This produces the following interaction:

```
Enter your age: 34
```

where the user enters the 34.

You can use the get from operator multiple times in the same statement:

```
int age;
float height;
cout << "Enter your age and height: ";
cin >> age >> height;
```

Here the user presses ENTER, SPACE, or TAB after each value before entering the next one. However, it's usually better to prompt the user for only one value at a time, to avoid any possibility of confusion.

Stream I/O

The techniques for input and output I've shown here are called *stream I/O*. A stream is a general term for a *flow of data*. As you'll see when you write a complete program, to use stream I/O, you need to include a file of declarations in your program. This file, IOSTREAM.H, is called a *header* or *include file*.

There is much more to be said about stream I/O in C++. I'll return to this topic in Chapter 10.

Old-Style C I/O

If you are a C programmer, you are familiar with a completely different style of input and output using `printf()`, `scanf()`, and similar library functions (declared in STDIO.H). You can use these functions in C++ as well, but the preferred approach is to use stream I/O. Why? First, it's easier to avoid mistakes. Have you ever used the wrong format specifier in `printf()` (e.g., `%d` instead of `%f`), so that data is displayed incorrectly? It's easy to do, and in `scanf()`, the wrong specifier can crash your program as well. Second, the stream I/O approach lets you use `cout` and `cin` with classes you write yourself. This allows you to perform I/O on any programming object the same way it's performed on basic data types. This is a very powerful technique, which is unavailable with standard C I/O. Some old-time C programmers can't get the hang of stream I/O and persist in using standard I/O, but they are missing out on some powerful and important features of C++.

QUIZ 5

1. Which of the following are true?
   a. `>>` means "get in."
   b. `<<` means "get out."
   c. `cfile` transfers data to files.
   d. `cout` represents the screen.
   e. `cout` represents the keyboard.

2. Which of the following will display "Nancy is 27" on the screen (assuming the variables have appropriate values)?
   a. `cin >> "Nancy is " >> 27;`
   b. `cin >> "Nancy is "`
      `cin >> age;`
   c. `cout << "Nancy is "; cout << age;`
   d. `cout << "Nancy is " << 27;`
   e. `cout >> "Nancy is ";`
      `cout >> age;`

3. The statement `cin >> name >> age >> height;` will
   a. potentially confuse the user.
   b. display name, age, and height.
   c. probably accept input of different types.
   d. require the user to separate constants with spaces or similar characters.
   e. display prompts.

4. Which statement or statements will create the display

   ```
   1    2
   3    4
   ```

   a. `cout << "1\t2\n3\t4\n";`
   b. `cout <<'1'<<'\t'<<'2'<<'\n'<<'3'<<'\t'<<'4'<<'\n';`
   c. `cout << "1\n2\t3\n4\t";`
   d. `cout <<1<<'\t'<<2<<'\n'<<3<<'\t'<<4<<'\n';`
   e. `cout << '1' << '\n' << '2' '\t'; cout << '3' '\n' '4' '\t';`

5. In a comparison of C++ I/O (stream I/O) and old-fashioned C I/O (standard I/O), which of the following is true?
   a. Stream I/O is faster.
   b. You can modify almost any object to use stream I/O but not standard I/O.

c. All objects know how to display themselves automatically in stream I/O.
d. Standard I/O is more intuitive.
e. Standard I/O allows you to avoid format specifiers.

EXERCISE 1

Thinking about the hot dog program, write a program fragment that displays the number of hot dogs and buns on hand. The output might look like this:

```
Hot dogs on hand = 125
Buns on hand = 133
```

EXERCISE 2

Write a program fragment that asks the user for the initial values of hot dogs and buns on hand, gets responses from the user, and then sets appropriately named variables to these values.

EXERCISE 3

Write a program fragment that does the following:

- Creates two variables, `num` and `denom`, that represent the numerator (top) and denominator (bottom) of a fraction.

- Asks the user to supply values for the numerator and denominator.

- Puts the values supplied into the variables.

- Displays the fraction in the format 2/3, with a slash between the two numbers.

Some sample interaction with this program fragment might look like this:

```
Enter the numerator: 4
Enter the denominator: 7
Fraction = 4/7
```

SESSION 6
MEMBER FUNCTIONS

Earlier in this chapter, I talked about basic data types. Data is one of the two parts of objects. Now I'll discuss the second part: member functions. Typically a program calls an object's member functions to tell the object to do something. This is why calling an object's member function is also called *sending a message* to the object.

In the hot dog stand example, there are three member functions: `initData()`, `SoldOneDog()`, and `displayData()`. Earlier, for simplicity, I showed these functions with empty function bodies. Now it's time to fill in these functions and see what they can actually do.

Initializing the Data

At the start of each day, you want to initialize the number of hot dogs and buns at a stand. Use the `initData()` function for this. This requires both `cout` (for the prompts) and `cin` statements. Here's how it looks:

```
void initData()
   {
   cout << "Enter dogs on hand: ";
   cin >> HotDogsOnHand;
   cout << "Enter buns on hand: ";
   cin >> BunsOnHand;
   }
```

An example of interaction with this function would be

```
Enter dogs on hand: 30
Enter buns on hand: 52
```

where the program displays the prompts and the user enters 30 and 52.

Recording a Sale

When a hot dog is sold, the stand operator calls Sally to tell her this fact. When she receives such a call, she wants the program to decrease both the number of hot dogs and the number of buns by one. Here's a member function that does the job:

```
void SoldOneDog()
   {
   HotDogsOnHand = HotDogsOnHand - 1;   // subtract 1 from variable
   BunsOnHand = BunsOnHand - 1;         // subtract 1 from variable
   }
```

Here there's no interaction with the user, only a little arithmetic.

Figure 1-14 shows how Sally interacts with an object of class `HotDogStand`, using its member functions.

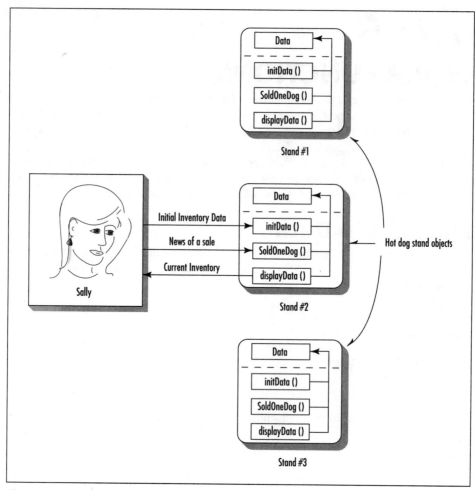

Figure 1-14   Interaction with HotDogStand object member functions

Displaying Data

Remember that a HotDogStand object records the numbers of hot dogs and buns on hand, in the variables HotDogsOnHand and BunsOnHand. You can use cout statements to display these values. The resulting displayData() function looks like this:

```
void displayData()
    {
    cout << "Hot dogs on hand = "
        << HotDogsOnHand << endl;
    cout << "Buns on hand = "
        << BunsOnHand << endl;
    }
```

The output from this function will be something like this:

```
Hot dogs on hand = 347
Buns on hand = 298
```

You've simply inserted two statements into the function. These statements make up the function body. (As you've seen, you could produce the same output with four `cout` statements or with only one.)

Arithmetic Operators

In the `SoldOneDog()` function, shown above, you used the subtraction operator (-) to subtract one from two values. C++ includes the usual four arithmetic operators plus a fifth, less common one, as shown in Table 1-6.

Operator	Purpose
+	Addition
–	Subtraction
*	Multiplication
/	Division
%	Remainder

Table 1-6 *Arithmetic operators*

The first four operators perform familiar operations. The remainder operator, `%` (also called the *modulus* operator), is used to calculate the remainder when one integer is divided by another. Thus the expression

```
20 % 3
```

evaluates to 2, because 20 divided by 3 is 6, with a remainder of 2.

You can use any of the arithmetic operators just as you would in normal arithmetic or algebra or most other programming languages. They are called *binary operators* because they operate on two quantities. That is, expressions involving them have the form `alpha+beta`, where the `+` operates on `alpha` and `beta`.

Of course, you can make arithmetic expressions as complicated as you want. For example,

```
c = (f-32) * 5 / 9;
```

converts a temperature in Celsius to one in Fahrenheit. Note that I use parentheses so the subtraction will be carried out first, despite its lower precedence. (The term *precedence* refers to the order in which operations are carried out. The `*` and `/` operators have higher precedence than the `+` and `–` operators.)

In C++, it's perfectly all right to mix different arithmetic types in the same expression. For example, in the above statements, `f` might be type `int` and `c` might be type `float`. The compiler would not complain. Instead, it would automatically convert the types appropriately before carrying out the arithmetic.

Increment and Decrement Operators

In programming, there always seems to be a need either to add 1 to something or to subtract 1 from something, just as there was in the example above. These situations are so common that C++ includes two special operators that perform the task in a much more compact form than using the normal addition and subtraction operators. The *decrement operator* subtracts 1 from a variable and the *increment operator* adds 1 to it.

Here's the `SoldOneDog()` function, rewritten to use the decrement operator:

```
void SoldOneDog()
    {
    --HotDogsOnHand;    // subtract 1 from HotDogsOnHand
    --BunsOnHand;       // subtract 1 from BunsOnHand
    }
```

The decrement operator consists of two minus signs together: `--`. If `HotDogsOnHand` were 30 and `BunsOnHand` were 52, then after executing this function, these two variables would be 29 and 51.

Similarly, the increment operator, `++`, increases the variable it's applied to by 1. The increment and decrement operators are called *unary operators* because they operate on only one variable. Their priority is higher than that of arithmetic operators, so in the expression `++x + 3`, the value of `x` will be incremented before the addition is carried out.

Now that I've defined some member functions, you may be wondering how I get them to do something; that is, how I *call* them or cause them to be executed. Be patient. You'll learn all about that in the next chapter.

1. The proper role of member functions is limited to
   a. performing stream I/O.
   b. allowing a class to alter its data.
   c. allowing a class to interact with the outside world.
   d. allowing objects to carry out any appropriate activity.
   e. performing arithmetic operations on instance data.

2. The member functions of the `HotDogStand` class can
   a. report to the user the number of buns and the number of hot dogs at a stand.
   b. calculate the profit made at each stand.
   c. record the sale of any number of hot dogs with a single function call.
   d. make change.
   e. carry out an arithmetic operation on a stand's inventory.

3. To what entities can the five basic C++ arithmetic operators be applied, assuming you don't overload these operators?
   a. objects
   b. integer variables
   c. floating-point constants

d. characters

e. classes

4. The expression `41 % 7` evaluates to

a. 7

b. 6

c. 5

d. 4

e. 1

5. If the value of `age` is 21, what statement (or statements) will change it to 23?

a. `++age;`

b. `age = ++age + 1;`

c. `age = 2 + --age;`

d. `++age; ++age;`

e. `--age; --age;`

EXERCISE 1

Start with the code fragment of Exercise 3 in Session 5, which sets values for the numerator and denominator of a fraction and displays them. Create two functions: one, `setFrac()`, to get values for *num* and *denom* from the user; the other, `showFrac()`, to display the fraction in the form 7/12.

EXERCISE 2

Imagine a class called `Employee` with two data items, `employee_number` and `employee_salary`, which record an employee's ID number and salary. Write statements to create these variables, the first type `int` and the second type `double`. Write a function, `get_emp()`, to get values for these variables from the user and another function, `put_emp()`, to display the values.

SESSION 7
SPECIFYING A CLASS

You now have all the pieces to write a complete class specification. You know how to declare variables of basic types, how to create member functions that interact with this data, and how to perform I/O so you can do something useful with these functions.

Here's a complete specification for the HotDogStand class:

```cpp
class HotDogStand
   {
   private:
      int HotDogsOnHand;          // dogs remaining
      int BunsOnHand;             // buns remaining
   public:
      void displayData()          // display data
         {
         cout << "Hot dogs on hand = "
              << HotDogsOnHand << endl;
         cout << "Buns on hand = "
              << BunsOnHand << endl;
         }
      void initData()             // get initial data from user
         {
         cout << "Enter dogs on hand: ";
         cin >> HotDogsOnHand;
         cout << "Enter buns on hand: ";
         cin >> BunsOnHand;
         }
      void SoldOneDog()           // adjust data to reflect sale
         {
         --HotDogsOnHand;
         --BunsOnHand;
         }
   };   // end of class HotDogStand
```

All I've done is to fill in the function bodies to complete the specification. However, it's easier now to see the relation between the class data and its member functions. The member functions all operate on the data, but in different ways. The displayData() function sends the values of the data (HotDogsOnHand and BunsOnHand) to cout so they will be displayed. The initData() function asks the user for values and inserts these values in to the data variables. The SoldOneDog() function decrements both data items by 1 to reflect the sale of a hot dog (with bun).

I'll devote the remainder of this lesson to the exercises, which will do more than anything to solidify your understanding of class specifications.

QUIZ 7

1. The **HotDogStand** class specification
   a. creates a number of **HotDogStand** objects.
   b. provides data and functions that will be accessed from **main()**.
   c. serves as part of an inventory program for hot dog stands.
   d. allows the creation of a number of hot dog stand objects.
   e. accomplishes nothing useful until other parts of the program are written.

2. The **SoldOneDog()** function
   a. hands the hot dog to the customer and makes change.
   b. decrements the number of buns and hot dogs.
   c. displays the number of buns and hot dogs.
   d. obtains the number of buns and hot dogs from the user.
   e. calculates the number of buns and hot dogs remaining.

3. When a member function in the **HotDogStand** class performs I/O with **cout** or **cin**, it is interacting with the user on behalf of
   a. a class.
   b. an object.
   c. a function.
   d. data.
   e. **main()**.

4. If you created a class where each object represented an aircraft, this class would likely include
   a. airport runway data.
   b. a function to change the aircraft's direction.
   c. the positions of other aircraft.
   d. the aircraft's altitude.
   e. luggage-handling capability.

5. In a traffic simulation program, it's most likely there would be a class of
   a. yellow school buses.
   b. highways.
   c. vehicles.
   d. acceleration characteristics of various vehicles.
   e. speeds.

EXERCISE 1

Rewrite the class specification for the **HotDogStand** class to include a data item for the cash on hand (you can call it **CashOnHand**), stored in dollars and cents format (e.g., 198.95). Assume the retail price of a hot dog (including the bun) is $1.95. Modify the member functions as follows:

Add statements to initData() so the user can specify the initial amount of cash on hand at the beginning of the day.

Add statements to SoldOneDog() that add the price of a hot dog from CashOnHand when a sale is made.

Add statements to displayData() that display the cash on hand along with the number of dogs and buns.

EXERCISE 2

Write a complete class specification, including member functions, for an elevator class. Each object of this class should include a data item that records the floor the elevator is currently on (e.g., from 1 at the bottom to 20 at the top). Write member functions that take the following actions:

Display the floor the elevator is on.

Move the elevator up one floor.

Move the elevator down one floor.

SESSION 8

CREATING AND INTERACTING WITH OBJECTS

You've learned how to specify a class using instance data and member functions. However, the purpose of a class specification is to serve as blueprint for creating objects. How do you actually create objects? And once you've created some, how do you interact with them so they do something useful?

Creating Objects from a Class Specification

As it turns out, you use the same syntax to create an object that you use to create a variable of a basic type such as int or float. This is no accident. In C++, objects are treated very much like variables and classes are treated very much like data types.

Here's how to create an object called stand1 of the class HotDogStand:

```
HotDogStand stand1;
```

What happens when this statement is executed? First, your program finds the specification for the HotDogStand class (which must have appeared earlier in your listing). It figures out how large such an object needs to be and sets aside enough memory to hold it. It then gives this memory space a name: `stand1`. This is exactly what it would do with a variable of a basic type. However, `stand1` is more complicated because it has several pieces of data and several member functions as well.

You can create as many objects as you need.

```
HotDogStand stand1;
HotDogStand stand2;
HotDogStand stand3;
```

Or (as with basic data types) you can also use a single statement to create multiple objects of the same type.

```
HotDogStand stand1, stand2, stand3;
```

So you see that, although writing a class specification may appear difficult or at least unfamiliar, *creating* objects based on this specification is simplicity itself.

Sending Messages to Objects

Once an object has been created, you need to interact with it. To do this, use its member functions, that is, the functions described in the class specification. You *call an object's member function*. This is the same as saying you *send a message to the object*.

A special syntax is used for this. When you send a message to an object, there are two things to consider. First, which object are you communicating with? In the case of the hot dog stands, is it `stand1`, `stand2`, or another stand? Second, what message are you sending to the object? This is the same as asking which of the object's member functions you are calling. Thus, you need a syntax with two parts: the name of the object and the name of the member function.

Here's how you would send a message to `stand1` asking it to display its data with `displayData()`:

```
stand1.displayData();
```

The object name and the function name are connected by the period symbol (.), which is called the *dot operator* or, more formally, the *class member access operator*. This rather ponderous name means that the operator allows you to access an object's member functions or data, but let's stick with the handier dot operator. Figure 1-15 shows how this looks.

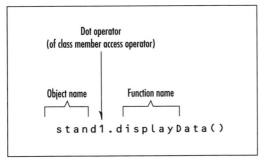

Figure 1-15 Syntax for sending a message

When this statement is executed, `stand1` will display its data

```
Hot dogs on hand = 347
Buns on hand = 298
```

(or whatever values are actually stored in its data variables). You can send the same message to a different object, for example, `stand2`.

```
stand2.displayData();
```

It will then display its data (which is probably not the same as that in `stand1`).

```
Hot dogs on hand = 74
Buns on hand = 82
```

Similarly, you could send a message to `stand3` telling it to get initial data values from the user.

```
stand3.initData();
```

When this statement is executed, `stand3` will call its `initData()` function and the following interaction with the user might take place:

```
Enter hot dogs on hand: 19
Enter buns on hand: 21
```

where the user enters the 19 and 21.

Once the `stand3` object has been given these initial values, you could call the `SoldOneDog()` function every time a hot dog is sold at this stand.

```
stand3.SoldOneDog();
```

This would cause the `HotDogsOnHand` and the `BunsOnHand` variables in `stand3` to be decremented, although nothing would appear on the screen. If you then executed

```
stand3.displayData();
```

you would see

```
Hot dogs on hand = 18
Buns on hand = 20
```

In other words, you can call member functions of specific objects to make the objects do useful work for us. This is what OOP is all about.

1. Creating an object normally involves
    a. declaring a variable.
    b. causing the compiler to designate memory space for the object.
    c. specifying what data and functions go in the object.
    d. using the object as a specification for a class.
    e. giving a name to the object.

2. Sending a message to an object normally involves
   a. modifying the object's data.
   b. calling one of the object's member functions.
   c. specifying the particular object and the message to be sent to it.
   d. using a dot (or other) operator to connect the object name and the member function name.
   e. changing the class specification.

3. If you create a class of aircraft named `acraft` and you want to tell an aircraft called `ac1` to turn right, you might say
   a. `ac1.rightTurn();.`
   b. `acraft.ac1.rightTurn();.`
   c. `rightTurn(ac1);.`
   d. `rightTurn().ac1;.`
   e. `acraft.rightTurn();.`

4. When you send a message to an object, the message content is determined by
   a. which object the message is sent to.
   b. the data in the object at the time.
   c. who sends the message.
   d. which member function you call.
   e. arguments to a member function.

5. To send a message to an object, you must always
   a. include the data to be placed in the object.
   b. name the class of the object.
   c. specify the member function you're calling.
   d. use the name of the object you are sending the message to.
   e. declare the object.

EXERCISE 1

Start with the elevator class specification of Exercise 2 in Session 7. Write statements that create an elevator object, display its position, move it up two floors, and display its new position.

EXERCISE 2

Start with the augmented `HotDogStand` class specification of Exercise 1 in Session 7. Write code that will allow the user to enter, for a particular stand, the hot dogs, buns, and cash on hand. Then tell the `HotDogStand` object to sell two hot dogs and display the same three variables.

SUMMARY: CHAPTER 1

Let's review the main points in this chapter. You've seen that the fundamental building blocks of C++ programs are objects, which are created using a class as a blueprint. Designing a program means figuring out what the objects will represent.

The two important constituents of objects are instance data and member functions. An object's data is usually made private, or inaccessible to all parts of the program except the object's own member functions. This makes it less likely the data will be corrupted by a programming error.

Once a class is specified and objects of that class are created, a program "sends messages" to the objects—that is, it calls their member functions—to cause them to carry out appropriate tasks, usually involving the object's own data.

In Chapter 2, you'll put together everything you've learned in this chapter, plus a few new details, to create a complete, working C++ program.

END-OF-CHAPTER DISCUSSION

Don: I think I'm starting to get it. Everything in the program is an object. A class specification describes how a bunch of similar objects will look. So the trick in designing a program is to figure out what the objects are going to be.

Estelle: That seems hard now, but I bet it'll get easier.

George: I think it's nuts. If I want to print a line of text, I've got to figure out what objects to use, write a specification for a class, define objects, and send one of them a message to print the text. You've got to be kidding! I can print a text with one statement in regular C code!

Don: So if all your program does is print one line, write it in C. The point is, most programs do more than that.

George: So *be* sarcastic. I'm just afraid all this OOP stuff will be so complicated it won't be worth the trouble, even for major programs.

Don: Lots of people seem to think it works fine for major programs.

Estelle: I've got a different question. I can't understand how anyone ever figured out that it would be a good idea to put data and functions together to make objects.

Don: I know, it's not exactly an obvious concept. It must have been a major inspiration.

George: More likely a lucky guess. If it works at all, which I doubt.

Estelle: It'll work. In the next chapter, we'll see a complete program.

George: It's about time!

CHAPTER 2

WRITING COMPLETE OOP PROGRAMS

o far, you've seen bits and pieces of a C++ program. In the beginning of this chapter, I'm going to put these pieces together and demonstrate a complete, working program. Then, in the next part of the chapter, I'll improve this program by using loops and decisions, the fundamental C++ control statements that allow your program to do something more than once and to do different things in different circumstances.

In the second half of this chapter, I'll introduce another complete C++ program—one that models time values. This is a completely new use for classes: modeling new data types rather than physical objects such as hot dog stands.

I'll show other improvements you can make to this program by introducing function arguments and function return values. Along the way, I'll touch on such topics as software reusability, output formatting, and creating temporary objects.

51

SESSION 1

THE COMPLETE HOT DOG STAND PROGRAM

I'll begin by showing the complete source file, or listing, for the hot dog stand program. Most of it should look familiar, but I'll also explain some important features that you haven't seen before: header files and the `main()` function.

Listing for the Hot Dog Stand Program

Listing 2-1 is the complete HOTDOG1 program.

Listing 2-1 HOTDOG1

```cpp
// hotdog1.cpp
// hot-dog stand inventory database program

#include <iostream.h>              // for cout, cin, etc.

class HotDogStand                  // class specification
     {
  private:
     int HotDogsOnHand;            // hot dogs on hand
     int BunsOnHand;               // buns on hand
  public:
     void displayData()            // display hot dogs and buns
        {
        cout << "\n    Hot dogs = " << HotDogsOnHand;
        cout << "\n    Buns = " << BunsOnHand;
        }
     void SoldOneDog()             // record sale of one dog
        {
        --HotDogsOnHand;
        --BunsOnHand;
        }
     void initData()               // set initial quantities
        {
        cout << "\n    Enter hot dogs on hand: ";
        cin >> HotDogsOnHand;
        cout << "    Enter buns on hand: ";
        cin >> BunsOnHand;
        }
     };  // end of HotDogStand class

//////////////////////////////////////////////////////////////
void main()
    {
    HotDogStand stand1;            // create hot-dog stand objects
    HotDogStand stand2;
```

```
                          // set initial data
cout << "\nInitialize data for stand 1";
stand1.initData();
cout << "\nInitialize data for stand 2";
stand2.initData();
                          // record some sales
cout << "\nSelling 2 dogs from stand1";
stand1.SoldOneDog();
stand1.SoldOneDog();
cout << "\nSelling 3 dogs from stand2";
stand2.SoldOneDog();
stand2.SoldOneDog();
stand2.SoldOneDog();
cout << endl;
                          // display current data
cout << "\nSupplies on hand, stand1";
stand1.displayData();
cout << "\nSupplies on hand, stand2";
stand2.displayData();
}
```

You've seen the specification for the HotDogStand class before. You've also seen the statements that create hot dog stand objects and that access their member functions. Let's look at two unfamiliar parts of the program.

The IOSTREAM.H Header File

To use I/O streams, you need to place in the program various class specifications from which the cin and cout objects, the << and >> operators, the endl manipulator, and so on are derived. These specifications, along with various other definitions, are stored in a file called IOSTREAM.H, which comes with your compiler. It's a text file, just like the .CPP source files you write yourself.

To insert the IOSTREAM.H file into your source file, place a line of text called a *preprocessor directive* into your code. It looks like this:

```
#include <iostream.h>
```

This directive inserts all the text from the file IOSTREAM.H into your source file (or at least the compiler treats it as if it had been inserted; actually your source file isn't altered).

Preprocessor Directives

Preprocessor directives are instructions to the *compiler*. By contrast, ordinary C++ statements, such as alpha=17; are instructions to the microprocessor, which the compiler translates into machine language that the microprocessor can understand. Preprocessor directives always start with a pound sign (#).

When the compiler encounters the #include preprocessor directive shown above, it starts to search for the file IOSTREAM.H. There is a particular subdirectory where such files are stored, usually called ...\INCLUDE\ (where the dots represent the first part of the path name, such as C:\BC5). This subdirectory is usually found in the general directory for the compiler you're using. The compiler should know where such a directory is located; if not, it may need to be told (see the appendix in this book that applies to your particular compiler). Once it finds the file, the compiler (actually a part of the compiler called the preprocessor) simply inserts its text into the source file in place of the #include directive.

If you want to see what's in IOSTREAM.H, you can go to the ...\INCLUDE\ directory and examine it with the compiler's editor or any other text editor. (Be careful not to change the file.) The contents won't make much sense at this point, but you will at least prove to yourself that IOSTREAM.H is a text file, written in normal ASCII characters.

There are other preprocessor directives besides `#include`; you'll encounter a few more as you go along.

I should note that there are two formats for specifying the file in an `#include` directive. Using the appropriate format speeds up the compiler's search for the file. In the example above, angle brackets are used to delimit the file name.

```
#include <filename.ext>
```

This causes the compiler's search for the file to start in the standard ...\INCLUDE\ directory. If quotes are used instead

```
#include "filename.ext"
```

then the search for the file will begin in the directory where the program's source files are stored. This is the format you would use if you had written the header file yourself, a situation you'll encounter in Chapter 11.

Other Header Files

There are many header files. Some are used with the C function library. For example, if you need to use mathematical functions such as `sin()` and `cos()`, you need to include a header file called MATH.H. If you're going to operate on strings, you'll need STRING.H; if you're going to perform certain kinds of data conversion, you may need to include STDLIB.H. Various specialized I/O functions may require CONIO.H or STDIO.H.

Other header files are needed for other kinds of class specifications. For example, your compiler may be bundled with a container class library. *Container* is a general name for a data structure, such as an array, a stack, a queue, or a linked list. The container class library contains classes that model these data structures, but if you want to use one, you'll need to include a header file specific to the particular container, such as ARRAYS.H, STACKS.H, or QUEUES.H.

Don't worry if there seems to be an endless number of header files. All you really need to know about header files at this point is that they are an important part of C++ programs and you'll need to include IOSTREAM.H to run any program that does stream I/O.

The `main()` Function

Everything must have a beginning, and your program begins executing in a function called `main()`. This is not a member function of a class; it's a special standalone function to which control is transferred from the operating system. The first statement in `main()`, whatever it may be, is the first statement in your program to be executed.

Here's how `main()` looks when it has no statements installed in it:

```
void main()
    {
    }
```

Every program must contain a `main()` function. If it doesn't, you'll get error messages from the linker when you try to compile and link your program.

Above I show `main()` with a return type of `void`. You can also use a return type of `int`. When you do, the value returned is a code, which is usually used to indicate whether the program ran successfully. (This is useful for batch files.) The example programs in this book don't return a code, so the return type of `main()` will always be void. You don't need to worry about return types now anyway.

The `main()` function can also take arguments, which are used when a program is called from the command line and has extra text, such as a file name, typed after the program name. However, I'll ignore this possibility as well.

Interaction with the Hot Dog Stand Program

Here's some typical interaction with this version of the hot dog stand program:

```
Initialize data for stand 1        <--Interaction with initData()
   Enter hot dogs on hand: 103     <--(User enters numbers)
   Enter buns on hand: 107
Initialize data for stand 2
   Enter hot dogs on hand: 223
   Enter buns on hand: 227

Selling two dogs from stand 1      <--Interaction with SoldOneDog()
Selling three dogs from stand 2

Supplies on hand, stand 1          <--Interaction with displayData()
   Hot dogs = 101                  <--(Program displays numbers)
   Buns = 105
Supplies on hand, stand 2
   Hot dogs = 220
   Buns = 224
```

As you've seen, the user enters the initial amounts by calling the `initData()` function for each object. The program then somewhat arbitrarily sells two dogs from stand 1 and three dogs from stand 2, and displays the resulting supplies on hand.

Of course, this kind of interaction isn't really very useful, because the program always causes the exact same number of hot dogs to be sold. A more practical program would allow the user to enter a sale for any hot dog stand at any time, and print out supplies on hand for a particular stand when requested. You'll see how to achieve this after you learn about loops and decisions later in this chapter.

Program Organization

Here's how your source file is usually arranged. Preprocessor directives such as `#include` come first, followed by class specifications, followed by `main()`. The `main()` function contains statements that define objects and send messages to them. Figure 2-1 shows what this looks like.

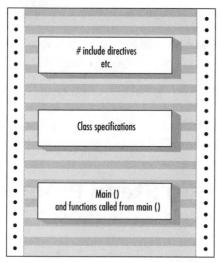

Figure 2-1   Source file organization

In larger programs, things may be a bit more complicated. There will probably be many files. Some will contain class specifications, whereas others will hold the code that uses these classes. Nevertheless, the simple arrangement I use here reveals the essentials of OOP.

1. Preprocessor directives
    a. tell the compiler to do something before translating the source file into machine code.
    b. give the compiler instructions that will be translated into machine code.
    c. are executed just before the program executes.
    d. are executed just before the program is compiled.
    e. are executed just before the program is linked.

2. Which of the following will most efficiently include the file CONIO.H, located in the compiler system's ...\INCLUDE\ directory, into your source file?
    a. `#include "conio.h"`
    b. `#include "..\include\conio.h"`
    c. `#include <conio.h>`
    d. `#include <..\include\conio.h>;`
    e. `#include "conio";`

3. The `main()` function
    a. must contain any class specifications.
    b. is a member function of all classes.
    c. may return `void` or `int`.
    d. is the first function to be executed when a program is executed.

e. may contain statements that create objects.

4. In HOTDOG1, the user can't interactively signal the program every time a hot dog is sold because
   a. such interaction is impossible in an object-oriented language.
   b. there is no member function to handle this activity.
   c. you haven't learned yet how to write loops and decisions in C++.
   d. the `main()` function does not include code to handle this activity.
   e. there are no I/O statements in the program.

5. The general scheme of program organization you've seen so far is that
   a. a class is specified outside of `main()` and objects of that class are created in `main()`.
   b. objects are defined outside of `main()` and told what to do within `main()`.
   c. all parts of the program are within `main()`.
   d. objects are told what to do inside of `main()`.
   e. classes tell objects what to do and when to do it.

EXERCISE 1

Write a complete C++ program based on the `elevator` class specification and instructions of Exercise 1 in Chapter 1, Session 8, which encouraged you to display the elevator's position, move it up two floors, and display its position again. Run this program. Its output should look like this:

```
Elevator location: floor 1
Elevator location: floor 3
```

EXERCISE 2

Start with Exercise 2 in Chapter 1, Session 8. This augmented hot dog stand class (`hotdogstand2`) included a cash-on-hand data item in addition to the number of hot dogs and buns. Create a complete program, with functionality similar to HOTDOG1, that uses the capabilities of this class. Create two hot dog stand objects from the `hotdogstand2` class. Interaction with the program should look something like this:

```
Initialize data for stand 1
   Enter hot dogs on hand: 103
   Enter buns on hand: 107
   Enter cash on hand: 100.00
Initialize data for stand 2
   Enter hot dogs on hand: 223
   Enter buns on hand: 227
   Enter cash on hand: 200.00

Selling two dogs from stand 1
Selling three dogs from stand 2
```

continued on next page

continued from previous page

```
Supplies on hand, stand 1
   Hot dogs = 101
   Buns = 105
   Cash = 96.10
Supplies on hand, stand 2
   Hot dogs = 220
   Buns = 224
   Cash = 194.15
```

SESSION 2

LOOPS

You can't write interesting programs without loops. A loopless program does something once, then exits. A program with a loop, on the other hand, can do something as many times as necessary. Now I'm going to introduce the three kinds of loops available in C++. If you already know C, you can probably skip this lesson, because loops are the same in C and in C++.

To determine how many times to cycle around a loop, all C++ loops check whether an expression is true or false. This tells them whether to cycle one more time or to exit the loop immediately. Thus, to understand loops you must first examine what makes an expression true or false, and how to construct such true/false expressions. Then you can examine specific kinds of loops: the `while` loop, the `do` loop, and the `for` loop.

True and False Values

Loops (and decisions, which I'll discuss next) make decisions based on values that can be either true or false. In C++, a value of 0 (zero) is false and any other value is true. Thus, the constant 0 is false by definition, but the constant 1 is true, as are -1, 275, and any other nonzero numbers. Some languages have a special Boolean data type to hold true/false values, but in C++ these values are simply stored in any of the integer data types (`char`, `int`, `short`, `long`, and their unsigned counterparts).

Sometimes the value of a single variable is used by a loop to decide whether to cycle again or exit. For example, a loop might check whether the variable `avar` is true or false (nonzero or zero), and quit when it becomes false. More often, however, loops check whether a *relationship* between two variables, or between a variable and a constant, is true or false. That is, a loop might want to continue cycling only if `j` is greater than 0; another loop might want to continue if `ch` is not equal to `'x'`. Being equal to, greater than, and so on are calculated with relational operators in C++, so let's examine these operators before examining examples of loops.

Relational Operators

Relational operators compare two values and evaluate to a true/false value, depending on whether the comparison is true or not. There are six such operators, as shown in Table 2-1.

Symbol	Meaning	Example
==	equal to	a == b
!=	not equal to	a != b
<	less than	a < b
>	greater than	a > b
<=	less than or equal to	a <= b
>=	greater than or equal to	a >= b

Table 2-1 *Relational operators*

The expressions in the Example column will be either true or false depending on the values of a and b. For example, suppose a is 9 and b is 10. Then a==b is not true, because 9 does not equal 10, but a!=b is true, as are a<b and a<=b. The expressions a>b and a>=b are false.

You can compare characters as well as numbers, because characters have underlying (ASCII) numerical values. Thus, it's true that 'a'<'b' and that 'A'==65, but not true that 'z'<='a' (because 'z' in fact has a higher ASCII value than 'a').

Now that you understand relational operators, let's look at the three kinds of C++ loops and see how they decide what to do based on expressions that use these operators.

while **Loops**

A while loop lets you do something over and over until a *condition* changes. The condition is something that can be expressed by a true/false value. For example, a while loop might repeatedly ask the user to enter a character. It would then continue to cycle until the user enters the character 'q' (for "quit").

Here's an example of a while loop that behaves just this way:

```
while(ch != 'q')
   {
   cout << "Enter a character: ";
   cin >> ch;
   }
```

If the user does not press 'q', the loop continues. Some sample interaction might look like this:

```
Enter a character: c
Enter a character: a
Enter a character: t
Enter a character: s
Enter a character: q
```

A while loop consists of the keyword while followed by a *test expression* (also called a *conditional expression* or *condition*) enclosed in parentheses. The body of the loop is delimited by braces (but no semicolon), just like a function. Figure 2-2 shows how this looks.

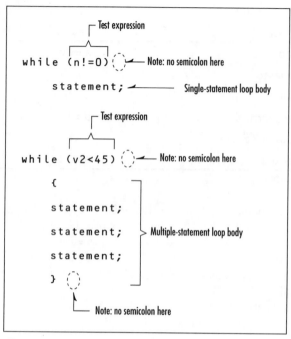

Figure 2-2   Syntax of the `while` loop

If the body of the loop consists of only one statement, you don't need the braces.

```
while(n < 100)
      n = n * 2;         <--One-statement loop body, so no braces
```

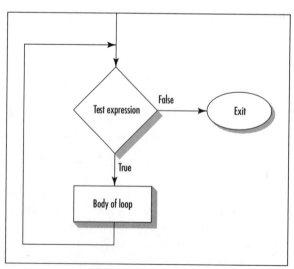

Figure 2-3   Operation of the `while` loop

This loop will keep doubling **n** until **n** is not less than (i.e., becomes greater than or equal to) 100; it will then terminate. If **n** has a value of 1 when the loop is entered, what value will it have when the loop terminates? That's right, 128. The values will go 1, 2, 4, 8, 16, 32, 64, and 128, at which point the loop terminates (i.e., control goes to the statement following the loop). Figure 2-3 is a flow chart of a **while** loop's operation.

Note that the test expression is checked before the body of the loop is executed. If the condition is false when the loop is entered, then the body of the loop will never be executed. This is appropriate in some situations, but it means you must be careful that a variable in the test expression has an appropriate value before you enter the loop. The **ch** in the first example must not have a value of **'q'** when you enter the loop, or the loop body will never be executed. The **n** in the second loop must be initialized to a value less than 100.

do **Loops**

The **do** loop (often called the **do while** loop) operates like the **while** loop except that the test expression is checked *after* the body of the loop is executed. This is nice when you always want something (whatever is in the body of the loop) done at least once, no matter what the initial true/false state of the condition is. Figure 2-4 shows how this looks.

Here's an example of a **do** loop. This fragment repeatedly performs addition on two numbers entered by the user. When the user enters 0 for the first number, the loop terminates.

```
do
    {
    cout << "\nEnter two numbers (to quit, set first to 0): "
    cin >> x >> y;
    cout << "The sum is " << x + y;
    } while(x != 0);
```

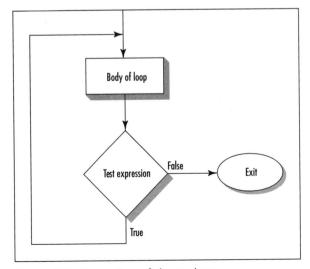

Figure 2-4   Operation of the **do** loop

A do loop begins with the keyword do, followed by the body of the loop in braces, then the keyword while, a test expression in parentheses, and finally a semicolon. This arrangement is shown in Figure 2-5. Note that the do loop is the only loop that is terminated with a semicolon. The semicolon is necessary because the test expression follows the loop body, so the closing brace of the loop body can't act as a delimiter for the entire loop.

The do loop has a slightly dubious reputation among C++ programmers because its syntax is not quite so clean and easy to read as that of the while loop. The consensus is to use a while loop unless there's a really good reason to use a do loop.

for **Loops**

In both the while and do loops, you usually don't know, at the time you enter the loop, how many times the loop will be executed. The condition that terminates the loop arises spontaneously inside the loop: The user answers 'n' instead of 'y', for example. This is not the case with for loops.

In a for loop, the number of times the loop will be executed is (usually) stated at the beginning of the loop. Here's a loop that prints 20 asterisks in a line across the page:

```
int j;                  // define the loop variable

for(j=0; j<20; ++j);    // cycle 20 times
    cout << '*';        // print asterisk
```

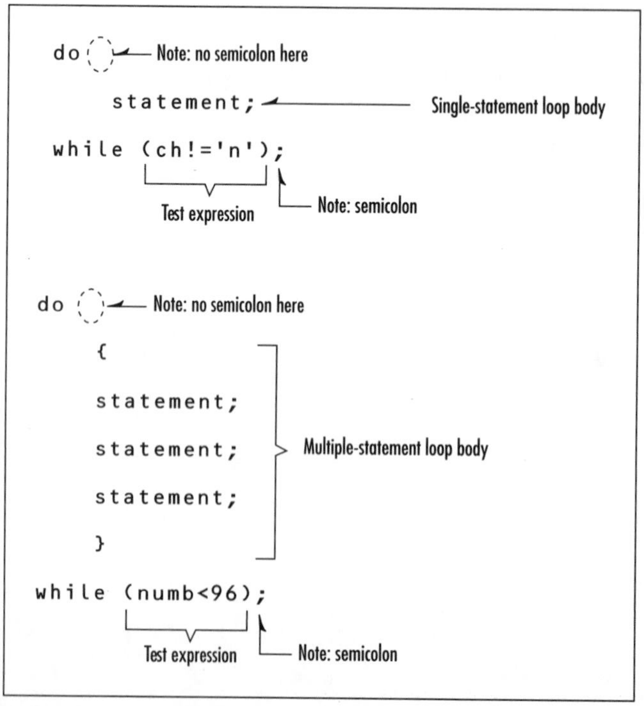

Figure 2-5 Syntax of the do loop

The parentheses following the keyword **for** contain three different expressions, separated by semi-colons. In the most common situation, these three expressions operate on a variable called the *loop variable*, which in this example is **j**. These three expressions are

- The *initialization expression*, which usually initializes the value of a loop variable.

- The *test expression*, which usually checks the value of the loop variable to see whether to cycle again or to quit the loop.

- The *increment expression*, which usually increments (or decrements) the value of the loop variable.

In the example, the loop variable **j** is given an initial value of 0, then the test expression is evaluated. If this expression is true (if **j** is less than 20), the body of the loop is executed and the increment expression is executed (**j**'s value is increased by 1). If the test expression is false, the loop terminates. Figure 2-6 shows the syntax of the **for** loop, and Figure 2-7 depicts its operation.

How many times will the loop in the example be executed? 20 times. The first time through the loop, **j** is 0; the last time, it's 19. (It does *not* run from 1 to 20, as you might expect.) Starting at 0 and continuing until the loop variable is 1 less than a constant is the most common arrangement in

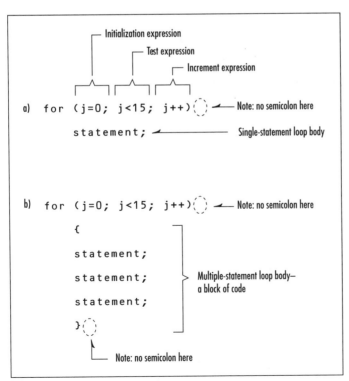

Figure 2-6 Syntax of the **for** loop

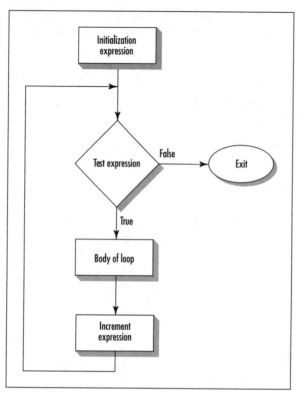

Figure 2-7 Operation of the `for` loop

`for` loops because, among other reasons, array indexes (which you'll learn about in Chapter 3) typically start at 0 and go up to 1 less than the size of the array.

If you *did* want the loop variable to run from 1 to 20, you could write

```
for(j=1; j<=20; ++j)
    // body of loop
```

where the less-than-or-equals operator is used instead of the less-than operator. However, this is not a common idiom in C++.

Notice that, as in the `while` loop, the test expression is evaluated before the loop body is executed the first time. Thus, the loop body may not be executed at all if the test expression is false to begin with.

Here's another example of a `for` loop, this one with multiple statements in the loop body. As in the other loops, multiple statements must be surrounded by braces.

```
int j;                     // define loop variable
int total = 0;             // define and initialize total

for(j=0; j<10; ++j)        // cycle 10 times
   {
   total = total + j;      // add j to total
   cout << total << ' ';   // display total
   }
```

This fragment will display the sequence

```
0 1 3 6 10 15 21 28 36 45
```

Notice that there is no rule that says that the loop variable must be increased by 1 each time through the loop. You can also decrease it by 1:

```
for(j=10; j>0; --j)
   cout << j << ' ';
```

which will display

```
10 9 8 7 6 5 4 3 2 1
```

or you can increase it or decrease it by any other amount. This code

```
for(j=0; j<100; j=j+10)
   cout << j << ' ';
```

will display

```
0 10 20 30 40 50 60 70 80 90
```

There is a surprising amount of flexibility in what you can put in the three expressions in a for loop. For example, you can use multiple statements in the initialization expression and the test expression. Here's an example of a for loop with such multiple statements:

```
for(j=0, total=0; j<10; ++j, total=total+j)
   cout << total << ' ';      // display total
```

This loop prints

```
0 1 3 6 10 15 21 28 36 45
```

as in the earlier example. However, here the variable total is set to 0 in the initialization expression instead of before the loop, and increased by j in the increment expression instead of in the loop body. The individual statements in these expressions are separated by commas.

Another option is to leave out any or all of the three for loop expressions entirely, retaining only the semicolons.

Generally, taking advantage of the flexibility of the for loop in these ways causes more confusion than it's worth, but big-time C gurus enjoy it.

Nested Loops

You can nest one loop inside another. For example, the following program fragment prints a 10 by 10 square of Xs, like this:

```
XXXXXXXXXX
XXXXXXXXXX
XXXXXXXXXX
XXXXXXXXXX
XXXXXXXXXX
XXXXXXXXXX
XXXXXXXXXX
XXXXXXXXXX
XXXXXXXXXX
XXXXXXXXXX
```

in the upper-left corner of the screen.

```
for(y=0; y<10; y++)        // outer loop, drops down line-by-line
   {
   for(x=0; x<10; x++)     // inner loop, goes across char-by-char
       cout << 'X';        // print 'X'
   cout << endl;           // go to new line
   }
```

Of course, you can embed any kind of loop inside any other kind of loop, and loops can be nested in loops that are nested in other loops, and so on.

Logical Operators

It's often convenient to test the true/false values of several expressions at the same time and combine the results into a single true/false value. For instance, you might want to create a true value any time both x<10 and y<5 are true.

True/false values can be operated on with *logical operators*. There are three logical operators in C++ (see Table 2-2). Two of them combine two true/false values, and the third negates a true/false value.

Logical Operator	Meaning	Example
&&	AND	x>0 && x<10
||	OR	x==3 || x<1
!	NOT	!x

Table 2-2 *Logical operators*

An AND expression is true only if the expressions on both sides of the && operator are true. Thus, the example in the table is true only if x is greater than 0 and also less than 10. The AND operator is often used to determine whether something is in a specified range. In the example in the table, the expression is true if x is in the range of 1 to 9. Similarly, the expression

```
ch >= 'a' && ch <= 'z'
```

is true if `ch` is a lowercase letter.

The OR (`||`) operator evaluates to true if *either* or both of its operands are true. For example,

`j==0 || ch == 'q'`

is true if either `j` is 0 or ch equals `'q'`, or if both are true.

The OR operator is often used to discover if a value is outside a specified range. The expression

`temp<65 || temp>75`

is true if temp is outside the 65 to 75 range (the "comfort zone" for Fahrenheit temperatures).

The `!` (NOT) operator negates the variable following it. Thus, `!alpha` is true if `alpha` is false, and false if `alpha` is true. (As you can see, this operator has an Alice in Wonderland quality.) It's often used when you want a `while` loop to continue until something is true, instead of continuing until it's false. For example,

```
while( !alpha )
    {
    }
```

will cycle until `alpha` becomes true (nonzero).

Logical expressions can often be written in several ways. The expression

`temp<65 || temp>75`

could also be written

`!(temp>=65 && temp<=75)`

because a value being *not in* range is the same as it's being *out* of range.

Precedence

In normal algebraic expressions, multiplication and division are carried out before addition and subtraction. For example, in the expression

`2*2+3*3`

the 2s are multiplied (which gives 4), then the 3s are multiplied (giving 9), and only then are these results added, yielding 13. The multiplications are carried out before the addition because the `*` operator has a higher *precedence* than the `+` operator.

If there was no precedence and the compiler just evaluated expressions blindly from left to right, the compiler would obtain a different answer. Multiplying the 2s gives 4, adding the 3 makes 7, and multiplying the result by 3 gives 21, which is not what you expect. Thus precedence is important in normal arithmetic expressions. It's also important when different C++ operators are used.

You may have wondered why, when I say

`temp<65 || temp>75`

how I can be sure that the true/false value of temp<65 and temp>75 are evaluated first, before being ORed together. If the processor proceeded from left to right, for example, temp<65 would be evaluated, ORed with `temp` (whatever that would mean, because `temp` is a number, not a true/false value), and the result compared with 75. This isn't what I want, of course.

The expression is evaluated correctly because relational operators have a higher precedence than logical operators.

How is the expression

```
n + 2 < x + 3
```

evaluated? You want to compare two arithmetic expressions, `n+2` and `x+3`. Is that what's happening? Yes, because arithmetic operators have a higher precedence than relational operators. Table 2-3 shows the precedence relations, with the higher precedence operators higher in the table.

Operators	Operator Types	Precedence
* / %	Multiplicative	Higher
+ –	Additive	
< > <= >= == !=	Relational	
&& ||	Logical	
=	Assignment	Lower

Table 2-3 *Precedence relations*

Notice that the assignment operator, =, has the lowest precedence of all; that is, it's applied after all the other operators. You'll see other examples of precedence relations as you go along.

QUIZ 2

1. True values and false values are represented in C++ by the numerical values _____ and _____, respectively.
   a. any number except 0, 0
   b. 0, any positive number
   c. 0, any negative number
   d. 0, 1
   e. 1, 0

2. Relational operators compare two
   a. true/false values and evaluate to a number (such as 77).
   b. numerical values and evaluate to a true/false value.
   c. logical values and evaluate to a true/false value.
   d. logical values and evaluate to a number.
   e. true/false values and evaluate to a logical value.

3. What expression(s) will cause the `while` loop to cycle as long as `j` is greater than 0 and `ch` is not `'q'`?
   a. `while( !(j<=0 || ch=='q') )`
   b. `while(j > (0 && ch) != 'q')`
   c. `while(j > 0 && ch != 'q')`
   d. `while(j <= 0 && ch == 'q')`
   e. `while( !(j <= 0) || !(ch == 'q') )`

4. If you want a loop variable to run from 12 to 36 (inclusive) in steps of 3, you might write
   a. `for(alpha==12, alpha<37, alpha=alpha+3)`
   b. `for(x==12; x<=37; x=x+3)`
   c. `for(b=12, b<37, b+b+3)`
   d. `for( gamma=12; gamma<37; gamma=gamma+3 )`
   e. `for(rad=12; rad<=36; ++rad, ++rad, ++rad)`

5. `while` loops and `do` loops differ in that
   a. a `do` loop is terminated by a condition arising within the loop.
   b. the number of times a `while` loop will cycle is known before the loop is entered.
   c. a `while` is terminated by a condition arising within the loop.
   d. the body of a `do` loop is always executed at least once.
   e. the loop variable may be incremented within a `do` loop.

EXERCISE 1

Write a loop that repeatedly asks the user to type a character and then displays the ASCII value of the character. Hint: You can cause a variable of type `char` to print as a number by converting it to type `int`. Use an expression such as `int(ch)`, which converts the variable `ch` to an `int`. Have the loop exit when the user enters the character `'q'`.

EXERCISE 2

Write a program fragment, probably consisting of some nested loops, that asks the user what character to use to create a 10 by 10 square on the upper-left corner of the screen. Then display this square and ask for another character. Exit from the outermost loop when the user enters `'q'`.

SESSION 3

SIMPLE DECISIONS

I'm going to cover decisions in two sessions rather than one. I'll examine simple decisions (`if` and `if...else`) now and advanced decisions (`else...if`, `switch`, and the conditional operator) in the next lesson. This relaxed pace will give you a chance to see how to improve the hot dog stand program with various kinds of decision statements.

The `if` Statement

The simplest way to make a decision in C++ is with the `if` statement. Here's an example of an `if` statement at work:

```
if(denominator == 0)
    cout << "Division by zero is illegal";
```

If a variable called `denominator` is 0, this fragment causes a message to be displayed. If `denominator` is not 0, then nothing happens.

As with loops, if you use more than one statement in the body of an if statement, you need to surround them with braces.

```
if(choice == 's')                // if user chooses "sold dog' option
   {
   cout << "Selling a dog";  // verify I sold the dog
   stand1.SoldOneDog();      // sell the dog
   }
```

An **if** statement consists of the keyword **if** followed by a test expression in parentheses. The loop body, which follows, consists of either a single statement or multiple statements surrounded by braces. (With the exception of the keyword, an **if** statement has the same syntax as a **while** statement.) Notice that there is no **then** keyword in C++, as there is in some other languages. The body of the loop follows immediately after the test expression.

Figure 2-8 shows the syntax of the **if** statement and Figure 2-9 show how it operates.

The `if...else` Statement

In a simple **if** statement, something happens if the condition *is* true, but if the condition is *not* true, nothing happens at all. Suppose you want something to happen either way: one action if the condition is true and a different action if the condition is false. To do this, you use an **if...else** statement. The following fragment takes the hour of the day, expressed in 24-hour time, and displays it in 12-hour time, with "am" or "pm" as appropriate:

```
if(hours < 12)
    cout << hours << " am";    // e.g., "7 am" if hours is 7
else
    cout << hours-12 << " pm";   // e.g., "3 pm" if hours is 15
```

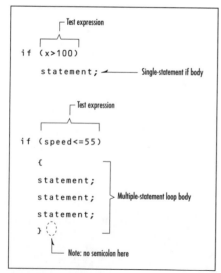

Figure 2-8 Syntax of the **if** statement

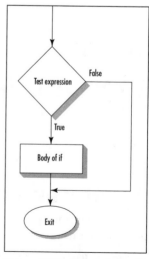

Figure 2-9 Operation of the **if** statement

Actually, this simple approach doesn't handle the situation very well when `hours` is 0 (midnight) or 12 (noon). You'll see how to deal with these cases in the next lesson.

As with other C++ constructions, the `if` body or the `else` body may consist of multiple statements surrounded by braces rather than the single statements I show here.

Test Expression

The test expression in an `if` or an `if...else` statement can be just as complicated as expressions in loops. For example, this `if...else` statement advances the day from February 28 to either March 1 or February 29, depending on whether the year is a leap year or not:

```
                         // if it's Feb 28 and it's a leap year
if(day==28 && month==2 && year%4==0 && year%100 != 0)
    day = 29;            // then the next day is the 29th
else                     // otherwise,
    {
    day = 1;             // next day is March 1st
    month = 3;
    }
```

Leap years occur when the year is divisible by 4 (e.g., 1996 is a leap year), but not divisible by 100 (so 1900 is *not* a leap year, although it is divisible by 4. The remainder operator (%) is used to find if the year is divisible by 4 (and by 100) with no remainder. The AND operators make sure that February 29 occurs only when all the conditions are true at once. (Yes, I know, leap years have other corrections as well.)

Nested `if...else` Statements

You can nest `if...else` statements within one another. Typically, the nested statements end up in the `else` body rather than in the `if` body. For example

```
if(age<2)
    cout << "\nInfant";
else
    if(age<18)
        cout << "\nChild";
    else                        // age >= 18
        cout << "\nAdult";
```

This `if...else` "ladder" prints an appropriate description of a person's age.

An insidious problem may arise when you nest `if...else` statements. Here's a program fragment that is intended to have a similar functionality to the one above, except it can't print the adult designation:

```
if(age>2)                   // if greater than 2
    if(age<18)              // and less than 18
        cout << "\nChild";  // it's a child
else
    cout << "\nInfant";     // ERROR: inappropriate response
```

Will this fragment print `"Infant"` when `age` is less than or equal to 2, as I want? Alas, no. `"Infant"` will be printed whenever `age` is greater than or equal to 18. Why? I have mislead you with the indentation, so it looks as if the `else` matches up with the first `if`. It doesn't. Here's the rule: An `else` is associated with the nearest preceding `if` that doesn't have its own `else`. The correct version of the fragment above would be

```
if(age>2)
   if(age<18)
      cout << "\nChild";
   else                    // the else goes with the preceding if
      cout << "\nAdult";   // appropriate response, age>=18
```

If you really want an `else` to be associated with an `if` that doesn't immediately precede it, you must surround the intervening `if` statement with braces

```
if(age>2)
   {
   if(age<18)
      cout << "\nChild";
   }
else                      // this else goes with the top if
   cout << "\nInfant";    // appropriate response
```

The braces make the entire `if` statement invisible to the `else`. (It would be nice if we could conceal ourselves from telemarketers this easily.)

The moral is to be careful with complicated `if...else` statements. Forgetting which `if` gets the `else` is a common source of annoying program bugs.

Improving the Hot Dog Program with `if`

Now that you know how to cause a program to do things more than once and make decisions, you can improve the hot dog stand program, HOTDOG1. Rewrite the `main()` part of the program so it runs continuously, waiting for the user to tell it a hot dog has been sold. For simplicity, work with only one hot dog stand, represented by the `stand1` object.

When first started, the program asks the user to enter the initial amounts of buns and hot dogs on hand. Then the program enters a `while` loop, waiting for user input. If the user enters `'s'`, the program records a sale. If the user enters `'q'`, the program displays the hot dogs and buns on hand and exits. Presumably, the user enters `'q'` when the last sale has been made and the hot dog stand has closed down for the day.

Notice that I use the `if` statement to see if the user has typed an `'s'`, and the `while` loop to check for `'q'`. Listing 2-2 shows HOTDOG2.

Listing 2-2 HOTDOG2

```
// hotdog2.cpp
// hot dog stand inventory database
// uses while loop and if statement

#include <iostream.h>            // for cout, cin, etc.

class HotDogStand                // class specification
      {
   private:
      int HotDogsOnHand;         // hot dogs on hand
```

```
      int BunsOnHand;                    // buns on hand
public:
   void displayData()                    // display hot dogs and buns
      {
      cout << "\n   Hot dogs = " << HotDogsOnHand;
      cout << "\n   Buns = "      << BunsOnHand;
      }
   void SoldOneDog()                     // record sale of one dog
      {
      --HotDogsOnHand;
      --BunsOnHand;
      }
   void initData()                       // set initial quantities
      {
      cout << "\n   Enter hot dogs on hand: ";
      cin >> HotDogsOnHand;
      cout << "    Enter buns on hand: ";
      cin >> BunsOnHand;
      }
}; // end of HotDogStand class

////////////////////////////////////////////////////////////
void main()
   {
   char choice = 'x';                 // user's letter choice

   HotDogStand stand1;                // create hot dog stand object
                                      // set initial data
   cout << "\nInitialize data";
   stand1.initData();

   while(choice != 'q')               // loop until 'q' typed
      {
      cout << "\nEnter s to record sale, q to quit: ";
      cin >> choice;
      if(choice == 's')               // if user entered 's'
         {                            // then sell a dog
         cout << "Selling a dog";
         stand1.SoldOneDog();
         }
      } // end while
                                      // display current data
   cout << "\nSupplies on hand";
   stand1.displayData();
   }
```

A Glimpse of Reusability

One of the most important things to notice about Listing 2-2 is that the specification for the HotDogStand class is exactly the same as it was in the HOTDOG1 program. I have made significant changes to the functionality of the program, but I have not altered the class at all. In an embryonic way, this demonstrates one of the major strengths of OOP. I have *reused* the HotDogStand class in a new program. I haven't worried about integrating or modifying the parts of the class; I simply insert-ed the entire class, just as I found it, into the new program. In a small program, the gain may not appear significant, but in larger programs, the savings in time and effort that result from being able to reuse already existing classes can be substantial. The savings may be especially large when an entire library of classes can be reused.

Of course, it is also possible to reuse code, especially functions, in old-fashioned procedural lan-guages such as C. However, the OOP approach, which reuses classes instead of functions, provides a more coherent and easily understood package for reuse, with both data and functions combined into a single entity. The interface between the class, which specifies how objects behave, and `main()`, which creates objects and sends messages to them, is cleaner and more easily understood than the relationship between some functions and some data that's unrelated to the functions and statements in `main()` that call functions and access the data.

1. The test expression in an `if` statement
   a. is an expression that counts how often the `if` statement body will be executed.
   b. may contain logical and relational operators.
   c. determines whether the `if` statement body will be executed.
   d. may be evaluated after the `if` statement body is executed.
   e. may be any expression that evaluates to a true/false value.

2. Which of the following are test expression(s) for an `if` statement that determine whether a character `ch` is a digit; that is, if it is in the range of characters from `'0'` to `'9'`.
   a. `if(ch>='0' && ch<='9')`
   b. `if ( ch >= 0 && ch <= 9 )`
   c. `if(ch>0) else (ch<9)`
   d. `if( ch < '0' || ch > '9' )`
   e. `if(ch > -1 && ch < 10)`

3. Which of the following are true?
   a. An `else` is associated with the `if` that has the same indentation as the `else`.
   b. An `else` is associated with the `if` that is closest to and above the `else`, if that `if` is not surrounded by braces.
   c. An `else` is associated with the `if` that is surrounded by braces and immediately precedes the `else`.
   d. The body of an `else` is executed if the test expression in the corresponding `if` is true.
   e. The body of an `else` is executed if the test expression following the `else` is true.

4. The interface between a class and the rest of a program normally includes
   a. the class sending messages to objects.
   b. the program creating objects.
   c. the program sending messages to objects.
   d. objects sending messages to `main()`.
   e. the program manipulating the objects' data.

5. OOP offers superior reusability because
    a. other parts of the program need not be concerned with how data is structured in an object.
    b. it's easier for objects to communicate with each other.
    c. every object is built to the same specification.
    d. other parts of the program need to relate only to one thing—objects—not to data and functions separately.
    e. the programmer need not be aware of the class specification.

Rewrite the program of Exercise 1 in Session 1 in this chapter so that it continuously waits for a character to be entered. The user should be able to make the elevator go up one floor by entering a '+' (pressing the '+' and (ENTER)) and go down one floor by entering a '-'. After each floor change, the program should display the floor the elevator is on. Pressing 'q' should terminate the program. Assume that the elevator starts on floor 1 and that the program informs the user of this fact when it is first started. Here's some sample interaction:

```
Elevator is now on floor 1
Enter choice: +
Elevator is now on floor 2
Enter choice: +
Elevator is now on floor 3
Enter choice: -
Elevator is now on floor 2
Enter choice: q
```

Rewrite the program of Exercise 2 in Session 1 in this chapter (which uses the `hotdogstand2` class with a `CashOnHand` variable) so that it has the same functionality as the HOTDOG2 program (Listing 2-2).

ADVANCED DECISIONS

In this session, I'll cover more advanced ways for a program to choose between different actions: the `else if` construction, the powerful `switch` statement, and the weird but compact conditional operator. I'll also apply the `switch` statement to the hot dog stand program to enhance its functionality.

The `else if` Construction

In the previous session, I showed an example of an `if...else` statement that displayed `"am"` or `"pm"` for hour values less than and greater than 12. I also acknowledged that this statement didn't handle the occasions when `hour` was 0 or 12. How can I fix this? I can check for these specific values of `hour` and respond accordingly. Here's how that looks with an `if...else` ladder:

```
if(hours == 0)                          // first-level indent
    cout << "Midnight";
else
    if(hours == 12)
        cout << "Noon";                 // second-level indent
    else
        if(hours < 12)
            cout << hours << " am";     // third-level indent
        else
            cout << hours-12 << " pm";
```

If the `hours` is 0, it's midnight, so the program displays an appropriate message and exits from the entire `if...else` ladder. If it isn't 0, the program goes on to the next `if...else`. It keep moving to more deeply nested `if...else` statements until it finds one whose test expression is true or it runs out of possibilities.

This arrangement does what I want, but it's hard for humans to read the multiple indentations. Here's a somewhat more easily understood way to rewrite the same code:

```
if(hours == 0)
    cout << "Midnight";
else if(hours == 12)
    cout << "Noon";
else if(hours < 12)
    cout << hours << " am";
else
    cout << hours-12 << " pm";
```

The `if` that follows each `else` is simply moved up onto the same line, thus creating a sort of artificial `else if` construction and removing the multiple levels of indentation. This arrangement not only saves space, it presents a clearer picture of the program's logic (at least, after you've gotten used to it).

Notice that the `else if` construction is not really a part of the syntax of the C++ language; it's merely a way to rewrite an `if...else` ladder by rearranging the whitespace on the page. You can do this because—as you know—the compiler doesn't care about whitespace.

Fine-Tuning Loops

This is a good place to introduce the `break` and `continue` statements, even though they pertain to loops, because they are used most effectively in conjunction with decisions. Also, `break` is an important feature in the `switch` statement, which I'll demonstrate next.

Usually loops work well with the straightforward syntax I showed in the last session. However, sometimes you need to fudge things a bit to make a loop behave as you want. The `break` and `continue` statements provide this added flexibility.

The break *Statement*

The `break` statement causes you to exit immediately from a loop, as shown in Figure 2-10.

The `break` statement is often used to handle unexpected or nonstandard situations that arise within a loop. For example, here's a code fragment that sets the variable `isPrime` to 1 if an integer `n` is a prime number or to 0 if `n` is not a prime number. (A prime number is divisible only by itself and 1.) To tell if `n` is prime, I use the straightforward approach of trying to divide it by all the numbers up to n-1. If any of them divide evenly (with no remainder), then it's not prime.

```
isPrime = 1;            // assume n is prime
for(j=2; j<n; ++j)      // divide by all integers from 2 to n-1
   {
   if(n%j == 0)         // if evenly divisible,
      {
      isPrime = 0;      // n is not a prime
      break;            // no point in looping again
      }
   }
```

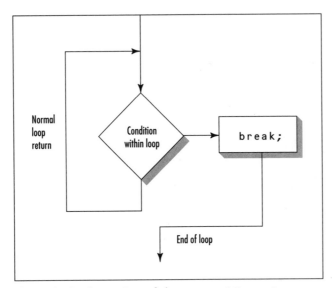

Figure 2-10 Operation of the `break` statement

I want to divide by all the numbers up to n-1, so I use a for loop with appropriate expressions. However, if one of the j values does divide evenly, there's no use remaining in the loop and dividing by the remaining the j values. As soon as the program finds the first number that divides evenly, it should set isPrime to 0 and then immediately exit from the loop. The break statement allows you to exit from the loop at any time.

The continue *Statement*

The continue statement is similar to the break statement in that it is usually activated by an unexpected condition in a loop. However, it returns control to the top of the loop—causing the loop to continue—rather than causing an exit from the loop. Figure 2-11 shows how this looks.

Whereas the break statement causes an exit from a loop, the continue statement causes part of the loop to be "short-circuited" or bypassed while the loop keeps running. That is, following a continue, control goes back to the top of the loop. Here's an example:

```
do
   {
   cout << "Enter dividend: ";
   cin >> dividend;
   cout << "Enter divisor: ";
   cin >> divisor;
   if(divisor == 0)                       // if user error,
      {
      cout << "Divisor can't be zero\n";
      continue;                           // go back to top of loop
      }
   cout << "Quotient is " << dividend / divisor;
   cout "\nDo another (y/n)? ";
   cin >> ch;
   } while(ch != 'n');
```

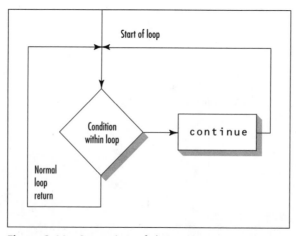

Figure 2-11 Operation of the continue statement

Division by zero is illegal, so if the user enters 0 for the divisor, control goes back to the top of the loop and the program prompts for a new dividend and divisor so the user can try again. To exit from the loop, the user must answer `'n'` to the `"Do another"` question.

The `switch` **Statement**

Now you're ready for perhaps the most powerful decision-making construction in C++. The `switch` statement checks a variable and routes program control to any of a number of different sections of code, depending on the value of the variable. Here's an example:

```
switch(diskSpeed)
   {
   case 33:                       // if diskSpeed is 33
      cout << "Long-playing album";
      break;
   case 45:                       // if diskSpeed is 45
      cout << "Single-selection";
      break;
   case 78:                       // if diskSpeed is 78
      cout << "Old single-selection";
      break;
   default:                       // if nothing matches
      cout << "Unknown format";
   }
```

The `switch` statement consists of the keyword `switch` followed by a variable name in parentheses. The body of the `switch` statement, enclosed in braces, follows. Within the body are a number of *labels*, which are names followed by a colon. In a `switch` statement, these labels consist of the keyword `case` followed by a constant and then the colon. When the value of the `switch` variable is equal to the constant following a particular `case`, control will go to the statements following this `case` label.

The above section of code prints different messages depending on the value of the `diskSpeed` variable. If `diskSpeed` is 33, control jumps to the label `case 33`. If `diskSpeed` is 45, control jumps to the label `case 45`, and so on. If `diskSpeed` doesn't match any of the `case`s, control jumps to the `default` label (or, if there is no `default`, falls through the bottom of the `switch`). Figure 2-12 shows the syntax of the `switch` statement and Figure 2-13 shows its operation.

The variable or expression used to determine which label is jumped to (`diskSpeed`, in this example) must be an integer or a character or must evaluate to an integer or a character. The values following the `case`s must be—or must evaluate to—integer or character constants. That is, you can use variable names or expressions, such as `alpha`, `j+20`, and `ch+'0'`, as long as `alpha`, `j`, and `ch` already have appropriate values.

Once control gets to a label, the statements following the label are executed one after the other from the label onward. In this example, the `cout` statement will be executed. Then what? If the `break` weren't there, control would continue down to the next `cout` statement, which is *not* what you want. Labels don't delimit a section of code, they merely name an entry point. The `break` causes control to break out of the `switch` entirely.

Here's another example that might be used in the hot dog stand program. It gives the user the choice of three stands for which to record the sale of a hot dog. The user types a digit from `'1'` to `'3'`, which is then used as the `switch` variable.

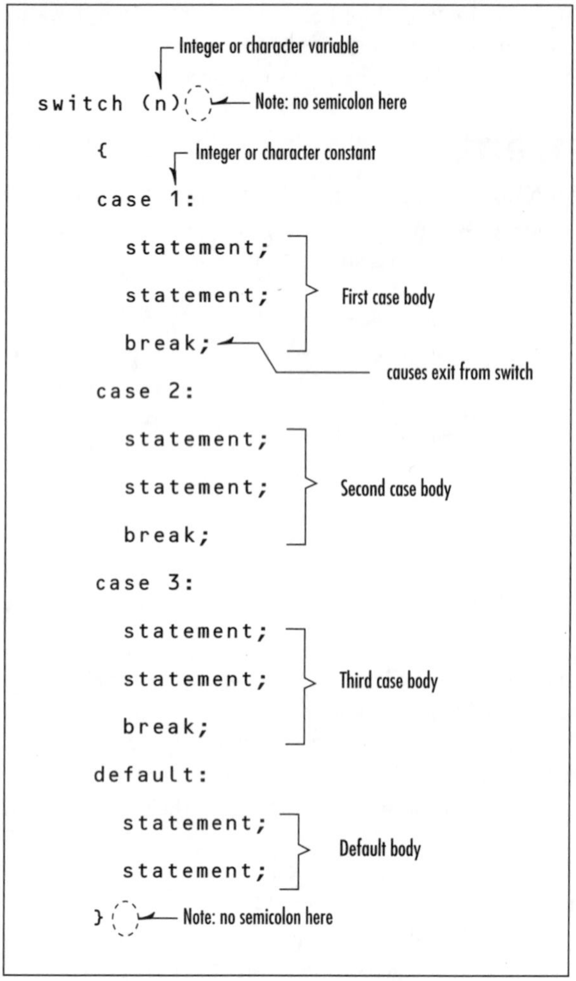

Figure 2-12 Syntax of the switch statement

```
cin >> choice;
switch(choice)
    {
    case '1';
        stand1.SoldOneDog();
        break;
    case '2';
        stand2.SoldOneDog();
        break;
    case '3';
        stand3.SoldOneDog();
        break;
    }
```

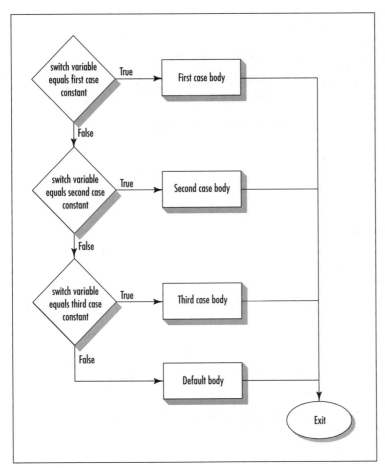

Figure 2-13 Operation of the `switch` statement

Improving the Hot Dog Program with `switch`

Let's put this `switch` construction into a complete program. A `while` loop will allow the user to repeatedly record the sale of hot dogs from the three stands. Listing 2-3 shows HOTDOG3.

Listing 2-3 HOTDOG3

```
// hotdog3.cpp
// hot dog stand inventory database
// uses while loop and switch statement

#include <iostream.h>              // for cout, cin, etc.

class HotDogStand                  // class specification
        {
    private:
```

continued on next page

continued from previous page

```
      int HotDogsOnHand;          // hot dogs on hand
      int BunsOnHand;             // buns on hand
   public:
      void displayData()          // display hot dogs and buns
         {
         cout << "\n   Hot dogs = " << HotDogsOnHand;
         cout << "\n   Buns = "    << BunsOnHand;
         }
      void SoldOneDog()           // record sale of one dog
         {
         --HotDogsOnHand;
         --BunsOnHand;
         }
      void initData()             // set initial quantities
         {
         cout << "\n   Enter hot dogs on hand: ";
         cin >> HotDogsOnHand;
         cout << "   Enter buns on hand: ";
         cin >> BunsOnHand;
         }
   };  // end of HotDogStand class

////////////////////////////////////////////////////////////
void main()
   {
   char choice = 'x';            // user's letter choice

   HotDogStand stand1;           // create hot dog stand objects
   HotDogStand stand2;
   HotDogStand stand3;
                                 // set initial data
   cout << "\nInitialize data for stand 1";
   stand1.initData();
   cout << "\nInitialize data for stand 2";
   stand2.initData();
   cout << "\nInitialize data for stand 3";
   stand3.initData();

   while(choice != 'q')          // loop until user enters 'q'
      {
      cout << "\nEnter stand number, or q to quit: ";
      cin >> choice;
      switch(choice)
         {
         case '1':
            cout << "Selling a dog at stand 1";
            stand1.SoldOneDog();
            break;
         case '2':
            cout << "Selling a dog at stand 2";
            stand2.SoldOneDog();
            break;
         case '3':
```

```
            cout << "Selling a dog at stand 3";
            stand3.SoldOneDog();
            break;
        }  // end switch
    }  // end while
                                // display current data
cout << "\nSupplies on hand at stand 1";
stand1.displayData();
cout << "\nSupplies on hand at stand 2";
stand2.displayData();
cout << "\nSupplies on hand at stand 3";
stand3.displayData();
}
```

The user can enter initial amounts of hot dogs and buns for three different stands, then record an arbitrary number of sales at each stand, and then, at the end of the day, display the remaining inventory before exiting from the program. Here's some sample interaction:

```
Initialize data for stand 1
   Enter hot dogs on hand: 100
   Enter buns on hand: 110

Initialize data for stand 2
   Enter hot dogs on hand: 200
   Enter buns on hand: 220

Initialize data for stand 3
   Enter hot dogs on hand: 300
   Enter buns on hand: 330

Enter stand number, or q to quit: 1        <--sell 3 dogs from stand 1
Selling a dog at stand 1
Enter stand number, or q to quit: 1
Selling a dog at stand 1
Enter stand number, or q to quit: 1
Selling a dog at stand 1
Enter stand number, or q to quit: 2        <--sell 2 dogs from stand2
Selling a dog at stand 2
Enter stand number, or q to quit: 2
Selling a dog at stand 2
Enter stand number, or q to quit: 3        <--sell 1 dog from stand 3
Selling a dog at stand 3
Enter stand number, or q to quit: q        <--quit program

Supplies on hand at stand 1
   Hot dogs = 97
   Buns = 107
Supplies on hand at stand 2
   Hot dogs = 198
   Buns = 218
Supplies on hand at stand 3
   Hot dogs = 299
      Buns = 329
```

In this example, the user enters initial amounts for the three stands and sells three hot dogs from stand 1, two from stand 2, and one from stand 3. Entering `'q'` displays the current inventory and exits the program.

Again, notice that I've altered the functionality of the program without changing the class specification.

The Conditional Operator

The conditional operator was invented because a particular construction occurs often in C++ programs and it is nice to shorten it. Here's an example of the lengthy version of the code:

```
if(alpha<beta)
    min = alpha;
else
    min = beta;
```

I have a variable `min` and I want to set it to `alpha` or `beta`, whichever is smaller. This `if...else` statement requires four lines of code. (I could put it all on one line, of course, but it would still be long and complicated.) However, using the conditional operator, I can shorten it to

```
min = (alpha<beta) ? alpha : beta;
```

The conditional operator is the only C++ operator that operates on three operands. It consists of two symbols: a question mark and a colon. First comes a test expression (with optional parentheses), then the question mark, then two values separated by the colon. If the test expression is true, the entire expression takes on the value before the colon (here it's `alpha`); if the test expression is false, the entire expression takes on the value following the colon (`beta`). Figure 2-14 shows the syntax of the conditional operator and Figure 2-15 shows its operation.

Here's another example. The statement

```
absvalue = (n<0) ? -n : n;
```

imitates an absolute value function. (The absolute value of a number is simply the number with any negative sign removed.) The result is `-n` if n is less than 0 and `+n` otherwise.

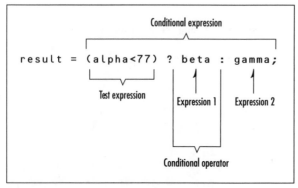

Figure 2-14 Syntax of the conditional operator

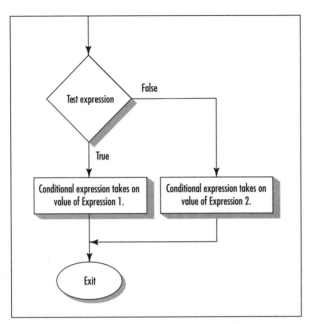

Figure 2-15   Operation of the conditional operator

1. Suppose you want to display **"Weekday"** if a variable **day** is between 1 (Monday) and 5 (Friday), but you want to display **"Saturday"** if **day** is 6 and **"Sunday"** if **day** is 7. Which of the following fragments might reasonably be part of the code for this task? Assume **day** is always in the range of 1 to 7.
   a. `if else(day==7) cout << "Sunday";`
   b. `else if(day==6) cout << "Saturday"; else cout << "Sunday";`
   c. `else if(day<6) cout << "Weekday"; else if(day==6);`
   d. `else cout << "Weekday";`
   e. `if(day<6) cout << "Weekday" else cout << "Saturday";`

2. Which of the following are true?
   a. **break** brings you back to the top of a loop, whereas **continue** continues on from the same point within the loop.
   b. **continue** brings you back to the top of the loop, whereas **break** takes you out of the bottom of the loop.
   c. **break** takes you out of all the loops in which you may be nested
   d. **continue** takes you immediately to the top of the innermost loop in which you're nested
   e. **break** takes you immediately out of an **if** statement body

3. What will be displayed if the following code is executed when `var` has the value `'b'`?

```
switch(var)
    {
    case 'a': cout << "Alpha ";
    case 'b': cout << "Beta ";
    case 'c':
        cout << "Gamma ";
        break;
    default:
        cout << "Not on list";
    }
```

     a. `Alpha`

     b. `Beta`

     c. `Gamma`

     d. `Alpha Beta`

     e. `Beta Gamma`

4. If you want to display `"Too slow"` if `speed` is less than 40, `"Too fast"` if `speed` is greater than 65, and nothing otherwise, it would be appropriate to use

     a. a `switch` statement.

     b. a series of `if` statements.

     c. nested `if...else` statements.

     d. an `else if` ladder.

     e. a conditional operator.

5. You want to send a message to each object in a group of objects. You already know the names of all the objects. The message would retrieve a certain item of instance data from each object. Your program would then display "Found one!" if this data item in any object was divisible by 7. You would be likely to use

     a. a `switch` in a `do` loop.

     b. nested `if...else` statements in a `while` loop.

     c. an `else if` ladder in a `do` loop.

     d. an `if` in a `for` loop.

     e. an `else if` ladder in a `for` loop.

EXERCISE 1

Rewrite the program of Exercise 1 in Session 3 in this chapter so that it uses a `switch` statement to distinguish among the user's choices.

EXERCISE 2

Rewrite the program of Exercise 2 in Session 3 in this chapter (which uses the `hotdogstand2` class with a `CashOnHand` variable) so that it has the same functionality as the HOTDOG3 program in this session and uses a `switch` statement to distinguish among the user's choices.

MIDCHAPTER DISCUSSION

Estelle: So George, what terrible negative thoughts do you have today?

George: No negative thoughts. I'm on top of the whole thing. I see how a C++ program fits together. It's like there are two halves: the class specification and `main()`. In the specification, you define what the objects are and how they'll act. In `main()`, you make objects based on the class and interact with them.

Don: Well said. I think I'm beginning to see something else, too. There's a philosophical difference between a class specification and the code in `main()`. The class is more general. You can imagine one programmer writing a class specification, and then a whole bunch of different programmers using the class for their own special purposes, each one writing a different `main()`. It's like someone designing a tool and other people using it in different ways.

Estelle: Anyone with a chain of hot dog stands is a potential customer for the `HotDogStand` class, but they might want to write their own `main()`.

Don: Exactly.

George: I'm also relaxed because all the material on `if` and `while` and `for` isn't exactly news to an old C programmer such as myself.

Estelle: Lucky you. Actually, I didn't think it was too hard either, except for the conditional operator, which has too much going on in too small a space. It'll take me all day to figure out a line of code if it's got one of those things in it.

George: You don't need to use a conditional operator if you don't want to; just use `if...else` instead.

Don: What I thought was silly is how in a `switch` statement you need to put `break` statements at the end of every `case`. Why not have control jump to the end of the `switch` automatically after a `case` is completed?

Estelle: It's a trade-off. The advantage of requiring a `case` is that, if you want, two `case`s can go to the same code.

Don: When would you ever do that?

Estelle: Hmm...oh, I know. Suppose you wanted your program to do the same thing if the user typed either an upper- or lowercase version of the same character. Then you could put two cases right after each other. Here, I'll write it on the board:

```
case 'a':
case 'A':
// do something
   break;
```

Don: I guess that's reasonable. But you know what I think is weird? The `continue` statement.

George: Don't worry about it. It doesn't come up that much in C programming, so I bet it doesn't in C++ either.

A CLASS TO REPRESENT TIME VALUES

In the first half of this chapter, I devoted attention to hot dog stands. Now, to prove how versatile OOP can be, I'm going to use a class to model something quite different: a new data type. This data type will represent time. In particular, it will represent the time used for airline flight reservation systems. This time has two data items: one for hours and one for minutes. There is (regrettably) no need for seconds in airline scheduling. I'll call this new data type `airtime`.

New Data Types

Why would you want to create a new data type? Don't `int` and `float` and the other basic types pretty much allow you to do anything you want? Well, not really. You may be able to do everything, but you can't do it very elegantly or quickly. It would be nice if you could treat `airtime` values just as though they were basic types and make statements such as

```
t1 = t2 + t3;        <--nice clean way to add times
```

where I add two `airtime` values and set the result equal to a third `airtime` value.

Of course, I could do this by using two `int` values for each time value: one for hours and one for minutes. But then I would need to use two addition operations to add two times.

```
h1 = h2 + h3;        <--more complicated way to add times
m1 = m2 + m3;
```

I would also need to worry about how to carry an hour when the sum of the minutes exceeds 60.

Or perhaps I could represent times as a single minutes values, obtained by adding the minutes value to the hours value multiplied by 60.

```
t2 = m2 + h2*60;     <--another complicated way to add times
t3 = m3 + h3*60;
t1 = t2 + t3;
```

However, this is not particularly elegant, because I need to convert from hours/minutes format to minutes-only format and back again. It turns out that it's far easier to write a program that uses time values if these values are represented by objects that can be treated like basic C++ variables.

Representing new data types is a major use for OOP languages. Other data types you might want to model using classes are

- Dates, which have separate values for year, month, and day

- Fractions, which have separate values for the numerator and denominator

- Points on the Cartesian plane, which have separate x and y coordinates

Complex numbers in mathematics, which have a real and an imaginary component

It will take several iterations before you're ready to use the + operator to add two values of a user-defined data type. Along the way, you'll learn to add such values using a member function, `add()`. But first, let's create a time class with no capability to add values and see what that looks like.

A Simple Version of the `airtime` Class

Let's first examine a simple version of the `airtime` class. This class does little more than handle input and output for `airtime` variables, but it will introduce the idea of user-defined data types. Note that `airtime` variables use 24-hour time, where 13:00 is 1:00 pm, and 23:59 is 11:59 pm. Listing 2-4 is the complete TIME1 program.

Listing 2-4 TIME1

```cpp
// time1.cpp
// a class that models a time data type

#include <iostream.h>

class airtime
    {
    private:
        int hours;          // 0 to 23
        int minutes;        // 0 to 59
    public:
        void set()
            {
            char dummy;     // for colon

            cout << "Enter time (format 23:59): ";
            cin >> hours >> dummy >> minutes;
            }
        void display()
            {
            cout << hours << ':' << minutes;
            }
    };

void main()
    {
    airtime t1, t2; // create two airtime variables

    cout << "For t1, ";
    t1.set();           // set t1
    cout << "For t2, ";
    t2.set();           // set t2

    cout << "\nt1 = ";
    t1.display();   // display t1
    cout << "\nt2 = ";
    t2.display();   // display t2
    }
```

The `airtime` class specifies two items of instance data, `hours` and `minutes`, and two member functions, `set()` and `display()`, which get an airtime value from the user and display a value. Here's some sample interaction with the program:

```
For t1, Enter time (format 23:59): 10:15
For t2, Enter time (format 23:59): 23:30

t1 = 10:15
t2 = 23:30
```

The user enters two times and the program displays them.

Considering that it creates a data type instead of a group of hot dog stands, this program is surprisingly similar to the HOTDOG1 program. But when you think about it, time quantities and hot dog stands share common characteristics. They both store data. Also, they should have similar capabilities: they should specify their initial data, modify it, and display it.

Assignment Statements with Objects

One of the easiest ways to demonstrate the power of using classes for data types is to assign the value of one object to another. You know how that works with basic types such as `int`. The statement

```
avar = 3;
```

gives the value 3 to the variable `avar`. Can you do the same thing with variables (objects) of data types (classes) that you've defined yourself? Absolutely. Here's a modification of the `main()` part of the TIME1 program. It gets a value for one `airtime` variable `t1`, assigns this value to `t2` with the statement

```
t2 = t1;
```

and then displays the value of `t2`.

```
void main()
   {
   airtime t1, t2; // create two airtime variables

   cout << "For t1, ";
   t1.set();        // set t1

   t2 = t1;         // make t2 equal to t1

   cout << "\nt2 = ";
   t2.display();    // display t2
   }
```

How can you set one object equal to another? The capability is built into C++. Although an `airtime` value contains two data items (`hours` and `minutes`), the compiler has no trouble transferring these two values from one variable to another. No matter how many items of instance data there are in an object, they will all be copied to another object during assignment. This may seem natural enough, but it's a pretty slick capability.

What's Really in an Object?

I've said that when you assign one object to another, its instance data is copied into the other object. Are its member functions copied as well? Conceptually, it's probably easiest to think of them being copied along with the data: Everything associated with one object is copied to another. You probably won't get into too much trouble if you assume this is true. However, that's not exactly what happens.

The truth is, no matter how many objects of a given class exist, there is only one image of each member function stored in memory. This makes sense, because the member functions are the same for each object, unlike instance data, which in general contains different values for each object. It would waste memory to duplicate the member functions, so all objects share the class member functions, as shown in Figure 2-16.

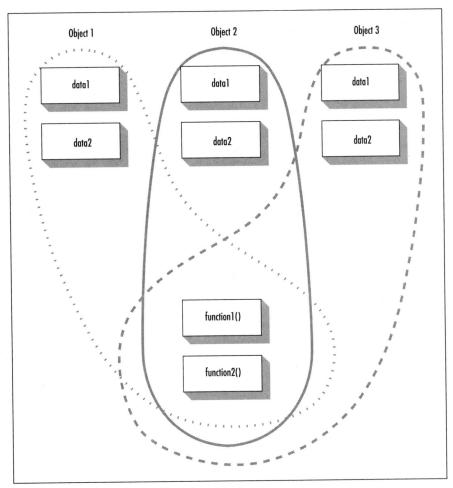

Figure 2-16   Objects, data, functions, and memory

When you call a member function for a certain object, as in

```
t2.display();    // display t2
```

you always call the same `display()` function, but it operates on different data, depending on what object called it. In this case, `display()` operates on the data stored in `t2`.

More Manipulators: Formatting Leading Zeros

As with most languages, there is a rich vocabulary in C++ for formatting output to the screen. So far I've ignored such possibilities, except for `endl` and escape characters such as `\n`. However, the `air-time` class suffers from an annoying drawback: It doesn't print the hours with leading zeros when appropriate. For example, in the `time1` program, you might have the following interchange:

```
For t1, Enter time (format 23:59): 12:00
For t2, Enter time (format 23:59): 3:05

t1 = 12:0
t2 = 3:5
```

We humans don't recognize 12:0 and 3:5 as time values. We want the times to be displayed with lead-ing zeros when appropriate, as the user entered them. Here's how to modify the `display()` member function to supply leading zeros:

```
void display()
   {
   cout << hours << ':'        // hours and colon
        << setfill('0')        // fill character is '0'
        << setw(2) << minutes;   // minutes is 2 chars wide
   }
```

This arrangement makes use of two new manipulators. Recall that a manipulator is an object that can be inserted into an I/O stream. You've already made the acquaintance of `endl`, a manipulator that takes no arguments.

The `setw()` manipulator takes one argument, which is the width in characters, of the field to be occupied by the next output value. Ordinarily, the field width is automatically adjusted to the num-ber of digits to be displayed (which does not include leading zeros). By setting a fixed width with `setw(2)`, I specify that I want `minutes` to be displayed as two characters, even if it has a value less than 10. The unused space will be filled with a *fill character*, which by default is a blank (`' '`). I want it to be a `'0'` character, so I set this with the `setfill('0')` manipulator. This arrangement always prints two digits, using 0 for the left one when appropriate.

With this revised version of the display function, the input shown above will display

```
t1 = 12:00
t2 = 3:05
```

as it should.

There is a subtle difference between the `setfill()` and `setw()` manipulators. The effect of `setfill()` lasts for the entire `cout` statement, no matter how many values are output. The effect of `setw()`, on the other hand, lasts only until the next value has been displayed. Thus, you must use `setw()` before every value if you want to change its field width.

There are other manipulators in C++; you'll see some in Chapter 10.

QUIZ 5

1. Data types are to variables as
    a. classes are to member functions.
    b. variables are to values.
    c. data is to values.
    d. variables are to member functions.
    e. classes are to objects.

2. The following are advantages of representing multivalued quantities (such as time or coordinates) by class objects rather than using separate variables.
    a. Arithmetic is faster on objects than on separate variables.
    b. It's easier to declare an object than several variables.
    c. It's easier to write a statement to perform an arithmetic operation on an object than on separate quantities.
    d. It's easier to write assignment statements for objects than for separate quantities.
    e. Objects take up less space in memory than using separate variables for each quantity.

3. If you wanted to line up three integer values (which would never exceed 32,767) in three columns, you might say

    a. `cout << endl << setw(4) << alpha1 <<< alpha2 << alpha3;`
    b. `cout << endl << setw(7) << alpha1 << alpha2 << alpha3;`
    c. `cout << endl << setw(7) << alpha1`
    `                       << setw(7) << alpha2`
    `                       << setw(7) << alpha3;`
    d. `cout << endl << setw(7) << alpha1`
    `               << endl << setw(7) << alpha2`
    `               << endl << setw(7) << alpha3;`
    e. `cout << endl << setfill('*')`
    `               << setw(7) << alpha1 << setw(7) << alpha2`
    `               << setw(7) << alpha3;`

4. If you developed a class called `AircraftPosition`, appropriate instance data might be
    a. latitude
    b. longitude
    c. speed
    d. altitude
    e. capacity

5. When you execute

    `alpha = beta;`

    (assuming that `alpha` and `beta` are objects of a user-specified class)
    a. the compiler checks that their instance data has the same values.
    b. `beta`'s data and member functions are copied to `alpha`.

c. beta's data but not its member functions are copied into alpha.

d. the compiler sets beta equal to alpha.

e. the compiler doesn't care if alpha and beta are of the same class.

EXERCISE 1

Rewrite the specification for the airtime class in the TIME1 program so it includes a seconds data member. The new class should work with the same main() that the old class did.

EXERCISE 2

Add a member function to the original airtime class that will advance the time by 1 minute. Handle the case where the minutes value is 59 and adding a minute will cause the hours value to be incremented. If the hours value becomes 24, set it back to 00.

SESSION 6
FUNCTION ARGUMENTS

The member functions you've looked at so far have always done exactly the same thing in the same way. I've asked them to display their object or to get input from the user or—in the case of the `SoldOneDog()` function—to decrement all inventory items. In none of these cases did I need to add additional details to a message when I sent it to an object. (Sending a message to an object is, as you recall, the same as calling one of the object's member functions.)

However, in most cases, you need to supply additional information to a function besides the mere fact that you've called it. This is done with *function arguments*, which are values passed to a function when it is called.

Adding Hours to an `airtime` Value

Suppose that I need to add a certain number of hours to variables of type `airtime`, described in the last session. I might do this to convert an airline departure or arrival to a different time zone. Something that happens at 12:30 in San Francisco happens at 15:30 in Philadelphia, for example. I would carry out this conversion by adding the integer 3 to the hours value of the `airtime` 12:30. I don't need to touch the minutes value at all.

However, I don't always want to increase the number of hours by 3. The time difference between Salt Lake City and Chicago is 1, but between Chicago and London it's 6. How do I convey the number of hours, which will be 1 or 3 or 6 or whatever, to the `airtime` object? As you've guessed, I use a function argument.

Sending a Message with an Argument

Assuming I am sending an `addhours()` message to the `t1` object, telling it to add 3 hours to itself, I would say

```
t1.addhours(3);
```

The argument is placed between the parentheses following the function name. Or I could use a variable name, provided it has already been given the appropriate value.

```
int diffhours = 3;
...
t1.addhours(diffhours);
```

Writing the Member Function

When I write a member function that takes an argument, I must place two things within the parentheses in the function definition: the data type and a variable name, as shown in Figure 2-17.

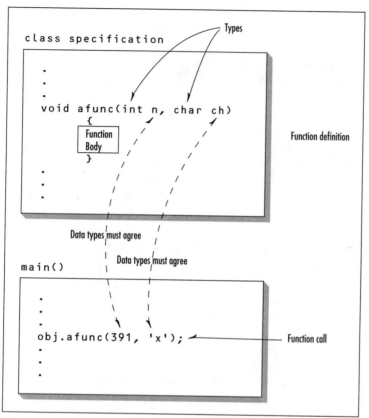

Figure 2-17   Syntax of a function call with arguments

Here's the definition of the `addhours()` member function of the `airtime` class:

```
void addhours(int h)
   {
   hours = hours + h;        // add hours
   if(hours > 23)            // if carry to next day,
      hours = hours - 24;    // subtract a day
   }
```

The `int` in

```
void addhours(int h)
```

specifies the type of data expected as an argument and the `h` is the name of the argument. This argument `h` is a variable that can be accessed anywhere in the function. However, note that `h` is visible (has meaning) *only* within the function; it is unknown to other parts of the program.

The `addhours()` function adds `h` to the hours value of its object. It then checks to see if the resulting hours value exceeds 23; if so, it subtracts 24. (Don't worry about the date.)

Listing for *HOURADD.CPP*

Let's put everything together to see how this new member function might be used in a program. Listing 2-5 is a revision of the TIME1 program that incorporates `addhours()` and lets the user exercise this function. This program is called HOURADD.

Listing 2-5 HOURADD

```
// houradd.cpp
// a class that models a time data type
// includes member function to add hours to a time

#include <iostream.h>
#include <iomanip.h>    // for setw(), etc.

class airtime
    {
    private:
        int hours;        // 0 to 23
        int minutes;      // 0 to 59
    public:
        void set()
            {
            char dummy;

            cout << "Enter time (format 23:59): ";
            cin >> hours >> dummy >> minutes;
            }
        void display()
            {
            cout << hours   << ':'
                << setfill('0')
                << setw(2) << minutes;
            }
        void addhours(int h)
            {
            hours = hours + h;        // add hours
            if(hours > 23)            // if carry to next day,
                hours = hours - 24;   // subtract a day
            }
    };

void main()
    {
    airtime t1;               // airtime
    int diffhours;            // hours
    char choice;              // user's choice: 'n' or 'y'

    do
        {
        cout << "For t1, ";
        t1.set();                  // set t1
        cout << "Enter hours to add: ";
        cin >> diffhours;
```

continued on next page

continued from previous page

```
      t1.addhours(diffhours);   // add hours to t1

      cout << "t1 = ";
      t1.display();              // display t1
      cout << "\nDo another (y/n)? ";
      cin >> choice;
      }
   while(choice != 'n');
   }
```

The user enters an `airtime` value and an hours value, and the program adds them. This continues until the user enters `'n'` to quit the loop.

```
For t1, Enter time (format 23:59): 10:45
Enter hours to add: 3
t1 = 13:45
Do another (y/n)? y

For t1, Enter time (format 23:59): 23:30
Enter hours to add: 5
t1 = 4:30
Do another (y/n)? n
```

Let's look at some other examples where function arguments are helpful.

The `set()` Member Function with Arguments

There's more than one way to design a class. In the `airtime` class (and the `hotdogstand` class as well), I initialized the values of an object's data members by having a member function request the values directly from the user. However, I could instead pass these values as arguments to the member function. This would shift the responsibility for getting user input from the class to the `main()` function. Depending on circumstances, this might be a superior choice.

Let's revise the `set()` member function from the `airtime` class, as seen in the TIME1 program, so that it obtains values as arguments rather than from the user. Let's also revise `main()` to handle user input, as shown in Listing 2-6.

Listing 2-6 TIME2

```
// time2.cpp
// a class that models a time data type
// uses arguments to the set() function

#include <iostream.h>

class airtime
   {
   private:
      int hours;        // 0 to 23
      int minutes;      // 0 to 59
   public:
      void set(int h, int m)    // set airtime value
         {                      // (values supplied by arguments)
         hours = h; minutes = m;
```

```
        }
    void display()              // display airtime value
        {
        cout << hours << ':' << minutes;
        }
    };

void main()
    {
    int hhs, mms;         // variables for user-supplied values
    char dummy;           // for colon
    airtime t1, t2;       // two airtime variables

    cout << "For t1, enter time (format 23:59): ";
    cin >> hhs >> dummy >> mms;
    t1.set(hhs, mms);  // set t1 values

    cout << "For t2, enter time (format 23:59): ";
    cin >> hhs >> dummy >> mms;
    t2.set(hhs, mms);  // set t2 values

    cout << "\nt1 = ";
    t1.display();          // display t1
    cout << "\nt2 = ";
    t2.display();          // display t2
    }
```

The set() member function now takes two arguments: h and m. The body of the function simply sets the hours and minutes instance data items to the values of these arguments.

```
void set(int h, int m)       // (values supplied by arguments)
    {
    hours = h; minutes = m;    // set airtime value
    }
```

Notice the breakdown of effort between the two parts of this program, the class specification and main(). Compared with the TIME1 program, the set() function is simpler, but main() has become more complicated. Actually, in this particular case, this is probably a mistake. The idea in OOP is that classes will be created once but will be used many times in many different programs. Thus it makes sense to embed as much functionality as possible within the class so that every program that uses the class can be simpler.

Arguments of Any Type

I've shown only arguments of type int, but arguments may be of any type, and there can be any number of arguments to a function. Here's the skeleton for a member function that takes three arguments of different types:

```
class Foo
    {
    ...
    void func(int ivar, float fvar, char cvar)  // define function
        {
```

continued on next page

continued from previous page

```
        }
    ...
    };

main()
    {
    Foo foo;                    // make an object
    int iarg = 17;              // make some variables
    float farg = 6.025e23;
    char carg = 'x';
    ...
    foo.func(iarg, farg, carg);  // call the function
    ...
    }
```

I specify a class `Foo` with a member function `func()` that takes three arguments of three different types. Then in `main()`, I create an object of class `Foo` and call `func()` for this object, with appropriate values for the arguments.

Other Uses for Functions

Because I'm focusing on the object-oriented approach to programming, using examples with simple classes and programs, I've shown only one situation involving function calls: from `main()` to a member function. However, functions may be called in all sorts of other situations as well. First, the `main()` part of the program may be divided up into many functions, all of which are called from `main()` or perhaps called from other functions that are called from `main()`. This is a way of organizing the program. Second, member functions within classes may call other functions. You'll see examples as we go along. In the meantime, keep in mind the comforting thought that things can always be more complicated than I show here.

Passing by Value

The method of passing arguments that I have shown here is called *passing by value*. This means that the function creates an entirely *new variable* (a place in memory with a name and a suitable size) to hold the value of each argument passed to it. In the skeleton example above, there are three variables in `main()`, `iarg`, `farg`, and `carg`. When the function is called, it creates three new variables, `ivar`, `fvar`, and `cvar`, and copies the values into them, as shown in Figure 2-18.

The function may modify the variables it has created, but doing so has no effect on the variables in `main()`. This provides a built-in protection mechanism: `main()` can use variables as arguments without worrying that they might be modified by the function it supplies them to.

Sometimes you *want* a function to be able to modify the variables passed to it. When this is the case, you can use a different approach: *passing by reference*. With this mechanism, the function operates on the original variables in `main()`. This approach is used less often, but sometimes it's essential, as you'll see later.

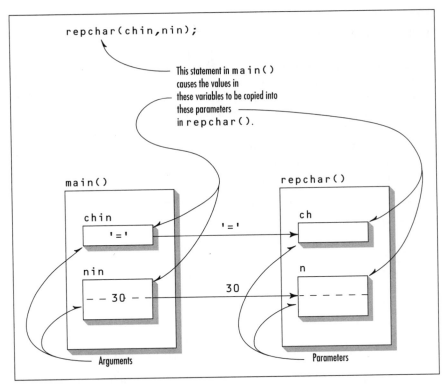

Figure 2-18 Passing by value

1. Function arguments are generally used to
   a. download responsibilities from a class to `main()`.
   b. create new variables that the function can use however it likes.
   c. make a copy of data in case of harm to the original.
   d. pass information to the function.
   e. make functions more versatile.

2. If `var1` is 11 and `var2` is 13, the statement `obj1.dotask(var1, var2);`
   a. assigns the values 11 and 13 to the variables `var1` and `var2` in the `dotask()` function.
   b. transmits 11 and 13 to the `dotask()` member function of `obj1`.
   c. writes 11 and 13 into the instance data of `obj1`.
   d. gets new values of `var1` and `var2` from `obj1`.
   e. assigns 11 and 13 to some other variables in the `dotask()` function of `obj1`.

3. Which of the following might be a reasonable way to tell an object of the `ship` class to locate itself at +120 degrees longitude and -17 degrees latitude? (In case you wondered, west longitude is plus and east is minus, north latitude is plus and south is minus).

   a. `RoyalStar.setPosition(120, -17);`

   b. `RoyalStar.setLongitude(120);`
     `RoyalStar.setLatitude(-17);`

   c. `RoyalStar.setPosition(longitude, lat);`

   d. `RoyalStar(120).setLongitude;`
     `RoyalStar(-17).setLatitude;`

   e. `RoyalStar.setLongitude120();`
     `RoyalStar.setLatitude-17();`

4. The keywords `int` and `float` in the function declarator

```
void afunc(int ivar, float fvar)
   {
   }
```

   a. are optional, because the function already knows the values and types being sent.

   b. specify the data type of the expected values, so the function can check that the correct types are passed.

   c. convert the values passed to the function to type `int` and type `float`, respectively.

   d. tell the function the types of two variables in `main()` so the function can access their values.

   e. create new variables of type `int` and `float`, called `ivar` and `fvar`.

5. When arguments are passed from `main()` by value, the called function

   a. cannot modify the variables whose names are supplied by `main()`.

   b. makes copies of the variables supplied by `main()` to hold the values passed.

   c. can modify the variables whose names are supplied by `main()`.

   d. cannot access the values passed to it.

   e. refers to the same variables as `main()` but uses different names.

EXERCISE 1

Rewrite the HOTDOG1 program so that the `initData()` member function takes two arguments, one for the number of hot dogs and one for the number of buns. To keep the same functionality, rewrite `main()` so it obtains this information from the user.

EXERCISE 2

Write a member function for the `airtime` class that will change the `seconds` data by an integer amount supplied as an argument to the function. You'll need to handle the cases where seconds overflow past 60 and hours overflow past 23. Write a `main()` program to test this new member function.

SESSION 7
ARITHMETIC FOR USER-DEFINED TYPES

You've seen that you can write a member function that will alter one of the data values of an object. (see the addhour() function in the HOURADD program). However, this is not the same as performing arithmetic on an entire object all at once. In fact, you can perform arithmetic on user-defined types just as you can on basic types like float; this is a powerful capability of C++. As examples, I'll show how to add two airtime values and how to multiply an airtime value by a number of type float. Along the way, you'll see how user-defined data types can be used in function arguments.

Adding airtime Values

The add() member function in the airtime class takes two time values as arguments, adds these values, and places the result in the object that called it. That is, if add() is called like this

```
t3.add(t1, t2);
```

then t1 will be added to t2 and the result placed in t3. For example, if t1 is 10:10 and t2 is 2:30, then the result placed in t3 will be 12:40. (Technically, this amounts to adding a time *interval*, not another time, to a time. Adding 2 o'clock to 3 o'clock doesn't really make much sense, but if you leave Denver at 10 minutes after 10 and it takes you 2 hours and 30 minutes to fly to Dallas, then it does makes sense to say you'll arrive there at 12:40.) Listing 2-7 shows TIMEADD.

Listing 2-7 TIMEADD

```cpp
// timeadd.cpp
// a class that models a time data type
// includes member function to add two times

#include <iostream.h>
#include <iomanip.h>      // for setw(), etc.

class airtime
    {
    private:
        int minutes;       // 0 to 59
        int hours;         // 0 t0 23
    public:
        void set()
            {
            char dummy;    // for colon

            cout << "Enter time (format 23:59): ";
            cin >> hours >> dummy >> minutes;
            }
        void display()
            {
            cout << hours   << ':'
                 << setfill('0')
```

continued on next page

continued from previous page

```
                    << setw(2) << minutes;
         }
      void add(airtime at1, airtime at2)
         {
         minutes = at1.minutes + at2.minutes;   // add minutes
         hours = at1.hours + at2.hours;          // add hours
         if(minutes > 59)                        // if carry,
            {
            minutes = minutes - 60;              // adjust minutes
            hours = hours + 1;                   // and hours
            }
         if(hours > 23)                          // if carry,
            hours = hours - 24;                  // adjust hours
         }
   };

void main()
   {
   airtime t1, t2, t3;       // create three airtime variables
   char choice;

   do
      {
      cout << "For t1, ";
      t1.set();              // set t1
      cout << "For t2, ";
      t2.set();              // set t2

      t3.add(t1, t2);        // add t1 and t2, result in t3

      cout << "t3 = ";
      t3.display();          // display t3
      cout << "\nDo another (y/n)? ";
      cin >> choice;
      } while(choice != 'n');
   }
```

Figure 2-19 shows how the function call `t3.add(t1, t2)` interacts with the the `add()` function.

It's important to notice that you can use function arguments of types (classes) you've defined your-self (`airtime` in this case) just as you can with basic types such as `int`. Here the `add()` member function takes two values of type `airtime` as arguments:

```
void add(airtime at1, airtime at2)
```

This is a powerful capability. Variables of a user-defined type can be treated almost exactly the same way as basic types in every aspect of C++ programming.

The `add()` function adds the minutes for the two `airtime` values, then adds the `hours`. If the sum of the `minutes` exceeds 59, then 1 hour is added to `hours` and 60 is subtracted from `minutes`. If the sum of the `hours` exceeds 23, then 24 is subtracted from `hours`. (Don't worry that the resulting `airtime` is the next day.)

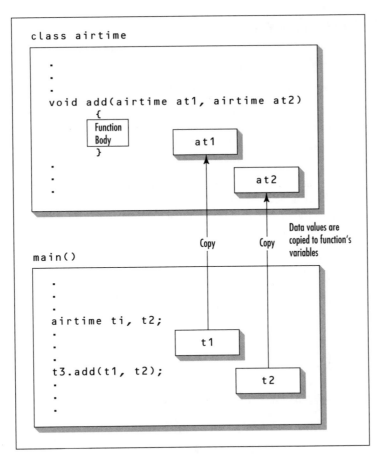

Figure 2-19 Operation of function call with arguments

If using functions such as **add()** to carry out arithmetic seems crude, rest assured that you will eventually learn how to perform arithmetic operations by overloading the arithmetic operators such as + and *. This will make for more natural-looking arithmetic expressions, like

```
t3 = t1 + t2;
```

instead of

```
t3.add(t1, t2);
```

Arithmetic Is Not for All Classes

It makes sense to add objects of type **airtime** because such objects represent a quantity that is basically numerical: time. (Assuming, as I noted, that you imagine adding a time *interval* to a time.) However, addition doesn't make sense for objects of all classes. If I add two objects of the **hotdogstand** class, for example, it's not clear what meaning the "sum" would have.

Access to Private Data

Notice that the `add()` member function can access the private data members of the objects passed to it as arguments. It receives copies of the data in `t1` and `t2` when it's called in the statement

```
t3.add(t1, t2);        // add t1 and t2, result in t3
```

These values are copied in the function's `at1` and `at2` objects. Statements within the function can then access individual data items using the names `at1.minutes`, and so on. This is done in the statements

```
minutes = at1.minutes + at2.minutes;  // add minutes
hours = at1.hours + at2.hours;        // add hours
```

As you may recall, private data items such as `at1.minutes` cannot be accessed by `main()` directly. Because they are private, they can be accessed only by member functions of their own class. However, member functions can access the private data, not only of the object for which they are called (`t3` in this example) but of *any* object, provided it's from the same class (as `t1` and `t2` are). An object's data is private to the outside world, but not to other objects of its own class. Figure 2-20 shows how this looks.

Let's try some sample interaction with the TIMEADD program.

```
For t1, Enter time (format 23:59): 10:10
For t2, Enter time (format 23:59): 10:50
t3 = 21:00
Do another (y/n)? y
For t1, Enter time (format 23:59): 23:59
For t2, Enter time (format 23:59): 0:01
```

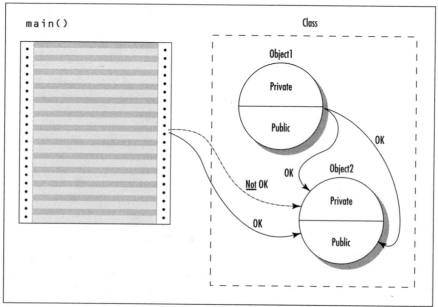

Figure 2-20   Accessing other objects

```
t3 = 0:00
Do another (y/n)? n
```

Converting Minutes to `airtime`

The `add()` member function operated on two variables. Let's look at a different function that operates on a single variable. This function will take as its only argument an `int` value representing minutes (which can be larger than 59). It converts this minutes value into an `airtime` value. This `airtime` value is then stored in the object that called the function. The result is a minutes-to-`airtime` conversion function. Listing 2-8 shows TIMECNV1.

Listing 2-8 TIMECNV1

```cpp
// timecnv1.cpp
// a class that models a time data type
// includes a member function to convert minutes to airtime

#include <iostream.h>
#include <iomanip.h>    // for setw(), etc.

class airtime
    {
    private:
        int minutes;        // 0 to 59
        int hours;          // 0 to 23
    public:
        void set()
            {
            char dummy;     // for colon

            cout << "Enter time (format 23:59): ";
            cin >> hours >> dummy >> minutes;
            }
        void display()
            {
            cout << hours   << ':'
                 << setfill('0') << setw(2) << minutes;
            }
                        // convert minutes to airtime
        void MinsToAirtime(int imins)
            {
            hours = imins / 60;
            minutes = imins - hours*60;
            }
    };

void main()
    {
    airtime t1;
    int iminutes;           //  minutes (can be > 59)
    char choice;
```

continued on next page

continued from previous page

```
    do
        {
        cout << "Enter minutes (for example, 241): ";
        cin >> iminutes;

        t1.MinsToAirtime(iminutes);

        cout << "t1 = ";
        t1.display();      // display t1
        cout << "\nDo another (y/n)? ";
        cin >> choice;
        } while(choice != 'n');
    }
```

In the class specification for `airtime`, I define the member function `MinsToAirtime()`, which converts an `int` minutes value to an `airtime` value. To do this, the function first divides the minutes by 60 to get the hours. The fractional part of this result (representing minutes) is chopped off when the number is converted to type `int` because integers don't have a fractional part. The resulting hours value becomes the `hours` instance data in the object that called `MinsToAirtime()`, which, as can be seen in `main()`, is `t1` in this example. To obtain minutes, the function subtracts the number of minutes in the `hours` variable (`hours*60`) from the original number of minutes and assigns this to the instance variable `minutes`.

In `main()`, I ask the user for a minutes value and then convert it to `airtime` by calling `MinsToAirtime()` for the `t1` object. The resulting value of `t1` is then displayed in the usual way with the `display()` member function, just to prove that the conversion works.

Nonautomatic Conversions

Conversions, such as the one from minutes to `airtime`, play an important role in C++ programs. Remember that C++ automatically converts basic types from one to another. For example, you can say

```
int ivar = 27;
float fvar;

fvar = ivar;
```

and the C++ compiler will arrange for the integer value 27 to be converted to the equivalent floating-point value, 27.0, for storage in `fvar`. Such conversions are completely automatic. The conversion routines are built into the compiler, and it knows how to use them.

However, when you convert between basic types and types you've specified yourself, such as `airtime`, there are no routines built into the compiler to handle the conversion. (After all, it doesn't know what type you might invent.) You must write the routines yourself, as I've done here with `MinsToAirtime()`. I'll be returning to the subject of conversions.

Multiplying an `airtime` Value

Let's look at another example of arithmetic on the user-defined data type `airtime`. Multiply an `airtime` value by a floating-point number. Such an operation might be handy if, for example, you want to know how long it would take an airplane mechanic to service 23 jet engines if it takes her 1 hour and 15 minutes to service one engine. Listing 2-9 shows TIMEMULT.

Listing 2-9 TIMEMULT

```cpp
// timemult.cpp
// a class that models a time data type
// includes a member function to multiply a time by a float

#include <iostream.h>
#include <iomanip.h>       // for setw(), etc.

class airtime
    {
    private:
        int minutes;        // 0 to 59
        int hours;          // 0 t0 23
    public:
        void set()
            {
            char dummy;     // for colon

            cout << "Enter time (format 23:59): ";
            cin >> hours >> dummy >> minutes;
            }
        void display()
            {
            cout << hours  << ':'
                 << setfill('0') << setw(2) << minutes;
            }
                         // multiply airtime by float
        void mult(airtime at1, int mplier)
            {                               // convert to minutes
            int im = at1.hours * 60 + at1.minutes;
            int ianswer = im * mplier;      // do the multiply
            hours = ianswer / 60;           // convert back to
            minutes = ianswer - hours*60;   // hours and minutes
            }
    };

void main()
    {
    airtime t1, t2;             // create airtime variables
    int m;                      // multiplier
    char choice;

    do
        {
        cout << "For t1, ";     // get t1 from user
        t1.set();               // set t1
        cout << "Enter multiplier: ";
        cin >> m;               // get multiplier

        t2.mult(t1, m);         // multiply t1 by m, result in t2

        cout << "t2 = ";
        t2.display();           // display t2
```

continued on next page

continued from previous page

```
        cout << "\nDo another (y/n)? ";
        cin >> choice;
        } while(choice != 'n');
    }
```

The user enters an `airtime` value and an integer to be used as a multiplier. Here's some sample interaction. As you can see, servicing the 23 engines will take 28 hours and 45 minutes.

```
For t1, Enter time (format 23:29): 1:01
Enter multiplier: 3
t2 = 3:03
Do another (y/n)? y
For t1, Enter time (format 23:29): 1:15
Enter multiplier: 23
t2 = 28:45
Do another (y/n)? n
```

The `mult()` member function takes two arguments, one of type `airtime` (which is `t1`) and one of type `int` (called `m`, for multiplier). It multiplies these together and stores the resulting `airtime` value in the object that called it (`t2`).

This function first converts the `t1` `airtime` value to an integer, `im`, representing minutes. It then multiplies this value by the multiplier `mplier` and saves the answer in `ianswer`. To convert this all-minutes value back to an hours-and-minutes `airtime` value, it uses the same approach shown in the TIMECONV1 program. As you can see, two different data type conversions are actually carried out in this one function: `airtime` to minutes and minutes to `airtime`.

Notice that in both the `sub()` and the `mult()` functions, the answer is stored in the `airtime` object that called the function. The answer to a calculation can be placed in other objects as well, as you'll see in the next lesson, on function return values.

Calling Each Other

A member function can call another member function. In the `mult()` function in TIMEMULT, I performed the same conversion from minutes to `airtime` that I did in the `MinsToAirtime()` function in the TIMECNV1 program. I could have saved myself the trouble of rewriting this conversion code by using the `MinsToAirtime()` function instead. Here's how I would rewrite `mult()` to do this:

```
// multiply airtime by int
void mult(airtime at1, int mplier)
    {                             // convert to minutes
    int im = at1.hours * 60 + at1.minutes;
    int ianswer = im * mplier;    // do the multiply
    MinsToAirtime(ianswer);       // convert back to airtime
    }
```

The `MinsToAirtime()` function, because it is being called from a member function, is smart enough to act on the same object as the function that called it. That is, it will operate on the `hours` and `minutes` data in `t3`. It doesn't need to be called with an object name and the dot operator, as member functions do in `main()`. Of course, the `MinsToAirtime()` function would also need to appear in the class specification.

```
                            // convert minutes to airtime
void MinsToAirtime(int imins)
    {
    hours = imins / 60;
    minutes = imins - hours*60;
    }
```

QUIZ 7

1. Performing arithmetic on user-defined types is useful
   a. when the user-defined type represents something that acts like a number.
   b. for the same reason it's useful to perform arithmetic on basic types such as int and float.
   c. because otherwise it's impossible to access an object's private data.
   d. in situations where the data in an object is numerical.
   e. any time two objects have similar data.

2. In the statement t3.add(t1, t2); found in the TIMEADD program in this lesson,
   a. the function add() could, if it were rewritten in the class specification, add the values of t1 and t3 and place the result in t2, without changing the format of the call.
   b. the arguments t1 and t2 are variables of a basic C++ type.
   c. the values in t1 and t2 are added and the result is placed in t3.
   d. the function add() is a member function of the t3 object.
   e. the add() function can access private data in three objects.

3. We use a member function of class A to perform arithmetic on objects of class A because
   a. the compiler won't let you call a function of class A from an object of any other class.
   b. only member functions of class A can access the private data of class A objects.
   c. only member functions of class A can access public parts of class A objects.
   d. functions in class A cannot access public data in class A.
   e. functions in other classes cannot access the private data of objects of class A.

4. A member function that converts a value from a basic data type to a user-defined data type
   a. is impossible because a user-defined type is not a number.
   b. can place the new value in the object that called the conversion function.
   c. can get the old value from the object that called the conversion function.
   d. can take the user-defined type as a pass-by-value argument.
   e. can take the basic type as a pass-by-value argument.

5. The statement t3.mult(t1, t2); in which the variables are all of class airtime (as defined in the TIMEMULT program in this lesson)
   a. will apparently cause t1 to be multiplied by t2.
   b. implies that the mult() function can modify data only in t1, t2, or t3.
   c. implies that the mult() function can modify data only in t1 or t2.
   d. implies that the mult() function can modify data only in t3.
   e. doesn't make sense, because multiplying two airtime values has no meaning.

EXERCISE 1

Write a `sub()` member function for the `airtime` class that subtracts one `airtime` value from another. Write a `main()` that allows the user to test this function. Assume that the smaller (earlier) time value will always be subtracted from the larger so that negative values will not arise.

EXERCISE 2

Write a minutes-to-airtime conversion member function for the `airtime` class. You can call it `MinsToAirtime()`. This function should take an all-minutes time value, which can have values such as 65 and 241, as its only argument. The function should convert this minutes value to an `airtime` value in hours and minutes and store these values in the object that called it. Write a `main()` that tests this function by asking the user for a minutes value, and then convert this quantity into an `airtime` and display it.

SESSION 8

FUNCTION RETURN VALUES

So far, all the functions I've used have been type `void`; that is, they have not returned a value. When a member function, such as `add()` or `MinsToAirtime()`, generated a value, this value was given to the object itself. But what happens if you need a function to generate a value of some other type? Then the value can't be inserted in the object that called the function. What can you do with it?

The function can return the value. This means that the call to the function actually takes on the new value and can be assigned or otherwise used as if it were a constant.

Converting `airtime` to Minutes

As an example of a function that returns a value, I'll develop a member function for the `airtime` class that's the opposite of `MinsToAirtime()`. That is, the new function, `AirtimeToMins()`, will convert an `airtime` value to a minutes value and will return this minutes value. (This minutes value can be greater than 59 because it represents both hours and minutes.) Listing 2-10 shows TIMECNV2.

Listing 2-10 TIMECNV2

```
// timecnv2.cpp
// a class that models a time data type
// includes member function to convert airtime to minutes

#include <iostream.h>
#include <iomanip.h>    // for setw(), etc.

class airtime
    {
```

```
    private:
        int minutes;        // 0 to 59
        int hours;          // 0 to 23
    public:
        void set()
            {
            char dummy;     // for colon

            cout << "Enter time (format 23:59): ";
            cin >> hours >> dummy >> minutes;
            }
        void display()
            {
            cout << hours   << ':'
                    << setfill('0') << setw(2) << minutes;
            }
        int AirtimeToMins()    // convert airtime to minutes
            {
            int imins = hours*60 + minutes;
            return imins;
            }
    };

void main()
    {
    airtime t1;
    int iminutes;                   //  minutes (can be > 59)
    char choice;

    do
        {
        cout << "For t1, ";      // get airtime value from user
        t1.set();
                                 // convert airtime to minutes
        iminutes = t1.AirtimeToMins();

        cout << "Minutes = "     // display minutes
            << iminutes;
        cout << "\nDo another (y/n)? ";
        cin >> choice;
        } while(choice != 'n');
    }
```

In `main()`, I obtain an `airtime` value from the user and store it in `t1`. Then I call `AirtimeToMins()` with `t1` as an argument. The return value from this function is the equivalent time in minutes, which is then displayed.

Notice how I treat the entire expression `t1.AirtimeToMins()` as if it were a value, assigning it to the variable `iminutes`.

The return Statement

Any function will return to the code that called it when control "falls through" the bottom of the function (passes from the last statement to the closing brace). However, this simple approach doesn't allow you to return a value. For a function to return a value, it must use a `return` statement. The keyword `return` can be followed by an expression that evaluates to the value to be returned. In `AirtimeToMins()`, I say

```
return imins;
```

which causes the minutes value, stored in `imins`, to be returned, as shown in Figure 2-21.

A `return` statement causes control to jump immediately out of the function and to return to the code that called it. The expression following `return` must be the same type as the type of the function. This expression is optional. If it's not included, then the function must be of type `void`, meaning it does not return a value. In `void` functions, a return statement is not necessary (as you've already seen in numerous examples), provided you want the function to end at its last statement. Using `return` gives you the option of exiting from the function anywhere.

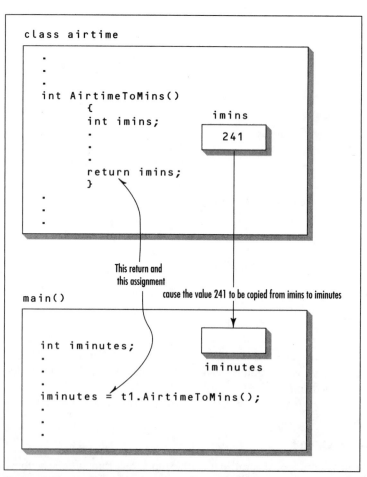

Figure 2-21   Operation of the `return` statement

Creating Automatic Variables

You've seen examples of variables that are defined in a function body. Mostly these definitions have occurred at the beginning of the function and defined a variable without giving it a value.

```
int somevar;
...
somevar = 3;
```

However, it's also possible to initialize a variable at the same time it's defined. Not only that, but the value used to initialize it can be calculated in the same statement. This is what I do in the `AirtimeToMins()` function.

```
int imins = hours*60 + minutes;
```

Defining a variable and calculating it in the same statement is not a common idiom in C, but it's used frequently in C++.

When a function returns to the program that called it, any automatic variables created within the function, such as `imins`, are destroyed. (That's why they're called automatic; they're created automatically when the function is called and destroyed automatically when the function returns.) In this case, the value of `imins` is returned just in time—as soon as the `return` statement has finished executing, the function returns and `imins` is destroyed.

The Stack

Automatic variables are stored in a part of computer memory called the *stack*. The stack grows and shrinks as functions are called and returned. It has a maximum size, usually several thousand bytes, so you can't use huge amounts of automatic data (unless you make special arrangements to enlarge the stack). When an automatic variable is first created, it has a random "garbage" value, probably not zero. This is because the stack has just expanded into an (often) previously occupied part of memory. The moral is: Don't trust that an automatic variable will have an initial value of 0; be sure to initialize it before you use it.

Nameless Automatic Variables

You can simplify the `AirtimeToMins()` function. You don't actually need to give a name to the variable that holds the result of the calculation. Instead, rewrite the function like this:

```
int AirtimeToMins()    // convert airtime to minutes
  {
  return hours*60 + minutes;
  }
```

The number of minutes will be calculated as before and assigned to a nameless variable. This variable will be type `int`, because that's the return type of the function. Its value will be returned and the nameless variable will be destroyed when the function returns, just as `imins` was in the original version of the function.

Returning a Value from add()

C++ is nothing if not versatile, and there are often many ways to carry out a given task. As an example, I'll rewrite the add() member function of airtime so that it returns a value instead of storing the result of its addition in the object that called it. As you may remember, add() in the TIMEADD program was called this way

```
t3.add(t1, t2);
```

where the values of t1 and t2, passed as arguments, were added and the result was stored in t3, the object that called add() in the first place.

However, if I use a version of add() that returns a value, I can rewrite this statement in a different way.

```
t3 = t1.add(t2);
```

This is a mixed blessing in terms of clarity. It's more natural to assign t3 the result of the addition, because that's closer to the way it would be written in normal algebra: t3=t1+t2. However, t1 and t2 are now treated differently: t1 is the object for which the function is called and t2 is an argument to the function. This looks odd, because t1 and t2 play the same kind of role.

Whether it's any clearer or not, this new version of add() works just as well as the old one. Listing 2-11 shows TIMERET.

Listing 2-11 TIMERET

```cpp
// timeret.cpp
// a class that models a time data type
// member function to adds times, returns time value

#include <iostream.h>
#include <iomanip.h>      // for setw(), etc.

class airtime
    {
    private:
        int minutes;      // 0 to 59
        int hours;        // 0 t0 23
    public:
        void set()
            {
            char dummy;    // for colon

            cout << "Enter time (format 23:59): ";
            cin >> hours >> dummy >> minutes;
            }
        void display()
            {
            cout << hours   << ':'
                 << setfill('0') << setw(2) << minutes;
            }
        airtime add(airtime at2)
            {
            airtime temp;
```

```
                temp.minutes = minutes + at2.minutes;   // add minutes
                temp.hours = hours + at2.hours;          // add hours
                if(temp.minutes > 59)                    // if carry,
                    {
                    temp.minutes = temp.minutes - 60;    // adjust minutes
                    temp.hours = temp.hours + 1;         // and hours
                    }
                if(temp.hours > 23)                      // if carry,
                    temp.hours = temp.hours - 24;         // adjust hours
                return temp;
                }
        };

void main()
    {
    airtime t1, t2, t3;        // create three airtime variables
    char choice;

    do
        {
        cout << "For t1, ";
        t1.set();              // set t1
        cout << "For t2, ";
        t2.set();              // set t2

        t3 = t1.add(t2);       // add t1 and t2, result in t3

        cout << "t3 = ";
        t3.display();          // display t3
        cout << "\nDo another (y/n)? ";
        cin >> choice;
        } while(choice != 'n');
    }
```

In the `add()` function, the program creates an object, called `temp`, of class `airtime`. This is an automatic variable and it will be destroyed when the function returns, just as any automatic variable is. Remember, the compiler treats all variables the same, whether they are of a built-in type or a type defined in the program.

You might wonder if there's a way to generate nameless temporary objects. There is, but to use them you'll need to learn about constructors, a topic I'll get to in Chapter 5.

Returning by Value

I should note that the `return` statements I examine in this session return *by value*. The actual value is passed back to the code that called the function. In other words, there will be—at least briefly— two variables holding the same value: one in the function and one in the code that called the function.

Another mechanism can be used to handle return values: returning *by reference*. In this case, the code that calls the function receives only a *reference* to the original variable in the function. However, you'll need to learn about constructors before I talk about returning by reference.

Library Functions

Now that you know about function arguments and return values, I can mention the existence of C-style library functions. These functions were developed for the C language, but can also be used in C++. Many of these functions are not as useful in C++ as they are in C (such as I/O functions, assuming you use the C++ stream classes). However, C library functions are still an essential aspect of C++ programming. There are library functions for input/output, data conversions, string handling, directory and file control, memory allocation, math, process control, and so on. You'll encounter many of these functions.

As an example, let's look at the `sqrt()` function, which returns the square root of a floating-point number. This skeleton code shows the essentials.

```
#include <math.h>          // needed for sqrt()
...
double answer, somenum;    // sqrt operates on type double
...
answer = sqrt(somenum);    // find the square root
```

To use a library function, you'll need to look it up either in your compiler's online help or in the manual. The first thing you'll need to know is the name of the appropriate header file. Every library function requires that a header file be included before the function is called; here it's MATH.H. Most of the math-related functions use this same header file.

The documentation will also tell you the data types of the function's arguments and return value. The `sqrt()` function takes a single argument of type `double` and returns the same type, so in this example, both `somenum` and `answer` are type `double`. Other examples of library functions will pop up in future lessons.

1. In the TIMECNV2 program, converting a value from `airtime` to minutes involves using a function that
   a. returns a minutes value.
   b. accesses a minutes value provided as an argument.
   c. accesses the private data of the `airtime` object that called it.
   d. accesses the private data of the `airtime` variable provided as an argument.
   e. cannot exist, because `airtime` values are not numbers.

2. Depending on how it's written, a `return` statement may cause
   a. control to return from a function when the closing brace is reached.
   b. control to return from a function immediately.
   c. control to return from a function once the return value is calculated.
   d. a function definition to assume a value.
   e. a function call to assume a value.

3. An automatic variable is created when which two events have occurred?
   a. The program loads.
   b. The program executes.
   c. The variable is defined.
   d. The variable is assigned a value.
   e. Control is transferred to the function in which the variable is defined.

4. Returning the answer from a function that adds two user-defined values is superior to putting the answer in the object that called the function because
   a. the object that called the function is destroyed when the function returns.
   b. you can use the equal sign as it's used in arithmetic.
   c. one of the values to be added is the object that called the function.
   d. one of the values to be added is an argument to the function.
   e. it's awkward to use an argument to send the answer back to the code that called the function.

5. Returning from a function *by value* means that
   a. a nameless temporary object (or variable) is always created in the function.
   b. a function call can be assigned to a variable.
   c. a reference to a variable defined in a function is returned.
   d. a reference to a variable defined outside a function is returned.
   e. the function must be of type `void`.

EXERCISE 1

Write statements to create variables called `LetterCode`, `SalePrice`, and `Quantity` of types `char` `double` and `long`.

EXERCISE 2

Write statements to set the three variables in Exercise 1 to `'V'`, 67.95 and 1,000,000, respectively.

SUMMARY: CHAPTER 2

In this chapter, you've seen two quite different kinds of complete, working C++ programs: one in which a class represents hot dog stand inventory data and another in which a class models a data type that represents time. Because time is a numerical entity, you can treat a class that models it as a new, user-defined C++ data type.

I also focused on some of the nuts and bolts of C++ programming: loops (`while`, `do`, and `for`), decisions (`if`, `if...else`, the `else if` construction, `switch`, and the conditional operator), and function arguments and return values. I used various kinds of loops and decisions in programs that further extend the capability of the hot dog stand and time programs.

A major focus was expanding the kinds of member functions you can write. You saw how to write member functions that perform arithmetic on objects and that convert from one data type to another.

Finally, I discussed several more subtle features of C++. You discovered that you can assign the value of one object to another the same way you can with basic C++ types. You also learned that, although it may be convenient to think of each object as containing both data and member functions, the member functions are actually shared by all objects of a class. The function examples you've seen so far pass arguments by value; that is, values are copied from the calling program to variables in the function. The functions also return by value, which means that a copy of a variable in the function is returned to the calling program.

You learned that member functions can access the object for which they are called. They can also access objects sent to them as arguments, provided these objects are of the same class as the member function.

Automatic variables or objects are created automatically when a function is called and are destroyed when the function returns. Automatic variables are stored on the stack. Some automatic variables have no name and are created temporarily to store the results of evaluating expressions.

C-style library functions are available to carry out many tasks. They are not object oriented but they are very helpful in some situations, such as mathematics operations.

END-OF-CHAPTER DISCUSSION

George: I was just getting used to the idea that objects represent things in the real world, and now it turns out they can represent data types. Anyway, doing arithmetic on objects is too weird. No one would do addition using a function!

Estelle: Poor George. I know you hate this answer, but again I think the payoff is going to come later.

Don: Right. It doesn't buy you much to add two `airtime` values with a function such as `add()`, but it'll be a lot more interesting to say `t3=t1+t2`, just like in ordinary arithmetic.

George: Yeah, that may be cute, but what good is it? I can calculate time values in C just by using separate variables for hours and minutes. I don't see that this `airtime` class is making my life any easier. These sample programs he's showing us are more complicated than a C program would need to be.

Estelle: That's because you're looking at both parts of the program: the class specification and the `main()` function. But suppose you bought a whole `airtime` class library. Then the class specification and all the member functions would already be written and you wouldn't need to put them in your listing, you could just use an #include. You probably wouldn't even need to look at the source files for the class. You'd just need to create objects and send them messages.

George: You mean define weird things and call their member functions.

Estelle: Whichever way you like to say it.

Don: You'd need a description of how the member functions worked, like what arguments and return values to use for `add()` and `display()` or whatever.

Estelle: Right, so you'd know how to use them. But looking up a short description of a function is a lot easier than trying to figure it out from the source code.

Don: Usually.

Estelle: And if you look at the listings of the programs we've seen so far, about half the lines of code are the class specification. If all you had to worry about was `main()`, things would be pretty easy.

George: Easy as chopping wood with a broom, as my granny used to say.

Estelle: Come on, George. Get with the program.

CHAPTER 3

ARRAYS AND STRINGS

Arrays are the most common way to combine a number of data items into a single unit. Most computer languages include array handling in their fundamental syntax, and C++ is no exception. Because arrays are such a fundamental data storage mechanism, I'll devote several sessions to them. Also, as it turns out, a text string in C++ is treated as an array of characters. So after you've seen what arrays can do in general, I'll introduce strings.

Arrays do have an important limitation: The variables stored in an array must all be of the same type. However, you can group variables of different types together in another storage mechanism called a structure, so I'll talk about structures as well. Finally, I'll introduce the enumerated data type, which is a sort of simple way to create your own data types. Along the way, you'll make the acquaintance of some new and surprising classes.

123

ARRAY FUNDAMENTALS

An array is a way to group together a number of variables of a single data type. Arrays are useful primarily because the individual variables stored in an array can be accessed using an *index number*. This makes it easy to cycle through the array, accessing one variable after another.

In this session, I'll look at the fundamentals of array syntax. Later in this chapter, you'll see how to put arrays to work, first as instance data in a class and then as an array of class objects.

Defining an Array

To define an array, you tell the compiler to set aside storage for a given number of data items of a specified type. You also tell the compiler the name of the array. Here's an example of an array definition that creates storage for four integers. I'll give this array the name `age`; perhaps it will be used to store the ages of four people.

```
int age[4];
```

The `int` specifies the type of data to be stored, `age` is the name of the array, and 4 is the size of the array; that is, the maximum number of variables of type `int` that it will hold. Brackets `[]` (*not* braces or parentheses) surround the size. It's the brackets that tell the compiler I'm defining an array and not something else, such as a function. Figure 3-1 shows the format of this array definition.

You can define arrays of any data type, of course. Here's an array of 100 variables of type `float`, called `foo`:

```
float foo[100];                 // 100 floats
```

There is also no problem defining arrays of types you have created yourself, using classes:

```
airtime DenverDepartures[50];   // array of 50 airtimes
```

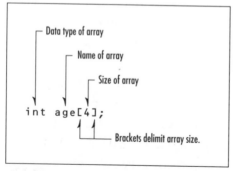

Figure 3-1 Syntax of array definition

The type of the array can be any kind of class, whether it behaves like a data type or not:

```
HotDogStand stands[6];          // array of 6 hot dog stands
```

Here you have an array of objects that represent physical objects, not data types. It doesn't matter to the compiler.

Array Elements

Each variable stored in an array is called an *element*. The elements are numbered. These numbers are called *index numbers* or *indexes*. Some people also refer to them as *subscripts*. The index of the first array element is 0, the index of the second is 1, and so on. If the size of the array is n, the last element has the index n-1. For example, in the `age` array, which has a size of 4, the elements are numbered 0, 1, 2, and 3. This numbering can be the source of some confusion. Keep in mind that the last element in an array has an index *one less* than the size of the array.

Figure 3-2 shows the array elements for the `age` array stored in memory. (Here each element is assumed to occupy 2 bytes.) The elements have been given the values 44, 16, 23, and 68. Don't confuse the *values* of the elements with their *index numbers* (0 to 3).

Accessing Array Elements

You refer to individual array elements using their index numbers and the array name. Somewhat confusingly, the brackets [ ] are used again, but in a different context than in defining an array. As you

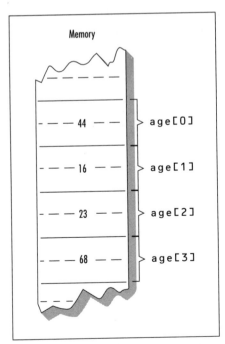

Figure 3-2 Array elements

can see in Figure 3-2, the first element is called age [0], the second is age [1], and so on. You can make statements such as

```
age[2] = 23;
```

which sets element age [2] to a value, and

```
cout << age[3];
```

which displays the value of age [3] (which is 68, given the data in Figure 3-2). Remember that the statement

```
int age[4];
```

defines an array of four elements, but the expression

```
age[2]
```

does not define an array of two elements; it refers to the third element of the array.

The real power of arrays comes from the fact that you can use a variable, rather than a constant such as 2, as an array index. For example, you can print out all the values in the age array with the code

```
int age[4];                  // define the array
...                          // (other code inserts values)
for(int j=0; j<4; ++j)       // cycle through four elements
    cout << age[j] << endl;  // display each element
```

Such code is a common idiom in C++. The for loop cycles through values of j from 0 to 3, which are simply the values of the array index needed to access each element. Notice that the expression j<4 uses the size of the array as a limit, but restricts j to one less than this value. The output from this fragment might be something such as

```
44
16
23
68
```

depending on what values had been inserted into the array. To set the elements of the array age to values obtained from the user, you might say

```
int age[4];
...
for(int j=0; j<4; ++j)
    {
    cout << "Enter the value of element " << j << ": ";
    cin >> age[j];
    }
```

Interaction with this fragment might be

```
Enter the value of element 0: 44    <--User enters 44, 16, etc.
Enter the value of element 1: 16
Enter the value of element 2: 23
Enter the value of element 3: 68
```

Initializing Array Elements

You can set array elements to a value when you first define the array. Here's an example:

```
int coins[6] = { 1, 5, 10, 25, 50, 100 };
```

The first element is initialized to 1, the second to 5, and so on. The equal sign connects the list of values to the array definition, the values are separated by commas, and the list is delimited by braces, as shown in Figure 3-3.

You could display these values with a **for** loop:

```
for(int j=0; j<6; ++j)
       cout << coins[j] << " ";
```

which would produce the output

```
1 5 10 25 50 100
```

Here's another example:

```
int days_per_month[12] = { 31, 28, 31, 30, 31, 30,
                           31, 31, 30, 31, 30, 31 };
```

A surprising feature of array initialization is that you don't need to count how many items are being initialized unless you want to. The definition

```
int coins[] = { 1, 5, 10, 25, 50, 100 };
```

works just as well as the earlier version, despite not specifying the array size. The compiler cleverly counts how many values there are and uses this for the array size.

What happens if you specify an array size but it disagrees with how many initialization values are actually on the list? If there are more values than the array size specified, the compiler complains. If there are fewer values in the list than the array size, the compiler will simply fill out the balance of the array with 0s. Thus if you want to initialize an array—of *any* size—with all 0s, you need only say

```
int anarray[10] = { 0 };    // initialize 10 ints to 0
```

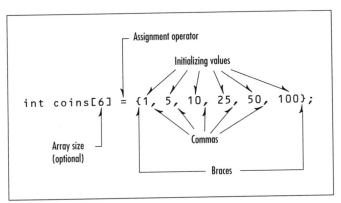

Figure 3-3 Syntax of array initialization

The first element is initialized to 0 explicitly and the remaining 9 are initialized to 0 because no value is given for them. If they are not initialized, the elements of arrays declared *inside* a function will have random (*garbage*) values. Arrays declared outside of a function or class—that is, as external variables—are initialized to zero automatically. You'll learn more about the external storage class in Session 5 in Chapter 4.

Multidimensional Arrays

So far, you've looked only at one-dimensional arrays. You can create arrays of as many dimensions as you like, and each dimension can be a different size. Here's the definition of a 4 by 3 array:

```
float sales[4][3];    // define two-dimensional array
```

Notice that each array dimension is surrounded by its own set of brackets. Don't write [4,3], as is done in some languages. If the first dimension represents sales districts (North, South, East, and West, say) and the second dimension represents the three months in a quarter, then I might represent this array as shown in Figure 3-4.

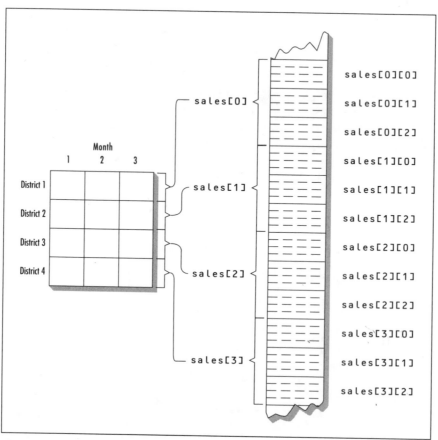

Figure 3-4 Two-dimensional array

Individual array elements are accessed using two indexes. Thus in Figure 3-4, the element in the upper-right corner of `sales` is `sales[0][2]` and the element in the lower-left corner is `sales[3][0]`. To display all the elements of such an array, you would probably use two nested `for` loops.

```
for(int y=0; y<3; ++y)              // step from row to row
   {
   for(int x=0; x<4; ++x)           // step from column to column
      cout << sales[x][y] << ' ';   // display value and a space
   cout << endl;                     // go to next line
   }
```

A two-dimensional array can be looked at as an *array of arrays*. The `sales` array is an array of four subarrays, each of which has three elements. The subarrays are one-dimensional arrays called `sales[0]`, `sales[1]`, and so on. This way of looking at things is important if you want to refer to the subarrays of an array, which is common in arrays of strings, as you'll see later.

To initialize a two-dimensional array, make a list of lists

```
float sales[4][3] = { { 1437.07,    234.50,    654.01},
                      {  322.00, 13838.32, 17589.88},
                      { 9328.34,    934.00,  4492.30},
                      {12838.29,  2332.63,     32.93} };
```

where each subarray is initialized with its own list of numbers separated by commas and delimited with braces; these four lists are in turn separated by commas and delimited with braces.

If you initialize an array as shown here and then use the nested `for` loops to display its contents, the output will be

```
1437.07, 234.50, 654.01
322.00, 13838.32, 17589.88
9328.34, 934.00, 4492.30
12838.29, 2332.63, 32.93
```

A three-dimensional array would be defined with the three dimensions in brackets

```
int cube[4][3][5];    // array of 60 ints
```

and its elements would be accessed with expressions such as `cube[1][2][3]`. Arrays of higher dimensions can be defined and accessed similarly.

Danger: Index Out of Range

You should be aware that C++ contains no built-in mechanism to prevent a program from using an incorrect index value. If your program generates an index value that is smaller than 0 or so large it points beyond the last element of the array, you may be in for big trouble. If you *read* data from nonexistent array elements (really memory outside your array), you will obtain meaningless data. However, if you *write* data into memory outside your array, you may write over other data, your program, or who knows what.

There are two morals here. The first is to be careful when programming arrays. The second is that it would be nice to have a "safe array," one that automatically checks all index values to be sure they are in bounds. As it turns out, you can use a class to create safe arrays. I'll return to this topic later.

Quiz 1

1. To specify an array of 30 variables of type `char` you would say
   a. `int[30] array_name;`
   b. `char array_name[30];`
   c. `array_name char[30];`
   d. `char[30] array_name;`
   e. `array_name[30];`

2. To access the last element of an `int` array `alpha` of 10 elements, you would say
   a. `int[10]`
   b. `int[9]`
   c. `int alpha[0]`
   d. `alpha[10]`
   e. `alpha[9]`

3. A `for` loop to access all the elements of an array of size 7 would most likely be written as
   a. `for(k=1; k<10; ++k)`
   b. `for(k=1; k<7; ++k)`
   c. `for(k=1; k<=10; ++k`
   d. `for(k=0; k<=7; ++k)`
   e. `for(k=0; k<7; ++k)`

4. To initialize an array to the squares of the first six integers, you could write
   a. `int squares[6] = { 1, 4, 9, 16, 25, 36 };`
   b. `int squares[6] = { [1], [4], [9], [16], [25], [36] };`
   c. `int squares[] = {1; 4; 9; 16; 25; 36};`
   d. `int squares{6} = {1, 4, 9, 16, 25, 36};`
   e. `int squares[] = ( 1, 4, 9, 16, 25, 36 );`

5. In the two-dimensional array defined as `int addr[2][20];` that represents the starting and ending locations (in that order) of 20 programs (don't worry about what "location" means), you would refer to the ending address of the third program as
   a. `addr[2][20]`
   b. `addr[1][2]`
   c. `addr[2][1]`
   d. `addr[2][3]`
   e. `addr[3][2]`

Since I am concentrating on syntax rather than complete programs in this session, there are no exercises.

SESSION 2
ARRAYS AS INSTANCE DATA

An array, like any other variable, can be used as instance data in classes. Let's look at an example in a class called **employee**. This class, as you might have guessed, models people who are employees of a company. In this version of the class, the information about the employees is not very complete; it is limited to a name and an employee serial number. A full-scale employee class would include other data, such as home address, salary, position, and date of first employment.

You may wonder, because you have not yet learned about strings (used in C++ for storing text), how I am able to store a name such as John Smith. In this program, I treat a name simply as an array of individual characters and I input and output each character separately. In other words, I make my own strings "by hand." This demonstrates how arrays work and may provide the motivation for learning how to handle strings in a more efficient way (by terminating a string with a zero), which I'll get to in Session 4. Figure 3-5 shows an example of a homemade string stored in memory.

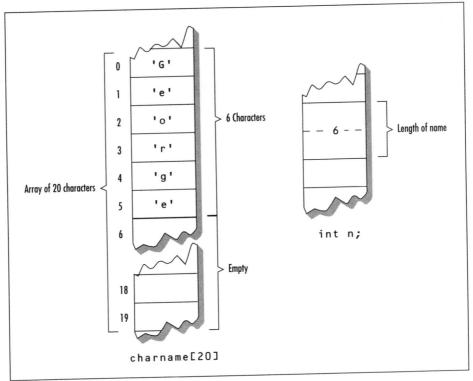

Figure 3-5 Text stored in a homemade string

The employee Class

The employee class contains three data items: an array of type char to hold the letters of a name, an integer n that specifies the length of the name (i.e., how many characters are currently stored in the array), and another integer for the employee serial number. The member functions that obtain and display this data for the user are called input() and output(), respectively. Listing 3-1 shows EMPLOY1.

Listing 3-1 EMPLOY1

```cpp
// employ1.cpp
// models an employee
// uses array of type char for name

#include <iostream.h>
#include <conio.h>                    // for getche()

class employee
    {
    private:
        char name[20];                // name (20 chars max)
        int n;                         // length of name
        int serial_number;
    public:
        void input()                  // get data from user
            {
            char ch;
            n = 0;
            cout << "   Enter name: ";
            do
                {
                ch = getche();        // get one char at a time
                name[n] = ch;         // store in "name" array
                ++n;
                } while(ch != '\r'); // quit if "Enter" key
            cout << "\n   Enter serial number: ";
            cin >> serial_number;
            }
        void output()                 // display employee data
            {
            cout << "   Name = ";
            for(int j=0; j<n; ++j)    // display one character
                cout << name[j];      // at a time
            cout << "\n   Serial number = " << serial_number;
            }
    };

void main()
    {
    employee e1, e2;

    cout << "Enter employee 1 data" << endl;
    e1.input();
```

```
cout << "Enter employee 2 data" << endl;
e2.input();

cout << "\nEmployee 1" << endl;
e1.output();
cout << "\nEmployee 2" << endl;
e2.output();
}
```

I must confess that this source file may elicit warning messages from the compiler, such as "Functions containing do are not expanded inline" and "Functions containing for are not expanded inline." (Your compiler may generate somewhat different messages.) The compiler prefers that I use standalone member functions when the functions contain loops. You'll see what this means when I discuss functions in Chapter 4. In the meantime, don't worry about these messages. The compiler will do the right thing.

In main(), the program creates two employee objects, gets the data from the user for each one, and then displays the data. Some sample interaction with the program looks like this:

```
Enter employee 1 data              <--User enters data
    Enter name: George Harrison
    Enter serial number: 1119
Enter employee 2 data
    Enter name: Paul McCartney
    Enter serial number: 2229


Employee 1                         <--Program displays data
    Name = George Harrison
    Serial number = 1119
Employee 2
    Name = Paul McCartney
    Serial number = 2229
```

Library Function getche()

I used a new library function in the EMPLOY1 program. A weakness of the stream I/O approach to C++ is that there's no way to input a character without pressing the [ENTER] key afterward. However, if you're typing a name, you don't want to press [ENTER] after every character. Fortunately, the C function library contains a function that does just what we want: getche(). This function waits until a single key is pressed on the keyboard and then returns with the ASCII value of the key. There's no need to press [ENTER] to get the character. The getche() function requires that the CONIO.H header file be included. I used this function in a do loop to obtain all the letters of the employee name.

```
do
    {
    ch = getche();         // get one char at a time
    name[n] = ch;          // store in "name" array
    ++n;                      // increment the array index
    } while(ch != '\r');   // quit if "Enter" key
```

Each time through the loop, the getche() function returns with a new character, which is then assigned to an array element. The index n starts at 0 and is incremented each time through the loop by the ++n; statement. (I'll show a more compact way to increment n in a moment.)

The [ENTER] Key

What is the ASCII code for the [ENTER] key? It turns out it's 13 (decimal), but you don't really need to know this, because the escape code `'\r'` (for carriage Return) represents this code. When the program encounters this code, it exits from the `do` loop. At this point, it obtains the serial number from the user, a simpler process.

Displaying a name is the reverse of storing it. The program goes through the array one character at a time, using a `for` loop, displaying each one.

```
for(int j=0; j<n; ++j)    // display one character
   cout << name[j];       // at a time
```

The program knows how long the name is because it counted the incoming characters with `n`, which is included as instance data for the class so it can be accessed by all member functions. (When I discuss real C strings, you'll see that you don't need to store a string length.)

Postfix Increment Operators

When I store characters in the array `name`, I want to start with the array index of 0, as usual, and then increment this index for each additional character. I do this with the code

```
name[n] = ch;    // store the character
++n;             // increment the index
```

The second line here is rather short; it's too bad I need to devote a whole line of code to it. In fact, it would be nice if I could cause `n` to be incremented inside the same statement in which it's used as the array index. Here's how this might look:

```
name[++n] = ch;
```

Can I actually do this? Well, it's perfectly legal syntax as far as the compiler is concerned. However, there's a glitch. The index `n` starts off at 0, and I want to put the first character in array element 0, so I don't want to increment `n` until *after* the contents of `ch` have been placed in the array. Unfortunately, `++n` causes `n` to be incremented *before* it is used. The result will be that the first character of the name will go in `name[1]` instead of in `name[0]`.

Is there a way to increment `n` after it's used? The designers of C and C++ anticipated just this situation and built the necessary capability into the increment and decrement operators. Here's the statement rewritten so it works properly:

```
name[n++] = ch;
```

When the `++` operator *follows* its operand, it's called a *postfix* operator. When it *precedes* its operand, as you've seen several times before, it's called a *prefix* operator. The prefix operator is applied before the value of the variable is used, whereas the postfix operator is used after the variable is used. This is summarized as follows.

```
++n    Prefix operator        Incremented before being used
n++    Postfix operator       Incremented after being used
```

Using the postfix operator, I can rewrite the `do` loop in EMPLOY1 as

```
do
    {
    ch = getche();      // get one char at a time
    name[n++] = ch;     // store in "name" array
    } while(ch != '\r'); // quit if "Enter" key
```

This saves a line of code, which is widely believed to make the listing more readable. You will not be surprised to learn that there is a postfix version of the decrement operator (`n--`) as well as of the increment operator.

The `Stack` Class

An array is a built-in way to store data, but arrays are inappropriate in many situations. A major task of programming is creating other data-storage structures such as linked lists, stacks, queues, hash tables, dictionaries, and vectors. (Here the word *structure* is used in a general sense to mean any mechanism that stores data, not in reference to the C++ `struct`, which you'll encounter later.) Each such storage structure has advantages and disadvantages. It's faster to access a random data item or easier to add an item using some containers, whereas using others, it's easier to search or sort the data.

As it turns out, data storage structures belong in another category that lends itself to being modeled by classes. Along with real-world objects such as hot dog stands and data types such as time, you can also model arrays, linked lists, and so on.

Let's look at an example in which a class models a *stack*. A stack is a data storage structure that is convenient when you want to access the most recently stored data item first. This is often referred to as LIFO, for Last In First Out. It's like a stack of trays in a cafeteria. The dishwasher puts trays on the stack and customers take them off. The last tray placed on the stack goes on top, so it's the first one to be removed. (That's why the tray you get is often still warm and damp; it's been recently washed. Trays at the bottom of the stack may have been there, unused, for weeks.)

Stacks are useful in many programming situations, such as parsing algebraic expressions like `2*x+4*(3+y)`, where they are convenient for storing intermediate results. Hewlett Packard calculators use a stack-based approach to calculations.

Pushing and Popping

Stacks can hold any kind of data, from basic types to complicated class objects. However, like an array, each stack usually holds only one kind of data, `int` or `float` or whatever, but not a mixture. (You can avoid this limitation if you use templates, which you'll encounter in Chapter 11.) When you place a value on a stack, you are said to *push* it; when you take a value off, it's called *popping* it. Figure 3-6 shows what this looks like.

In this example, I use an array, as instance data of the `Stack` class, to store a number of integers. Listing 3-2 shows STACK1, which specifies the `Stack` class and then tests it by creating a stack, pushing three integers on it, and then popping them back off and displaying them.

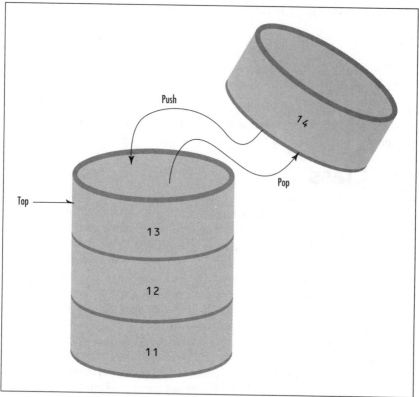

Figure 3-6   Pushing and popping from a stack

Listing 3-2 STACK1

```
// stack1.cpp
// class models a stack

#include <iostream.h>

class Stack                    // a stack holds up to 20 ints
   {
   private:
      int st[20];              // integers are stored in array
      int top;                 // index of last item pushed
   public:
      void init()              // initialize index
         {
         top = -1;
         }
      void push(int var)       // place an item on the stack
         {
         st[++top] = var;
         }
      int pop()                // remove an item from the stack
```

```
        {
        return st[top--];
        }
    };

void main()
    {
    Stack s1;                     // create a stack object

    s1.init();                    // initialize it
    s1.push(11);                  // push 3 items onto stack
    s1.push(12);
    s1.push(13);

    cout << s1.pop() << endl;     // pop 3 items and display them
    cout << s1.pop() << endl;
    cout << s1.pop() << endl;
    }
    }
```

When you pop items off a stack, they appear in reversed order. Thus the output from this program is

```
13
12
11
```

Notice that I use both prefix and postfix operators to manipulate the array index. This instance variable, top, represents the top of the stack. (Think of a pointer to the top cafeteria tray.) It's initialized to -1 with the init() member function when main() first starts. When items are pushed, top is incremented first (++top), and only then used as the index, so top always points one place beyond the last item pushed. When items are popped, they are accessed first and then the index is decremented (top--), so top again points just above the top of the stack.

An Array Disguised as a Stack

The actual instance data, st, which is used as the storage mechanism in an object of the Stack class, is an ordinary array of type int. However, to the user, a Stack object seems to operate like a stack: Data is added and removed with the push() and pop() member functions, rather than with index numbers as in an array. The Stack class wraps an array with class member functions so it looks, to the user, like a completely different storage mechanism.

This is a common theme in OOP classes: They create a new *interface* between the programmer and the data. An example of this is the use of classes to wrap the basic Windows Application Program Interface (API) functions in a new and presumably easier-to-use set of classes and member functions.

Not a Constructor

Initializing top to -1 using a function like init(), as I do in the STACK1 program, is not the favored approach in OOP. One reason is that the programmer who writes main() must remember to call this init() function every time an object (in this example, the Stack object s1) is created. According to Murphy's law, anything that *can* be forgotten, *will* eventually be forgotten, so init() is not a good idea. The solution to this is the *constructor*, which I'll discuss in Chapter 5.

QUIZ 2

1. To insert into an array the characters that constitute a name (such as John Smith) entered by the user, you might say

   a. `j=0; while(ch != ' ') { ch=getche(); charray[++j]=ch; }`

   b. `j=1; while( ch != '\r' ) { ch=getche(); charray[++j]=ch; }`

   c. `j=0; while(ch != '\r') { ch=getche(); charray[j++]=ch; }`

   d. `j=1; while( ch != ' ' ) { ch=charray[j++]; getche(ch); }`

   e. `j=0; while(ch != 13) { ch=charray[++j]; getche(ch); }`

2. The `employee` class in the EMPLOY1 program

   a. contains an instance data item that holds the names of all the employees.

   b. stores data for a number of employees in each object.

   c. includes a member function that displays an employee's name and serial number.

   d. requires the length of the `name` data item to be initialized to -1.

   e. requires that `main()` create an array of `employee` objects.

3. Data storage structures such as stacks and linked lists

   a. can be implemented with classes.

   b. must be implemented with classes.

   c. should not be implemented with classes.

   d. exist because an array isn't always the most useful approach to data storage.

   e. can store data using a different approach than an array.

4. When you push a data item onto a stack in the STACK1 program, you are actually

   a. creating an object.

   b. reading data.

   c. calling an object's member function.

   d. inserting the data item in array position 0.

   e. storing the data item in an array.

5. Which of the following arrangements of `stack` class member functions would work together properly, without wasting space?

   ```
   a. void init()          { top = 1; }
      void push(int var)   { st[--top] = var; }
      int  pop()           { return st[top++]; }
   b. void init()          { top = 0; }
      void push(int var)   { st[++top] = var; }
      int  pop()           { return st[top--]; }
   c. void init()          { top = -1; }
      void push(int var)   { st[++top] = var; }
      int  pop()           { return st[top--]; }
   d. void init()          { top = 0; }
      void push(int var)   { st[top++] = var; }
      int  pop()           { return st[--top]; }
   ```

```
e. void init()        { top = -1; }
   void push(int var)  { st[++top] = var; }
   int  pop()          { return st[--top]; }
```

EXERCISE 1

Seven years after an employee leaves the Amalgamated Widgets company, the employee records are purged of all information about that employee. Add a member function called **purge()** to the **employee** class of the EMPLOY1 program. It should write over the existing data for an employee so that when displayed, the name will have no characters and the serial number will be 0. Modify **main()** so it tests this function.

EXERCISE 2

Sometimes it's useful to examine the data item at the top of a stack without actually popping the item off the stack. (That is, after you've read its value, the item remains at the top of the stack.) A member function that does this is traditionally called **peek()**. Write such a function that works with the **Stack** class of the STACK1 program. Modify **main()** to check it out.

SESSION 3

ARRAYS OF OBJECTS

Just as there can be objects with arrays in them, there can also be arrays of objects. This is a particularly useful construction. You will often want to treat a large number of objects of the same class in a similar way. For example, you may want to display the data from 100 **employee** objects. Placing the objects in an array and using a loop with a member function in it is a simple way to carry out this task.

Defining an Array of Objects

The syntax for defining an array of objects is the same as that for defining an array of a basic type. Of course, you must place the class specification in your file before you try to define any arrays of objects (or single objects, for that matter). If you have already created the specification for the **Xerxes** class, for example, then you can define an array of objects of this class, called **Xarray**, like this:

```
Xerxes Xarray[5];    // array of 5 Xerxes objects
```

All the data for each object in the array is stored contiguously in memory. If you assume that the specification for the **Xerxes** class looks like this:

```
class Xerxes
```

continued on next page

continued from previous page

```
    {
private:
    int ivar;
    float fvar;
public:
    // member functions go here
};
```

then the elements of the array `Xarray`, each of which is an object of the class `Xerxes`, will look as shown in Figure 3-7.

New Syntax for Access

As it happens, you need to learn a new syntax, or at least a variation on some old syntax, to reference member functions of objects stored in an array. Suppose you have a specification for a class `X` like this:

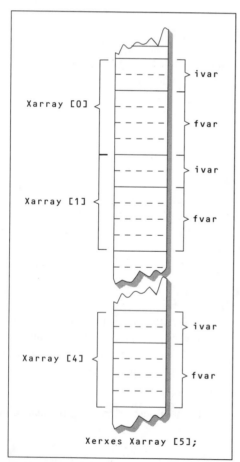

Figure 3-7 Elements of `Xarray` in memory

```
class Xerxes
    {
    ...
    public:
        void afunc()
            {
            // does something here
            }
    };
```

and further suppose that in `main()`, you've defined an array to 10 objects of class **X**

```
Xerxes xa[10];    // array xa of 10 objects of class Xerxes
```

Now the question is, how do you call the member function `afunc()` for the object that is in, say, the third element of the array **xa**? You know you can't say

```
xa.afunc();    // no good; xa is an array, not a single variable
```

because this gives no indication of which element in the **xa** array is calling the function. You need to mix array notation with the dot operator, like this:

```
xa[2].afunc();    // accesses afunc() for the third object in xa
```

This syntax is straightforward, although it looks a little odd at first. Notice that the subscript operator (`[]`) has higher precedence than the dot operator, so the expression is interpreted as `(xa[2]).afunc()` and not as `xa([2].afunc())`. Let's see how this syntax is used in an actual program.

Array of `airtime` Objects

I'll use the same `airtime` class I introduced in the TIMERET program in Chapter 2. In `main()` the program defines an array of `airtime` objects, obtains data for as many such objects as the user wants to type, and finally, when the user has finished with input, the program displays all the data. Listing 3-3 shows ARRAYAIR.

Listing 3-3 ARRAYAIR
```
// arrayair.cpp
// creates array of airtime objects

#include <iostream.h>
#include <iomanip.h>    // for setw(), etc.

class airtime
    {
    private:
        int minutes;    // 0 to 59
        int hours;      // 0 to 23
    public:
        void set()
            {
            char dummy;    // for colon

            cout << "Enter time (format 23:59): ";
```

continued on next page

continued from previous page

```
            cin >> hours >> dummy >> minutes;
            }
        void display()
            {
            cout << hours   << ':'
                    << setfill('0') << setw(2) << minutes;
            }
    };

void main()
    {
    airtime at[20];         // array of 20 airtime objects
    int n=0;                // number of airtimes in array
    char choice;

    do
        {                               // get time from user
        cout << "Airtime " << n << ". ";
        at[n++].set();                  // and insert in array
        cout << "Do another (y/n)? ";
        cin >> choice;
        } while(choice != 'n');

    for(int j=0; j<n; ++j)          // display every airtime
        {                           // in the array
        cout << "\nAirtime " << j << " = ";
        at[j].display();
        }
     }
```

Some sample interaction with the program looks like this:

```
Airtime 0. Enter time (format 23:59): 1:01
Do another (y/n)? y
Airtime 1. Enter time (format 23:59): 23:30
Do another (y/n)? y
Airtime 2. Enter time (format 23:59): 10:00
Do another (y/n)? n

Airtime 0 = 1:01
Airtime 1 = 23:30
Airtime 2 = 10:00
```

The important statements in ARRAYAIR are

```
at[n++].set();      // insert data into object in array
```

which calls the set() member function so the user can enter data for the object in the array at index n (and which subsequently increments n) and

```
at[j].display();    // display data from object in array
```

which calls the display() member function to display the data for the object stored at index j.

Array of employee **Objects**

In a similar way, I can define an array of objects of type employee, last seen in the EMPLOY1 program earlier in this chapter. Listing 3-4 shows ARRAYEMP.

Listing 3-4 ARRAYEMP

```
// arrayemp.cpp
// models an employee
// uses array of employees

#include <iostream.h>
#include <conio.h>                // for getche()

class employee
    {
    private:
        char name[20];            // name (20 chars max)
        int n;                    // length of name
        int serial_number;
    public:
        void input()              // get data from user
            {
            char ch;
            n = 0;
            cout << "   Enter name: ";
            do
                {
                ch = getche();         // get one char at a time
                name[n++] = ch;        // store in "name" array
                } while(ch != '\r');   // quit if "Enter" key
            cout << "\n   Enter serial number: ";
            cin >> serial_number;
            }
        void output()             // display employee data
            {
            cout << "   Name = ";
            for(int j=0; j<n; ++j)    // display one character
                cout << name[j];      // at a time
            cout << "\n   Serial number = " << serial_number;
            }
    };

void main()
    {
    employee emps[100];       // array of employee objects
    int n = 0;                // number of objects in array
    char choice;

    do
        {
        cout << "Enter employee " << n << " data" << endl;
        emps[n++].input();             // get data
```

continued on next page

continued from previous page

```
        cout << "Do another (y/n)? ";
        cin >> choice;
        } while(choice != 'n');

    for(int j=0; j<n; j++)
        {
        cout << "\nData for employee " << j << endl;
        emps[j].output();              // display data
        }
    }
```

There should be no surprises in the operation of this program. The class specification for
`employee` is the same as in earlier examples, and the array of objects is handled as it was in ARRAYAIR.
Sample interaction with the program looks like this:

```
Enter employee 0 data
    Enter name: Henry James
    Enter serial number: 1119
Do another (y/n)? y
Enter employee 1 data
    Enter name: Nathaniel Hawthorne
    Enter serial number: 2229
Do another (y/n)? y
Enter employee 2 data
    Enter name: Edgar Allan Poe
    Enter serial number: 3339
Do another (y/n)? n

Data for employee 0
    Name = Henry James
    Serial number = 1119
Data for employee 1
    Name = Nathaniel Hawthorne
    Serial number = 2229
Data for employee 2
    Name = Edgar Allan Poe
    Serial number = 3339
```

One trouble with arrays is that you must declare an array that can hold the largest number of objects
that you will ever expect to be placed in it. Most of the time, the array will hold fewer objects, so memory space is wasted. A linked list, or an array of pointers to objects, can reduce this kind of memory
extravagance, as you'll see later .

QUIZ 3

1. The member function f() takes no arguments. To call this function for the fourth element in
   an array arr of objects of type X, you would say
   a. f().arr[3];
   b. f(X).arr[3];
   c. arr.f(X);

d. `arr[3].f();`
e. `X arr.f()[3];`

2. Suppose you have a two-dimensional array of `airtime` values, defined as

   `airtime aat[50][100];`

   How would you call the `display()` member function for the `airtime` variable located at the 25th element in the 20th subarray?
   a. `aat[19, 24].display();`
   b. `aat[19][24].display();`
   c. `aat[24][19].display();`
   d. `aat.display([24][19]);`
   e. `aat[25][20].display();`

3. An array of objects is useful when
   a. there are many objects of the same class.
   b. a number of objects of different classes must be stored and accessed.
   c. a number of objects will all have the same values in their instance data.
   d. there are many variables of the same basic type to store as class instance data.
   e. a number of objects all have the same member functions.

4. Assume that n is 5 just before the statement `emps[n++].input();`, taken from the ARRAYEMP program, is executed. You can conclude that
   a. the sixth element of the array will be accessed.
   b. the statement contains a subtle bug.
   c. no additional statement is necessary to move the index to the next array element.
   d. no elements of `emps` will be modified.
   e. data will be obtained from the user and placed in an object of type `employee`.

5. In the ARRAYEMP program, assume the user has entered three employees called Henry James, Nathaniel Hawthorne, and Edgar Allan Poe (as in the example). How many bytes of memory are allocated to storing names?
   a. 45
   b. 2,000
   c. 48
   d. 60
   e. 51

EXERCISE 1

Start with the program HOTDOG3 from Session 4 in Chapter 2. Write a program that uses the `HotDogStand` class, allows the user to enter data for up to 10 hot dog stands, and then displays the data for all the stands, as in the `arrayemp` program. Use an array to hold the `HotDogStand` objects.

EXERCISE 2

Starting with the program in Exercise 1, modify `main()` so the user can choose what action to take by entering one of four letters: `'i'` to initialize the data at a particular stand, `'s'` to record a sale at a particular stand, `'r'` to report the current data for all the stands, or `'q'` to quit the program. You may want to use a `switch` statement to select among these choices and a `while` or `do` loop to cycle repeatedly through the `switch`.

SESSION 4

STRINGS

You learned in Session 2 in this chapter that text—such as a name—can be treated strictly as an array of characters. Loops can be used to input and output the text from such arrays, one character at a time. This is all a little awkward. Text is so common in computer programs that having to program a loop every time text must be handled is not acceptable. Fortunately, C++ provides a sophisticated repertoire of ways to simplify text handling.

The C++ method of text handling treats text as a *string*, which is a sequence of characters terminated by a special character. This approach to text was developed in C, long before the arrival of OOP, so such strings are not object oriented. I will sometimes call them *C strings* to avoid confusion with more sophisticated string classes, which can be created only in C++. However, in most cases the context is clear, and I'll simply call them strings.

Although they are old fashioned, strings are a key feature of both C and C++ programming, and often form the foundation of more sophisticated string classes. It's therefore important to learn about strings, which is what you'll do in the next few lessons.

String Variables

A *string* is a sequence of characters in which the last character has a numerical value of 0 (zero). As a character, this value can be represented by the escape sequence `'\0'`. It is often called the *null character*. Using a special value like this to indicate the end of a text string means that there is no reason to store the length of the text as a separate integer value, as I did in the EMPLOY1 program. Instead, string-handling routines look for the `'\0'` to determine when the string ends.

A *string variable* is an array of type `char`. Like other variables, it may or may not contain a value at any given time. Here's how you would define a string variable called `str`:

```
char str[80];    // string variable; can hold up to 80 characters
```

When the string variable is first created, no value is stored in it. Unlike variables of basic types, string variables can be different sizes; this one can hold a string of up to 80 characters.

Although they are really arrays of type `char`, C++ treats strings in some ways like a basic data type such as `int`. For one thing, `cin` and `cout` know how to handle strings, so you can use ordinary stream

I/O to input or output a string with a single statement. Here's how you would create a string variable, read some text into it from the keyboard, and then display this same text:

```
char str[80];    // create a string variable str

cin >> str;      // get text from user, store in str
cout << str;     // display text entered by user
```

The user types the characters of the string and then presses ENTER. (As you know, this is called *entering* the text.) Figure 3-8 shows how the array `str` looks in memory after the user has entered the string `"Amanuensis"` (which means one employed to copy manuscripts).

String Constants

You can initialize a string variable to a value when you define it, just as you can with other variables. Here's one way to initialize a string variable called `name` to the string `"George"`:

```
char name[20] = {'G', 'e', 'o', 'r', 'g', 'e', '\0'};
```

This is the format used to initialize arrays of other types: a list of values separated by commas. However, typing all those quotes and commas is inefficient to say the least, so the designers of C and C++ took pity on us and acknowledged that strings were slightly more than arrays of type `char` by allowing this kind of initialization:

```
char name[20] = "George";
```

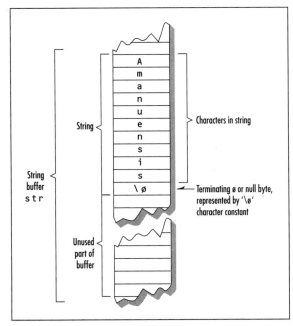

Figure 3-8 String stored in string variable

where double (not single) quotes delimit text. A sequence of characters surrounded by double quotes like this is called a *string constant*. Although you can't see it, a null (`'\0'`) is included as the last character of this string constant `"George"`; it's inserted automatically by the compiler. Thus, although there are only six characters in the name George, there are seven characters in the string constant `"George"`: six letters and the `'\0'` character. If you're creating a string variable, you must keep this in mind. The array you define must be large enough to hold the largest number of characters you will ever store in it *plus one more* for the null character.

```
char name[6] = "George";   // not OK, the '\0' won't fit
char name[7] = "George";   // OK, it just fits
```

A string constant is a value that can be placed in a string variable. You might wonder whether this means you can say

```
name = "George";   // illegal
```

Alas, this doesn't work. In this situation, C++ thinks of a string variable as an array, and you can't use the equal sign to *assign* a whole bunch of values to an array, even though the equal sign is used to *initialize* an array. (Later you'll see that you can make the equal sign do anything you want by overloading it.)

As with any array, you don't need to specify the number of elements in a string variable if you initialize it when you define it. You can say

```
char somestring[] = "Four score and seven years ago";
```

and the compiler will make `somestring` just the right length to hold the string constant (including the null character). This can save you a lot of counting.

Improved String I/O

I've mentioned that you can use `cout` and `cin` for strings.

```
char str[80];

cin >> str;      // get string from user, store in str
cout << str;     // display string entered by user
```

Some sample interaction with this program fragment might look like this:

```
Caramba!    <--user enters this
Caramba!    <--program displays this
```

Used in this way, with the overloaded `>>` operator, `cin` has an unfortunate drawback. Once it encounters a space (the `' '` character) typed by the user, it stops reading the input, so you might have the following interchange with this program:

```
Law is a bottomless pit.
    Law
```

Only the word `"Law"` is stored in `str`. Everything else the user typed is lost. To fix this, you must resort to another construction: the `get()` member function of the `istream` class. I won't explore stream classes in detail until Chapter 10, but you can use their member functions without knowing much about them. To read a string that may contain blanks, you can use this construction:

```
char str[80];

cin.get(str, 80);      // get string from user
cout << str;           // display string
```

Not only does `get()` handle input that contains blanks, it also provides an easy way to ensure that the user won't overflow the string array. The first argument to `get()` is the name of the array where the string will be stored; the second is the maximum length of the string that can be accepted. This length includes the null character, so you can use the same number here that you use for the size of the array. You can then input strings of up to, in this case, 79 characters.

Using `const` Variables

The code fragment just shown provides the motivation to introduce a new keyword. Notice that the number 80 appears in two places: as the size of the array `str` and as the maximum number of characters that can be placed in that array by `cin.get()`. These numbers should be the same; if they're not, the input from `get()` may overflow the array, or—less seriously—space may be wasted in the array because `get()` can't fill it up.

To ensure that these numbers are the same, it's desirable to use a variable instead of a numerical constant, like this:

```
int size = 80;          // array size

char str[size];         // define array

cin.get(str, size);     // get string from user
cout << str;            // display string
```

Now if you change the value of `size` in the first statement, making `size` equal to 40, for example, then both the array size and the character limit in `cin.get()` will be changed automatically, ensuring they remain the same.

This is a safer way to program, but I can go further. An array size cannot be modified during the course of a program. This implies that the variable `size` should be a constant, so that the programmer is prevented from inadvertently modifying it. But how can a variable be a constant? I can mandate this seeming contradiction using the keyword `const`. This keyword is used in the definition of a variable that *cannot change its value* during the course of the program. Here's how you might use `const`:

```
const int SIZE = 80;    // array size: cannot be changed

char str[SIZE];         // define array

cin.get(str, SIZE);     // get string from user
cout << str;            // display string
```

I use all uppercase letters as a reminder that `SIZE` is a constant. Now I can change the value of `SIZE` if I want, but only by rewriting its declaration and recompiling the program. Attempts by other program statements to modify it will elicit a compiler error. Because it cannot be changed, a `const` variable must be initialized to a value when it's first defined.

Old-time C programmers may remember when a preprocessor directive, #define, was used to create constants, as in

```
#define SIZE 80
```

This construction can also be used in C++, but it has fallen out of favor because no data type can be applied to the name, which means the compiler can't verify that the correct type is used. This makes programs potentially more error prone.

The const keyword can be used to improve program reliability in a variety of other situations, notably with function arguments. I'll explore these possibilities in Session 7 in Chapter 5.

Eating Extra Characters

Nothing is perfect, and sometimes when you mix cin.get() with cin >>, a problem arises (at least with some compilers). For example, suppose you say

```
cout << "Enter the patient's age: ";
cin >> age;                          // get a number
cout << "Enter the patient's name: "
cin.get(name, SIZE);                 // get a string
```

The name may not be obtained from the user. Instead, the program appears to skip right over the last statement. Why is this? Because, following the input of the number age, a newline character ('\n') is left behind in the input buffer. When cin.get() is executed, it reads the new line from the buffer, assumes this is all there is to read, and exits. To get rid of this new line, I can employ another member function of istream, called ignore(). Here's the revised code:

```
cout << "Enter the patient's age: ";
cin >> age;                          // get a number
cin.ignore(10, '\n');                // eat the newline
cout << "Enter the patient's name: "
cin.get(name, SIZE);                 // get a string
```

Here the ignore() function reads and discards up to 10 characters (which probably won't be there) and the new line. The moral: If you're having trouble using cin.get(), try using cin.ignore() to eat any extra new lines first.

Real Strings for the employee Class

Earlier in this chapter, I showed several programs that used the employee class. In this class, I stored the employee's name as a simple array of characters, not as a real null-terminated string. Let's rewrite this class to use real strings. This will simplify input and output, because I can use cin and cout for text, instead of for loops. I'll also add a switch statement to main() so the user can operate the program interactively, choosing repeatedly from a list of options. Listing 3-5 shows STREMP.

Listing 3-5 STREMP

```
// stremp.cpp
// models database of employees
// uses switch statement for user choice

#include <iostream.h>
```

```
const int SMAX = 21;        // maximum length of strings
const int EMAX = 100;       // maximum number of employees

class employee
    {
    private:
        char name[SMAX];        // name (20 chars max)
        int serial_number;
    public:
        void input()            // get data from user
            {
            cout << "    Enter name: ";
            cin.get(name, SMAX);
            cout << "    Enter serial number: ";
            cin >> serial_number;
            }

        void output()           // display employee data
            {
            cout << "    Name = " << name;
            cout << "\n    Serial number = " << serial_number;
            }
    };

void main()
    {
    employee emps[EMAX];        // array of employee objects
    int n = 0;                  // current number of objects in array
    int j;                      // loop variable
    char choice = 'x';          // (ensure it's not 'q')

    while(choice != 'q')                // exit on 'q'
        {
        cout << "\n'a' to add an employee"
                "\n'd' to display all employees"
                "\n'q' to quit program"
                "\nEnter letter choice: ";
        cin >> choice;                  // get user's choice
        cin.ignore(10, '\n');           // eat extra '\n'

        switch(choice)
            {
            case 'a':                           // get employee data
                cout << "Enter data for employee " << (n+1) << endl;
                emps[n++].input();
                break;
            case 'd':                           // display all employees
                for(j=0; j<n; j++)
                    {
                    cout << "\nData for employee " << (j+1) << endl;
                    emps[j].output();
                    }
                break;
            case 'q':                           // let the while loop
```

continued on next page

continued from previous page

```
        break;                          // terminate the program
      default:
        cout << "Unknown command";
        break;
    }  // end switch
  }  // end while
}  // end main()
```

String I/O

Notice how using real strings simplifies the `input()` and `output()` member functions of `employee`. The `do` and `for` loops have vanished.

I use `cin.get()` to read the employee's name in the `input()` member function. This requires that I use `cin.ignore()` in `main()` to eat the `'\n'` after the user's letter choice so `cin.get()` won't become confused.

The `switch` statement embedded in a `while` loop makes the program interactive. It displays a list of possible letter choices; when the user enters one, the program carries out the appropriate task before returning to the list of choices. Here's some sample interaction with STREMP:

```
'a' to add an employee
'd' to display all employees
'q' to quit program
Enter letter choice: a

Enter data for employee 1          <--input employee 1
   Enter name: James Joyce
   Enter serial number: 1117

'a' to add an employee
'd' to display all employees
'q' to quit program
Enter letter choice: a

Enter data for employee 2          <--input employee 2
   Enter name: Henry James
   Enter serial number: 2227

'a' to add an employee
'd' to display all employees
'q' to quit program
Enter letter choice: d             <--display all employees

Data for employee 1
   Name = James Joyce
   Serial number = 1117
Data for employee 2
   Name = Henry James
   Serial number = 2227

'a' to add an employee
'd' to display all employees
'q' to quit program
Enter letter choice: q             <-- quit the program
```

External Variables

I should mention that SMAX and EMAX are defined in a new way. The variables you've seen before have been defined either inside a class or inside the main() function. SMAX and EMAX, on the other hand, are defined outside of everything: There are no braces surrounding them. Variables defined this way are called *external variables*. External variables are accessible to all parts of the program, whereas variables defined within a class are accessible only within the class and variables defined inside a function are accessible only within the function. I'll delve into external variables Session 5 in Chapter 4.

1. In C and C++, a string constant
   a. has a character with a numerical value of 0 (zero) at the end.
   b. has a character count stored in memory along with it.
   c. can be assigned to any string variable using the = operator.
   d. is terminated by the null character '\n'.
   e. must be manipulated one character at a time for input/output.

2. Which of the following correctly defines a string variable?
   a. `char stringvar[8] = "piggyback";`
   b. `char stringvar[8];`
   c. `char "piggyback";`
   d. `stringvar[8] = "piggyback";`
   e. `char stringvar[80] = "rolling stone";`

3. The expression `cin.get(buff, MAX)`
   a. displays characters.
   b. reads from the keyboard.
   c. obtains up to MAX characters and places them in buff.
   d. implies that buff should be an array of MAX characters.
   e. is identical to `cin >> buff`.

4. The keyword const, used when declaring a variable,
   a. implies that the variable's value can be changed only by member functions of the const class.
   b. implies that the variable's value cannot be assigned to another variable.
   c. implies that the variable must be given a value at the same time it's defined.
   d. creates variables that can be used for storing keyboard input.
   e. implies that the variable's value won't be changed by other program statements.

5. The architecture of an interactive program, where the user enters one-letter choices, might reasonably involve
   a. a switch in a while loop.
   b. a switch in a for loop.
   c. an else if ladder in a for loop.
   d. an else if ladder in a do loop.
   e. no loops at all.

EXERCISE 1

Modify the **employee** class in the STREMP program of this lesson so that it includes an additional item of instance data to hold the employee's title, such as "Editorial Assistant", "Vice-president of Marketing", "Laborer", and so forth. This modified class should work with the same **main()** found in STREMP.

EXERCISE 2

Write a class called **book** that contains the data necessary to manage books in a bookstore. This includes the title, publisher, price, and quantity on hand. Write a **main()** that stores book objects in an array and allows the user to add a book to the array interactively, display all the books, and sell a book by decrementing the number on hand.

MIDCHAPTER DISCUSSION

Don: Well, at least arrays are pretty straightforward.

George: Except for that little detail about the last element being numbered one less than the size of the array. Or was it one more? I can never remember. Anyway, whatever happened to 10 apples numbered from 1 to 10? That's the natural way to number things.

Estelle: But then you waste the place for number 0. In computers, the first address, or the first anything, is always 0. It's more logical.

Don: You could do it either way, but in C++, arrays just happen to start with 0. You better get used to it.

George: No need to get huffy.

Estelle: How come I learned about two different kinds of strings?

George: Huh?

Estelle: You know, I started off with "homemade" strings, as in the EMPLOY1 program in Session 2. Then I learned about "real" C++ strings, which are terminated with a zero.

George: I didn't know there was a difference.

Estelle: Uh, oh. You're in trouble.

Don: The homemade strings just showed how to treat text as as array of characters. But doing that isn't practical, because you need loops to handle the characters individually. Real C strings are a lot easier to use.

Estelle: You can use a single operator such as `cout` `<<` to output a real string all at once, instead of doing it one character at a time.

Don: And real strings are null terminated, instead of having to store a separate character count.

George: Is that good?

Don: Well, probably. It's another deal where either way would work. A C string is always one character longer than the number of characters, but on the other hand, you don't need an extra integer variable to specify the length.

Estelle: Isn't there a lot of stuff about strings I don't know how to do? Adding strings together, copying them, and comparing them? Are there operators built into C++ to do all that?

Don: I think they use library functions instead of operators, and I bet we'll get to them soon.

SESSION 5

STRING LIBRARY FUNCTIONS

The function library that accompanies most C and C++ compilers includes dozens of functions that operate on strings. Functions copy strings, compare them, search them for other strings, and so on. You'll look at a few of these library functions in this lesson: the most common ones and those that will be useful later in this book. Then you'll put some of these library functions to work to create a simple string class, which can replace ordinary C strings.

Library Functions for Strings

As with all library functions, you can find out more about the string functions by looking them up in your compiler's documentation or online help. What I cover here is just enough to get you started and give you an idea what's available. These string-oriented library functions all require the header file STRING.H.

Finding String Lengths

The `strlen()` function returns the length of a string used as an argument. Here's a fragment in which a string variable `s1` is initialized to `"Songs"` and the `strlen()` function is applied to `s1`:

```
char s1[] = "Songs";
cout << "Length of s1 = "
     << strlen(s1);
```

The output would be

```
Length of s1 = 5
```

Notice that the terminating `'\0'` character is not included in the length reported by `strlen()`. Nevertheless, that character is there in `s1`, taking up space in memory. The array `s1` is actually 6 bytes long.

Copying Strings

You can copy a string variable or constant to another string variable using the `strcpy()` function.

```
char src[] = "Songs";       // string initialized to a value
char dest[80];              // empty string variable

strcpy(dest, src);          // copies the contents of src into dest
```

After this statement has been executed, `dest` will contain `"Songs"`. The string `src` will not be changed. Notice that `strcpy()` causes the string named in its right argument to be copied to the string in its left argument. If this right-to-left direction seems backward to you, remember that it's how the assignment operator (=) works: The value on the right is copied into the variable on the left.

Appending Strings

Appending strings might be called *adding* strings. If you append the string `"hurry"` onto the string `"You better "` the result is `"You better hurry"`. Here's how that might look as a program fragment:

```
char s1[80] = "You better ";
char s2[] = "hurry";
strcat(s1, s2);
```

The string `s1` is now `"You better hurry"`. The library function `strcat()` appends one string to another. The *cat* in `strcat()` stands for *concatenate*, another word for append (although some writers use concatenate to mean that a third string is created that consists of the other two).

Some languages allow you to concatenate strings using the + operator, as in `s1+s2`; this isn't permitted with ordinary C strings. (However, as I'll demonstrate later, you can do this by overloading the + operator in user-defined string classes.)

Let's make a slight change in the previous code fragment. Will these statements operate correctly?

```
char s1[] = "You better ";   // s1 is 12 bytes long
char s2[] = "hurry";         // s2 is 6 bytes
strcat(s1, s2);              // Error: now s1 needs to be 17 bytes
```

No, because the compiler makes `s1` just large enough to hold `"You better "` and concatenating anything else onto it will overflow `s1`, leading to unpredictable but probably unpleasant results. The moral is, when you put a string anywhere, you'd better be sure there's enough space for it.

Comparing Strings

It's often useful to compare strings—in checking passwords, for example. The `strcmp()` function compares two strings and returns a number indicating that the strings are the same or, if they aren't the same, which comes first alphabetically. This function is case sensitive, so `"Smith"` is not the same as `"smith"`.

```
char name[] = "Smith";
n1 = strcmp(name, "Renaldo");    <--returns 1 (first argument follows second)
n2 = strcmp(name, "Smith");      <--returns 0 (first argument same as second)
n3 = strcmp(name, "Townsend");   <--returns -1 (first argument precedes second)
```

Some string functions have close cousins that perform similar but not quite identical tasks. For example, the `stricmp()` function compares two strings in the same way that `strcmp()` does but is not case sensitive; the `i` stands for case *in*sensitive. Thus it will tell you that `"Blue"` and `"blue"` are identical. The `strncmp()` function is also similar to `strcmp()`, except that it looks only at a specified number of characters in the strings it's comparing. Many other string functions have similar variations, signaled by the addition of a letter in the function name.

Some string functions cannot be used effectively without an understanding of pointers, which you'll encounter in Chapter 8. These include functions that search a string for a given character and search a string for another string.

Because the C++ function library was inherited from C, it is not based on classes. However, most C++ compilers also include a class library that contains a string class. For example, Borland C++ includes a class called `cstring`. I'm going to ignore such prebuilt classes for the moment, because it will be more educational to develop our own string class as we go along.

A Homemade String Class

The motivation for creating a string class arises from the deficiencies of ordinary C strings and string functions. What are these deficiencies? Here are a few:

- You must define an array, not a single variable, to store a string.

- You can't copy one string to another with the assignment operator (=).

- The string functions don't warn you if you overflow a string array.

- You can't concatenate strings with the + operator.

- You can't compare strings with the ==, !=, <, and > operators.

In this section, I'm going to take a first step toward creating a homemade string class. I'll address the first two items on the list here; the last three require that you know how to overload C++ operators, so I'll defer them until later.

I'll name the string class `xString`. Its instance data consists of an ordinary string and it includes member functions to initialize itself to an ordinary string, get a string from the user, display its own contents, and append one string to another. A surprising benefit of making a string into a class is that you can use the equal sign to set one xString object equal to another. Listing 3-6 shows STRCLASS.

Listing 3-6 STRCLASS

```
// strclass.cpp
// uses a class to models strings

#include <iostream.h>
#include <string.h>              // for strlen(), strcpy(), etc.

const int MAX = 80;             // maximum length of xStrings

class xString
   {
   private:
      char str[MAX];            // ordinary C string
   public:
      void init( char s[] )     // initialize with string
         {
          strcpy(str, s);
         }
      void input()              // get string from user
         {
         cin.get(str, MAX);
         }
      void display()            // display string
         {
          cout << str;
         }
      void append(xString xs)   // append argument string
         {
         if(strlen(str) + strlen(xs.str) < MAX-1)
             strcat(str, xs.str);
         else
             cout << "\nError: xString too long" << endl;
         }
   };

void main()
   {
   xString s1, s2, s3;          // make xString objects

   s1.init("Greetings, ");      // initialize s1

   cout << "Enter your name: ";
   s2.input();                  // get s2 from user

   s1.append(s2);               // append s2 to s1
   s3 = s1;                     // set s3 to s1
   s3.display();                // display s3
   }
```

In `main()`, the program creates three `xString` objects. It initializes `s1` to an ordinary string using the function `init()`, gets text from the user for `s2` with the `input()` function, appends `s2` to `s1` with `append()`, sets `s3` equal to `s1` using the assignment operator, and finally displays `s3` with `display()`. This may not be exactly what you would want to do with three string objects, but it does provide a chance to exercise all the member functions of the `xString` class.

Now let's look at some features of this program.

Library Functions

I use the `strcpy()`, `strlen()`, and `strcat()` library functions to copy, find the length of, and append ordinary C strings. As you can see, these functions are far more convenient than writing your own loops to do the same thing character by character.

Clean Format

You can see how easy it is to create `xString` objects. You don't need to define arrays, only simple variables (or what look like simple variables but are actually user-defined class objects).

Data Conversions

As I've noted, the `init()` function is a rather clumsy way to initialize an object. You'll learn a more elegant approach when I talk about constructors. However, the `init()` function does do something interesting and useful: It acts as a conversion function, converting an ordinary C string into an `xString` object. The C string is given as an argument to `init()`, which assigns its value to the `xString` object that called it. Converting from one data type to another is an important topic in OOP; I'll return to it later.

Appending

The member function `append()` appends its argument to the object that called it. In this example, whatever name the user enters into `s2` is appended to `"Greetings, "`.

Assignment

Perhaps surprisingly, the assignment operator (=) works with objects (at least these objects). The program sets `s3` equal to `s1`; when it displays `s3`, you can sees that `s3` has indeed taken on the value of `s1`. How can the equal sign work with objects that contain arrays, when it doesn't work with arrays? It seems odd at first, but makes sense when you think about it. For one thing, because all objects of the same class are identical (except for their contents), it's easy to copy the data from one into another, whereas one array may be a different size than another.

Overflow Protection

The `input()` member function provides built-in protection against the user overflowing the `xString` storage buffer (the `str` array). The programmer doesn't need to take any special precautions, such as specifying a buffer size. Also, the `append()` function checks that the two strings that it's about to append won't exceed the size of an `xString`. Thus the `xString` class is safer to use than ordinary C strings.

Of course there's a downside to this safety: All `xStrings` must be the same length. This may waste a lot of memory space for short `xStrings` and precludes using long strings. (Later I'll show how objects of a string class can be made exactly as large as they need to be using dynamic memory allocation.)

Wrapping

Imagine that the xString class was created by one programmer, but another programmer must write a main() that makes use of this class. The main() programmer could use ordinary C strings and library functions such as strcpy(), or she could choose to use the xString class instead. Thus, although the xString class itself uses ordinary C strings and string library functions internally, these are invisible to the main() programmer, who instead sees xString objects and member functions such as input() and append(). This is another example of *wrapping* one set of functions with another to create a new user interface.

QUIZ 5

1. String library functions such as strlen() and strcpy()
   a. work with user-defined class objects.
   b. are useful for ordinary C strings.
   c. are used exclusively with null-terminated strings.
   d. are member functions.
   e. cannot be applied to nonstring arrays of characters.

2. To use the strcpy() library function to copy the string s1 to the string s2, you would say
   a. s1.strcpy(s2);
   b. s2.strcpy(s1);
   c. strcpy(s1, s2);
   d. strcpy(s2, s1);
   e. s2 = strcpy(s1);

3. Which of these statements are true?
   a. The chief task of the single equal sign (=) in C++ is to assign a value to a variable.
   b. You can assign one C string variable to another with a function.
   c. You can assign one C string variable to another with an equal sign.
   d. You can assign any object to another of the same class with the strcpy() function.
   e. You can assign any object to another of the same class with the = operator (assume that = is not overloaded).

4. A string class can reasonably be expected to be superior to ordinary C strings for which of the following reasons:
   a. It's less error prone.
   b. It's easier to program.
   c. It can do more things.
   d. It executes faster.
   e. It takes less memory to store a string.

5. One might want to use a class to "wrap" a group of functions and data in a different group of functions because
   a. there were flaws in the way the original functions operated.

b. different program design goals may favor a new approach.
c. the idea of classes is easier to understand.
d. using classes is generally more efficient than using library functions.
e. the programmer's interface can be made easier or more capable.

EXERCISE 1

For the **xString** class, create a member function called **compare()** that compares an **xString** given to it as an argument with the **xString** that called it. This function should return -1 if the argument comes before the object alphabetically, 0 if the two are the same, and 1 if the argument comes after the object.

EXERCISE 2

For the **xString** class, create a member function that takes two **xString** objects as arguments, concatenates them, and places the resulting value in the object that called the function. You can name this function **concat()**. Add some statements to **main()** to test it.

SESSION 6

ARRAYS OF STRINGS

A commonly used construction is an array of strings. Such arrays can hold lists of employee names, passwords, file names, and so on. In this session, I'm going to create a class based on an array holding the names of the days of the week. First, however, I'll review the syntax of an array of strings.

Syntax of Arrays of Strings

You can create an array of empty string variables using a simple two-dimensional array. Because a string is an array, an array of strings is an array of arrays.

Arrays of Empty Strings

Suppose you don't know yet what strings you want to store but you want to create space for them. To store five strings, each of which can be up to 10 characters long, you would define an array this way:

```
char names[5][10];    // array of 5 strings
```

Notice that the number of strings is always the first dimension given. The length of the strings (which, because this is an array, must all be the same) is the second dimension. Figure 3-9 shows how this looks.

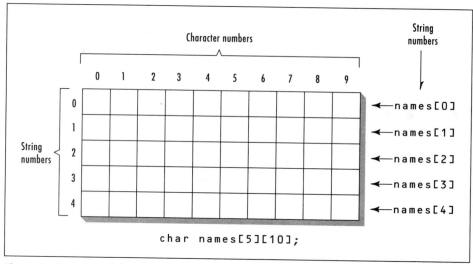

Figure 3-9 Array of empty strings

You might write some code so the user could enter names into this array:

```
for(j=0; j<5; j++)
   {
   cout << "Enter name (or press Enter to exit loop): ";
   cin.get(names[j], 10);
   if( strlen(names[j])==0 )     // if user presses [Enter],
      break;                     // exit from loop
   }
```

Here the `for` loop won't let the user enter more than five names. By pressing ENTER and thus inserting a 0-length name into the array, the user can exit the loop after entering fewer than five names.

Notice that a single string is referred to as `names[j]`, with only one index. As I mentioned earlier, this is how you refer to one subarray in a two-dimensional array.

Arrays of Initialized Strings

You can initialize the strings in an array of strings when you create them. Here's an example in which I store the days of the week:

```
const int MAX = 10;      // maximum length of day name, +1
const int DPW = 7;       // days per week

const char day_name[DPW][MAX] =        // array of day names
                { "Sunday", "Monday", "Tuesday",
                  "Wednesday","Thursday", "Friday",
                  "Saturday"};
```

The string constants used for initialization are separated by commas and surrounded by braces, just as constants are in one-dimensional arrays. This causes each string constant to be installed in the appropriate subarray of `day_name`. Figure 3-10 shows how this looks.

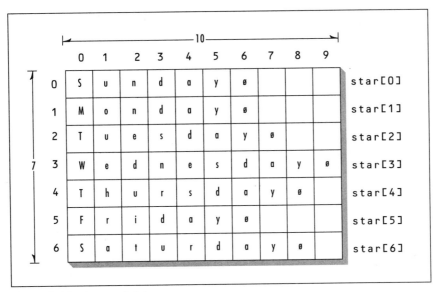

Figure 3-10   Array of strings

  Note in Figure 3-10 that there is some space wasted at the ends of the shorter string constants because all the string variables are the same length. You can avoid this if you use pointers, as you'll see later.

I've used the variable names **MAX** and **DPW** for the array dimensions and made them type `const`, as discussed earlier. I've also made the entire array type `const` because presumably the days of the week will never need to be changed.

The weekday Class

I'll turn the weekday names into a class. Because I don't want to duplicate the `day_name` array in every object, I'll make it an external variable. (I could also have made it a static variable within the class. I'll discuss static variables, along with external variables, in Chapter 4. For the moment, all you need to know is that external variables can be accessed from anywhere in the program.) Listing 3-7 shows WEEKDAYS.

Listing 3-7 WEEKDAYS

```
// weekdays.cpp
// creates a class of days of the week objects

#include <iostream.h>
#include <string.h>       // for stricmp()

const int MAX = 10;       // maximum length of day name, +1
const int DPW = 7;        // days per week

const char day_name[DPW][MAX] =        // array of day names
```

continued on next page

continued from previous page

```
                              { "Sunday", "Monday", "Tuesday",
                                "Wednesday","Thursday", "Friday",
                                "Saturday"};

class weekday                       // class of day names
    {
    private:
        int day_number;             // Sunday=0, etc.
    public:
        void inday()                // user inputs day name
            {
            char tempday[MAX];      // holds user input
            int gotit = 0;          // match found? (0=false)
            int j;                  // loop variable

            while( !gotit )         // cycle until user enters
                {                   // a correct name
                cout << "Enter day of week (e.g., Friday): ";
                cin >> tempday;
                for(j=0; j<DPW; j++)  // compare user input
                    {                 // with list of names
                    if( stricmp(tempday, day_name[j])==0 )
                        {             // if there's a match,
                        gotit = 1;    // set flag,
                        break;        // break out of for loop
                        }
                    }  // end for
                day_number = j;     // record what day it was
                }  // end while
            }  // end inday()

        void outday()               // display the day name
            {
            cout << day_name[day_number];
            }
        void outnumber()            // display the day number
            {
            cout << (day_number + 1);
            }
        void add(int days)          // add days to
            {                       // this weekday
            day_number += days;     // add days
            day_number %= DPW;      // ensure not > 7
            }
    };  // end weekdays class

/////////////////////////////////////////////////////////////
void main()
    {
    weekday wd;                     // make a weekday object

    cout << "What day is it?" << endl;
    wd.inday();                     // user gives it a value
```

```
cout << "You entered ";
wd.outday();                          // display its day name
cout << "\nThat's day number ";
wd.outnumber();                       // display its day number
wd.add(10);                           // add 10 days to it
cout << "\nTen days later is ";
wd.outday();                          // display its day name
}
```

In `main()`, the program creates an object of the `weekday` class, `wd`. Then it gets a name from the user and compares it with all the weekday names in the `day_name` array. If there's a match, it stores the number of the day in the object. Then it tells this object to display its day name and day number.

I've added a member function to the `weekday` class to enable the user to add a number of days to a `weekday` object. In `main()`, the program tells `wd` to add 10 days to itself, and then reports what day of the week `wd` has become (10 days after Wednesday is a Saturday). Here's the output from WEEK-DAYS:

```
What day is it?
Enter day of week (e.g., Friday): wednesday
You entered Wednesday
That's day number 4
Ten days later is Saturday
```

There are several new wrinkles in the operation of WEEKDAYS. It uses a variation of the string function `strcmp()` and it uses a new kind of operator.

The stricmp() Function

Notice in the interaction with the program that the user typed "wednesday" with a lowercase 'W'. The `weekday` class recognizes this as a legitimate weekday name because it uses the `stricmp()` comparison function, which ignores case. This provides a more forgiving approach to user input.

Arithmetic Assignment Operators

You may find the two lines in the `add()` member function somewhat puzzling. To add a fixed number of days to the `day_number` variable, you might expect a statement such as

```
day_number = day_number + days;
```

where `days` is provided by the argument to the `add()` function. However, what I use instead is the statement

```
day_number += days;
```

What's this all about? The designers of C and C++ considered brevity a good thing and so developed this shorthand format. Both statements have exactly the same effect, but the `day_number` variable is named only once in the second statement. This is made possible by the arithmetic assignment operator `+=`. This operator takes the value on its right and adds it to the variable on its left, leaving the result in the variable on its left. Figure 3-11 shows how this looks when the value of `item` is added to the value of `total` and the result is stored in `total`.

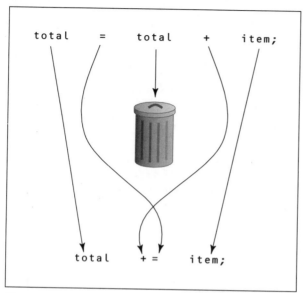

Figure 3-11 Arithmetic assignment operator

It turns out that there are arithmetic assignment operators for all the arithmetic operations.

```
a += b;     // same as a = a + b
a -= b;     // same as a = a - b
a *= b;     // same as a = a * b
a /= b;     // same as a = a / b
a %= b;     // same as a = a % b
```

There are a few other assignment operators as well, but you can ignore them for now.

In the WEEKDAYS program, I use the last of these operators, %=, to make sure that `day_number` is always in the range of 0 to 6, no matter how many days you add to it.

```
day_number %= DPW;
```

This sets `day_number` to the remainder produced when `day_number` is divided by 7.

Arithmetic assignment operators provide a way to make your listing look less cumbersome, possibly at the expense of some clarity for newcomers to C++.

1. Which of the following statements define(s) an array of 100 empty strings, each of which can hold up to 80 characters?
   a. `char strarray[100];`
   b. `char strarray[80][100];`
   c. `int strarray[80, 100];`

   d. `char strarray[100, 80];`
   e. `char strarray[100][80];`

2. If you initialize an array of strings called `names`,
   a. each character is placed in a one-dimensional subarray of `names`.
   b. each string constant is placed in a one-dimensional subarray of `names`.
   c. each character is placed in an element of a one-dimensional subarray of `names`.
   d. each string constant is placed in an element of a one-dimensional subarray of `names`.
   e. all the string constants are placed in a subarray of `names`.

3. The `weekday` class
   a. models the number of work hours in each day of the week.
   b. must have access to the `day_name` array.
   c. can convert from a day name such as `"Monday"` to a number and back again.
   d. stores the name of a day of the week as instance data.
   e. stores a number as instance data.

4. If an external variable is defined at the beginning of a file, and there is only one file for the program, the variable is
   a. not accessible by any statement in the program.
   b. accessible by statements in member functions in the program.
   c. accessible by statements in `main()`.
   d. accessible by statements that are neither in standalone functions such as `main()` nor in member functions.
   e. not accessible unless it's made into a class.

5. Arithmetic assignment operators such as `+=` and `*=`
   a. exist to shorten and simplify the program listing.
   b. perform arithmetic only on imaginary numbers.
   c. combine the tasks of the equal sign (`=`) and another binary operator.
   d. perform arithmetic on two variables and leave the result in a third.
   e. assign something and then perform arithmetic on it.

EXERCISE 1

Add a member function called `difference()` to the `weekday` class. This function should subtract the day number of the object that called it from the day number of its argument and return an integer representing the number of days between these two days of the week. Here's how it might be called from `main()`:

```
cout << "Enter the starting day: "
start_day.inday();
cout << "Enter the ending day: "
end_day.inday();
cout << "\nThe project will take ";
cout << start_day.difference(end_day);
cout << " days";
```

EXERCISE 2

Create a class called `ordinal` that models the names of the ordinal numbers, "first", "second", "third", "fourth", "fifth", and so on, up to "twelfth". Provide input and output member functions that get and display such values using either of two formats: ordinary integers (1, 2, and so on) or ordinals. Also, provide an `add()` function that allows you to add a fixed integer to objects of the class. Assume that no number larger than 12 or less than 1 will be represented.

SESSION 7

STRUCTURES

A C++ *structure* is a way to group together several data items that can be of different types. An array, by contrast, groups a number of data items of the same type. Structures are typically used when several data items form a distinct unit but are not important enough to become a class. Structures are more important in C, where there are no classes. In C++, a class plays many of the roles filled by structures in C. Nevertheless, there are still many situations where structures are useful.

Specifying a Structure

Here's an example of a structure specification:

```
struct part
    {
    int modelnumber;
    int partnumber;
    float cost;
    };
```

A structure consists of the keyword `struct`, followed by the structure name (also called the *tag*) and braces that surround the body of the structure. It is terminated with a semicolon. The body of the structure usually consists of various data items, which may be of different types. These individual data items are called *members*. (As you recall, the individual data items within an array are called elements.) Figure 3-12 shows the syntax.

As you can see, a structure is quite similar syntactically to a class. However, structures and classes are usually used in quite different ways. Typically, a class contains both data and member functions, whereas a structure contains only data. I'll return to the relationship between structures and classes at the end of this lesson.

As with a class, a structure specification does not actually create a structure. It merely specifies how a structure will look when it's created.

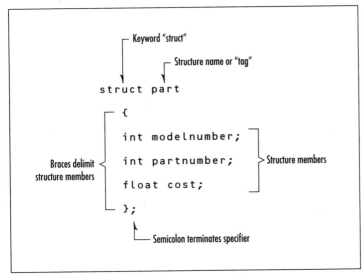

Figure 3-12 Syntax of the structure specifier

Defining Structure Variables

To define variables of type `struct part`, you would say something like

```
part cp1, cp2;
```

Figure 3-13 shows the relation between a structure specifier and the variables created by using the specification as a blueprint.

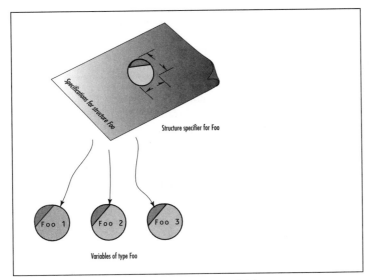

Figure 3-13 Structures and structure variables

I should mention for completeness that there's a shortcut for defining structure variables. The variable names are telescoped into the structure specification, like this:

```
struct part
    {
    int modelnumber;
    int partnumber;
    float cost;
    } cp1, cp2;
```

This code specifies the structure and creates two variables of that structure at the same time. A peculiarity of this format is that you can remove the structure name or tag (`part`); it's not needed because the variables already know what structure they're based on.

This shortcut format is not as easy to understand as using separate statements for the specification and the definition, so I'll avoid it in the example programs.

Accessing Structure Members

The dot operator is used to access structure members, just as it's used to access member functions from objects. Here's how that looks:

```
struct part                     // specify structure
    {
    int modelnumber;
    int partnumber;
    float cost;
    };


part cp1;                       // define structure variable

cout << "Enter model number: "
cin >> cp1.modelnumber;         // access data member in structure
cout << "Enter part number: ";
cin >> cp1.partnumber;          // access data member in structure
cout << "Enter cost: ";
cin >> cp1.cost;                // access data member in structure
```

The variable name precedes the dot and the name of the member data follows it: `cp1.cost`. Figure 3-14 shows how this looks if the user enters 6244, 373, and 217.55 for the model number, part number, and cost; Figure 3-15 shows how the variable name and member data name are related to what's stored in memory.

Initializing Structure Variables

You can provide initial values for structure variables just as you can for arrays. Here's how you would initialize a structure variable of type `part` to the same values seen in Figure 3-14:

```
part cp1 = { 6244, 373, 217.55 };
```

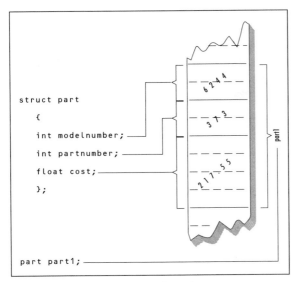

Figure 3-14   Structure members in memory

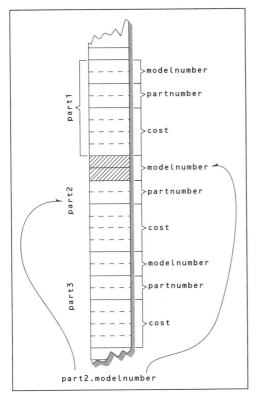

Figure 3-15   The dot operator

Structure Usage

Let's modify an earlier example program so that it uses a structure. Notice in the STACK1 program, from Session 2 in this chapter, that the array that stores data items and the index to this array (the top of the stack) are closely related. You might find it convenient to combine these two data items into a structure, and then use the structure as a single data member of the **Stack** class. Listing 3-8 shows how this might look.

Listing 3-8 STRUSTAK

```
// strustak.cpp
// class models a stack, uses struct for array and index

#include <iostream.h>

struct stackette               // structure
   {
   int arr[20];                // storage array
   int top;                    // index of top of stack
   };

class Stack                    // class
   {
   private:
      stackette st;            // structure variable
   public:
      void init()              // initialize index
         {
         st.top = -1;
         }
      void push(int var)       // place an item on the stack
         {
         st.arr[++st.top] = var;
         }
      int pop()                // remove an item from the stack
         {
         return st.arr[st.top--];
         }
   };

void main()
   {
   Stack s1;                   // create a stack object

   s1.init();                  // initialize it
   s1.push(11);                // push 3 items onto stack
   s1.push(12);
   s1.push(13);

   cout << s1.pop() << endl;   // pop 3 items and display them
   cout << s1.pop() << endl;
   cout << s1.pop() << endl;
   }
```

Here the structure **stackette** holds the array of integers and the index that points to the top of the stack (the last item placed in the array).

```
struct stackette
   {
   int arr[20];        // storage array
   int top;            // index of top of stack
      };
```

The only item of instance data in the **Stack** class is now a variable of class **stackette**.

```
   stackette st;
```

Member functions of **Stack** now refer to individual data members of **st**, using the dot operator

```
st.top = -1;
```

and

```
st.arr[++st.top] = var;
```

Notice that **main()** is identical to the **main()** in the STACK1 program. I've modified the class but kept the class interface the same, so no rewriting is necessary for the functions that use the class.

It's doubtful whether in this particular programming example the use of a structure provides significant simplification. However, once I discuss pointers, you'll encounter examples where the use of structures as class members can indeed clarify the workings of a program. (See the linked list example in Session 7 in Chapter 8.)

Structures versus Classes

I've emphasized the use of structures as aggregates of data items. This is the way structures are usually used. With this emphasis, structures appear quite different from classes. We might say that a structure is a passive grouping of data items, whereas a class is an active combination of data and functions. Of course, classes are far more important in C++ than structures are. Classes form the very basis of object-oriented programming, whereas structures are a minor part of C++ usage.

However, these differences obscure the fact that the syntax of structures and classes is almost identical. You can install member functions within a structure just as you can in a class, and conversely you can remove the member functions from a class so that it acts like a structure.

There is only one real syntactical difference between a structure and a class: The members of a structure are public by default, whereas the members of a class are private by default. That is, if you don't use the keywords **public** or **private**, class members are private.

```
class Foo
   {                   // no need for keyword, private by default
      int george;
      int harry;
   public:             // public must be specified
      void init()
         { }
      void display()
         { }
   };
```

For clarity, I'll always use the keyword `private` in class specifications in the example programs, but in fact it's optional. In structures, the situation is reversed.

```
struct Bar
   {                      // no need for keyword, public by default
   void init()
       { }
   void display()
       { }
private:                  // private must be specified
   int george;
   int harry;
   };
```

In structures, you usually want all the data members to be public, so you normally leave out this keyword.

These syntax distinctions are all rather academic because in most situations, using a structure as a class or vice versa would simply cause confusion. No doubt, the designers of C++ borrowed the syntax of C structures when they invented classes and then—perhaps to make compiler design easier—augmented structures to make them as similar as possible to classes.

QUIZ 7

1. Specifying a structure
   a. uses syntax similar to a class specification.
   b. creates a structure variable.
   c. requires the use of the keyword `public`.
   d. usually involves a number of member data items.
   e. usually involves a number of member functions.

2. Structures are normally used
   a. as an alternative way to create classes and objects.
   b. to group data items of the same type.
   c. to group data items of different types.
   d. to combine data items that are closely related into a single unit.
   e. to increase memory efficiency.

3. Accessing a structure's member data
   a. is normally carried out using the structure's member functions.
   b. is normally carried out by a function located somewhere outside the structure.
   c. uses a similar format to accessing member functions in classes.
   d. is easy because the data is public by default.
   e. requires the dot operator (ignore pointers).

4. In the STRUSTAK program,
   a. statements in **main()** access the **stackette** structure using the dot operator.
   b. a structure variable is included in the **Stack** class.
   c. a structure specification is included in the **Stack** class.
   d. there is only one member data item in the **Stack** class.
   e. member functions in **Stack** need not be modified when a **stackette** structure is inserted in the class in place of individual data items of basic types.

5. Structures and classes differ in that
   a. the public versus private distinction is applicable to classes but not to structures.
   b. structures are usually used only for data, not for data and functions.
   c. data members may be accessed using the dot operator in classes, but not in structures.
   d. structures use brackets, whereas classes use braces.
   e. both data and function members are public by default in structures, but private by default in classes.

EXERCISE 1

In Exercise 2 in Session 2 in this chapter, I suggested you create a **peek()** function, which would access the item on the top of the stack without removing it. Modify this function so it works with the version of **Stack** in the STRUSTAK program.

EXERCISE 2

Modify the EMPLOY1 program from Session 2 in this chapter so that the array **name** and the integer **n**, used as instance data in the **employee** class, are combined into a structure. Substitute a variable of this structure type for these two member data items and make whatever modifications are necessary for the **employee** class to work as it did in EMPLOY1.

SESSION 8

enum AND bool

I'll cover two short topics in this lesson. An enumerated data type—specified by the keyword **enum**—allows the programmer to invent a data type and then specify exactly what values are allowed for the type. The **bool** keyword and the related literals **true** and **false** are used in situations involving logic tests. These topics are related in that **bool** type was typically, until a recent change in the C++ draft standard, implemented using an **enum** type.

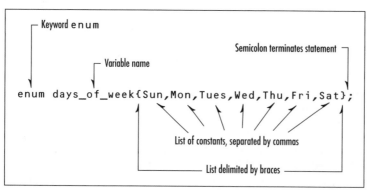

Figure 3-16   Syntax of enum specifier

Enumerated Data Types

Creating a new type using enumerated data types is akin to creating a new type using a class, as I did in programs that used the `airtime` class. However, enumerated data types are much more limited than types created using classes. You can't create member functions to specify the operation of `enum` types; instead, they always behave more or less like integers. Enumerated types existed in C long before OOP was invented. You can think of them as a sort of poor person's approach to creating one's own data types. However, given the right situation, they work well and they are simpler to implement than classes. Enumerated types are usually used when a variable has only a few allowable values, because every value must be named.

Specifying an Enumerated Type

In the WEEKDAYS example (Listing 3-7), I used a class to define a new data type consisting of days of the week. This type also lends itself to being specified by an enumerated type. Here's how that would look:

```
enum days_of_week {Sun, Mon, Tue, Wed, Thu, Fri, Sat };
```

They keyword `enum` is followed by the name of the type, `days_of_week` in this example, and then by braces enclosing a list of comma-separated value names. Figure 3-16 shows the format.

Enumerated means that all the values are listed explicitly. This is unlike the specification of an `int`, for example, which has a *range* of possible values (such as -32,768 to 32,767). In an `enum`, you must give a specific name to every allowable value. This is potentially confusing. Remember, the names used for `enum` values are *not* the names of variables. An `int` has values 0, 1, 2, and so on. The `enum` shown above has the values `Sun`, `Mon`, and so on up to `Sat`. Figure 3-17 shows the difference between an `int` and an `enum`.

As with classes and structures, specifying an enumerated type is not the same as actually creating variables of that type. That step requires a separate statement.

Creating and Using Enumerated Variables

Here's how you might create and give values to some enumerated variables:

```
// specify a type
```

```
enum days_of_week {Sun, Mon, Tue, Wed, Thu, Fri, Sat };

days_of_week day1, day2;    // create variables of that type

day1 = Mon;                 // give them values
day2 = Wed;
```

One of the advantages of using enumerated types is that attempting to assign a nonspecified value will cause a compiler error, alerting you to program bugs. For example, even if Easter is defined as an int variable,

```
day1 = Easter;
```

will not compile because day1 is a variable of type days_of_week and Easter is not on the list of possible values for days_of_week.

They're Really Integers

The compiler actually stores enumerated values as integers, starting with 0 for the first name specified. In the previous figure, north is 0, south is 1, east is 2, and west is 3. In the days-of-the-week example Sun is 0, Mon is 1, Tue is 2, and so on. Alternatively, you can specify that the series begins on a value other than 0. For example, you could say

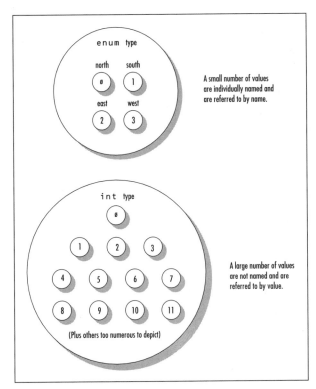

Figure 3-17   Usage of ints and enums

```
enum ordinal { first=1, second, third };
```

where first is 1, second is 2, and third is 3. Or you can specify separate values for all the names.

```
enum coin { penny=1, nickel=5, dime=10,
            quarter=25, halfdollar=50, dollar=100 };
```

A Card Game Program

Let's look at a lengthy example that uses arrays, structures, and enumerated types. This program features a class, card, that models the playing cards used in games such as bridge, hearts, and poker. Each object of this class represents a single card. Instance data records the card's number (2 through 10, jack, queen, king, and ace) and suit (clubs, diamonds, hearts, spades). Member functions are provided to give the card an initial value and to display its value.

In main(), the program defines an array of 52 objects of type card and calls it deck. It then gives appropriate values to all these cards in order and displays the result. Next, it shuffles the deck by exchanging each card with another in a random location in the deck array. Finally, it displays the resulting shuffled deck. Listing 3-9 shows CARDARAY.

Listing 3-9 CARDARAY

```cpp
// cardaray.cpp
// cards as objects

#include <iostream.h>
#include <stdlib.h>         // for randomize(), rand
#include <time.h>           // for randomize()
#include <conio.h>          // for getche()

enum Suit { clubs, diamonds, hearts, spades };

const int jack = 11;        // from 2 to 10 are
const int queen = 12;       // integers without names
const int king = 13;
const int ace = 14;

class card
    {
    private:
        int number;         // 2 to 10, jack, queen, king, ace
        Suit suit;          // clubs, diamonds, hearts, spades
    public:
        void init(int n, Suit s)    // initialize card
            { suit = s; number = n; }
        void display()              // display the card
            {
            if( number >= 2 && number <= 10 )
                cout << number;
            else
                switch(number)
                    {
                    case jack:  cout << "J"; break;
                    case queen: cout << "Q"; break;
```

```
                 case king:   cout << "K"; break;
                 case ace:    cout << "A"; break;
                 }
         switch(suit)
             {
             case clubs:     cout << 'c'; break;
             case diamonds:  cout << 'd'; break;
             case hearts:    cout << 'h'; break;
             case spades:    cout << 's'; break;
             }
         }  // end display()
    }; // end class card

void main()
    {
    card deck[52];                      // deck of cards
    int j = 0;                          // counts thru deck
    int num;                            // card number

    cout << endl;
    for(num=2; num<=14; num++)          // for each number
        {
        deck[j].init(num, clubs);        // set club
        deck[j+13].init(num, diamonds);  // set diamond
        deck[j+26].init(num, hearts);    // set heart
        deck[j++ +39].init(num, spades); // set spade
        }

    cout << "\nOrdered deck:\n";
    for(j=0; j<52; j++)             // display ordered deck
        {
        deck[j].display();
        cout << "   ";
        if( !( (j+1) % 13) )       // newline every 13 cards
            cout << endl;
        }

    randomize();                   // seed random number generator
    for(j=0; j<52; j++)            // for each card in the deck,
        {
        int k = random(52);        // pick another card at random
        card temp = deck[j];       // and swap them
        deck[j] = deck[k];
        deck[k] = temp;
        }

    cout << "\nShuffled deck:\n";
    for(j=0; j<52; j++)            // display shuffled deck
        {
        deck[j].display();
        cout << "   ";
        if( !( (j+1) % 13) )       // newline every 13 cards
            cout << endl;
```

continued on next page

continued from previous page

```
        }
    getch();                    // wait for keypress
    }   // end main
```

This program uses two library functions that may not exist on all compilers. These are `random-ize()`, which seeds a random number generator (using the current time), and `random()`, which returns a random number. These functions exist in Borland compilers but other compilers use slight variations, so you may need to modify the source code to get this program to run.

Here's the output from CARDARAY. First the deck is displayed in the order it was initialized. Then it's displayed after shuffling.

```
Ordered deck:
2c 3c 4c 5c 6c 7c 8c 9c 10c Jc Qc Kc Ac
2d 3d 4d 5d 6d 7d 8d 9d 10d Jd Qd Kd Ad
2h 3h 4h 5h 6h 7h 8h 9h 10h Jh Qh Kh Ah
2s 3s 4s 5s 6s 7s 8s 9s 10s Js Qs Ks As

Shuffled deck:
3c 5c Qc 9s Ah Kd 6h 7h 4s As 2h 5d Ks
7c Js 3s 10h 8s Jc Jh Ac 5s 7s Qs 10d 2c
Jd 8d 4d 2d 6s 4h 10s 6d 4c Ad Qh 7d 6c
10c 9c 3h 8c 5h 2s Kc 9h Qd 8h 3d 9d Kh
```

The program uses an `enum` type for the suit because there are only four possible values: clubs, diamonds, hearts, and spades. This makes it impossible for the program to assign any value other than these four. If you try to use an integer value, for example, the compiler will issue a warning.

The `enum` approach would be unwieldy for the card number, so I use an integer that can have a value from 2 to 14, with the special names `jack`, `queen`, `king`, and `ace` given to the values 11, 12, 13, and 14. The `display()` member function uses `switch` statements to figure out the appropriate display, given the suit and number of each card.

The `bool` Keyword

Until recently, there was no Boolean type in C++. Such a type (named after George Boole, a British mathematician), has only two values: true and false. Variables of this type are used to store the results of logic tests, such as the answer to such questions as, "Is `alpha` less than 10?".

Until recently, C and C++ programmers either used an integer type for a Boolean value or had to create their own using an `enum`.

```
enum boolean (false, true);   // false is 0, true is 1
```

Then later in the program, variables of this type could be defined

```
boolean flag;
```

and set to one of the two permissible values

```
if(alpha<10)
    flag = false;
```

However, this homemade Boolean type is now unnecessary. A recent revision to the C++ draft standard introduces a new keyword to specify Boolean variables, `bool`, and two new predefined literal values for it, `true` and `false`. A variable of type `bool` must have one of these two values.

Thus, to define a Boolean variable `flag`, simply say

```
bool flag;
```

There's no need for an `enum`.

You can convert `bool` values to integers: `true` becomes 0 and `false` becomes 1. You can also convert integers to `bool` values: 0 becomes `false` and all other values become `true`.

In the WEEKDAYS program in Session 6 in this chapter, I used an integer variable, `gotit`, to indicate whether or not the user had typed a correct day name. I used the value 0 to indicate false and 1 to indicate true. That's not as clear or elegant as it might be. The new `bool` type allows you to use a type designed for true/false values. Listing 3-10 shows WEEKDAYS rewritten to use a `bool` type for the `gotit` flag.

Listing 3-10 BOOL

```
// bool.cpp
// creates a class of days of the week objects
// uses bool for logic value

#include <iostream.h>
#include <string.h>        // for stricmp()

const int MAX = 10;        // maximum length of day name, +1
const int DPW = 7;         // days per week
const char day_name[DPW][MAX] =        // array of day names
                { "Sunday", "Monday", "Tuesday",
                  "Wednesday","Thursday", "Friday",
                  "Saturday"};

class weekday                          // class of day names
    {
    private:
        int day_number;                // Sunday=0, etc.
    public:
        void inday()                   // user inputs day name
            {
            bool gotit = false;        // match found?
            int j;                     // loop variable
            char tempday[MAX];         // holds user input

            while( gotit==false )      // cycle until user enters
                {                      // a correct name
                cout << "Enter day of week (e.g., Friday): ";
                cin >> tempday;
                for(j=0; j<DPW; j++)   // compare user input
                    {                  // with list of names
                    if( stricmp(tempday, day_name[j])==0 )
                        {              // if there's a match,
                        gotit = true;  // set flag,
                        break;         // break out of for loop
```

continued on next page

continued from previous page

```
                        }
              }  // end for
           day_number = j;              // record what day it was
           }  // end while
        }  // end inday()

     void outday()                       // display the day name
        {
        cout << day_name[day_number];
        }
     void outnumber()                    // display the day number
        {
        cout << (day_number + 1);
        }
     void add(int days)                  // add days to
        {                                // this weekday
        day_number += days;              // add days
        day_number %= DPW;               // ensure not > 7
        }
  };  // end weekday class

//////////////////////////////////////////////////////////////
void main()
   {
   weekday wd;                           // make a weekday object

   cout << "What day is it?" << endl;
   wd.inday();                           // user gives it a value
   cout << "You entered ";
   wd.outday();                          // display its day name
   cout << "\nThat's day number ";
   wd.outnumber();                       // display its day number
   wd.add(10);                           // add 10 days to it
   cout << "\nTen days later is ";
   wd.outday();                          // display its day name
   }
```

1. The **enum** keyword specifies
    a. a list of variable names.
    b. a new data type
    c. a list of values.
    d. a list of data types.
    e. the numerical equivalent for each name on a list.

2. Enumerated data types are useful when
    a. only a small number of variables of a certain type will be used.

b. you will redefine how arithmetic works with variables of the type.

c. you want to ensure that a variable is not given an incorrect value.

d. a variable can take on a limited number of values.

e. a variable contains instance data of several basic types.

3. Declaring a variable of an enumerated type

a. requires you to use the `int` basic type.

b. involves specifying a list of possible values.

c. requires that the variable be simultaneously initialized to a value.

d. has the same syntax as declaring an object of a class.

e. creates a variable that is represented in computer memory by an integer.

4. In the CARDARAY program, a `card` object

a. can display its number and suit.

b. must be initialized to an appropriate `card` value when it is defined.

c. represents a deck of 52 cards.

d. can be moved to a different location in the array `deck`.

e. might have the value `{ jack, hearts }`.

5. The keyword `bool`

a. represents an `enum` type.

b. is used to create variables that can have only one of two values.

c. represents an integer type.

d. is a value given to variables.

e. defines variables used to store the results of logic tests.

EXERCISE 1

Revise the `main()` part of the CARDARAY program so that, after shuffling the deck, it deals a hand of 13 cards to each of four players (as in bridge). A player can be represented by an array holding that player's cards. After dealing the four hands, display them.

EXERCISE 2

Revise the `airtime` class in the ARRAYAIR program in Session 3 in this chapter so it works with 12-hour time. In other words, 1:30 should be displayed as 1:30 am and 13:30 should be displayed as 1:30 pm. Create an enumerated data type called `meridian` that has two possible values: `am` and `pm`. Rewrite the `set()` and `display()` functions so they use this type to help handle the 12-hour format.

SUMMARY: CHAPTER 3

In this chapter, I've focused on arrays and strings, with brief looks at structures and enumerated types. An array is a way to group a number of variables of the same type and to refer to them using an index number or subscript. The index number is represented by a number in brackets, such as [5]. Arrays are the most commonly used data storage structure, but they do not warn the programmer when an array index is out of bounds, so it's easy to make programming mistakes that cause serious malfunctions.

The increment and decrement operators, ++ and --, can be placed either before or after their operands. If placed before (++x), the operand is incremented (or decremented, if -- is used) before its value is used in an expression. If placed after (x++), the operand is incremented (or decremented) after its value is used.

A string is a group of characters terminated with a null character, '\0', which has the numerical value 0. A string variable is an array of type char used for storing strings. A string constant is defined using double quotes: "George Smith". Special library functions exist for processing strings. Strings (i.e., ordinary C strings) have nothing to do with classes and OOP. However, string classes can be created that act like strings and improve upon them in various ways.

A variable defined with the const modifier must be initialized to a value when it's defined; this value cannot be modified during the course of the program.

A structure is, from a syntax standpoint, almost identical to a class; the only difference is that a structure's members are public by default, whereas a class's are private. However, a structure usually does not have member functions; it's used only as a way to group data items together. In many cases in C++, a class replaces a structure.

Enumerated types allow the programmer to specify a new data type that can be given only a small number of values whose names are specified. This can aid in clarity and safety.

END-OF-CHAPTER DISCUSSION

George: Great. Now I have *three* kinds of strings to worry about. Homemade, regular, and classes. When do you use what?

Estelle: Forget about homemade strings. No one would use them in a real program; that was just a teaching device.

Don: In C++, assuming you have a string class, it's easier to use strings that are class objects than ordinary C strings.

Estelle: Why?

Don: Because you can define whatever string operation you want, using member functions. But to write the class in the first place, you need to use C strings. They're the fundamental way to handle text.

George: So you need to understand both?

Don: Ideally. But in your case, I'd stick with one or the other. No use getting confused.

George: A wise guy, eh?

Estelle: I don't understand why I need structures. It seems like classes do everything structures do and then some.

Don: I don't think structures are as important in C++ as they are in C, for just that reason. But every now and then you probably want to stick some data items together without going to the trouble of making it a full-blown class.

George: What about enumerated types? What are they really for?

Don: I bet if they hadn't already been part of C when C++ was invented, no one would have bothered. For sure you can use a class to do everything that enumerated types do. At least, I think so. But because they're in the language, you may as well use them.

George: Use them when?

Estelle: Whenever some variable is going to have just a small number of possible values.

George: What's the advantage?

Don: It makes the listing clearer and makes it easier for the compiler to find bugs in your program. If you assign an incorrect value to an enumerated type, the compiler lets you know.

George: Who needs that? I never make programming mistakes anyway.

Estelle: Oh, right.

CHAPTER 4

FUNCTIONS

Functions are important not only because they are one of the two major components of objects but also because they are one of the basic ways to organize C++ programs.

I'll first summarize what you've learned about functions so far. Then I'll examine a new way to write member functions outside of the class specification. I'll look at the advantages of overloading functions, which means giving the same name to different functions, and default arguments, which allow a function to be called with fewer arguments than it really has.

In the second half of this chapter, I'll switch gears to a related topic: storage classes. You'll see how variables acquire different characteristics from two sources: first, from the location of the variable with regard to functions and classes and second, from the use of special keywords. Finally, I'll examine references, a new way to pass arguments to functions and to return values from them.

187

SESSION 1

FUNCTION REVIEW AND FUNCTION DECLARATION

This session begins with a brief review of what you've learned so far (or maybe just assumed!) about functions and function syntax. It then introduces the function declaration, which provides information to the compiler about how a function should be called.

Review

I've been using functions all along. So far, you've seen them in three different situations.

First, I introduced *member functions*, which are one of the two fundamental components of classes, along with instance data.

Second, functions appear independently in the listing, outside of any class specification. An important function in this category is `main()`, which is the function to which control is transferred when a C++ program starts to run. At the end of this lesson, you'll see that `main()` can, in effect, be divided into many functions.

Third, you've seen examples of C library functions such as `getche()` and `strlen()`, which are called from `main()` or from member functions. The programmer does not need the source code for library files; instead, object (.OBJ) or library (.LIB) files are linked to user-written object files to create the final .EXE file. Library functions require that the appropriate header file (e.g., CONIO.H for the `getche()` function) be included in the source file.

Now let's look in more detail at the various aspects of functions.

Function Calls

A function is a section of code. It is typically *called* (made to execute) from a statement in another part of the program. The statement that does this is a *function call*. The function call causes control to jump to the start of the function. As part of the function call, arguments also may be passed to the function. After the code in the function has been executed, control returns to the statement following the function call; at this time, the call can return a value from the function.

Here's an example of a function call:

```
func1();
```

This call causes the function `func1()` to be executed. This particular call takes no arguments and does not return a value. It consists of the name of the function followed by parentheses. Note that, like any other program statement, it is terminated with a semicolon.

Functions, along with classes, serve as one of the important organizing principles of C++ programs. They also increase memory efficiency: A function can be executed many times without the need for inserting duplicates of its code into the listing. Figure 4-1 shows how three different statements cause the same section of code to be executed.

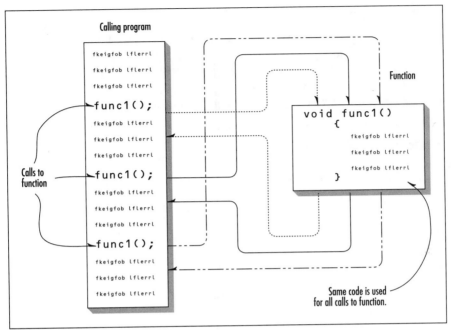

Figure 4-1 Flow of control to a function

Function Definitions

A *function definition* consists mostly of the function's code, that is, the statements that make up the function and cause it to do something. When I say *function*, I usually mean the function definition. The function definition starts with a line called the *declarator*, which specifies the function name, its return type, and the types and names of arguments. Parentheses follow the function name and enclose the arguments, if any. The function's statements, which are the function *body*, are enclosed in braces. Figure 4-2 shows a typical function definition.

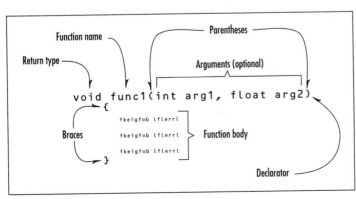

Figure 4-2 Syntax of a function definition

Arguments

Arguments are the mechanism by which information may be passed from a function call to the function itself. As an example, say that somewhere in your program is a function called `repchar()`, whose purpose is to display a given character a certain number times. The character to be displayed and the number of times to display it are passed as arguments to the function. If you want to display 10 x's in a line, for example, you might call the function this way:

```
repchar('x', 10);  // display 10 x's
```

Here's the definition of the function `repchar()`:

```
// repchar()
// displays n characters with value ch

void repchar(char ch, int n)   <--This line is the declarator
   {
   for(int j=0; j<n; j++)
   cout << ch;
   }
```

This function will output the character `ch` exactly `n` times in a row. These variables are assigned whatever values appeared in the function call. If the function is executed by the function call shown above, it will display 10 x's. If it is called with the statement

```
repchar('=', 30);
```

it will display 30 equal signs.

When data is passed as arguments in this way, the data is copied and the duplicate values are stored in separate variables in the function. These variables are named in the function declarator. This is called *passing by value*. Figure 4-3 shows how this looks.

Technically, the term *arguments* means the values specified in the function call, whereas the term *parameters* is given to the variables in the function definition into which the values are copied. However, argument is often used loosely for both meanings.

Return Values

A function can return a value to the statement that called it. Here's a function that converts pounds (lbs) to kilograms (kg). It takes one argument, a value in pounds, and returns the corresponding value in kilograms.

```
// lbstokg()
// converts pounds to kilograms
float lbstokg(float pounds)         <--declarator
   {
   float kilograms = 0.453592 * pounds;
   return kilograms;
   }
```

The type of the value returned, in this case `float`, must precede the function name in the function declarator. As I've mentioned, if a function does not return any value, `void` is used as a return type to indicate this.

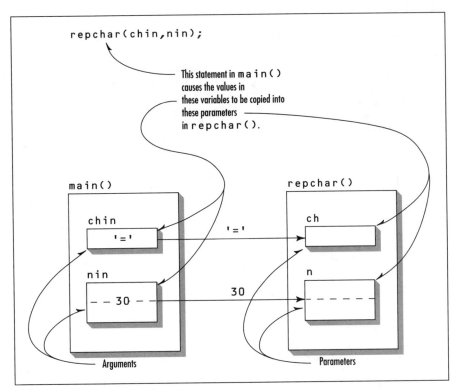

Figure 4-3 Passing by value

If a function does return a value, the **return** statement must be used. The value to be returned is specified following the keyword **return**.

```
return kilograms;
```

This statement causes control to return immediately to the function call, even if it is not the last statement in the function definition. It also causes the entire function call expression to take on the value of the returned variable **kilograms**.

This function might be called this way:

```
kgs = lbstokg(lbs);
```

The function call expression, **lbstokg(lbs)**, itself takes on the value returned and can be assigned to a variable, in this case, **kgs**.

If the **pounds** variable happens to be 165.0 when this call is made, then the value 74.84 (i.e., 165.0 times 0.453592) is assigned to **kgs** when the function returns. Figure 4-4 shows how this value is copied from the **kilograms** variable in the function to the **kgs** variable in **main()**.

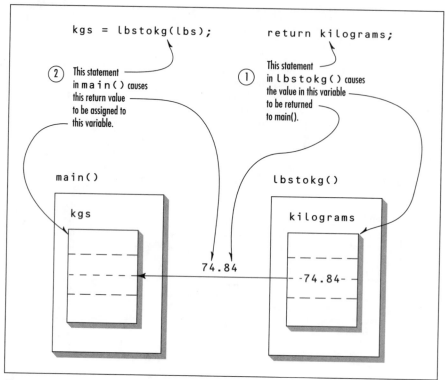

Figure 4-4   Returning by value

Function Declarations

In the example programs you've seen so far, all the functions were member functions of a class, the main() function itself, or library functions. However, there are many other possibilities. For one thing, main() can call other functions. Or, member functions may call other functions located inside or outside the class.

When the compiler generates the machine language instructions for a function call, it needs to know the name of the function, the number and types of arguments in the function, and the function's return value. If the function was defined someplace *before* the function call, this isn't a problem. The compiler will have taken note of these characteristics and stored them away for reference. However, if the function definition *follows* the function call, the compiler won't know how to handle the call and you'll get an "undefined function" error message.

To keep this from happening (and assuming it's not convenient to rearrange things so the function definition precedes all calls to it), you must *declare* the function before any function call. If you do this, the function can be defined anywhere. A function declaration is a single line that tells the compiler the name of the function, the number and types of arguments, and the return type. Here's how you would declare the lbstokg() function:

```
float lbstokg(float);  // function declaration or prototype
```

The declaration looks very much like the declarator (the first line of the function definition). However, it is followed by a semicolon because it is a standalone statement. Also, you don't need the names of the arguments, only the types.

Remember that a function declaration does not specify anything about what will go inside the function body. All it tells is the name of the function, its return type, and the number and types of its arguments. Function declarations are also called *prototypes* because they serve as a sort of nonoperative model of how the function will be called.

Arguments

Although they aren't necessary, argument names can be used in the declaration.

```
float lbstokg(float pounds);    // function declaration
```

These names need not be the same as those in the definition; in fact, they are "dummy" names, and the compiler ignores them (although they may be referred to in error messages). Sometimes, however, they're helpful for human readers. For example, suppose the arguments x and y represent screen coordinates for a function that displays a dot on the screen.

```
void draw_dot(int, int);        // function declaration
```

This declaration is fine for the compiler, but the programmer may not know which is the x coordinate and which is the y. So it's helpful to write

```
void draw_dot(int X, int Y);    // function declaration
```

Functions Called from main()

Here's a typical situation where you would need to use function declarations. Suppose the main() function has gotten so big that I want to break it up into several different functions. In this example, the only purpose of main() is to call these other functions, func1() and func2(). Here's part of a source file in which this happens:

```
void func1();       // function declarations
void func2();

void main()
   {
   func1();         // call to func1()
   func2();         // call to func2()
   }

void func1()        // definition of func1()
   {
   // statements here
   }

void func2()        // definition of func2()
   {
   // statements here
   }
```

The functions follow `main()`, so they must be declared before they can be called. Here they're declared outside of `main()`, but they could be declared inside as well, like this:

```
void main()
    {
    void func1();        // function declarations
    void func2();

    func1();             // call to func1()
    func2();             // call to func2()
    }
```

Functions Called from Member Functions

Often a member function will need to call a user-written function that is not part of the class. This also requires a declaration. Here's an example:

```
class alpha
    {
    ...
    void member_func()   // member function
        {
        void afunc();     // declaration of afunc()
        ...
        afunc();          // call to afunc()
        ...
        }
     };
void afunc()             // definition of afunc()
    {
    // statements
    }
```

Again, the declaration could be placed outside the class entirely, as long as it appears in the listing before the function is called.

Library Functions

Perhaps you are wondering where the function declarations for library functions are located. For example, if I call `getche()` from somewhere in the program, how does the compiler know this function's characteristics, such as how many arguments it takes? The answer, of course, lies in the header files: They hold the function declarations for a group of related functions. By including the header file in your listing, you cause all these functions to be declared.

The Rule

I can summarize the necessity for function declarations in the following rule: If you call a function before its definition appears in the listing, then you must insert a declaration somewhere before the call. In practice, it's best to place function declarations at the beginning of your source file or sometimes at the beginning of the particular function from which calls are made. (As you'll see in Chapter 11, Session 7, declarations are typically placed in header files in large program functions.)

1. The function _____ transfers control to the function; the function _____ is the function itself; the function _____ is surrounded by braces; and the first line of the definition is called the _____.
   a. definition, declarator, call, body
   b. definition, body, definition, call
   c. call, definition, body, declarator
   d. call, declarator, definition, body
   e. call, declarator, body, definition

2. When a function returns a certain value,
   a. the function must use a **return** statement.
   b. the function can return other values at the same time.
   c. the function call must supply the return value.
   d. the function call expression can be treated as a constant with that value.
   e. the function must not be of type **void**.

3. A function declaration has the same relationship to a function definition that
   a. a class specification has to an object definition.
   b. an object declaration has to an object.
   c. a variable has to a variable declaration.
   d. a variable declaration has to the variable itself.
   e. none of the above.

4. A function declaration
   a. creates the code for a function.
   b. must be placed at the beginning of the file.
   c. must be placed in the same function as the call.
   d. must precede any calls to the function.
   e. tells the compiler how to create a call to the function.

5. Library function declarations
   a. are located in .LIB library files.
   b. are located in .H header files.
   c. are not necessary.
   d. must be inserted into the source file by hand.
   e. must not be inserted into the source file by hand.

Because this session is theoretical and concerned with the big picture, it does not include any exercises.

SESSION 2

STANDALONE MEMBER FUNCTIONS

From time to time, the example programs have included member functions that contain loops or decisions. This has elicited warning messages from the compiler, such as `Functions containing for are not expanded inline`. What does this mean? In this lesson, I'll examine the difference between ordinary functions and inline functions; this will lead me into a discussion of how member functions can be defined outside the class specification.

Inline Functions

There are two quite different ways for the compiler to construct a function. I described the normal approach in the last session: A function is placed in a separate section of code and a call to the function generates a jump to this section of code. When the function has finished executing, control jumps back from the end of the function to the statement following the function call, as depicted in Figure 4-1.

The advantage of this approach is that the same code can be called (executed) from many different places in the program. This makes it unnecessary to duplicate the function's code every time it is executed. There is a disadvantage as well, however. The function call itself, which requires not only a jump to the function but also the transfer of the arguments, takes some time, as does the return from the function and the transfer of the return value. In a program with many function calls (especially inside loops), these times can add up to sluggish performance.

For large functions, this is a small price to pay for the savings in memory space. For short functions (a few lines or so), however, the savings in memory may not be worth the extra time necessary to call the function and return from it. The designers of C++ therefore came up with another approach: the *inline function*. An inline function is defined using almost the same syntax as an ordinary function. However, instead of placing the function's machine-language code in a separate location, the compiler simply inserts it into the normal flow of the program at the location of the function call. Figure 4-5 shows the difference between ordinary functions and inline functions.

For inline functions, there is no time wasted in "calling" the function because it isn't actually called.

Specifying an Inline Function

You can request the compiler to make any function an inline function by using the keyword `inline` in the function definition.

```
inline void func1()
   {
   // statements
   }
```

In other respects, the function is defined in the same way as an ordinary function.

If you need to use a function declaration, it must reflect the `inline` as well.

```
inline void func1();  // declaration
```

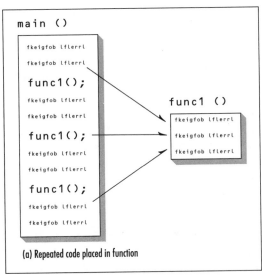

main ()

func1 ();

func1 ();

func1 ();

func1 ()

(a) Repeated code placed in function

Figure 4-5 Ordinary functions versus inline functions

However, calls to the function are made in the normal way:

```
func1();
```

When Should You Inline a Function?

The decision to inline a function must be made with some care. If a function is more than a few lines long and is called many times, then inlining it may require much more memory than an ordinary function. It's appropriate to inline a function when it is short, but not otherwise. If a long or complex function is inlined, too much memory will be used and not much time will be saved.

Actually, you seldom need to define a function explicitly as inline. In the most obvious place to do this, it's already done for you by the compiler, as you'll see next.

Member Functions Defined Within a Class

Here is the (somewhat surprising) situation: Member functions defined within the class specification (such as those shown in all the examples so far) are *inline by default*. That is, they are inline whether you use the `inline` keyword or not.

```
class anyClass
    {
    public:
        void anyfunc()      // this function is inline by default
            {
            // statements
            }
    };
```

Ordinary nonmember functions, on the other hand, are *not* inline unless inlining is explicitly specified with the `inline` keyword.

```
void afunc();   // declaration

void main()
   {
   afunc();     // call to function
   }

void afunc();   // definition -- NOT an inline function
   {
   }
```

The `main()` function, of course, is never inline; what would it be in line with?

Member Functions Defined Outside a Class

What happens if you want to define a member function that is too large to make inline? C++ provides an entirely different syntax for this arrangement. The function is *declared* within the class but *defined* outside it. Here's how that looks:

```
class anyClass         // class specification
   {
   public:
      void anyfunc();   // declaration only
   };

void anyClass::anyfunc()   // definition outside class
   {                       // this function is NOT inline
   // statements
   }
```

Member functions defined outside the class are ordinary–*not* inline–by default. (However, you can force them to be inline using the `inline` keyword.)

The Scope Resolution Operator

When it is defined outside a class, the name of a member function must incorporate the name of the class of which it's a member; otherwise there would be no way for the compiler to know which class that was. Of course, the function must use its own name as well, so these two names must be combined. The operator used to join these names is called the *scope resolution operator*. It consists of a double colon. In the previous example, the complete function name would be

`anyclass::anyfunc()`

The scope resolution operator can appear in various other contexts as well. It's used whenever you want to tell what class something is when you're outside the class specification.

The Compiler Has Its Own Ideas

Even if you define a member function *within* a class specification, the compiler may not allow it to be an inline function. As you saw in earlier examples where I used a loop in a member function, the compiler treats such member functions as ordinary functions, issuing warning messages when it does so.

Thus you can see that defining a function within a class specification (or using the keyword `inline` explicitly, for that matter) is merely a *suggestion* to the compiler to make a function inline. If the compiler thinks the function is too complicated, it will make it an ordinary function no matter what you've told it to do.

Revised WEEKDAYS **Program**

Let's see how these new member function definitions look in an actual program. The WEEKDAYS program in Chapter 3, Session 6, elicited a compiler warning that `Functions containing switch statements are not expanded inline`. In addition, the `inday()` function, in which the offending `switch` statements were embedded, is indeed rather large to be inline. So let's do what the compiler did for us anyway and define the `inday()` function outside of the class. Listing 4-1 shows the WEEKOUT program.

Listing 4-1 WEEKOUT

```
// weekout.cpp
// creates a class of days of the week objects
// uses member function external to class

#include <iostream.h>
#include <string.h>      // for stricmp()

const int MAX = 10;      // maximum length of day name, +1
const int DPW = 7;       // days per week

const char day_name[DPW][MAX] = // array of day names
                { "Sunday", "Monday", "Tuesday",
                  "Wednesday","Thursday", "Friday",
                  "Saturday"};

class weekday                    // class of day names
   {
   private:
      int day_number;            // Sunday=1, etc.
   public:
      void inday();              // NOTE: declaration

      void outday()              // display the day name
         {
         cout << day_name[day_number];
         }
      void outnumber()           // display the day number
         {
         cout << (day_number + 1);
         }
      void add(int days)         // add days to
         {                       // this weekday
         day_number += days;     // add days
         day_number %= DPW;      // ensure not > 7
         }
```

continued on next page

continued from previous page

```
};   // end weekdays class


                                    // NOTE: definition
void weekday::inday()               // user inputs day name
    {
    int j;
    char tempday[MAX];              // holds user input
    int gotit = 0;                  // match found? (0=false)

    while( !gotit )                 // cycle until user enters
        {                           // a correct name
        cout << "Enter day of week (e.g., Friday): ";
        cin >> tempday;
        for(j=0; j<DPW; j++)        // compare user input
            {                       // with list of names
            if( stricmp(tempday, day_name[j])==0 )
                {                   // if there's a match,
                gotit = 1;          // set flag,
                break;              // break out of for loop
                }
            }  // end for
        day_number = j;             // record what day it was
        }  // end while
    }  // end inday()

//////////////////////////////////////////////////////////////
void main()
    {
    weekday wd;                     // make a weekday object

    cout << "What day is it?" << endl;
    wd.inday();                     // user gives it a value
    cout << "You entered ";
    wd.outday();                    // display its day name
    cout << "\nThat's day number ";
    wd.outnumber();                 // display its day number
    wd.add(10);                     // add 10 days to it
    cout << "\nTen days later is ";
    wd.outday();                    // display its day name
    }
```

This program is the same as WEEKDAYS except `inday()` is defined outside the class specification. The other member functions, `outnumber()` and `add()`, which are quite short, have been kept inline.

Move 'em Out?

All member functions of more than a few lines should be written outside the class specification, as shown for `inday()` in WEEKOUT. From now on, the examples will conform to this usage.

Some programmers go further and recommend defining *all* member functions, no matter what size, outside the class. This has the advantage of simplifying the class specification and it may be a good idea when writing function libraries. However, for small programs such as the examples in this book, defining short member functions within the class avoids some extra program lines and makes the listings easier to read.

Macros

In C, in the olden times, it was customary to use something called a *macro* to accomplish what inline functions accomplish in C++. For example, in C++ you might have a function that returns the smaller of two integers.

```
int min(int a, int b)
    {
    return (a<b) ? a : b;
    }
```

This function uses the conditional operator to compare its two arguments. If **a** is less than **b**, it returns **a**; otherwise, it returns **b**.

A macro uses the preprocessor directive **#define**, with arguments, to simulate a function. The **min()** function, implemented as a macro, would look something like this:

```
#define MIN(A, B) ((A<B) ? A : B)
```

The **#define** directive basically causes the text on the right, **((A<B) ? A : B)**, to be substituted for the name on the left (**MIN**) wherever this name occurs in the source file. It's like a word processor doing a global search and replace, except that it also uses arguments. If you "call" the macro from your program like this,

```
cout << MIN(3, 5);
```

the statement will print out 3, the smaller of the two numbers. How does it work? The preprocessor expands this statement into

```
cout << ((3<5) ? 3 : 5);
```

before it goes to the compiler. Thus, a macro causes a short section of code to be generated and placed inline whenever it's called. This has the same advantage inline functions do—it eliminates the overhead of a function call and return.

However, macros are potentially dangerous. For one thing, they don't perform type checking, so they can't tell if the types of the arguments are correct. On the whole, the compiler is better at catching mistakes than the preprocessor is. Also, macros have some built-in problems (such as the need to surround all variables with parentheses) that can generate particularly troublesome bugs. My advice, even for old-time C programmers: Don't use macros, use inline functions instead.

QUIZ 2

1. Member functions, when defined within the class specification,
   a. are always inline.
   b. are inline by default, unless they're too big or too complicated.
   c. are inline only if the compiler thinks it's a good idea.

       d. are not inline by default.

       e. are never inline.

2. The code for an inline function

       a. is inserted into the program in place of each function call.

       b. is not generated by the compiler itself, but by the preprocessor.

       c. may be repeated many times throughout the program.

       d. occurs only once in a program.

       e. is merely symbolic; it is not actually executed.

3. The scope resolution operator

       a. joins a function name on the left and a variable name on the right.

       b. joins a function name on the left and a class name on the right.

       c. joins an inline function name and an ordinary function name.

       d. consists of a semicolon.

       e. comprises two semicolons.

4. In the WEEKDAYS program, there is a(n) _____ for `inday()` within the class specification, a(n) _____of this function following the class specification, and a(n) _____ to the function within `main()`.

       a. function body, declaration, assignment

       b. declaration, definition, call

       c. definition, member function, declaration

       d. assignment, call, member function

       e. declaration, function body, call

5. Member functions should be defined outside the class when

       a. they are more than a few lines long.

       b. they contain switches or loops.

       c. they contain I/O statements.

       d. they are short.

       e. they are simple.

EXERCISE 1

Start with the STREMP program from Chapter 3, Session 4, and move both the `input()` and `output()` member functions definitions outside the `employee` class.

EXERCISE 2

Start with the CARDARAY program from Chapter 3, Session 8, and move the `display()` member function outside the card class. This will eliminate the warning message from the compiler about `switch` statements not being expanded inline.

SESSION 3

OVERLOADED FUNCTIONS

One really nice convenience built into C++ is *function overloading*. This means that you can use the same name for different functions. You could, for example, have three functions all called `afunc()`, but each one would have a separate function definition. It may not seem obvious why you would want to do this, so I'll explain.

Need for Function Overloading

Suppose there is a function that calculates the average of an array of numbers of type `int`. Such a function might look like this:

```
int iaverage(int array[], int size);
   {
   int total = 0;              // set total to 0
   for(int j=0; j<size; j++)   // for every array member,
      total += array[j];       //    add it to total
   return total/size;          // return total div by array size
   }
```

The statement that calls this function passes the array name and the number of elements in the array as arguments:

```
avg = iaverage(int_array, 50);
```

Now, what happens if I want a function that averages arrays of type `long`? Such a function might look like this:

```
long laverage(long array[], int size);
   {
   long total = 0;             // set total to 0
   for(int j=0; j<size; j++)   // for every array member,
      total += array[j];       //    add it to total
   return total/size;          // return total div by array size
   }
```

The call to the function would be similar:

```
avg = laverage(long_array, 50);
```

There might be a similar function `faverage()` for type `float` and `daverage()` for type `double`. This arrangement works all right, but notice that, even though `iaverage()`, `laverage()`, and so on do the same thing–average numbers–they have different names. This is too bad, because the programmer must remember all the names. In a reference book, each name requires a separate section or messy cross-referencing. The multiplicity of names makes everyone's life harder.

Using different names for functions that do the same thing to different types is common in the C language library. For example, the function that returns the absolute value of a number is `abs()` for type `int`, `fabs()` for type `double`, `labs()` for type `long`, and so on. This is called *name proliferation*.

How Does It Know?

C++ avoids the pitfalls of name proliferation by making it possible for several different functions to have the same name. Thus, the `iaverage()`, `laverage()`, and similar functions can be called `average()`.

You may wonder how the compiler knows which function definition to call when the user writes a statement such as

```
avg = average(larray, 20);
```

The compiler looks at the type and number of the function's arguments to figure out what function is intended. Here the second argument is always `int`, but the first argument varies with the type of data to be averaged. In this statement, the type of `larray` is `long`, so the compiler calls the `average()` function that operates with the `long` type. If I say

```
avg = average(iarray, 20);
```

where `iarray` is type `int`, the compiler will call the average function that works with the `int` type. Figure 4-6 shows how the argument types determine which function is called.

How does the compiler distinguish one function from another that has the same name? It engages in a process called *name mangling*. ("What's the charge, officer?" "Name mangling, your honor.")

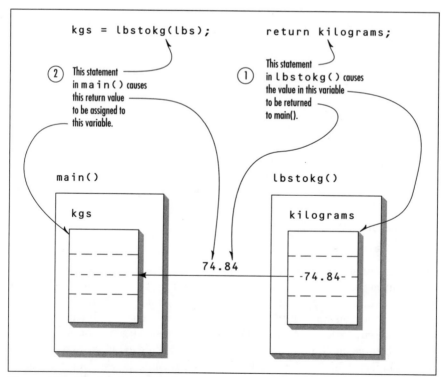

Figure 4-6 Overloaded functions

This consists of creating a new name by combining a function's name with the types of its arguments. The exact syntax varies from one compiler to another, and in any case is normally hidden from the programmer. However, I can speculate that the `average()` function for type `int` might be mangled into something like `average_int_int()`, whereas the `average()` function for type `long` might become `average_long_int()`. Notice, by the way, that the function's return type is *not* part of its mangled name. The compiler can't distinguish between two functions on the basis of return type.

A Member Function Example

Let's examine an example in which three different member functions all have the same name. Suppose I want a class that handles the display of text in various fancy ways. The objects will contain text strings, and member functions will display them. In particular, I want a set of functions that display text with a "box" around it. For simplicity, boxes will consist of a line above the text and a line below. The lines can be composed of various kinds of characters, such as dashes, asterisks, or equal signs. (This is a text-only example, so it can't draw real lines.)

Different versions of the member function `box_display()` will create boxes of varying degrees of sophistication. The first function will always display lines of 40 dashes. The second will also display lines 40 characters long, but will draw them using any specified character. The third will allow the user to specify both the character and the length of the lines. Listing 4-2 shows OVERFUN.

Listing 4-2 OVERFUN

```cpp
// overfun.cpp
// overloaded  functions

#include <iostream.h>
#include <string.h>                   // for strcpy()

const int MAX_LENGTH = 40;            // maximum length of text

class fancy_text                      // class displays text
    {
    private:
        char text[MAX_LENGTH];        // text to be displayed
    public:
        void set_text(char tx[])      // set the text
            {
            strcpy(text, tx);
            }
        void box_display();           // line of dashes
        void box_display(char);       // line of characters
        void box_display(char, int);  // line of n characters
    };

void fancy_text::box_display()        // line of 40 dashes
    {
    cout << "----------------------------------------";
    cout << endl << text << endl;
    cout << "----------------------------------------";
    }
                                      // line of 40 characters
```

continued on next page

continued from previous page

```
void fancy_text::box_display(char ch)
   {
   int j;
   for(j=0; j<MAX_LENGTH; j++)
      cout << ch;
   cout << endl << text << endl;
   for(j=0; j<MAX_LENGTH; j++)
      cout << ch;
   }
                                      // line of n characters
void fancy_text::box_display(char ch, int n)
   {
   int j;
   for(j=0; j<n; j++)
      cout << ch;
   cout << endl << text << endl;
   for(j=0; j<n; j++)
      cout << ch;
   }


void main()
   {
   fancy_text ft1;

   ft1.set_text("Gone with the Wind");

   ft1.box_display();          // display text with default lines
   cout << endl << endl;

   ft1.box_display('=');       // default length and equal signs
   cout << endl << endl;

   ft1.box_display('=', 18);   // equal signs; length matches text
   cout << endl << endl;
   }
```

In `main()`, the program creates a `fancy_text` object and gives it the text `Gone with the Wind`. Then it displays this text using three different versions of `box_display()`. First the program uses the default version, which always prints lines of 40 dashes. Then it uses the version that allows the specification of the type of character to use in the lines; it chooses equal signs. Finally, it uses the version that allows it to select both the character and the length; it uses equal signs again, but matches the length to the length of the text, which is 18 characters. The output from OVERFUN looks like this:

```
----------------------------------------
Gone with the Wind
----------------------------------------


========================================
Gone with the Wind
========================================


==================
Gone with the Wind
==================
```

Notice that I've defined all the `box_display()` functions outside the class. The function declarations within the class show, with commendable brevity, the differences between the three versions of the function:

```
void box_display();           // uses two lines of dashes
void box_display(char);        // uses two lines of characters
void box_display(char, int);   // uses two lines of n characters
```

Remember that, even though they have the same name, these three functions are completely different as far as the compiler is concerned. The compiler has even invented separate names for each function by mangling the argument type names into the function name. (Actually, although you don't need to know this, the class name is mangled into member function names as well so the compiler can distinguish member functions that have the same name but are in different classes, such as the ubiquitous `init()`.)

QUIZ 3

1. Function overloading is desirable because
   a. you don't need to define as many functions.
   b. in a reference book that's arranged in alphabetical order, all the functions that do the same thing will be in the same place.
   c. one overloaded function can be made to do the work of several ordinary functions.
   d. when functions that do the same thing all have the same name, it's clearer and easier to remember, even if they do it to different types of data.
   e. you don't need to make up a lot of slightly different function names.

2. In the OVERFUN program, once the code is compiled into machine language, how many versions of the `box_display()` function actually exist?
   a. 1.
   b. 3.
   c. There must always be the same number as there are function definitions.
   d. There must always be the same number as there are function calls.
   e. There must always be the same number as the number of arguments.

3. Name mangling of a member function involves
   a. creating a name for internal use by the compiler.
   b. creating a name for use by the programmer.
   c. incorporating the name of the object that called the function into the function name.
   d. incorporating the function's argument types into the function name.
   e. incorporating the class name into the function name.

4. Assuming the statements shown here are all in the same `main()`, which ones can potentially compile properly and not interfere with each other?
   a. `intvar1 = get_number();`
   b. `floatvar1 = get_number();`
   c. `intvar1 = get_number(intvar2);`

   d. `floatvar1 = get_number(floatvar2);`
   e. `intvar1 = get_number(intvar2, intvar3);`

5. It might be reasonable to use a set of overloaded member functions to
   a. perform the five basic arithmetic operations on type `float`.
   b. exit from a class in different ways.
   c. draw different shapes.
   d. display information about different kinds of employees.
   e. play the roles of `strcpy()`, `strcat()`, `strlen()`, and so on in a string class.

EXERCISE 1

Write a set of overloaded functions (not necessarily member functions) that return the smaller of two numbers passed to them as arguments. Make versions for `int`, `long`, and `float`.

EXERCISE 2

In the HOURADD program in Chapter 2, Session 6, is a member function called `addhours()` This function adds a specified number of hours to an `airtime` object. Change the name of this function to `add()` and write another member function, also called `add()`, that uses an `airtime` value as an argument and adds this argument to the `airtime` object that called the function. Change `main()` to check out these overloaded functions.

SESSION 4

DEFAULT ARGUMENTS

Default arguments are another convenience feature in C++. Like overloaded functions, they make things easier for the programmer by reducing the number of function names that must be remembered. However, where overloaded functions give a number of functions the same name, default arguments allow a single function to operate as if it were several functions.

A Power Example

Suppose I write a function called `power()` whose purpose is to raise a number of type `float` to a power, that is, to multiply the number by itself a given number of times. For simplicity, I'll restrict the power to whole numbers. To raise 2.0 to the power of 3, for example, I would call the function like this:

```
answer = power(2.0, 3);
```

Here `answer` should be 2.0 cubed, or 8.0. The definition for such a function might look like this:

```
float power(float fpn, int pow)
    {
```

```
float product = 1.0;
for(int j=0; j<pow; j++)    // multiply fpn by itself pow times
    product *= fpn;
return product;
}
```

This is fine so far, but let's further suppose that I want the same function to handle a special case somewhat differently. If no second argument is specified, I want it to find the square of a number (multiply the number by itself).

```
answer = power(9.0);            // should square the number
```

Here the answer should be 9.0 times 9.0, or 81.0.

To achieve this result, I could overload `power()` so I have two separate functions, one that takes a single argument, which it multiplies by itself and one that takes two arguments and raises the first to the power of the second. However, there's a simpler approach.

Default arguments allow you to leave out one or more arguments when you call a function. Seeing that arguments are missing, the function declaration supplies fixed values for the missing arguments. Let's see how that looks with the `power()` example.

```
float power(float, int=2);      // function declaration
...                             // (supplies default argument)
void main()
    {
    ...
    answer = power(9.0);        // call with one argument
                                // (2.0 is supplied as 2nd arg)

    ...
    answer = power(2.0, 3);     // call with two arguments

    }

float power(float fpn, int pow) // function definition
    {                           // (doesn't know about defaults)
    float product = 1.0;
    for(int j=0; j<pow; j++)
        product *= fpn;
    return product;
    }
```

The function declaration is used to supply the default argument. The equal sign indicates that a default argument will be used; the value following the equal sign specifies the value of this argument. The function definition is not changed at all. It doesn't know whether it's receiving real arguments or default arguments; it just does what it's told. In `main()`, the program calls `power()` both ways, first with one argument and then with two. Figure 4-7 shows how the definition supplies the values of the default arguments.

I should note that there is a family of C library functions, `pow()`, `powl()`, `pow10()`, and so on, that raise one number to the power of another. However, being written in C, they cannot use function overloading or default arguments.

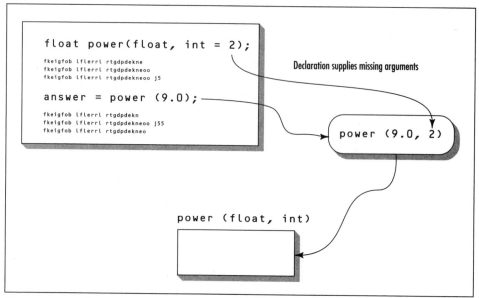

Figure 4-7   Default arguments

A Member Function Example

Let's modify the `fancy_text` class from the OVERFUN example in the last lesson so that the `box_display()` member function uses default arguments instead of overloading. Depending on how many arguments are sent to this function, it will display lines of 40 dashes, lines of 40 user-chosen characters, or lines of characters with both the length and the character selected by the class user. Listing 4-3 shows DEFARGS.

Listing 4-3 DEFARGS

```
// defargs.cpp
// default arguments

#include <iostream.h>
#include <string.h>                  // for strcpy()

const int MAX_LENGTH = 40;           // maximum length of text

class fancy_text                     // class displays text
    {
    private:
        char text[MAX_LENGTH];       // text to be displayed
    public:
        void set_text(char tx[])     // set the text
            {
            strcpy(text, tx);
            }

                                     // set default values
```

```
        void box_display(char ch='-', int n = MAX_LENGTH);
    };

// line of n characters ch, or default values for n and/or ch
void fancy_text::box_display(char ch, int n)
    {
    int j;
    for(j=0; j<n; j++)                    // line of n ch's
        cout << ch;
    cout << endl << text << endl;         // line of text
    for(j=0; j<n; j++)                    // line of n ch's
        cout << ch;
    }

void main()
    {
    fancy_text ft1;

    ft1.set_text("Gone with the Wind");

    ft1.box_display();           // display text with default lines
    cout << endl << endl;

    ft1.box_display('=');        // default length and equal signs
    cout << endl << endl;

    ft1.box_display('=', 18); // equal signs; length matches text
    cout << endl << endl;
    }
```

There are three ways to call `box_display()`: You can leave out both arguments, leave out only the second one, or supply them both. Here are examples of these three approaches. Each displays a line of characters, a line of text, and another line of characters:

```
ft1.box_display();           // two lines of 40 dashes
ft1.box_display('=');        // two lines of 40 '=' characters
ft1.box_display('=', 18);    // two lines of 18 '=' characters
```

The output from this program is the same as that from OVERFUN:

```
----------------------------------------
Gone with the Wind
----------------------------------------

========================================
Gone with the Wind
========================================

==================
Gone with the Wind
==================
```

Note also that the `main()` part of the program is identical to that of OVERFUN. I've changed a member in the class from using overloaded functions to using default arguments, but this has not affected the interface between `main()` and the class.

The `cin.getline()` Function

Another example of default arguments in action can be seen in the C++ library function `cin.getline()`. I've already used the `cin.get()` function to acquire text from the keyboard. The `cin.getline()` function is similar, but it uses a default argument for the termination character—the character the user types to terminate input. You can call the function much as you can call `cin.get()`:

```
cin.getline(str, 80);        // get up to 80 chars, place in str
```

When used this way, the function will return when the user presses ENTER. However, you can also add a third argument:

```
cin.getline(str, 80, '$');    // get up to 80 chars, place in str
```

In this case, the function will not terminate when the user presses ENTER but will continue to accept input from the keyboard until the user presses the dollar sign ($).

The declaration of `getline()` in the IOSTREAM.H header file, somewhat simplified, looks like this:

```
istream getline(char, int, char = '\n');    // simplified declaration
```

The third argument is given a default value of `'\n'`, which is the character returned when the user presses ENTER. By specifying a third argument, I can change the terminating character to anything I want.

Limitations

Only the arguments at the end of the argument list can have default arguments. If one argument has a default argument, it must be the last one. If two arguments do, they must be the last two, and so on. You can't insert a default argument in the middle of a list of normal arguments because the compiler would lose track of what arguments went where. In other words, you can't say

```
void badfunc(int, int=2, int);    // no good
```

because the default argument is not the last one. However

```
void okfunc(int, int=2, int=10);    // ok
```

is all right because both default arguments are at the end of the list (i.e., on the right).

If you call a function such as `okfunc()` that has two default arguments and you leave one argument out, it must be the last one. Otherwise, the function won't be able to figure out which value matches up with which argument.

You can't change the values of the default arguments midway through your program by using additional function declarations. Attempting to do so will elicit a complaint from the compiler.

When to Do What

I've explored two ways to make one function name do the work of several. Overloaded functions are actually separate functions with the same name but different numbers and/or types of arguments. A function that has default arguments is only one function, but it can take different numbers of arguments.

Overloaded functions are typically used when a similar operation must be performed on different data types. Default arguments are used in cases where a simplified or default version of a function can be used in certain circumstances. Default arguments are also useful in functions that are under development. They can serve as place holders for arguments that are not yet installed in a function definition but are planned for some time in the future. The defaults allow existing function calls to operate correctly, but allow future calls to take advantage of a revised function that uses more arguments.

1. A default argument is an argument that
   a. can be of different types in different calls to the function.
   b. must always have the same value.
   c. can be used, or not used, in a function call.
   d. will cause control to be routed to different functions, depending on whether it's supplied or not.
   e. can be supplied with a value, but not by the function call.

2. The values for nonexistent default arguments are specified in
   a. the function body.
   b. the function declaration.
   c. the function definition.
   d. the function call.
   e. class member data.

3. Given the following function declaration

   ```
   void afunc(float, int=2, char='x');
   ```

   which of the following are correct calls to the function?

   a. `afunc(3.14159);`
   b. `afunc(19, 'a');`
   c. `afunc(12.2, 19, 'a');`
   d. `afunc(12.2, 'a');`
   e. `afunc(12.2, 19);`

4. Which of the following are valid declarations for functions that use default arguments?
   a. `void afunc(char, float=3.14159, int=10);`
   b. `void afunc(char='x', float, int);`
   c. `void afunc(char ch, float fpn, int intvar=77);`

```
    d. void afunc(char ch=3.14159, float fpn=3.14159, int intvar);
    e. void afunc(char, float, int);
```

5. It is appropriate to use default arguments when
   a. you want to pass an array of data to a sorting function `sort()`, but the data can be of any type.
   b. you want a function `log()` that usually calculates logarithms to the base 10, but you occasionally want to specify a different base.
   c. you want to average the contents of `int` arrays of varying sizes.
   d. the type of the arguments will vary.
   e. the value of one of the arguments will often be a particular fixed value.

EXERCISE 1

Using the `getche()` function to read the characters, write your own version of the `cin.getline()` function described in this lesson. Include the default argument for the terminating character.

EXERCISE 2

Revise the `box_display()` function in the `fancy_text` class so it boxes in the left and right ends of the displayed text as well as on the top and bottom, like this:

```
|===================|
| Gone with the Wind |
|===================|
```

Add a fourth argument to the function so the user can determine the character to be used for the box ends. Make this a default argument, which, if it's not supplied, causes the function to use the | character shown in the example output.

MIDCHAPTER DISCUSSION

George: Overloaded functions, default arguments, what do they buy you? Is it really that hard to remember a bunch of different function names?

Estelle: I don't think it's a major feature of the language, like classes or something. It's just a convenience.

Don: Right. Remember, with OOP we've got programmers who are class creators and other programmers who are class users. I think overloaded functions is a way to make things a little easier for the class users. If you've got a whole lot of member functions for a new class you're learning about, overloading means you've got fewer names to remember.

Estelle: Does everyone get the difference between function declarations and definitions?

George: The definition *is* the function, and the declaration is just the instructions to the compiler about how to make a function call.

Don: Very good, George. You're getting sharper and sharper.

George: Well, I read the assignment, for a change. But I still don't see why you don't just put all the function definitions first. Then you wouldn't need any declarations.

Estelle: Lots of programmers like to put the more important functions, such as `main()`, first and less important ones later. But the important ones tend to call the unimportant ones.

Don: Or a program could be divided into different files. When you call a function that's in a different file, then you better have the declaration in your file or the compiler won't know how to handle it.

Estelle: There sure are a lot of ways to use functions.

George: I don't see any reason to use anything but `main()` and member functions.

Don: That's true in the little example programs we've seen in these sessions. But you need more flexibility in big programs. That's why you've got to be able to call a function that's in another part of the file or in a different file.

George: If you say so.

SESSION 5

STORAGE CLASSES

As I noted earlier, functions, along with classes, are an important organizing principle in the design of C++ programs. Dividing a program into functions and classes gives rise to the concept of *storage classes*, which allow you to specify various features of data variables. (Incidentally, the word *class* in *storage class* is used in its generic sense; it has nothing to do with C++ classes.) Storage classes are a major tool in the design of C++ programs. They allow the programmer to *manage* variables. This can help save memory, make the program run faster, simplify it, and avoid variable name clashes. In this session, I'll explore storage classes and several other fundamental aspects of variable usage.

Some of the material in this lesson may seem theoretical or obscure. Don't worry if you don't understand it all. You can come back to this lesson later when questions about storage classes arise in future discussions.

Before you learn about storage classes, you need to firm up your understanding of two words: declaration and definition.

Declarations and Definitions

Thus far, I have used the terms declaration and definition as they apply to data variables without explaining exactly what they mean. In many cases, these words are used in much the same way, but there is an important distinction.

A *declaration* specifies a name and a data type. This is all a declaration is required to do. Its job is to impart information to the compiler; it does not cause the compiler to take any action.

A *definition*, on the other hand, causes the compiler to allocate a specific place in memory for the variable.

I've already noted these distinctions with regard to functions, where a function can be declared or defined:

```
void afunc();      // function declaration

void afunc()       // function definition
   {
   // statements
   }
```

The declaration is for information only, whereas the definition is the "real thing"; it is turned into code that is installed in memory. The same is true for variables: At a single point in a program, a definition causes memory to be set aside for each variable but the variable can be declared—that is, its name and type can be specified—in several different places.

Two Kinds of Declarations

Confusingly, most writers consider a definition to be a *kind of* declaration. That is, some declarations cause memory to be allocated, whereas some don't. Other writers try to use the word declaration only when a definition is *not* taking place. Thus the word declaration is potentially confusing. In any case, the word definition always means that memory is being allocated. And, fortunately, the context usually makes it clear whether the word declaration means declaration as opposed to definition or declaration that may or may not be a definition.

All the variable declarations you've seen so far have been definitions as well. However, when I discuss the external storage class in a moment, you'll see that some variable declarations are not definitions.

Lifetime and Visibility

Storage class determines two key characteristics of a variable. The first, called *visibility*—or *scope*—relates to which parts of the program can "see" or access the variable. The second, the *lifetime*, is the period of time during which the variable exists. Variables can be visible within a class, a function, a file, or a number of files. A variable's lifetime can coincide with that of an object, a function, or an entire program.

Each storage class provides a different combination of lifetime and visibility. You've already made the acquaintance of several storage classes (although I have not dwelled on the implications). These are automatic variables and external variables. I'll first look at these storage classes from the standpoint of lifetime and visibility. Then I'll introduce some new storage classes; finally, I'll summarize lifetime and visibility for all the storage classes.

Automatic Variables

Automatic variables are declared inside a function, like this:

```
void anyfunc()
    {
    int ivar;       // automatic variables
    float fvar;
    }
```

They are called automatic variables because they are automatically created when a function is called. When the function returns, its automatic variables are destroyed. For the technically minded, automatic variables are pushed onto the stack when a function first starts to execute and popped off when it returns. Thus, the lifetime of automatic variables coincides with the time the function is actually executing.

Automatic variables are visible only within the function. Statements in any other function cannot access them. Thus, a variable defined as j in one function is a completely different variable than one defined as j in another function.

You can use the keyword auto to specify an automatic variable, but because variables defined within a function are automatic by default, there is seldom a reason to do this.

Automatic variables are not initialized by default, so unless you initialize them explicitly, they will have a random "garbage" value when they first come into existence.

Figure 4-8 shows the visibility of variables of various storage classes. The wide arrows indicate the parts of the program where a variable is visible.

Register Variables

A *register variable* is a specialized kind of automatic variable. Register variables require the keyword register. The idea is that the compiler will attempt to place register variables in CPU registers rather than in memory. Because registers are more quickly accessed, they should make a program with commonly used variables more efficient. A typical variable that would profit from this treatment is the innermost loop variable in a set of nested loops. You are usually limited to one or two register variables in a given function.

Actually, modern compilers are so efficient at figuring out—on their own—what variables should be register variables that it's questionable whether there is much point in specifying this storage class. I'll ignore it in this book. If you have a loop in which your program spends a great deal of time, you might experiment to see if making the loop variables register speeds things up.

Blocks

Automatic variables can be defined not only within a function but also within a *block*, which is any section of code enclosed in braces. The body of a loop or an if statement is a block, for example. Variables defined within a block have *block scope*; that is, they are visible only within the block.

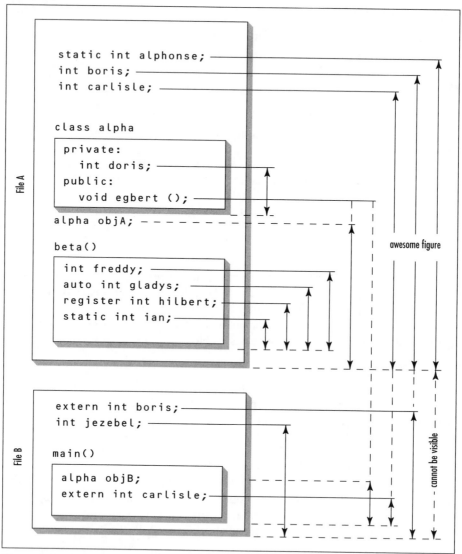

Figure 4-8 Visibility of storage classes

External Variables

As you've seen, most variables are declared either as class instance data (usually private) or as automatic variables inside functions. However, you've also seen a few examples of variables declared outside any class or function, most recently the **MAX_LENGTH** variable in the OVERFUN program in Session 3 in this chapter. Such variables are called *external variables*. Here's an example:

```
// start of file (e.g., somename.cpp)
```

```
int xvar;          // external variable

void afunc()
   {
   ...
   }

class aclass
   {
   ...
   };

// end of file
```

External variables are visible to all statements throughout the file from the point where the variable is declared onward. The lifetime of external variables is the life of the program. External variables, unlike automatic variables, are automatically initialized to 0, unless they are initialized explicitly.

External Variables and Multiple Files

All but the smallest C++ programs are typically divided into several files. For simplicity, in this book most of the example programs consist of a single file, although I'll delve into multiple-file programs on Chapter 11, Session 7. In the meantime, it's useful to understand how external variables can be made visible or invisible in multiple files.

You've already seen that an external variable is known throughout the file in which it's defined from the point of the declaration onward. An external variable that is defined in one file is not normally accessible in other files; it is invisible outside its own file. However, it can be made accessible by using a declaration, with the keyword extern, in any other file that wants to access the variable. Here's an example that consists of three files:

```
// file #1
int ivar;          // definition
// ivar is known in this file
// end of file #1

// file #2
extern int ivar;   // declaration
// ivar is also known in this file
// end of file #2

// file #3
// ivar is not known in this file
// end of file #3
```

The variable ivar is defined in file 1, declared in file 2, and not declared in file 3. This variable is thus visible in files 1 and 2, but not in 3.

In any program, a variable can have only one *definition*. It can exist in memory in only one place, and only one statement can cause this memory to be allocated. However, a variable can be *declared* in many places. In the example above, ivar can be declared in any number of other files, each time using the keyword extern.

You can also restrict an external variable so it is invisible in other files even if they attempt to access it using an `extern` declaration. To do this, use the keyword `static`, which doesn't really mean *static* in this context as much as it means *restricted scope*.

```
// file #1
static int ivar;          // definition
// ivar can be known ONLY in this file
// end of file #1

// file #2
extern int ivar;          // useless declaration
// end of file #2
```

Here the compiler will think that `ivar` refers to some other variable that hasn't been defined yet; when the linker encounters this reference, it will complain that `ivar` is undefined.

External Variables in the Doghouse

Now that I've discussed external variables, I must note that their use is somewhat suspect in C++. There are several problems with them. The first is that they are open to accidental alteration. Because they are visible to all the functions in the program, it's easy for a function to alter an external variable by mistake. It's like leaving your address book on the sidewalk. Who knows what might happen to it?

The second problem has to do with name control. Variable names defined inside a class or function do not conflict with the same names used for different variables inside another class or function. That is, you can define a variable `count` inside `func1()`, a different variable `count` inside `func2()`, and a third variable `count` inside `class X`. These names will not conflict because the names are not visible outside their function or class.

External variables, on the other hand, are visible everywhere, so there can be only one external variable called `count` in the entire program (or file, if it's static). This can lead to name clashes, especially in large programs where different sections of the program are created by different programming teams.

Look long and hard at any external variables in your program; you may not really need them. Often you should use static instance data, which I'll look at in the next session, instead of external variables.

Local Static Variables

Sometimes you want a function to be able remember something between one call to the function and the next. For example, suppose you want a function (perhaps called `average()`) to add a value to a running total every time it is called and to return with the updated average of all the numbers it has been called with, including all the values from previous calls as well as the present call.

Such a function would need to store the total and the number of times the function has already been called so it could calculate the new average. However, this can't be done with normal automatic variables because they are destroyed and their contents are lost every time the function returns. The solution is to make these variables static:

```
float average(float item)
  {
  static int n = 0;         // number of times we've been called
  static float total = 0.0; // running total
```

```
total += item;          // add argument to running total
return total/n++;       // find average, increment count
}
```

Local static variables exist for the lifetime of the program, so they don't lose their existence or their values when the function returns. They are initialized to 0.0 automatically, but doing so explicitly, as I show here, helps clarify for the programmer what's happening.

Local static variables are not used as much in C++ as they are in C. In C++, objects have taken over the role of functions that use local static variables. Both an object and such a function contain data that continues to exist even when the function is not executing. Because objects are more powerful and versatile than functions (that's why OOP was invented), it makes sense to use a class instead of a function and static variables. If you find yourself needing to use static variables in a standalone (nonmember) function, it's probably time to turn the function into a class by making the static data into instance data.

The Storage Class Table

Table 4-1 summarizes the scope and lifetime attributes of the various storage classes.

Storage Class	Specifier (Keyword)	Visibility (Scope)	Lifetime
Automatic	None (or `auto`)	Function	Function
Register	`register`	Function	Function
Local static	`static`	Function	Program
External (definition)	None	File (can be declared in other files)	Program
External (declaration)	`extern`	File	Program
External static	`static`	File (cannot be declared in other files)	Program

Table 4-1   Storage class, visibility, and lifetime

Objects

Remember that objects are treated almost the same as variables in C++. (The difference is that objects must have a class specification, whereas the specifications for basic types are built into the language.) Objects can be created in any of the storage classes described in Table 4-1: automatic, external, and so on. Like variables, they can be defined or only declared. (The exception is the storage class `register`, which doesn't make any sense for objects because an object cannot be placed in a register.)

Visiblity of Instance Data

What about the visibility of instance data within classes? The variables I have used thus far in class specifications have all been private. As you've learned, this means that such variables cannot be "seen" or accessed except by statements in that class's member functions. Private class data is invisible outside the class. Here's an example:

```
class someclass
   {
   private:
       int ivar;        // private instance data
       float fvar;
   public:
       // member functions can access ivar and fvar
   };
```

In this class specification, the variables `ivar` and `fvar` are visible only to statements between the braces that delimit the `someclass` class. The visibility of private class data is the class.

Public class members (usually functions) are visible to all functions and classes throughout the entire file—at least from the point of the class specification onward—provided they are called in conjunction with an actual object of that class. This requires the dot operator (or something similar) to link the object and the function, as in

```
anobj.memfunc(); // member functions must be called by an object
```

Lifetime of Instance Data

What is the lifetime of class instance data? Such data doesn't exist until an actual object of that class is defined. Then the variables that make up the instance data for *that particular object* (but not for any other objects) are defined as well. By *defined*, I mean that specific locations in memory are set aside for these variables.

When an object ceases to exist, all its variables are destroyed along with it. (I'll discuss in Chapter 5 how objects may cease to exist.) Thus, the lifetime of class instance data, whether public or private, is the lifetime of its object.

QUIZ 5

1. Storage classes are concerned with
    a. which variable a value is stored in.
    b. which data type a value is stored in.
    c. a special class whose objects are variables of basic types.
    d. whether a variable can retain its value when a function returns.
    e. how long a variable stays in existence.

2. A declaration _____, whereas a definition _____.
    a. may be a definition, can never be a declaration.
    b. specifies only a name and a data type, also allocates memory space.
    c. specifies a data type, specifies a name.
    d. specifies a name, specifies a data type.
    e. allocates only memory space, also specifies a name and a data type.

3. Instance data exists for the life of
   a. a block.
   b. a function.
   c. an object.
   d. a file.
   e. the entire program.

4. Automatic variables are visible only in the _____ in which they are declared.
   a. class
   b. function
   c. object
   d. file
   e. program

5. To make an external variable accessible in a file other than the one in which it is defined,
   a. is impossible.
   b. it must be defined again.
   c. the keyword `extern` must be used.
   d. the keyword `static` must be used.
   e. it must be declared.

Due to the largely theoretical nature of this lesson, there are no exercises.

SESSION 6

STATIC MEMBERS

In this lesson, I'll introduce a C++ feature that's related to storage classes and that casts some light on the nature of class members.

Static Member Data

So far, the data members I've used in classes have been *instance data*, meaning that one copy of the data exists for each instance of an object that is created. In other words, instance data is associated with a particular object. But what if you need a variable that applies to the class as a whole, rather than to particular objects?

For example, suppose I have a class of race cars in a game program. Such things as the position of each car and its speed are clearly instance data because they apply to each individual car. However, other data applies to the race track, such as the length of the track, and any obstructions that might suddenly appear on it, like an oil slick or the yellow caution flag. This sort of data is not

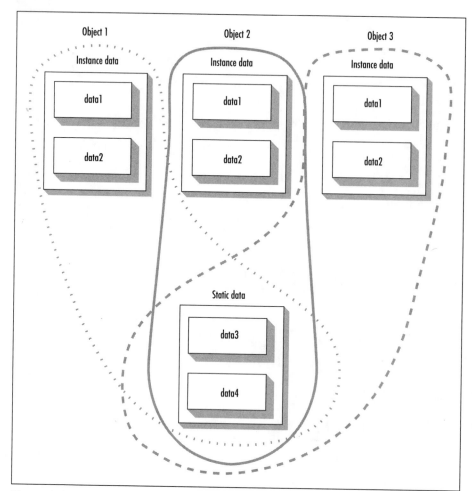

Figure 4-9   Instance data and static data

specific to each car, but is related to the entire class of race cars. All the cars in the class access the same variable to determine if the yellow flag is up; this data isn't duplicated for each car.

I could use external variables for such data, but external variables are not associated with the particular class and have other problems as well, as mentioned in the last session. I want a class variable, but one that is not duplicated for each object.

Static member data solves this problem. One copy of such data exists for the entire class, as shown in Figure 4-9.

Creating Static Data

The syntax for creating static member data is unusual. You must have separate statements to declare a variable within a class and to define it outside the class. Here's an example:

```
class aclass
    {
    private:
        static int stavar;     // declaration
    ...
    };

int aclass::stavar = 77;     // definition
```

The declaration uses the keyword **static**. The definition uses the class name connected to the variable name with the scope resolution operator (::). This double-barreled approach to creating a static variable makes some kind of sense if you assume that data defined *inside* the class specification is always instance data, duplicated for each object. To define a data item that exists only once for the entire class, you define it *outside* the class, although you declare it inside the class so it will be visible to other class members.

The static data member can be initialized when it's defined, as I showed here. If it's not explicitly initialized, it's automatically set to 0. Once it's defined, static class data can be accessed only by class member functions; it has class scope.

Accessing Static Data

You can access static member data from an ordinary member function. However, it usually makes more sense to use a special kind of function that, like static data, applies to an entire class rather than a particular object. This is called a *static function*.

Static Functions

A static member function is defined using the keyword **static**. Otherwise, it looks like any other member function. However, function calls to member functions are made without referring to a particular object. Instead, the function is identified by connecting it to the class name with the scope resolution operator. Here's how that looks:

```
class aclass
    {
    private:
        ...
    public:
        static int stafunc()  // function definition
            {
            // can access only static member data
            }
    };

main()
    {
    ...
    aclass::stafunc();          // function call
    ...
    }
```

A static member function cannot refer to any nonstatic member data in its class. Why not? Because static functions don't know anything about the objects in a class. All they can access is static, class-specific data. You can call a static function even before you've created any objects of a class.

Count-the-Objects Example

Sometimes individual objects in a class, or nonmember functions such as main(), need to know how many objects of a class exist at any given time. A race car, for example, might want to know how many other race cars are left on the track after various crashes and engine failures.

The example program creates a class of widgets (small devices of obscure purpose). Each widget is given a serial number, starting with 10,000. The class uses a static variable, total_widgets, to keep track of how many widgets have been created so far. It uses this total to generate a serial number and to place it in the instance variable widget_number when a new widget is created.

A static member function is used in main() to access the total number of widgets. This allows the program to access the total before it has created any widgets and again when it has created three. Listing 4-4 shows STATIC.

Listing 4-4 STATIC

```
// static.cpp
// demonstrates static data and functions

#include <iostream.h>

class widget
    {
    private:
        int widget_number;          // a widget's serial number
        static int total_widgets;   // all widgets made so far
                                    // NOTE: declaration only
    public:
        void init()                 // initialize one widget
            {
            widget_number = 10000 + total_widgets++;
            }
        int get_number()            // get a widget's number
            {
            return widget_number;
            }
        static int get_total()      // get total widgets
            {
            return total_widgets;
            }
    };

int widget::total_widgets = 0;      // NOTE: definition

void main()
    {
    cout << "Total widgets = " << widget::get_total() << endl;
```

```
widget w1, w2, w3;        // create widgets
w1.init();                // initialize them
w2.init();
w3.init();

cout << "w1=" << w1.get_number() << endl;
cout << "w2=" << w2.get_number() << endl;
cout << "w3=" << w3.get_number() << endl;

cout << "Total widgets = " << widget::get_total() << endl;
}
```

The program calls `get_total()` before creating any widgets, creates three widgets, numbers them by calling `init()` for each one, displays each widget's number, and then calls `get_total()` again. Notice that the nonstatic member function `init()` can access the static variable `total_widgets` (it increments it), but static member function `get_total()` *cannot* access nonstatic (instance) data.

Here's the output of the STATIC program:

```
Total widgets = 0
w1 = 10000
w2 = 10001
w3 = 10002
Total widgets = 3
```

I've noted before how clumsy it is to use a function such as `init()` to initialize each object to a certain value just after it's created. I'll fix this in the next chapter, when you learn about constructors.

1. Which of the following would be reasonable uses for static member data in a class where each object represents an elevator in a high-rise building?
   a. The location of each elevator.
   b. A request from the 17th floor to go up.
   c. The number of riders in an elevator.
   d. The number of elevators in the building.
   e. Pushing the button for the 17th floor while inside an elevator.

2. A static member variable in a class
   a. is duplicated within each object.
   b. does not really exist, in the sense of being defined.
   c. has only one copy for the entire class.
   d. is duplicated in each member function.
   e. represents something about the class as a whole.

3. Static member functions
   a. must be declared inside the class specification, but defined outside it.
   b. must be called using an object of the class.

c. have only one copy for the entire class.
d. can access only static data.
e. can access any object's data.

4. Calling a static member function from `main()` requires
   a. the dot operator.
   b. the scope resolution operator.
   c. no operator.
   d. the function to be public.
   e. the class name.

5. In the STATIC program,
   a. the `get_number()` function can access static variables.
   b. the `get_total()` function can access static variables.
   c. the `get_number()` function can access nonstatic variables.
   d. the `get_total()` function can access nonstatic variables.
   e. `widget_total` can be assigned a new value by a statement in `main()`.

EXERCISE 1

Add a `price_per_widget` member data variable (type `float`) to the `widget` class. Should it be static? Also add a member function that will return the total value of all widgets created to date; call it `get_value()`. Make this function static.

EXERCISE 2

Start with the elevator program from Exercise 1 in Chapter 2, Session 1. The `elevator` class has member functions to display the floor the elevator is on, to move it up one floor, and to move it down one floor. To this program add a static member variable that represents how many floors there are in the building. Modify the existing member functions so they use this value to check whether moving the elevator up or down will cause it to go higher than the highest floor or lower than the lowest floor (which you can assume is 1). Don't move the elevator if these conditions occur.

SESSION 7

REFERENCE ARGUMENTS

What's a reference? The short and enigmatic definition is that it's another name—an *alias*—for a variable. Why would anyone want a different name for a variable? The most important reason has to do with function arguments.

Recall that when I pass an argument to a function by value (as you've seen many times already), this value originates in a variable in the code that calls the function and is then *copied into another variable* in the function itself. The function then operates on its own copy of the variable; it cannot access the original variable.

But what happens if I *want* the function to operate on the original variable? When this is the case, I must use a different approach to specifying the name the function uses for an argument. By doing this, I can make the name used by the function refer to the original variable in the code that called the function, instead of referring to a newly created copy of the variable within the function.

I'll first show a simple example of this, using integers. Then I'll show how the technique can be applied to objects. Finally, you'll see that references don't need to be used exclusively with function arguments (or with return values, as you'll see in the next lesson), although they usually are.

Swapping Integers

Suppose you have two integer variables in your program and you want to call a function that swaps (exchanges) their values. For example, suppose you've defined two variables this way:

```
int alpha = 2;          // initialize two ints
int beta = 7;
```

Passing by Value

Now you want to call a function that will swap 7 into `alpha` and 2 into `beta`. Will the following function definition have the desired effect?

```
void swap(int a, int b)  // function swaps values???
   {
   int temp = a;
   a = b;
   b = temp;
   }
```

This function swaps the values of `a` and `b`. However, if you call this function in the usual way, like this,

```
swap(alpha, beta);       // try to swap their values
```

hoping it will swap the values of `alpha` and `beta`, you will be disappointed. If you print out the values of `alpha` and `beta` after calling the function, you will find that they are unchanged. Why? Because normal function arguments in C++ are *passed by value*, as I noted. The function automatically creates completely new variables, called `a` and `b` in this example, to hold the values passed to it (2 and 7) and operates on these new variables. So when the function terminates, although it's true that `a` has been changed to 7 and `b` has been changed to 2, unfortunately the variables `alpha` and `beta`, in the code that called the function, remain stubbornly unchanged.

Passing by Reference

We need a way for the function to reach back into the original variables (`alpha` and `beta`) and manipulate *them* instead of creating new variable. That's what passing by reference accomplishes.

Syntactically, to cause an argument to be passed by reference, simply add an ampersand (**&**) to the data type of the argument in the function definition (and the function declaration, if one is needed). Here's how you can rewrite the **swap()** function to use reference arguments:

```
void swap(int&, int&);      // function declaration,
                            // (note ampersands)
...
int alpha = 2;              // initialize two ints
int beta = 7;
...
swap(alpha, beta);          // swap their values (declaration)
...
void swap(int& a, int& b)   // function swaps values
   {                        // (note ampersands)
   int temp = a;
   a = b;
   b = temp;
   }
```

If you print out the values of **alpha** and **beta** following the call to this version of **swap()**, you'll find that they have indeed been exchanged: **alpha** is 7 and **beta** is 2.

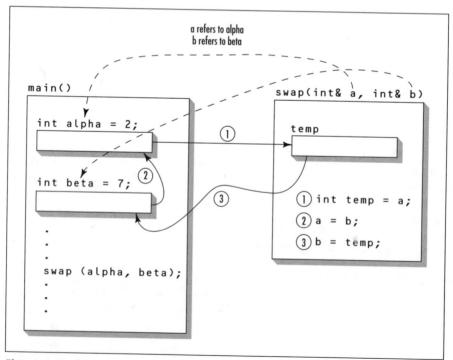

Figure 4-10   Passing by reference

Note

The ampersands follow the ints in both the declaration and the definition. They tell the compiler to pass these arguments by reference. More specifically, they specify that a is a reference to alpha and that b is a reference to beta. (As you can see, ampersands should *not* be used in the function call itself.) Figure 4-10 shows how the function swap() operates on the variables alpha and beta in main(); the function has no variables a and b of its own because they are only aliases for alpha and beta.

A Reference Is a Different Name

What exactly is a reference? From the programmer's standpoint, it is simply another name for the same variable. The name a refers to exactly the same location in memory as alpha, and b refers to the same location as beta.

Swapping Objects

Listing 4-5 shows a complete program, SWAPOBJ, that uses a swap() function to exchange two objects. I'll use the employee class, last seen in the STREMP program in Chapter 3, Session 4.

Listing 4-5 SWAPOBJ

```
// swapobj.cpp
// function swaps employee objects

#include <iostream.h>

const int SMAX = 21;        // maximum length of strings

class employee
    {
    private:
        char name[SMAX];       // name (20 chars max)
        int serial_number;
    public:
        void input()           // get data from user
            {
            cout << "   Enter name: ";
            cin >> name;
            cout << "   Enter serial number: ";
            cin >> serial_number;
            }
        void output()          // display employee data
            {
            cout << "   Name = " << name;
            cout << "\n   Serial number = " << serial_number;
            }
    };
```

continued on next page

continued from previous page

```
void main()
    {
    void swap(employee&, employee&);          // declaration

    employee e1, e2;
    cout << "Enter data for employee 1" << endl;
    e1.input();
    cout << "Enter data for employee 2" << endl;
    e2.input();
    cout << "Swapping employee data";
    swap(e1, e2);                             // swap employees
    cout << "\nData for employee 1" << endl;
    e1.output();
    cout << "\nData for employee 2" << endl;
    e2.output();
    }  // end main()

void swap(employee& emp1, employee& emp2)     // definition
    {
    employee temp = emp1;
    emp1 = emp2;
    emp2 = temp;
    }
```

In `main()`, the program creates two `employee` objects and asks the user to supply the data for them. Then it calls the `swap()` function to exchange the data in the two objects. This works because the objects are passed by reference. Finally, the program displays the data. Here's some interaction with this program. (You can't use multiple-word names because I simplified the input routine in the interest of brevity.)

```
Enter data for employee 1
    Enter name: Bernard
    Enter serial number: 111
Enter data for employee 2
    Enter name: Harrison
    Enter serial number: 222

Swapping employee data

Data for employee 1
    Name = Harrison
    Serial number = 222
Data for employee 2
    Name = Bernard
        Serial number = 111
```

Notice that the `swap()` function doesn't need to be a member function of `employee` because it doesn't deal with private `employee` instance data.

Standalone References

Let's perform a little experiment to clarify what references are. So far, you've seen references used only as function arguments. References can also be used as standalone variables. (Although it's not clear why you would want to do this in a real program.)

First, I'll create a variable of type `int`, initialized to a value:

```
int intvar = 7;
```

Now I'll create a reference:

```
int& intref = intvar;   // make a reference to intvar
```

When you create a reference you must also, in the same statement, initialize it to the variable it refers to. Here I specify that `intref` is a reference to `intvar`. If you don't initialize a reference, the compiler will complain. (This initialization is handled automatically for function arguments that are references, as you saw above.)

What happens if you now display the values of the original variable and the reference?

```
cout << "\nintvar=" << intvar;   // 7
cout << "\nintref=" << intref;   // 7
```

The numbers in the comments show the output. Both statements print the same value. This isn't surprising because they are actually referring to exactly the same variable. If you change the value of the original variable and display its—and the reference's—contents, you'll see they've both changed:

```
intvar = 27;                     // assign value to variable
cout << "\nintvar=" << intvar;   // 27
cout << "\nintref=" << intref;   // 27
```

I can also turn things around and use the reference to assign a new value to the variable:

```
intref = 333;                    // assign value to reference
cout << "\nintvar=" << intvar;   // 333
cout << "\nintref=" << intref;   // 333
```

This again causes the same output from both statements because both the reference and the original variable name refer to the same part of memory.

After it's defined and initialized, you cannot change a reference to refer to a different variable. If you try to do this, the compiler will think you're simply trying to assign the reference (and the variable it already refers to!) to the *value* of the new variable:

```
int intvar2 = 3;
intref = intvar2;  // gives intref (really intvar) the value 3
```

In any case, such arcane matters are hardly worth pondering because, as I noted, the use of references is almost always restricted to passing arguments to functions and returning values from functions. In this context, references are essential to creating overloaded operators and copy constructors, which you'll be meeting later on.

Behind the Scenes

Behind the scenes, the compiler uses the *address* of the original variable as the value assigned to a reference when it's initialized. As a programmer, you don't need to know anything about this. However, grizzled C hackers will recognize that references are similar to pointers. References have advantages over pointers, however. The notation is simpler because you don't need to dereference anything, and the compiler forces you to initialize a reference, so you have less excuse to make the dangling pointer mistake. On the other hand, although references are easier to use and safer than pointers, they are less powerful. You'll learn more about pointers in Chapter 8.

Advantages of Passing by Reference

The advantage of passing by value is that a function cannot accidentally corrupt the original values of the variables in the code that called it. Passing by value is often preferable when passing data of basic types. However, when working with objects, passing by reference is often a better choice. Why? Because when you pass by value, a copy of the object is created and stored in a new variable, which is created in the function for that purpose.

There are several disadvantages to creating unnecessary copies of an object. The most obvious is that some objects can be quite large (much larger than variables of basic types), so extraneous copies waste memory space. Also, creating a copy of an object is often not as straightforward as simply copying the values of all the instance data. Special member functions (constructors) may need to be executed to create the copy; this takes time and may cause unexpected side effects.

Passing by reference avoids these problems because nothing is copied; the only thing that's passed to the function is the reference to the original object.

1. A reference is
   a. the contents of a variable.
   b. the address of a variable.
   c. another name for a data type.
   d. another name for a variable.
   e. a recommendation, usually laudatory.

2. When you declare a reference,
   a. the variable used to initialize the reference must itself already be initialized.
   b. the variable used to initialize the reference must itself be declared.
   c. it must have the same type as the variable used to initialize it.
   d. you use the ampersand following the data type of the reference.
   e. you use the ampersand following the name of the reference.

3. Passing function arguments by reference allows the function to
   a. receive values passed from the function call, but not alter them.
   b. perform input/output.

c. operate on variables that are not defined within the function.
d. access the variables named in the function definition.
e. access the variables named in the function call.

4. If you have a reference `floref` to the variable `flovar` and you execute the statement

```
floref = 12.7;
```

you are actually

a. telling `floref` to refer to a different variable.
b. causing no change to the contents of any variable.
c. assigning the value 12.7 to `floref`.
d. assigning the value 12.7 to `flovar`.
e. creating two different copies of 12.7 in memory, one for `floref` and one for `flovar`.

5. A standalone reference (one not used for function arguments)
a. must be initialized, usually to a variable.
b. must be initialized, usually to a value.
c. must be initialized, usually to a function.
d. is used for function arguments.
e. is seldom used.

EXERCISE 1

Write an ordinary (nonmember) function called `divrem()` that takes three arguments of type `int`. This function should divide the first argument by the second, return the quotient (the answer; which is also type `int`), and send the remainder back using the third argument, which is passed by reference. A call to such a function might look like this:

```
quotient = divrem(dividend, divisor, remainder);
```

EXERCISE 2

Write a member function called `move()` for the employee class that, instead of exchanging two employee objects as the `swap()` function did in this session, moves the contents of one object to another. That is, the function will set its first argument equal to its second argument and then set the second argument to an empty employee. An empty employee has the name "" (the null string) and a serial number of 0. The original value in the first argument will be lost. To simplify the programming, you can have the user enter the values for the empty employee.

RETURNING BY REFERENCE

If you thought reference arguments were strange, hang onto your hat. *Returning by reference* will definitely raise your eyebrows.

One important reason for returning by reference is that the function call expression can be used on the *left side* of the equal sign and assigned a value as if it were a variable. For example, if you have an object `om1` and a member function `getnset()` you can say

```
om1.getnset() = 1088;   // function call on the left side
```

This looks very strange. Ordinarily you can't do this, because the compiler does not think of a function call as a variable—something that can be given a value. Instead it thinks of it as a constant—a value that can only be given to something else. You can't ordinarily use a function call on the left for the same reason you can't say

```
3 = avar;   // doesn't mean anything
```

Because the number 3 is a constant, it can't appear on the left of the equal sign. There are names to express these concepts. Something that can be given a value is called an *lvalue,* because it normally appears on the left side of the equal sign, whereas something that can't be given a value, like a constant, is called an *rvalue* because it normally appears on the right side of the equal sign.

Setting an Object to a Value

Listing 4-6 shows the RETREF program, which demonstrates how, by defining a function to return by reference, I can put the function on the left side of the equal sign and thereby assign a value to an object.

Listing 4-6 RETREF

```
// retref.cpp
// demonstrates returning by reference
#include <iostream.h>

class omega
    {
    private:
       int data;
    public:
       int& getnset()          // returns OR SETS data
          {                     // (note ampersand)
          return data;
          }
    };

void main()
    {
    omega om1;                  // make an object
```

```
om1.getnset() = 92;      // give it a value (!)

cout << "om1 = "
     << om1.getnset();  // get the value and display it
}
```

In `main()`, the `getnset()` member function is called twice. The second call is a normal one: The function call goes on the right side of the equal sign and it returns the value from the instance variable `data`, which is then displayed.

However, the first call to `getnset()` is placed on the left side of the equal sign in the expression

```
om1.getnset() = 92;
```

What does this do? It assigns the value 92 to the variable `data` in the `om1` object. Two things are necessary for this to happen. First, the function `getnset()` must be defined as returning by reference. This is accomplished by inserting an ampersand following the data type of the return value:

```
int& getnset()
```

Second, the function must return the variable `data`, which is the variable I want to set to a value. The statement

```
return data;
```

takes care of this. The arrangement is shown in Figure 4-11.

The return value of 92 goes from `main()` to the function, the opposite direction from normal return values, which are passed back from the function to `main()`. The output of the program is

```
om1 = 92
```

which shows that `genset()` can both set an object and get its value.

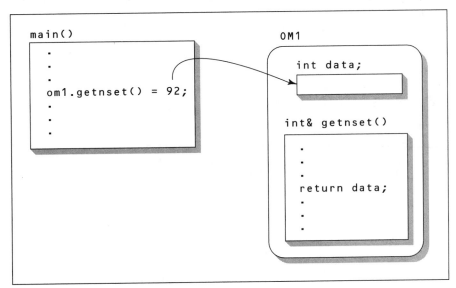

Figure 4-11 Value returned by reference

Cautions

Don't try to return an automatic variable (one defined within the function) by reference. Such variables cease to exist when the function terminates, so you would be assigning a value to some random location in memory. For example, don't write a member function like this:

```
int& badret()        // returns by reference
   {
   int somevar;      // local variable
   ...
   return somevar;   // don't do this
   }
```

If in `main()` you then said something like

```
anObj.badret() = 1066;
```

you would be assigning `somevar` a value, but `somevar` would have already been destroyed because the function had returned. Fortunately, the compiler won't let you get away with this.

What's It For?

Returning by reference was created to solve a particular problem in C++: how to handle return values from overloaded operators. It probably doesn't have much use otherwise, because there are more straightforward ways to set an object's instance data to a value. However, for those cases where it does make sense, it's invaluable. I'll use this technique when I explore overloaded operators in Chapter 6.

1. Anything you place on the left side of the equal sign must be a variable because
   a. the variable shouldn't go on the right side, where constants go.
   b. only a variable can be given a value.
   c. only a constant can be given a value.
   d. functions are always variables.
   e. only variables can be equal to anything.

2. Syntactically, returning by reference involves inserting
   a. in the function definition an ampersand following the data type of the return value.
   b. in the function definition an ampersand following the name of the return value.
   c. in the function call an ampersand following the name of the return value.
   d. in the function definition a statement that returns the variable whose value is passed to the function.
   e. in the class instance data a variable that can be assigned a value.

3. An lvalue is
   a. always an object.
   b. always a constant.
   c. always a variable.
   d. a variable that must appear on the left side of an equal sign.
   e. anything that can appear on the left side of an equal sign.

4. You can't return a local variable by reference because
   a. the local variable is unknown to the `return` statement in the function.
   b. the local variable is unknown to the statement calling the function.
   c. local variables become inaccessible when the function terminates.
   d. local variables cease to exist when the function terminates.
   e. local variables are private.

5. Returning by reference is usually used in relation to
   a. objects.
   b. arguments passed by reference.
   c. overloaded functions.
   d. overloaded operators.
   e. standalone member functions.

There are no exercises for this lesson because returning by reference can't be used for anything meaningful until you learn about overloaded operators.

SUMMARY: CHAPTER 4

Functions are used for a variety of purposes. A function is basically a section of code that can be called from elsewhere in the program. This saves memory space. However, functions are also used to divide a program into more manageable sections. Whereas member functions in classes are a key way to organize C++ programs, standalone functions divide up parts of the program that are not parts of objects.

Overloading allows several functions to have the same name. These functions are distinguished by the number and types of their arguments. Default arguments enable a single function to act as if it were several functions. Arguments not supplied by the function call are supplied by the function declaration.

Storage classes determine the lifetime and visibility of variables. The lifetime is the period of time when a variable is in existence, whereas visibility (or scope) is concerned with which other parts of the program can access the variable. Storage classes include automatic, register, and local static within functions, external and static external outside of functions, and class data and functions.

A reference is an alias for a variable name. References are mostly used to pass arguments to functions. In this system, an alias to a variable in the calling program is passed to the function, rather than a value. This allows the function to operate on the variables in the calling program and avoids the need to copy the argument's value, which may require much time and space if the argument is a large object. Returning values by reference is more esoteric and enables a function call to be used on the left side of the equal sign. This will be important later for overloaded operators.

END-OF-CHAPTER DISCUSSION

Estelle: I think we've spent the last half of this chapter basically learning how to fine-tune a program.

Don: That's a good way to put it. You don't desperately need all these storage classes and references unless you want to make your program more efficient.

George: Huh?

Estelle: It's all a question of trade-offs. If a variable stays around too long, it takes up too much memory. So automatic variables disappear when the function returns. But you need some variables to last longer so different functions can access them. That's why variables can be local static, external, or external static. That way they can last the life of the program.

George: Why not just have one life-of-the-program category?

Don: So you can avoid name clashes.

George: Sorry, I don't follow you.

Estelle: You want to be able to use the same name for different variables in different places in your program. Otherwise, you could use **j** only for a loop variable in one function in the program.

Don: Again, the bigger the program the more useful that kind of thing is.

George: Umm. Well, one thing's for sure. Count me out on references. I didn't get that at all.

Don: References are really just another way to optimize your program. With a reference, the function can manipulate the variables in the function that called it without having to make them external variables.

Estelle: And the point of that is that you don't have to copy reference arguments when you pass them, which is faster and saves memory.

Don: Which is especially important with objects, because they can be so big.

George: I thought it was so the function could change variables in the code that called it.

Don: That too.

Estelle: What about static members?

Don: More of the same. If you didn't have static members, you'd need to use external variables, and that would spread class data out all over the place, which is what classes were supposed to avoid in the first place.

George: Really, I'm so glad you guys understand all this.

Don: If you don't like that explanation about references, remember they're going to be used later for overloaded operators. I'm sure it'll all be clearer then.

George: I can hardly wait.

CHAPTER 5

CONSTRUCTORS

n this chapter I'm going to discuss constructors, which are special member functions used to create and initialize objects. I'll also briefly demonstrate their counterpart, destructors, which carry out clean-up tasks when an object is destroyed.

I'll show constructors that take no arguments and constructors that do, and a special case: the copy constructor, which takes one argument that is a member of its own class. Along the way, you'll encounter some other C++ features, such as `const`.

SESSION 1

INTRODUCING CONSTRUCTORS

A *constructor* is a special member function that's used to initialize an object. You may remember that in several previous programs, I used a member function called `init()` when I wanted to give a certain value to an object just after it was created. For example, in the STACK1 program in Chapter 3, Session 2, I used an `init()` to set the top-of-the-stack array index to -1. This had to be done before the first item could be pushed onto the stack. In the STRCLASS program in Chapter 3, Session 5, I used an `init()` to set an `xString` object to a specified string constant. (Of course, I didn't need to name the initialization function `init()`; it could have been `initialize()` or `CallMeFirst()` or anything else.)

Initialization

In these programs, the use of a function such as `init()` was somewhat suspect. What's wrong with using `init()`? First of all, it's possible for the class user to forget to call the `init()`, thereby leaving an object uninitialized. Second, initialization should be a one-step process, just as it is when you define an external variable and it's set to zero automatically. But when you use `init()`, you have a two-step process: creating the object and then initializing it. This may seem like a theoretical distinction. However, initializing an object automatically when it's created can pay big dividends in making a program more error free and more understandable.

The role of the user-written constructor, then, is to carry out any initialization that's necessary for the object. When you define an object in your program, like this:

```
aClass anObj;    // make an object
```

the compiler arranges for the class constructor to be called when this statement is executed.

Creation

Whether you've written an explicit constructor or not, the compiler generates the code necessary to create the object, allocate memory for it, and perform other kinds of behind-the-scenes initialization. This happens automatically, just as it does for variables of basic types such as `int`. Confusingly, the term constructor is often used to refer not only to the user-written initialization function, but also to this compiler-generated behind-the-scenes activity.

Destructors

Every object that is created must eventually be destroyed. Automatic objects (those created within the body of a function) are destroyed (automatically!) when the function returns. This is true of `main()`, just as it is with other functions. Conversely, objects declared as external or static variables are destroyed only when the program ends.

The class creator can write an explicit *destructor* for a class. This destructor typically takes care of deallocating whatever was allocated by the constructor. Think of a destructor as the object's last will and testament.

Whether the programmer writes a destructor or not, the compiler supplies a routine to deallocate the memory occupied by an object and to perform other clean-up operations when the object is destroyed. This code is often included in the meaning of the term destructor.

Constructors and Destructors in Action

Let's look at a very simple example that shows what constructors and destructors look like. In this program, objects of the class Omega have no purpose except to announce when they are initialized and when they are destroyed. Listing 5-1 shows CONDEST.

Listing 5-1 CONDEST

```cpp
// condest.cpp
// demonstrates constructors and destructors
#include <iostream.h>

class Omega
    {
    public:
        Omega()         // constructor
            {
            cout << "I am the constructor" << endl;
            }
        ~Omega()        // destructor
            {
            cout << "I am the destructor" << endl;
            }
    };

void main()
    {
    cout << "Starting main()" << endl;

    Omega om1, om2, om3;    // create three objects

    cout << "Ending main()" << endl;
    }
```

Same Name as the Class

A constructor always has exactly the same name as the class. Why? Well, it has to be given a standard and distinctive name. Using the class name helps avoid name clashes, because you aren't likely to use this name for one of your own member functions. In any case, that's how the compiler knows you're defining a constructor.

The destructor has the same name as the class, but it is preceded by a tilde (~).

No Return Value

Constructors have no return value, not even void. It's hard to imagine what a constructor would return, and to whom, because it's called automatically. The same is true of destructors. (Because a destructor is called to do away with an object, it's hard to imagine what message a destructor would return to the code that called it. Maybe You'll be sorry!)

What They Do

In the CONDEST example, the constructor doesn't actually initialize anything. It simply displays a message announcing that it's executing. Likewise, the destructor doesn't clean up anything, it displays a message. Here's the output when you run this program:

```
Starting main()
I am the constructor
I am the constructor
I am the constructor
Ending main()
I am the destructor
I am the destructor
I am the destructor
```

Notice that there are no function calls in `main()`, or anywhere else, to the constructor or destructor. They are called automatically. The constructor is called when each object is created. This happens three times in the statement

```
Omega om1, om2, om3;
```

When `main()` ends, by dropping through the closing brace, the three objects go out of scope and are automatically destroyed. The destructor is called for each one just before it's destroyed, as can be seen from the output. Notice that, like messages from the grave, these announcements from the destructor appear after `main()` has terminated.

Initializing Variables

Let's look at a more realistic example, where a constructor actually performs a useful activity. I'll rewrite the STACK1 program from Chapter 3, Session 2, to use a constructor instead of the `init()` function. Listing 5-2 shows STACKCON.

Listing 5-2 STACKCON

```
// stackcon.cpp
// class models a stack; uses a constructor

#include <iostream.h>

class Stack                      // a stack holds up to 20 ints
   {
   private:
      int st[20];                // integers are stored in array
      int top;                   // index of last item pushed
   public:
      Stack() : top(-1)          // constructor
         { }
      void push(int var)         // place an item on the stack
         {
         st[++top] = var;
         }
      int pop()                  // remove an item from the stack
         {
```

```
            return st[top--];
            }
   };

void main()
   {
   Stack s1;                    // create a stack object
                                // (no need to initialize it)
   s1.push(11);                 // push 3 items onto stack
   s1.push(12);
   s1.push(13);

   cout << s1.pop() << endl;    // pop 3 items and display them
   cout << s1.pop() << endl;
   cout << s1.pop() << endl;
   }
```

Notice that I have not only eliminated the `init()` member function, I've also eliminated all the calls to it that I needed in `main()` in STACK1. The constructor handles the initialization automatically, which is a considerable convenience.

Initialization List

The purpose of the constructor is to set the `top` variable in each object to –1 when the object is first created. You might expect code like this:

```
Stack()                 // constructor, incorrect approach
   {
   top = -1;
   }
```

This version of the constructor actually does the job, at least in this particular program. However, it is not the preferred approach to initializing variables within the object. Some variables cannot be initialized with ordinary assignment statements. As a somewhat recursive example, suppose that one of the member variables in your class is an object from some other class. This object should be initialized with a constructor, not a separate function such as `init()`, so you don't even have the option of initializing by calling a member function.

Instead, a new syntax is used that causes actual initialization (rather than assignment) of specified variables. A colon follows the class name and the variables to be initialized are listed following the colon (separated by commas, if there is more than one). This is called the *initialization list* (or *initializer list*). The value used to initialize each variable on the list is placed in parentheses following the name, as shown in Figure 5-1.

In this example, the constructor's declarator initializes the variable `top`:

```
Stack() : top(-1)      // creates and initializes top
   { }
```

The body of the constructor is empty because all the initialization has already been taken care of on the initialization list. An empty function body is not unusual in a constructor. However, many constructors carry out other tasks in the function body. Also, some variables, such as arrays, cannot be initialized in the initialization list.

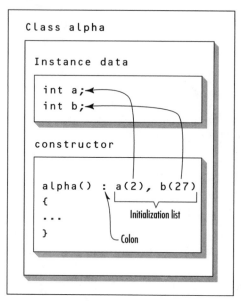

Figure 5-1 Syntax of constructor initialization

I didn't define a destructor for the **stack** class because the constructor doesn't allocate any system resources or do anything else that needs unusual cleaning up.

Default Constructor

A constructor that takes no arguments, such as the one in the STACKCON program, is called a *default constructor*. As you'll see in the next session, other constructors do take arguments.

1. A constructor will typically _____ when an object is created.
   a. allocate system resources
   b. free system resources
   c. initialize instance variables
   d. destroy instance variables
   e. cause **main()** to terminate

2. A constructor is preferable to a function like **init()** because
   a. it has a unique name.
   b. the programmer doesn't need to remember to call the constructor, as is true with **init()**.
   c. the constructor executes before the object is defined.
   d. some instance variables must be initialized rather than assigned a value.
   e. the constructor has no return value.

3. Destructors typically
   a. deallocate system resources.
   b. initialize instance variables.
   c. return zero if all went well.
   d. are called when the class specification is no longer visible.
   e. are executed automatically when their object is destroyed.

4. The function call to a constructor
   a. looks like any function call, except there is no return value.
   b. may take arguments, as in `aclass(2, 4);`.
   c. creates but cannot initialize an object.
   d. is made automatically when an object is defined.
   e. happens whenever an object's instance data changes.

5. The preferred syntax for initializing an instance variable, using a constructor,
   a. uses an assignment statement in the function body.
   b. uses parentheses to surround the value.
   c. inserts the variable name following a colon that follows the function body.
   d. actually assigns the variable a value, as opposed to simply initializing it.
   e. can be used for only one variable.

EXERCISE 1

Start with the TIME1 program from Chapter 2, Session 5. Add a constructor to the `airtime` class that initializes both the `hours` and `minutes` member variables to zero. This will help avoid errors when using the class, because an object will always have a valid time value when created. Without the constructor, if you used `display()` without first using `set()`, impossible time values would be displayed, such as 14203:2491.

EXERCISE 2

Start with the STATIC program from Chapter 4, Session 6. Change the `init()` function to a constructor. (Note that you can do simple arithmetic in the expression that initializes an instance variable in the constructor.)

Session 2

CONSTRUCTOR ARGUMENTS

It's nice to initialize objects to fixed values when they're created, but it's even more useful to initialize them to values that you supply when you create them. In this lesson, you'll see how to do this. Special cases occur in the case of one-argument and no-argument constructors, so I'll begin with a more generic two-argument constructor and then look at the no-argument constructor. I'll examine the one-argument constructor in the next lesson.

A Two-Argument Constructor

Remember the `airtime` class from the TIME1 program in Chapter 2, Session 5? (You should; it's prominently featured in Exercise 1 of the last session.) Let's see how to use constructor arguments to initialize an `airtime` to any specified value when it's created. Listing 5-3 shows TIMECON.

Listing 5-3 TIMECON

```
// timecon.cpp
// class models time data type; uses constructor

#include <iostream.h>

class airtime
   {
   private:
      int hours;          // 0 to 23
      int minutes;        // 0 to 59
   public:                // two-argument constructor
      airtime(int h, int m) : hours(h), minutes(m)
         {
         }
      void display()
         {
         cout << hours << ':' << minutes;
         }
   };

void main()
   {
   airtime t1(7, 54);      // initialize t1

   cout << "\nt1 = ";
   t1.display();           // display t1
   }
```

The output from this program is

```
t1 = 7:54
```

I've successfully initialized **t1** to an **airtime** value. Because an **airtime** object has both hours and minutes components, a two-argument constructor is required.

Arguments look much the same in the constructor definition as they do in any other function. The data type is followed by a name and the arguments are separated by commas:

```
airtime(int h, int m)    // looks like an ordinary function
```

Of course, you can tell this is a constructor because there's no return type.

The Wrong Way

I could make the constructor look more like a normal function by using assignment statements within the function body:

```
airtime(int h, int m)    // still looks like an ordinary function
   {
   hours = h;
   minutes = m;
   }
```

However, assignment is not the proper way to initialize member variables.

The Right Way

Instead, I use the initialization list, following the colon, with the arguments as the initial values:

```
airtime(int h, int m) : hours(h), minutes(m)
   {
   }
```

Visually, you may find this a bit topheavy: a long declarator and an empty function body. You can put the initializers on a separate line if you want:

```
airtime(int h, int m) :
        hours(h), minutes(m)
   {
   }
```

but it still looks strange. You'll get used to it. In any case, it causes **hours** to be initialized to the value of **h** and **minutes** to be initialized to the value of **m**. Figure 5-2 shows a similar situation.

"Calling" the Constructor

Now you know how to write the constructor. However, because the constructor is called automatically, you can't use a normal function call to pass it the argument values. So how should you pass it the values? By placing them in the object definition, like this:

```
airtime t1(7, 54);
```

This looks like a function call. As with function arguments, the values are placed in parentheses and separated by commas. However, don't be confused: This is the definition of an object. It creates the **airtime** object **t1** and initailizes its **hours** variable to 7 and its **minutes** to 54.

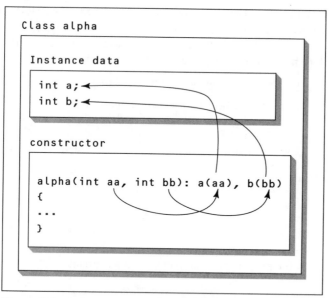

Figure 5-2   Arguments used as initializers

A No-Argument Constructor

If you don't explicitly define any constructors, the compiler automatically generates a default constructor for you, that is, a constructor that takes no arguments. This is why it's called the default constructor. I relied on this automatic creation of a default constructor in the program examples in previous chapters. For example, there is no problem saying

```
employee emp1, emp2;
```

even if I have not explicitly defined any constructors at all for the `employee` class.

However, once you've defined even one kind of constructor, no matter how many arguments it takes, the compiler will no longer create the default no-argument constructor for you. You must do it yourself. Suppose I rewrite `main()` in TIMECON this way, without changing the class:

```
void main()
    {
    airtime t2;              // can't do this
                             //    without a no-arg constructor
    airtime t1(7, 54);       // initialize t1

    cout << "\nt1 = ";
    t1.display();            // display t1
    }
```

This would cause an error like

```
Could not find a match for airtime::airtime()
```

because there isn't any no-argument constructor to handle the creation of `t2`. (The `airtime::airtime()` format means "the no-argument constructor of class `airtime`.") The compiler does not supply a default constructor because there's another (two-argument) constructor. However, it's easy to create a no-argument constructor. It could look like this:

```
airtime()
    { }
```

Although it doesn't do anything, this constructor tells the compiler that I did not forget to write the constructor, I know what I'm doing, and not to worry.

1. Using a constructor with arguments (as opposed to the default constructor) allows you to create objects
   a. and at the same time specify what class they are.
   b. with their own constructors.
   c. whose instance data can be initialized to values supplied by the class user.
   d. and modify their existing instance data.
   e. and assign values to the program's external data variables.

2. Which of the following make(s) sense as an object definition?
   a. `horse george;`
   b. `horse george(hands_high);`
   c. `horse george(float hands_high);`
   d. `point3d p(int x, int y, int z);`
   e. `point3d p(0, 0, 0);`

3. Which is the preferred two-argument constructor for class `x`?
   a. `X(int v1, float v2) { }`
   b. `X(int v1, float v2) : var1(v1), var2(v2) { }`
   c. `X(int v1, float v2) : var1(v1), var2(v2) { var1=v1; var2=v2; }`
   d. `X(int v1, float v2) { var1=v1; var2=v2; }`
   e. `X(int v1, float v2) : { var1(v1), var2(v2) }`

4. Calling a constructor with arguments is implemented by
   a. a normal function call.
   b. a normal function call, but with no return value.
   c. a normal function call with arguments but no return value.
   d. the definition of an object.
   e. the specification of a class.

5. Which complete list of constructors, whose definitions you insert in a class, will compile properly if you create objects using the syntax

```
aclass anobj;
```

a. no-argument constructor, one-argument constructor
b. one-argument constructor
c. no-argument constructor, two-argument constructor
d. one-argument constructor, two-argument constructor
e. no constructors at all

EXERCISE 1

Write a two-argument constructor for the `employee` class in the STREMP program in Chapter 3, Session 4. It should allow you to define an `employee` object and at the same time initialize it with appropriate values for the name and serial number. Ask yourself whether, within the constructor, there is a difference in the way you should set `name` and `serial_number` to the values passed as arguments.

EXERCISE 2

Start with the CARDARAY program from Chapter 3, Session 8. Change the `init()` function to a two-argument constructor, which should have an empty function body. Remove all the references to an array of type `card` in `main()` and test the constructor by initializing a few cards and displaying them. The initializations should look like this:

```
card c1(jack, diamonds);
```

THE ONE-ARGUMENT CONSTRUCTOR

A constructor with one argument plays a special role in object-oriented programming: It can be used to convert an object from one class to another. This is usually done for classes that represent data types, where a one-argument constructor can be used to convert a value of one data type to another. Another name for such a constructor is a *conversion function*. Figure 5-3 shows the idea.

Conversions

As a barebones example, let's look at a class called `typeA`. This class has a constructor that takes a single argument of the basic type `int`. Here's how that looks:

```
class typeA
    {
    typeA(int i)   // 1-argument constructor
        {
        // convert the int value to a typeA value
        }
    };
```

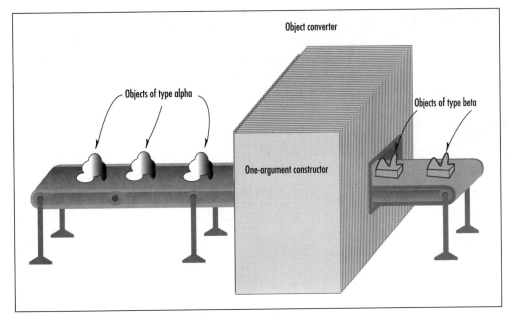

Figure 5-3 Conversion function

This constructor can be used to convert a variable of type `int` to an object of class `typeA`. Remember, saying a variable is of a certain *data type* is the same as saying an object is of a certain *class*.

There are two ways to write such a conversion. The most familiar way is for the `typeA` object to be initialized with an `int` value in parentheses following the name of the object:

```
void main()
   {
   int intv = 27;      // an integer with a value

   typeA ta(intv);     // initialize typeA object with int
   }
```

This causes the one-argument constructor to be called. Alternatively, you can use an equal sign instead of the parentheses:

```
typeA ta = intv;     // exactly the same as typeA ta(intv);
```

This is completely equivalent to the syntax with parentheses. Although it looks like an assignment statement, the equal sign is not assigning anything; it's initializing `ta` to the value of `intv`. It also causes the one-argument constructor to be called.

A real assignment statement,

```
ta = tb;
```

does not cause a constructor to be called. Initialization is *not* the same as assignment. This is an important distinction, as you'll see later.

Converting Strings to xStrings

Let's look at a more fully developed example of data conversion. In Chapter 3, Session 5, I introduced the STRCLASS program, which used the **xString** class to model text strings. I'll modify this program by installing a one-argument constructor that can be used to convert an ordinary null-terminated string to an **xString** object. Listing 5-4 shows STRCON.

Listing 5-4 STRCON

```
// strcon.cpp
// class models strings; uses constructors

#include <iostream.h>
#include <string.h>              // for strlen(), strcpy(), etc.

const int MAX = 80;             // maximum length of xStrings

class xString
   {
   private:
      char str[MAX];            // ordinary C string
   public:
      xString()                 // no-arg constructor
         {
         strcpy(str, "");       // make null string
         }
      xString( char s[] )       // 1-arg constructor
         {
         strcpy(str, s);        // initialize with string
         }
      void input()              // get string from user
         {
         cin.get(str, MAX);
         }
      void display()            // display string
         {
         cout << str;
         }
      void append(xString xs)   // append argument string
         {
         if(strlen(str) + strlen(xs.str) < MAX-1)
            strcat(str, xs.str);
         else
            cout << "\nError: xString too long" << endl;
         }
};

void main()
   {
   xString s2, s3;              // make xString objects
   xString s1("Greetings, ");   // make and initialize s1

   cout << "Enter your name: ";
```

```
s2.input();              // get s2 from user

s1.append(s2);           // append s2 to s1
s3 = s1;                 // set s3 to s1
s3.display();            // display s3
}
```

This program is similar to STRCLASS. Here's some sample interaction with it:

```
Enter your name: Kubla Khan
Greetings, Kubla Khan
```

However, STRCON uses a one-argument constructor instead of an `init()` function to give an `xString` object a string value. In the definition

```
xString s1("Greetings, ");
```

the C string `"Greetings"` is converted to an `xString` called `s1`.

Notice that, as I mentioned earlier, I need to define a no-argument (default) constructor explicitly because I also define a one-argument constructor. The no-argument constructor simply copies the null string (a string of zero length) to its object. It's probably a good idea to use the no-argument constructor to initialize the `xString`. If you use the `display()` member function on an object that's been initialized to the null string, nothing will be printed; whereas, in the STRCLASS program, displaying an uninitialized `xString` would produce a garbage string value, such as `"x!8*tEv$#^%"`.

Of course, the two `xString` constructors in STRCON have the same name. This is simply another example of function overloading. As long as the number or type of arguments is different for each one, you can have as many constructors as you want.

Note that you can't initialize the `str` instance data in the one-argument constructor:

```
xString( char s[] ) : str(s[])   // can't do this --
    {                            // s is an array
    }
```

Because you're dealing with an array, you must copy its elements one by one using the `strcpy()` library function:

```
xString( char s[] )      // 1-arg constructor
    {
    strcpy(str, s);      // initialize with string
    }
```

Converting Meters to English Distances

As another example involving a one-argument constructor, let's create a class that models distances in feet and inches. I'll call this class `English`, because feet and inches are part of the English measurement system, in which a foot is divided into 12 inches. An English value of 6 feet 2 inches is displayed as 6'-2", with a single quote for feet and a double quote for inches and the two quantities separated by a dash. There are 3.280833 feet in a meter.

The one-argument constructor will convert meters to an `English` object, which stores feet and inches separately. I'll also use a two-argument constructor to convert an `int` value for feet and a `float` value for inches into an `English` value. (The `float` type allows me to use fractional values for inches, such as 6.5.) With these constructors, I'll also need a no-argument constructor, which will set feet and inches to zero. Listing 5-5 shows ENGLCON.

Listing 5-5 ENGLCON

```cpp
// englcon.cpp
// demonstrates constructors with English class
#include <iostream.h>

class English                           // English distances
    {
    private:
        int feet;
        float inches;
    public:                             // no-argument constructor
        English() : feet(0), inches(0.0)
            { }
        English(float meters)           // 1-argument constructor
            {
            const float MTF = 3.280833; // meters to feet
            float fltfeet = MTF * meters; // get decimal feet
            feet = int(fltfeet);        // integer part is feet
            inches = 12 * (fltfeet-feet); // remainder is inches
            }
        English(int f, float i) :       // 2-argument constructor
                feet(f), inches(i)
            { }
        void display()                  // display
            {
            cout << feet << "\'-" << inches << '\"';
            }
    };

void main()
    {
    English E1(5, 2.5);                 // call 2-arg constructor
    cout << "\nE1 = ";
    E1.display();

    English E2(2.0);                    // call 1-arg constructor
    English E3;                         // call no-arg constructor
    E3 = E2;
    cout << "\nE3 = ";
    E3.display();
    }
```

Meters to English Objects

The English object E1 is initialized to a feet and inches value. The object E2 is initialized to a value in meters; then E3, created with the no-argument constructor, is set equal to E2. Here's the output of this program:

```
E1 = 5'-2.5"
E3 = 6'-6.73999"
```

The one-argument constructor converts meters to feet and inches by converting first to decimal feet (2.0 meters is 6.56 decimal feet), then taking the integer part of this (6), and subtracting it from the total and multiplying by 12 to get the inches value (6.56 - 6 is 0.56, times 12 is about 6.7 inches).

Escape Characters

The single quote (') and the double quote (") are special characters, used to delimit characters and string constants respectively, so they can't be displayed as normal characters without being preceded by the escape character (\).

```
cout << feet << "\'-" << inches << '\"';
```

Thus, \' causes a single quote to be displayed (indicating feet) and \" causes a double quote to be displayed (indicating inches).

Not Always Appropriate

I mentioned that one-argument constructors work best on classes that represent data types. As an example of a class that doesn't represent a data type, consider the employee class, seen in such examples as the STREMP program in Chapter 3, Session 4. What value would you put in a one-argument constructor? An employee can't be boiled down into a single number, so this sort of conversion doesn't make much sense. Generally, if objects of a class represent physical, real-world objects, such as employees or elevators or airplanes, then conversions with one-argument constructors aren't appropriate. Conversions work when objects represent variables.

More Conversions to Come

Conversions are an important part of working with C++ classes that represent quantities, but I haven't covered all there is to know about this topic. For example, you've seen how to convert a basic type to a class object, but what about going the other way? Suppose you want to convert an object of class English to a float type representing meters? Or suppose you want to convert one kind of object to another kind of object? You'll learn more about these topics in Chapter 6.

1. The purpose of data conversion is
   a. to display data in different ways.
   b. to exercise the one-argument constructor.
   c. to convert a class of one type to a class of another type.
   d. to convert a value of one type to a value of another type.
   e. to convert a variable of one type to a variable of another type.

2. A one-argument constructor is the most appropriate constructor for data conversions because
   a. the no-argument constructor can work only with the value zero.
   b. you want to convert the value of a single variable into another variable.
   c. the two-argument constructor can be used only with feet and inches.
   d. it can convert an object to a basic type.
   e. it doesn't require a no-argument constructor to be defined.

3. Converting a C string to an xString requires
   a. a C string constructor.
   b. a C string object.
   c. a C string value.
   d. an xString constant.
   e. an xString variable.

4. The two-argument constructor in the English class converts
   a. feet and inches to English.
   b. feet and inches to meters.
   c. English to meters.
   d. English to English.
   e. English to feet and inches.

5. Converting from meters to an English distance value
   a. requires you to multiply the number representing the value of the English object by 3.280833.
   b. requires you to multiply the feet part of the English object by 3.280833.
   c. is more complicated than a. or b.
   d. results in a single number.
   e. results in two numbers.

EXERCISE 1

Write a one-argument constructor for the airtime class of the TIMECON program in this chapter. It should convert decimal hours (type float) to an airtime value in hours and minutes, that is, 1.5 hours becomes 1 hour and 30 minutes. Test it out by initializing some airtime values to decimal hours values in main().

EXERCISE 2

Change the one-argument constructor in the ENGLCON program in this session so that it accepts a floating-point quantity in inches rather than meters and converts it into a feet and inches English value.

SESSION 4
ARRAYS AS INSTANCE DATA

Arrays pose some interesting problems when used with constructors. In this session, I'll begin by investigating the question of how to size an array that's being using as instance data. I'll start with several approaches that don't work or are nonoptimum, but are nevertheless instructive.

Array Sized with Constant

In the STACKCON program in Session 1 in this chapter, I committed a stylistic *faux pas* by sizing the array with a constant:

```
class Stack
   {
   private:
      int st[20];    // really bad
      int top;
   ...
   };
```

What's wrong with this? It compiles and runs fine, but at some point in the development of the Stack class, I will probably need to use this same number 20 in a member function. Suppose I want to ensure, for example, that I don't push too many objects onto the stack. I might say

```
void push(int var)
   {
   if(top+ > 20)                // if beyond end of array,
      cout << "Illegal push";   // error message
   else
      st(++top) = var;
   }
```

Now the constant 20 appears in two (or perhaps more) places in the class and, by Murphy's law, someone (perhaps myself) will change one without changing the other, leading to problems. Also, the number 20 doesn't tell me very much about its own purpose. A name such as `size` (or better yet, especially in larger programs, `array_size` or even `stack_array_size`) is more infomative.

Array Sized with External `const`

To have only one definition for a constant such as 20, I have recommended in other contexts the use of external `const` variables at the beginning of the listing. Here's what that might look like, applied to the Stack class:

```
const int size = 20;
...
class Stack
   {
   private:
      int st[size];   // better
```

continued on next page

continued from previous page
```
    int top;
...
};
```

This works, but it's not in the spirit of OOP because it doesn't encapsulate the data for the class within the class specification. Ideally, the variable `size` should be declared within the class so it is invisible outside the class and therefore impervious to accidental alteration by other parts of the program.

Initializing Member Variables

Can I move the `const` variable into the class? A first attempt at that solution might look something like this:

```
class Stack
    {
    private:
        const int size = 20;   // illegal initialization
        int st[size];
        int top;
...
};
```

Sorry. I can't initialize member data this way whether it's `const` or not. The compiler will say something like `Cannot initialize a class member here`. Instance data must be initialized from the constructor's initialization list, not in the variable declaration. Let me digress for a moment to explore this rule.

Instance Data Initialization

Why can't you initialize instance data with an equal sign, as in

```
const int size = 20;   // not OK in instance data
```

as you can with nonmember data? Because instance variables are specific to each object. The same variable within different objects can have different values. Therefore, *instance data can only be initialized when an object is created*. How do you do that? In the constructor, which is executed once for each object, when it's created. The correct approach is to put the variable on the initialization list:

```
class aClass
    {
    private:
        const int var;
    public:
        aClass(int v) : var(v)   // v initializes var
            { }
...
};
```

Initialization Is Not Assignment

Incidentally, you cannot use an assignment statement in the body of the constructor to initialize a `const` variable because assignment means changing an existing variable, not initializing it, and `const` variables can't be changed:

```
class aClass
   {
   private:
      const int var;
   public:
      aClass(int v)
         {
         var = v;   // can't do this
         }
   ...
   };
```

Arrays Sized at Compile Time

Suppose I go ahead and initialize the `size` variable properly with the constructor. Unfortunately, I still can't use this value to size the array:

```
class Stack
   {
   private:
      const int size;   // legal
      int st[size];      // illegal--not known at compile time
      int top;
   public:
      Stack() : size(20), top(-1)   // size initialized here
         {  }
   ...
   };
```

The trouble is that the size of an array must be known to the compiler *at compile time*. It's not something the program can figure out for itself when it's running. So I can't use normal instance data, whether it's `const` or not, for an array size.

The `enum` Hack

To solve the problem of initializing array sizes, many programmers have in the past used something called the *enum hack* (where the word "hack" indicates that the solution works, but it isn't as elegant as it might be). Here's how it looks:

```
class Stack
   {
   private:
      enum { size=20 };   // established at compile time
      int st[size];        // OK
      int top;
   ...
   };
```

You encountered the `enum` data type in Chapter 3, Session 8. As you recall, `enum` provides a way to create a new data type whose values are all listed and given names and—optionally—values. In the expression:

```
enum { size=20 };
```

Here the idea isn't to specify a new data type; it's simply to give a name to a value. I do this by leaving out the `enum` type name, specifying only one value name, and giving this name a value. Because this value will be fixed at compile time, the compiler is happy to use it as an array size. I'm happy too because I've created a value that can't be changed, yet is visible only within the class specification.

Static Constant Variables

Because the `enum` hack is so inelegant, the ANSI/ISO C++ working group has recently added a new construction to the language: initialization of static constant instance variables. This solves all the problems discussed in the sections above. Here's the idea:

```
class Stack
    {
    private:
        static const int size = 20;   // static constant
        int st[size];
        int top;
    ...
    };
```

Here the variable `size` is a constant so it can't be changed, but because it's static, it's given a value at compile time, so it can be used to size the array.

This is now the preferred approach to sizing arrays that are instance variables. However, not all compilers have been updated to handle this new construction, and older compilers will produce errors if you try it. So you'll probably see the `enum` hack being used for quite a while. You may even catch me using it myself.

The Improved STACK Program

Listing 5-6 shows the new improved version of the STACK program, incorporating the static constant approach.

Listing 5-6 STATICON

```
// staticon.cpp
// class models a stack
// uses static constant for member array size

#include <iostream.h>

class Stack                       // a stack holds up to 20 ints
    {
    private:

        static const int size = 20;   // array size
        int st[size];                 // integers are stored in array
        int top;                      // index of last item pushed
    public:
        Stack() : top(-1)             // constructor
```

continued on next page

continued from previous page

```
    { }
  void push(int var)         // place an item on the stack
    {
    st[++top] = var;
    }
  int pop()                  // remove an item from the stack
    {
    return st[top--];
    }
};

void main()
  {
  Stack s1;                  // create a stack object

  s1.push(11);               // push 3 items onto stack
  s1.push(12);
  s1.push(13);

  cout << s1.pop() << endl;  // pop 3 items and display them
  cout << s1.pop() << endl;
  cout << s1.pop() << endl;
  }
```

This program works the same way its predecessors did and produces the same output:

```
13
12
11
```

Note that if you wanted to make several different **Stack** objects of different sizes, you wouldn't be able to use arrays at all. Instead, you would need to include the size as an argument in a constructor and then allocate space for the array dynamically, using **new**. I'll explore dynamic allocation and **new** in Chapter 8.

Initializing a Member Array

How can you initialize the elements of an array that's declared as instance data in a class? For example, in the WEEKOUT program in Chapter 4, Session 2, the array **day_name** was defined outside the class weekday. However, it should be instance data, because it's specific to the class. If it were instance data, could it be initialized to the days of the week?

Unfortunately, you can't initialize array elements in a constructor's initialization list:

```
weekday() : day_name[0]("Sunday"), day_name[1]("Monday"), ...   // no good
  {
  }
```

The compiler can handle only individual variables in the initialization list, not arrays. How about initializing the array when it's defined? Alas, as you've seen, you can't initialize nonstatic instance data either:

```
class weekday
  {
```

continued on next page

continued from previous page

```
   private:
       char day_name[DPW][MAX] =
               { "Sunday", "Monday", ...};   // no good
       ...
   };
```

In the particular situation of the WEEKOUT program, the array should be static, because it's the same for all objects and there's no use duplicating it in each object. When an array is static, it can be initialized in its definition (not the declaration):

```
class weekday
   {
   private:
       static const char day_name[DPW][MAX];      // declaration
   ...
   };
...
const char weekday::day_name[DPW][MAX] =          // definition
               { "Sunday", "Monday", "Tuesday",
                 "Wednesday", "Thursday",
                 "Friday", "Saturday" };
```

This approach solves this particular problem. I'll leave it as an exercise to put this together into a working program.

1. Constants such as 20 should be avoided in your program listing because
   a. such numbers have no specified data type.
   b. their lifetime is too long.
   c. if you change one 20 then you must change any others as well.
   d. the number itself isn't very informative about its purpose.
   e. constants are visible throughout the program.

2. External variables should not be used to supply constant values for use in class member functions because
   a. their visibility does not correspond to that of the class.
   b. their lifetime does not correspond to that of objects.
   c. they can't be initialized at compile time.
   d. they can't be initialized at all.
   e. they can't be made `const`.

3. You can't use a statement such as

   ```
   const int size = 20;
   ```

   to initialize instance data in a class specification because
   a. the assignment operator can't be used to give values to data.
   b. a constructor must be used to initialize instance data.

c. `const` variables can't be initialized.

d. `const` variables must be initialized at compile time.

e. `const` variables must be initialized outside the class.

4. Why can't you use `const` instance data to size an array?
   a. `const` variables can never be used to size an array.
   b. Array sizes must be declared outside the class.
   c. Arrays must be declared outside the class.
   d. Arrays are sized at compile time.
   e. Arrays aren't sized until after the data is declared.

5. The `enum` hack
   a. associates a name and a value when an object is defined.
   b. uses the name of a value of an `enum` variable to name a constant.
   c. uses the name of an `enum` variable to name a constant.
   d. uses the value of an `enum` variable as a constant.
   e. cannot be used to size an array that is not instance data.

EXERCISE 1

Rewrite the STRCON program from Session 3 in this chapter so that it uses a static constant value for the array size `MAX`.

EXERCISE 2

Rewrite the WEEKOUT program from Chapter 4, Session 2, so the array `day_name` is declared inside the class. How will you insert the day names into the array? You should make the array type `static`, because it is shared by all objects. This has repercussions on the variables used for the array size: `DPW` and `MAX`. Where and how should they be declared?

MIDCHAPTER DISCUSSION

George: I can't believe I spent so much time on constructors. All they do is initialize objects. It shouldn't be that much more complicated than initializing an `int`.

Don: Well, whereas an `int` just has one value, objects can have many data items and you may want to initialize different data items in different ways. That's why C++ lets you write your own constructors: It gives you complete control over the initialization process.

Estelle: I can see that. It's not like basic types, where you either initialize a variable to a certain number or you don't. What I didn't get was the conversion function thing.

Don: With basic types, all that conversion stuff happens automatically. The compiler knows how to convert `int` to `float` and you don't need to think about it. But if you want to convert `int` to `airtime`, the compiler can't do it because it's never heard of `airtime` values. So you need to write a one-argument constructor.

George: Why a constructor? Why not just a function?

Estelle: Good question.

Don: Well, I guess you could use any old function for conversions, but the constructor makes it easier to create a variable and initialize it to some simple value at the same time. It's really just a convenience.

Estelle: Isn't it a safety feature, too? It forces the class user to remember to initialize every object.

Don: Right. That's what I meant.

Estelle: You know, I'm not sure I see the advantage of this `English` class having separate numbers for feet and inches. Why not just store one number, representing fractional feet?

George: Or fractional inches.

Don: Hmm. Well, suppose you have, like, 6 feet 4 inches. You can represent that exactly if you store both those numbers. But if all you store is 6.333333 feet, then it's not a nice round number any more and you get round-off errors.

George: Big deal. Who cares about a ten-thousandth of a foot?

Don: I guess you could do it with a single number if you wanted, but it wouldn't be as pretty.

Estelle: Also you'd need to convert back and forth whenever there was input or output. It would be slower for some functions.

George: I hope I never hear another word about constructors.

Don: Good luck.

Session 5

COPY CONSTRUCTORS

Copy constructors provide another way to create objects: by making a copy of an existing object. I can use copy constructors overtly in my own programs, but the compiler also uses them behind the scenes, sometimes in unexpected ways. In this session, you'll learn what copy constructors are and how to make them work for you.

Copying Variables

You've seen numerous examples where I created an object or a variable from scratch. Where before there was no object, now suddenly there is one:

```
sigma sigobj;          // create an object of class sigma
```

The data in the object is initialized to zero or other appropriate beginning values. This is the familiar approach to object creation, but there's another one. You can also create an object that's a *copy of an existing object*. Do this with variables of basic types without thinking too much about it:

```
int alpha = 27;      // create an int with value 27
int beta = alpha;    // create another int that's a copy of beta
```

With basic types, copying means making a new variable of the same type and giving it the same value. It's not too complicated because there's only one value to worry about and it's always copied as is into the new object.

Remember that in the two statements above, the *equal signs are not assignment operators*. The equal signs in these statements don't mean I'm *assigning* a value to an existing variable, they mean I'm *initializing* a variable—as it's being created—to a value. There is an important distinction between assignment and initialization.

Equivalent Syntax

As I noted, a different but equivalent notation can be used for copying one variable to another. I can also say

```
int beta(alpha);    // copy alpha to beta
```

This has exactly the same effect as

```
int beta = alpha;    // copy alpha to beta
```

However, the fact that there is no equal sign helps avoid confusion between assignment and initialization. This is sometimes called *functional notation*. (It's also used in constructors, in the initialization list, as you've seen.)

Copying Objects

You can copy objects as well as variables of basic types:

```
sigma sigalpha;             // create sigalpha
sigalpha.getdata();         // put some data in sigalpha
sigma sigbeta(sigalpha);    // create sigbeta by copying sigalpha
```

Here I create `sigalpha` and give it some data by calling the member function `getdata()`. Then I copy `sigalpha` to `sigbeta`. Another way of saying this is that I create `sigbeta` and initialize it with `sigalpha`. Whatever data was placed in `sigalpha` by the `getdata()` function is presumably transferred automatically into `sigbeta` when it's initialized. I could say that I've *cloned* the `sigalpha` object. Figure 5-4 shows how this looks.

Not the Normal Constructor

When you create an object from scratch,

```
sigma sigobj;               // create an object of class sigma
```

a constructor is invoked to initialize `sigobj`. It may take arguments and it may not. But if you copy an object,

```
sigma sigbeta(sigalpha);   // uses copy constructor to create sigbeta
```

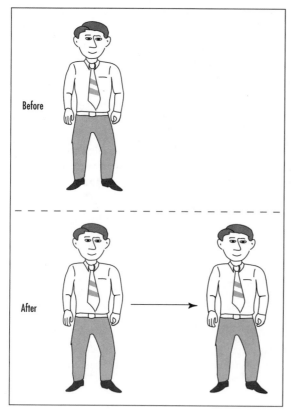

Figure 5-4   Effect of the copy constructor

what entity is responsible for initializing **sigbeta**? This also requires a constructor, but a very special one with a unique argument type. It's called the *copy constructor*.

The Default Copy Constructor

If you don't explicitly define your own copy constructor, the compiler creates one for you. This default copy constructor carries out what's called a *memberwise copy* of all the data from one object to another. Memberwise means that the default copy constructor makes no effort to change or interpret any of the data; it simply copies the value of each member into the corresponding member in the other object.

Many times this memberwise copy is just what you want and there's no need to create your own copy constructor. However, when you want the new object to be different in some way from the one it's copied from or when you want the act of copying to cause some other side effect, then you must explicitly define your own copy constructor.

You'll see how to do this in a moment. First, however, I must digress briefly to show how function arguments can be **const**. This is important because copy constructors typically use a **const** argument.

const **for Function Arguments**

A major advantage of passing function arguments by value is that, because it works with a copy of the argument, the function cannot access, and therefore cannot accidentally change, the original variable used as an argument in the function call. This is an important safety device.

Passing by Reference

However, as I've noted, creating extra copies of an object, which may be arbitrarily large and complex, is not always a great idea. Unnecessary copies of large objects may use too much memory, and the copying process itself takes time and in some cases may introduce other problems as well. For these reasons, it's often preferable to pass objects by reference (see Chapter 4, Session 7). This is the case in copy constructors, as you'll see.

One of the advantages (at least sometimes) of passing by reference is that the function can modify the arguments in the function call. But suppose you *don't* want to modify them. Maybe you want the other advantages of passing by reference, but don't want to give up the guaranteed safety of the original arguments that you get automatically when passing by value.

You can, when passing by reference, reinstate the guarantee that the original arguments won't be modified. All you need to do is declare these arguments as const. Listing 5-7 shows PASSCON, which shows how that looks for arguments of basic types.

Listing 5-7 PASSCON

```
// passcon.cpp
// demonstrates passing const variables

class omega
    {
    private:
        int omdata;
    public:
        void getdata(const int& i)  // guarantees not to change i
            {
            omdata = i;   // this is fine
//          i = 44;       // error: can't modify const variable
            }
    };

void main()
    {
    omega om1;
    int ivar = 77;        // I don't want getdata() to modify ivar

    om1.getdata(ivar);    // perfectly safe
    }
```

I want to guarantee that the getdata() member function, when called from main() with ivar as a reference argument, will not modify ivar. To do this, I make the argument const in getdata():

```
void getdata(const int& i)  // guarantees not to change argument
    {
    ...
    }
```

Here, although `ivar` is passed by reference and given the alias `i` in the function, `getdata()` can't modify it, because it's `const`.

Using `const` for reference arguments is an important technique for avoiding program bugs. You should always make reference arguments `const` unless there is a specific reason for not doing so (perhaps you *want* to modify the original variables).

Passing by Value

Notice that there is no point in using `const` for arguments that are passed by value. Passing by value is already a guarantee that the original variable is safe because the original variable isn't passed at all; the function has access only to its own copy of the variable. Using `const` would be gilding the lily.

A Simple Example of a Copy Constructor

Now that you know how to use `const` with function arguments, you can look at a real copy constructor. Listing 5-8, COPYCON, is very simple.

Listing 5-8 COPYCON

```
// copycon.cpp
// demonstrates copy constructors
#include <iostream.h>

class omega
    {
    private:
        int intvar;
    public:
        omega(int v) : intvar(v)      // one-arg constructor
            { }
        omega(const omega& om)        // copy constructor
            {
            intvar = om.intvar;
            cout << "\nI am the copy constructor";
            }
    };

void main()
    {
    omega om1(27);               // uses one-arg constructor

    omega om2=om1;               // uses copy constructor
    omega om3(om1);              // uses copy constructor
    }
```

There are two constructors for a class called **omega**: a one-argument constructor and the copy constructor. You've already seen examples of one-argument constructors so it should be familiar, but the copy constructor has some new features.

Just Another Constructor

The copy constructor is in many ways just another one-argument constructor. It has the same name as the class and it has no return value. However, its argument is always of the same class the function is a member of. The argument represents the object to be copied.

COPYCON uses the copy constructor twice: when it makes om2 and when it makes om3:

```
omega om2=om1;                  // uses copy constructor
omega om3(om1);                 // uses copy constructor
```

Both statements initialize a new object to the value of om1 by calling the copy constructor. As I noted, the two syntax are equivalent. The copy constructor prints a message each time it's called. Here's the output of the program:

```
I am the copy constructor    <--when om2 is created
I am the copy constructor    <--when om3 is created
```

The statement in the copy constructor

```
intvar = om.intvar;   // copy the data item
```

is necessary to copy the data from one object to another. If you *don't* define a copy constructor at all, the compiler will generate a default constructor that will take care of all this data copying automatically, using a memberwise copy. But if you *do* define a copy constructor, then you are responsible for carrying out the copy operation for every data item yourself. In omega, there's only one such item, intvar, so copy it.

If you checked the contents of the new objects, om2 and om3, following their creation, you would see that they both have intvar values of 27.

You might wonder, if the compiler will make copy constructors for you, why worry about them at all? In this simple example, the user-written copy constructor doesn't accomplish anything the compiler-generated (default) version would not have. However, as you'll see in the next session, there are times when a "smart" copy constructor—which does things the default cannot do—is necessary.

Argument Must Be Passed by Reference

The copy constructor takes as its only argument an object of the same class as itself. This argument *must* be passed by reference. (You'll see why in the next session, when I show how the compiler calls the copy constructor automatically.)

Argument Should Be const

The argument to the copy constructor should be const. There's seldom any reason for the copy constructor to modify anything in the object it's copying from, and guaranteeing that it can't perform such modifications is an important safety feature. You don't absolutely need to use const, but it's a good idea.

QUIZ 5

1. A copy constructor
   a. takes no arguments.
   b. takes one argument.
   c. takes an arbitrary number of arguments.
   d. creates a new object that later may be assigned the data of an existing object.
   e. creates an object initialized with the same data as an existing object.

2. The statement `aclass obj2 = obj1;` causes _____ to be executed.
   a. no constructor
   b. a one-argument constructor that must be written by the user
   c. a one-argument constructor that must copy data
   d. the copy constructor
   e. an assignment operator

3. To prevent the possibility that a function will modify the object or variable passed to it as an argument,
   a. the argument may be passed by value.
   b. the argument may be made `const` and passed by reference.
   c. the function may be made `const`.
   d. the function may not refer to the variable.
   e. the function call must use the keyword `const`.

4. A copy constructor is always called when
   a. an object is initialized with another object of the same class when it's created.
   b. an object is initialized with another object of any class when it's created.
   c. an object is initialized with a variable of a basic type when it's created.
   d. an object is not initialized when it's created.
   e. an object is returned from a function by value.

5. The argument to a class copy constructor must be passed by reference because otherwise
   a. the copy constructor would not return.
   b. the integrity of the argument object could not be guaranteed.
   c. the integrity of the object being created could not be guaranteed.
   d. too many objects would be created.
   e. the copy constructor could not be identified by the compiler.

EXERCISE 1

Write a copy constructor for the `airtime` class from Exercise 1 of Session 1 in this chapter. Have it perform a memberwise copy of all data. Write statements in `main()`, using two different syntax, that exercise this copy constructor. Do you really need an explicit copy constructor in this situation?

EXERCISE 2

One reason for an explicit copy constructor is to check that the arguments used to initialize the new object have reasonable values. Modify the copy constructor in Exercise 1 so it checks that the **hours** and **minutes** values are within appropriate ranges and displays error messages if they are not. While you're at it, modify the constructor to perform the same check.

SESSION 6

COPY CONSTRUCTORS AT WORK

In this session, I'll extend your understanding of copy constructors in two ways. First I'll look at a situation where defining your own copy constructor is necessary. Then you'll see several examples of how the compiler arranges for the copy constructor to be called even when it may not be obvious that an object is being copied.

Numbering the Objects

Remember the STATIC program in Chapter 4, Session 6? Objects of the **widget** class in this program numbered themselves as they were created, using a static member variable to record the total number of objects created to date.

However, suppose I create one widget object by initializing it with another:

```
widget w2(w1);    // clone w2 from w1
```

If I have not written my own copy constructor, this will result in **w2** being given exactly the same widget number as **w1**, because the data is simply copied from one object to another. Also, the count of all the existing objects won't be incremented, because the normal constructor is not called and the default copy constructor doesn't know anything about the count.

An Intelligent Copy Constructor

To fix this, I must define my own copy constructor. For this example, I'll use the **omega** class from the COPYCON program in the last session. Its instance data will include a serial number and a static count of all objects, as in the **widget** class, but it will also include a string representing a name. The argument to the one-argument constructor will be a string that gives each object whatever name the class user wants. However, I'll arrange things so that the copy constructor copies the **name** variable—without alteration—into a new object. The object's **number** variable, on the other hand, will be handled as it is in the **widget** class: Each object will get a new **number** no matter how it's created. An object created with the copy constructor will therefore have the same **name**, but a different **number** than the object it was copied from. Listing 5-9 shows COPYCON2.

Listing 5-9 COPYCON2

```
// copycon2.cpp
// demonstrates copy constructors,
// using objects that number themselves
```

continued on next page

continued from previous page

```
#include <iostream.h>
#include <string.h>            // for strncpy()

class omega
    {
    private:

        static const int size = 20;
        char name[size];
        static int total;
        int number;
    public:                     // one-arg constructor
        omega(char str[]) : number(++total)
            {
            strncpy(name, str, size);
            cout << "\nI am the 1-arg constructor. I have "
                 << "created object " << name << "-" << number;
            }
                                // copy constructor
        omega(const omega& om)
            {
            strncpy(name, om.name, size);
            number = ++total;
            cout << "\nI am the copy constructor. I have "
                 << "created object " << name << "-" << number;
            }
    };
int omega::total = 0;

void main()
    {
    omega om1("Harriet");       // uses one-arg constructor

    omega om2=om1;              // uses copy constructor
    omega om3(om1);            // uses copy constructor
    }
```

In main(), I create one object of class omega, called om1, and give it the name Harriet. Because it is the first object created in the program, it's given the number 1 automatically by the constructor.

The second and third objects, om2 and om3, are created by copying om1 with the copy constructor. They have the same name variable as om1 because the copy constructor simply copies name. However, they have different number variable values because the copy constructor does the same things the one-argument constructor does: It increments the total count and uses the result for the new number value. Here's the output from COPYCON2:

```
I am the 1-arg constructor. I have created object Harriet-1
I am the copy constructor. I have created object Harriet-2
I am the copy constructor. I have created object Harriet-3
```

This shows that, if you write your own copy constructor, you can pretty much do whatever you want to intialize the instance data in the new object. You can copy data directly from the old object or you can modify the data or you can generate entirely new data.

Initialization List

Remember that the strange-looking initialization list syntax in the constructor:

```
omega(char str[]) : number(++total)  <--initialization
   {
   ...
   }
```

has almost the same effect as would a similar statement in the function body:

```
omega(char str[])
   {
   number = ++total;  <--assignment
   ...
   }
```

However, the first construction *initializes* `number` to a value, whereas the second *assigns* `number` a value.

A Variation on `strcpy()`

Incidentally, I've used a new library function, `strncpy()`, to copy the name from the constructor argument to the object. This function is similar to `strcpy()`, but it includes an argument that specifies the size of the buffer being copied to. It won't permit any more characters than this to be copied, thus offering insurance against buffer overflow.

Other Reasons for Using Copy Constructors

When do you write your own copy constructor? In Exercise 2 in the last session, you saw that a copy constructor could be used to check the correctness of the data being passed to the new object. Also, as you'll see when I talk about pointers in Chapter 8, copy constructors are often used when memory or other system resources are allocated during object creation, for instance in string classes. (In fact, classes containing pointers used for *any* purpose may need copy constructors so that the pointer points to things in its own object instead of in the object it was copied from.)

Copy Constructor Invoked in Pass by Value

I have intimated that copy constructors are sometimes invoked in strange and mysterious situations. There are two of these: when an argument is passed to a function by value and when a function returns by value. In this section, I'll look at the first of these situations.

Passing by Value Creates a Copy

Why should the copy constructor be invoked when an object is passed by value? Because a copy of the object is created for use by the function. It doesn't matter whether you create a copy explicitly by defining a new object or whether the compiler creates a copy implicitly because you've passed an argument by value. Either way, the copy constructor is invoked. Listing 5-10, COPYCON3, demonstrates this process.

Listing 5-10 COPYCON3

```
// copycon3.cpp
// demonstrates copy constructors
// passes objects to functions by value
```

continued on next page

continued from previous page

```cpp
#include <iostream.h>
#include <string.h>              // for strncpy()

class omega
    {
    private:

        static const int size = 20;  // array size
        char name[size];             // array for name string
        static int total;            // total number of omegas
        int number;
    public:                          // one-arg constructor
        omega(char str[]) : number(++total)
            {
            strncpy(name, str, size);
            cout << "\nI am the 1-arg constructor. I have "
                 << "created object " << name << "-" << number;
            }
                                // copy constructor
        omega(const omega& om)
            {
            strncpy(name, om.name, size);
            number = ++total;
            cout << "\nI am the copy constructor. I have "
                 << "created object " << name << "-" << number;
            }
    };
int omega::total = 0;

void main()
    {
    void func(omega);          // declaration

    omega om1("Harriet");      // uses one-arg constructor
    omega om2("Nancy");

    func(om1);                 // call the function
    func(om2);                 // call it again
    }

void func(omega og)            // argument passed by value
    {
    }
```

This program uses the same `omega` class as COPYCON2. However, it adds a function called `func()` that is called twice from `main()`. This function takes one argument: an object of type `omega`. The function doesn't do anything and it doesn't return anything. (The fact that it doesn't do anything with its argument generates a warning message, which you can ignore.)

In `main()`, I create two objects of type `omega` with the instance data names `Harriet` and `Nancy`. Each time I create an object, the one-argument constructor is invoked. After creating the objects, `main()` calls `func()` with the first object as an argument; it then calls it again with the second. Each time I call this function, the copy constructor is invoked to create a new `omega` object, using data from the argument passed to it. Thus the first object, `Harriet-1`, is cloned to `Harriet-3` and the second object, `Nancy-2`, is cloned to `Nancy-4`. Here's the output from the program:

```
I am the 1-arg constructor. I have created object Harriet-1
I am the 1-arg constructor. I have created object Nancy-2
I am the copy constructor. I have created object Harriet-3
I am the copy constructor. I have created object Nancy-4
```

The copy is created when the function starts to execute, as shown in Figure 5-5.

The new object has the same instance data name as the original (such as `Harriet`), because the copy constructor merely copies the name. However, the new object has a different number, because the copy constructor, using the same process as the original constructor, gives every object a unique number.

Why the Copy Constructor Must Use a Reference Argument

You're now ready to think about why a copy constructor must take a reference argument rather than one passed by value. What happens when an argument is passed by value? The copy constructor is called to create a copy. But if the function I'm calling is the copy constructor, it must call itself to create the copy. When it calls itself, a new copy of the object must be created and the copy constructor calls itself again to create the copy. In fact, it calls itself an infinite number of times, or at least until the computer's stack overflows and the program grinds to a halt, perhaps taking the entire operating system with it. To avoid this unfortunate scenario, the copy constructor avoids making copies by passing its argument by reference.

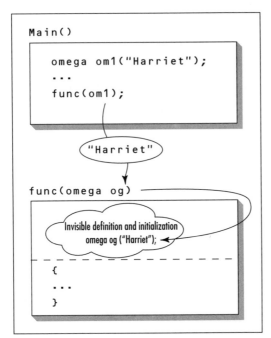

Figure 5-5 The copy constructor and passing by value

Copy Constructor Invoked in Return by Value

The copy constructor is also invoked when a function returns by value. In the next example, I use the same class `omega` but the function `retfunc()`, called from `main()`, creates a new object, `temp`, and returns it. What does returning the object entail? It means that a copy of the object is created and installed in the code that called the function. Listing 5-11 shows `copycon4`.

Listing 5-11 COPYCON4

```cpp
// copycon4.cpp
// demonstrates copy constructors
// function returns object by value
#include <iostream.h>
#include <string.h>          // for strncpy()

class omega
    {
    private:

        static const int size = 20;  // array size
        char name[size];        // array for name string
        static int total;       // total number of omegas
        int number;
    public:                     // one-arg constructor
        omega(char str[]) : number(++total)
            {
            strncpy(name, str, size);
            cout << "\nI am the 1-arg constructor. I have "
                 << "created object " << name << "-" << number;
            }
                                // copy constructor
        omega(const omega& om)
            {
            strncpy(name, om.name, size);
            number = ++total;
            cout << "\nI am the copy constructor. I have "
                 << "created object " << name << "-" << number;
            }
    };
int omega::total = 0;

void main()
    {
    omega retfunc();           // function declaration

    retfunc();                 // call the function
    }

omega retfunc()                // return by value
    {
    omega temp("Pandora");     // uses one-arg constructor
    return temp;               // uses copy constructor
    }
```

In `main()`, the function call itself,

```
retfunc();
```

takes on the value of the object being returned.

Although I don't show it here (to avoid complicating things too much), the function call can be used, like a constant, on the right side of an equal sign:

```
void main()
  {
  omega retfunc();        // function declaration
  omega om1;              // create a new object

  om1 = retfunc();        // call the function, assign to om1
  }
```

To do this, however, I would need a no-argument constructor, which I haven't shown before, and three objects would be created: `om1` in `main()`, `temp` in the function `retfunc()`, and the unnamed object created when the function returns. The value of this unnamed object is then assigned to `om1`.

Here's the output from the program:

```
I am the 1-arg constructor. I have created object Pandora-1
I am the copy constructor. I have created object Pandora-2
```

The one-argument constructor is called when the function creates the temp object. The copy constructor is called when the function returns and creates a copy for use by the code that called the function. This is shown in Figure 5-6.

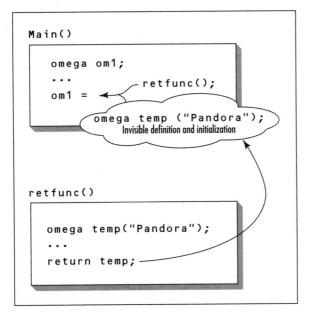

Figure 5-6 The copy constructor and returning by value

1. The copy constructor can't modify the data in the object that's being copied from, because
   a. the data is declared `const` in the class specification.
   b. constructors have no return value.
   c. the argument to the copy constructor is passed by value.
   d. the argument to the copy constructor is passed by reference.
   e. the argument to the copy constructor is `const`.

2. A copy constructor written by the class creator
   a. must copy all data without modification from one object to another.
   b. must copy all data, possibly modifying it, from one object to another.
   c. must copy data from one object to another, modify it before copying, or create new data.
   d. is not necessary if all the member data is to be copied as is from one object to another.
   e. is necessary if there is a one-argument constructor.

3. When an object is passed by value to a function,
   a. the function must access the object's data using member functions.
   b. the original object is accessed by the function.
   c. a copy of the object is created in the function.
   d. the object's copy constructor is invoked.
   e. the object is not copied.

4. An object constructed by a copy constructor
   a. is only temporary.
   b. lasts for the life of the program.
   c. may not have a name.
   d. is local to a member function.
   e. must be identical to the object from which it was copied.

5. When a function returns an object by value,
   a. the copy constructor is called.
   b. the data to be returned is copied into a temporary object.
   c. the function call can be used on the left side of an assignment operator.
   d. no additional objects are created.
   e. two additional objects are created.

Start with the program in Exercise 2 in Session 5 in this chapter, which included a constructor and a copy constructor that checked that correct values were passed to any newly created `airtime` object. Write a standalone function, called from `main()`, that takes an `airtime` as an argument passed by value. Check that the copy constructor works by attempting to pass bad data to the function.

EXERCISE 2

Write another function, similar to that in Exercise 1, but have this one return an **airtime** by value. Again, attempt to return bad data and verify that the copy constructor won't allow it.

SESSION 7

const OBJECTS

I've described how **const** variables of basic types are used in several contexts. I've used them to define constants such as array sizes and, in the last lesson, I discussed **const** reference arguments. Constant variables provide an important safety feature, helping to save programmers from themselves when they inadvertently attempt to modify a value that should remain fixed.

Perhaps you've wondered whether it's possible to use **const** not only with basic types but with objects of user-defined classes as well. In other words, can you say

```
const zclass zobj;    // declare a constant object of class zclass
```

This might be useful for the same reason it's useful to use **const** with basic types: You want to guarantee that the data in an object cannot be changed. In this section, I'll digress from my focus on constructors to examine the idea of **const** objects.

The Wandering Noon

As an example, think about the **airtime** class, last seen in the TIMECON program in Session 2 in this chapter. Suppose you want an **airtime** object called **noon** that always has the value {12, 0}, that is, 12:00 in 24-hour time. It would be nice to guarantee that this noon object could not change its value. Can you do this by making it **const**?

```
const airtime noon(12, 0);
```

This is possible, but to make it work, you must make some modifications to the class specification.

Let's start off with a program that defines an **airtime** object **noon** but does *not* use const. Listing 5-12 shows CONSTA1.

Listing 5-12 CONSTA1

```
// consta1.cpp
// class models time data type

#include <iostream.h>

class airtime
   {
   private:
      int hours;            // 0 to 23
      int minutes;          // 0 to 59
   public:                  // constructor
```

continued on next page

continued from previous page

```
        airtime() : hours(0), minutes(0)
           { }
                                // copy constructor
        airtime(int h, int m) : hours(h), minutes(m)
           { }

        void display();        // declaration
        void get();            // declaration
   };  // end class airtime

void airtime::display()    // output to screen
   {
   cout << hours << ':' << minutes;
   }

void airtime::get()      // input from user
   {
   char dummy;           // for colon
   cout << "\nEnter time (format 12:59): ";
   cin >> hours >> dummy >> minutes;
   }

void main()
   {
   airtime noon(12, 0);       // create noon

   cout << "noon = ";
   noon.display();            // display noon

   noon.get();                // change noon (bad!)
   cout << "noon = ";
   noon.display();            // display noon
   }
```

The problem here is that there's nothing to stop the class user from calling a member function that changes noon, as happens in the line

```
noon.get();
```

which gets a new `airtime` value from the user and inserts it in **noon**. The output from the program might be

```
noon = 12:00
Enter time(format 12:59): 1:23
noon = 1:23
```

Not so good: Noon should not occur early in the morning. The most obvious way to fix this might appear to involve adding a `const` to the definition of **noon**:

```
const airtime noon(12, 0);
```

But now every time a member function of airtime is called in `main()`, as in

```
noon.display();
```

the compiler issues a warning along the lines of

```
Non-const function airtime::display() called for const object.
```

Apparently, the compiler wants me to use something called a const *function*.

const **Functions**

What is a const function? It's a member function that guarantees that it won't change the object for which it's called. Specify such a function by placing the keyword const in the definition (and the declaration too, if there is one) just after the parentheses that follow the function name. Here's how that looks for the display() member function of airtime:

```
class airtime
   {
   ...
   void display() const;          // const in declaration
   ...
   };

void airtime::display() const    // const in definition
   {
   cout << hours << ':' << minutes;
   }
```

Only member functions that *do not change an object's data* should be made const. In this example, only display() is const. What about get()? Well, you should never use get() with a const airtime object, because get() is expressly designed to modify the object. You *want* an error message if you try to use get() with a const object, so don't make this function const.

You might think you should put the const before the function name, rather than after it:

```
const void display();   // not a const function
```

but this has a different meaning: It specifies that the return value of the function is const (which doesn't make sense here, because the return type is void).

In the example, I show the functions defined outside the class specification. If you define the function within the class specification, then there's only one place to put the const. However, you must use const with any declaration because const becomes part of the function name. The function void display() const is not the same as the function void display().

Constructors are never const because the creation of an object requires const to be changed.

The Fixed Noon

The next example shows how the parts of the program fit together when the display() function is made const. Listing 5-13 shows CONSTA2.

Listing 5-13 CONSTA2
```
// consta2.cpp
// class models time data type
// demonstrates const airtime objects
#include <iostream.h>
```

continued on next page

continued from previous page
```
class airtime
   {
   private:
      int hours;          // 0 to 23
      int minutes;        // 0 to 59
   public:                // constructor
      airtime() : hours(0), minutes(0)
         { }
                          // copy constructor
      airtime(int h, int m) : hours(h), minutes(m)
         { }

      void display() const; // declare constant function
      void get();           // declare non-constant function
   };  // end class airtime

void airtime::display() const   // output to screen
   {                            // can be called for const objects
   cout << hours << ':' << minutes;
// hours = 2;               // error: can't modify const object
   }

void airtime::get()          // input from user
   {                         // cannot be called for const objects
   char dummy;               // for colon
   cout << "\nEnter time (format 12:59): ";
   cin >> hours >> dummy >> minutes;
   }

void main()
   {
   const airtime noon(12, 0);  // create noon

   cout << "\nnoon = ";
   noon.display();          // display noon
// noon.get();              // warning: attempt to change noon

   airtime at1;             // create at1
   at1.get();               // OK: at1 is not a const object
   cout << "at1 = ";
   at1.display();           // display at1
   }
```

Two airtime variables are defined in main(). The first one, noon, is const, whereas the second one, at1, is not. The display() member function is const, because it does not modify its object, but the get() member function does modify its object, so it's not const. You can call get() for at1 but not for noon. Here's the output from the program:

```
noon = 12:00
Enter time (format 12:59): 1:30
at1 = 1:30
```

I can modify the nonconstant object **at1** but not the constant **noon**. Attempting to call a non-**const** function for a **const** object leads to a warning from the compiler, as you saw above. However, I can call a non-**const** function for any object, whether **const** or not.

Within a **const** function such as **display()**, it's illegal to modify any of the class data. You can verify this by uncommenting the line

```
hours = 2;
```

in the **display()** function and recompiling. The compiler will tell you something like

```
Cannot modify a const object in function "airtime::display() const"
```

If the use of **const** with objects is to be meaningful, the class creator must have made **const** those member functions that are *not* intended to modify their object. Then if the class user attempts to call such a member function with a **const** object, a warning results.

QUIZ 7

1. A **const** object is one whose
   a. member functions can change only non-**const** variables.
   b. member functions can change only **const** variables.
   c. **const** member functions cannot be called.
   d. instance data cannot be changed.
   e. instance data can only be changed by non-**const** member functions.

2. Which of the following are appropriate **const** objects?
   a. An object of class **employee** that represents the company president.
   b. An object of the **xString** class that represents the null string.
   c. Any object of the **Stack** class.
   d. An object of the **airtime** class that represents pm (times after noon).
   e. An object of the **airtime** class that represents a time entered by the user.

3. Which of these statements has (have) the correct syntax for a constant function?
   a. `const int func(int);`
   b. `int const func(int);`
   c. `int func(const int);`
   d. `int func(int const);`
   e. `int func(int) const;`

4. A nonconstant member function of a constant object
   a. can always modify the object's instance data.
   b. can modify the object's instance data if the data not **const**.
   c. guarantees not to modify the object's data.
   d. can always be called.
   e. should never be called.

5. Statements in a `const` member function
   a. can modify a `const` object's data.
   b. can modify any object's data.
   c. cannot modify a `const` object's data.
   d. cannot modify any object's data.
   e. cannot modify their own local variables.

EXERCISE 1

Create a `const` object called `midnight` for the `airtime` class (as in the CONSTA2 example in Session 7 in this chapter). Write some statements to exercise this object.

EXERCISE 2

Assume you want to make some `const` objects of the `weekday` class, as seen in WEEKOUT in Chapter 4, Session 2. Modify the class specification appropriately, make some `const` objects, and test to be sure you can't modify them.

SESSION 8

VISUALIZING CONSTRUCTION AND DESTRUCTION

I'll end this chapter by focusing on how constructors and destructors interact with different storage classes. The class in the example program contains constructors and destructors that display data about the objects they're creating or destroying. This program is an aggrandizement of the COPYCON3 program from Session 6 in this chapter. It doesn't present any new concepts, but it does use most of the C++ features I've discussed in this chapter, so it's a good chance to review what you've learned.

Two Kinds of Total

I've split the `total` variable from the COPYCON3 program, a static member variable of class `omega`, into two kinds of total. One, `total_ever`, records how many `omega` objects have ever been created (since the program started running). The other, `total_now`, is the number of currently existing `omega` objects. The `total_now` variable can be less than `total_ever` if objects are destroyed. Both constructors increment both totals, whereas the destructor decrements `total_now` but not `total_ever`. The `total_ever` variable is used to number each object as it's created, as `total` did in COPYCON3.

I kept the function `func()` from COPYCON3. Calling it demonstrates how arguments passed by value cause the creation of a local object within the function. I also created a local object explicitly within the function. Finally, I defined an `omega` object as an external variable. All this leads to interesting activity on the part of `omega`'s constructors and destructor.

This is a fairly complex program, but the resulting output rewards a bit of study. Listing 5-14 shows DESTRU.

Listing 5-14 DESTRU

```cpp
// destru.cpp
// demonstrates constructors, destructors,
// and storage classes
#include <iostream.h>
#include <string.h>              // for strncpy()

class omega
    {
    private:

        static const int size = 20;  // array size
        char obname[size];           // array for obname string
        static int total_now;    // objects in existence now
        static int total_ever;   // objects ever created
        int snumber;             // serial number of this object
    public:
                                // one-arg constructor
        omega(char str[]) : snumber(++total_ever)
            {
            strncpy(obname, str, size);
            cout << "\n   1-arg constructor creating "
                << obname << "-" << snumber
                << ". Total=" << ++total_now;
            }
                                  // copy constructor
        omega(const omega& om) : snumber(++total_ever)
            {
            strncpy(obname, om.obname, size);
            cout << "\n   Copy constructor creating  "
                << obname << "-" << snumber
                << ". Total=" << ++total_now;
            }
        ~omega()                      // destructor
            {
            cout << "\n   Destructor destroying       "
                << obname << "-" << snumber
                << ". Total=" << --total_now;
            }
    };  // end class omega

int omega::total_now = 0;
int omega::total_ever = 0;

omega om0("Adam");                // external object

//////////////////////////////////////////////////////////
void main()
    {
    cout << "\nmain() starting";
```

continued on next page

continued from previous page

```
    void func(omega);              // declaration

    omega om1("Jane");             // uses one-arg constructor
    omega om2("Paul");
    omega om3(om2);                // uses copy constructor
    cout << "\nmain() calling func(om1)";
    func(om1);
    cout << "\nmain() calling func(om2)";
    func(om2);
    cout << "\nmain() terminating";
    }

void func(omega og)                // argument passed by value
    {
    cout << "\nfunc() starting";
    omega om4("Mike");             // object is local to func()
    cout << "\nfunc() terminating";
    }
```

The output from DESTRU looks like this:

```
    1_arg constructor creating Adam-1. Total=1
main() starting
    1_arg constructor creating Jane-2. Total=2
    1_arg constructor creating Paul-3. Total=3
    Copy constructor creating  Paul-4. Total=4
main() calling func(om1)
    Copy constructor creating  Jane-5. Total=5
func() starting
    1_arg constructor creating Mike-6. Total=6
func() terminating
    Destructor destroying      Mike-6. Total=5
    Destructor destroying      Jane-5. Total=4
main() calling func(om2)
    Copy constructor creating  Paul-7. Total=5
func() starting
    1_arg constructor creating Mike-8. Total=6
func() terminating
    Destructor destroying      Mike-8. Total=5
    Destructor destroying      Paul-7. Total=4
main() terminating
    Destructor destroying      Paul-4. Total=3
    Destructor destroying      Paul-3. Total=2
    Destructor destroying      Jane-2. Total=1
    Destructor destroying      Adam-1. Total=0
```

The indented lines are printed by the constructors and the destructor. The nonindented lines show what part of **main()** or **func()** is executing. The total shown in the last column is the value of the **total_now** variable. As you can see, it shows how many objects exist at a given moment.

Remember that the object's name, **obname**, is copied without change by the copy constructor. That's why several different objects can have the same name, such as Paul. However, each object's serial number, **snumber**, is set equal to the current **total_ever** value, so it is unique. It is only possible for there to be one number object numbered 3 in the entire program, although there can be both

Paul-3 and Paul-4 objects. The distinction between numbers and names makes it easier to follow which objects are created by the one-argument constructor and which are created by the copy constructor.

Program Features

Let's examine some important points demonstrated in DESTRU.

External Variables

I use the one-argument constructor to define `om0`, which I initialize as `Adam-1`, as an external variable. The output shows that it's created before `main()` starts to execute. External variables are destroyed after all the variables defined in `main()` have been destroyed and after `main()` itself has terminated, as can be seen in the last line of the output.

Variables in `main()`

Within `main()`, the one-argument constructor is also used to create `om1` (Jane-2) and `om2` (Paul-3). Then the copy constructor copies `om2`, creating `om3` (Paul-4). All this is reflected in the output. When `main()` terminates, these three variables are destroyed in the opposite order they were created.

Passing by Value

As you saw in Session 6 in this chapter, passing an argument to a function by value causes the object's copy constructor to be called, implicitly, to create a copy for use by the function. This happens twice in DESTRU: the two calls from `main()` to `func()`. In the first call, Jane-5 is copied from Jane-2. In the second, Paul-7 is copied from Paul-2.

I don't show an example of returning by value, but if I did, the copy constructor would create an extra copy there as well.

Local Variables

The function `func()` creates a local variable, `om4`. The first time it's called, it creates Mike-6; the second time, it creates Mike-8. These variables are destroyed as soon as `func()` returns so, like the argument variable created by the copy constructor, they don't stay around very long.

1. Static member data is _____ by a copy constructor.
   a. copied automatically to the new object
   b. ignored
   c. copied, but only if there are appropriate assignment statements,
   d. copied, but only if there are specific items on the initialization list,
   e. set to zero

2. In the DESTRU program, the `total_ever` variable _____, whereas the `total_now` variable _____.

    a. is static, is nonstatic

    b. is decremented when a function returns, is not decremented when a function returns

    c. records the number of objects created with the copy constructor, records the number of objects created with the one-argument constructor

    d. is not decremented by the destructor, is decremented by the destructor

    e. lasts for the life of the program, lasts for the life of an object

3. Variables created as a result of passing to a function by value

    a. have the same lifetime as the function.

    b. have the same lifetime as the variable named as the argument in the function call.

    c. are created by the one-argument constructor.

    d. are created by the assignment operator.

    e. are created by the copy constructor.

4. Instance data variables in a class

    a. have the same lifetime as the program.

    b. have the same lifetime as `main()`.

    c. have the same lifetime as the object of which they are a part.

    d. have the same lifetime as the class of which they are a part.

    e. may be created by a copy constructor.

5. External variables defined at the beginning of the program are created before _____ and destroyed after _____.

    a. the operating system starts execution, the operating system terminates

    b. each function starts execution, each function terminates

    c. local variables in `main()`, local variables in `main()`

    d. `main()` starts execution, `main()` terminates

    e. static instance variables, static instance variables

EXERCISE 1

Insert some more external variables of type `omega` and some more local variables in `func()` in the DESTRU program. What can you conclude about the order in which external and local objects are created and destroyed?

EXERCISE 2

Change the `func()` function in the `omega` class in the DESTRU program so it returns an `omega` object by value. Notice what effect this has on the output. The destructor is very busy. You may want to insert `getch()` statements in `main()` to pause the program in several places, because the output becomes rather lengthy.

SUMMARY: CHAPTER 5

In this chapter, I've focused, for the most part, on constructors. A constructor is a special member function whose purpose is to initialize the instance data in an object. A no-argument constructor (called the default constructor) initializes all objects to the same value. Constructors that take arguments can initialize objects to specified values. A special constructor is the copy constructor, which creates a copy of an object. If you don't write your own copy constructor, the compiler supplies one that performs a memberwise (member-by-member) copy.

Copy constructors usually pass a `const` value by reference. Doing this keeps the function from modifying the value named in the function call.

A `const` object, like a `const` variable of a basic type, is one that can't be modified. To make this work with classes, member functions that do not modify any instance data are declared `const` and can be called for `const` objects. Member functions that are not `const` cannot be called for `const` objects.

END-OF-CHAPTER DISCUSSION

George: That's just terrific. There are two ways to write a definition that initializes an object with another object, they both do the same thing, but one looks like an assignment statement. Why don't these guys get their act together?

Estelle: Life's tough, George.

Don: I'm impressed with copy constructors. It's all so flexible and there are so many options. There's a copy constructor built in, which you use normally and the compiler uses it too, for stuff like passing arguments by value. But if you write your own copy constructor, then you can use it and the compiler will use it too.

Estelle: It's pretty amazing that the compiler executes programmer-written routines. It puts the shoe on the other foot.

Don: There's a lot more interaction between the compiler and the programmer in C++ than there is in Pascal.

George: Or C.

Don: Or BASIC.

Estelle: It's almost like you can write parts of the compiler yourself.

Don: Right. When you write a class specification you're creating your own data types and telling the compiler how to operate with them. With basic types that are built into the compiler, all that's invisible; you don't even need to think about it.

CHAPTER 6

OPERATOR OVERLOADING

You've seen how functions can be overloaded so that calls to a single function *name* can actually invoke different *functions*, provided the arguments are different. This has advantages for the class user, such as not needing to remember so many names.

It is also possible to overload the built-in C++ operators such as **+**, **>=**, and **++** so that they too invoke different functions, depending on their operands. That is, the **+** in **a+b** will call one function if **a** and **b** are integers, but will call a different function if **a** and **b** are objects of a class you've created. Operator overloading is another C++ convenience feature that can make your program easier to write and to understand.

In this chapter, you'll find out how to overload the C++ operators so you can define their operation for objects of your own classes. I'll begin with binary arithmetic operators such as +, -, * and / then move on to comparison operators such as < and >= and assignment operators such as +=. Next, I'll talk about unary operators such as ++, --, and the negative sign (as in -a).

The topic of data conversion is closely related to that of overloaded operators. You've seen that you can use one-argument constructors to convert from basic types to class types. To go the other way, from objects to basic types, you can overload the built-in *cast operators* such as int(), float(), and long().

The assignment operator (=) is an important special case of operator overloading, so I'll discuss it in some detail. I'll also show you how to overload the subscript operator, [], so you can make your own kinds of arrays. Finally, I'll introduce some techniques that make overloaded operators safer and more efficient.

OVERLOADING BINARY ARITHMETIC OPERATORS

The C++ operators can be divided roughly into binary and unary. Binary operators take two arguments. Examples are a+b, a-b, a/b, and so on. Unary operators take only one argument: -a, ++a, a--. (There is also one ternary operator—meaning it takes three arguments—in C++, the *conditional operator* (?:), but we won't worry about overloading it).

For a discussion of overloaded operators, it makes sense to discuss the binary operators first, because they are the most straightforward, and then move on to the somewhat more obscure unary operators.

Why Overload Operators?

An overloaded operator, when applied to objects (not to basic types), can carry out whatever operation the class creator wants. The + operator can concatenate two xString objects, add two airtime objects, and so on.

Why would you want to overload operators? The basic reason is that you want to make your listing easier to read. Perhaps the most familiar operator is the plus sign (+), so I'll begin my exploration of overloading with that. Suppose you want to add two values of type airtime and to assign the result to another airtime variable. It's considerably easier to understand what's happening when you see

```
at3 = at1 + at2;
```

than when the same operation is expressed as

```
at3 = at1.sum(at2);
```

or the even less obvious

```
at3.sum(at1, at2);
```

You Could Do It with Functions

Overloading doesn't actually add any capabilities to C++. Everything you can do with an overloaded operator you can also do with a function. However, by making your listing more intuitive, overloaded operators make your programs easier to write, read, and maintain. They are also a lot of fun to create and to use.

You might think of overloaded operators as a way to transfer some of the labor from the class user to the class creator. If the class creator spends a little time overloading operators for appropriate tasks, the class user can spend less time writing the code that invokes these tasks, because the operations will be more intuitive.

Not for All Classes

Some kinds of classes lend themselves to using overloaded operators, but others don't. If you're talking about objects of class **employee**, for example, it probably doesn't make sense to say

```
emp3 = emp1 + emp2;
```

After all, what would it mean to add two employees together? Of course, if you do come up with a reasonable meaning for the + operator in this context, you are free to overload it. In general, however, overloaded operators are best used with classes that represent numerical data types. Examples are times, dates, imaginary numbers (x+iy), and geographical positions. String classes can also profit from overloaded operators.

You Can't Overload Everything

Incidentally, you can't overload operators that don't already exist in C++. You can't make up a ****** operator for (say) exponentiation or a **<-** operator for some other obscure purpose. You can overload only the built-in operators. Even a few of these, such as the dot operator (**.**), the scope resolution operator (**::**), the conditional operator (**?:**), and several others you haven't encountered yet, can't be overloaded.

The `operatorX()` Function

Let's see how to overload the + operator for **airtime** objects. Suppose you want to arrange things so that

```
at3 = at1 + at2;
```

has the same effect as

```
at3 = at1.sum(at2);
```

How do you write an equivalent of the **sum()** member function that will enable the + sign to carry out the addition operation? C++ uses a new keyword called **operator**, which is followed by the operator itself, to form a function name. To overload the + operator, the name is **operator+** (to which you normally append parentheses to show that it's a function). Here's an **operator+()** member function for the **airtime** class, in skeleton form:

```
airtime operator+(airtime right)
    {
    // needs function body
    }
```

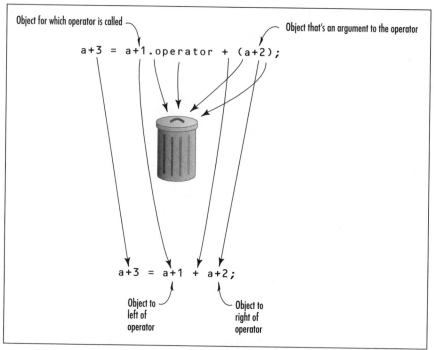

Figure 6-1 Syntax of overloaded operator

Now, you might think you need to invoke this member function in the ordinary way, like this:

```
at3 = at1.operator+(at2);
```

This actually works—it adds **at2** to **at1** and returns the result—but it doesn't gain much in terms of readability. The payoff comes when you rearrange the syntax, as shown in Figure 6-1.

The dot operator, the word operator itself, and the parentheses surrounding the function argument aren't necessary. They can all be removed, leaving only

```
at3 = at1 + at2;
```

This same syntax holds true for any binary operator x. The function `operatorX()` enables the operator to be used alone, with the other parts of the syntax being understood.

Adding airtime Objects

Let's look at a complete program that overloads the + operator for the **airtime** class. Listing 6-1 shows ADDAIR.

Listing 6-1 ADDAIR

```
// addair.cpp
// class models time data type
// overloads the + operator
#include <iostream.h>
```

```
class airtime
    {
    private:
        int hours;              // 0 to 23
        int minutes;            // 0 to 59
    public:
        void display() const    // output to screen
            {
            cout << hours << ':' << minutes;
            }

        void get()                  // input from user
            {
            char dummy;
            cout << "\nEnter time (format 12:59): ";
            cin >> hours >> dummy >> minutes;
            }
                                    // overloaded + operator
        airtime operator + (airtime right)
            {
            airtime temp;           // make a temporary object
            temp.hours = hours + right.hours;   // add data
            temp.minutes = minutes + right.minutes;
            if(temp.minutes >= 60)              // check for carry
                {
                temp.hours++;
                temp.minutes -= 60;
                }
            return temp;            // return temporary object
            }

    };  // end class airtime

void main()
    {
    airtime at1, at2, at3;
    cout << "Enter first airtime: ";
    at1.get();
    cout << "Enter second airtime: ";
    at2.get();

    at3 = at1 + at2;            // overloaded + operator
                               //     adds at2 to at1
    cout << "sum = ";
    at3.display();             // display sum
    }
```

Notice how easy it is to understand what's going on in main(). The overloaded + makes the addition look just like addition with basic types.

Arguments

The `operator+()` function in the `airtime` class works like the `add()` function in the TIMEADD program (see Chapter 2, Session 7). It adds the hours, adds the minutes, and checks if the minutes overflow past 59. (For brevity, I've left out the code that checks if the hours exceed 23.)

However, notice where the input operands are placed in `operator+()`. The `airtime` variable on the right of the + operator, which is called `at2` in `main()`, becomes the single argument to `operator+()`.

Where does `at1`, the variable on the left side of the + operator in `main()`, show up in `operator+()` in the class specification? It's the object for which `operator+()` was called. That is, it's the object to which the `operator+()` message was sent. This message tells `at1` to add itself to `at2` and to return the result. Notice that there will always be one less argument to `operator+()` than there are operands to an   `operator x`. That's because one operand (the one on the left, for binary operators) is the object for which the function was called. (This rule doesn't apply to friend functions, which I'll introduce in   Chapter 9.)

Return Value

In `main()`, the return value from the addition is assigned to `at3` in the usual way. In the `operator+()` function, this is accomplished by returning the local `airtime` object, `temp`, by value. The result of an addition of two `airtime` values is another `airtime` value, so this must be the return value of `operator+()`. The `temp` object is used to hold the results of the calculations and is the object that is returned.

Creating a temporary object as I do with `temp` is not very efficient. The object's constructor must be called, and its destructor must be called when the function terminates and the object goes out of scope. Also, because this object is returned by value, the copy constructor must be called when the function returns. I can make some improvements in the way things are handled, as you'll see later in this chapter.

Adding `xString` Objects

For a nonnumeric example, I'll overload the + operator so it can be used to concatenate two `xString` objects (last seen in the STRCON program in Chapter 5, Session 3). That is, if you have two `xStrings`, "dog" and "fish", they will be concatenated to form "dogfish" (a kind of small shark). The result will be returned from the operator, where it can be assigned to another `xString` object. Listing 6-2 shows STRPLUS.

Listing 6-2 STRPLUS

```
// strplus.cpp
// overloads + operator to concatenate xStrings
#include <iostream.h>
#include <string.h>                    // for strlen(), strcpy(), etc.

class xString
   {
   private:
      enum {MAX=80};                   // maximum length of xStrings
      char str[MAX];                   // ordinary C string
   public:
      xString()                        // no-arg constructor
```

```
         { strcpy(str, ""); }
     xString( char s[] )        // 1-arg constructor
         { strcpy(str, s); }
     void input()               // get string from user
         { cin.get(str, MAX); }
     void display()             // display string
         { cout << str; }
                                // concatenate two strings
     xString operator+(xString right)
         {
         xString temp;                    // temporary xString
         if(strlen(str) + strlen(right.str) < MAX-1)
             {
             strcpy(temp.str, str);       // copy us to temp
             strcat(temp.str, right.str); // concatenate argument
             }
         else
             cout << "\nError: xString too long" << endl;
         return temp;                     // return temporary
         }
     };

void main()
    {
    xString s1("Greetings, ");
    xString s2, s3;

    cout << "Enter your name: ";
    s2.input();              // get s2 from user

    s3 = s1 + s2 + ".";  // concatenate period to s2, s2 to s1
    s3.display();            // display s3
    }
```

The `operator+()` function creates a temporary xString object, temp, because it needs a "work area" and it doesn't want to modify its own object (or its argument). It first checks to be sure there's room for the concatenated string. Then it copies its own object to temp with the strcpy() library function, concatenates the argument onto temp with strcat(), and returns temp.

In main(), the program initializes the xString s1 to "Greetings"; gets another string, s2, from the user; concatenates them; and assigns the result to s3. Then it displays s3. Here's some sample interaction:

```
Enter your name: George Bernard Shaw
Greetings, George Bernard Shaw.
```

Other Binary Arithmetic Operators

You can overload the other binary arithmetic operators, such as -, *, and /, in similar ways. The exercises in this session include several examples and you'll encounter others later on.

QUIZ 1

1. Which of the following are valid reasons for overloading an operator?
   a. To make it possible to perform arithmetic on objects of user-defined classes.
   b. To have fun.
   c. To clarify the listing.
   d. To speed up the program.
   e. To make the program more memory efficient.

2. What is the name of the function that overloads the + operator for the `airtime` class?
   a. `add`
   b. `airtime add`
   c. `+`
   d. `operator+`
   e. `operator`

3. The argument to an overloaded binary operator function such as `operator+()`
   a. represents the operand on the left side of the + operator.
   b. represents the operand on the right side of the + operator.
   c. is the variable to which the sum is assigned.
   d. is the temporary variable that is returned from the function.
   e. is not necessary.

4. In the ADDAIR program, the return value of `operator+()` is
   a. an `airtime` value.
   b. type `void`.
   c. an `int` value.
   d. assigned to `at3` in `main()`.
   e. actually serves no purpose, because the results of the addition are placed in the object for which the function was called.

5. The named temporary object `temp`, defined in `operator+()` in the `airtime` class in ADDAIR,
   a. is used as a dummy variable and never contains valid data.
   b. would need to be of the `widget` class if you were adding two `widget` objects.
   c. is returned by reference.
   d. is an instance variable.
   e. must be constructed and destroyed whenever `operator+()` is called.

EXERCISE 1

Overload the subtraction operator to subtract one `airtime` value from another. Write some statements in `main()` to exercise this function. Assume that the earlier (smaller) time will always be subtracted from the later (larger) one, so you don't need to consider negative times.

EXERCISE 2

It doesn't make sense to multiply one `airtime` value by another. After all, there's no such thing as time squared (that I know about, anyway). However, it's perfectly reasonable to multiply an `airtime` value by an ordinary number, say of type `float`. This lets you calculate things like how long an airplane has been in the air since its last inspection or if it has made 36 one-way flights between Austin and Boston, each of which lasted 3 hours and 45 minutes. Overload the `*` operator for the `airtime` class so it multiplies an `airtime` by a `float`. Write some statements in `main()` to test it.

SESSION 2

OVERLOADING OTHER BINARY OPERATORS

The overloaded arithmetic operators typified by `operator+()`, which I discussed in the last session, perform an operation on two values of some type and return another value of the same type. They are used, at least in this example, by calling them for the object on the left of the operator, with the object on the right of the operator as an argument. (Later I'll show how both operands can be made into arguments by using friend functions, but don't worry about that now.)

Neither the object for which they are called nor their argument is modified. This is one scenario and it applies to some operators, notably the arithmetic operators. However, there is a wide variety of other ways to use overloaded binary operators. They may return values of types other than their class or take arguments of types other than their class. (Exercise 2 in the last session showed one possibility, with an argument of type `float`.)

In this session, I'll show several other common ways that binary operators are used and discuss the relational operator `<` and the assignment operator `+=`.

Relational Operators

When you compare integers with a relational operator, the answer returned is a true/false value; in C++, false is 0 and true is any other value. You can use a simple `int` variable to hold true/false values, but this is a little obscure. It's clearer and more self-explanatory to use an `enum` declaration to give names to such true/false values:

```
enum boolean {false=0, true};
```

I'll use this declaration in the next example, which overloads the `<` operator to compare two `airtime` values and return a value of type `boolean`. The skeleton for this operator looks like this:

```
boolean operator< (const airtime& right)
    {
    // statements
    }
```

When it's called for an object, this operator compares its own object with its argument, called right, and returns true if its object is less than right and false otherwise. Listing 6-3 shows COMPAIR.

Listing 6-3 COMPAIR

```cpp
// compair.cpp
// overloads the < operator
#include <iostream.h>

class airtime
    {
    private:
        int hours;              // 0 to 23
        int minutes;            // 0 to 59
    public:
        void display() const    // output to screen
            {
            cout << hours << ':' << minutes;
            }
        void get()              // input from user
            {
            char dummy;
            cout << "\nEnter time (format 12:59): ";
            cin >> hours >> dummy >> minutes;
            }
                                // overloaded < operator
        bool operator<(const airtime& right)
            {
            if(hours < right.hours)
                return true;
            if(hours == right.hours && minutes < right.minutes)
                return true;
            return false;
            }
    };  // end class airtime

void main()
    {
    airtime at1, at2;
    cout << "Enter first airtime: ";
    at1.get();
    cout << "Enter second airtime: ";
    at2.get();

    if(at1 < at2)
        cout << "\nfirst less than second";
    else
        cout << "\nfirst not less than second";
    }
```

In main(), the program uses the relational operator < to compare two airtime values in the expression

```cpp
if(at1 < at2)
```

The overloaded < operator makes this look like a normal comparison with basic types. As you can see by experimenting with this program, it tells you which of two `airtime`s is less than the other. Here's a sample interaction:

```
Enter first airtime:
Enter time (format 12:59): 3:59
Enter second airtime:
Enter time (format 12:59): 4:00

first less than second
```

How It Works

The member function `operator<()` first compares the `hours` member for its own object and its argument object. If its own object's `hours` is less, then it knows its whole `airtime` value is less than its argument. Otherwise, it checks the `minutes` value. If the `hours` are equal and the `minutes` are less, then again its own object is less. In all other cases, its own object is equal to or larger than its argument. The function returns the appropriate `boolean` true/false value to reflect this fact.

Passing the Argument by `const` *Reference*

I pass this argument by reference because I don't want an unnecessary copy of it to be created. Then, to prevent `operator+()` from accidentally modifying the original object, I make the argument `const`, as I've discussed before. In the programs in the last session, ADDAIR and STRPLUS, I passed the argument to the `operator+()` function by value to simplify the listings. However, for maximum efficiency, they should also have been passed by constant reference.

Notice that, in the COMPAIR example, no constructors are needed in the `airtime` class. The `operator<()` function doesn't use them. This is unlike the `operator+()` function in the examples in Session 1 in this chapter, which required a constructor to create a temporary object to be returned. Figure 6-2 shows the difference.

Assignment Operators

Another important category of operators that can be overloaded is the assignment operators, which include +=, -=, *=, /=, and other more obscure operators. In the example, I'll examine +=. The major difference between "normal" binary operators such as + and assignment operators such as += is that assignment operators modify the object for which they are called. If you say

```
at1 += at2;
```

then the function `operator+=()` is called for the `at1` object and `at1` is modified (by having `at2` added to it). You're sending a message to `at1` saying, "Add this argument to yourself." By contrast, the message with the normal addition `operator+()` is "add yourself to this argument and return the result."

Although the primary purpose of an assignment operator is to modify the object for which it was called, it's common for it to return a value as well. You want to be able to say

```
at3 = at1 += at2;
```

where the result of the += operation is assigned to `at3` as well as `at1`. Assignment operators typically return a value of their own class to make this sort of chaining possible, even though this return value is not always used.

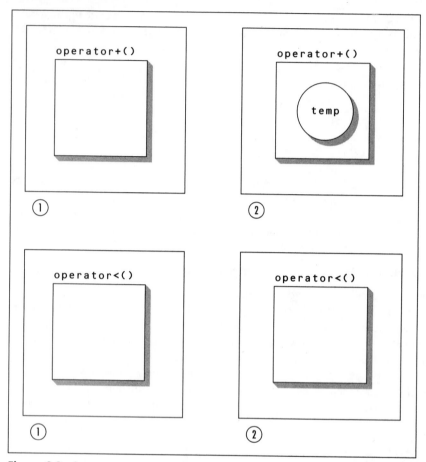

Figure 6-2   Some operators create a new object

The example, PLEQAIR, following a long tradition, will overload the += operator for the airtime class. Listing 6-4 shows PLEQAIR.

Listing 6-4 PLEQAIR

```
// pleqair.cpp
// overloads the += operator
#include <iostream.h>

class airtime
    {
    private:
        int hours;          // 0 to 23
        int minutes;        // 0 to 59
    public:
                            // no-arg constructor
        airtime() : hours(0), minutes(0)
```

```
      { }
                              // 2-arg constructor
   airtime(int h, int m) : hours(h), minutes(m)
      { }

   void display() const      // output to screen
      {
      cout << hours << ':' << minutes;
      }

   void get()                // input from user
      {
      char dummy;
      cout << "\nEnter time (format 12:59): ";
      cin >> hours >> dummy >> minutes;
      }
                              // overloaded += operator
   airtime operator += (const airtime& right)
      {
      hours += right.hours;         // add argument to us
      minutes += right.minutes;
      if(minutes >= 60)             // check for carry
         { hours++; minutes -= 60; }
      return airtime(hours, minutes);   // return our new value
      }
}; // end class airtime

void main()
   {
   airtime at1, at2, at3;
   cout << "Enter first airtime: ";
   at1.get();
   cout << "Enter second airtime: ";
   at2.get();

   at1 += at2;                // overloaded += operator
                              // adds at2 to at1
   cout << "\nat1+=at2 = ";
   at1.display();            // display result

   at3 = at1 += at2;         // do it again, use return value
   cout << "\nat3 = ";
   at3.display();           // display result
   }
```

In main(), I show the assignment operator used twice: once where no value is returned and once where one is. Here's some interaction:

```
Enter first airtime:
Enter time (format 12:59): 10:30
Enter second airtime:
Enter time (format 12:59): 0:10
```

continued on next page

continued from previous page
```
at1+=at2 = 10:40
at3 = 10:50
```

In a similar way, you can overload the other assignment operators `-=`, `*=`, `/=`, and so on. Overloading the assignment operator `=`, however, is a somewhat more complex operation that I'll discuss in Session 6 in this chapter.

Avoiding Temporary Objects

Notice how the program returns the result of the addition in the `operator+=()` function in PLEQAIR:

```
return airtime(hours, minutes);
```

This is a very special kind of statement. It looks like a constructor, and you might think it will cause the creation of a new `airtime` object. However, the C++ compiler, which is sometimes unnervingly clever, realizes that all I want to do here is return a value. Consequently, it doesn't create a temporary object within the function. The only object that's created is the return value in `main()`, which is always necessary when returning by value. The first time `operator+=()` is called, this return value is not used; the second time, it's assigned to `at3`.

Avoiding the creation of a temporary object within `operator+=()` saves time and memory space and is clearly a good idea. Why didn't I do this in `operator+()` in the last lesson? Because I needed a place to store intermediate calculations (the addition results before I checked for a carry). However, I could have created temporary `int` variables for this purpose instead:

```
                        // overloaded + operator
airtime operator + (const airtime& right)
   {
   int thrs = hours + right.hours;    // add data
   int tmins = minutes + right.minutes;
   if(tmins >= 60)                     // check for carry
      { thrs++; tmins -= 60; }
   return airtime(thrs, tmins);        // return unnamed
   }                                   // temporary object
```

This could be a better approach, if creating and destroying individual member data items is faster than creating and destroying a complete object.

1. In the overloaded `<` operator for `airtime` values in COMPAIR, the `operator<()` function
   a. returns a value of type `boolean`.
   b. returns a value of type `int`.
   c. returns an `airtime` object.
   d. compares two objects passed as arguments.
   e. compares the object for which it was called with the object passed as an argument.

2. Why did I not construct a temporary `airtime` object in the `operator<()` function in the COMPAIR program, as I did for the `operator+()` function in the ADDAIR program?
   a. A comparison doesn't require a value to be returned, whereas addition does.

b. A comparison returns a `boolean`, whereas addition returns an `airtime`.
c. Constructing a temporary object would have worked just as well.
d. The result of the comparison was not an object.
e. I hadn't yet learned how inefficient such temporary objects were.

3. The `operator +=()` function in the `airtime` class in the PLEQAIR program
   a. alters an unnamed temporary object.
   b. alters the value of the object for which it was called.
   c. performs addition on two `airtime` objects.
   d. returns the value of the object that called it.
   e. returns the sum of two `airtime` objects.

4. Every time you overload the `+=` operator for a class, you necessarily give this operator the ability to
   a. add an object to the object for which the operator was called.
   b. add the argument to `operator+=()` to itself.
   c. add two objects without modifying them.
   d. return the result of an addition.
   e. create a new numerical value.

5. Returning an unnamed temporary object from a member function using a statement such as

   ```
   return classname(arg1, arg2);
   ```

   causes a call to

   a. the two-argument constructor and the destructor, before the function terminates.
   b. the two-argument constructor, to make an object in `main()`.
   c. the copy constructor, when the function is called.
   d. the copy constructor, when the function returns.
   e. the two-argument constructor twice, once to create the temporary object and once to create the return value.

EXERCISE 1

Overload the `>=` operator in the `airtime` class. Write some statements in `main()` to demonstrate that it works correctly.

EXERCISE 2

Overload the `*=` operator for the `airtime` class. Write some statements in `main()` to demonstrate that it works correctly.

SESSION 3

OVERLOADING UNARY OPERATORS

Unary operators operate on a single operand. Examples are the increment (++) and decrement (--) operators; the unary minus, as in -28; and the logical not (!) operator. The most commonly overloaded unary operators are the increment and decrement operators. I'll show how the ++ operator is overloaded; the -- operator is similar. As you know, these operators can be used in either prefix or postfix form. I'll show the prefix version first and the unary minus later.

Prefix Version of Operator ++

Unary operators take no arguments (at least in the member function versions I show here; they take one argument if you use friend functions, which you'll encounter in Chapter 9). They operate on the object for which they were called. Normally, this operator appears on the left side of the object, as in !obj, -obj, and ++obj. Most of the unary operators can appear only with the object on the left, but the ++ and -- operators can be either on the left (prefix) or on the right (postfix). The prefix version is thus the "normal" one and the postfix version is the exception.

Listing 6-5 shows PREFIX, in which the prefix version of the ++ operator is overloaded for the airtime class.

Listing 6-5 PREFIX

```
// prefix.cpp
// overloads the ++ operator, prefix version
#include <iostream.h>

class airtime
    {
    private:
        int hours;              // 0 to 23
        int minutes;            // 0 to 59
    public:
                                // no-arg constructor
        airtime() : hours(0), minutes(0)
            {  }
                                // 2-arg constructor
        airtime(int h, int m) : hours(h), minutes(m)
            {  }

        void display() const    // output to screen
            {
            cout << hours << ':' << minutes;
            }

        void get()              // input from user
            {
            char dummy;
            cout << "\nEnter time (format 12:59): ";
```

```
            cin >> hours >> dummy >> minutes;
            }

       airtime operator++ ()   // overloaded prefix ++ operator
            {
            ++minutes;            // increment this object
            if(minutes >= 60)
               {
               ++hours;
               minutes -= 60;
               }              // return new value
            return airtime(hours, minutes);
            }
    };   // end class airtime

void main()
    {
    airtime at1, at2;          // make two airtimes
    at1.get();                 // get value for one

    ++at1;                     // increment it
    cout << "\nat1=";
    at1.display();             // display result

//  at1++;                     // error: postfix

    at2 = ++at1;               // increment again, and assign
    cout << "\nat2=";
    at2.display();             // display assigned value
    }
```

The first use of ++ in main() adds 1 minute to the airtime object for which it was called, handling the carry if necessary. (Of course, you can define an overloaded operator however you want. You could increment the hours, if you wish, and leave the minutes alone, as happens when you change time zones.)

Do I return the old value of the object before it was incremented, or the new value? Because it's a prefix operator, which increments the operand *before* it's used in any other calculations, I return the new value.

Here's some interaction when the user enters 7:35 into the program:

```
Enter time(format 12:59): 7:35
at1=7:36
at2=7:37
```

In main(), the program gets a time, at1, from the user (7:35 in this example), increments it, and displays the result (7:36). The commented-out statement shows that the compiler will issue a warning if you try to use the postfix version of an operator when you have defined only the prefix version. Next, the program increments at1 again and in the same statement assigns it to at2. Then it displays at2. Because at1 is incremented *before* the assignment, at2 is assigned the new value of 7:37.

Postfix Version of Operator ++

The next example demonstrates the postfix version of the overloaded ++ operator. How does the compiler distinguish between the prefix and the postfix versions of operator++()? The answer is rather arbitrary and not very elegant: A dummy argument with a data type of int is inserted to indicate the postfix version.

```
airtime operator++ ()        // prefix version
airtime operator++ (int)     // postfix version
```

You don't actually supply a value for this dummy argument; the mere inclusion of the int is enough to let the compiler know it's postfix. Listing 6-6 shows POSTFIX, which includes both prefix and postfix versions of the ++ operator.

Listing 6-6 POSTFIX

```cpp
// postfix.cpp
// overloads the ++ operator, postfix and prefix versions
#include <iostream.h>

class airtime
   {
   private:
      int hours;              // 0 to 23
      int minutes;            // 0 to 59
   public:
                              // no-arg constructor
      airtime() : hours(0), minutes(0)
         { }
                              // 2-arg constructor
      airtime(int h, int m) : hours(h), minutes(m)
         { }

      void display() const    // output to screen
         {
         cout << hours << ':' << minutes;
         }

      void get()              // input from user
         {
         char dummy;
         cout << "\nEnter time (format 12:59): ";
         cin >> hours >> dummy >> minutes;
         }

      airtime operator++ ()   // overloaded prefix ++ operator
         {
         ++minutes;           // increment this object
         if(minutes >= 60)
            {
            ++hours;
            minutes -= 60;
            }                 // return incremented value
```

```
        return airtime(hours, minutes);
        }

    airtime operator++ (int)          // overloaded postfix ++ operator
        {
        airtime temp(hours, minutes);  // save original value
        ++minutes;                     // increment this object
        if(minutes >= 60)
            {
            ++hours;
            minutes -= 60;
            }
        return temp;                   // return old original value
        }
    };  // end class airtime
/////////////////////////////////////////////////////////////////////
void main()
    {
    airtime at1, at2;        // make two airtimes
    at1.get();               // get value for one

    at2 = ++at1;             // increment it (prefix) and assign
    cout << "\nat2=";
    at2.display();           // display result

    at2 = at1++;             // increment (postfix) and assign
    cout << "\nat1=";
    at1.display();           // display incremented value
    cout << "\nat2=";
    at2.display();           // display assigned value
    }
```

The postfix function `operator++(int)` operates differently from the prefix function `operator++()`. The postfix version must remember the original value of its object, increment the object, and then return the original value, not the new value. This is accomplished by creating a temporary object, `temp`, that is initialized to the original value of the object. After the object is incremented, `temp` is returned. Figure 6-3 shows how this compares with the prefix version.

Here's some sample interaction with POSTFIX:

```
Enter time (format 12:59): 7:35
at2=7:36
at1=7:37
at2=7:36
```

The user enters a time for `at1`. The program increments it with the prefix operator, assigns it to `at2`, and displays `at2`. Because `at1` was incremented before being assigned, `at2` reflects the new value of 7:36. Now the program increments `at1` again, this time with the postfix operator, and assigns it to `at2`. This time, because it was assigned before being incremented, `at2` retains the original value of 7:36, whereas `at1` is now 7:37.

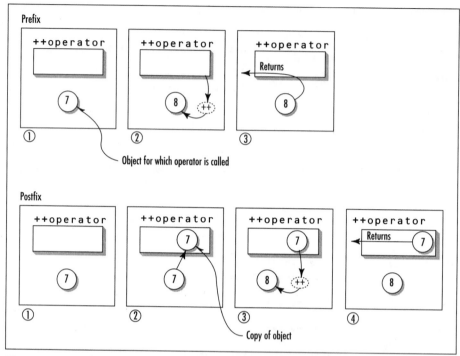

Figure 6-3   Prefix and postfix versions of ++ operator

The Unary Minus Operator

I'll close this session with a look at another unary operator: the negative sign. When you say something like

```
alpha = -beta;
```

you're assigning the negative of **beta** to **alpha**. You know what it means to change the sign of an ordinary number. If beta is an **int** with a value of 7, then **alpha** will be -7. But what does the negative sign do with class objects? If you're the class creator, you can handle it however you like.

Let's look at an example using the **English** class. Perhaps you plan to subtract one English value from another, so you want to be able to handle negative English values. We'll assume negative values are indicated by making the **feet** member, but not **inches**, negative. (There are other options: You could make **inches** negative, or make both **feet** and **inches** negative, or use a third member, possibly **boolean**, to indicate a negative value.)

Listing 6-7 shows NEGENGL, which overloads both the binary subtraction operator and the unary minus.

Listing 6-7 NEGENGL

```
// negengl.cpp
// overloads the unary minus for English class
```

```cpp
#include <iostream.h>

class English                         // English distances
    {
    private:
        int feet;
        float inches;
    public:                           // no-argument constructor
        English() : feet(0), inches(0.0)
            {  }
                                      // 2-argument constructor
        English(int f, float i) : feet(f), inches(i)
            {  }

        void get()                    // user input
            {
            cout << "   Enter feet: ";   cin >> feet;
            cout << "   Enter inches: "; cin >> inches;
            }

        void display()                // display
            {
            if(feet<0)
                cout << "-(" << -feet << "\'-" << inches << "\")";
            else
                cout << feet << "\'-" << inches << '\"';
            }

        English operator-()           // negation operator
            {                         // (unary minus)
            return English(-feet, inches);
            }
                                      // subtraction operator
        English operator-(English right)
            {
            int tfeet = feet - right.feet;
            int tinches = inches - right.inches;
            if(tinches < 0)
                {
                tinches += 12.0;
                tfeet -=1;
                }
            return English(tfeet, tinches);
            }
    };  // end English class

void main()
    {
    English man(6, 2.0);
    English horse(7, 0.0);
    English difference;

    difference = man - horse;         // subtraction
```

continued on next page

continued from previous page
```
cout << "\ndifference = ";
difference.display();

difference = -difference;      // unary minus
cout << "\n-difference = ";
difference.display();
}
```

The job of the unary minus function `operator-()` is to return the value of the object for which it was called, but with the sign of the `feet` member changed. This operator does not change the value of its own object.

The subtraction function `operator-(English)` works like the addition functions you've seen for the `airtime` class. It subtracts the appropriate values, checks for a carry, and returns the result without changing either its own object or the argument.

I've changed the `display()` member function so it can print out negative English values. The format for this is to surround the value with parentheses and to precede the result with a minus sign, as in `-(1'-2")`, which means minus the distance one foot two inches.

In `main()`, the program initializes two English variables and subtracts one from the other, yielding a negative result, which it places in a third English variable, `difference`. It displays `difference`, negates it with the unary minus operator, and displays it again. Here's the output from NEGENGL:

```
difference = -(1'-2")
-difference = 1'-2"
```

The unary plus operator (as in `+alpha`) can be overloaded in a way similar to that of the unary minus, except that it (usually) doesn't need to do anything. Plus is the default sign, so applying it causes no change.

QUIZ 3

1. A unary operator x
   a. is called "unary" because `operatorX()` takes only one argument.
   b. is called "unary" because x takes only one operand.
   c. always changes the object for which it's called.
   d. usually returns a value.
   e. is normally written immediately following a variable name.

2. The prefix version of the `++` operator, overloaded as a member function of class x, probably has the declarator
   a. `void operator++(X)`
   b. `void operator++()`
   c. `void operator++(int)`
   d. `X operator++(int)`
   e. `X operator++()`

3. The postfix and prefix versions of the `++` operator for the `airtime` class differ in that
   a. the prefix version returns its object's value after it has been incremented.

   b. the postfix version increments the object and then returns its value.
   c. the prefix operator is applied after the object is used in other calculations.
   d. the prefix version increments the value passed as an argument.
   e. the postfix version increments the value for which it was called.

4. Overloading the unary minus operator (-) for the `airtime` class
   a. could be handled in much the same way as it was in the `English` class.
   b. would lead to syntactic difficulties.
   c. would probably require a way to display negative `airtime` values.
   d. could never make sense, because there is no such thing as "minus time."
   e. would be handled similarly to overloading the binary + operator.

5. The unary minus operator, overloaded as a member function for class x,
   a. changes the object for which it was called to the negative of its former value.
   b. returns a value that is the negative of the object for which it was called.
   c. negates its argument.
   d. subtracts its argument from the object for which it was called.
   e. can perform "negation" however it wants.

EXERCISE 1

Overload the decrement (--) operator for the `English` class and write some statements in `main()` to check that it operates correctly.

EXERCISE 2

Overload the unary minus (-at) for the `airtime` class and write some statements in `main()` to check that it operates correctly.

CONVERSION FROM OBJECTS TO BASIC TYPES

It's surprising how important the topic of data conversion becomes when class objects are being discussed. When you operate exclusively on basic types (as in C or other non-object-oriented languages), you don't notice this conversion process so much. Partly that's because it's automatic. If you say

```
floatvar = intvar;
```

where `floatvar` is type `float` and `intvar` is type `int`, the conversion takes place invisibly, with no complaint from the compiler. The appropriate conversion routines for basic types are built in.

This is not the case with classes. If I write a class and I want to convert between basic types and class objects, or between objects of different classes, then I must write the conversion routines myself.

Conversions can be divided into several categories. These are

- From basic types to objects

- From objects to basic types

- From objects to objects of another class

You've already seen several examples of converting basic types to objects. This conversion is conveniently handled by the one-argument constructor, where the argument is the basic type. In Chapter 5, Session 3, you saw how ordinary strings were converted to `xString` objects in STRCON and how a type `float` quantity representing meters was converted to an `English` object in ENGLCON.

The second category, conversion from objects to basic types, is the subject of this session. Conversion from objects of one class to objects of a different class is discussed in the next session.

Type Casting: Conversion for Basic Types

Before you see how to convert objects to basic types, let's see how to use explicit conversion operators to convert one basic type to another. The same format is used in both cases.

As I noted, conversions between basic types often take place automatically, with no intervention from the programmer. However, there are times when the programmer needs to tell the compiler to make a conversion explicitly. As an example, let's look at a small function that breaks a floating-point number into a whole number part and a fractional part. If I give this function, which I'll call `parts()`, the number 123.45, for example, it will break it into a whole number part of 123.0 and a fractional part of 0.45. All these numbers are type `float`. Here's how the function looks:

```
float parts(const float& orig, float& fracpart)
   {
   float wholepart = int(orig);      // find whole part
   fracpart = orig - wholepart;      // find fractional part
   return wholepart;                 // return whole part
   }
```

The first argument to the function is the original number. The second argument is where the function will place the fractional part. The function will return the whole number part. You can call the function this way:

```
wpart = parts(original_number, fpart);      // call to function
```

The key to the operation of this function is the statement

```
float wholepart = int(orig);    // find whole part
```

which strips off the fractional part of the floating-point number `orig` and assigns the remaining whole number part to `wholepart`. How does it get rid of the fractional part? By converting `orig` to a type `int`, which has no fractional part. This conversion is accomplished by *casting* `orig` to type `int`. A cast is an explicit conversion of one type to another. Here the keyword `int` is used as if it were a function name; it's called the `int` operator. The variable to be converted is its argument and the return value is the type implied by its name. Figure 6-4 shows the syntax. Casting can be used this way to convert any basic type to any other basic type.

Type casting is a semidangerous practice. Why? For one reason, you may lose information (e.g., converting from `long` to `int` may entail the loss of significant digits). More importantly, *typing*, or making sure that variables interact only with variables of their own type, is an important technique in preventing errors. If you find yourself assigning a `float` to an `int`, you may be making a conceptual mistake. Casting should therefore never be done merely for the sake of expediency, to fix something that doesn't seem to work, but only when it's obviously necessary.

I should mention that there's another format for type casting. Besides using the so-called "functional" syntax (because it looks like a function),

```
var2 = long(var1);  // "functional" syntax
```

to convert `var1` to type `long`, you can also say

```
var2 = (long)var1;  // alternative syntax (not recommended)
```

This second form is the old-fashioned syntax used in C. It is not the preferred approach, but occasionally it works in situations where the preferred syntax does not.

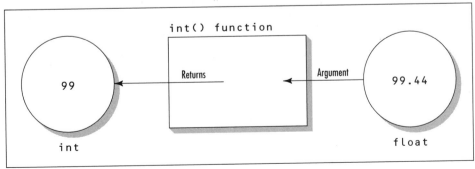

Figure 6-4   Casting from one type to another

Conversion from `English` to `float`

You can use the cast syntax to convert a class object to a basic type. The only difference is that the class creator must write the routine to handle the conversion. This is done using the same `operator` keyword I've used before to overload operators. For example, here's how you'd write a member function to convert a class object to type `long`:

```
operator long()
   {
   // conversion performed here
   return longvar;
   }
```

Although this function returns a `long`, no return type is specified; it's implied in the name of the function. As you've seen, this `long()` operator works for basic types, but you can overload it to work with your own classes.

As an example, we'll see how to convert an `English` object (feet and inches) to a `float` type (representing meters), using the overloaded `float()` operator. Listing 6-8 shows ENGLCONV.

Listing 6-8 ENGLCONV

```
// englconv.cpp
// converts English objects to meters

#include <iostream.h>

class English                           // English distances
   {
   private:
      int feet;
      float inches;
      static const float MTF;           // meters to feet, declaration
   public:                              // no-argument constructor
      English() : feet(0), inches(0.0)
         { }

      English(float meters)             // 1-argument constructor
         {
         float fltfeet = MTF * meters;  // get decimal feet
         feet = int(fltfeet);           // integer part is feet
         inches = 12 * (fltfeet-feet);  // remainder is inches
         }
                                        // 2-argument constructor
      English(int f, float i) : feet(f), inches(i)
         { }

      void get()                        // user input
         {
         cout << "   Enter feet: ";   cin >> feet;
         cout << "   Enter inches: "; cin >> inches;
         }

      void display()                    // display
```

```
     {
     cout << feet << "\'-" << inches << '\"';
     }
   operator float()                    // convert English to float
     {
     float fracfeet = inches/12;       // inches to feet
     fracfeet += float(feet);          // add the feet
     return fracfeet/MTF;              // convert to meters
     }                                 // and return
};   // end English class

const float English::MTF = 3.280833;   // meters to feet,
                                       // definition
void main()
  {
  English engman(1.9);                 // meters to English
  cout << "\nengman = ";
  engman.display();                    // display English

  float metman;
  metman = float(engman);              // English to meters
  cout << "\nmetman = " << metman;     // display meters
  }
```

The `English` class includes both a one-argument constructor, to convert from `float` to `English`, and the `float()` function, to convert from `English` to `float`.

In `main()`, the program converts from a `float` value of 1.9 meters to `English` when constructing the `engman` variable. This `English` value, 6'-2.803", is displayed, then converted back to `float` in the statement

```
metman = float(engman);  // English->float conversion
```

The program then displays the meters value, which should be the same one we started with, 1.9. Here's the output from ENGLCONV:

```
engman = 6'-2.803"
metman = 1.9
```

Conversion Function Invoked Automatically

Other syntaxes will also invoke the `float()` member function. If you say

```
metman = engman;  // also causes the English->float conversion
```

the compiler will realize it can't assign an `English` value to a `float` value without converting it first, so it will look for a way to do this. It will find the `float()` member function and carry out the conversion, even though you have not explicitly asked for it.

The `float()` function will also be invoked in initializations:

```
float metman(engman);
```

Here `metman` is not assigned a value; it's *initialized* to a value. But because the value is `English`, the compiler will call the `float()` function automatically. (Lord Wormsley always said that English values were the best.)

Casting for Clarity

I used the cast syntax in two places in ENGLCONV where it's not really necessary. In the one-argument constructor, I said

```
feet = int(fltfeet);
```

This conversion would have happened automatically even without the `int()`, because `feet` is an `int` variable. However, using an explicit conversion makes it clearer to someone reading the listing that I intended to perform the conversion. Similarly, in the `float()` function, I said

```
fracfeet += float(feet);
```

This conversion from `int` to `float` would also have been carried out automatically.

Note that the `float()` function that converts from `int` is not the same as the `float()` function that converts from `English`. The first is built in; the second is written by the class creator.

A Static Constant

The MTF member variable is the conversion factor for converting meters to feet. I make this variable `static` because it can be used by all objects and I make it `const` because it should not be changed.

Conversion from xString to String

As another example of converting from a class type to a basic type, let's see how to convert an `xString` object to an ordinary C string. (You last saw the `xString` class in the STRPLUS program in Session 1 in this chapter.) Listing 6-9 shows STRCONV.

Listing 6-9 STRCONV

```
// strconv.cpp
// converts xString to normal C string
#include <iostream.h>
#include <string.h>              // for strlen(), strcpy(), etc.

class xString
   {
   private:
      enum {MAX=80};             // maximum length of xStrings
      char str[MAX];             // ordinary C string
   public:
      xString()                  // no-arg constructor
         { strcpy(str, ""); }
      xString( char s[] )        // convert string to xString
         { strcpy(str, s); }
      void input()               // get string from user
         { cin.get(str, MAX); }
      void display()             // display string
         { cout << str; }

      operator char*()           // convert xString to string
         {
```

```
            return str;
            }
    };

void main()
    {
    xString s1("George");          // constructor converts
                                   //     string to xString

    xString s2;
    cout << "Enter your name: ";
    s2.input();                    // get s2 from user

                                   // convert s1, s2 to strings
    if( strcmp(s1, s2)==0 )        // compare them with strcmp()
        cout << "You're George!";
    else
        cout << "You aren't George.";
    }
```

Why would you want to convert xString objects to ordinary null-terminated C strings? Well, for one thing, there's a large library of functions that work with C strings. If I have a conversion function, I can use these library functions on xStrings.

That's what STRCONV does in main(), where it calls the strcmp() library function to compare two xString objects, s1 and s2. When the compiler sees that the arguments to strcmp() are xStrings, but that this function requires C strings, it looks for a conversion function. Finding that the char*() operator has been overloaded for the xString class, the compiler uses it to convert s1 and s2 to C strings and then calls strcmp(), which returns 0 if the strings are the same. Here's some sample interaction with STRCONV:

```
Enter your name: Dan
You aren't George.
```

You might be wondering what the asterisk means in the member function operator char*(). It indicates a pointer, which I have not yet discussed. However, the asterisk has the same effect here as brackets ([]): It indicates (approximately) an array of type char or, in other words, a normal C string. Thus, the operator char*() function converts an xString to a string.

The static_cast Approach

You may be interested to know that there is another, considerably more lengthy, syntax that you can use to perform type casting. To draw an example from the ENGLCONV program, instead of the statement

```
feet = int(fltfeet);
```

which was used in the one-argument constructor to convert float to int, you can substitute

```
feet = static_cast<int>(fltfeet);
```

This has the same effect, but makes it much more obvious that a data conversion is taking place. It also makes it easier to find all such conversions in your listing by searching for the keyword static_cast. The target type is inserted between angle brackets following static_cast and the variable to be converted is inserted in parentheses in the usual way.

This format also works with conversions you have written yourself, so for the statement

```
metman = float(engman);
```

(again from the ENGLCONV program), which converts `English` to `float`, you can substitute

```
metman = static_cast<float>(engman);
```

This is a rather ponderous syntax, and you won't normally use it. However, if you're trying to write the most error-free and maintainable code you can, you might consider it a helpful feature.

QUIZ 4

1. Conversions from basic types to class objects
   a. are carried out using a constructor.
   b. are carried out using an overloaded operator.
   c. are carried out using a member function of the basic type.
   d. are carried out using a cast operator member of the class.
   e. are not possible.

2. Conversions from class objects to basic types
   a. are carried out using a constructor.
   b. are carried out using an overloaded operator.
   c. are carried out using a member function of the basic type.
   d. are carried out using a cast operator member of the class.
   e. are not possible.

3. In the ENGLCONV program, `operator float()`
   a. returns type `English`.
   b. returns type `float`.
   c. has no return value.
   d. converts from a decimal-feet value.
   e. converts from a meters value.

4. The declarator of a member function to convert from type `airtime` to type `float` might be
   a. `airtime float()`
   b. `float(airtime at)`
   c. `float static_cast(airtime at)`
   d. `operator float(airtime at)`
   e. `operator float()`

5. The member function `operator char*()` in the `xString` class in the STRCONV program
   a. takes a C string as an argument.
   b. takes an `xString` as an argument.
   c. returns an `xString`.
   d. returns a C string.
   e. returns an array of type `char*`.

EXERCISE 1

Write a member function for the `airtime` class that converts `airtime` values to type `long`, where the `long` variable represents the number of seconds since midnight (e.g., 1:05 would convert to 65). You can start with the ADDAIR program in Session 1 in this chapter. Write some statements in `main()` to exercise this function.

EXERCISE 2

Write another member function for the `airtime` class, but have this one convert `airtime` values to type `float`, where the `float` variable represents the number of hours since midnight. For example, 2:30 would convert to 2.5.

MIDCHAPTER DISCUSSION

George: I really like overloaded operators. I haven't been so excited since I got my first C program to print "Hello, world."

Don: Yeah, I like them too. You can define whole new number systems. How about doing arithmetic in hexadecimal? Or making up a class of really huge numbers, like integers with hundreds of digits?

Estelle: I like being able to apply operators to nonarithmetic stuff, like concatenating strings.

George: I bet you can overload the plus sign to add one file to another and the equal sign to copy files. Just type `file1 = file2` at the C prompt.

Don: Wait a minute. The idea is for the class user, the programmer, to use these operators, not the end user.

George: Nobody ever likes my ideas.

Estelle: Poor boobie.

SESSION 5
CONVERSIONS BETWEEN CLASSES

Why would you want to convert from an object of one class to an object of another class? For many classes, such conversions wouldn't make any sense. It's hard to imagine converting an `airtime` object to an `employee` object, for example. Even when both classes represent numerical quantities, a conversion may be hard to justify. Why convert `airtime` to `English`? One is time and one is distance. However, when both classes represent numerical quantities that measure the same thing, class-to-class conversions may be reasonable. In this session, I'll demonstrate such conversions by concocting a new class, `FracFeet`, and converting between it and the `English` class.

There are two ways to convert from one class to another. You saw in Chapter 5 that you can use a one-argument constructor to convert from a basic type to a class object, and you saw in Session 4 in this chapter how to overload operators such as `float()` and `int()` to convert from a class object to a basic type. These same two techniques are used to convert between objects of different classes.

A Short Example

Let's look first at a skeleton program that reduces the conversion operations to their fundamentals. This program contains two classes, `alpha` and `beta`, and includes the necessary functions to convert from `alpha` to `beta` and from `beta` to `alpha`. Both the conversion functions are located in `beta`. One is a constructor that takes an `alpha` object as an argument; the other is the `operator alpha()` function, which returns an `alpha`. Listing 6-10 shows TWOTEST.

Listing 6-10 TWOTEST

```
// twotest.cpp
// tests conversions between two classes

class alpha
    {
    private:
        int ia;
    public:
        alpha(int i)             // converts int to alpha
            { ia = i; }
        int get_ia()             // "peek" function
            { return ia; }
    };

class beta
    {
    private:
        int ib;
    public:
        beta(alpha a)            // converts alpha to beta
            { ib = a.get_ia(); } // uses alpha get_ia()
        operator alpha()         // converts beta to alpha
```

```
      { return alpha(ib); } // uses alpha 1-arg constr
  };

void main()
   {
   alpha a(11);    // alpha 1-arg constructor; int to alpha
   beta b(a);      // beta 1-arg constructor; alpha to beta
   a = b;          // beta operator alpha(); beta to alpha
   }
```

Both classes contain a single data item of type int. Class alpha contains a one-argument constructor that converts an int to an alpha (or initializes an alpha with an int, to put it another way). It also contains a "peek" function that gives other parts of the program read-only access to its data item. Such access is necessary for the conversion function, the one-argument constructor, in beta.

This one-argument constructor in beta converts an alpha to a beta. It does this by calling the get_ia() peek function in alpha to obtain alpha's data and assigning this data to its own object. (Of course, a more practical class would probably need to change the data in some way.)

The second member function in beta is the operator alpha(), which converts the beta for which it was called into an alpha, which it returns. It performs this conversion by calling the alpha constructor with its own int data as the argument.

In this scenario, both conversion functions—the constructor and the class operator—are in beta. However, you could also handle the conversions using similar functions in class alpha. Figure 6-5 shows the relationship of functions in the two classes.

In main(), the program tests the conversions by initializing a beta with an alpha and setting an alpha equal to a beta. There's no output.

Notice that it's important to put class alpha first in the listing. The beta class needs to know about alpha's member functions, but alpha doesn't need to know anything about beta's.

The FracFeet Class

Let's move on to a more realistic example. The new class is called FracFeet. It stores distances in feet and fractions of a foot. More specifically, it has three member data items that represent whole feet, the numerator of a fraction, and the denominator of a fraction. It displays its value like this: 5-1/2 ft, which means five and one-half feet. An interaction with the input routine for this class looks like this:

```
Enter feet: 7
Enter fraction (format 2/3): 3/4
```

Here the user has entered 7-3/4 ft (seven and three-quarters feet).

Why would you ever need both an English class and a FracFeet class in the same program? After all, they both store distances using the English system. If you were designing a program from scratch, it might not make sense to create both classes. Suppose, however, that an architectural firm works with data in the feet and inches format and someone has already written the English class to handle this kind of data. One day this firm buys another company that stores data in the feet and fractions format. Now you need to modify the program to store this new kind of data in addition to the English kind, so you invent the FracFeet class. (This situation might also be a candidate for inheritance, which I'll cover in Chapter 7.)

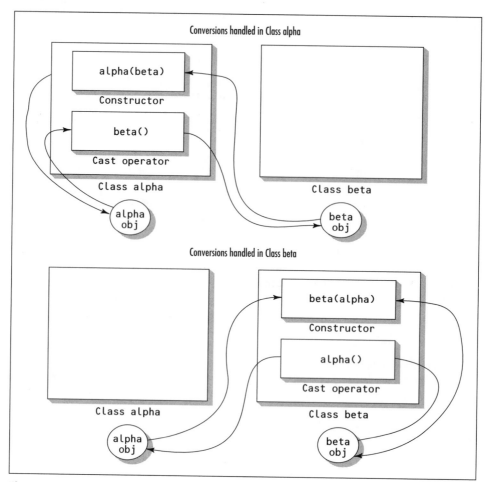

Figure 6-5 Class-to-class conversions

I'll use roughly the same arrangement for the conversion functions that I did in the TWOTEST program, with both conversion functions in the new `FracFeet` class. These will be a constructor that takes as its single argument an object of the `English` class and an `English()` function that converts its `FracFeet` object to an `English` value.

I've added two member functions, `get_feet()` and `get_inches()`, to the `English` class; they return the `feet` and `inches` values of an English object. These peek functions provide the only way for functions outside the `English` class to access its data. The `English` class also has a two-argument constructor taking feet and inches as arguments.

The `FracFeet` **Program**

Because it includes two classes, this program is somewhat longer than the usual examples. However, you've seen the `English` class before, and that's half the program. The classes are separated by slashed lines. Listing 6-11 shows FRACFEET.

Listing 6-11 FRACFEET

```cpp
// fracfeet.cpp
// converts between English and FracFeet
#include <iostream.h>
//////////////////////////////////////////////////////////////
class English                       // feet-and-inches class
   {
   private:
      int feet;
      float inches;
   public:                          // no-argument constructor
      English() : feet(0), inches(0.0)
         { }
                                     // 2-argument constructor
      English(int f, float i) : feet(f), inches(i)
         { }

      void get()                     // user input
         {
         cout << "   Enter feet: ";   cin >> feet;
         cout << "   Enter inches: "; cin >> inches;
         }

      void display()                 // display
         { cout << feet << "\'-" << inches << '\"'; }

      // these functions needed for conversions
      int getfeet()                  // return feet
         { return feet; }
      float getinches()              // return inches
         { return inches; }
   };  // end English class
//////////////////////////////////////////////////////////////
class FracFeet                       // fractional feet class
   {
   private:
      int wfeet;                     // whole feet
      int numer;                     // numerator
      int denom;                     // denominator
   public:                           // no-argument constructor
      FracFeet() : wfeet(0), numer(0), denom(1)
         { }

      FracFeet(English);             // one-argument constructor
                                     // (declaration)
      void get()                     // user input (never use 0
         {                           // in denominator)
         char dummy;
         cout << "   Enter feet: ";
         cin >> wfeet;
         cout << "   Enter fraction (format 2/3): ";
         cin >> numer >> dummy >> denom;
         }
```

continued on next page

continued from previous page

```
      void display()                    // display
         {
         cout << wfeet;
         if(numer != 0)                 // if numerator 0, no fraction
            cout << '-' << numer << '/' << denom;
         cout << " ft";
         }
      operator English()               // convert FracFeet to English
         {                             // inches = 12 * n / d
         float temp_inches = 12.0 * float(numer) / float(denom);
         return English( wfeet,  temp_inches);
         }
   };  // end class FracFeet
/////////////////////////////////////////////////////////////////
FracFeet::FracFeet(English e)           // one-argument constructor
   {                                    // convert English to FracFeet
   wfeet = e.getfeet();                 // feet are the same
   int i = int( e.getinches() );        // convert inches to integer
                                        // find fraction
   if(i==6)              { numer=1;    denom=2; }    // 1/2
   else if(i==2 || i==10) { numer=i/2; denom=6; }    // 1/6, 5/6
   else if(i==3 || i== 9) { numer=i/3; denom=4; }    // 1/4, 3/4
   else if(i==4 || i== 8) { numer=i/4; denom=3; }    // 1/3, 2/3
   else                  { numer=i;    denom=12;}    // i/12
   }
/////////////////////////////////////////////////////////////////
void main()
   {
   FracFeet ff;
   English eng;

   cout << "\nFracFeet value\n";
   ff.get();                            // get FracFeet from user
   cout << "FracFeet = ";
   ff.display();                        // display FracFeet

   eng = ff;                            // convert FracFeet to English
   cout << "\nEnglish = ";
   eng.display();                       // display equivalent English

   cout << "\n\nEnglish value\n";
   eng.get();                           // get English from user
   cout << "English = ";
   eng.display();                       // display English

   ff = eng;                            // set English to FracFeet
   cout << "\nFracFeet = ";
   ff.display();                        // display equivalent FracFeet
   }
```

In `main()`, the program tests both kinds of conversions. First, a `FracFeet` object gets data from the user and displays itself. Then the program sets an `English` object equal to the `FracFeet` object and displays it, proving that the `FracFeet` to `English` conversion works. Second, an `English` object gets data from the user and displays itself. The program sets the `FracFeet` object equal to the `English` object and displays it, thus demonstrating the `English` to `FracFeet` conversion. Here's some interaction with FRACFEET:

```
FracFeet value
    Enter feet: 7
    Enter fraction (format 2/3): 3/4
FracFeet = 7-3/4 ft
English = 7'-9"

English value
    Enter feet: 3
    Enter inches: 8
English = 3'-8"
FracFeet = 3-2/3 ft
```

Notice that the `FracFeet` class specification follows the `English` class specification in the listing. This ordering is necessary, because the conversion functions reside in `FracFeet`. These conversion functions must access member functions in the `English` class, so `English` must be specified first.

The English() Operator

The `English()` operator in the `FracFeet` class converts `FracFeet` to `English` by supplying values to the `English` class two-argument constructor. The feet value is supplied as is; it's the same in both classes. The fraction of a foot is converted to inches by converting both numerator and denominator to type `float`, dividing them, and then multiplying by 12.0.

The One-Argument Constructor

The one-argument constructor for the `FracFeet` class converts an `English` object to a `FracFeet` object. To do this, it must access the private data inside the `English` object. This isn't possible unless the `English` class includes public functions that allow such access. The member functions `get_feet()` and `get_inches()` do this. In `FracFeet`, the one-argument constructor calls these functions to get `feet` and `inches` values from the `English` object passed as the argument.

The `English` inches must be converted to the numerator and denominator of a fraction in the `FracFeet` class. The constructor does this somewhat inelegantly in an `else...if` ladder by selecting values for the numerator and denominator, depending on how many inches there are. (A more elegant approach is to call a function that finds the lowest common divisor of two numbers and to use it to reduce a fraction to its lowest terms, but that takes you too far afield.)

I'll return to the topic of conversions when we encounter friend functions in Chapter 9. Friends provide increased flexibility for conversions in several ways.

QUIZ 5

1. Conversions between classes
   a. are never a good idea.
   b. can always be carried out, no matter what the classes are.
   c. normally make the most sense for classes representing numerical types.

    d. can usually make use of an overloaded `cast` operator.

    e. can always be handled with existing constructors.

2. To convert from class **A** to class **B**, you could use

    a. a constructor in class **A**.

    b. a constructor in class **B**.

    c. an `operator A()` in class **A**.

    d. an `operator B()` in class **B**.

    e. an `operator B()` in class **A**.

3. You can't exchange the order of the **English** and **FracFeet** class specifications in the FRACFEET program because

    a. **FracFeet** objects are defined earlier in **main()** than **English** objects.

    b. the **English** two-argument constructor needs to access data in **FracFeet**.

    c. the **FracFeet** one-argument constructor needs to access member functions in **English**.

    d. the `operator English()` function needs to call the **English** two-argument constructor.

    e. the `operator English()` function needs to call the **FracFeet** one-argument constructor.

4. In the FRACFEET program, inches are converted to

    a. feet and fractions of a foot.

    b. feet and inches.

    c. a numerator and denominator.

    d. a fraction of an inch.

    e. a fraction of a foot.

5. The one-argument constructor in **FracFeet** gets the values it needs from

    a. "peek" member functions of the **English** class.

    b. a locally stored list.

    c. its single argument.

    d. the constructor in the **English** class.

    e. the `operator English()` function.

EXERCISE 1

Rearrange the FRACFEET program so that the conversions are carried out in the **English** class rather than in the **FracFeet** class. Use a one-argument constructor that takes a **FracFeet** object as an argument and an `operator FracFeet()` function.

EXERCISE 2

Create a class called **Time** that stores three data items: **hours**, **minutes**, and **seconds**, all of type **int**. Include the **Time** class in the same program as the **airtime** class. (See the ADDAIR program in Session 1 in this chapter.) Create the necessary functions to convert between **Time** and **airtime** and between **airtime** and **Time**.

SESSION 6

OVERLOADING THE ASSIGNMENT OPERATOR (=)

You can overload the assignment operator (=) just as you can other operators. However, the assignment operator plays a larger role than most operators because it performs such a fundamental operation and is used so frequently. It and the copy constructor can be thought of as twins. They both copy data from one object to another. If, when you do this, you need to copy any data item in other than a simple memberwise fashion, then you will probably need to overload both the copy constructor and the assignment operator.

Syntax of the Overloaded Assignment Operator

Here's one way to write an overloaded assignment operator (OAO):

```
void operator=(const omega& right)    // overloaded assignment
   {
   // copy data if appropriate
   }
```

This function takes one argument of its own class (here called `omega`), which is usually passed as a `const` reference. When there's a `void` return value, as I show here, you can't chain the assignment operator (as in `a=b=c`). We'll see how to fix this later.

The comment `copy data if appropriate` means that the OAO is responsible for copying each data member from one object to another *unless* there's a good reason to do otherwise. Typically, there is a good reason to do something other than a memberwise copy on at least one data item; otherwise, you wouldn't need to overload the assignment operator in the first place.

Notice how similar the OAO is to the copy constructor, which often performs exactly the same operation on the data:

```
omega(const omega& om)    // copy constructor
   {
   // copy data if appropriate
   }
```

The difference between the assignment operator and the copy constructor is that the copy constructor actually creates a new object before copying data from another object into it, whereas the assignment operator copies data into an already existing object. Figure 6-6 shows how this looks.

Remember that the use of an equal sign in a definition is not the same as assignment:

```
omega beta = alpha;    // construction and initialization
                       // uses copy constructor

beta = alpha;          // assignment
                       // uses assignment operator
```

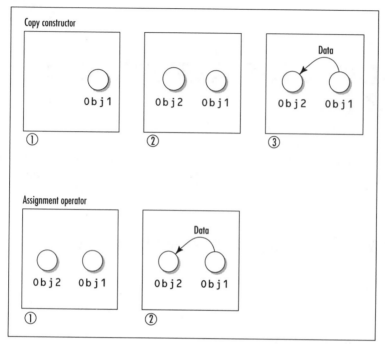

Figure 6-6 Operation of the overloaded assignment operator

The assignment operator is not used in the first statement, only in the second.

A Simple Assignment Operator Example

As with the copy constructor, you typically need to overload the assignment operator when the creation of an object causes resources (such as memory) to be allocated, or when objects use pointers, or when objects do something unusual such as counting or numbering themselves. I'll return to the issues of pointers and memory allocation in Chapter 8. For now, you'll see how to overload the assignment operator for the omega class, which counts and numbers its objects. You encountered this class in the COPYCON2 program in Chapter 5, Session 6.

In the omega class, I adopted the (somewhat arbitrary) convention that each new object, when it's first created, is given a unique and permanent serial number. Because this number can't change, it's *not* copied by either the copy constructor or the assignment operator. Each object is also given a name (such as Harriet) that *is* copied by the copy constructor and the assignment operator. An object's name thus indicates from which other object it was copied. Listing 6-12 shows ASSIGN.

Listing 6-12 ASSIGN

```
// assign.cpp
// demonstrates overloaded assignment operator
// using objects that number themselves
```

```
#include <iostream.h>
#include <string.h>              // for strncpy()

class omega
    {
    private:
        enum { size=20 };
        char name[size];
        static int total;
        const int number;
    public:                      // one-arg constructor
        omega(char str[]) : number(++total)  // number the object
            {
            strncpy(name, str, size);        // give it a name
            cout << "\n1-arg constructor has "
                 << "created " << name << "-" << number;
            }
                                 // overloaded assignment operator
        void operator=(const omega& right)
            {
            cout << "\n" << right.name << "-" << right.number
                 << " assigned to " << name << "-" << number;

            strncpy(name, right.name, size);  // copy the name

            cout << ", making " << name << "-" << number;
            }

    };
int omega::total = 0;            // (no objects when program starts)

void main()
    {
    omega om1("Harriet");        // uses one-arg constructor
    omega om2("Bernard");

    om2 = om1;                   // assignment
    }
```

There are three data items in the omega class. The OAO copies only one of these, name, using the strncpy() library function.

The second item, total, is static. Static data is never copied by an OAO (or a copy constructor) because it applies to the class as a whole, not to individual objects.

I don't copy the number data item either, because each object's serial number is permanent from the time it's first created. I reinforce this by making number a const data item. After const member data is initialized in the constructor, the compiler won't allow it to be changed. (Incidentally, it follows that when an object has a const data item, you *must* overload the assignment operator and copy constructor, because the compiler can't use the default memberwise copy, which would involve changing the unchangeable const variable.)

In `main()`, the program creates two objects and then uses the assignment operator to copy one to the other. Both the constructor and the OAO display messages to tell what they're doing. Here's the output from the program:

```
1-arg constructor has created Harriet-1
1-arg constructor has created Bernard-2
Harriet-1 is assigned to Bernard-2, making Harriet-2
```

The `om2` object, which started out as Bernard-2, becomes Harriet-2; its name is changed but not its number. (This is similar to a person being able to change his or her name legally but not his or her social security number.)

An Assignment Operator That Allows Chaining

You can chain the default memberwise assignment operator:

```
var3 = var2 = var1;
```

For this to work, the result of one assignment operation, the one on the right, must be made available to the one on its left. This requires the assignment operator to return the value of the operand on its left. In the case of an OAO, this is the object for which it was called. Here's how an OAO that permits chaining looks in skeleton form:

```
omega operator=(const omega& right)      // overloaded assignment op
   {
   // copy data if appropriate
   return omega(name);                    // returns by value; uses
   }                                      // 1-arg constructor
```

The `return` statement uses the one-argument constructor to create a new temporary "copy" of the object for which the OAO was called, which is the object to the left of the = sign in `main()`. Listing 6-13, ASSIGN2, shows how this looks.

Listing 6-13 ASSIGN2

```cpp
// assign2.cpp
// overloaded assignment operator with self-numbering objects
// returns a value
#include <iostream.h>
#include <string.h>              // for strncpy()

class omega
   {
   private:
      enum { size=20 };
      char name[size];
      static int total;
      int number;
   public:
                              // one-arg constructor
      omega(char str[]) : number(++total)
         {
         strncpy(name, str, size);
```

```
        cout << "\n1-arg constructor has "
             << "created " << name << "-" << number;
        }
    ~omega()
        {
        cout << "\nDestructor has "
             << "destroyed " << name << "-" << number;
        }
                            // overloaded assignment operator
    omega operator=(const omega& right)
        {
        cout << "\n\n" << right.name << "-" << right.number
             << " assigned to " << name << "-" << number;
        strncpy(name, right.name, size);
        cout << ", making " << name << "-" << number;
        return omega(name);
        }
    };
int omega::total = 0;       // no objects when program starts

void main()
    {
    omega om1("Harriet");       // uses one-arg constructor
    omega om2("Bernard");
    omega om3("Damien");

    om3 = om2 = om1;            // chained assignment
        }
```

The output from the program looks like this:

```
1-arg constructor has created Harriet-1
1-arg constructor has created Bernard-2
1-arg constructor has created Damien-3

Harriet-1 assigned to Bernard-2, making Harriet-2
1-arg constructor has created Harriet-4

Harriet-4 assigned to Damien-3, making Harriet-3
1-arg constructor has created Harriet-5

Destructor has destroyed Harriet-5
Destructor has destroyed Harriet-4

Destructor has destroyed Harriet-3
Destructor has destroyed Harriet-2
Destructor has destroyed Harriet-1
```

The first three lines are created by the first three invocations of the one-argument constructor in main(). Then the chained assignment statement is executed:

```
om3 = om2 = om1;
```

Each of the two assignment operators in this statement causes an assignment of the `name` variable and the invocation of the one-argument constructor to create the temporary variable that will be assigned. These temporary objects are Harriet-4 and Harriet-5. Both are destroyed at the end of the assignment statement.

When the program ends, the three original objects with their new names (Harriet-1, Harriet-2, and Harriet-3) are destroyed as well. All the objects end up with the name Harriet because either they all have been assigned to Harriet-1 or have been assigned to an object that was itself assigned to Harriet-1.

Future Improvement

In the ASSIGN2 program, the OAO is returned by value, using the one-argument constructor. This is not very efficient, because it requires the creation (and destruction) of a new object every time you use the assignment operator. It's better to be able to return by reference, which does not require the creation of a new object. But you can't return a local object by reference, because local objects are destroyed when the function returns.

It would be really nice to return a *reference* to the object that called the OAO (return a reference to myself). How can you do that? The magic expression `*this` solves the problem; I'll mention it again in Session 8 at the end of this chapter. For now, keep in mind that the current version of the OAO can be improved.

Another improvement to OAOs that you can make later, when you learn about pointers, is to check for *self-assignment*: that is, assigning an object to itself:

```
obj1 = obj1;   // uh, oh
```

If nothing else, such a statement may indicate that the class user made a mistake; for some classes, it can cause serious internal problems. For now, assume that class users don't make this mistake.

1. Overloading the assignment operator is the only way to
   a. chain assignment operators in a single statement, such as `a=b=c=d`.
   b. perform assignment on objects.
   c. assign one object to another when not all the data should be copied.
   d. assign an object of one type to an object of another type.
   e. initialize an object with another object when it's created.

2. Classes in which an overloaded assignment operator might be helpful include those
   a. that contain pointers as member data.
   b. that number each object.
   c. with `static` data.
   d. with `const` data.
   e. that allocate system resources such as memory.

3. An overloaded assignment operator
   a. is used to initialize objects in statements such as `alpha b = a`;
   b. copies all the data without modification from the source object to the target object.
   c. copies data or does not copy it, as appropriate, from the source object to the target object.
   d. performs any action the class creator wants when one object is assigned to another.
   e. operates the same way as the default assignment operator, except for large objects.

4. Returning an object from an OAO makes it possible to
   a. chain assignment operators, as in `a=b=c=d`.
   b. assign an object of one type to an object of another type.
   c. assign one object to another even when not all the data should be copied.
   d. display information from within the OAO.
   e. exit from the OAO.

5. Returning an object by value from an OAO
   a. cannot be done with objects that number themselves.
   b. is not a perfect solution.
   c. is not acceptable to the compiler.
   d. causes a temporary object to be created.
   e. returns the object for which the function was called.

EXERCISE 1

It's not really necessary, but overload the assignment operator for the `airtime` class.

EXERCISE 2

Remove the `name` variable from the `omega` class and create overloaded versions of the assignment operator and copy constructor for the new version of the class.

SESSION 7

OVERLOADING THE [ ] OPERATOR

The subscript operator, [ ], which is normally used to access array elements, can be overloaded. This is useful if you want to modify the way arrays work in C++. For example, you might want to make a "safe" array: one that automatically checks the index numbers you use to access the array to ensure they are not out of bounds. That's what I'll do in this example.

Access with access( ) Function

To show that things aren't as mysterious as they might seem, I'll first introduce a program that uses a normal member function, called access( ), to read and write the elements of a safe array. This function returns by reference. As you learned in the RETREF program in Chapter 4, Session 8, you can use the same member function both to insert data into an object and to read it out if the function returns the value from the function by reference. A function that returns by reference can be used on the left side of the equal sign, like this:

```
afunc() = 3;    // possible if function returns by reference
```

The example program creates a class called safearay whose only member data is an array of int values. The access( ) function in this class takes as its only argument the index of the array element to be accessed. It checks that this index is within bounds and then either assigns a new value to the array element at this index or retrieves the element's value, depending on which side of the equal sign it finds itself on.

The main( ) function tests the class by creating a safe array, filling it with values (each equal to 10 times its array index), and then displaying them to assure the user that everything is working as it should. Listing 6-14 shows ARROVER1.

Listing 6-14 ARROVER1

```
// arrover1.cpp
// creates safe array (index values are checked before access)
// uses access() function for put and get
#include <iostream.h>
#include <process.h>                    // for exit()

class safearay
   {
   private:
      enum {SIZE=100};               // array size
      int arr[SIZE];                 // ordinary array
   public:
      int& access(const int& n);     // function declaration
   };

int& safearay::access(const int& n)    // access() function
   {                                   // returns by reference
   if( n< 0 || n>=SIZE )
```

```
        { cout << "\nIndex out of bounds"; exit(1); }
    return arr[n];  // return the value by reference
    }

void main()
    {
    int j;
    int temp;
    safearay sa;                    // make a safe array
    const int LIMIT = 20;           // amount of data

    for(j=0; j<LIMIT; j++)          // insert elements
        sa.access(j) = j*10;        // *left* side of equals

    for(j=0; j<LIMIT; j++)          // display elements
        {
        temp = sa.access(j);        // *right* side of equals
        cout << "\nElement " << j << " is " << temp;
        }
    }
```

In `main()`, the statement

```
sa1.access(j) = j*10;
```

causes the value `j*10` to be placed in array element `arr[j]`, the return value of the function. Here the function appears on the left of the operator. The statement

```
temp = sa.access(j);
```

causes the value of `arr[j]` to be assigned to `temp`. Here the function appears to the right of the operator.

One Size Fits All

For simplicity, all `safearay` objects are the same size: They can store 100 `ints`. This wouldn't be too practical in a real-world situation. You'll see in Chapter 8 how such a class can be designed so the user can determine the size of a safe array, either when it's first defined or, dynamically, as more data is added to it.

Note that in `main()`, only 20 `int` values are stored in the safe array. Thus, there's plenty of space left over. Here's the output from ARROVER1 (with most of the lines omitted for brevity):

```
Element 0 is 0
Element 1 is 10
Element 2 is 20
...
Element 18 is 180
Element 19 is 190
```

The output shows that the data has been successfully inserted and retrieved from the safe array.

Errors Are Reported

The `access()` function will display the error message `Index out of bounds` if the index sent to it as an argument is not between 0 and SIZE-1. Try changing `LIMIT` to 101 and see if the error-detection device works. After the error message is displayed, the `exit()` library function is executed, which causes the immediate termination of the program.

Access with Overloaded [ ] Operator

The `access()` function works fine, but it would be a convenience to the programmer, and to anyone else trying to read the listing, to access the elements of the safe array using the same subscript (`[ ]`) operator as normal C++ arrays. To do this, I overload the `[ ]` operator in the `safearay` class, using the `operator[]()` function. With the `access()` function, I would write

```
temp = sa.access(j);        // get element j of array sa
```

With the `operator[]` function, this could be rewritten as

```
temp = sa.operator[](j);   // get element j of array sa
```

but of course C++ allows you to use the simplified syntax

```
temp = sa[j];               // get element j of array sa
```

where the dot operator, the keyword `operator`, and the parentheses disappear and the index `j` moves from inside the parentheses to inside the brackets so as to replicate normal array syntax, as shown in Figure 6-7.

Like the `access()` function in ARROVER1, `operator[]()` must return by reference so it can be used on the left of the equal sign. Listing 6-15 shows ARROVER2.

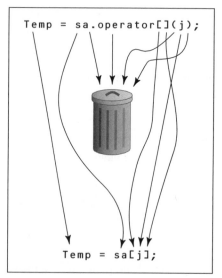

Figure 6-7 Syntax of the overloaded [ ] operator

Listing 6-15 ARROVER2

```
// arrover2.cpp
// creates safe array (index values are checked before access)
// uses overloaded [] operator for put and get

#include <iostream.h>
#include <process.h>              // for exit()

class safearay
    {
    private:
        enum {SIZE=100};          // array size
        int arr[SIZE];            // ordinary array
    public:
        int& operator [](int n);  // function declaration
    };

int& safearay::operator [](int n)    // overloaded []
    {                                // returns by reference
    if( n< 0 || n>=SIZE )
        { cout << "\nIndex out of bounds"; exit(1); }
    return arr[n];
    }

void main()
    {
    int j;
    int temp;
    safearay sa;                  // make a safe array
    const int LIMIT = 20;         // amount of data

    for(j=0; j<LIMIT; j++)        // insert elements
        sa[j] = j*10;             // *left* side of equal sign

    for(j=0; j<LIMIT; j++)        // display elements
        {
        temp = sa[j];             // *right* side of equal sign
        cout << "\nElement " << j << " is " << temp;
        }
    }   // end main()
}   // end program
```

In this version of `main()`, I can use the natural subscript expressions

```
sa[j] = j*10;
```

and

```
temp = sa[j];
```

for input and output to the safe array. They are used in exactly the same way as normal subscript operators are. The output from ARROVER2 is the same as that from ARROVER1.

Of course, you don't need to use `operator[]` exactly as I've shown here. If you're only going to read from an array, for example, there's no reason for it to return by reference. Feel free to adapt any of the overloaded operators to do exactly what you want.

QUIZ 7

1. Overloading the subscript operator allows you to
   a. access elements of normal C++ arrays, such as `intarray[10]`.
   b. use the array name on the right side of the equal sign.
   c. access elements of an array object, using `[]`.
   d. make an array class that, to a class user, acts like a normal C++ array.
   e. make an array that, internally, behaves differently than a normal C++ array.

2. In `arrover1`, all array objects of the `safearay` class hold the same amount of data because
   a. overloaded operators can't handle large amounts of data.
   b. that's how `LIMIT` is defined in `main()`.
   c. that's the size specified within the class.
   d. all objects of the same class are necessarily the same size.
   e. other options would require dynamic memory allocation.

3. An overloaded subscript operator should
   a. take one argument and return a value by reference.
   b. take no arguments and return a value by reference.
   c. take no arguments and return `void`.
   d. take no arguments and return by value.
   e. calculate the index of the element to be accessed.

4. Returning by reference from an overloaded subscript operator means that
   a. you can use the operator on the left side of the equal sign.
   b. you can use the operator on any data type.
   c. no copy is made of the returned data item.
   d. only objects can be returned.
   e. only objects of the same class as the operator can be returned.

5. You might reasonably want to create an array class that
   a. uses an overloaded subscript operator that always returns the last item inserted in the array.
   b. expands automatically as you add data.
   c. automatically sorts data as you enter it.
   d. allows the user to choose the size of the array when it's defined.
   e. models a write-only array.

EXERCISE 1

Add a one-argument constructor to the safearay class so the user can specify the highest element that will be used in the array. (For example, on ARROVER2, only the first 20 elements are used.) Then have the overloaded subscript operator check that the index does not exceed this limit (called LIMIT in ARROVER2), rather than checking if it exceeds the total size of the array.

EXERCISE 2

Modify the safearay class by adding a new member function, called add(), that allows the class user to insert a value at the end of the array, where "end" is defined as the highest-numbered element to have been accessed. In other words, if elements 0 to 6 are already filled, then

```
sa.add(127);
```

will insert the value 127 into element 7. This function is convenient because the user doesn't need to supply an index number. You'll probably need a new member data item (called top?) that records the number of the highest element accessed.

SESSION 8

FINE-TUNING OVERLOADED OPERATORS

In the operator overloading examples you've seen so far in this chapter, I've left out some refinements. I did this to simplify the listings and to avoid muddying the waters while introducing the basic concepts of overloaded operators. Now it's time to return to some of these earlier examples and retrofit them with the latest in OOP technology. I'll demonstrate two such features: making overloaded operators into constant functions and using appropriate return types. I'll begin by reviewing what you've learned about constant arguments.

Constant Arguments

I already discussed (in Chapter 4, Session 7) the desirability of passing arguments, when they are objects, by reference. Because an object may be large, passing by reference avoids the time and memory space necessary to create the copy of an object that's generated automatically when an argument is passed by value.

An argument passed by reference should be passed as a const to guarantee that it won't be accidentally altered by the function. (Of course, this isn't true if the function is *supposed* to modify the argument.) Almost all arguments to overloaded operators are objects and should be passed by const reference. I've done this in most of the examples in this chapter.

An argument that is a basic type such as `int` can be passed by value without incurring significant overhead. As I've noted, arguments passed by value can't be modified by the function and so don't need to be `const`.

Constant Functions

I discussed making an entire function `const` in Chapter 5, Session 7. A `const` function guarantees not to modify the object for which it is called. You can call a `const` member function, but not a non-`const` one, for a `const` object. A constant function is indicated by the keyword `const` following the parentheses of the function name:

```
void afunc() const      // constant function
    { }                 // won't modify its object
```

Constant Overloaded Operators

How does this apply to overloaded operators? Any overloaded operator, if it does not modify the object for which it was called, should be made `const`. This allows the class user to define `const` objects that are guaranteed to be unalterable.

Binary operators such as +, *, <, and == should be `const`, because they don't modify the object for which they were called (the object on the left side of the operator); neither do the unary + and – (with these operators, the object is on the right). However, assignment operators such as = and += do modify their object, as do the ++ and -- unary operators, so they should not be `const`. The subscript operator [ ] may modify its object, so it should not be `const` either.

Adding Constant `airtime` Objects

Let's modify the ADDAIR example from Session 1 in this chapter. I'll make `operator+()` into a `const` function and use it to add an `airtime` to a `const airtime`. Listing 6-16 shows ADDAIRCO.

Listing 6-16 ADDAIRCO

```
// addairco.cpp
// overloads the + operator for airtime class,
// using const function
#include <iostream.h>

class airtime
    {
    private:
        int hours;          // 0 to 23
        int minutes;        // 0 to 59
    public:
                            // no-arg constructor
        airtime() : hours(0), minutes(0)
            { }
                            // two-arg constructor
        airtime(int h, int m) : hours(h), minutes(m)
            { }

        void display() const    // output to screen
            {
```

```
          cout << hours << ':' << minutes;
          }

      void get()                  // input from user
          {
          char dummy;
          cout << "\nEnter time (format 12:59): ";
          cin >> hours >> dummy >> minutes;
          }
                              // overloaded + operator
      airtime operator + (const airtime& right) const
          {
          airtime temp;         // make a temporary object
          temp.hours = hours + right.hours;   // add data
          temp.minutes = minutes + right.minutes;
          if(temp.minutes >= 60)              // check for carry
              {
              temp.hours++;
              temp.minutes -= 60;
              }
          return temp;                // return temporary object by value
          }
   };   // end class airtime

void main()
    {
    airtime at1, at2;
    const airtime noon(12, 0);              // constant object

    cout << "Enter first airtime: ";
    at1.get();

    at2 = noon + at1;                       // overloaded + operator
                                            //      adds at1 to noon
    cout << "sum = ";
    at2.display();                          // display sum
    }
```

In main(), the airtime object noon is declared to be const. The statement

```
at2 = noon + at1;
```

adds another airtime value, at1, to noon. Because operator+() is a const function, it's all right to call it for a const airtime. If this operator were not const, attempting to use it on a const object would elicit a compiler warning. This mechanism keeps an overloaded operator from accidentally modifying a const object for which it is called.

Notice that, whether operator+() is const or not, it's perfectly all right to say

```
at2 = at1 + noon;
```

because in this case, the operator is called for the nonconstant object at1, whereas noon is the argument to the function and is already declared const.

Return Values

When an operator produces a new value, an object must be created to hold this value. For example, in the ADDAIRCO program, `operator+()` adds its argument to its object and must store the sum somewhere. Usually it's stored in a temporary object defined in the function. Because it's temporary, this object cannot be returned by reference, but must be returned by value. For this reason, the overloaded arithmetic operators return by value, as `operator+()` does for the `airtime` class.

However, things are simplified for some other kinds of operators because they can return a copy of themselves. This is true when the result of an operation is placed in the object for which the operator is called. This happens in the assignment operators and a few others.

Returns from Assignment Operators

If `answer`, `a` and `b` are class objects and you say

```
answer = a += b;
```

the `operator+=()` function is called for `a` and the result of the `a+b` operation is assigned to `a`. The return value of the operation `a+=b` is thus simply `a`. It's this value that is assigned to `answer`.

When the object that called a function itself takes on the result of the calculation performed by the function, then the function can return by reference. Why? Because, unlike a local object created within the function, the object itself will be in existence after the function returns. (Objects, not surprisingly, are longer lived than local variables defined within their member functions.) Thus, `operator+=()` can return by reference, whereas `operator+()` must return by value.

Should this reference return for assignment operators be `const` or non-`const`? In most cases, it probably doesn't make any difference. However, in some obscure situations a nonconstant reference allows more flexibility. I'll refrain from making any recommendation about applying `const` to return values and I'll leave it out in the examples. You're free to use a `const` return if it works best in your own situation.

The Amazing *this Object

But what, exactly, do I return by reference if I want to return my own object? In previous examples (e.g., in `operator+=()` in PLEQAIR in Session 2 in this chapter), when I've needed to return the value of the object for which a function was called, I've used the construction

```
return airtime(hours, minutes);
```

where hours and minutes are the data from my own object. This creates a temporary object with the same data as my object. Because it's temporary, I return it by value. As I noted in Session 2 in this chapter, the compiler is clever enough to create only one temporary object in this situation, so it is fairly efficient to execute. However, if I can figure out a way to return by reference, I won't need to create any temporary objects at all.

To return the value of our own object by reference, we need to know about a magic name called `*this`. In any member function, this name stands for the object for which the function was called. That is, if in `main()` you say

```
anobj.afunc();
```

then within **afunc()**, the expression ***this** refers
does in **main()**.

The ***this** expression is passed implicitly (i.e.,
I am a member function, I always know how to refer
phrase Pogo, we have met ***this**, and it is us!)

You don't need to know anything about pointers
pointer notation, you'll recognize the asterisk (*) as
the address of the object that called the function; ***t**
addresses in greater detail in Chapter 8.

It follows that if a member function needs to retu

```
return *this;
```

and the deed is done. If the return is by reference, no
cient than that.

The += *Operator Revisited*

Let's modify the PLEQAIR example from Session 2 in this chapter so that **operator+=()** returns by
reference, using ***this**. Listing 6-17 shows PLEQRET.

Listing 6-17 PLEQRET

```cpp
// pleqret.cpp
// overloads the += operator, uses *this
#include <iostream.h>

class airtime
    {
    private:
        int hours;              // 0 to 23
        int minutes;            // 0 to 59
    public:
                                // no-arg constructor
        airtime() : hours(0), minutes(0)
            {  }
                                // 2-arg constructor
        airtime(int h, int m) : hours(h), minutes(m)
            {   }

        void display() const    // output to screen
            {
            cout << hours << ':' << minutes;
            }

        void get()              // input from user
            {
            char dummy;
            cout << "\nEnter time (format 12:59): ";
            cin >> hours >> dummy >> minutes;
            }
                                // overloaded += operator
        airtime& operator += (const airtime& right)
```

continued on next page

```
                ...t.hours;                  // add argument to us
                right.minutes;
              ...s >= 60)                     // check for carry
            ...ours++; minutes -= 60; }
          ...rn *this;                        // return by reference

       ... end class airtime

   ...main()
   {
   airtime at1, at2, at3;
   cout << "Enter first airtime: ";
   at1.get();
   cout << "Enter second airtime: ";
   at2.get();

   at1 += at2;                  // overloaded += operator
                                //    adds at2 to at1
   cout << "\nat1+=at2 = ";
   at1.display();              // display result

   at3 = at1 += at2;           // do it again, use return value
   cout << "\nat3 = ";
   at3.display();             // display result
   }
```

The main() here is the same as in PLEQAIR. The class user won't need to change anything to use the improved operator +=() function, but the function is more efficient. Notice that operator +=() itself cannot be made const because the object for which it is called (i.e., a in a+=b) is modified. You can't call this operator for a constant object.

The Increment Operator Revisited

The POSTFIX program in Session 3 in this chapter demonstrated both prefix and postfix versions of the overloaded increment (++) operator. Let's bring this program up to date. Listing 6-18 shows PFIXRET.

Listing 6-18 PFIXRET

```
// pfixret.cpp
// overloads the ++ operator, prefix version uses *this
#include <iostream.h>

class airtime
   {
   private:
      int hours;                  // 0 to 23
      int minutes;                // 0 to 59
   public:
                                  // no-arg constructor
      airtime() : hours(0), minutes(0)
         {  }
                                  // 2-arg constructor
```

```
        airtime(int h, int m) : hours(h), minutes(m)
          { }

        void display() const      // output to screen
          {
          cout << hours << ':' << minutes;
          }

        void get()                // input from user
          {
          char dummy;
          cout << "\nEnter time (format 12:59): ";
          cin >> hours >> dummy >> minutes;
          }
        airtime& operator++ ()    // overloaded prefix ++ operator
          {
          ++minutes;
          if(minutes >= 60)
             {
             ++hours;
             minutes -= 60;
             }
          return *this;           // return our object by reference
          }
        airtime operator++ (int) // overloaded postfix ++ operator
          {
          airtime temp(hours, minutes);  // save original value
          ++minutes;              // increment this object
          if(minutes >= 60)
             {
             ++hours;
             minutes -= 60;
             }
          return temp;            // return old original value
          }
     };  // end class airtime
/////////////////////////////////////////////////////////////
void main()
     {
     airtime at1, at2;           // make two airtimes
     at1.get();                  // get value for one

     at2 = ++at1;                // increment (prefix) and assign
     cout << "\nat2=";
     at2.display();              // display assigned value

     at2 = at1++;                // increment (postfix) and assign
     cout << "\nat1=";
     at1.display();              // display incremented value
     cout << "\nat2=";
     at2.display();              // display assigned value
     }
```

The prefix version of ++ increments its object before its value is used so it can return its own value. But where before I used

```
return airtime(hours, minutes);
```

I can now say

```
return *this;
```

This allows me to use a reference return and to avoid copying any objects at all.

As I noted earlier, the postfix version must return the value its object had *before* it was incremented, so there's no choice but to save this value in a temporary object and return this object after the real object has been incremented. Because a temporary object is being returned, it must be returned by value, so I can't make a corresponding improvement in the postfix ++ operator.

Summary of Fine-Tuning for Overloaded Operators

Table 6-1 shows the recommended approach to overloaded operators as regards their return value, how their argument (if any) is passed, and whether they are themselves declared const. Note that this table applies only to operators used as member functions, as I've shown in this chapter, not to operators that are friend functions.

Type of Overloaded Operator	Return	Argument Passed by	Function
*Arithmetic (+, -, *, /)	by value	const reference	const
Assignment (=, +=, -=)	by reference (*this)	const reference	non-const
*Comparison (<, ==)	by value (boolean)	const reference	const
Unary prefix (++, --)	by reference (*this)	none	non-const
Unary postfix (++, --)	by value	value (dummy int)	non-const
Unary (-, +)	by value	none	const
Subscript ([ ])	by reference	value (integer)	non-const

Table 6-1 *Recommended functions, return values, and arguments for overloaded operators as member functions*

Binary operators other than assignments are marked with asterisks to show that, ideally, they should be friend functions rather than member functions. When they're friends, you can use a basic type on the left of the operator as well as on the right, in classes where this is appropriate. However, except in this case, they work fine as member functions.

1. Which of the following are advantages of declaring an overloaded operator to be a `const` function?
   a. It cannot modify the object for which it was called.
   b. Its return value cannot be modified.
   c. It can be called for a constant object.
   d. It cannot modify its argument.
   e. It cannot modify any objects of its class.

2. In the `airtime` class, the `operator+()` function
   a. adds the object that called it to its argument.
   b. adds its argument to the object that called it.
   c. should return by reference.
   d. returns the value of its own object.
   e. returns the result of the addition.

3. Within a member function, the expression `*this` always refers to
   a. the object passed as an argument to the function.
   b. the address of an object.
   c. a temporary object created within the function.
   d. the object that called the function.
   e. the object that will be returned from the function.

4. In the overloaded assignment operator `+=`,
   a. the object for which the operator is called may be modified.
   b. the argument to the operator may be modified.
   c. nothing is modified but the return value.
   d. the return value is the sum of the object that called the operator and its argument.
   e. the return value is the same as that of the object that called the operator.

5. The prefix version of the increment operator `++`
   a. can return by reference.
   b. modifies the object that called it.
   c. returns the value of the object that called it.
   d. returns a temporary object that has been incremented.
   e. returns a temporary object that has not been incremented.

Overload the `>=` operator for the `airtime` class, using the various improvements shown in this session.

EXERCISE 2

Overload the `*=` operator for the English class, again using the various improvements shown in this session. Multiply by type `int` (how many feet and inches in five boards 2'-6" long?) because it gets complicated to generate square feet, which are not the same as feet.

SUMMARY: CHAPTER 6

You've seen how the normal C++ operators, such as `+`, `+=`, `<`, and `++`, can be made to work with class objects as well as with basic C++ types such as `int` and `float`. This involves overloading the operators so they cause different functions to be executed, depending on the data type of their operands.

The advantage of operator overloading is purely visual: Source code may be easier to read and write when operators are used instead of functions such as `add()`. However, using equivalent functions produces the same results. It follows that overloaded operators should not be used unless they make the listing easier to read. They are not helpful when they do something that is not intuitively similar to their operation on basic types. Using the `+` operator to display something or, worse yet, to subtract two objects is a bad idea.

With binary operators, as in `a+b`, the object that calls the overloaded function is to the left of the operator; the object to the right is an argument to the operator. Unary operators may appear on either side of the object that calls them: `++a` and `a++`. Unary operators take no argument.

Various techniques can be used to make overloaded operators safer and more efficient. Most arguments should be `const` and passed by reference, to avoid the creation of extraneous object copies. The operators themselves should be `const` whenever they don't modify the object that called them. The `*this` expression allows the value of the object that called the operator to be returned by reference, which again avoids the creation of additional copies.

As you will find when you learn about friend functions, you can make an additional improvement to overloaded binary operators. Also, you'll see in Chapter 10 how the `<<` and `>>` operators can be overloaded to perform input and output with class objects, as they do with basic types.

END-OF-CHAPTER DISCUSSION

Estelle: There's some pretty subtle stuff going on. I like overloaded operators, but I don't like worrying about the most efficient possible way to write them.

George: Yeah, it's a drag. You've got to think about every little thing. Does an operator modify its own object? Does it modify its argument? Can it return the value of its own object or does it create a new value? It's really too much.

Don: Well, you don't need to worry about all that stuff if you don't want to. Pass all your arguments by value, return everything by value, don't make anything `const`, forget `*this`, and it'll still work.

George: Really?

Don: I wouldn't kid you. It just makes your program faster and smaller and safer if you do it right.

Estelle: Why are we talking about all this efficiency stuff now? Don't these rules apply to regular functions as well as overloaded operators?

Don: Sure. But it's easier to be specific about overloaded operators because they do pretty much the same thing no matter what class they're in.

Estelle: It seems like there are situations where you can do something several different ways. Like when you convert one class to another, you could use a constructor in one class or an overloaded cast operator in the other class.

George: You could probably overload the equal operator, too.

Don: I don't think there are any rules about which approach to use. It depends on the circumstances, like which class is already written, or which class you have the source code for, or which classes have peek functions.

Estelle: The nice thing about C++ is you can try out stuff and the compiler will pretty much tell you if it's right.

Don: It's a lot smarter than the C compiler. If you can compile it error free in C++, it'll probably run.

INHERITANCE

nheritance is the second central concept behind object-oriented programing, after classes themselves. In fact, although conceptually inheritance is secondary to the idea of classes, practically it is the driving force behind OOP. Why? Because inheritance makes reusability possible. Reusability means taking an existing class and using it in a new programming situation. By reusing classes, you can reduce the time and effort needed to develop a program, and make software more robust and reliable. If you develop software for money, you can't afford to overlook the savings made possible by reusability.

Inheritance also plays a major role in OOP design. It allows you to conceptualize a complex program using a new relationship between program elements.

357

In this chapter, I'll first discuss the conceptual underpinning of inheritance and then I'll delve into some of the slippery details, including how to handle constructors in inheritance and multiple inheritance. Along the way, you'll see plenty of examples of how to use this key feature of OOP.

INTRODUCTION TO INHERITANCE

In this first session, I'll start by considering the two principal motivations for inheritance: how it aids reusability and how it provides a new basis for program organization. I'll finish the session by introducing the syntax used to make one class inherit from another.

Reusability

To understand why inheritance is important, you need to look back at the history of reusability. Programmers have always tried to avoid writing the same code twice, or "reinventing the wheel." Inheritance is the latest solution to this problem, and the most powerful.

Rewriting Code

The earliest approach to reusability was simply rewriting existing code. You have some code that works in an old program, but doesn't do quite what you want in a new project. You paste the old code into your new source file, make a few modifications to adapt it to the new environment, and you're off and running. Except that the modifications you made, in all probability, have introduced new bugs. Now you must debug the code all over again. Often you're sorry you didn't just write new code.

Function Libraries

To reduce the bugs introduced by modification of code, programmers attempted to create self-sufficient program elements in the form of functions. The hope was that functions could be written that were general enough that they could be used without modification in a variety of programming situations. Software companies gathered groups of such functions together into *function libraries* and sold them to other programmers.

Function libraries were a step in the right direction, but, as I discussed in Chapter 1, functions don't model the real world very well, because they don't include important data. All too often, functions require modification to work in a new environment; it was common for the purveyors of function libraries to provide source code to make such modifications easier. But again, the modifications introduced bugs.

Class Libraries

A powerful new approach to reusability appears in OOP: the class library. Because a class more closely models a real-world entity, it needs less modification than functions do to adapt it to a new situation. More importantly, OOP provides a way—in effect—to modify a class without changing its code. This apparent contradiction is achieved by using inheritance to derive a new class from the old one. The old class (called the *base class*) is not modified, but the new class (the *derived class*) can use all the features of the old one and additional features of its own. Figure 7-1 shows how this looks.

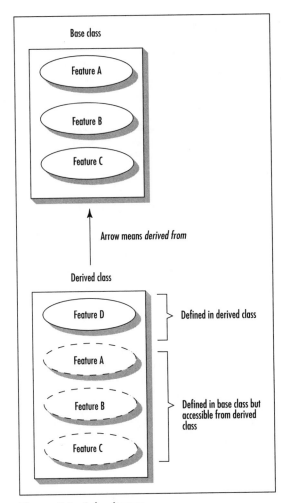

Figure 7-1 Inheritance

Inheritance and Program Design

Besides making it easier to modify existing program components, inheritance has another benefit. It provides a new way of relating one program component to another. This new relationship gives added flexibility to program design and allows program architecture to mirror real-world relationships more accurately. Inheritance is sometimes referred to as a "kind of" relationship. To see what this means, let's first examine another relationship, *composition*, which you can think of as a "has a" relationship.

Composition: A "Has a" Relationship

You've already used composition many times. Every time you place instance data in a class, you are creating a "has a" relationship. If there is a class `employee` and one of the data items in this class is the employee's name, I can say that an `employee` object *has a* name. The `employee` object may also have a salary, ID number, and so on. This sort of relationship is called *composition* because the `employee` object is composed of these other variables.

Similarly, in a `stack` class, member data may include an array (to hold the stack's data) and an index to the top of the stack. I can say that a `stack` object is composed of an array and a stack-top index.

Class member data can contain objects of other classes as well as variables of basic types. I might use `airtime` objects called `Departure` and `Arrival` in an airline's `FlightInformation` class. Or you can imagine a `bicycle` class, in which each `bicycle` object includes a `frame` object, two `wheel` objects, and a `handlebar` object (among other things). Composition in OOP models the real-world situation in which objects are composed of other objects.

Old-fashioned procedural languages such as C and Pascal model this "has a" relationship using structures. A structure can be composed of variables and other structures. However, there is another relationship procedural languages cannot model: the "kind of" relationship.

Inheritance: A "Kind of" Relationship

Inheritance in OOP mirrors the concept that we call *generalization* in the real world. If I have a racing bicycle, a mountain bicycle, and a child's bicycle, I can say that these are all specific instances of a more general concept called a bicycle. Every kind of bicycle has certain features: two wheels, a frame, and so on. But a racing bike, in addition to these general features, has narrow tires and a low weight. A mountain bike also has all the features of a bicycle, but in addition has fat knobbly tires and powerful brakes.

Similarly, there may be laborers, executives, scientists, and clerks on a company's payroll. These are all specific examples of a more general category of employees.

We use generalization in our everyday perception of the world. I know that cats, sheep, and humans are kinds of mammals; trucks, cars, and buses are kinds of vehicles; that PCs and Macintoshes are kinds of computers. This sort of relationship is so common in ordinary life that it makes sense to model it in computer programs. That's what inheritance does. As you'll see as we go along, this turns out to be a surprisingly useful tool in program design.

Not Exactly a Family Tree

Inheritance is often compared to family relationships; hence the name. However, inheritance in OOP is not quite the same thing as inheritance in human families. For one thing, a class can—and usually does—inherit from a single parent. Also, derived classes tend to have more features than base classes, whereas human children, as is well known, often lack qualities possessed by their parents.

Inheritance Syntax

The simplest example of inheritance requires two classes: a base class and a derived class. The base class does not need any special syntax. The derived class, on the other hand, must indicate that it's derived from the base class. This is done by placing a colon after the name of the derived class, followed by a keyword such as `public` and then the base class name, like this:

```
class Base
    {
    // member data and functions
    };

class Derv : public Base
    {
    // member data and functions
    };
```

The colon (like the arrow in inheritance diagrams) means "is derived from." Thus, the class `Derv` is derived from the class `Base` and inherits all the data and functions that `Base` has (although I don't show any here). I'll leave an explanation of the keyword `public` until later. (It's called an *access specifier*, and the other possibilities are `private` and `protected`, but `public` is by far the most commonly used.) Figure 7-2 shows the syntax used in inheritance.

Let's look at a more detailed example. Listing 7-1 has a `Parent` class, and a `Child` class derived from it.

Listing 7-1 INHERIT

```
// inherit.cpp
// skeleton classes demonstrate inheritance
#include <iostream.h>

class Parent
    {
    private:
        float flov;                    // Parent's data
    public:
        void pget()                    // get Parent's data
            {
            cout << "\n   Enter float value: ";
            cin >> flov;
            }
        void pdisplay()                // display Parent's data
            {
            cout << "flov=" << flov;
```

continued on next page

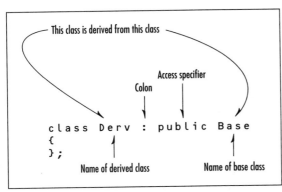

Figure 7-2   Derived class syntax

continued from previous page

```
         }
    };

class Child : public Parent
    {
    private:
        int intv;                    // Child has its own data
    public:
        void cget()                  // get data for Child
          {
          pget();                    // call function in Parent
          cout << "   Enter integer value: ";
          cin >> intv;               // get Child-specific data
          }
        void cdisplay()
          {
          pdisplay();                // call function in Parent
          cout << ", intv=" << intv; // show Child-specific data
          }
    };

void main()
    {
    Child ch;                        // make a child object

    cout << "Requesting data for child object";
    ch.cget();                       // get data for it

    cout << "Data in child object is ";
    ch.cdisplay();                   // display its data
    }
```

The Parent class has a data item flov, along with pget() and pdisplay() member functions. The Child class has a data item intv and similar cget() and cdisplay() functions.

In main(), the program creates an object of class Child, gets data for it from the user, and then displays the data. Here's how the interaction with the program looks:

```
Requesting data for child object
   Enter float value: 456.789
   Enter integer value: 123
Data in child object is flov=456.789, intv=123
```

This may seem mysterious. Although the object ch of class Child contains only an integer data item, the output shows it has successfully stored and retrieved a float item as well. How does this happen?

Inheriting Attributes

An object of a derived class *inherits all the member data and functions of the base class*. Thus the Child object ch contains not only a data item intv, but a data item flov as well. The ch object can also access, in addition to its own member functions cget() and cdisplay(), the member functions from Parent, which are pget() and pdisplay().

Accessing Base Class Data

Although an object of a derived class may contain data defined in the base class, it doesn't necessarily follow that this data is *accessible* from the derived class. Assuming that I want the `cdisplay()` function in `Child` to display `Parent`'s `flov` data as well as its own `intv`, could I rewrite `cdisplay()` this way?

```
class Child
   {
   ...
   void cdisplay()
      {
      cout << "flov=" << flov;       // error: private Parent member
      cout << ", intv=" << intv;
      }
   };
```

No, I can't access `flov` from the `Child` class, because `flov` is a *private* member of `Parent`. As is usual in C++, public members (data and functions) can be accessed from outside the class, but private members cannot.

It's true that the derived class occupies a strange new position with regard to the base class. Derived class functions aren't actually in the base class, but they are more closely related to the base class than functions in some completely unrelated class. Nevertheless, they can't access private members of the base class. (You'll see later that a special category, `protected`, does allow such access.)

Calling a Base Class Function

Fortunately, I don't need to access the base class data `flov` from functions in `Child` objects directly. Unlike `flov`, which is private, the member functions of `Parent` are public, so I can call them to handle `flov`. From `cget()` I call `pget()`, which asks the user to enter a value for `flov`. From `cdisplay()` I call `pdisplay()`, which displays the value of `flov`. The derived class need never access `flov` directly.

Function Overloading in Base and Derived Classes

In the INHERIT program, there are separate functions to get user input in the base and derived classes: `pget()` for `Parent` and `cget()` for `Child`. Similarly, `pdisplay()` displays the data item in `Parent` and `cdisplay()` displays the item in `Child`. It's somewhat confusing, and not in the spirit of OOP, to use different function names for functions that do essentially the same thing. It would be nice if both these functions had the same name, so the name would be clearer and easier to remember (among other benefits).

It turns out that it's perfectly all right to overload functions in base and derived classes. If I name both functions `display()`, we'll have a situation like this:

```
class Parent
   {
   void display()
      { }
   };
class Child : public Parent
```

continued on next page

continued from previous page

```
    {
    void display()
        {
//      display();          // bad: calls display() in Child
        Parent::display();  // good: calls display() in Parent
        }
    };
```

The compiler has no trouble distinguishing the two versions of display() because they're in different classes.

However, if I use the name display() in a derived class function, the compiler assumes I mean the function of that name *in the derived class*. That would be disastrous from within display(), because a function calling itself over and over would eventually crash the program. In the derived class, to refer to the version of the function that's in the base class, I must use the scope resolution operator and the base class name:

```
Parent::display();
```

This makes it clear to the compiler which function I mean. Listing 7-2, a revised version of the INHER-IT example, shows how it looks when I overload the member functions, calling both display functions display() and both input functions get().

Listing 7-2 INHERIT2

```
// inherit2.cpp
// skeleton classes demonstrate inheritance
// uses overloaded functions
#include <iostream.h>

class Parent
    {
    private:
        float flov;
    public:
        void get()
            {
            cout << "\n    Enter float value: ";
            cin >> flov;
            }
        void display()
            {
            cout << "flov=" << flov;
            }
    };

class Child : public Parent
    {
    private:
        int intv;
    public:
        void get()
            {
            Parent::get();
            cout << "    Enter integer value: ";
```

```
            cin >> intv;
            }
        void display()
            {
            Parent::display();
            cout << ", intv=" << intv;
            }
        };

void main()
    {
    Child ch;

    cout << "Requesting data for child object";
    ch.get();

    cout << "Data in child object is ";
    ch.display();
    }
```

This program operates the same way as INHERIT, but using overloaded functions makes it easier for the class user to remember the function names.

Table 7-1 summarizes how overloaded and normal functions can be accessed from base and derived classes. I assume there's a `basefunc()` member function in the base class, a `dervfunc()` function in the derived class, and an overloaded `func()` in both classes.

Function Is Member of	Overload Status	To Access Function from Base Class	To Access Function from Derived Class
Base class	Different names	`basefunc()`	`basefunc()`
Base class	Overloaded	`func()`	`Base::func()`
Derived class	Different names	Function is unknown	`dervfunc()`
Derived class	Overloaded	Function is unknown	`func()`

Table 7-1 *Function accessibility from base and derived classes*

If functions are not overloaded, the derived class can access functions in the base class using their name alone. For overloaded functions, the derived class must use the scope resolution operator to access functions in the base class.

Of course, inheritance only works one way. The base class doesn't know anything about the derived class and can't access any of its members.

QUIZ 1

1. Inheritance facilitates reusability because
    a. child objects cannot be modified.
    b. the base class need not be modified to derive a new class.

    c. programming objects are more like real-world objects.

    d. objects of the base class can be treated as objects of the derived class.

    e. derived class objects inherit only the desirable features of the base class.

2. Inheritance helps with program organization by

    a. allowing the use of "gives birth to" arrows in organization diagrams.

    b. modeling the "has a" relationship.

    c. exactly replicating human family trees.

    d. providing a new kind of relationship between objects.

    e. allowing a class to consist of objects of other classes.

3. If you want the functions in a derived class to access the data in a base class directly, you must

    a. make the base class data private.

    b. not make the base class data private.

    c. use a private base class function.

    d. use a nonprivate base class function.

    e. make the data public and call a public access function.

4. To access a public nonoverloaded base class function `bafunc()`, a statement in a derived class function `defunc()` uses the expression

    a. `Base::bafunc();`

    b. `Derv::bafunc();`

    c. `bafunc();`

    d. `defunc();`

    e. "I'm outta luck."

5. To access the public function `func()` in the base class, a statement in the derived class function `func()` uses the statement

    a. "This is impossible."

    b. `Base();`

    c. `Derv();`

    d. `func();`

    e. `Base::func();`

Due to its abstract nature, this session has no exercises.

SESSION 2

PROGRAM DESIGN: THE employee CLASS

Let's look at a somewhat more realistic example of inheritance. I'll start with the **employee** class of the EMPLOY1 program from Chapter 3, Session 2. This program emphasizes the program design aspect of inheritance: that is, using inheritance as a basic way to relate program components. It is less relevant to the concept of reusability, which I'll focus on in the next session.

Suppose I want to program a database of company employees. It's common for employees to be divided into different categories. In this particular imaginary company, I'll assume there are managers, scientists, and laborers. (Forget for the moment about secretaries, salespeople, accountants, and so on.)

Class Hierarchy

When you encounter a situation in which different categories of things can be described as kinds of something else, you're looking at a situation that can be modeled in a program as inheritance. Managers, scientists, and laborers are kinds of employees. Here's how that looks in C++ in skeleton form:

```
class employee
    { ... };

class manager : public employee
    { ... };

class scientist : public employee
    { ... };

class laborer : public employee
    { ... };
```

The three classes **manager**, **scientist**, and **laborer** are derived from the **employee** class.

All employees, no matter what derived class they belong to, share some common elements. For purposes of the database, let's assume that they all have a name and an ID number. In inheritance, such common elements are placed "upstream," in the base class. The derived classes have their own individual characteristics. The characteristics that are important about managers are titles, such as "President" or "Vice-President," and golf club dues. For scientists, the important data is the number of publications for which the scientist has written scholarly articles. Laborers have no distinguishing characteristics other than their name and ID number. (A database program does not always mirror the diversity of real people, with all their hopes and dreams.) Figure 7-3 shows how this looks.

The EMPINH Program

The full-scale program is rather lengthy, but the similarities of the classes make it easier to understand than it might seem at first sight. Listing 7-3 shows EMPINH.

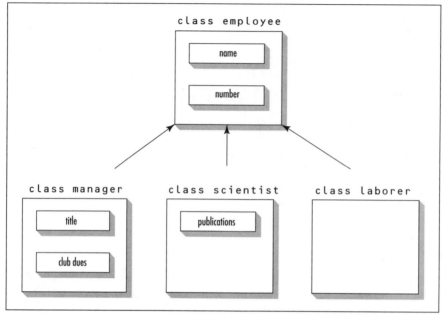

Figure 7-3 Class hierarchy in EMPINH

Listing 7-3 EMPINH

```
// empinh.cpp
// models employee database using inheritance
#include <iostream.h>

class employee                 // employee class
    {
    private:
        enum { LEN=30 };        // maximum length of names
        char name[LEN];         // employee name
        unsigned long number;   // employee number
    public:
        void getdata()
            {
            cout << "\n   Enter last name: "; cin >> name;
            cout << "   Enter number: ";      cin >> number;
            }
        void putdata()
            {
            cout << "\n   Name = " << name;
            cout << "\n   Number = " << number;
            }
    };

class manager : public employee      // management class
    {
    private:
```

```
        enum { LEN=40 };   // maximum length of titles
        char title[LEN];   // "vice-president" etc.
        double dues;       // golf club dues
    public:
        void getdata()
            {
            employee::getdata();
            cout << "    Enter title: ";           cin >> title;
            cout << "    Enter golf club dues: "; cin >> dues;
            }
        void putdata()
            {
            employee::putdata();
            cout << "\n    Title = " << title;
            cout << "\n    Golf club dues = " << dues;
            }
    };
class scientist : public employee       // scientist class
    {
    private:
        int pubs;       // number of publications
    public:
        void getdata()
            {
            employee::getdata();
            cout << "    Enter number of pubs: "; cin >> pubs;
            }
        void putdata()
            {
            employee::putdata();
            cout << "\n    Number of publications = " << pubs;
            }
    };

class laborer : public employee       // laborer class
    {
    };

void main()
    {
    manager m1, m2;
    scientist s1;
    laborer l1;

    cout << endl;
    cout << "\nEnter data for manager 1";     // get data for
    m1.getdata();                              // several employees

    cout << "\nEnter data for manager 2";
    m2.getdata();

    cout << "\nEnter data for scientist 1";
    s1.getdata();
```

continued on next page

continued from previous page

```
    cout << "\nEnter data for laborer 1";
    l1.getdata();

    cout << "\nData on manager 1";          // display data for
    m1.putdata();                           // several employees

    cout << "\nData on manager 2";
    m2.putdata();

    cout << "\nData on scientist 1";
    s1.putdata();

    cout << "\nData on laborer 1";
    l1.putdata();
    }
```

The member functions of `manager` and `scientist` call base class functions in `employee` to get the employee name and number from the user and to display them. They also handle their own particular data, title, and dues for managers and number of publications for scientists. The `laborer` class relies completely on `employee` for all data and member functions.

Abstract Classes

You might think I could simply use `employee` objects instead of `laborer` objects, because they have the same data and functions. However, this violates the spirit of the program's organization. As used here, the `employee` class is not one from which actual objects will be instantiated. The only purpose of `employee` is to serve as a general class from which other classes are derived. All real employees are members of a more specific category.

As an analogy, imagine you own a specific animal called Toby. If someone asked you what Toby is, you probably wouldn't say, "Oh, he's a mammal." Everyone would say, "Yes, but what kind of mammal?" All real animals must come from a more specific category than simply mammals. (It turns out Toby is a hamster.) Mammal is a category that has no members itself, but serves only as a generalization.

A class from which you don't intend to instantiate any objects, but is used only as a base class for other classes is called an *abstract class*. One of the advantages of using an abstract class for `employee` is that if you decide, sometime after the `employee` class hierarchy is designed, to add a data item to the `laborer` class, then you can modify `laborer` without modifying `employee`, which would potentially affect all `employee`'s derived classes.

Abstract classes are a powerful concept in OOP, and I'll return to them later.

Interaction with EMPINH

In `main()`, the program creates four employees: two managers, a scientist, and a laborer. It then gets the data for these four employees from the user and displays it. Here's some sample interaction with EMPINH. First the user enters the data:

```
Enter data for manager 1
   Enter last name: Montegue
   Enter number: 111
```

```
    Enter title: President
    Enter golf club dues: 500000

Enter data for manager 2
    Enter last name: Blakley
    Enter number: 222
    Enter title: Vice-President
    Enter golf club dues: 100000

Enter data for scientist 1
    Enter last name: Lee
    Enter number: 333
    Enter number of pubs: 99

Enter data for laborer 1
    Enter last name: Jones
            Enter number: 87647162
```

Then the program plays it back:

```
Data on Manager 1
    Name = Montegue
    Number = 111
    Title = President
    Golf club dues = 500000

Data on Manager 2
    Name = Blakley
    Number = 222
    Title = Vice-President
    Golf club dues = 100000

Data on Scientist 1
    Name = Lee
    Number = 333
    Number of publications = 99

Data on Laborer 1
    Name = Jones
    Number = 87647162
```

1. The purpose of the EMPINH program is to demonstrate
    a. inheritance.
    b. composition.
    c. classes.
    d. the "kind of" relationship.
    e. reusability.

2. In EMPINH, the _____ class is _____ the _____ class(es).
    a. `scientist`, the base class for, `employee`
    b. `laborer`, derived from, `employee`
    c. `employee`, composed of, `manager`, `scientist`, and `laborer`
    d. `employee`, derived from, `laborer`
    e. `laborer`, the same as, `employee`

3. An object of the `scientist` class contains instance data representing
    a. the employee name, employee number, and number of publications.
    b. only the number of publications.
    c. only the employee name and employee number.
    d. the title and golf club dues.
    e. the location of the object.

4. From the `manager` class, you call the `putdata()` function in `employee` to
    a. display all the data on a manager.
    b. satisfy the formal requirements of the compiler.
    c. display the manager's name and number.
    d. display the manager's title and golf club dues.
    e. let the compiler know you're dealing with an object derived from the `employee` class.

5. An abstract class is
    a. one whose objects are identical to those of some derived class.
    b. one from which no objects will be instantiated.
    c. one that contains common elements of derived classes.
    d. any base class.
    e. any derived class.

EXERCISE 1

Add a `secretary` class to the hierarchy in EMPINH. The quality unique to this class is typing speed in words per minute, an integer value. In `main()`, create two objects of this class and input and output appropriate data.

EXERCISE 2

Create a class hierarchy with a vehicle base class. Derived classes will be trucks, cars, buses, and motorcycles. All vehicles have instance data representing the vehicle identification number (type `long`) and the gross vehicle weight. In addition, trucks have a load capacity (in pounds, type `float`), cars have a body style (a string, such as "sedan", "sports car", or "station wagon"), and busses have a passenger capacity (type `int`). Motorcycles have no additional instance data.

SESSION 3

REUSABILITY: AN IMPROVED
Stack CLASS

In the last session, we examined a program in which inheritance served as a major design element. In this session, I'll demonstrate a program where inheritance allows reusability. I'll start with the Stack class, last seen in the ENUMSIZE program from Chapter 5, Session 4.

As you may recall, the previous versions of the Stack class did not warn the class user if too many items were placed on the stack or too many items were removed. Let's remedy this situation by deriving a new class from Stack that checks for stack overflow and underflow. I'll call this derived class (with a certain lack of inventiveness) Stack2.

Reusability

Imagine that one company (or group of programmers) developed the original Stack class. It spent many years developing and debugging the class, and the class is now a reliable programming component. Later, another programming group in another company obtains a library containing the Stack class. It is impressed with the class's speed and versatility, but the company discovers that it needs better error protection. This second group therefore derives a new class from the old one. Because it doesn't change anything in the original Stack class, the original features will continue to work well. The new class simply adds some new features; it is only these that need to be debugged.

The STACKINH Program

In a real-world situation, I would be dealing with multiple files, but for simplicity I'll show both the base class and derived class as part of the same source file. Listing 7-4 shows STACKINH.

Listing 7-4 STACKINH

```
// stackinh.cpp
// improved stack created using inheritance
#include <iostream.h>
#include <process.h>          // for exit()

class Stack                    // a stack holds up to SIZE ints
   {
   protected:
      enum {SIZE=20};          // capacity of stack
      int st[SIZE];            // integers are stored in array
      int top;                 // index of last item pushed
   public:
      Stack()                  // no-arg constructor
         { top = -1; }
      void push(int var)       // place an item on the stack
         { st[++top] = var; }
      int pop()                // remove an item from the stack
```

continued on next page

continued from previous page

```
          { return st[top--]; }
   };
//////////////////////////////////////////////////////////////
class Stack2 : public Stack
   {
   public:
   void push(int var)
      {
      if(top >= SIZE-1)
         { cout << "Error: stack overflow"; exit(-1); }
      Stack::push(var);        // call push() in Stack class
      }
   int pop()
      {
      if(top<0)
         { cout << "Error: stack underflow"; exit(-1); }
      return Stack::pop();     // call pop() in Stack class
      }
   };
//////////////////////////////////////////////////////////////
void main()
   {
   Stack2 s;                   // create a Stack2 object

   s.push(11);                 // push 3 items onto it
   s.push(12);
   s.push(13);

   cout << s.pop() << endl;    // pop items and display them
   cout << s.pop() << endl;
   cout << s.pop() << endl;
   cout << s.pop() << endl;    // oops, popped one too many
   }
```

A Smarter Object

The `Stack2` class has no data of its own. Its role is to "wrap" the `pop()` and `push()` functions of the `Stack` class with its own improved `pop()` and `push()`. These improved functions start with `if` statements that check to be sure the class user is not popping or pushing too many items. Then they call the base class versions of `pop()` or `push()` to carry out the actual data storage and retrieval.

The accessible members of a class are called its *interface*, because they're what the class user interacts with. Here the interface for `Stack2` is just the same as for `Stack`. The `Stack2` class has in effect disguised itself as the `Stack` class. However, a `Stack2` object is smarter internally.

In `main()`, the program creates a `Stack2` object and pushes three items onto it. Then, mistakenly, it pops four items off. Fortunately it's using the new improved `Stack2` class, which duly complains. Here's the output from STACKINH:

```
13
12
11
Error: stack underflow
```

The Base Class Constructor

Notice that there is a constructor in the base class **s t a c k** but not in the derived class **s t a c k 2**. When you create an object of the derived class, the compiler checks to see if it has a constructor. If it does, the constructor arranges for it to be called; if there is no derived class constructor, the compiler calls the base class constructor instead. (This is only true of no-argument constructors, as you'll see in the next session.) In **s t a c k**, this constructor's job is to initialize the **t o p** index to the top of the empty stack.

The p r o t e c t e d **Access Specifier**

Actually, as you may have noticed, it's not true that I made absolutely no alterations to the base class **s t a c k** before deriving **s t a c k 2** from it. Can you spot the change? I altered the access specifier for **s t a c k**'s data from **p r i v a t e** (which I've used for member data in all previous examples) to **p r o t e c t e d**. What effect does this have?

I've noted that a **p r i v a t e** access specifier allows access only by member functions that are within the class itself. A **p u b l i c** specifier, on the other hand, allows access by any function in the program. The **p r o t e c t e d** specifier has a role in between. It allows access to functions that are *either* members of the class or members of its derived classes. Thus, **p r o t e c t e d** is the family-oriented access specifier.

The creators of **s t a c k** would need to make its data **p r o t e c t e d** when the class was first created so that, if anyone else wanted to derive other classes from it, they could access the data.

Actually, there's a disadvantage to making class data **p r o t e c t e d** in that it's not quite as safe as if it were **p u b l i c**. I'll return to this point when I focus on access specifiers in Session 5 in this chapter.

Functions That Aren't Inherited

Before we go any farther, I should mention that a few special functions aren't automatically inherited. What does this mean? As you learned in Session 1 in this chapter, if you have a function **f u n c ( )** in a base class **a l p h a** and it's not overloaded in a derived class **b e t a**, then an object of a derived class can call this base class function:

```
beta bb;
bb.func();
```

The function **f u n c ( )** is automatically inherited by **b e t a**. The assumption is that **f u n c ( )** operates only on base class data; it doesn't need to interact with the derived class.

With a few functions, however, you know in advance that they will need to do different things in the base class and the derived class. They are the overloaded = operator, the destructor, and all constructors.

Consider a constructor. The base class constructor must create the base class data, and the derived class constructor must create the derived class data. Because the derived class and base class constructors create different data, one constructor cannot be used in place of another. Thus, constructors cannot be automatically inherited.

Similarly, the = operator in the derived class must assign values to derived class data, and the = operator in the base class must assign values to base class data. These are different jobs, so this operator is not automatically inherited.

Finally, in the same way, a derived class destructor destroys derived class data. It can't destroy the base class object; it must call the base class constructor to do this. Again, these destructors do different jobs, so they can't inherit.

If you explicitly define one of these noninheritable functions in the base class, the = operator, say, and don't explicitly define the same function in the derived class, the compiler will generate a default version for you. The default copy constructors and the default = operator perform memberwise copying and assignment.

QUIZ 3

1. The purpose of the STACKINH example is to demonstrate
   a. inheritance.
   b. composition.
   c. the "kind of" relationship.
   d. a class hierarchy.
   e. reusability.

2. The class creator may make the data in the **Stack** class **protected**
   a. so that it cannot be accessed by functions in other classes.
   b. so that it can be accessed by objects of derived classes.
   c. if other classes will be derived from **Stack**.
   d. if **Stack** is derived from another class.
   e. to prevent other classes from being derived from **Stack**.

3. The interface between a class and the class user consists of
   a. the class member functions accessible from a derived class.
   b. the class's public member functions or data.
   c. the class specification.
   d. any class member functions and variable definitions.
   e. calls in **main()** to class member functions.

4. Which of the following are true?
   a. If the base class has a constructor, the derived class must also have one.
   b. If the derived class has a constructor, the base class must also have one.
   c. If the base class has no constructor, the derived class constructor will be called.
   d. If the derived class has no constructor, the base class constructor will be called.
   e. The compiler will look for multiple approaches to a problem.

5. The **protected** access specifier
   a. allows access to functions in the program.
   b. allows access to functions in the class.
   c. allows access to functions in derived classes.
   d. is used in the base class.
   e. is used in the derived class.

EXERCISE 1

In Exercise 2 in Chapter 3, Session 2, I discussed a `peek()` function that allows the user of a stack to read the data item from the top of the stack without popping it off. Write such a function for the `Stack` class and then write an overloaded version for the `Stack2` class that checks to be sure the stack is not empty.

EXERCISE 2

A queue is like a stack except that it works on a first-in-first-out (FIFO) principle instead of the last-in-first-out (LIFO) principle of a stack. It's like the line at a bank teller's window: The first person to join the tail of the line is the first person to reach the head of the line and be removed. Rewrite the `Stack` and `Stack2` classes in the STACKINH program so they model queues instead of stacks; you can call the new classes `Queue` and `Queue2`. You'll need two index variables, `head` and `tail`, instead of `top`. The head index will be incremented when an item is pushed onto the queue, and the tail index will be incremented when an item is popped off. These indexes will follow each other through the array as items are pushed and popped. When either one gets to the end of the array, it must wrap around to the beginning.

SESSION 4

CONSTRUCTORS AND INHERITANCE

As you've seen, constructors are rather special functions. It's not surprising, therefore, that they play an unusual role in inheritance. In this session, I'll examine that role, show you when you need constructors and when you don't, and explain how one constructor can call another using a special syntax.

The Great Chain of Constructors

When you define an object of a derived class, not only is its constructor executed but the constructor in the base class is executed as well. In fact—perhaps surprisingly—the base class constructor is executed first. This is because the base class object is a *subobject*—a part—of the derived class object, and you need to construct the parts before you can construct the whole. Figure 7-4 shows the relationship between objects and subobjects.

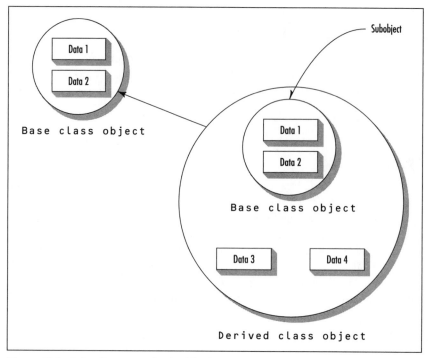

Figure 7-4 Inheritance and subobjects

The constructors for all the subobjects of an object are called before the constructor for the object itself. The next example demonstrates this point. Listing 7-5 shows INCONDES.

Listing 7-5 INCONDES

```
// incondes.cpp
// tests constructors and destructors in inheritance
#include <iostream.h>
/////////////////////////////////////////////////////
class Parent
    {
    public:
        Parent()
            { cout << "\n    Parent constructor"; }
        ~Parent()
            { cout << "\n    Parent destructor"; }
    };
/////////////////////////////////////////////////////
class Child : public Parent
    {
    public:
        Child()
            { cout << "\n    Child constructor"; }
        ~Child()
            { cout << "\n    Child destructor"; }
    };
```

```
/////////////////////////////////////////////////////
void main()
    {
    cout << "\nStarting";
    Child ch;                      // create a Child object
    cout << "\nTerminating";
    }
```

This program specifies a Parent class and a Child class derived from Parent. In main(), it then creates an object of the Child class. I've installed explicit constructors and destructors in both classes that identify themselves when they execute. Here's the output from INCONDES:

```
Starting
    Parent constructor
    Child constructor
Terminating
    Child destructor
    Parent destructor
```

As you can see, the base class constructor is called first; then the derived class constructor is called. When the Child object goes out of scope at the end of the program, the destructors are called in reverse order: The derived object is destroyed first, then the base class object.

The compiler arranges for all these constructors and destructors to be called automatically, so you don't need to worry about it. Even if you haven't defined explicit constructors and destructors as I did here, the compiler will call the implicit (invisible) ones that actually create and destroy objects and subobjects. You should be aware that this activity is taking place, whether or not you write your own explicit constructors and destructors.

Incidentally, an object's implicit constructor is always called before the explicit one you define. When your explicit constructor starts to execute, your object and all its subobjects already exist and have been initialized.

When Are Derived Class Constructors Necessary?

You saw in the STACKINH program in the last session that you don't need to write a no-argument (default) constructor for the derived class if the base class already has such a constructor. It turns out this is about the *only* time you can get away without explicitly writing a constructor in the derived class.

No Arguments

You can't use a constructor with arguments unless it's explicitly defined in the specific class from which you're instantiating an object. That is, even if there's an *n*-argument constructor in the base class, you must still write an *n*-argument constructor in the derived class. Listing 7-6, CONSINH1, shows how this works.

Listing 7-6 CONSINH1
```
// consinh1.cpp
// demonstrates constructors and inheritance
/////////////////////////////////////////////////////////////////
```

continued on next page

continued from previous page

```
class Mu                          // base class
    {
    private:
        int mudata;               // data
    public:
        Mu() : mudata(0)          // no-arg constructor
            { }
        Mu(int m) : mudata(m)     // one-arg constructor
            { }
    };
/////////////////////////////////////////////////////////////
class Nu : public Mu              // derived class
    {                             // no constructors
    };
/////////////////////////////////////////////////////////////
void main()
    {
    Nu n1;          // can use the no-arg constructor in Mu
//  Nu n2(77);      // error: cannot use one-arg constructor
    }
```

You can write the specification for class `Nu`, which is derived from `Mu`, without any constructors; the compiler doesn't complain. You can also define an object of `Nu` if you don't use any arguments, as seen in the first statement in `main()`. But you can't define a `Nu` object that takes arguments unless there's an appropriate constructor in `Nu` itself. The compiler won't substitute the constructor from the base class because it can't be sure how you want to handle the arguments.

Arguments

If you add an explicit one-argument constructor to the derived class `Mu`, then you must also add a no-argument constructor, just as you must with any class (assuming you're actually going to create objects with this constructor). Listing 7-7 shows the previous program, rewritten as CONSINH2, with these additional constructors.

Listing 7-7 CONSINH2

```
// consinh2.cpp
// demonstrates constructors and inheritance
class Mu
    {
    private:
        int mudata;               // data
    public:
        Mu() : mudata(0)          // no-arg constructor
            { }
        Mu(int m) : mudata(m)     // one-arg constructor
            { }
    };
/////////////////////////////////////////////////////////////
class Nu : public Mu
    {
    public:
        Nu()                          // no-arg constructor
```

```
        { }
    Nu(int n) : Mu(n)          // one-arg constructor
        { }
};
/////////////////////////////////////////////////////////////////
void main()
    {
    Nu n1;                     // calls no-arg constructor
    Nu n2(77);                 // calls 1-arg constructor
    }
```

In `main()`, the program successfully defines `Nu` objects using both the no-argument and the one-argument constructors. The one-argument constructor passes its argument along to the constructor in `Mu` using a new syntax: the initializer list.

The Initializer List

The derived class constructor `Nu(int)` calls the base class constructor `Mu(int)` using a syntax that may appear strange and yet familiar:

```
Nu(int n) : Mu(n)          // one-arg constructor
        { }
```

Everything following the colon is the *initializer list,* where initializations are carried out before the constructor starts to execute. This is the same syntax used by constructors to initialize variables of basic types, but here it's used to call a constructor. Actually these operations are conceptually identical, so it's not surprising they use the same syntax. In one case, a class object is initialized and in the other, a variable of a basic type is initialized, but C++ treats class objects and basic-type variables in the same way.

Here the derived class constructor simply passes the argument `n` along to the base class constructor. It takes no action of its own, so the braces are empty. This is a common situation in derived classes: Constructors have an empty function body because all their work is done in the initialization list.

Adding Functionality to the Derived Class Constructor

Not all derived class constructors have an empty function body. Suppose I want to add an additional feature to the `airtime` class (last seen in the ADDAIRCO program in Chapter 6, Session 8). I want to prevent the class user from initializing `airtime` objects with hours or minutes values that are too large. Hours should be less than 24, and minutes should be less than 60. (Of course, they should both be greater than 0 as well, but I won't worry about that now.) That is, if the class user writes

```
airtime Departure(11, 65);
```

I want the constructor to complain because minutes can't be greater than 59.

To add this new feature to `airtime`, I'll derive a new class called `airtime2`, with the requisite error-checking code in its two-argument constructor. Listing 7-8 shows AIRINH.

Listing 7-8 AIRINH

```
// airinh.cpp
// constructors and inheritance in the airtime class
#include <iostream.h>
#include <process.h>            // for exit()

class airtime
    {
    protected:
        int hours;              // 0 to 23
        int minutes;            // 0 to 59
    public:
                                // no-arg constructor
        airtime() : hours(0), minutes(0)
            {  }
                                // two-arg constructor
        airtime(int h, int m) : hours(h), minutes(m)
            {  }

        void display() const  // output to screen
            { cout << hours << ':' << minutes; }

    };  // end class airtime
/////////////////////////////////////////////////////////////
class airtime2 : public airtime
    {
    public:                     // no-arg constructor
        airtime2() : airtime()
            {  }                // two-arg constructor
        airtime2(int h, int m) : airtime(h, m)
            {
            if(minutes>59 || hours>23)
                { cout << "\nError: invalid airtime value "
                    << hours << ':' << minutes; exit(-1); }
            }
    };  // end class airtime2
/////////////////////////////////////////////////////////////
void main()
    {
    airtime2 at0;               // ok (no-arg constructor)
    cout << "\nat0 = ";
    at0.display();

    airtime2 at1(10, 45);       // ok (2-arg constructor)
    cout << "\nat1 = ";
    at1.display();

    airtime2 at2(10, 65);       // user error (2-arg constructor)
    cout << "\nat2 = ";
    at2.display();
    }
```

In the `airtime2` class, I create explicit no-argument and two-argument constructors. The two-argument constructor calls the two-argument constructor in the base class and then checks the values provided to it. If either hours or minutes is too large, it prints an error message and causes an exit from the program.

In `main()`, the program creates three `airtime2` objects. The first uses the no-argument constructor; the second uses the two-argument constructor with appropriate argument values; and the third uses the two-argument constructor with a `minutes` value that's too large. Here's the output from AIRINH:

```
at0 = 0:00
at1 = 10:45
Error: invalid airtime value 10:65
```

As you can see, the `airtime2` constructor has successfully detected the out-of-range minutes value for `at2` and notified the user.

1. Which of the following are true?
  a. A derived class constructor is executed before the base class constructor.
  b. A derived class constructor is executed after the base class constructor.
  c. A derived class destructor is executed before the base class destructor.
  d. A derived class destructor is executed after the base class destructor.
  e. Derived and base class constructors are executed simultaneously.

2. For a derived class constructor with arguments to call a base class constructor, it must
  a. make the call in the usual way from within its function body.
  b. finish executing before calling the base class constructor.
  c. use any arguments to itself in the call to the base class constructor.
  d. place the call to the base class constructor on its initialization list.
  e. make no explicit call, because the system will handle it automatically.

3. If there's a constructor with arguments in a derived class, then you must have
  a. at least a no-argument constructor in the base class.
  b. a constructor with the same number of arguments in the base class.
  c. a no-argument derived class constructor (assuming you'll substantiate objects without arguments).
  d. a no-argument base class constructor (assuming you'll substantiate objects without arguments).
  e. instantiated objects of the base class.

4. The initializer list in a constructor typically
  a. initializes variables of basic types in its own class.
  b. calls a constructor in a base class.
  c. initializes variables of basic types in a base class.
  d. calls other constructors in its own class.
  e. assigns values to existing variables.

5. A derived class constructor
  a. need not call a base class constructor.

b. can do more than simply call the base class constructor.

c. must call the base class constructor that has the same number of arguments.

d. creates an object of the derived class.

e. creates a subobject of the base class.

EXERCISE 1

Augment the two-argument constructor to the `airtime2` class in the AIRINH program so it checks for values of hours and minutes that are too small (less than 0) as well as too large.

EXERCISE 2

Rewrite the STACKINH program from Session 3 in this chapter so the `stack2` class, in addition to checking for stack overflow and underflow, also provides a one-argument constructor that can create stacks of different sizes, with the value of the argument (type `int`) specifying the size. Actually, the array used will always be the same size, but the stack will *act* as if it's a smaller size in that it will report stack overflow if the user tries to push too many items.

MIDCHAPTER DISCUSSION

George: Does this reusability business work in the real world? I mean, do software companies actually see any improvement in the bottom line because of inheritance?

Don: Absolutely. Although I hear it takes a while for the payoff. First the programmers have to learn C++. And then they need to write the first major application in C++. After that, they start to be much more productive, because they can reuse classes from the first project for all the projects that follow.

Estelle: Well, I bet it takes a while to learn. Things are getting pretty complicated, aren't they? All these rules about constructors, when you need them and when you don't. Who can remember all that?

Don: I've been trying out some of this stuff at home, and...

George: Oh, aren't you the overachiever! You better not learn this stuff too fast, or you'll make the rest of us look bad.

Don: ...and the surprising thing is that the compiler really helps you get it right. If you need a constructor and you don't have one, the compiler lets you know. So it's a lot easier to program than you might think. It's like the compiler is on your side, for a change.

Estelle: Sounds like you need to experiment a lot.

Don: Absolutely. Writing code is even more important for learning C++ than it is for procedural languages. Wump on those keys!

George: Oh, for Pete's sake. You wump on the keys. I'm gonna watch TV.

Session 5

ACCESS CONTROL

You've already been introduced to the `public`, `protected`, and `private` access specifiers and seen how they control access to base class members. In this session, I'll take a longer look at access specifiers and when to use which one. I'll also look at another access situation: public, protected, and private inheritance.

Access Review

Let's review what you've already learned about access. When inheritance is not involved, class member functions have access to anything in the class, whether public or private, but objects of that class have access only to public members, as shown in Figure 7-5.

Once inheritance enters the picture, other access possibilities arise for derived classes. Member functions of a derived class can access public and protected members of the base class, but not private members. Objects of a derived class can access only public members of the base class (assuming it's publicly derived; more on this at the end of the session). This situation is shown in Table 7-2.

Access Specifier	Accessible from Own Class	Accessible from Derived Class	Accessible from Objects Outside Class
public	yes	yes	yes
protected	yes	yes	no
private	yes	no	no

Table 7-2   *Inheritance and accessibility*

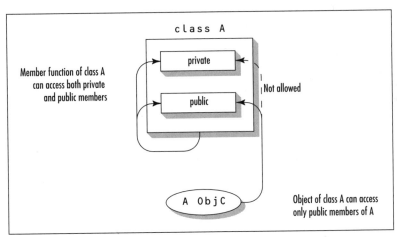

Figure 7-5   Access specifiers without inheritance

Even though a class is derived from the base class, the situation for the base class members and objects is unchanged, because they know nothing about the derived class. Figure 7-6 shows these relationships.

Keeping Data Private

Should data in the base class be protected or private? I've shown examples of both approaches. For example programs, making base class data protected has the advantage of simplicity: No additional base class functions need to be written to access data from the derived class. However, this is not usually the best approach.

In general, class data should be private. (Of course, there are legitimate exceptions to this rule.) Public data is open to modification by any function anywhere in the program and should almost always be avoided. Protected data is open to modification by functions in any derived class. Anyone can derive one class from another and thus gain access to the base class's protected data. It's safer and more reliable if derived classes can't access base class data directly.

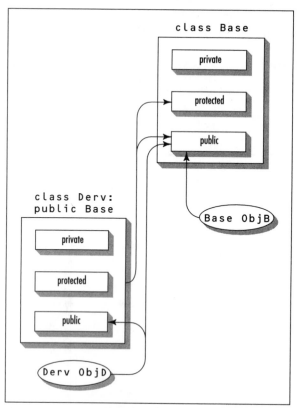

Figure 7-6   Access specifiers with inheritance

Recall that an interface consists of the functions used to access something. Design your classes to provide two interfaces: a public interface for use by objects of the class and a protected interface for use by derived classes. Neither of these interfaces should have direct access to data. One advantage of keeping base class data private is that you can change it without breaking (causing the failure of) derived classes. As long as the interface remains the same, you can modify the underlying data.

Although it may be a good idea to prevent derived class functions from modifying base class data, such functions must often *read* base class data. To provide this read-only access, you can write simple functions as I demonstrated earlier (e.g., in the `get_ia()` function in TWOTEST in Chapter 6, Session 5). These functions should be protected, because they are part of the protected interface used by derived classes and should not be accessible to nonderived classes.

A Stack Example

The next example shows this arrangement of private data and protected access functions. It's a modification of the STACKINH program in Session 3 in this chapter. Listing 7-9 shows STAPROFU.

Listing 7-9 STAPROFU

```cpp
// staprofu.cpp
// superior stack created using inheritance,
// base class data private; uses protected member function
#include <iostream.h>
#include <process.h>              // for exit()
//////////////////////////////////////////////////////////////////
class Stack                       // a stack holds up to SIZE ints
   {
   protected:
      enum {SIZE=20};             // capacity of stack
   private:
      int st[SIZE];               // integers are stored in array
      int top;                    // index of last item pushed
   protected:
      int get_top() const         // return current top
         { return top; }
   public:
      Stack()                     // no-arg constructor
         { top = -1; }
      void push(int var)          // place an item on the stack
         { st[++top] = var; }
      int pop()                   // remove an item from the stack
         { return st[top--]; }
   };
//////////////////////////////////////////////////////////////////
class Stack2 : public Stack
   {
   public:
      void push(int var)
         {
         if(get_top() >= SIZE-1)
            { cout << "Error: stack overflow"; exit(-1); }
         Stack::push(var);        // call push() in Stack class
```

continued on next page

continued from previous page

```
          }
      int pop()
         {
         if(get_top() < 0)
            { cout << "Error: stack underflow"; exit(-1); }
         return Stack::pop(); // call pop() in Stack class
         }
   };
///////////////////////////////////////////////////////////////
void main()
   {
   Stack2 s;                      // create a Stack2 object

   s.push(11);                    // push 3 items onto stack
   s.push(12);
   s.push(13);

   cout << s.pop() << endl;       // pop 3 items and display them
   cout << s.pop() << endl;
   cout << s.pop() << endl;
   cout << s.pop() << endl;       // oops, popped one too many
   }
```

As you can see, the array `st` and the index `top`, which constitute the main data items in `Stack`, are now private. Only member functions of `Stack` can access them. When I derive `Stack2` from `Stack`, `Stack2`'s `push()` and `pop()` can call `Stack`'s `push()` and `pop()` functions to store and retrieve data. However, in `Stack2` I also need to read the value of `top` so I can check if the stack is full. To make this possible, I install a `get_top()` function in `Stack`. This function is protected, so derived classes can execute it; to ensure they can't use it to alter anything in `Stack`, it's a `const` function.

To the normal class user, `Stack2` works just the way it did in STACKINH. (Note that `main()` looks almost the same as it did when only `Stack` existed.) However, in STAPROFU, `Stack`'s data is safe from harm by class users who code incorrectly.

In general, this is a better approach than making `Stack`'s data protected. For brevity, I'll continue to show some program examples with protected data, but you should be aware that this is often a second-choice approach.

Notice that I've made the `enum` constant `SIZE` protected so it can be used by `Stack2`. Because `SIZE` must be defined before `st`, which is private, I use two protected sections of data in `Stack`.

A Graphics Example

Let's look at another example where data is made private in the base class. In this program, inheritance is used as a design element rather than for reuse. The purpose of the program is to draw shapes on the screen. To avoid becoming embroiled in the graphics library of any particular compiler, I'll simulate graphics activity by drawing shapes made of Xs on the character display. The OOP principles are the same as if I used functions that draw in graphics mode.

A Hierarchy of Shapes

The program consists of a base class, `shape`, and three derived classes, `square`, `cap`, and `bowl`. A *cap* is a triangle with the point facing up (a pyramid), whereas a *bowl* is a triangle with the point facing down. Other shapes, such as circles and polygons, would be fun, but would take us too far afield.

You can create shapes of any size and position them (with certain restrictions) anywhere on the screen. Specify a shape's position and size with arguments to its constructor. For example,

```
square(15, 2, 6);
```

creates an X-filled square, 6 lines high and 6 characters wide, with its upper-left corner 15 columns from the left edge of the screen and 2 rows down from the last position of the cursor. The object looks something like this:

```
XXXXXX
XXXXXX
XXXXXX
XXXXXX
XXXXXX
XXXXXX
```

Alas, in my rather crude implementation, you can put only one shape on any given row and each shape must be drawn below the previous shape. (You could fix this by storing the shapes in an array before displaying them, but again this would complicate the example.)

The Classes

The shape class contains elements that are common to all shapes. These are the position of the object on the screen, represented by the coordinates xCo and yCo, and its size, represented by size. Both position and size are measured in characters. The position has two parts: the distance from the left edge of the screen to the left edge of the object and the distance from the top of the screen to the top of the object. Size is the height of the object.

Shape also contains protected member functions that permit read-only access to its private data. Because Shape is an abstract base class that will never be instantiated itself, its constructor can be protected along with these access functions. The square, cap, and bowl classes contain constructors that call the base class constructor, and member functions to draw themselves. Listing 7-10 shows the SHAPES program.

Listing 7-10 SHAPES

```
// shapes.cpp
// draws shapes made from Xs on character-based display
// base class data is private; uses protected access functions
#include <iostream.h>
/////////////////////////////////////////////////////////////
class shape
    {
    private:
        int xCo, yCo;          // coordinates of shape
        int size;              // size of shape
    protected:                 // read-only functions
        int getx() const { return xCo; }
        int gety() const { return yCo; }
        int getz() const { return size; }
        void down() const;     // declaration
                               // 3-arg constructor
        shape(int x, int y, int s) : xCo(x), yCo(y), size(s)
            { }
    };
```

continued on next page

continued from previous page

```
void shape::down() const          // move cursor down to top of shape
   {
   for(int y=0; y<yCo; y++)
      cout << endl;
   }
//////////////////////////////////////////////////////////////////
class square : public shape       // square shape
   {
   public:                        // 3-arg constructor
      square(int x, int y, int s) : shape(x, y, s)
         { }
      void draw() const;          // declaration
   };

void square::draw() const         // draw a square
   {
   shape::down();                 // position y at top of shape
   for(int y=0; y<getz(); y++)    // move y down across shape
      {
      int x;
      for(x=1; x<getx(); x++)     // space over to shape
         cout << ' ';
      for(x=0; x<getz(); x++)     // draw line of Xs
         cout << 'X';
      cout << endl;
      }
   }
//////////////////////////////////////////////////////////////////
class cap : public shape          // cap (pyramid) shape
   {
   public:                        // 3-arg constructor
      cap(int x, int y, int s) : shape(x, y, s)
         { }
      void draw() const;          // declaration
   };

void cap::draw() const            // draw a cap
   {
   shape::down();
   for(int y=0; y<getz(); y++)
      {
      int x;
      for(x=0; x < getx()-y+1; x++)
         cout << ' ';
      for(x=0; x<2*y+1; x++)
         cout << 'X';
      cout << endl;
      }
   }
//////////////////////////////////////////////////////////////////
class bowl : public shape      // bowl (inverted pyramid) shape
   {
```

```
   public:                      // 3-arg constructor
      bowl(int x, int y, int s) : shape(x, y, s)
         { }
      void draw() const;        // declaration
   };

void bowl::draw() const        // draw a bowl
   {
   shape::down();
   for(int y=0; y<getz(); y++)
      {
      int x;
      for(x=0; x < getx()-(getz()-y)+2; x++)
         cout << ' ';
      for(x=0; x < 2*(getz()-y)-1; x++)
         cout << 'X';
      cout << endl;
      }
   }
//////////////////////////////////////////////////////////////////
void main()
   {
   bowl bw(10, 0, 3);          // make a bowl
   bw.draw();                  // draw it

   square sq(20, 1, 5);        // make a square
   sq.draw();                  // draw it

   cap cp(30, 1, 7);           // make a cap
   cp.draw();                  // draw it
   }
```

In `main()`, I create and draw three shapes: a bowl 3 units high, a square 5 units high, and a cap 7 units high. Here's the output from SHAPES:

```
XXXXX
 XXX
  X


      XXXXX
      XXXXX
      XXXXX
      XXXXX
      XXXXX


             X
            XXX
           XXXXX
          XXXXXXX
         XXXXXXXXX
        XXXXXXXXXXX
       XXXXXXXXXXXXX
```

A member function of `shape`, called `down()`, is responsible for moving the cursor down to the top of the shape to be drawn. This function is called by each of the `draw()` functions in the derived classes. The `draw()` functions for each shape move the cursor down line by line through the shape and on each line space over from the left edge of the screen to the object, and then display the appropriate number of Xs. How far to space over and the number of Xs to draw depend on the shape being drawn, its size, and its location. I won't dwell on the details of how the functions figure this out. The point of this program is the relationship between the classes and the use of public and private members in the base class.

Public and Private Inheritance

I've discussed how different access specifiers can be applied to base class data to control access from the derived class. Now let's look at a different use for access specifiers: controlling the way classes are inherited.

In inheritance, you usually want to make the access specifier `public`.

```
class alpha
   { };
class beta : public alpha
   { };
```

This is called *public inheritance* (or sometimes *public derivation*). With this kind of inheritance, objects of the derived class can access public members of the base class, as shown in the left side of Figure 7-7.

In public inheritance, the implication—as I've noted before—is that an object of the B class is a "kind of" object of the A class. A derived class object has all the features of the base class, plus some of its own.

The Compiler and Public Inheritance

The compiler takes the "kind of" relationship in public inheritance quite seriously. It will let you use a derived class object in many situations where a base class object is expected simply because the derived class object is a kind of base class object. The next example program, KINDOF, demonstrates this tolerant approach (see Listing 7-11). (Incidentally, this program has no definition for `anyfunc()` and is not meant to be linked or executed.)

Listing 7-11 KINDOF
```
// kindof.cpp
// a derived class object is a kind of base class object

class alpha                    // base class
   {
   public:
      void memfunc()           // public member function
         { }
   };

class beta : public alpha      // derived class
   { };
```

```
void main()
  {
  void anyfunc(alpha);   // declaration; takes alpha argument
  alpha aa;              // object of type alpha
  beta bb;               // object of type beta

  aa = bb;               // beta object assigned to alpha variable
  anyfunc(bb);           // beta object passed as alpha argument
  }
```

As you already know, an object of a derived class can call a member function in the base class, as long as the function has public access:

```
bb.memfunc();
```

However, you may be surprised to see that you can assign an object of a derived class to a variable of the base class:

```
aa = bb;
```

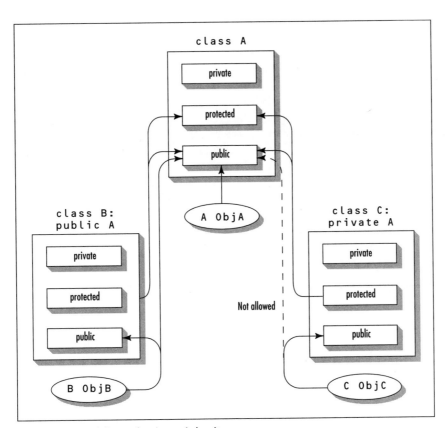

Figure 7-7 Public and private inheritance

The compiler is happy with this, because `bb` is a kind of `alpha`. Similarly, you can pass a derived class object to a function that expects a base class argument:

```
anyfunc(bb);
```

The real payoff from this flexibility comes when you learn about pointers and virtual functions, but this brief introduction hints at the possibilities.

Incidentally, it doesn't work the other way. You can't, for example, say

```
bb = aa;
```

because an `alpha` object is not a kind of `beta` object.

Private Inheritance

Now that you've seen how the compiler treats public inheritance, let's look at private inheritance, which looks like this:

```
class alpha
    {  };
class beta : private alpha
    {  };
```

By substituting `private` for `public`, you are changing the entire inheritance relationship in a surprising way. (I'll ignore the possibility of using `protected` for the moment; it's quite similar to `private`.)

Basically, when a class is privately inherited, its objects can't access anything in the base class, no matter what access specifier was used for the base class members. This is shown on the right side of Figure 7-7.

The effect is that the base class is entirely hidden from objects of the derived class. As far as derived class objects are concerned, there *is no* base class. (Of course, as in public inheritance, statements within derived class member functions can access protected and public members of the base class.)

Thus, objects of the derived class don't see themselves as a "kind of" base class object; they don't know anything about the base class, even though the base class is part of the derived class. This is more like composition—a "has a" relationship. (I introduced composition in Session 1 in this chapter.) The derived class "has an" object of the base class, but objects of the derived class don't know about it.

Because private inheritance is so much like composition, it's usually better to use composition instead. In the fragment shown above, you would simply install an object of class `alpha` in class `beta` and forget about inheritance:

```
class alpha
    {  };

class beta
    {
    private:
       alpha obj;
    };
```

The `alpha` object is made private, so it is still concealed from `beta` objects. Composition results in a cleaner, less complicated relationship between the two classes and, as far as derived class objects are concerned, works the same way. You'll see an example of composition in Session 7 in this chapter.

The Compiler and Private Inheritance

The compiler understands that private inheritance is more like composition than it is like inheritance. Accordingly, the compiler is no longer tolerant of derived class objects being used in place of base class objects. An expanded version of the KINDOF program shows both public and private inheritance. Listing 7-12 shows KINDOF2.

Listing 7-12 KINDOF2

```
// kindof2.cpp
// a derived class object is a kind of base class object,
// but not if it's privately derived

class alpha                    // base class
    {
    public:
        void memfunc()         // public member function
            { }
    };

class beta : public alpha      // public derivation
    { };

class gamma : private alpha    // private derivation
    { };

void main()
    {
    void anyfunc(alpha);  // function takes alpha argument
    alpha aa;             // object of type alpha
    beta bb;              // object of type beta
    gamma gg;             // object of type gamma

    bb.memfunc();         // ok
    gg.memfunc();         // error: 'memfunc() not accessible'

    anyfunc(bb);          // ok
    anyfunc(gg);          // error: 'cannot convert gamma to alpha'

    aa = bb;              // ok
    aa = gg;              // error: 'cannot convert gamma to alpha'
    }
```

A new class `gamma` is privately derived from `alpha`. The compiler will not allow you to call an `alpha` member function from a `gamma` object, pass a `gamma` object to a function expecting an `alpha` argument, or assign a `gamma` object to an `alpha` variable.

Protected Inheritance

Protected inheritance is similar to private inheritance: they're both like composition (the "has a" relationship). However, statements in member functions of a protected derived class *can* access public and protected members of the base class, whereas—as you've seen—statements in member functions of a privately derived class cannot.

Protected inheritance is not used often and is included in the language mostly for completeness.

Access Summary

Let's summarize what you've learned about accessibility and the different kinds of inheritance. Table 7-3 shows the access to base class members (usually data) that is allowed to member functions of the derived class. Private members are never accessible, and private inheritance makes all members inaccessible.

	Private Inheritance	Protected Inheritance	Public Inheritance
Private base class data	Not accessible	Not accessible	Not accessible
Protected base class data	Not accessible	Accessible	Accessible
Public base class data	Not accessible	Accessible	Accessible

Table 7-3 *Access by members of the derived class*

Table 7-4 shows the access to base class members (usually functions) allowed to derived class objects that are defined outside the class specifications, as in `main()`. Only publicly derived public members are accessible.

	Private Inheritance	Protected Inheritance	Public Inheritance
Private base class data	Not accessible	Not accessible	Not accessible
Protected base class data	Not accessible	Not accessible	Not accessible
Public base class data	Not accessible	Not accessible	Accessible

Table 7-4 *Access by objects of the derived class*

1. In public inheritance, a derived class object can call, say from `main()`, a
   a. public member function of the base class.
   b. public member function of the derived class.
   c. protected member function of the base class.
   d. protected member function of the derived class.
   e. private member function of the derived class.

2. Making data protected in the base class
   a. is the preferred approach.
   b. is not acceptable to the compiler.
   c. makes it easy to access this data from derived class objects.
   d. typically requires the use of special functions to access base class data.
   e. can cause problems because the data can be mistakenly altered by functions in a poorly written derived class.

3. In the **Stack** class in the STAPROFU program,
   a. **SIZE** is protected so it can be used to define **Stack**'s array **st**.
   b. **push()** and **pop()** are·public because they are called from **Stack2** objects.
   c. the important data is private because this is the safest approach.
   d. the **get_top()** function is necessary because **push()** and **pop()** are public.
   e. member functions of **Stack2** can find out what **top** is, but can't modify it.

4. In a "kind of" relationship, you can
   a. do anything with a derived class object that you can with a base class object.
   b. assign a derived class object to a base class object.
   c. assign a base class object to a derived class object.
   d. call a derived class function from a base class object.
   e. call a base class function from a derived class object.

5. When a class **beta** is privately derived from a class **alpha**, **beta**'s public member functions
   a. can access private data in **alpha**.
   b. can access protected data in **alpha**.
   c. can access public data in **alpha**.
   d. are visible to objects of class **beta**.
   e. are visible to objects of class **alpha**.

EXERCISE 1

Add a class called **line** to the SHAPES program. A line **object** displays itself as a line of Xs, running either vertically or horizontally. (Other angles aren't allowed.) Member data should include the x and y coordinates of the starting point, the line direction (down or right), and the length. Create some sample **line** objects in **main()** and display them.

EXERCISE 2

Start with Exercise 2 of Session 3 in this chapter. Modify the **Queue** class to use private data and provide the necessary access to **Queue2** through protected member functions, as in the STAPROFU program in this session.

SESSION 6

GRANDPARENTS

As you have perhaps surmised, there can be more than two levels of inheritance. Not only can a class beta be derived from a class alpha, but a class gamma can be derived from beta, a class delta can be derived from gamma, and so on, as long as you like (or, in this example, until you run out of Greek letters).

```
class alpha                    // first generation
   { };

class beta : public alpha      // second generation
   { };

class gamma : public beta      // third generation
   { };

class delta : public gamma     // fourth generation
   { };
```

Everything works as you would expect. The relationship between delta and gamma is just the same as that between beta and alpha.

A class has access to all its ancestors. In public inheritance, member functions of delta can access public or protected data in gamma, beta, and alpha. They can't, of course, access private members of any class except their own.

Deriving foreman from laborer

In the EMPINH program in Session 2 in this chapter, I examined a program in which several kinds of employees were derived from the employee class. Let's add a foreman to this program. A foreman is a special kind of laborer, so the foreman class is derived from the laborer class, as shown in Figure 7-8.

Foremen oversee the laborers who operate the dangerous widget-stamping presses. Foremen are responsible for the widget production quota for their group. A foreman's ability is measured by the percentage of production quotas he or she successfully meets. The quotas data item in the foreman class represents this percentage (e.g., a typical foreman meets 72.5 percent of the quotas). Listing 7-13 shows EMPGRAND.

Listing 7-13 EMPGRAND
```
// empgrand.cpp
// more than two levels of inheritance
// foreman derived from laborer
#include <iostream.h>

const int LEN = 80;              // maximum length of names

class employee
```

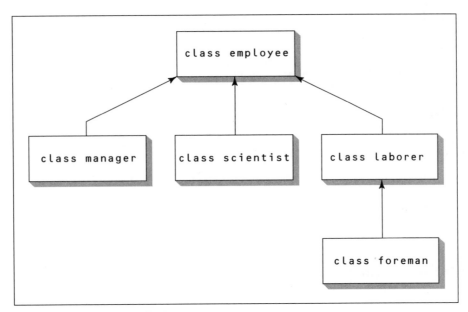

Figure 7-8 Class hierarchy in EMPGRAND

```
   {
   private:
      char name[LEN];          // employee name
      unsigned long number;    // employee number
   public:
      void getdata()
         {
         cout << "\n   Enter last name: "; cin >> name;
         cout << "   Enter number: ";        cin >> number;
         }
      void putdata()
         {
         cout << "\n   Name = " << name;
         cout << "\n   Number = " << number;
         }
   };

class manager : public employee    // management class
   {
   private:
      char title[LEN];  // "vice-president" etc.
      double dues;      // golf club dues
   public:
      void getdata()
         {
         employee::getdata();
         cout << "   Enter title: ";           cin >> title;
         cout << "   Enter golf club dues: ";  cin >> dues;
         }
```

continued on next page

continued from previous page

```cpp
      void putdata()
         {
         employee::putdata();
         cout << "\n    Title: " << title;
         cout << "\n    Golf club dues: " << dues;
         }
   };
class scientist : public employee        // scientist class
   {
   private:
      int pubs;        // number of publications
   public:
      void getdata()
         {
         employee::getdata();
         cout << "    Enter number of pubs: "; cin >> pubs;
         }
      void putdata()
         {
         employee::putdata();
         cout << "\n    Number of publications: " << pubs;
         }
   };

class laborer : public employee          // laborer class
   {
   };

class foreman : public laborer           // foreman class
   {
   private:
      float quotas;        // percent of quotas met successfully
   public:
      void getdata()
         {
         laborer::getdata();
         cout << "    Enter quotas: "; cin >> quotas;
         }
      void putdata()
         {
         laborer::putdata();
         cout << "\n    Quotas: " << quotas;
         }
   };

void main()
   {
   laborer labo;
   foreman fore;

   cout << endl;
   cout << "\nEnter data for laborer";
```

```
labo.getdata();
cout << "\nEnter data for foreman";
fore.getdata();

cout << endl;
cout << "\nData on laborer";
labo.putdata();
cout << "\nData on foreman";
fore.putdata();
}
```

Notice that a class hierarchy is not the same as an organization chart. A class hierarchy results from generalizing common characteristics. The more general the class, the higher it is on the chart. A laborer is a more general type of employee than a foreman, so the `laborer` class appears above the `foreman` class in the class hierarchy. On a company's organization chart, the foreman would appear above the laborer, because, on an organization chart, the employees with the most authority have the highest positions. Here's some sample interaction with EMPGRAND:

```
Enter data for laborer
    Enter last name: Jones
    Enter number: 246137

Enter data for foreman:
    Enter last name: Smith
    Enter number: 4781
    Enter quotas: 78.5

Data for laborer
    Name = Jones
    Number = 246137

Data for foreman:
    Name = Smith
    Number = 4781
    Quotas = 78.5
```

Constructors

When there are more than two levels in the class hierarchy, handling constructors with initialization lists can become rather clumsy looking. Listing 7-14, INHCON, shows an example of such constructors.

Listing 7-14 INHCON
```
// inhcon.cpp
// tests constructors with arguments, in inheritance
#include <iostream.h>

class Gparent
    {
    private:
        int intv;
```

continued on next page

continued from previous page

```
        float flov;
    public:
        Gparent(int i, float f) :
            intv(i), flov(f)                // initialize Gparent
            { }
        void display()
            { cout << intv << ", " << flov << "; "; }
    };

class Parent : public Gparent
    {
    private:
        int intv;
        float flov;
    public:
        Parent(int i1, float f1, int i2, float f2) :
            Gparent(i1, f1),                // initialize Gparent
            intv(i2), flov(f2)              // initialize Parent
            { }
        void display()
            {
            Gparent::display();
            cout << intv << ", " << flov << "; ";
            }
    };

class Child : public Parent
    {
    private:
        int intv;
        float flov;
    public:
        Child(int i1, float f1,
              int i2, float f2, int i3, float f3) :
            Parent(i1, f1, i2, f2),         // initialize Parent
            intv(i3), flov(f3)              // initialize Child
            { }
        void display()
            {
            Parent::display();
            cout << intv << ", " << flov;
            }
    };

void main()
    {
    Child ch(1, 1.1, 2, 2.2, 3, 3.3);
    cout << "\nData in ch = ";
    ch.display();
    }
```

A Child class is inherited from a Parent class, which is in turn inherited from a Gparent class. Each class has one int and one float data item. The constructor in each class takes enough arguments to initialize the data for the class and all ancestor classes. This means two arguments for the `Gparent` class constructor, four for `Parent` (which must initialize `Gparent` as well as itself), and six for `Child` (which must initialize `Gparent` and `Parent` as well as itself). Each constructor calls the constructor of its base class, which in turn calls the constructor for *its* base class.

In `main()`, I create an object of type `Child`, initialize it to six values, and display it. Here's the output from INHCON:

```
Data in ch = 1, 1.1; 2, 2.2; 3, 3.3
```

The `Child` object `ch`, the `Parent` subobject within the `Child` object, and the `Gparent` subobject within that `Parent` subobject, are all initialized before the `Child` constructor starts to execute. That's why all the calls to subobject constructors appear on the initialization list: They must be initialized before the opening brace of the constructor. Thus, when your constructor starts to execute, you're guaranteed that all the subobject's you're working with are created and initialized.

Incidentally, you can't skip a generation when you call an ancestor constructor in an initialization list. In the following modification of the `Child` constructor:

```
Child(int i1, float f1,
     int i2, float f2, int i3, float f3) :
   Gparent(i1, f1),       // error: can't initialize Gparent
   intv(i3), flov(f3)     // initialize Child
   { }
```

the call to `Gparent()` is illegal because the `Gparent` class is not the immediate base class of `Child`.

Summary

Let me attempt to summarize some of the access situations in multigenerational inheritance.

- Private data is never accessible outside its class.

- Private derivation makes *all* data in the base class, whether public, protected, or private, inaccessible to all generations of derived classes.

- Protected derivation makes protected and public data in the base class accessible to all generations of derived classes, no matter what kind of inheritance is used to derive subsequent generations from each other.

- Protected members of the base class are accessible to members of publicly derived and protectedly derived classes, and to publicly derived and protectedly derived classes of these derived classes.

- An object of a derived class that is defined outside the class hierarchy can access members of the base class only if the base class member is public and the derivation from the base class is public from each generation to the next. That is, if any of the derivations is not public, the member will not be accessible.

Tables 7-5 and 7-6 show how this looks with three generations: a first generation base class, a second generation derived class, and a third generation derived class.

TABLE 7-5

Type of Inheritance from Class A to Class B								
Private			Protected			Public		
Type of Inheritance from Class B to Class C								
Priv	Prot	Pub	Priv	Prot	Pub	Priv	Prot	Pub
A's data private								
No	No	No	No	No	No	No	No	No
A's data protected								
No	No	No	Yes	Yes	Yes	Yes	Yes	Yes
A's data public								
No	No	No	Yes	Yes	Yes	Yes	Yes	Yes

Table 7-5 *Access by members of third generation class C to members in first generation class A*

TABLE 7-6

Type of Inheritance from First to Second Generation								
Private			Protected			Public		
Type of Inheritance from Second to Third Generation								
Priv	Prot	Pub	Priv	Prot	Pub	Priv	Prot	Pub
A's functions private								
No	No	No	No	No	No	No	No	No
A's functions protected								
No	No	No	No	No	No	No	No	No
A's functions public								
No	No	No	No	No	No	No	No	Yes

Table 7-6 *Access by third generation objects to first generation members*

1. If a class C is derived from a class B, which is derived from a class A, all through public inheritance, then a class C member function can access
   a. protected and public data only in C and B.
   b. protected and public data only in C.
   c. private data in A or B.
   d. protected data in A or B.
   e. public data in A or B.

2. Assume a class C is derived from a class B, which is derived from a class A. To call a nonoverloaded member function `afunc()` in class A from a member function in class C, you would need to
   a. use the expression `A::B::afunc();`
   b. use the expression `A::afunc();`
   c. use the expression `afunc();`
   d. create an object of class A, say `aObj`, and use the function call `aObj.func();`
   e. create an object of class A, say `aObj`, and use the function call `aObj.A::func();`

3. In an inheritance diagram,
   a. a scientist specializing in metal alloys would be shown above a laborer.
   b. a racing bicycle would be shown above a bicycle.
   c. a lion would be shown above a mammal.
   d. a vehicle would be shown above a car.
   e. a flea would be shown below a lion.

4. In an inheritance situation, when a constructor for a derived class is called,
   a. constructors of all subobjects, and subobjects of subobjects, are called automatically.
   b. only the members of the object itself are initialized, but not those of its subobjects.
   c. every subobject, and every subobject in a subobject, is initialized before the constructor begins to execute.
   d. as many objects and subobjects are created as there are ancestor classes.
   e. only a subobject of the base class is created.

5. If a class C is derived from a class B, which is derived from a class A, then a class C constructor's
   a. arguments can be used to initialize only class C members.
   b. arguments can be used to initialize members of any ancestor class.
   c. initialization list may contain a call to any ancestor's constructor.
   d. initialization list may contain a call only to the constructor in the immediate base class.
   e. initialization list may be used to initialize class C data members.

EXERCISE 1

Start with the EMPGRAND program in this session and add a `manager` class. Managers oversee all the foremen in a particular factory. Like all employees, managers have a name and number, and like foremen they have a `quotas` data member, which is the average of the `quotas` members for all the foremen in their factory. In addition, managers have an `absenteeism` data member, type `float`, which is the average percentage of work time missed by their foremen and laborers. Situate the `manager` class appropriately in the inheritance diagram.

EXERCISE 2

From the `line` class in Exercise 1 in Session 5 in this chapter, derive a `horizLine` class and a `vertLine` class. The arguments to the constructors for these classes should comprise the starting coordinates of the line and its length.

SESSION 7

COMPOSITION

Composition is putting one object inside another object or, from the programmer's viewpoint, defining an object of one class inside another class specification. I've already mentioned composition several times in this chapter: in Session 1 and in Session 5, where I compared composition and private inheritance. Here's the composition example I used then:

```
class alpha
    { };

class beta
    {
    private:
        alpha aObj;
    };
```

Of course, I've used a rudimentary kind of composition every time I placed instance data of basic types such as `int` and `char` in an object. Because class objects can be considered data types, there's no conceptual difference between using class objects and variables of basic types as data in other classes. However, when I speak of composition, I'm usually talking about embedding a class object in the specification for another class.

Embedding `airtime` Objects in a `flight` Class

Here's a typical example of composition. You've already seen numerous examples of the `airtime` class, which represents hours and minutes time values. Now suppose I'm developing an airline scheduling program and I want to work with objects representing airline flights (as in, "Flight 962 to Atlanta is now ready for boarding at gate 32.").

For simplicity, I'll include only three data items in the flight class: the flight number and the departure and arrival times, which are stored as `airtime` values. (One could imagine including the origination city and destination city, among other data, but I'll forego this in the interest of a smaller listing.) Member functions in `flight` will get values for these three items from the user and display them. Listing 7-15 shows AIRSCHED.

Listing 7-15 AIRSCHED

```
// airsched.cpp
// demonstrates composition: airtime objects in flight class
#include <iostream.h>
/////////////////////////////////////////////////////////////////
class airtime
    {
    private:
        int hours;              // 0 to 23
        int minutes;            // 0 to 59
    public:
                                // no-arg constructor
```

```
      airtime() : hours(0), minutes(0)
         { }
                              // two-arg constructor
      airtime(int h, int m) : hours(h), minutes(m)
         { }

      void display() const     // output to screen
         {
         cout << hours << ':' << minutes;
         }

      void get()               // input from user
         {
         char dummy;
         cout << "\n   Enter time (format 12:59): ";
         cin >> hours >> dummy >> minutes;
         }
   };   // end class airtime
//////////////////////////////////////////////////////////////
class flight
   {
   private:
      long fnumber;            // flight number
      airtime departure;       // airtime
      airtime arrival;         // objects
   public:
      flight() : fnumber(0)    // no-arg constructor
         { }
      void get()               // input from user
         {
         char dummy;
         cout << "\nEnter flight number: ";
         cin >> fnumber;
         cout << "   Departure";
         departure.get();
         cout << "   Arrival";
         arrival.get();
         }
      void display() const     // output to screen
         {
         cout << "Flight number = " << fnumber;
         cout << "\n   Departure = ";
         departure.display();
         cout << "\n   Arrival = ";
         arrival.display();
         }
   };   // end class flight
//////////////////////////////////////////////////////////////
void main()
   {
   flight flarr[100];          // array holds 100 flight objects
   int total = 0;              // number of flights in array
   char ch;                    // for 'y' or 'n'
```
continued on next page

continued from previous page

```
    do                              // get data for flights
        {
        flarr[total++].get();
        cout << "Enter another flight (y/n)? ";
        cin >> ch;
        }
    while(ch != 'n');

    for(int j=0; j<total; j++)  // display data for flights
        {
        cout << endl;
        flarr[j].display();
        }
    }
```

In `main()`, the program lets the user enter data for as many flights as desired. It stores these flights in an array. It then displays the data for all flights stored in the array. Here's some sample interaction when two flights are entered:

```
Enter flight number: 940
    Departure
    Enter time (format 12:59): 22:15
    Arrival
    Enter time (format 12:59): 23:35
Enter another flight (y/n)? y

Enter flight number: 1474
    Departure
    Enter time (format 12:59): 10:45
    Arrival
    Enter time (format 12:59): 16:33
Enter another flight (y/n)? n

Flight number = 940
    Departure = 22:15
    Arrival = 23:35
Flight number = 1474
    Departure = 10:45
    Arrival = 16:33
```

In the AIRSCHED program, composition seems like a natural choice; I use `airtime` as you would a `float`. I would probably not even be tempted to use inheritance to connect the `airtime` class with the `flight` class, because `airtime` objects are so much like variables of basic types. However, not all situations are so clear.

A `safearay` **Object in a** `Stack` **Class**

Here's an example where the object being placed in another class doesn't seem at all like a variable of a basic type: It's the `safearay` class developed in the ARROVER2 program in Chapter 6, Session 7. As you no doubt recall, this class modeled an array and overloaded the `[]` operator to check that index values supplied by the class user were in bounds.

I'm going to place a `safearay` object in the `Stack` class, last seen in the STACKINH program in Session 3 in this chapter. In previous examples, the `Stack` class used a normal C++ array to store data, but if I use a `safearay` object instead, I can incorporate its error-checking benefits into the stack.

In this situation, it's not quite so clear whether `Stack` should use composition, by including a `safearay` object as member data, or inherit the `safearay` class. However, composition is probably the better approach. Why? Because the `safearay` is used in the *internal* workings of the `Stack` class. It is completely hidden from the class user, who will therefore have no reason to consider a `Stack` to be a "kind of" `safearay`.

Listing 7-16 shows SAFESTAK.

Listing 7-16 SAFESTAK
```
// safestak.cpp
// creates stack using safe array object as a member of Stack
#include <iostream.h>
#include <process.h>              // for exit()
//////////////////////////////////////////////////////////////
class safearay
    {
    private:
        enum {SIZE=100};          // array size
        int arr[SIZE];            // ordinary array
    public:
        int& operator [](int n);  // function declaration
    };

int& safearay::operator [](int n)     // overloaded []
    {                                 // returns by reference
    if( n< 0 || n>=SIZE )
        { cout << "\nIndex out of bounds"; exit(1); }
    return arr[n];
    }
//////////////////////////////////////////////////////////////
class Stack                           // stack stores ints in safe array
    {
    private:
        safearay st;                  // safe array object
        int top;                      // index of last item pushed
    public:
        Stack()                       // no-arg constructor
            { top = -1; }
        void push(int var)            // place an item on the stack
            { st[++top] = var; }
        int pop()                     // remove an item from the stack
            { return st[top--]; }
    };
//////////////////////////////////////////////////////////////
void main()
    {
    Stack s;                          // create a Stack object

    s.push(11);                       // push 3 items onto stack
```

continued on next page

continued from previous page
```
    s.push(12);
    s.push(13);

    cout << s.pop() << endl;    // pop items and display them
    cout << s.pop() << endl;
    cout << s.pop() << endl;
    cout << s.pop() << endl;    // woops, popped one too many
    }
```

The `Stack` class works just the same as before, but now, even though no bounds-checking mechanism is built into `Stack` itself (as there was in the `Stack2` class in the STACKINH example), errors are caught by the `safearay` object. Here's some sample output, in which the class user attempts to pop one too many items:

```
13
12
11
Index out of bounds
```

The `safearay` object within `Stack` spots the incorrect value of `top` and complains.

Could I use inheritance to derive `Stack` from `safearay`? I could, but it's not a great idea. If I used public inheritance, then the user of the `Stack` class could access member functions in the `safearay` class directly, leading to usage such as

```
Stack s;
s[3] = 77;
```

where a `Stack` object is treated as if it were an array. This subverts the purpose of a stack, which is to restrict data access to the LIFO approach. I could make `safearay` invisible using private inheritance, but this still leaves an unnecessarily complex relationship between `Stack` and `safearay`. To make things simple and to minimize surprises, use composition.

Should a scientist "Have an" employee?

When is it better to use inheritance than composition? When the "kind of" relationship between classes is important. Suppose you have an array of type `employee`. It would be nice to be able to store any kind of employee in this array—manager, scientist, foreman, or whatever—like this:

```
employee emparray[SIZE];
emparray[0] = laborer1;
emparray[1] = scientist1;
emparray[2] = laborer2;
...
```

The only way you can do this is to inherit the various kinds of employees from `employee`. Composition doesn't create the necessary relationships between the classes. (Being able to store objects of different derived classes in an array of the base class is an important feature of C++, but, as I noted earlier, the reason it's so important won't be clear until I discuss virtual functions in Chapter 9.)

The same "kind of" relationship is true of the `Shape` class in the SHAPES program in Session 5 in this chapter. If you used composition to place a `shape` object in `square`, `cap`, and `bowl`, you couldn't treat a `square` as a kind of `shape`.

Summary

It may be helpful to summarize the various characteristics of composition, as well as the three kinds of inheritance. Table 7-7 attempts to do this.

	Composition	Private Inheritance	Protected Inheritance	Public Inheritance
Relationship of base class to derived class	"Has a"	"Has a"	"Kind of" to derived classes; "Has a" to class user	"Kind of"
Derived class members can access base class members that are	Public	Public Protected	Public Protected	Public Protected
Syntax for derived class access to base class functions	Base b; b.func();	Base::func();	Base::func();	Base::func();
Can derived class objects access the public base class interface?	No	No	No	Yes
Can derived class objects be treated as a base class object?	No	No	No	Yes
Recommendation	Use when derived class objects don't need to see the base class interface and will not be treated as a kind of base class object.	Not recommended: Base class protected data is exposed.	Not recommended: Base class protected data is exposed. Use when derived class members must have access to base class members.	Use when derived class objects will be treated as a kind of base class object and you need to see the base class interface.

Table 7-7 *Characteristics of composition and inheritance*

1. Composition means
    a. private inheritance.
    b. member functions of one class operating on objects of another class.
    c. using a class specification for one class inside another class.
    d. using a variable of a basic type as instance data in another class.
    e. using a class object as instance data in another class.

2. You would probably use composition to relate
    a. `wing`, `tail`, `window`, and `landing_gear` classes to an `airplane` class.
    b. `lion`, `tiger`, `ocelot`, and `cheetah` classes to the `feline` class.
    c. `int`, `float`, and `long` types to the `ship` class.
    d. `living`, `dining`, `basement`, and `hall` classes to the `room` class.
    e. `hockey`, `baseball`, and `tennis` to the `sport` class.

3. Composition
    a. is a "has a" relationship.
    b. is a "kind of" relationship.
    c. is a "is a" relationship.
    d. allows you to put objects of the derived class in an array of the base class type.
    e. allows you to hide objects of one class from the user of another class.

4. Assume `aObj` is an object of class `alpha` and `bObj` is an object of class `beta`. When composition is used to place an `alpha` in `beta`, to access a member function `afunc()` of `alpha` from the class `beta`, you would say
    a. `alpha::afunc();`
    b. `beta::afunc();`
    c. `aObj.afunc();`
    d. `bObj.afunc();`
    e. a member function of `beta` must be used.

5. Objects of a class `alpha`, used as private instance data in a class `beta`,
    a. are named in `alpha`.
    b. are named in `beta`.
    c. are named in `main()`.
    d. can be accessed from `beta`.
    e. can be accessed from `main()`.

Assume you want to store `flight` objects (as in the AIRSCHED program) in a `safearay` object (as seen in the SAFESTAK program). Modify `safearay` so this is possible. (You'll see a way to avoid this kind of modification when you learn about templates in Chapter 11.) In `main()`, create a safearay object, get flight data from the user, and store it in the safearay. You'll need to decide what relationship to use between flight and safearay.

EXERCISE 2

Suppose you want to store objects of class flight in an object of class Stack, which uses the safearay class for its array. Write a program that lets you do this. You'll need to modify safearay to store flight objects. In main(), create a Stack object, get flight data from the user, store it on the stack, and then display the contents of the stack. Don't worry about why anyone would want to store flight data on a stack.

SESSION 8

MULTIPLE INHERITANCE

Multiple inheritance occurs when a class inherits from two or more base classes, like this:

```
class Base1
    {  };

class Base2
    {  };

class Derv : public Base1, public Base2
    {  };
```

Derv is derived from both Base1 and Base2. In the specification for the derived class, the base classes are separated by a comma (or commas, if there are more than two base classes) and each base class has its own access specifier. The derived class Derv inherits all the instance data and member functions from both Base1 and Base2.

Two Base Classes: employee **and** student

Let's look at a situation in which multiple inheritance is used with the employee class, last seen in the EMPGRAND program in Session 6 in this chapter. Suppose I'm developing the employee class hierarchy and I decide I need to include the educational qualifications of certain kinds of employees (namely, everyone except laborers). Fortunately, the local university has developed a student class that incorporates all this educational data, along with member functions to get and display it.

How can I combine the student and employee classes? One way is through multiple inheritance. Those classes that need educational data can inherit from both employee and student. Here's a shorthand version of how that looks:

```
class student
    { ... };
class employee
    { ... };
```

continued on next page

continued from previous page

```
class manager : public employee, public student
    { ... };
class scientist : public employee, public student
    { ... };
class laborer : public employee
    { ... };
```

The `manager` and `scientist` classes inherit from both `employee` and `student`, but `laborer` inherits only from `employee` (the elitist assumption being that the educational achievements of laborers are irrelevant).

Now let's look at a full-scale version of this program, EMPMULT, shown in Listing 7-17.

Listing 7-17 EMPMULT

```cpp
// empmult.cpp
// multiple inheritance with employees and students
#include <iostream.h>

const int LEN = 80;

class student                  // educational background
    {
    private:
        char school[LEN];      // name of school or university
        char degree[LEN];      // highest degree earned
    public:
        void getedu()
            {
            cout << "   Enter name of school or university: ";
            cin >> school;
            cout << "   Enter highest degree earned \n";
            cout << "   (Highschool, Bachelor's, Master's, PhD): ";
            cin >> degree;
            }
        void putedu()
            {
            cout << "\n   School or university = " << school;
            cout << "\n   Highest degree earned = " << degree;
            }
    };

class employee
    {
    private:
        char name[LEN];          // employee name
        unsigned long number;    // employee number
    public:
        void getdata()
            {
            cout << "\n   Enter last name: "; cin >> name;
            cout << "   Enter number: ";      cin >> number;
            }
        void putdata()
            {
```

```
            cout << "\n   Name = " << name;
            cout << "\n   Number = " << number;
            }
    };

class manager : public employee, public student   // management
    {
    private:
        char title[LEN];   // "vice-president" etc.
        double dues;       // golf club dues
    public:
        void getdata()
            {
            employee::getdata();
            cout << "   Enter title: ";            cin >> title;
            cout << "   Enter golf club dues: ";  cin >> dues;
            student::getedu();
            }
        void putdata()
            {
            employee::putdata();
            cout << "\n   Title = " << title;
            cout << "\n   Golf club dues = " << dues;
            student::putedu();
            }
    };
class scientist : public employee, public student   // scientist
    {
    private:
        int pubs;       // number of publications
    public:
        void getdata()
            {
            employee::getdata();
            cout << "   Enter number of pubs: "; cin >> pubs;
            student::getedu();
            }
        void putdata()
            {
            employee::putdata();
            cout << "\n   Number of publications = " << pubs;
            student::putedu();
            }
    };

class laborer : public employee                    // laborer
    {
    };

void main()
    {
    manager m1;
    scientist s1, s2;
    laborer l1;
```

continued on next page

continued from previous page

```
      cout << endl;
      cout << "\nEnter data for manager 1";      // get data for
      m1.getdata();                              // several employees

      cout << "\nEnter data for scientist 1";
      s1.getdata();

      cout << "\nEnter data for scientist 2";
      s2.getdata();

      cout << "\nEnter data for laborer 1";
      l1.getdata();

      cout << "\nData on manager 1";             // display data for
      m1.putdata();                              // several employees

      cout << "\nData on scientist 1";
      s1.putdata();

      cout << "\nData on scientist 2";
      s2.putdata();

      cout << "\nData on laborer 1";
      l1.putdata();
      }
```

Notice that, if there is a function with the same name in both base classes (`employee` and `student`), then in a derived class, the scope resolution operator must be used to specify which function is meant, for example, `employee::getdata()` or `student::getdata()`. Some sample interaction with the program might look like this:

```
Enter data for manager 1
   Enter last name: Webley
   Enter number: 111
   Enter title: President
   Enter golf club dues: 50000
   Enter name of school or university: Yale
   Enter highest degree earned
   (Highschool, Bachelors, Masters, PhD): Bachelors

Enter data for scientist 1
   Enter last name: Frish
   Enter number:222
   Enter number of pubs: 99
   Enter name of school or university: MIT
   Enter highest degree earned
   (Highschool, Bachelors, Masters, PhD): PhD

Enter data for scientist 2
   Enter last name: Wong
   Enter number:333
   Enter number of pubs: 204
```

```
    Enter name of school or university: Stanford
    Enter highest degree earned
    (Highschool, Bachelors, Masters, PhD): Masters
Enter data for laborer 1
    Enter last name: Jones
    Enter number: 482562

Data for manager 1
    Name = Webley
    Number = 111
    Title = President
    Golf club dues = 50000
    Name of school or university = Yale
    Highest degree earned
    (Highschool, Bachelors, Masters, PhD) = Bachelors

Data for scientist 1
    Name = Frish
    Number = 222
    Number of pubs = 99
    Name of school or university = MIT
    Highest degree earned
    (Highschool, Bachelors, Masters, PhD) = PhD

Data for scientist 2
    Name = Wong
    Number = 333
    Number of pubs = 204
    Name of school or university = Stanford
    Highest degree earned
    (Highschool, Bachelors, Masters, PhD) = Masters

Data for laborer 1
    Name = Jones
    Number = 482562
```

Repeated Base Classes

Incidentally, although it's not clear why you would want to do this, you can't repeat the same base class when deriving another class:

```
class Base1
    { };

class Derv : public Base1, public Base1
    { };
```

The compiler would not be happy about this arrangement.

It's Controversial

Multiple inheritance is controversial. In the simple case shown in EMPMULT, multiple inheritance works as expected. In more complicated class hierarchies, however, problems may arise. One of these problems results from the following kind of inheritance situation:

```
class Gparent
   { };

class Mother : public Gparent
   { };

class Father : public Gparent
   { };

class Child : public Mother, public Father
   { };
```

Both `Mother` and `Father` inherit from `Gparent`, and `Child` inherits from both `Mother` and `Father`. This forms a diamond-shaped pattern. Recall that each object created through inheritance contains a subobject of the base class. A `Mother` object and a `Father` object will contain subobjects of `Gparent`, and a `Child` object will contain subobjects of `Mother` and `Father`, so a `Child` object will also contain two `Gparent` subobjects, one inherited via `Mother` and one inherited via `Father`, as shown in Figure 7-9.

Ambiguous Subobjects

This is a strange situation. There are two subobjects when really there should be one. Suppose there's a data item in `Gparent`:

```
class Gparent
   {
   protected:
      int gdata;
   };
```

and you try to access this item from `Child`:

```
class Child : public Mother, public Father
   {
   public:
      void Cfunc()
         {
         int temp = gdata;   // error: ambiguous
         }
   };
```

The compiler will complain that the reference to `gdata` is ambiguous. It doesn't know which version of `gdata` to access: the one in the `Gparent` subobject in the `Mother` subobject or the one in the `Gparent` subobject in the `Father` subobject.

Virtual Base Classes

You can fix this using a new keyword, `virtual`, when deriving `Mother` and `Father` from `Gparent`:

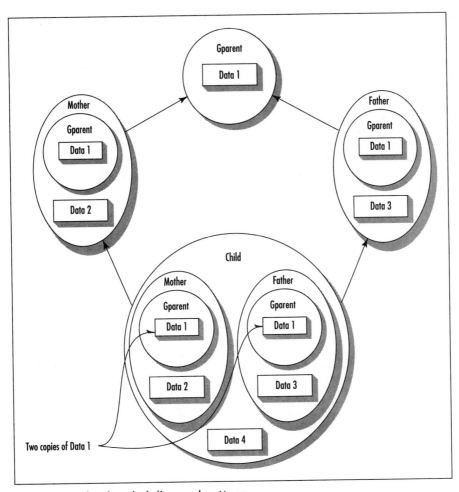

Figure 7-9 The dreaded diamond pattern

```
class Gparent
    { };

class Mother : virtual public Gparent
    { };

class Father : virtual public Gparent
    { };

class Child : public Mother, public Father
    { };
```

The **virtual** keyword tells the compiler to inherit only one subobject from a class into subsequent derived classes. That fixes the ambiguity problem, but other more complicated problems arise that are too complex to delve into here.

In general, you should avoid multiple inheritance, although if you have considerable experience in C++, you might find reasons to use it in unusual situations. In a simple program like EMPMULT, you probably won't get into too much trouble if you do use it. However, in a programming project of any size, where classes may be used—perhaps at some time in the future—in ways you don't anticipate today, it's a good idea to steer clear of multiple inheritance.

Composition to the Rescue

You can almost always avoid multiple inheritance. Perhaps the most common and effective substitute is composition. I could create a variation of the EMPMULT program that uses composition, rather than multiple inheritance, to place objects of the **student** class in appropriate derived classes of **employee**. The **student** and **employee** classes would be unchanged, but **manager** and **scientist** would incorporate a **student** object. I won't show the entire program, but here's how a revised version of the **manager** class would look:

```
class manager : public employee   // management
   {
   private:
      char title[LEN];   // "vice-president" etc.
      double dues;       // golf club dues
      student stu;       // NOTE: student object
   public:
      void getdata()
         {
         employee::getdata();
         cout << "   Enter title: ";           cin >> title;
         cout << "   Enter golf club dues: ";  cin >> dues;
         stu.getedu();   // send message to student object
         }
      void putdata()
         {
         employee::putdata();
         cout << "\n   Title = " << title;
         cout << "\n   Golf club dues = " << dues;
         stu.putedu();   // send message to student object
         }
   };
```

The student object **stu** is placed in the **manager** class data using composition, and its member functions are called using the dot operator. The **scientist** class would be modified similarly. The **main()** part of the program would be unchanged, and any user interaction with the program would be the same as well.

Including the **student** class by composition makes sense conceptually because, although a manager and a scientist are kinds of employees, they aren't really kinds of students (although they may have been in their younger days).

1. Which of the following are examples of multiple inheritance?
   a. Class **B** is derived twice from class **A**.
   b. Class **C** is derived from class **B**, which is derived from class **A**.
   c. Class **D** is derived from classes **C** and **B**, which are both derived from class **A**.
   d. Class **C** is derived from class **B** and class **A**.
   e. Class **B** is derived from class **A**.

2. Which of the following are true?
   a. No more than two classes can be used as base classes in multiple inheritance.
   b. A member function name cannot be used in more than one multiply-inherited base class.
   c. A comma is used to separate multiple base classes in the specification of a derived class.
   d. A **manager** object in EMPMULT could be treated as a kind of **student**, but a **laborer** object could not.
   e. The class creator in EMPMULT decided that no educational data was needed for the **laborer** class.

3. Multiple inheritance is controversial because
   a. it's too complicated to imagine inheritance from more than one class.
   b. ambiguities may arise if a diamond-shaped inheritance diagram is created.
   c. the resulting objects would be too large.
   d. it doesn't make sense for an object to be a "kind of" **A** and a "kind of" **B** at the same time.
   e. hybrid objects are more prone to failure.

4. Virtual base classes
   a. solve all problems associated with multiple inheritance.
   b. are used as a programming convenience, but do not actually exist.
   c. have base classes of their own.
   d. specify that only one copy of a multiply-inherited subobject will be created in subsequent derived classes.
   e. have only one copy of each subobject, even if they have inherited from two classes, each containing that object.

5. Which of the following can often be used instead of multiple inheritance?
   a. single inheritance
   b. integration
   c. composition
   d. virtual functions
   e. the scope resolution operator

EXERCISE 1

Rewrite the entire EMPMULT program to use composition instead of multiple inheritance, following the example shown above for the manager class.

EXERCISE 2

Write a class DervStak that inherits from both the Stack class, from which the array has been removed, and the safearay class (see the SAFESTAK program in Session 7 in this chapter). The DervStak class should have the same interface as the Stack class in SAFESTAK.

SUMMARY: CHAPTER 7

Inheritance is the creation of a new class from an existing class without modifying the existing class. The new class usually has additional features that the old class does not. The new class is a specialized version of the old class. Inheritance can be thought of as a "kind of" relationship, where a new class object is a *kind of* old class object. This is different from composition, which is a "has a" relationship: One class *has* objects of another class embedded in it.

Inheritance can be used in the design of a program to specify a "kind of" relationship between classes. It can also be used to create improved or specialized versions of existing classes. An object of a derived class contains a subobject of the base class. This subobject contains the base class data.

The constructors of derived classes, if they need to call the constructors of their base classes, do so by placing the call on the initialization list following a colon in the constructor declarator. This ensures that all subobjects in an object are initialized before the constructor starts to execute.

Access specifiers determine whether class members will be accessible to derived classes. Public and protected members are accessible to functions in derived classes, but private members are not. Only public members are accessible to objects of derived classes.

Inheritance itself can be public, protected, or private. Public inheritance is the normal approach. In private inheritance, derived class objects are not a "kind of" base class object, but, as in composition, they are a "have a" base class object.

There can be several levels of inheritance, with the base class of one class being derived from another class.

Composition, like inheritance, can be used to relate classes. Composition means using objects of one class as instance data in another class. Composition is cleaner and less complicated to use because there are fewer connections between the classes involved, but the "kind of" relationship, which you will discover later is important in OOP, is possible only with inheritance.

Multiple inheritance means that a derived class has more than one base class. Multiple inheritance should normally be avoided and composition should be used instead.

END-OF-CHAPTER DISCUSSION

George: Correct me if I'm wrong, but I'd say it all boils down to two simple rules. First, always use private data in a base class, with protected functions to access it from derived classes. And second...

Estelle: Always use public inheritance.

George: Exactly.

Don: Well, that's about right. Of course those are just guidelines. You may find situations where you need protected base class data, or even public data. Or where nothing works but private inheritance.

Estelle: But it's easy to get into trouble by not following Rule 1 and Rule 2.

Don: Actually there's a third rule. Something like use composition unless you really need the "kind of" relationship.

Estelle: It's too bad multiple inheritance turns out to be so messy. It would be fun to create some really weird mixtures of classes.

George: Like what?

Estelle: I don't know. What would happen if you inherited a scientist object from both an employee object and a computer object? Wouldn't you have a supersmart scientist?

George: The mind boggles.

Don: Don't get carried away. Classes aren't exact models of things in the real world; they're just programming constructs used for managing data.

Estelle: Too bad. I was hoping for a little Frankenstein action, sewing different things together to make androids and monsters.

Don: Pointers are coming up in the next chapter, and lots of people think they're the Frankenstein of C++ programming.

George: Oh, fine, like it could get any more complicated. I'm going into something simple, like astrophysics.

CHAPTER 8

POINTERS

Pointers have a reputation for being hard to understand. Fortunately, only some of this reputation is deserved. In this chapter I'll introduce pointers slowly and gently and prove that, at least in concept, they really aren't that tough.

I'll spend the first several sessions discussing pointers in the abstract, mostly using basic types (rather than objects) as examples. Once you have a firm grasp of the fundamentals, I'll show how pointers are typically used in the C++ environment.

One important use for pointers is in the dynamic allocation of memory, carried out in C++ with the keyword `new` and its partner `delete`. I'll examine this issue in several examples. You'll also learn about a very special pointer called `this` that points to its own object.

Pointers are used to create complex structures for storing data. Toward the end of this chapter, I'll introduce examples of a memory-efficient string class, a linked list, and a kind of array that is self-sorting.

SESSION 1
ADDRESSES AND POINTERS

The basic ideas behind pointers are not complicated. You need to know about memory addresses and you need to know that addresses can be stored, like variables. I'll explore these fundamental ideas in this session.

Addresses (Pointer Constants)

Every byte in the computer's memory has an *address*. Addresses are numbers, just as they are for houses on a street. The numbers start at 0 and go up from there—1, 2, 3, and so on. If you have 1MB of memory, the highest address is 1,048,575; for 16 MB of memory, it is 16,777,215. Those would be large numbers for street addresses, but computers, as you know, enjoy large numbers.

Any program, when it is loaded into memory, occupies a certain range of these addresses. That means that every variable and every function in your program starts at a particular address. Figure 8-1 shows how this looks.

The addresses in the figure are numbered from the top down. To some people this seems backward (actually upside down) because they think higher numbers should be higher on the page. However, there is also logic in putting lower numbers at the top in that you read text from the top down. In any case, in whatever format it appears on the page, phrases such as *higher addresses* and *high memory* mean larger numbers, not higher on the page.

The Address of Operator &

You can find out the address occupied by a variable by using the *address of* operator &. Listing 8-1 shows a short program, VARADDR, that demonstrates how to do this.

Listing 8-1 VARADDR
```
// varaddr.cpp
// addresses of variables
#include <iostream.h>

void main()
    {
    int var1 = 11;          // define and initialize
    int var2 = 22;          // three variables
    int var3 = 33;

    cout << endl << &var1    // print out the addresses
        << endl << &var2    // of these variables
        << endl << &var3;
        }
```

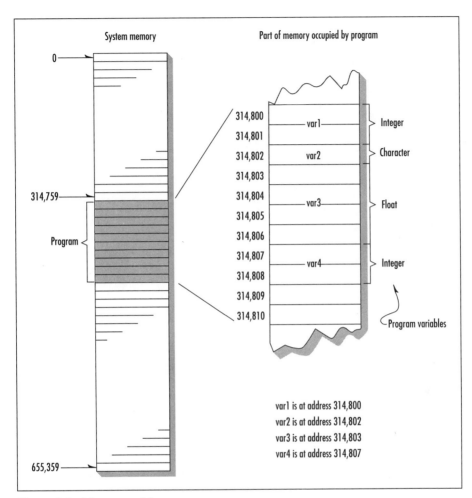

Figure 8-1 Memory addresses

This simple program defines three integer variables and initializes them to the values 11, 22, and 33. It then prints out the addresses of these variables.

The actual addresses occupied by the variables in a program depend on many factors, such as what computer the program is running on, the size of the operating system, and whether any other programs are currently in memory. For these reasons, you probably won't get the same addresses I did when you run this program. Here's the output on my machine:

```
Ox8f4ffff4     <--address of var1
Ox8f4ffff2     <--address of var2
Ox8f4ffff0     <--address of var3
```

Remember that the *address of* a variable is not the same as its *contents*. The contents of the three variables are 11, 22, and 33. Figure 8-2 shows the three variables in memory.

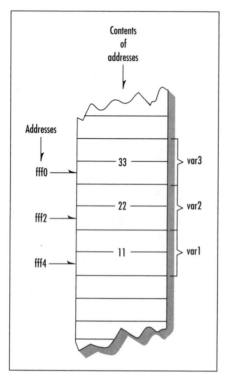

Figure 8-2   Addresses and contents
of addresses

The insertion operator (<<) displays the addresses in hexadecimal notation, as indicated by the prefix **0x** before each number. The address of **var1** is 8f4ffff4. This is the usual way to show memory addresses. If you aren't familiar with the hexadecimal number system, don't worry. All you really need to know is that each variable starts at a unique address. However, you might note in the output above that each address differs from the next by exactly 2 bytes. That's because, on my machine, integers occupy 2 bytes of memory. If I had used variables of type **char**, they would have adjacent addresses, because **chars** occupy 1 byte; if I had used type **double**, the addresses would have differed by 8 bytes.

The addresses appear in descending order because automatic variables (those defined within a function) are stored on the stack, which grows downward (from higher to lower addresses) in memory. If I had used external variables (defined outside of any function), the variables would have had ascending addresses, because external variables are stored on the heap, which grows upward. Again, you don't need to worry too much about all this because the compiler keeps track of the details for you.

Incidentally, don't confuse the address of operator **&**, which precedes a variable name, with the reference operator **&**, which follows the type name in a function prototype or definition. (References are discussed in Chapter 4.)

Pointer Variables

Addresses by themselves are rather limited. It's nice to know that you can find out where things are in memory, as I did in VARADDR, but printing out address values is not really that useful. The potential for increasing programming power requires an additional idea: *variables that hold address values.* You've seen variable types that store characters, integers, and floating-point numbers. An address is a number too, and it can be stored in a variable. A variable that holds an address value is called a *pointer variable*, or simply a *pointer*. If a pointer contains the address of a variable, I can say the pointer *points to* the variable; hence the name.

What is the data type of pointer variables? It's not the same as the variable whose address is being stored; a pointer to int is not type int. You might think a pointer data type would be called something like pointer or ptr. However, things are slightly more complicated.

Pointers to Basic Types

Listing 8-2, PTRVAR, shows the syntax for pointer variables that hold the addresses of variables of the basic type int.

Listing 8-2 PTRVAR

```
// ptrvar.cpp
// pointers (address variables)
#include <iostream.h>
void main()
   {
   int var1 = 11;              // two integer variables
   int var2 = 22;
   cout << endl << &var1       // print addresses of variables
        << endl << &var2;

   int* ptr;                   // pointer to integers

   ptr = &var1;                // pointer points to var1
   cout << endl << ptr;        // print pointer value

   ptr = &var2;                // pointer points to var2
   cout << endl << ptr;        // print pointer value
       }
```

This program defines two integer variables, **var1** and **var2**, and initializes them to the values 11 and 22. It then prints out their addresses. So far, this is similar to the VARADDR program.

The program next defines a pointer variable in the line

```
int* ptr;
```

To the uninitiated, this may seem a rather bizarre syntax. The asterisk means *pointer to*. Thus (reading from right to left, which is the proper way), the statement defines the variable **ptr** as a *pointer to* int. This is another way of saying that this variable can hold the addresses of integer variables.

What's wrong with the idea of a general-purpose pointer type that holds addresses to *any* data type? If I called it, for example, type **pointer**, I could write declarations such as

```
pointer ptr3;
```

The problem is that the compiler needs to know *what kind of variable the pointer points to*. (You'll see why when I talk about pointers and arrays later in this chapter.) The compiler designers could have come up with a bunch of new names, such as `pointer_to_int` and `pointer_to_char`, but they used a more compact notation that involves learning only one new symbol. Here's the syntax used in C++. It allows you to declare a pointer to any type, using only the type name and an asterisk:

```
char* cptr;        // pointer to char
int* iptr;         // pointer to int
float* fptr;       // pointer to float
```

and so on. The asterisk (in this context) is shorthand for *pointer* or, more completely, *pointer to the type on my left*.

Syntax Quibbles

Many programmers write pointer definitions with the asterisk closer to the variable name than to the type:

```
char *cptr3;
```

It doesn't matter to the compiler, but placing the asterisk next to the type helps emphasize that the asterisk is part of the type (pointer to `char`), and not part of the name itself.

If you define more than one pointer of the same type on one line, you need to insert the type pointed to only once, but you must place an asterisk before each variable name:

```
char* ptr1, * ptr2, * ptr3;   // three variables of type char*
```

Or you can use the asterisk-next-to-the-name approach:

```
char *ptr1, *ptr2, *ptr3;   // three variables of type char*
```

Pointers Must Have a Value

An address such as 0x8f4ffff4 can be thought of as a *pointer constant*. Once a variable is placed at a particular address in memory, it doesn't move. (If it does, because of swapping by the operating system, the effect is invisible to the programmer). Address values are therefore constant as long as the program continues to run.

On the other hand, a pointer such as `ptr` can be thought of as a *pointer variable*. Just as the integer variable `var1` can be assigned the constant value 11, so can the pointer variable `ptr` be assigned the constant value 0x8f4ffff4.

When I first define a variable, it holds no value (unless I initialize it at the same time). It may hold a garbage value, but this has no meaning. In the case of pointers, a garbage value is the address of *something* in memory, but probably not something that I want. So before a pointer is used, a specific address must be placed in it. In the PTRVAR program, `ptr` is first assigned the address of `var1` in the line

```
ptr = &var1;   <--put address of var1 in ptr
```

Then the program prints out the value contained in `ptr`, which should be the same address printed for `&var1`. The same pointer variable `ptr` is then assigned the address of var2 and this value is printed out. Figure 8-3 shows the operation of the PTRVAR program.

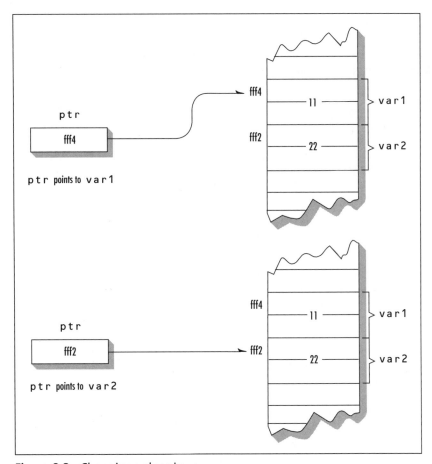

Figure 8-3 Changing values in `ptr`

Here's the output of PTRVAR:

```
0x8f51fff4      <--address of var1
0x8f51fff2      <--address of var2
0x8f51fff4      <--ptr set to address of var1
0x8f51fff2      <--ptr set to address of var2
```

To summarize: A pointer can hold the address of any variable of the correct type; it's a receptacle awaiting an address. However, it must be given *some* value or else it will point to an address you don't want it to point to, such as into program code or the operating system. Rogue pointer values can result in system crashes and are difficult to debug because the compiler gives no warning. The moral: Make sure you give every pointer variable a valid address value before using it.

Pointers to Objects

Objects are stored in memory, so pointers can point to objects just as they can to variables of basic types. For example, you can define an object and then place its address in a pointer:

```
employee emp1;              <--define object of class employee
employee* ptrobj = &emp1;   <--place object's address in ptrobj
```

The `ptrobj` variable is of type `employee*`, or pointer to `employee`. Let's rewrite the PTRVAR program to work with objects of class `employee`. Listing 8-3 shows PTROBJ.

Listing 8-3 PTROBJ

```cpp
// ptrobj.cpp
// pointers to class objects
#include <iostream.h>
#include <string.h>               // for strcpy()
/////////////////////////////////////////////////////////////////
class employee                    // employee class
   {
   private:
      enum {LEN=30};              // length of name
      char name[LEN];            // employee name
      unsigned long number;      // employee number

   public:                       // 2-arg constructor
      employee(char* na, unsigned long nu) : number(nu)
         { strcpy(name, na); }
   };
/////////////////////////////////////////////////////////////////
void main()
   {                             // employee objects
   employee emp1("Donlevy", 123123L);
   employee emp2("LeBlanc", 234234L);

   cout << "Address values";
   cout << endl << &emp1         // print addresses of objects
        << endl << &emp2;

   employee* ptr;                // pointer to employees

   cout << "\nPointer values";
   ptr = &emp1;                  // pointer points to emp1
   cout << endl << ptr;          // print pointer value

   ptr = &emp2;                  // pointer points to emp2
   cout << endl << ptr;          // print pointer value
         }
```

The operation of this program is analogous to that of PTRVAR. However, you can see from the output that `employee` objects occupy more space than `int` variables:

```
Address values
0x29072222
0x29072200
Pointer values
0x29072222
0x29072200
```

If you subtract 200 from 222, you get 22 hexadecimal, which is 34 decimal. This makes sense because an `employee` object contains a 30-character string and a 4-byte `unsigned long` number.

Accessing the Variable Pointed To

Suppose I don't know the name of a variable but I do know its address. Can I access the contents of the variable? (It may seem like mismanagement to lose track of a variable's name, but, as you'll see, there are many variables whose names we don't know.)

There is a special syntax to access the value of a variable by using its address instead of its name. Listing 8-4, PTRACC, shows how it's done.

Listing 8-4 PTRACC

```
// ptracc.cpp
// accessing the variable pointed to
#include <iostream.h>
void main()
   {
   int var1 = 11;              // two integer variables
   int var2 = 22;

   int* ptr;                   // pointer to integers

   ptr = &var1;                // pointer points to var1
   cout << endl << *ptr;       // print contents of pointer (11)

   ptr = &var2;                // pointer points to var2
   cout << endl << *ptr;       // print contents of pointer (22)
      }
```

This program is very similar to PTRVAR, except that instead of printing the address value in `ptr`, it prints the integer value *stored at* the address that's stored in ptr. Here's the output:

```
11
22
```

The expression that accesses the variables `var1` and `var2` is `*ptr`, which occurs in each of the two `cout` statements.

When the asterisk is used to the left of a variable name, as it is in the `*ptr` expression, it is called the *indirection operator*. It means *the value of the variable pointed to* by the variable on its right. Thus, the expression `*ptr` represents the value of the variable pointed to by `ptr`. When `ptr` is set to the address of `var1`, the expression `*ptr` has the value 11 because that's the value of `var1`. When `ptr` is changed to the address of `var2`, the expression `*ptr` acquires the value 22 because `var2` is 22. The indirection operator is sometimes called the *contents of* operator, which is another way of saying the same thing. Figure 8-4 shows how this looks.

You can use a pointer not only to display a variable's value, but to perform any operation you would perform on the variable directly. Listing 8-5 shows a program, PTRTO, that uses a pointer to assign a value to a variable and then to assign that value to another variable.

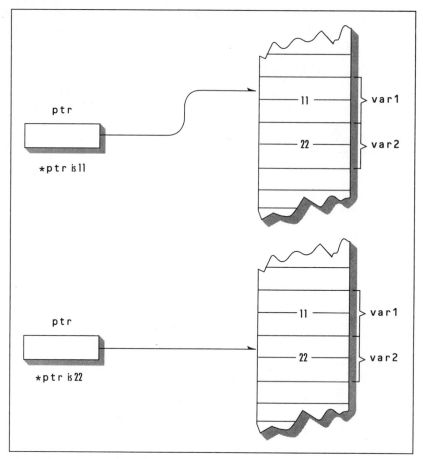

Figure 8-4   Access via pointer

Listing 8-5 PTRTO

```
// ptrto.cpp
// other access using pointers
#include <iostream.h>

void main()
    {
    int var1, var2;         // two integer variables
    int* ptr;               // pointer to integers

    ptr = &var1;            // set pointer to address of var1
    *ptr = 37;              // same as var1=37
    var2 = *ptr;            // same as var2=var1

    cout << endl << var2;   // verify var2 is 37
            }
```

Remember that the asterisk used as the indirection operator has a different meaning than the asterisk used to declare pointer variables. The indirection operator precedes the variable name and means *value of the variable pointed to by*. The asterisk used in a declaration means *pointer to*.

```
int* ptr;    // declaration:
*ptr = 37;   // indirection:
```

Using the indirection operator to access the value stored in an address is called *indirect addressing*, or sometimes *dereferencing*, the pointer.

Here's a capsule summary of what you've learned so far:

```
int v;       // defines variable v of type int
int* p;      // defines p as a pointer to int
p = &v;      // assigns address of variable v to pointer p
v = 3;       // assigns 3 to v
*p = 3;      // also assigns 3 to v
```

The last two statements show the difference between normal or *direct addressing*, where you refer to a variable by name, and pointer or *indirect addressing*, where you refer to the same variable using a pointer that holds its address.

These two approaches are vaguely analogous to delivering a letter to a friend. If you drive to the friend's house and stick the letter in the mail slot, that's direct addressing. You can also write the address on the envelope and put the letter in a public mailbox. The mail personnel will read the address and see that the letter gets to the right place. That's indirect addressing because it is directed by a third party.

In the example programs I've shown so far in this chapter, there's really no advantage to using the pointer expression to access variables because I can access them directly. Pointers come into their own when you can't access a variable, as you'll see.

Pointer to `void`

Before I go on to show pointers at work, I should note one peculiarity of pointer data types. Ordinarily, the address that you put in a pointer must be the same type as the pointer. You can't assign the address of a `float` variable to a pointer to `int`, for example. However, there is an exception to this rule. There is a sort of general purpose pointer that can point to *any* data type. It's called a pointer to `void`, and it is defined like this:

```
void* ptr;    // ptr can point to any data type
```

Such pointers have certain specialized uses, such as passing pointers to functions that operate on several different data types.

The next example uses a pointer to `void` and also shows that, if you don't use `void`, you must be careful to assign pointers an address of the same type as the pointer. Listing 8-6 shows PTRVOID.

Listing 8-6 PTRVOID
```
// ptrvoid.cpp
// pointers to type void
#include <iostream.h>

void main()
```

continued on next page

continued from previous page

```
   {
   int intvar;              // integer variable
   float flovar;            // float variable

   int* ptrint;             // define pointer to int
   float* ptrflo;           // define pointer to float
   void* ptrvoid;           // define pointer to void

   ptrint = &intvar;        // ok, int* to int*
// ptrint = &flovar;        // error, float* to int*

// ptrflo = &intvar;        // error, int* to float*
   ptrflo = &flovar;        // ok, float* to float*

   ptrvoid = &intvar;       // ok, int* to void*
   ptrvoid = &flovar;       // ok, float* to void*
   }
```

You can assign the address of `intvar` to `ptrint` because they are both type `int*`, but you can't assign the address of `flovar` to `ptrint` because the first is type `float*` and the second is type `int*`. However, `ptrvoid` can be assigned any pointer type, such as `int*` or `float*`, because it is a pointer to `void`.

Whenever possible you should avoid `void` (sorry about that). The insistence of C++ that pointers contain only addresses of a specific type is an important way of avoiding programming mistakes. Using `void` circumvents this safety feature. However, it's occasionally important, as you'll see.

QUIZ 1

1. The address of a variable `temp` of type `float` is
   a. `*temp`
   b. `&temp`
   c. `float& temp`
   d. `float* temp`
   e. `float temp&`

2. If the statements

```
airtime at1;
airtime* x = &at1;
```

   have been executed, then
   a. x is an `airtime` object.
   b. the contents of x can be changed.
   c. `&at1` is a variable.
   d. x is a pointer to type `airtime`.
   e. `&at1` is the address of an `airtime` object.

3. If the statements

```
float fv;
fv = 3.14159;
```

```
float* holdaddr = &fv;
```

have been executed, which expressions have the value 3.14159?

a. `&holdaddr`

b. `*holdaddr`

c. `holdaddr`

d. `&fv`

e. None of the above

4. If the statements

```
int j, k;
j = 123;
k = 234;
int* q, * r;
cout << *q << ' ' << *r;
```

are executed, what will be displayed?

a. The values in q and r.

b. The addresses of q and r.

c. The addresses of j and k.

d. 123, 234.

e. None of the above.

5. If these statements are executed:

```
employee emp1;
airtime air1;
void* p;
employee* d = &emp1;
airtime* q = &air1;
```

which of the following statements will compile correctly?

a. `p = d;`

b. `p = &emp1;`

c. `p = &d;`

d. `q = &d;`

e. `q = p;`

Due to the theoretical nature of this session, there are no exercises.

POINTERS, ARRAYS, AND FUNCTIONS

Pointers are used in some situations you may find surprising. Two interesting ones occur when pointers are used to access array elements and when they are used as function arguments. Putting these two situations together, I will show that pointers can be very useful when arrays are passed as function arguments.

Pointers and Arrays

There is a close association between pointers and arrays. You saw in Chapter 3 how array elements are accessed. The following program fragment provides a review:

```
int intarray[5] = { 31, 54, 77, 52, 93 };   // array

for(int j=0; j<5; j++)                       // for each element,
    cout << endl << intarray[j];             // print value
```

The `cout` statement prints each array element in turn. For instance, when `j` is 3, the expression `intarray[j]` takes on the value `intarray[3]`, which is the fourth array element, the integer 52. Here's the output of ARRNOTE:

```
31
54
77
52
93
```

Array Elements and Pointer Notation

Surprisingly, array elements can be accessed using pointer notation as well as array notation. The next example is similar to the previous one except it uses pointer notation:

```
int intarray[5] = { 31, 54, 77, 52, 93 };   // array

for(int j=0; j<5; j++)                       // for each element,
    cout << endl << *(intarray+j);           // print value
```

The expression `*(intarray+j)` here has exactly the same effect as `intarray[j]` in the first example, and their output is identical. But how do we interpret the expression `*(intarray+j)`? Suppose `j` is 3, so the expression is equivalent to `*(intarray+3)`. I want this to represent the contents of the fourth element of the array (52). Remember that the name of an array represents its address. The expression `intarray+j` is thus an address with something added to it. You might expect that `intarray+3` would cause 3 bytes to be added to `intarray`. But that doesn't produce the result we want: `intarray` is an array of integers, and 3 bytes into this array is the middle of the second element, which is not very useful. We want to obtain the fourth *integer* in the array, not the fourth byte, as shown in Figure 8-5.

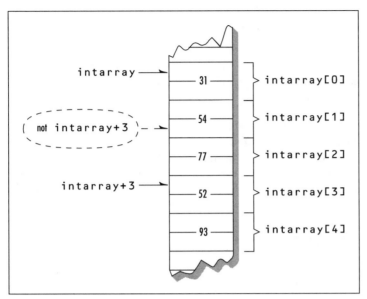

Figure 8-5 Counting by integers

The C++ compiler is smart enough to take the size of the data into account when it performs arithmetic on data addresses. It knows that intarray is an array of type int because it was declared that way. When it sees the expression intarray+3, it interprets it as the address of the fourth *integer* in intarray, not the fourth byte.

But I want the *value* of this fourth array element, not the *address*. To take the value, I use the indirection operator *. The resulting expression, when j is 3, is *(intarray+3), which is the contents of the fourth array element, or 52.

Now you see why a pointer declaration must include the type of the variable pointed to. The compiler needs to know whether a pointer is a pointer to int or a pointer to double so it can perform the correct arithmetic to access elements of the array. It multiplies the index value by 2 in the case of type int, but by 8 in the case of double.

Pointer Constants and Pointer Variables

Suppose that, instead of adding j to intarray to step through the array addresses, I want to use the increment operator. Could I write *(intarray++)?

The answer is no, and the reason is that I can't increment a constant (or indeed change it in any way). The expression intarray is the address where the system has chosen to place the array. The array will remain at this address until the program terminates; thus, intarray is a constant. I can't say intarray++ any more than I can say 7++.

However, although I can't increment an address, I can increment a pointer that holds an address. The next code fragment shows how:

```
int intarray[] = { 31, 54, 77, 52, 93 }; // array

int* ptrint;                             // pointer to int
```

continued on next page

continued from previous page

```
ptrint = intarray;                  // points to intarray
for(int j=0; j<5; j++)              // for each element,
    cout << endl << *(ptrint++);    // print value
```

Here I define a pointer to `int`—`ptrint`—and give it the value `intarray`, the address of the array. Now I can access the contents of the array elements with the expression

```
*(ptrint++)
```

The variable `ptrint` starts off with the same address value as `intarray`, thus allowing the first array element, `intarray[0]`, which has the value 31, to be accessed as before. But, because `ptrint` is a variable and not a constant, it can be incremented. After it is incremented, it points to the second array element, `intarray[1]`. The expression `*(ptrint++)` then represents the contents of the second array element, or 54. The loop causes the expression to access each array element in turn. The output of PTRINC is the same as that for PTRNOTE.

Pointers and Functions

In Chapter 4 I noted that there are three ways to pass arguments to a function: by value, by reference, and by pointer. If the function is intended to modify variables in the calling program, then these variables cannot be passed by value because the function would obtain only a copy of the variable. However, either a reference argument or a pointer argument can be used by the function to modify a variable in the calling program.

Passing Simple Variables

I'll first review how arguments are passed by reference and then compare this to passing pointer arguments. This fragment shows passing by reference:

```
void main()
    {
    void centimize(double&);    // prototype
    double var = 10.0;          // var has value of 10 inches

    cout << endl << "var=" << var << " inches";
    centimize(var);             // change var to centimeters
    cout << endl << "var=" << var << " centimeters";
    }

void centimize(double& v)
    {
    v *= 2.54;                  // v is the same as var
    }
```

Here I want to convert a variable `var` in `main()` from inches to centimeters. I pass the variable by reference to the function `centimize()`. (Remember that the `&` following the data type `double` in the prototype for this function indicates that the argument is passed by reference.) The `centimize()` function multiplies the original variable by 2.54. Notice how the function refers to the variable. It simply uses the argument name `v`; `v` and `var` are different names for the same thing.

Once it has converted `var` to centimeters, `main()` displays the result. Here's the output:

```
var=25.4 centimeters
```

The next example shows an equivalent situation using pointers:

```
void main()
    {
    void centimize(double*);        // prototype
    double var = 10.0;              // var has value of 10 inches

    cout << endl << "var=" << var << " inches";
    centimize(&var);                // change var to centimeters
    cout << endl << "var=" << var << " centimeters";
    }

void centimize(double* ptrd)
    {
    *ptrd *= 2.54;                  // *ptrd is the same as var
    }
```

The output is the same as before. The function `centimize()` is declared as taking an argument that is a pointer to `double`:

```
void centimize(double*);    // argument is pointer to double
```

When `main()` calls this function, it supplies the address of a variable as the argument:

```
centimize(&var);
```

Remember that this is not the variable itself, as it is in passing by reference, but the variable's address. Because the `centimize()` function is passed an address, it must use the indirection operator, `*ptrd`, to access the value stored at this address:

```
*ptrd *= 2.54;  // multiply the contents of ptrd by 2.54
```

Of course, this is the same as

```
*ptrd = *ptrd * 2.54;  // multiply the contents of ptrd by 2.54
```

where the standalone asterisk means multiplication. (The asterisk symbol really gets around.)

Because `ptrd` contains the address of `var`, anything done to `*ptrd` is actually done to `var`. Figure 8-6 shows how changing `*ptrd` in the function changes `var` in the calling program.

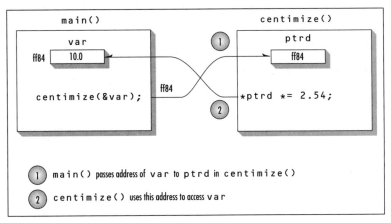

Figure 8-6 Pointer passed to function

Passing a pointer as an argument to a function is in some ways similar to passing a reference. They both permit the variable in the calling program to be modified by the function. However, the mechanism is different. A reference is an alias for the original variable, whereas a pointer is the address of the variable.

Passing Arrays as Arguments

You've already seen examples of arrays passed as arguments to functions and their elements being accessed by the function. This was done using array notation (at least until this chapter), because you had not yet learned about pointers. However, it's more common to use pointer notation instead of array notation when arrays are passed to functions. The following fragment shows how this looks:

```
const int MAX = 5;            // number of array elements
void main()
   {
   void centimize(double*);   // prototype
   double varray[MAX] = { 10.0, 43.1, 95.9, 59.7, 87.3 };

   centimize(varray);         // change elements of varray to cm
   for(int j=0; j<MAX; j++)   // display new array values
      cout << endl << "varray[" << j << "]="
           << varray[j] << " centimeters";
   }
void centimize(double* ptrd)
   {
   for(int j=0; j<MAX; j++)
      *ptrd++ *= 2.54;        // ptrd points to elements of varray
         }
```

The prototype for the function is the same in both examples; the function's single argument is a pointer to double. In array notation, this is written

```
void centimize(double[]);
```

That is, double* is equivalent here to double[], although the pointer syntax is more commonly used.

Because the name of an array is the array's address, there is no need for the address operator & when the function is called:

```
centimize(varray);  // pass array address
```

In centimize(), this array address is placed in the variable ptrd. To point to each element of the array in turn, I need only increment ptrd:

```
*ptrd++ *= 2.54;
```

Figure 8-7 shows how the array is accessed.

The output of both these examples is the same:

```
varray[0]=25.4 centimeters
varray[1]=109.474 centimeters
varray[2]=243.586 centimeters
varray[3]=151.638 centimeters
varray[4]=221.742 centimeters
```

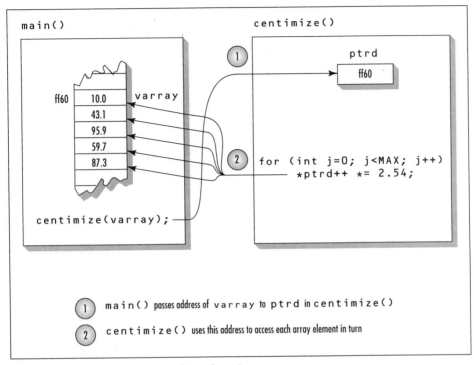

Figure 8-7 Accessing an array from function

Here's a syntax question: How do you know that the expression `*ptrd++` increments the pointer and not the pointer contents? In other words, does the compiler interpret it as `*(ptrd++)`, which is what I want, or as `(*ptrd)++`? It turns out that the asterisk `*` (at least when used as the indirection operator) and `++` have the same precedence. However, operators of the same precedence are distinguished in a second way: by associativity. Associativity is concerned with whether the compiler performs operations starting with an operator on the right or an operator on the left. If a group of operators have *right associativity*, the compiler performs the operation on the right side of the expression first, then it works its way to the left. The unary operators such as `*` and `++` do have right associativity, so the expression is interpreted as `*(ptrd++)`, which increments the pointer, not what it points to. That is, the pointer is incremented first and the indirection operator is applied to the result.

1. The expression `sales[month]`, expressed in pointer notation, is
   a. `sales[month]` (the same as in array notation)
   b. `sales + *month`.
   c. `&sales+month`.
   d. `sales+month`.
   e. `*(sales+month)`.

2. If the name of an array is `jules`, an expression that can be made to represent the address of each element of `jules` is
   a. `jules`.
   b. `jules++`.
   c. `jules+index`.
   d. `*(jules++)`.
   e. `*(jules+index)`.

3. The essential difference between array notation and pointer notation is that
   a. the compiler understands array notation more completely.
   b. they are written differently.
   c. a function that an array is passed to can modify only array elements using pointer notation.
   d. a function that an array is passed to can modify only array elements using array notation.
   e. there is no difference.

4. If a value is stored in a variable, then passing it by pointer differs from passing it by reference in that you pass _____ of the variable rather than _____.
   a. the contents, an alias
   b. the address, an alias
   c. the contents, the value
   d. the value, an alias
   e. the address, the value

5. If you have the following function declaration:

```
float rigel(float* alpha);
```

then, within `rigel()`, to refer to the `float` value being passed to it, you would use the expression
   a. `*alpha`.
   b. `alpha`.
   c. `&alpha`.
   d. `float* alpha`.
   e. `float& alpha`.

EXERCISE 1

Write a function that takes two variables, passed to it by pointer, and swaps (interchanges) their values. Write a `main()` to test this function.

EXERCISE 2

Write a function that will take every element of an array of type `float`, whose address is passed to it, and, using pointer notation, average the elements and return the average. Write a `main()` that calls the function.

Session 3

POINTERS AND STRINGS

As I noted in Chapter 3 in my introduction to arrays, strings are simply arrays of type `char`. Thus, pointer notation can be applied to the characters in strings just as it can to the elements of any array. This is a common idiom in C++, as for example in the declarations of string library functions such as `strcpy()`. In this session I'll examine several aspects of the relationship between strings and pointers.

Pointers to String Constants

Here's an example in which two strings are defined, one using array notation as you've seen in previous examples, and the other using pointer notation:

```
char str1[] = "Defined as an array";
char* str2 = "Defined as a pointer";

cout << endl << str1;        // display both strings
cout << endl << str2;

// str1++;                   // can't do this; str1 is a constant
   str2++;                   // this is OK, str2 is a pointer

cout << endl << str2;        // now str2 starts "efined..."
```

In many ways, these two types of string constants are equivalent. You can print out both strings as the example shows, use them as function arguments, and so on. But there is a subtle difference: `str1` is an address—that is, a pointer *constant*—whereas `str2` is a pointer *variable*. So `str2` can be changed, whereas `str1` cannot, as indicated in the program. Figure 8-8 shows how these two kinds of strings look in memory.

I can increment `str2` because it is a pointer, but once I do, it no longer points to the first character in the string. Here's the output:

```
Defined as an array
Defined as a pointer
efined as a pointer      <--following str2++
```

A string defined as a pointer is considerably more versatile than one defined as an array. The following examples make use of this flexibility.

Strings as Function Arguments

Here's an example that shows a string used as a function argument. The function `dispstr()` simply prints the string defined in `main()` by accessing each character in turn:

```
void main()
   {
   void dispstr(char*);      // prototype
```

continued on next page

continued from previous page

```
char str[] = "Idle people have the least leisure.";
dispstr(str);                // display the string
}

void dispstr(char* ps)
   {
   cout << endl;             // start on new line
   while( *ps )              // until null character,
      cout << *ps++;         // print character
            }
```

The array address `str` is used as the argument in the call to function `dispstr()`. This address is a constant but because it is passed by value, a copy of it is created in `dispstr()`. This copy is a pointer, **ps**. A pointer can be changed so the function increments **ps** to display each character in the string. The expression ***ps++** returns the successive characters. The loop cycles until it finds the null character (**'\0'**) at the end of the string. Because this character has the value 0, which represents *false*, the **while** loop terminates at that point. Such space-saving idioms are common in C++ (and even more common in C).

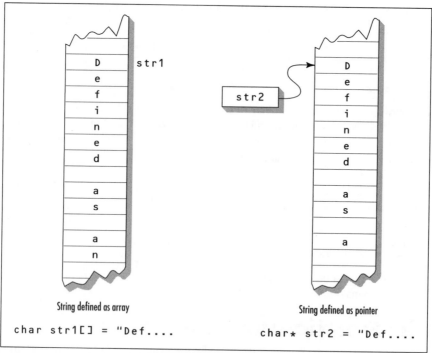

Figure 8-8 Strings as arrays and pointers

Copying a String Using Pointers

I just showed an example of a pointer that obtained character values from a string array. Pointers can also be used to insert characters into a string. The next code fragment demonstrates a function that copies one string to another:

```
void main()
    {
    void copystr(char*, char*);    // prototype

    char* str1 = "Self-conquest is the greatest victory.";
    char str2[80];                 // empty string

    copystr(str2, str1);           // copy str1 to str2
    cout << endl << str2;          // display str2
    }

void copystr(char* dest, char* src)
    {
    while( *src )                  // until null character,
        *dest++ = *src++;          // copy chars from src to dest
    *dest = '\0';                  // terminate dest
    }
```

Here the `main()` part of the program calls the function `copystr()` to copy `str1` to `str2`. In this function, the expression

```
*dest++ = *src++;
```

takes the character value at the address pointed to by `src` and places it in the address pointed to by `dest`. Both pointers are then incremented, so the next time through the loop the next character will be copied. The loop terminates when a null character is found in `src`; at this point, a NULL is inserted in `dest` and the function returns. Figure 8-9 shows how the pointers move through the strings.

Library String Functions

Many of the library functions I have already used for strings have string arguments that are specified using pointer notation. As an example, look at the description of `strcpy()` in your compiler's documentation (or in the STRING.H header file). This function copies one string to another, so you can compare it with my homemade `copystr()` function. Here's the syntax for a typical `strcpy()` library function:

```
char* strcpy(char* dest, const char* src);
```

This function takes two arguments of type `char*`. What is the effect of the `const` modifier in the second argument? It indicates that `strcpy()` cannot change the characters pointed to by `src`. (It does not imply that the `src` pointer itself cannot be modified. To do that, the argument declaration would be `char * const src`. I'll talk more about `const` and pointers in Session 5.)

The `strcpy()` function also returns a pointer to `char`; this is the address of the `dest` string. In other respects, this function works very much like the homemade `copystr()` function.

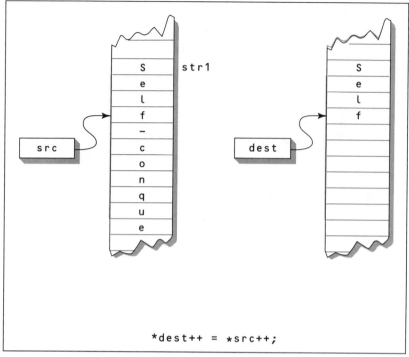

*dest++ = *src++;

Figure 8-9 Copying a string using pointers

Arrays of Pointers to Strings

Just as there are arrays of variables of type int or type float, there can also be arrays of pointers. A common use for this construction is an array of pointers to strings.

In Chapter 3, Session 6, I demonstrated an array of strings. As I noted, there is a disadvantage to using an array of strings in that the subarrays that hold the strings must all be the same length, so that space is wasted when strings are shorter than the length of the subarrays (see Figure 3-10).

Let's see how to use pointers to solve this problem. I'll modify the code fragment from the earlier session to create an array of pointers to strings, rather than an array of strings:

```
char* arrptrs[DAYS] = { "Sunday", "Monday", "Tuesday",
                "Wednesday", "Thursday",
                "Friday", "Saturday"  };

for(int j=0; j<DAYS; j++)     // display every string
        cout << arrptrs[j] << endl;
```

Here's the output of this fragment:

```
Sunday
Monday
Tuesday
Wednesday
```

```
Thursday
Friday
Saturday
```

When strings are not part of an array, C++ places them contiguously in memory so there is no wasted space. However, there must be an array that holds pointers to the strings to find them. A string is itself an array of type `char`, so an array of pointers to strings is an array of pointers to `char`. That is the meaning of the definition of `arrptrs` in the code above. Now recall that a string is always represented by a single address: the address of the first character in the string. It is these addresses that are stored in the array. Figure 8-10 shows how this looks.

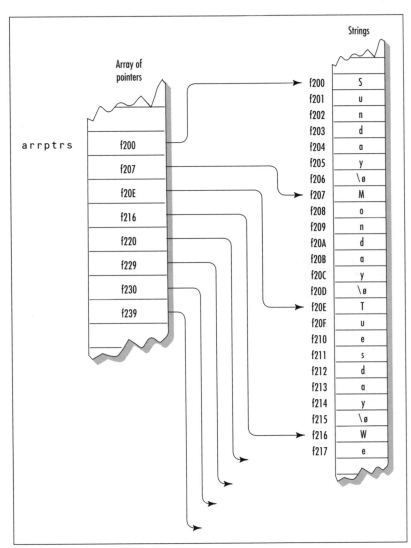

Figure 8-10   Array of pointers to strings

An array of pointers is a powerful construction in C++. I'll explore many examples of this in future sessions.

Membership Access Operator (->)

The next topic, although not exactly related to strings, nevertheless should be mentioned before the next session. Here's the question: Suppose you know that a pointer points to an object. Can you access the object's member functions using only the pointer? The following example demonstrates how to do this. First, I demonstrate the usual way, using the object name itself and the dot operator. Then I show the pointer approach. Listing 8-7 shows DASHGRAT.

Listing 8-7 DASHGRAT

```
// dashgrat.cpp
// demonstrates access to members using pointer
// and dash greater-than (->) operator
#include <iostream.h>

class English                   // English   class
   {
   private:
      int feet;
      float inches;
   public:
      void getdist()            // get length from user
         {
         cout << "\nEnter feet: ";   cin >> feet;
         cout << "Enter inches: ";   cin >> inches;
         }
      void showdist()           // display distance
         { cout << feet << "\'-" << inches << '\"'; }
   };

void main()
   {
   English edist;               // make English object

   English* ptreng = &edist;    // make pointer to object

   edist.getdist();             // access object members
   edist.showdist();            //    with dot operator

   ptreng->getdist();           // access object members
   ptreng->showdist();          //    with -> operator
         }
```

You might guess that you could use the dot (.) membership access operator with pointers as well as with objects, as in

```
ptreng.getdist();    // won't work; ptreng is not an object
```

but this won't work. The dot operator requires the identifier on its left to be an object. Because `ptreng` is a pointer to an object, we need another syntax. One approach is to dereference (get the object pointed to by) the pointer:

```
(*ptreng).getdist();   // ok but inelegant
```

The expression `*ptreng` is an object, not a pointer, so I can use it with the dot operator. However, this syntax is a bit cumbersome. A more concise approach is furnished by the membership access operator `->`, which consists of a hyphen and a greater-than sign:

```
ptreng->getdist();     // better approach
```

The `->` operator works with pointers to objects in just the same way that the dot operator works with objects.

QUIZ 3

1. Which of the following are differences between a string constant defined as (1) an array and as (2) a pointer?
   a. You can display (1) normally, but (2) must be dereferenced.
   b. You cannot increment (1) but you can increment (2).
   c. The data type of (1) is `char[]`, whereas the data type of (2) is `char*`.
   d. An individual array element in (1) is a character, whereas in (2) it's a pointer.
   e. There are no differences except for the notation.

2. If a string is passed by value as a function argument, then the function
   a. works with the original address of the string.
   b. works with a copy of the address.
   c. works with a pointer.
   d. cannot access individual characters.
   e. cannot access the string as a whole.

3. The loop `while(*ps)` can be made to terminate at the end of the string pointed to by `ps` because
   a. *ps is always 0.
   b. ps is the length of the string.
   c. *ps is 0 at the end of the string.
   d. '\0' is false.
   e. `ps` can be made to point to each character in turn.

4. The definition

   ```
   char* julio[4] = { "one", "two", "three", "four" };
   ```

   means that
   a. "one", "two", and so on are elements of an array.
   b. the addresses of "one", "two", and so on are elements of an array.
   c. the array `julio` holds pointers to characters.

d. the array `julio` holds strings.

e. the array `julio` holds pointers to strings.

5. If `ptrobj` is a pointer that points to an object, and `func()` is one of that object's member functions, then

a. `ptrobj` must contain the address of an object.

b. `func()` must be a member function of `ptrobj`.

c. you can call `func()` with the syntax `ptrobj->func()`.

d. you can call `func()` with the syntax `ptrobj.func()`.

e. you can't call `func()` unless you know an object's name.

EXERCISE 1

Write a homemade string function that is similar to `copystr()` in the example above, except that it concatenates one string to another rather than copying it. That is, if `str1` is "dog" and `str2` is "fight", the execution of this function:

```
concatstr(str1, str2);
```

will cause `str1` to become "dog fight". Assume there's enough space in `str1` to hold the new string. Use pointer notation throughout.

EXERCISE 2

Write a function that contains a list of passwords in the form of an array of pointers to strings. A string representing a potential password is passed to this function and the function returns true if the string is on the list and false otherwise. Write a `main()` that repeatedly gets a sample string from the user, calls this function to see if the string is on the list of approved passwords, and then displays `Accepted` or `Denied`, as appropriate.

SESSION 4

MEMORY MANAGEMENT WITH new AND delete

The most commonly used mechanism for storing a large number of variables or objects is the array. You've seen many examples in which arrays are used to allocate storage. The statement

```
int arr1[100];
```

reserves memory for 100 integers. Arrays are a useful approach to data storage, but they have a serious drawback: You must know at the time you write the program how large the array will be. You can't wait until the program is running to specify the array size. The following approach won't work:

```
cin >> size;      // get size from user
int arr[size];    // error; array size must be a constant
```

The compiler requires the array size to be a constant.

Unfortunately, in many situations you don't know how much memory you need until runtime. You might want to let the user enter data for a number of employee objects, for example, and you can't predict how many such objects the user might want to enter.

The `new` Operator

C++ provides another approach to obtaining blocks of memory: the `new` operator. This operator allocates memory of a specific size from the operating system and returns a pointer to its starting point. The following code fragment shows how `new` might be used to obtain memory for a string:

```
char* str = "Idle hands are the devil's workshop.";
int len = strlen(str);      // get length of str

char* ptr;                  // make a pointer to char
ptr = new char[len+1];      // allocate memory: size = str + '\0'

strcpy(ptr, str);           // copy str to new memory area

cout << "ptr=" << ptr;      // show that str is now in ptr

delete[] ptr;               // release ptr's memory
```

In the expression

```
ptr = new char[len+1];
```

the keyword `new` is followed by the type of the variables to be allocated and then, in brackets, the number of such variables. Here I'm allocating variables of type `char` and I need `len+1` of them, where `len` is the length of `str` (which I found with the `strlen()` library function) and the 1 creates an extra byte for the null character that terminates the string.

The `new` operator returns a pointer that points to the beginning of the section of memory. Figure 8-11 shows the syntax of a statement using the `new` operator.

When using `new`, remember to use brackets around the numerical size; the compiler won't object if you use parentheses, but the results will be incorrect. Figure 8-12 shows the memory obtained by `new` and the pointer to it.

In the code above, the program uses `strcpy()` to copy string `str` to the newly created memory area pointed to by `ptr`. Because I made this area equal in size to the length of `str`, the string fits exactly. The program then displays the contents of `ptr`. The output is

```
ptr=Idle hands are the devil's workshop.
```

The `new` operator obtains memory *dynamically*; that is, while the program is running. This memory is allocated from an area called the *heap* (or sometimes the *free store*). The heap is the third area of memory commonly used in C++ programs. As you've learned, automatic variables are stored in the *stack* and static and external variables are stored in the *static storage area*.

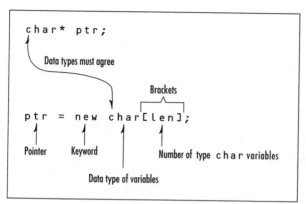

Figure 8-11 Syntax of the new operator

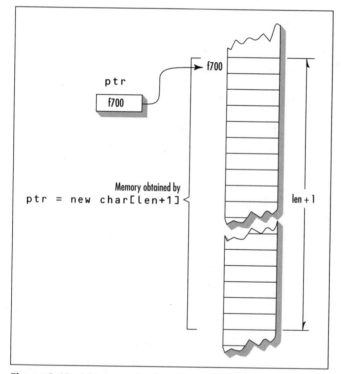

Figure 8-12 Memory obtained by new operator

C programmers will recognize that new plays a role similar to the malloc() family of library functions. However, the new approach is far superior. When you use new with objects, it not only allocates memory for the object, it also *creates* the object in the sense of invoking the object's constructor. This guarantees that the object is correctly initialized, which is vital for avoiding programming errors. Also, new returns a pointer to the appropriate data type, whereas malloc()'s pointer must be cast to the appropriate type. You should always use new for objects, never malloc().

The `delete` **Operator**

If your program reserves many chunks of memory using `new`, eventually all the available memory will be reserved and the system will crash. To ensure safe and efficient use of memory, the `new` operator is matched by a corresponding `delete` operator that releases the memory back to the operating system. In the code shown above, the statement

```
delete[] ptr;
```

returns to the system whatever memory was pointed to by `ptr`.

Actually, in this example there is no need for `delete`, because memory is automatically released when the program terminates. However, suppose you use `new` in a function. If the function uses a local variable as a pointer to newly acquired memory, then when the function terminates, the pointer will be destroyed but the memory will continue to be owned by the program. The memory will become an orphan, taking up space that is forever inaccessible. Thus, it is always good practice to delete memory when you're through with it.

Deleting the memory doesn't delete the pointer that points to it (`str` in the example) and doesn't change the address value in the pointer. However, this address is no longer valid; the memory it points to may be changed to something entirely different. Be careful that you don't use pointers to memory that has been deleted.

The brackets following `delete` in the example indicate that I'm deleting an array. If you create a single variable with `new`, you don't need the brackets when you delete it:

```
ptr = new int;   // allocate a single int variable

. . .

delete ptr;      // no brackets following delete
```

However, don't forget the brackets when deleting arrays of objects. Using them ensures that all the members of the array are deleted and that the destructor is called for each one. If you forget the brackets, only the first element of the array will be deleted.

A String Class That Uses `new`

The `new` operator often appears in constructors. As an example, let's modify the `xString` class, last seen in examples such as STRPLUS in Chapter 6, Session 1. You may recall that a potential defect of that class was that all `xString` objects occupied the same fixed amount of memory. A string shorter than this fixed length wasted memory, and a longer string—if one were mistakenly generated—could crash the system by extending beyond the end of the array. The next example uses `new` to obtain exactly the correct amount of memory. Listing 8-8 shows NEWSTR.

Listing 8-8 NEWSTR

```
// newstr.cpp
// using new to get memory for strings
#include <iostream.h>
#include <string.h>        // for strcpy(), etc

class xString            // user-defined string type
    {
```

continued on next page

continued from previous page

```
    private:
        char* str;                        // pointer to string
    public:
        xString(char* s)                  // constructor, one arg
            {
            int length = strlen(s);       // length of string argument
            str = new char[length+1];     // get memory
            strcpy(str, s);               // copy argument to it
            }
        ~xString()                        // destructor
            {
            delete[] str;                 // release memory
            }
        void display()                    // display the xString
            {
            cout << str;
            }
    };   // end class xString

void main()
    {                                     // uses 1-arg constructor
    xString s1("Who knows nothing doubts nothing.");

    cout << endl << "s1=";                // display string
    s1.display();
            }
```

The xString class has only one data item: a pointer to char, called str. This pointer will point to the ordinary string held by the xString object. However, there is no array within the object to hold the string. The string is stored elsewhere; only the pointer to it is a member of xString.

Constructor in NEWSTR

The one-argument constructor in this example takes a normal (char*) string as its argument. It obtains space in memory for this string with new and sets the member str to point to the newly obtained memory. The constructor then uses strcpy() to copy the string into this newly obtained space.

Destructor in NEWSTR

You haven't seen many destructors in the examples so far, but now that I'm allocating memory with new, destructors become increasingly important. If you allocate memory when you create an object, it's important to deallocate the memory when the object is no longer needed. As you may recall from Chapter 5, a destructor is a routine that is called automatically when an object is destroyed. The destructor in NEWSTR looks like this:

```
~String()
   {
   delete[] str;
            }
```

This destructor gives back to the system the memory obtained when the object was created. Objects (like other variables) are typically destroyed when the function in which they were defined terminates. This destructor ensures that memory obtained by the string object will be returned to the system. If it weren't explicitly returned to the system, such memory would become inaccessible (at least until the system was rebooted) and would constitute a "memory leak," which, if repeated often enough, would eventually crash the system.

Glitch in xString *Class*

I should note a potential glitch in using destructors as shown in NEWSTR. If you copy one xString object to another, say with a statement like s2 = s1, you're really only copying the pointer to the actual (char*) string, because the pointer is the only data that's actually in the object. Both objects now point to the same string in memory. But if you now delete one xString, the destructor will delete the char* string, leaving the other object with an invalid pointer. This can be subtle, because objects can be deleted in nonobvious ways, such as when a function, in which a local object has been created returns. In Session 6, you'll see how to make a smarter destructor that counts how many xString objects are pointing to a string and doesn't delete the string until there are no more xStrings pointing to it.

Creating Objects with new

Objects, as well as variables of basic types, can be created with the new operator. You've seen many examples of objects defined and given memory by the compiler:

```
English dist;  // definition
```

Here an object called dist is defined to be of the English class.

Sometimes, however, you don't know at the time you write the program how many objects you want to create. When this is the case, you can use new to create objects while the program is running. As you've seen, new returns a pointer to an unnamed object. Listing 8-9 shows a short example program, ENGLPTR, that demonstrates this use of new.

Listing 8-9 ENGLPTR

```cpp
// englptr.cpp
// accessing member functions by pointer
#include <iostream.h>

class English             // English class
   {
   private:
      int feet;
      float inches;
   public:
      void getdist()        // get distance from user
         {
         cout << "\nEnter feet: ";   cin >> feet;
         cout << "Enter inches: ";   cin >> inches;
         }
      void showdist()       // display distance
         { cout << feet << "\'-" << inches << '\"'; }
   };

void main()
   {
```

continued on next page

continued from previous page

```
      English* distptr;          // pointer to English
      distptr = new English;     // points to new English object
      distptr->getdist();        // access object members
      distptr->showdist();       //    with -> operator
      delete distptr;            // delete object from memory
      }
```

The program creates an object of type `English` using the `new` operator and returns a pointer to it called `distptr`. It uses this pointer with the `->` operator to access `getdist()` and `showdist()`. Here's the output of the program:

```
Enter feet: 6
Enter inches: 4.75
6'-4.75"
```

Note that, just before the program terminates, it explicitly deletes the `English` object obtained earlier with `new`. As I discussed, it is always good practice to ensure that anything allocated with `new` is eventually deallocated with `delete`.

An Array of Pointers to Objects

A common OOP construction is an array of pointers to objects. This arrangement allows easy access to a group of objects and is more flexible than placing the objects themselves in an array. (For instance, in Session 8 I'll show how a group of objects can be sorted by rearranging the pointers to them, rather than moving the objects themselves.)

Listing 8-10, PTROBJS, creates an array of pointers to the `person` class.

Listing 8-10 PTROBJS
```
// ptrobjs.cpp
// array of pointers to objects
#include <iostream.h>

class person                      // class of persons
    {
    protected:
        char name[40];            // person's name
    public:
        void setName(void)        // set the name
            {
            cout << "Enter name: ";
            cin >> name;
            }
        void printName(void)      // get the name
            {
            cout << "\n   Name is: "
                 << name;
            }
    };

void main(void)
    {
    person* persPtr[100];         // array of pointers to persons
```

```
int n = 0;                          // number of persons in array
char choice;

do                                  // put persons in array
   {
   persPtr[n] = new person;         // make new object
   persPtr[n]->setName();           // set person's name
   n++;                             // count new person
   cout << "Enter another (y/n)? "; // enter another person?
   cin >> choice;
   }
while( choice=='y' );               // quit on 'n'

for(int j=0; j<n; j++)              // print names of
   {                                //     all persons
   cout << "\nPerson number " << (j+1);
   persPtr[j]->printName();
   }   while(n)                     // delete all persons
   delete persPtr[--n];            //     from memory
      }   // end main()
```

The class `person` has a single data item, `name`, that holds a string representing a person's name. Two member functions, `setName()` and `printName()`, allow the name to be set and displayed.

At the end of the program, I use a `while` loop to delete the objects pointed to by all the pointers in the `persPtr` array.

Program Operation

The `main()` function defines an array, `persPtr`, of 100 pointers to type `person`. In a `do` loop, it then uses `new` to create a person object. It then asks the user to enter a name and gives this name to the new person object. The pointer to the person object is stored in the array `persPtr`. To demonstrate how easy it is to access the objects using the pointers, `main()` then prints out the `name` data for each `person` object, using a simple `for` loop.

Here's some sample interaction with program:

```
Enter name: Stroustrup          <--user enters names
Enter another (y/n)? y
Enter name: Ritchie
Enter another (y/n)? y
Enter name: Kernighan
Enter another (y/n)? n
Person number 1                 <--program displays all names stored
   Name is: Stroustrup
Person number 2
   Name is: Ritchie
Person number 3
   Name is: Kernighan
```

Accessing Member Functions

I need to access the member functions `setName()` and `printName()` in the `person` objects pointed to by the pointers in the array `persPtr`. Each of the elements of the array `persPtr` is specified in array notation to be `persPtr[j]` (or equivalently by pointer notation to be `*(persPtr+j)`). The elements are pointers to objects of type `person`. Also, as you know, to access a member of an object using a pointer, you use the `->` operator. Putting this all together, we have the following syntax for `getname()`:

```
persPtr[j]->getName()
```

This statement executes the `getname()` function for the `person` object pointed to by element `j` of the `persPtr` array. (It's a good thing we don't have to write programs using English syntax.)

1. The `new` operator
   a. is used to declare objects or variables.
   b. can create and initialize an object.
   c. names an object or variable.
   d. returns a pointer to an object or variable.
   e. can allocate an appropriate amount of memory for an object or variable.

2. The `delete` operator
   a. deallocates memory obtained with a variable or object definition.
   b. deallocates memory obtained when a variable or object is created with `new`.
   c. can destroy an object.
   d. can destroy a variable.
   e. must be used with brackets, as in `delete[]`.

3. If you define and initialize an `xString` object with a copy constructor, like this:

```
xString x2(x1);
```

   then it's true that
   a. the value of the pointer `str` in `x1` will be copied to `str` in `x2`.
   b. both `xString` objects will refer to the same `char*` string.
   c. the `char*` string will be copied from `x1` to `x2`.
   d. `x2` is an alias for `x1`.
   e. you can change the text in `x1` without affecting `x2`.

4. If you've created a new object using the statement

```
p = new X;
```

   then to access a normal member function `f()` in the new object, you would say
   a. `X.f();`
   b. `X->f();`
   c. `p.f();`
   d. `p->f();`
   e. `X::f();`

5. If you have an array `A` of pointers to objects, then to call a member function `f()` for the fourth object in the array you would say

   a. `A.f(3)`

   b. `A->f(3)`

   c. `A[3].f()`

   d. `A->f()`

   e. `A[3]->f()`

EXERCISE 1

Write a program along the lines of the PTROBJS example in this session, but make it work with `airtime` objects rather than with `person` objects. The program should allow the user to enter an arbitrary number of `airtime` objects. It should then display them.

EXERCISE 2

Create a class that obtains storage for integers. It should have a `store()` function to insert an `int` value at the next available location and a `get()` function to read the value in any specified location. To conserve memory, the class should use `new` to get memory one chunk at a time. For example, a chunk could store 10 `int` values. When `store()` is called for the 11th value, it must obtain another chunk of memory using `new`. To the class user, the chunks are invisible; it appears as if the integers are stored contiguously, as they would be in an array. The class, however, maintains an array of pointers to chunks and accesses any given value by figuring out what chunk it's in and what number it has in the chunk.

MIDCHAPTER DISCUSSION

George: I *hate* pointers! When I look at code that has pointers in it, my mind just goes blank.

Estelle: I know what you mean. All those asterisks.

Don: Actually I think the asterisks are a big part of the problem. The idea behind pointers is simple, but the notation is obscure. If they'd just used a keyword like `pointer_to` to define each pointer, and maybe a operator like `contents_of()` to get the contents of a pointer, things would be a lot more understandable for beginners.

George: Why have both pointer notation and array notation for accessing array elements?

Don: There's not much point in actually accessing array elements with pointer notation. It's just educational to see that *(array+j) is the same as array[j]. The assembly language code generated by the compiler actually works with pointers, but it's easier for humans to work with arrays.

Estelle: Then what are pointers really for?

Don: I think the most critical use is connecting together the parts of complex data structures.

George: Like what?

Don: Linked lists and stuff like that, which I suppose we'll get to later in this chapter. We've already seen an array of pointers to objects, and the pointer returned from `new` is important. I don't know how you would access dynamically allocated memory without a pointer.

SESSION 5

t h i s **AND** c o n s t

In this session, I discuss two short and somewhat unrelated topics: the `this` pointer, with which a member function can access the object that called it, and `const` used with pointers.

The t h i s **Pointer**

If you're an object, can you find out where you're located in memory? You can, and being able to do so has some surprising benefits.

The member functions of every C++ object have access to a sort of magic pointer named `this`, which points to the object itself. Thus, any member function can discover the address of the object that invoked it. Listing 8-11 is a short example, WHERE, that shows the mechanism.

Listing 8-11 WHERE

```
// where.cpp
// the this pointer
#include <iostream.h>

class where
    {
    private:
        char charray[10];    // occupies 10 bytes
    public:
        void reveal()
            { cout << "\nMy object's address is " << this; }
    };

void main()
    {
    where w1, w2, w3;    // make three objects
    w1.reveal();         // see where they are
    w2.reveal();
    w3.reveal();
    }
```

The main() program in this example creates three objects of type where. It then asks each object to print its address using the reveal() member function. This function prints out the value of the this pointer. Here's the output:

```
My object's address is Ox8f4effec
My object's address is Ox8f4effe2
My object's address is Ox8f4effd8
```

Because the data in each object consists of an array of 10 bytes, the objects are spaced 10 bytes apart in memory (EC minus E2 is 10 decimal, and so is E2 minus D8).

Incidentally, I should note that the this pointer is not available in static member functions, because they are not associated with a particular object but with the class as a whole.

Accessing Member Data with this

When you call a member function, it comes into existence with the value of its this pointer set to the address of the object for which it was called. The this pointer can be treated like any other pointer to an object, and can thus be used to access the data in the object it points to, as shown in the DOTHIS program (Listing 8-12).

Listing 8-12 DOTHIS

```
// dothis.cpp
// the this pointer referring to data
#include <iostream.h>

class what
    {
    private:
        int alpha;
    public:
        void tester()
            {
            this->alpha = 11;      // same as alpha = 11;
            cout << this->alpha;  // same as cout << alpha;
            }
    };

void main()
    {
    what w;
    w.tester();
            }
```

This program simply prints out the value 11. The tester() member function accesses the variable alpha using the expression

```
this->alpha
```

which has exactly the same effect as referring to alpha directly. This syntax works, but there is no reason for it except to show that this does indeed point to w, the object that invoked the member function tester().

Using this *for Returning Values*

A more practical use for **this** is returning values from member functions and overloaded operators. What help is **this** in such situations?

As I've noted before, it's always a good idea to return by reference when returning an object, because this avoids the creation of unnecessary objects. However, you've seen that you can't return an automatic (defined within the function) variable by reference, because such variables are destroyed when the function returns and the reference would refer to something that no longer existed. For example, in the ASSIGN2 program in Chapter 6, Session 6, I could not return the object by reference.

It would be nice to have something more permanent than a local object if I'm going to return it by reference. What about returning the object for which a function was called? An object is more permanent than its individual member functions. Member functions are created and destroyed every time they're called, but the object itself endures until it is destroyed by some outside agency (e.g., when it is **deleted**). Thus, returning the object that called a member function is a better bet than returning a temporary object created within the function. The **this** pointer makes this easy.

Let's rewrite the ASSIGN2 program from Chapter 6 to demonstrate returning an object. Listing 8-13 shows ASSIGN3, in which the **operator=()** function returns by reference the object that invoked it.

Listing 8-13 ASSIGN3

```
// assign3.cpp
// returns contents of the this pointer
#include <iostream.h>

class alpha
    {
    private:
        int data;
    public:
        alpha()                      // no-arg constructor
            { }
        alpha(int d)                 // one-arg constructor
            { data = d; }
        void display()               // display data
            { cout << data; }

        alpha& operator = (alpha& a)  // overloaded = operator
            {
            data = a.data;            // (not done automatically)
            cout << "\nAssignment operator invoked";
            return *this;             // return ref to this alpha
            }
    };

void main()
    {
    alpha a1(37);
    alpha a2, a3;

    a3 = a2 = a1;                        // invoke overloaded =
```

```
cout << "\na2="; a2.display();  // display a2
cout << "\na3="; a3.display();  // display a3
        }
```

In this program, I declare the overloaded = operator as

```
alpha& operator = (alpha& a)
```

which returns by reference. The last statement in this function is

```
return *this;
```

Because `this` is a pointer to the object that invoked the function, `*this` is that object itself, and the statement returns this object. Here's the output of ASSIGN3:

```
Assignment operator invoked
Assignment operator invoked
a2=37
a3=37
```

Each time the equal sign is encountered in

```
a3 = a2 = a1;
```

the overloaded `operator=()` function is called, which displays `Assignment operator invoked`. The three objects all end up with the same value, as shown by the output.

Returning by reference from member functions and overloaded operators is a powerful and commonly used approach that avoids the creation of unnecessary objects. This makes your program smaller, faster, and less prone to errors.

Pointers and the const Modifier

I'll finish this session with a different topic: the application of the `const` modifier to pointers. I'll begin by recalling how `const` is used with nonpointer variables, and then go on to show how `const` can apply to either the address in the pointer or the contents of the variable at that address.

const *Variables*

You've seen that if you want an ordinary (nonpointer) variable to be unchanged for the duration of the program, you make it `const`. For example, following the definition

```
const int var1 = 123;
```

any attempt to modify `var1` will elicit an error message from the compiler. It will have the value 123 throughout the program.

Two Places for const

Things get more complicated when pointers enter the picture. When you define a pointer, you can specify that the pointer itself is `const`, or that the value of what it points to is `const`, or both. Let's look at these possibilities. I'll start with an ordinary variable and define three pointers to it:

```
int a;                  // int variable

const int* p = &a;      // pointer to constant int
```

```
++p;                      // ok
++(*p);                   // error: can't modify a const a

int* const q = &a;        // constant pointer to int
++q;                      // error: can't modify a const q
++(*q);                   // ok

const int* const r = &a;  // constant pointer to constant int
++r;                      // error: can't modify a const r
++(*r);                   // error: can't modify a const a
```

If const is placed before the data type (as in the definition of p), the result is a pointer to a constant *variable*. If const is placed after the data type (as in the definition of q), the result is a constant *pointer* to a variable. In the first case, you can't change the value in the variable the pointer points to; in the second, you can't change the address in the pointer. Using const in both places (as in the definition of r) means that neither the pointer nor the variable it points to can be modified.

You should use const whenever possible. If a pointer value should never change, make the pointer const. If the pointer should never be used to change what it points to, make it a pointer to const.

All this may not seem vital in this example, because the variable a itself isn't const. Why worry about modifying it with a pointer if it can be modified directly? Things become more realistic when you have a variable that's already const and you want to define a pointer to it:

```
const int b = 99;     // const variable
int* r = &b;          // error: can't convert const to non-const
const int* s = &b;    // ok
int* const t = &b;    // error: can't convert const to non-const
```

The compiler protects you from writing statements that could lead to the value of a const variable being changed, even if the change takes place via a pointer. You can't assign the address of a const variable such as b to a pointer unless it's defined as a pointer to a constant variable (as is pointer s in the example). This maintains "constness" because you can't use such a pointer to modify the original const variable:

```
++(*s);                 // error:can't modify a const
```

Function Arguments *and* const

One place the use of const is important is when passing pointers to functions. The code calling the function often wants to be sure that the function won't modify whatever the pointer points to. The function can guarantee this by specifying a pointer to a constant variable:

```
void func(const int* p)
   {
   ++p;       // ok
   ++(*p);    // error: can't modify a constant int
   }
```

Better yet, the function can guarantee that both the pointer *and* what it points to will be unchanged:

```
void func(const int* const p)
   {
   ++p;        // error: can't modify a constant pointer
```

```
++(*p);    // error: can't modify a constant int
}
```

These techniques help reduce unexpected side effects when you call a function.

Returning const *Values*

To put the shoe on the other foot, a function that *returns* a pointer is in danger of having the code that called the function mistakenly use the pointer to modify the constant that the pointer points to. (This is only an issue with static or external variables, because variables local to the function are automatically destroyed when the function returns.)

To avoid this, the compiler requires you to use a const return value for a function returning a pointer to a constant. For example, if you define an external constant j:

```
const int j = 77;
```

then you can't say

```
int* func()
    {
    return &j;    // error: can't convert const to non-const
    }
```

because this would allow you to use the pointer returned by the function to modify j:

```
int* p = func();
*p = 88;               // bad; modifies j
```

Instead, you must declare the function as

```
const int* func()
    {
    return &j;    // ok
            }
```

Then the code that calls the function must assign the return value to a const:

```
const int* p = func()    // ok
```

Because you can't modify the contents of what **p** points to, j continues to be safe from modification. Constness is preserved.

This discussion of const may seem complicated, but the reason for using const is simple: It keeps constant variables from being modified. The beauty of this approach is that mistakes are caught by the compiler, so there's seldom any need for the debugging session that's necessary when you find your constants are being mysteriously modified at runtime.

Of course, you don't absolutely need to use const with pointers (or anywhere else), but it is an important aid in creating more robust and error-free programs.

QUIZ 5

1. The **this** pointer
   a. must never be accessed directly by the programmer.
   b. must be initialized by the programmer.
   c. is different in different versions of the same member function that are invoked by different objects.
   d. is different in different member functions called by the same object.
   e. points to the object that invoked a member function.

2. When you return ***this** from a function,
   a. the return type of the function must be the same class as the object that invoked the function.
   b. the return type of the function must be a pointer to the same class as the object that invoked the function.
   c. you can usually return by reference.
   d. you cannot return by value.
   e. the object that invoked the function is destroyed.

3. By using **const** appropriately, you can define a pointer that prevents any change to
   a. the variable the pointer points to.
   b. the contents of the pointer.
   c. the address of the pointer.
   d. the address of what the pointer points to.
   e. the contents of what the pointer points to.

4. If a function is declared as

   ```
   void f(const int* arg1);
   ```

   a. it can't change the contents of **arg1**.
   b. it can't change the value of the variable whose address is in **arg1**.
   c. it can't access the contents of **arg1**.
   d. it can't access the value of the variable whose address is in **arg1**.
   e. the compiler will flag an error.

5. If a function is declared as

   ```
   const int* f();
   ```

   a. it can return a pointer to a constant variable.
   b. it cannot return a pointer to a nonconstant variable.
   c. the return value can't be changed.
   d. the value pointed to by the return value can't be changed.
   e. the return value must be assigned to a **const** variable.

Due to its theoretical nature, this session contains no exercises.

SESSION 6
A MEMORY-EFFICIENT STRING CLASS

In this session, I'll put together some of what you've learned about pointers, and many other topics besides, to make an improved version of the oft-encountered xString class.

To Copy or Not to Copy?

The versions of the xString class shown in previous chapters were not very powerful. For example, they lacked an obvious feature of a good string class: overloading the = operator so that the class user can assign the value of one xString object to another with a statement such as

```
s2 = s1;
```

The next example will contain an xString class with an overloaded = operator. Before I can write this operator, however, I need to decide how I will handle the actual string (the variable of type char*), which is the principal data item in the xString class.

One possibility is for each xString object to have its own char* string. If I assign one xString object to another (from s1 into s2 in the statement above), I simply copy the string from the source into the destination object. The problem with this is that the same string now exists in two (or maybe more) places in memory. This is not very efficient, especially if the strings are long. Figure 8-13 shows the situation.

Instead of having each xString object contain its own string, I could arrange for each xString object to contain only a *pointer* to a string. Now, if I assign one xString object to another, I need only copy the pointer from one object to another. Both pointers will point to the same string. This saves space because only a single copy of the string itself needs to be stored in memory. Figure 8-14 shows how this looks.

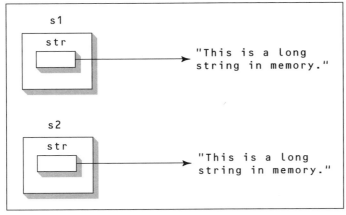

Figure 8-13 Replicating strings

However, if I use this system, I need to be careful when I destroy an **xString** object. If an **xString**'s destructor uses **delete** to free the memory occupied by the string, and if there are other objects with pointers pointing to the same string, then these other objects will be left with pointers pointing to memory that no longer holds the string they think it does; they become dangling pointers.

To use pointers to strings in **xString** objects successfully, I need a way to keep track of how many **xString** objects point to a particular string so I can avoid deleting the string until the last **xString** that points to it is itself deleted. In the following section, you'll see an example program, STRIMEM, that shows one way to do this.

A String Counter Class

Suppose I have several **xString** objects pointing to the same string and I want to keep a count of how many **xStrings** point to the string. Where will I store this count?

It would be cumbersome for every **xString** object to maintain a count of how many of its fellow **xStrings** were pointing to a particular string, so I don't want to use a member variable in **xString** for the count. Could I use a static variable? This is a possibility; I could create a static array and use it to store a list of string addresses and counts. However, this requires considerable overhead. It's more efficient to create a new class to store the count. Each object of this class, which I'll call **strCount**, contains a count and also a pointer to the string itself. Each **xString** object contains a pointer to the appropriate **strCount** object. Figure 8-15 shows the arrangement.

A **strCount** object manages the **char*** string. Its constructor uses **new** to create the string, and its destructor uses **delete** to delete it. To provide **xString** objects with access to the count and the string within their **strCount** object, I supply **strCount** with a number of short member functions: **getstr()**, **getCount()**, **incCount()**, and **decCount()**.Listing 8-14 shows STRIMEM.

Listing 8-14 STRIMEM

```
// strimem.cpp
// memory-saving xString class
// the this pointer in overloaded assignment
#include <iostream.h>
#include <string.h>                    // for strcpy(), etc
```

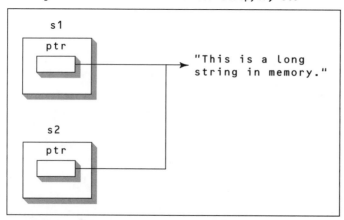

Figure 8-14 Replicating pointers to strings

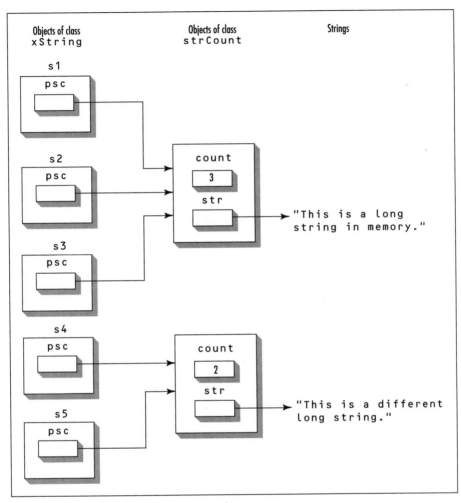

Figure 8-15 xString and strCount classes

```
/////////////////////////////////////////////////////////
class strCount                      // keep track of number
   {                                // of unique strings
   private:
      int count;                    // number of xStrings
      char* str;                    // pointer to string
   public:
      strCount(const char* const s) // one-arg constructor
         {
         int length = strlen(s);    // length of string argument
         str = new char[length+1];  // get memory for string
         strcpy(str, s);            // copy argument to it
         count=1;                   // start count at 1
         }
```

continued on next page

continued from previous page

```
      ~strCount()                     // destructor
         { delete[] str; }
      char* getstr()                  // get string
         { return str; }
      int getCount()                  // get count
         { return count; }
      void incCount()                 // increment count
         { ++count; }
      void decCount()                 // decrement count
         { --count; }
   };  // end class strCount
///////////////////////////////////////////////////////////////
class xString                         // xString class
   {
   private:
      strCount* psc;                   // pointer to strCount
   public:
      xString()                        // no-arg constructor
         {
         psc = new strCount("NULL");
         }
      xString(const char* const s)     // 1-arg constructor
         {
         psc = new strCount(s);
         }
      xString(const xString& S)        // copy constructor
         {
         cout << "\nCOPY CONSTRUCTOR";
         psc = S.psc;
         psc->incCount();
         }
      ~xString()                       // destructor
         {
         if(psc->getCount()==1)        // if we are its last user,
            delete psc;                // delete our strCount
         else                          // otherwise,
            psc->decCount();           // decrement its count
         }
      void display()                   // display the xString
         {
         cout << psc->getstr();                // print string
         cout << " (addr=" << psc << ")";      // print address
         }
                                       // assignment operator
      xString& operator = (const xString&  S)
         {
         cout << "\nASSIGNMENT";
         if(psc->getCount()==1)        // if we are its last user,
            delete psc;                // delete our strCount
         else                          // otherwise,
            psc->decCount();           // decrement its count
         psc = S.psc;                  // use argument's strCount
         psc->incCount();              // increment count
```

```
        return *this;                // return this object
        }
    }; // end class xString
///////////////////////////////////////////////////////////
void main()
    {                                // 1-arg constructor
    xString s1 = "When the fox preaches, look to your geese.";
    cout << "\ns1="; s1.display();   // display s1

    xString s2;                      // define s2
    s2 = s1;                         // set equal to s1
    cout << "\ns2="; s2.display();   // display s2

    xString s3(s1);                  // initialize s3 to s1
    cout << "\ns3="; s3.display();   // display s3
    }
```

In the `main()` part of STRIMEM, the program defines an `xString` object, `s1`, to contain the proverb `"When the fox preaches, look to your geese."` It defines another `xString` `s2` and sets it equal to `s1`; then it defines `s3` and initializes it to `s1`. Setting `s2` equal to `s1` invokes the overloaded assignment operator, and initializing `s3` to `s1` invokes the overloaded copy constructor. The program displays all three `xString`s and the address of the `strCount` object pointed to by each object's `psc` pointer to show that they all refer to the same `strCount` object (and hence the same `char*` string). Here's the output from STRIMEM:

```
s1=When the fox preaches, look to your geese. (addr=0x8f510e3e)
ASSIGNMENT
s2=When the fox preaches, look to your geese. (addr=0x8f510e3e)
COPY CONSTRUCTOR
s3=When the fox preaches, look to your geese. (addr=0x8f510e3e)
```

Notice how short and simple `main()` is. Once you've written the classes, using them is easy. The duties of the `xString` class are divided between the `xString` and `strCount` classes. Let's see what they do.

The strCount *Class*

As I noted, the `strCount` class contains the pointer to the actual string and the count of how many `xString` class objects point to this string. Its single constructor takes a pointer to a string as an argument and creates a new memory area for the string. It copies the string from the argument into this area and sets the count to 1, because just one `xString` points to it when it is created. The destructor in `strCount` frees the memory used by the string. I use `delete[]` with brackets because a string is an array. You'll see in a moment under what circumstances the `strCount` object is destroyed.

The xString *Class*

The `xString` class has three constructors. If a new string is being created, as in the zero- and one-argument constructors, a new `strCount` object is created to hold the string and the `psc` pointer is set to point to this object. If an existing `xString` object is being copied, as in the copy constructor and the overloaded assignment operator, then the pointer `psc` is set to point to the old `strCount` object and the count in this object is incremented. The overloaded assignment operator must also delete the old **strCount** object pointed to by **psc**. (Here I don't need brackets on **delete** because I'm deleting only a single **strCount** object.) Figure 8-16 shows the action of the overloaded assignment operator, and Figure 8-17 shows the copy constructor.

Returning *this by Reference

To make possible the chaining of multiple assignment operators for **xString** objects, as in the statement

```
s4 = s5 = s6;
```

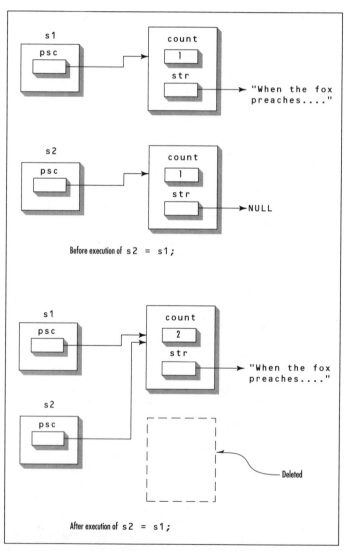

Figure 8-16 Assignment operator in STRIMEM

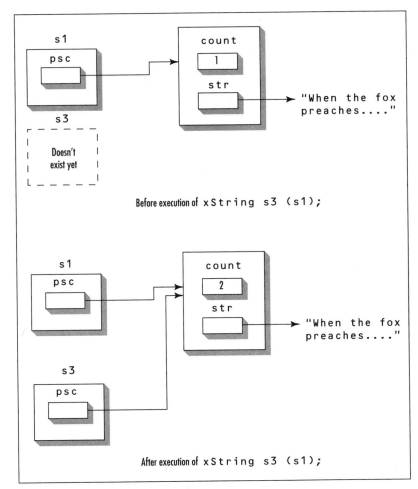

Figure 8-17   Copy constructor in STRIMEM

I provide a return value from the **operator=()** function. Using the **this** pointer, I can return by reference, thus avoiding the creation of extra objects.

In this program, I provide communication between **xString** and **strCount** using member functions in **strCount**. Another approach is to make the **xString** class a *friend* of the **strCount** class. This obviates the need for the access functions like **getstr()** and **incCount()** in **strCount**. You'll learn about friend classes in Chapter 9.

1. The advantage of the **xString** class in the STRIMEM program, compared with earlier versions

of xString, is that
a. memory is saved.
b. the + operator is overloaded.
c. you can set one xString object equal to another.
d. objects can be initialized more quickly.
e. if you set one object equal to another, you can delete one without invalidating the other.

2. When you set one xString object from STRIMEM equal to another, as in

s2 = s1;

a. s1 is copied memberwise into s2.
b. a char* string is copied from s1 to s2.
c. a pointer is copied from s1 to s2.
d. the pointer-to-strCount in s2 is changed.
e. the count in the strCount pointed to by s1 is changed.

3. The count stored in objects of the strCount class represents
a. how many xString objects the strCount object points to.
b. how many char* strings the strCount object points to.
c. the number of xString objects in the program.
d. the number of xString objects using that strCount.
e. how many times the corresponding xString object has been referenced.

4. The const in the argument in the copy constructor declarator for xString in STRIMEM means that
a. the object for which the copy constructor is invoked can't be modified.
b. the object for which the copy constructor is invoked will point to the same strCount as the argument to the copy constructor.
c. the newly initialized object is const.
d. the copy constructor can't modify the original object.
e. the copy constructor can't modify the new object.

5. The fact that the overloaded = operator uses a reference return for the object that invoked it means that
a. the = operator can be chained.
b. no extra xString objects are created if the = operator used, whether it assigns the return value to a variable or not.
c. no extra xString objects are created if the = operator is chained.
d. the = operator can be used to set one xString equal to another.
e. the copy constructor can use the same code as the = operator.

EXERCISE 1

Create a member function of xString, called mid(), that returns a new xString that is a substring from the middle part of the xString that invoked the function The first argument to this function is the character number where the substring starts (starting at 0 on the left), and the second argument is the number of characters in the substring. For example, if **s2** is "dogs and chickens", then the statement

```
s1 = s2.mid(5, 3)
```

will set **s1** to "and".

EXERCISE 2

Overload the + operator in the **xString** class so you can concatenate **xString** objects. For example, if **s1** is "Harry", **s2** is " ", and **s3** is "Brown" and you execute

```
name = s1 + s2 + s3;
```

then **name** should have the value "Harry Brown".

SESSION 7

A LINKED LIST CLASS

The next example demonstrates a simple *linked list*. What is a linked list? It's another way to store data. You've seen numerous examples of data stored in arrays and examples of arrays of pointers to data objects. Both the array and the array of pointers suffer from the necessity to declare a fixed-size array before running the program. The linked list allows you to use exactly as much memory as you need, even when you don't know how much this will be until the program is running.

A Chain of Pointers

The linked list provides a more flexible storage system in that it doesn't use arrays at all. Instead, space for each data item is obtained as needed with **new** and each item is connected, or *linked*, to the next item using a pointer. The individual items don't need to be located contiguously in memory as array elements are; they can be scattered anywhere there's room for them.

In the example, the entire linked list is an object of class **linklist**. The individual data items, or links, are represented by structures of type **link**. (I could have used class objects for the links, but there's no point because they don't need member functions.) Each such structure contains an integer—representing the object's single data item—and a pointer to the next link. The **linklist** object itself stores a pointer to the link at the head of the list; this is its only data item. The arrangement is shown in Figure 8-18.

The **linklist** class contains member functions that allow the class user to add a link to the list and to display the data in all the links. Of course, in a real program there would be much more data than a single **int** stored in each link. A link might contain a complete personnel file or the inventory data on a car part, for example. Listing 8-15 shows LINKLIST.

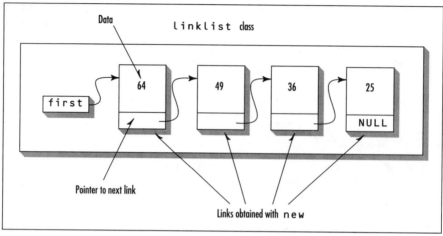

Figure 8-18   A linked list

Listing 8-15 LINKLIST

```
// linklist.cpp
// linked list
#include <iostream.h>

struct link                          // one element of list
   {
   int data;                         // data item
   link* next;                       // pointer to next link
   };

class linklist                       // a list of links
   {
   private:
      link* first;                   // pointer to first link
   public:
      linklist()                     // no-argument constructor
         { first = NULL; }           // no first link yet
      void additem(int d);           // add data item (one link)
      void display();                // display all links
   };

void linklist::additem(int d)        // add data item
   {
   link* newlink = new link;         // make a new link
   newlink->data = d;                // give it data
   newlink->next = first;            // it points to next link
   first = newlink;                  // now first points to this
   }

void linklist::display()             // display all links
   {
   link* current = first;            // set ptr to first link
```

```
    while( current != NULL )        // quit on last link
        {
        cout << endl << current->data;  // print data
        current = current->next;    // move to next link
        }
    }

void main()
    {
    linklist li;        // make linked list

    li.additem(25);     // add four items to list
    li.additem(36);
    li.additem(49);
    li.additem(64);

    li.display();       // display entire list
        }
```

The linklist class has only one member data item: the pointer to the start of the list. When the list is first created, the constructor initializes this pointer, first, to NULL. The NULL constant is defined in the mem.h header file (which is #included in the iostream.h file) to be 0. This value serves as a signal that a pointer does not hold a valid address. In the program, a link whose next member has a value of NULL is assumed to be at the end of the list.

Adding an Item to the List

The additem() member function adds an item to the linked list. A new link is inserted at the beginning of the list. (I could write the additem() function to insert items at the end of the list, but that would be a more complex program because I would need to step through the list to the end before inserting the new item.) Let's look at the steps involved in inserting a new link in additem().

First, a new structure of type link is created by the line

```
link* newlink = new link;
```

This creates memory for the new link structure with new and saves the pointer to it in the newlink variable.

Next, I want to set the members of the newly created structure to appropriate values. A structure is just like a class in that when it is referred to by pointer rather than by name, its members are accessed using the -> member access operator. The following two lines set the data variable to the value passed as an argument to additem() and the next pointer to point to whatever address was in first, which holds the pointer to the start of the list.

```
newlink->data = d;
newlink->next = first;
```

Finally, I want the first variable to point to the new link:

```
first = newlink;
```

The effect is to uncouple the connection between first and the old first link and insert the new link, moving the old first link into the second position. Figure 8-19 shows this process.

Displaying the List Contents

Once the linked list is created, it's easy to step through all the members, displaying them (or performing other operations). All I need to do is follow from one `next` pointer to another until I find a `next` that is `NULL`, signaling the end of the list. In the function `display()`, the line

```
cout << endl << current->data;
```

prints the value of the data, and

```
current = current->next;
```

moves me along from one link to another, until

```
current != NULL
```

in the `while` expression becomes false. Here's the output of LINKLIST:

```
64
49
36
25
```

Linked lists are perhaps the most commonly used data storage arrangements after arrays. As I noted, they avoid the wasted memory space engendered by arrays. The disadvantage is that finding a particular item on a linked list requires following the chain of links from the head of the list until the desired link is reached. This can be time-consuming. An array element, on the other hand, can be accessed quickly, provided its index is known in advance.

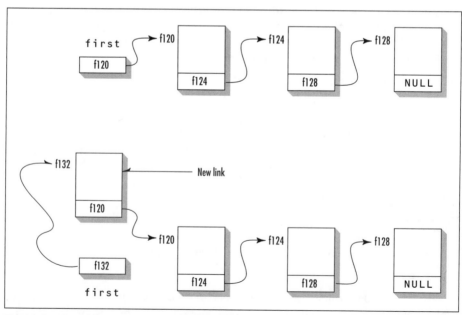

Figure 8-19 Adding a link to a linked list

Self-Containing Classes

I should note a possible pitfall in the use of self-referential classes and structures. The `link` structure in LINKLIST contained a pointer to the same kind of structure. You can do the same with classes:

```
class sampleclass
   {
   sampleclass* ptr;  // this is fine
   };
```

However, although a class can contain a *pointer* to an object of its own type, it cannot contain an *object* of its own type:

```
class sampleclass
   {
   sampleclass obj;  // can't do this
   };
```

This is true of structures as well as classes.

Augmenting the `linklist` Program

The general organization of LINKLIST can be used in a more complex situation than that shown. As I noted, there could be more data in each link. Instead of an integer, a link could hold a number of data items or it could hold a pointer to a structure or object.

Additional member functions of the `linklist` class could perform such activities as adding and removing links from an arbitrary location in the chain. Another important member function is a destructor. As I mentioned, it's important to delete blocks of memory that are no longer in use. A destructor that performs this task would be a highly desirable addition to the `linklist` class. It could go through the list using `delete` to free the memory occupied by each link.

Containers

The `linklist` class is an example of a *container class*. Container classes are used for storing (*containing*) data. In Chapter 12 I'll investigate the Standard Template Library (STL), which includes such containers as vectors, lists, sets, and deques.

The linked list stores integers and only integers. Most commercial container classes (including the STL) allow containers to store any kind of object or basic type by implementing the container as a *template*. You'll learn more about templates in Chapter 11.

1. Which of the following are advantages of a linked list as a data-storage device?
   a. You can quickly access an item with specified characteristics.
   b. The size of the data storage area can expand and contract dynamically.

c. You can quickly insert a new item.

d. You can quickly delete an existing item with specified characteristics.

e. The first item entered is the first to be removed.

2. The end of the linked list is signaled by

a. the current link number equaling the total number of links.

b. a 0 value in the data item in any link.

c. a **NULL** value in the **next** variable of the last link.

d. a **NULL** value in the **first** variable in **linklist**.

e. a pointer pointing back to **first**.

3. To add a new link to the linked list, using the scheme in LINKLIST, a member function must

a. ask the program's user to enter the data that will be stored in the link.

b. change **first** so it points to the new link.

c. leave the value of **first** unchanged.

d. set the **next** pointer in the new link so it points to the last link.

e. set the **next** pointer in the new link so it has whatever value was previously in **first**.

4. If a member function of **linklist**'s purpose is to delete a link that held specific data, this function would need to

a. step through the list, looking for the link to be deleted.

b. create a temporary link with a **NULL** pointer.

c. use **delete** to delete a link.

d. put the address of the deleted link in **first**.

e. rearrange the pointer in the previous link to bypass the deleted link.

5. Suppose you define a **linklist** object, as specified in the LINKLIST program above, as an automatic variable in a standalone (nonmember) function **f()**. Then, within **f()**, you add numerous links to the list. Which of the following will happen when **f()** terminates?

a. The **linklist** object will continue to occupy memory.

b. The **first** pointer will point to an invalid address.

c. The links will continue to occupy memory.

d. The data in the links can be accessed by calling **f()** again and creating a new **linklist** object.

e. The list can be accessed from some other function.

EXERCISE 1

Write a **destroy_list()** member function for the **linklist** class. It should follow the chain from link to link, deleting each link as it goes, and set **first** to **NULL**.

EXERCISE 2

Write a `remove_item()` member function for the `linklist` class. It should chain through the list, looking for a link with a data item that matches a value supplied by the program's user. When `remove_item()` finds this link, it should delete it and rearrange the pointers so the previous link points to the next link. (That is, if you delete link 6, then the pointer in link 5 should end up pointing to link 7.)

SESSION 8

A SORTED ARRAY CLASS

In this session I'll examine another container class. This one, called `SortedArray`, models an array that automatically arranges its elements in sorted order. The meaning of "sorted" depends on what's stored in the array. In this example, I store pointers to objects of class `employee`. The data in each employee object includes an employee number; the `SortedArray` object will ensure that the pointers-to-`employee` are arranged in order of increasing employee number.

Inserting Objects in Sorted Order

When you insert a new `employee` object in `SortedArray`, its pointer is automatically placed in the appropriate location and the pointers above it in the array are moved up to give it room, as shown in Figure 8-20.

Listing 8-16 shows SORTEMPS.

Listing 8-16 SORTEMPS

```
// sortemps.cpp
// sorted array class holds sorted employee objects
#include <iostream.h>
///////////////////////////////////////////////////////////
class employee                   // employee class
   {
   private:
      enum { LEN=30 };           // maximum length of names
      char name[LEN];            // employee name
      unsigned long number;      // employee number
   public:
      void getdata()             // get data from user
         {
         cout << "\n   Name: "; cin >> name;
         cout << "   Number: "; cin >> number;
         }
      void putdata() const       // display data
         {
         cout << "\n   Name = " << name;
         cout << "\n   Number = " << number;
```

continued on next page

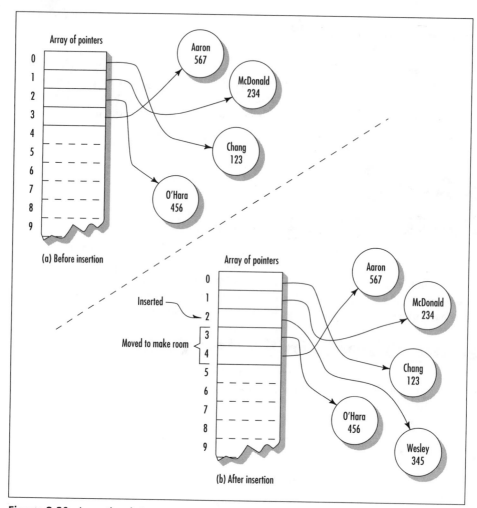

Figure 8-20 Insertion into a `SortedArray`

continued from previous page

```
            }
        unsigned long get_number() const   // return emp number
            { return number; }
    };
//////////////////////////////////////////////////////////////////
class SortedArray
    {
    private:
        enum {SIZE=100};
        employee* arr[SIZE];        // array of pointers to emps
        int total;                  // number of emps in array
    public:
        SortedArray() : total(0)    // no-arg constructor
            { }
```

```
      employee* operator[](int) const;   // declarations
      void insert(employee*);
  };
                                // read data from element n
employee* SortedArray::operator[](int n) const
   { return arr[n]; }
                                // insert in sorted order
void SortedArray::insert(employee* data)
   {
   int j = 0;
   while(j < total &&              // find correct place
                  data->get_number() > arr[j]->get_number() )
       j++;
   for(int k=total; k>j; k--)      // move higher elements up
      arr[k] = arr[k-1];
   arr[j] = data;                  // insert new data
   total++;                        // now it has one more element
   }
////////////////////////////////////////////////////////////
void main()
   {
   SortedArray sa;                // a sorted array
   employee* ptr;                 // utility pointer
   char answer;                   // 'y' or 'n'
   int total = 0;                 // number of employees in array

   do
      {
      ptr = new employee;         // make an employee
      cout << "Enter data for employee " << ++total << ": ";
      ptr->getdata();             // get employee data from user
      sa.insert(ptr);             // put employee in sorted array
      cout << "Do another (y/n)? ";
      cin >> answer;
      }
   while(answer != 'n');

   cout << "\nCONTENTS SORTED BY NUMBER" << endl;
   for(int j=0; j<total; j++)     // display data in order
      {
      cout << "\nEmployee " << (j+1);
      sa[j]->putdata();
      }
   }
```

Here's some sample interaction with SORTEMPS in which the user enters data for five employees:

```
Enter data for employee 1:
   Name: Wesley
   Number: 456
Do another (y/n)? y
Enter data for employee 2:
   Name: McDonald
```

```
    Number: 234
Do another (y/n)? y
Enter data for employee 3:
    Name: O'Hara
    Number: 345
Do another (y/n)? y
Enter data for employee 4:
    Name: Chang
    Number: 123
Do another (y/n)? y
Enter data for employee 5:
    Name: Aaron
    Number: 567
Do another (y/n)? n

CONTENTS SORTED BY NUMBER

Employee 1
    Name = Chang
    Number = 123
Employee 2
    Name = McDonald
    Number = 234
Employee 3
    Name = Wesley
    Number = 345
Employee 4
    Name = O'Hara
    Number = 456
Employee 5
    Name = Aaron
    Number = 567
```

The program has three parts: the `employee` class, the `SortedArray` class, and `main()`.

The employee *Class*

The data in class `employee` consists of a name (a `char*` string) and the employee number. A `getdata()` member function gets data for an `employee` object from the user, and a `putdata()` function displays the data. There's also a `get_number()` function, which is needed by the `SortedArray` class to find an employee's number. It uses the number to insert new employees in the correct location.

The SortedArray *Class*

The important data item in the `SortedArray` class is an array of pointers to `employees`. There's also an integer, `total`, that indicates how many objects are stored in the sorted array. A no-argument constructor sets `total` to 0 because the array starts out empty.

There are two member functions in `SortedArray`. The overloaded `[]` operator allows access to the element with a specified index. This is a read-only operator; it can't be used to set the value of a specified element. That's because the `SortedArray` itself, rather than the user, determines where each element will be inserted. If the user could insert an object at an arbitrary location, the order could be disrupted.

To insert an element in the `SortedArray`, the user calls the `insert()` member function. This function's only argument is a pointer to the object to be inserted. First, `insert()` examines the `employee` objects that are pointed to by the pointers in its array. The pointers are arranged in order of increasing employee numbers in the objects they point to.

When `insert()` finds an object with a higher employee number than the one it's trying to insert, it knows it should insert the new object just before this one. But first, `insert()` must move all the pointers that have higher employee numbers up one space to create room for the new element. This is handled by the `for` loop. Finally, a pointer to the new object is inserted in the newly vacated element.

In `main()`

The `main()` program creates a sorted array; then, in a `do` loop, it repeatedly creates `employee` objects, using `new`, and asks the user to fill them with data. The address of each `employee` object is then inserted into the sorted array. When the user is done inserting employees, the contents of the entire sorted array are displayed. Because they were inserted in sorted order, it's easy to display them in sorted order by accessing each element in turn.

Searching for a Specific Element

One of the advantages of a sorted array is that you can quickly locate a data item with a particular value for some variable (provided the array has been sorted using this same variable). In the next example, I'll show how you can search for an `employee` object with a specified employee number.

In a sorted array, you can use a *binary search* to locate the specified element. A binary search is very fast. In an array of 1,000 elements, for example, a binary search would require you to examine only 10 elements; whereas if the array were *not* sorted, you would need to look through all the elements one by one, requiring, on average, the examination of 500 elements, a lengthy process.

A binary search consists of repeatedly dividing the array in half. An analogy is when someone asks you to guess a number between, say, 1 and 100, and the person agrees to tell you if your guess is too big or too small. You start by guessing 50. If that guess is too small, you guess 75 (halfway between 50 and 100). If that's too big, you guess 62 (halfway between 50 and 75). If that's too big, you guess 56 (halfway between 50 and 62); if that's too small, you guess 59; if that's too small, you guess 60, and either that or 61 must be the answer. The process is shown in Figure 8-21.

In the `SortedArray` of `employee` objects, you first examine the object in the middle of the array. If the employee number you're looking for is larger than that contained in this middle element, you can forget the bottom half of the array and concentrate on the top half. Or, if the number you're looking for is less than the middle element, you can concentrate on the bottom half. You repeat this process, dividing the relevant half into quarters, and the relevant quarter into eighths, and so on, until you've narrowed the search to a single element. If this element doesn't have a matching number, the search fails. Listing 8-17 shows FINDEMP.

Listing 8-17 FINDEMP

```
// findemp.cpp
// sorted array class holds sorted employee objects
```

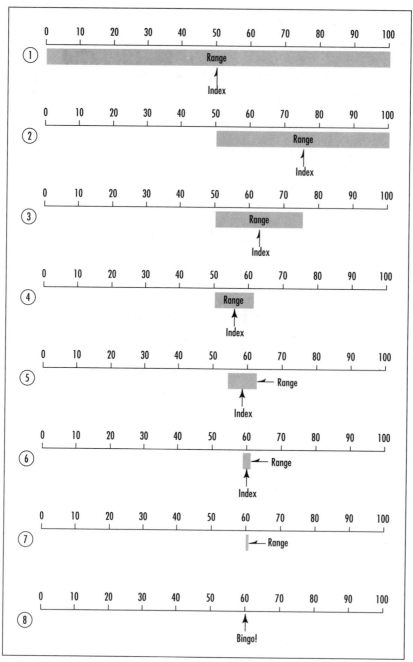

Figure 8-21 A binary search

```
// finds employee with binary search
#include <iostream.h>
```

```
#include <string.h>
/////////////////////////////////////////////////////////////////
class employee                      // employee class
    {
    private:
        enum { LEN=30 };            // maximum length of names
        char name[LEN];             // employee name
        unsigned long number;       // employee number
    public:
                                    // 2-arg constructor
        employee(char* na, unsigned long nu) : number(nu)
            { strcpy(name, na); }

        void putdata() const        // display data
            {
            cout << "\n   Name = " << name;
            cout << "\n   Number = " << number;
            }
                                    // return employee number
        unsigned long get_number() const
            { return number; }
    };
/////////////////////////////////////////////////////////////////
class SortedArray
    {
    private:
        enum {SIZE=100};            // size of array
        employee* arr[SIZE];        // define array
        int total;                  // number of objects in array
    public:
        SortedArray() : total(0)
            { }
        employee* operator[](int) const;
        void insert(employee*);
        employee* search(unsigned long);
    };
                                    // read data from element n
employee* SortedArray::operator[](int n) const
    { return arr[n]; }
                                    // insert in sorted order
void SortedArray::insert(employee* data)
    {
    int j = 0;
    while(j < total &&             // find correct place
                    data->get_number() > arr[j]->get_number() )
        j++;
    for(int k=total; k>j; k--)     // move higher elements up
        arr[k] = arr[k-1];
    arr[j] = data;                 // insert new data
    total++;                       // now it has one more element
    }

// binary search for employee with specified employee number
```

continued on next page

continued from previous page

```
employee* SortedArray::search(unsigned long num_to_find)
   {
   int lower = 0;                    // range of index numbers
   int upper = total;                // to be searched
   int index;                        // place to look

   while(upper > lower)
      {
      if(upper-lower > 1)
         index = lower + (upper-lower)/2;   // find middle
      else                                  // side-by-side
         index = upper = lower;             // merge them

      employee* ptr = arr[index];           // get ptr to emp
      unsigned long num = ptr->get_number();   // get emp number
      if(num == num_to_find)                // if exactly right,
         return ptr;                        // return pointer to emp
      if(num < num_to_find)                 // if emp number too low,
         lower = index;                     // move lower bound up
      else                                  // if too high,
         upper = index;                     // move upper bound down
      }
   return NULL;                             // no match
   }
//////////////////////////////////////////////////////////////
void main()
   {
   int j;
   SortedArray sa;                   // a sorted array
   unsigned long number;             // number to find
   employee* pemp;                   // ptr to found employee
   const int LIMIT = 10;             // number of employees

   employee emparr[LIMIT] =          // array of employees
     { employee("Webley", 468L),     // (note use of constructors
       employee("Suzuki", 672L),     // for initialization)
       employee("Smith", 371L),
       employee("Gonzalez", 274L),
       employee("Wong", 431L),
       employee("LeMonde", 789L),
       employee("Weinstein", 147L),
       employee("DeCarlo", 223L),
       employee("Nguyen", 390L),
       employee("O'Grady", 573L) };

   for(j=0; j<LIMIT; j++)            // insert address of each
      sa.insert(emparr+j);          // employee into SortedArray

   for(j=0; j<LIMIT; j++)           // display data in order
      {
      cout << "\nEmployee " << (j+1);
      sa[j]->putdata();
      }
```

```
cout << "\n\nEnter employee number to search for: ";
cin >> number;
pemp = sa.search(number);    // search for employee
if(pemp != NULL)
    {
    cout << "\nEmployee with that number is";
    pemp->putdata();
    }
else
    cout << "\No such employee number in database.";
}
```

The Binary Search

The `search()` member function of `SortedArray` carries out the binary search. It takes as its only argument the number of the employee to be found. If it succeeds in finding the desired employee, it returns a pointer to it. If it can't find a match, it returns NULL.

The function begins by defining a range specified by an upper bound and a lower bound (the variables `lower` and `upper`). It also defines an index (`index`) that is set to the midpoint of the range. It's the element at this index whose `employee` number will be examined. Initially, the range is the entire array, but each time the function finds that the element at the index has an employee number greater or less than the one it's looking for, it changes either the upper or the lower bound to be the same as the index. This divides the range in half, and the function then sets index to the middle of the new range and examines the object there. When the upper and lower bounds differ by only one element, it sets them equal, and after one more comparison, the loop ends whether a match has been found or not.

You could also use a binary search in the `insert()` member function in `SortedArray` to find where to insert a new member. This would speed up the insertion process, especially for large arrays.

Constructors Used to Initialize Array

In this program, rather than ask the user to supply employee data, I provide an ordinary C++ array of `employee` objects already initialized to values. This requires a two-argument constructor in `employee`:

```
employee(char* na, unsigned long nu) : number(nu)
    { strcpy(name, na); }
```

This constructor is called for each element when I define the array in `main()`:

```
employee emparr[LIMIT] =
    { employee("Webley", 468L),
      employee("Suzuki", 672L),
      ...
      employee("O'Grady", 573L) };
```

You might think you could initialize an array of objects as you would a structure:

```
employee emparr[LIMIT] = { {"Webley", 468L},          // not
```

```
{"Suzuki", 672L},        // a
    . . .                // legal
{"O'Grady", 573L} };     // syntax
```

However, this won't work. When you initialize a class object, its constructor must always be called.

1. Suppose pointers to **person** objects are placed in a sorted array according to a characteristic called **height**, with lower **height** values occupying lower array indexes. This is a good arrangement if
   a. the **height** of many **person** objects is not known when they are inserted in the array.
   b. no two objects have the same value for **height**.
   c. the array index occupied by an object must reflect the order in which it was inserted.
   d. single objects will be retrieved using their **height** characteristic.
   e. all the objects in the array will be accessed in order, from shortest to tallest.

2. Storing pointers to objects in an array, rather than storing the objects themselves, has the advantage that
   a. objects stored in an array take up less space than those allocated with **new**.
   b. an object with a given index can be accessed more quickly.
   c. the objects can be sorted more easily.
   d. it's quicker to organize storage for a new object.
   e. an object with a specified characteristic can be accessed more quickly.

3. In the FINDEMP program, when you insert a pointer to a new **employee** object into a **SortedArray** object,
   a. you must examine every array element with an employee number less than the one you're going to insert.
   b. the **total** member of **SortedArray** is incremented.
   c. the pointer goes at the smallest empty index.
   d. you must move the pointers to all objects that have employee numbers greater than that of the new object.
   e. you must move all the pointers that have index values greater than that of the new object.

4. In a binary search of a sorted array,
   a. each comparison divides the range to be searched into thirds.
   b. from an efficiency standpoint, it doesn't really matter whether the array contains objects or pointers to objects.
   c. if the array has 32 elements, you'll need to do about 6 (or possibly fewer) comparisons.
   d. from an efficiency standpoint, it doesn't really matter whether the array is sorted or not.
   e. the array should be sorted using the same characteristic that's being searched for.

5. To initialize three objects of class **X**, which require a one-argument constructor and are elements in an array **A**, you might say

a. `X A[SIZE] = { 121, 232, 343 };`

b. `X A[SIZE] = { X(121), X(232), X(343) };`

c. `X A[SIZE] = { A(121), A(232), A(343) };`

d. `X A[SIZE] = X( 121, 232, 343 );`

e. The objects can be initialized only after the array is defined.

EXERCISE 1

Change the `insert()` member function in `SortedArray` so it uses a binary search to find where to insert a new element, rather than simply stepping through all the elements from the beginning.

EXERCISE 2

Change the `SortedArray` class in FINDEMP so the array is sorted according to employee name rather than number. The names should be in alphabetical order. You can use the `strcmp()` library function to compare two names.

SUMMARY: CHAPTER 8

In this chapter I've introduced pointers and shown some typical uses for them.

A pointer is a variable that holds the memory address of some other variable. Pointers are a way of connecting parts of a program: A pointer in one part of a program points to another part of the program. For example, the **new** operator returns a pointer to a section of memory. Links in a linked list contain a pointer to the next link. An array of pointers allows access to any object whose pointer is in the array, and so on.

The **this** pointer, generated by the compiler, is automatically defined within most member functions and always points to the object that invoked the function. For example, if you say

```
objA.func();
```

then when `func()` is executed, it will contain a **this** pointer to **objA**.

It's good to use **const** wherever possible to avoid mistakenly changing values that shouldn't be changed. A pointer can be **const** in two different ways: The variable pointed to by the pointer may be **const** or the address in the pointer, specifying what variable is pointed to, may be **const**.

END-OF-CHAPTER DISCUSSION

Estelle: The `this` pointer is just as cute as can be.

Don: It is useful for returning objects.

George: Why is it such a big deal to keep from making extra copies of objects?

Estelle: Objects can be a lot bigger than basic type variables, so copying them takes time and memory.

Don: And there can be weird side effects to making copies. Some programs really care how many objects there are and get confused if there are extra ones.

Estelle: That's why it's nice to pass and return objects by reference, and that's why you need to return `*this`, so you have a more or less permanent object to return by reference. If you don't mind making a copy, you can make a temporary object and return it by value.

George: Putting `const` everywhere sure clutters up the listing. I never use it; it makes things look too messy.

Estelle: Well, in small programs you can get away with not using `const`. But when projects get big and hairy and complicated, you really want the compiler to help you find errors. The more you use `const`, the more the compiler can stop you from trying to change a constant.

Don: Absolutely. But if `const` bothers you, it probably doesn't hurt to write the code first without it and then go back and put it in later after you've conceptualized everything.

George: All of a sudden we're spending all our time talking about container classes. What's that got to do with C++?

Don: You need to know about data storage structures whether you're using a procedural language or OOP. But in C++, containers make really good examples. You can make them into objects and put other objects in them.

Estelle: And you learn a lot about pointers when you write a container class.

Don: That's for sure. But don't worry too much if you don't follow all the details of the containers. It's the stuff you'd normally learn in a Data Structures and Algorithms class in computer science. In the real world, you'll probably buy a set of containers from someone or use the ones that come with your compiler. In the meantime, just try to follow the OOP aspects of containers.

George: Yeah, well, I'll get to that as soon as I figure out what all these asterisks mean.

CHAPTER 9

VIRTUAL FUNCTIONS AND FRIEND FUNCTIONS

The first and largest part of this chapter is concerned with virtual functions, one of the major features of C++. Virtual functions make it possible to change the overall architecture of programs in surprising and powerful ways. The ideas involved in virtual functions are not trivial, so I'll introduce them gradually, covering the fundamentals first, then showing some expanded examples of their use, and then covering some additional features.

Later in this chapter, I'll examine friend functions and classes. Friends are a C++ concession to reality. Strict encapsulation and data hiding are usually highly desirable, but occasionally situations arise where an exception to the rules makes life easier. Friends provide an organized approach to liberalizing C++ strictness and, as it turns out, don't compromise data integrity in a serious way. I'll show the common situations in which friends are used.

495

SESSION 1

INTRODUCTION TO VIRTUAL FUNCTIONS

There are three major concepts in object-oriented programming. The first is classes and the second is inheritance. You've already seen these ideas at work. In this chapter I'll examine the third major concept: *polymorphism*, which is implemented in C++ by *virtual functions*.

Polymorphism

In real life, there is often a collection of different kinds of things that, given identical instructions, should take different actions. Take students, for example. There may be many kinds of students in a university: language students, premed students, computer science majors, athletes. Suppose you are the dean of this university and you want to send a directive to all students: "Fill out your registration forms!" Different kinds of students have different registration forms because they're in different departments. But as the dean, you don't need to send a different message to each group ("Fill out the premed registration form" to the premed students; "Fill out the engineering registration form" to engineers; and so on). One message works for everyone because everyone knows how to fill out his or her own particular version of the registration form.

Polymorphism means "taking many shapes." The dean's single instruction is polymorphic because it looks different to different kinds of students. To the premed student, it's an instruction to fill out the premed form, whereas to the English major, it's an instruction to fill out the liberal arts form.

Typically, polymorphism occurs in classes that are related by inheritance. In C++, polymorphism means that a call to a member function will cause a different function to be executed depending on the type of object that invokes the function.

This sounds a little like function overloading, but polymorphism is a different, and much more powerful, mechanism. One difference between overloading and polymorphism has to do with which function to execute when the choice is made. With function overloading, the choice is made by the compiler. With polymorphism, it's made while the program is running. Function overloading is merely a convenience for a class user, whereas polymorphism affects the entire architecture of a program.

This is all rather abstract, so let's start with some short programs that show parts of the situation, and put everything together later. In practice, virtual functions are associated with pointers to objects, so let's see how they work together.

Normal Member Functions Accessed with Pointers

The first example shows what happens when a base class and derived classes all have functions with the same name and these functions are accessed using pointers but *without* using virtual functions. Listing 9-1 shows NOTVIRT.

Listing 9-1 NOTVIRT

```
// notvirt.cpp
// normal member functions accessed using pointers to objects
#include <iostream.h>

class Base                          // base class
   {
   public:
      void show()                   // normal function
         { cout << "\nBase"; }
   };
class Derv1 : public Base           // derived class 1
   {
   public:
      void show()
         { cout << "\nDerv1"; }
   };
class Derv2 : public Base           // derived class 2
   {
   public:
      void show()
         { cout << "\nDerv2"; }
   };
void main()
   {
   Derv1 dv1;          // object of derived class 1
   Derv2 dv2;          // object of derived class 2
   Base* ptr;          // pointer to base class

   ptr = &dv1;         // put address of dv1 in pointer
   ptr->show();        // execute show()

   ptr = &dv2;         // put address of dv2 in pointer
   ptr->show();        // execute show()
   }
```

The `Derv1` and `Derv2` classes are derived from class `Base`. All three classes have a member function `show()`. In `main()`, the program creates objects of class `Derv1` and `Derv2` and a pointer to class `Base`. Then it puts the address of a derived class object in the base class pointer in the line

```
ptr = &dv1;  // derived class address in base class pointer
```

Remember that it's perfectly all right to assign an address of one type (`Derv1`) to a pointer of another (`Base`), because pointers to objects of a derived class are type compatible with pointers to objects of the base class.

Now the question is, when you execute the next statement

```
ptr->show();
```

what function is called? Is it `Base::show()` or `Derv1::show()`?

I can ask the same question after I put the address of an object of class `Derv2` in the pointer and again try to execute its `show()` function:

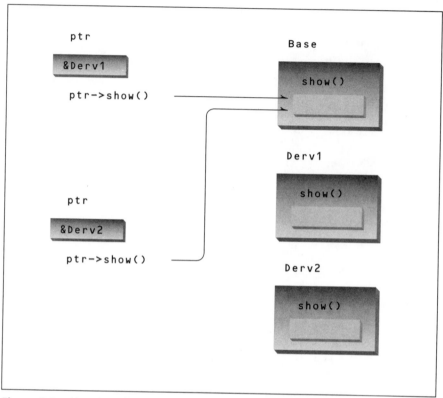

Figure 9-1   Nonvirtual pointer access {Fig 13-1 in "OOP in C++"}

```
ptr = &dv2;             // put address of dv2 in pointer
ptr->show();
```

Which of the `show()` functions is called here: `Base::show()` or `Derv2::show()`? The output from the program answers these questions:

```
Base
Base
```

The function in the base class is executed in both cases. The compiler ignores the *contents* of the pointer `ptr` and chooses the member function that matches the *type* of the pointer, as shown in Figure 9-1.

Virtual Member Functions Accessed with Pointers

Let's make a single change in the program: I'll place the keyword `virtual` in front of the declarator for the `show()` function in the base class. Listing 9-2 shows the resulting program, VIRT.

Listing 9-2 VIRT

```
// virt.cpp
// virtual functions accessed from pointer
#include <iostream.h>

class Base                          // base class
    {
    public:
        virtual void show()         // virtual function
            { cout << "\nBase"; }
    };
class Derv1 : public Base           // derived class 1
    {
    public:
        void show()
            { cout << "\nDerv1"; }
    };
class Derv2 : public Base           // derived class 2
    {
    public:
        void show()
            { cout << "\nDerv2"; }
    };
void main()
    {
    Derv1 dv1;          // object of derived class 1
    Derv2 dv2;          // object of derived class 2
    Base* ptr;          // pointer to base class

    ptr = &dv1;         // put address of dv1 in pointer
    ptr->show();        // execute show()

    ptr = &dv2;         // put address of dv2 in pointer
    ptr->show();        // execute show()
    }
```

The output of this program is

```
Derv1
Derv2
```

Now the member functions of the derived classes, not the base class, are executed. I change the contents of ptr from the address of Derv1 to that of Derv2, and the particular instance of show() that is executed also changes. So the same function call,

```
ptr->show();
```

executes different functions, depending on the contents of ptr. The compiler selects the function based on the *contents* of the pointer ptr, not on the *type* of the pointer, as in NOTVIRT. This is polymorphism at work. I've made show() polymorphic by designating it virtual. Figure 9-2 shows how this looks.

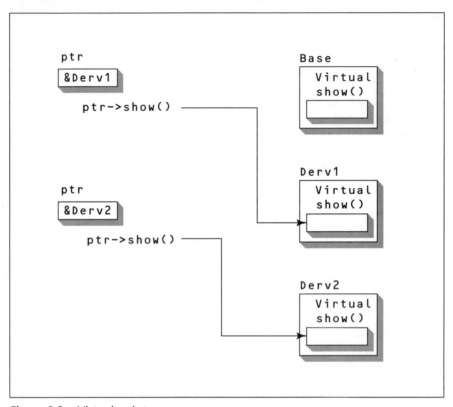

Figure 9-2   Virtual pointer access

Late Binding

The astute reader may wonder how the compiler knows what function to compile. In NOTVIRT, the compiler has no problem with the expression

```
ptr->show();
```

It always compiles a call to the `show()` function in the base class. But in VIRT, the compiler doesn't know what class the contents of `ptr` may be a pointer to. It could be the address of an object of the `Derv1` class or the `Derv2` class. Which version of `draw()` does the compiler call? In fact, at the time it's compiling the program, the compiler doesn't know what to do, so it arranges for the decision to be deferred until the program is running.

At runtime, when the function call is executed, code that the compiler placed in the program finds out the type of the object whose address is in `ptr` and calls the appropriate `show()` function: `Derv1::show()` or `Derv2::show()`, depending on the class of the object.

Selecting a function at runtime is called *late binding* or *dynamic binding*. (*Binding* means connecting the function call to the function.) Connecting to functions in the normal way, during compilation, is called *early binding* or *static binding*. Late binding requires a small amount of overhead (the call to the function might take something like 10 percent longer) but provides an enormous increase in power and flexibility, as you'll see.

How It Works

You now know the bare bones of using virtual functions, but sometimes it's nice to understand a little of what goes on behind the scenes.

Remember that, stored in memory, a normal object—that is, one with no virtual functions—contains only its own data, nothing else. When a member function is called for such an object, the compiler passes to the function the address of the object that invoked it. This address is available to the function in the **this** pointer, which the function uses (usually invisibly) to access the object's data. The address in **this** is generated by the compiler every time a member function is called; it's not stored in the object and does not take up space in memory. The **this** pointer is the only connection that's necessary between an object and its normal member functions.

With virtual functions, things are more complicated. When a derived class with virtual functions is specified, the compiler creates a table—an array—of function addresses called the *virtual table*. (It is named something like **vtbl** or **vtable**, depending on the compiler.) In the VIRT example, the **Derv1** and **Derv2** classes each have their own virtual table. There is an entry in each virtual table for every virtual function in the class. Because they are both derived from **Base**, **Derv1** and **Derv2** have the same virtual functions. The virtual table arrays for **Derv1** and **Derv2** can therefore contain entries for the same function names, arranged in the same order. However, the addresses in the table are different for the two classes. Figure 9-3 shows this arrangement. It also shows additional functions in each class, **func1()** and **func2()**, to make it clear that the virtual tables each have many entries (pointers to the appropriate member functions).

Every object of **Derv1** or **Derv2**, when it's constructed, contains an extra pointer in addition to its own data. This is true of any object of a class that has one or more virtual functions. This pointer, called something like **vptr** or **vpointer**, contains the address of the class virtual table. Thus, objects of classes with virtual functions are slightly larger than normal objects.

Including the address to a class specific **vtbl** in an object's **vptr** amounts to allowing an object to "know" what class it is. In the example, when a virtual function is called for an object of **Derv1** or **Derv2**, the compiler, instead of specifying what function will be called, creates code that will first look at the object's **vptr** and then uses this to access the appropriate member function address in the class **vtable**. Thus, for virtual functions, the object itself determines what function is called, rather than the compiler.

The VIRT example is not very realistic in that the pointers to objects used with virtual functions are not usually stored in standalone variables, but in arrays. The next example shows a more typical situation.

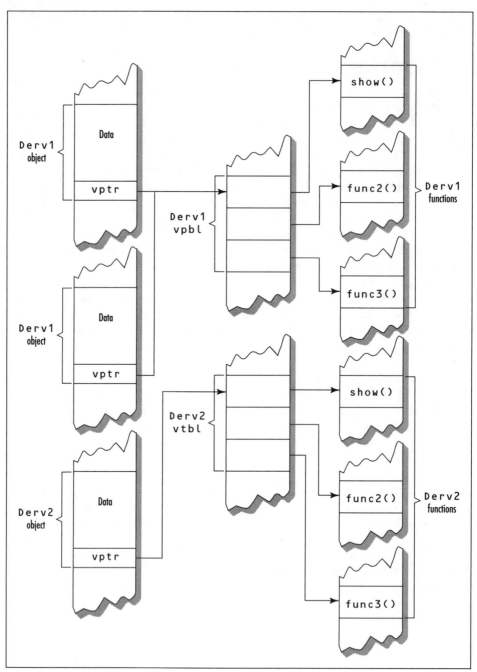

Figure 9-3   Virtual function linkage

Arrays of Pointers to Objects

Perhaps the most common way to use virtual functions is with an array of pointers to objects. Listing 9-3 shows a version of the VIRT program modified to demonstrate this arrangement. The classes are the same, but `main()` is different. The program is called ARRVIRT.

Listing 9-3 ARRVIRT

```
// arrvirt.cpp
// array of pointers to objects with virtual functions
#include <iostream.h>

class Base                          // base class
   {
   public:
      virtual void show()           // virtual function
         { cout << "\nBase"; }
   };
class Derv1 : public Base           // derived class 1
   {
   public:
      void show()
         { cout << "\nDerv1"; }
   };
class Derv2 : public Base           // derived class 2
   {
   public:
      void show()
         { cout << "\nDerv2"; }
   };
void main()
   {
   Base* arrBase[2];                // array of pointers to Base
   Derv1 dv1;                       // object of derived class 1
   Derv2 dv2;                       // object of derived class 2

   arrBase[0] = &dv1;               // put address of dv1 in array
   arrBase[1] = &dv2;               // put address of dv2 in array

   for(int j=0; j<2; j++)           // for all array elements,
      arrBase[j]->show();           //    execute show()
   }
```

I've put the addresses of the objects `dv1` and `dv2` into the array `arrBase`, which is of type `Base`. As in the VIRT program, the compiler uses the type of the pointers stored in the array, not the type of the array, to figure out which version of `show()` to call. The output is

```
Derv1
Derv2
```

Notice how easy it is for the `for` loop in `main()` to call `show()` for any number of objects. This is the heart of polymorphism: A single function call can invoke many different functions, depending on the type of object doing the calling.

Don't Try This with Objects

Be aware that the virtual function mechanism works only with pointers to objects (and, as you'll see later, with references), not with objects themselves. You can't rewrite `main()` in ARRVIRT to use an array of objects, like this:

```
void main()
   {
   Base arrObjs[2];           // array holds base class objects
   Derv1 dv1;                 // object of derived class 1
   Derv2 dv2;                 // object of derived class 2

   arrObjs[0] = dv1;          // put dv1 object in array
   arrObjs[1] = dv2;          // put dv2 object in array

   for(j=0; j<2; j++)         // for all array elements,
      arrObjs[j].show();      //    execute show()
   }
```

Although the compiler will let you put a derived class object in a base class array, the results probably won't be what you hoped for. The output from this version of `main()` is

```
Base
Base
```

Why aren't the derived class versions of `show()` executed? Well, for one thing, objects of a derived class may not be the same size as objects of the base class. They're usually bigger (although not in this example) because they include additional data that makes them a "kind of" base class object. Thus, they don't fit in the base class array. If you try to stick a derived class object in a base class array, the parts of the object that are specific to the derived class will be sliced off, leaving you with a base class object. Even if there's no size difference, the compiler regards derived class objects as base class objects. The moral is, never put derived class objects in base class variables; they'll forget what they are.

Pointers, on the other hand, are the same size no matter what class they point to, so you don't lose any information putting a derived class address in an array of base class pointers. The moral: To use polymorphism, invoke virtual functions with *pointers to objects* (or with references, which are pointers in disguise), but not with *objects*.

1. If you put the address of a derived class object into a variable whose type is a pointer to the base class, then the object, when accessed using this pointer,

   a. continues to act like a derived class object.

   b. acts like a base class object.

   c. will cause the compiler to issue an error message.

   d. continues to act like a derived class object if virtual functions are called.

   e. can determine which of several virtual functions to call.

2. Virtual functions are appropriate when
    a. you don't know, at the time you write the program, what class to use.
    b. pointers (or references) to objects are used to access the object.
    c. the function bodies are empty.
    d. objects of different types should respond to the same message in different ways.
    e. objects of the base class will never be invoked.

3. Late binding
    a. concerns connecting a function call to a function.
    b. relies on an object to know what its own member functions are.
    c. happens at compile time.
    d. happens at link time.
    e. happens at runtime.

4. If you have an array of pointers to objects called `arr_of_ptrs_to_objs`, and this array is of type `alpha*`, and there is a class `beta` derived from `alpha`, and `alpha` and `beta` have a virtual function called `mayday()`, then which of the following statements are reasonable?
    a. `alpha->mayday();`
    b. `beta->mayday();`
    c. `arr_of_ptrs_to_objs[3]->mayday();`
    d. `beta* arr_of_ptrs_to_objs[77];`
    e. `alpha arr_of_ptrs_to_objs[77];`

5. When you put a derived class object in a base class variable
    a. it continues to act like a derived class object.
    b. it starts to act like a base class object.
    c. the compiler issues an error message.
    d. only the object's virtual functions can be executed.
    e. only the object's nonvirtual functions can be executed.

Due to its theoretical nature, this session contains no exercises.

EXAMPLES OF VIRTUAL FUNCTIONS

Now that you understand the mechanics of virtual functions, let's look at some situations where it makes sense to use them. I'll introduce two programs in this session. In the first, you'll discover which kinds of people are outstanding; in the second, you'll see how to use the same function to draw different shapes. In both examples, the use of virtual functions significantly simplifies the programming.

A Personnel Example

This example models the kinds of people one finds in a school or university. The major categories are students and teachers. Noticing that these categories have some features in common, I'll arrange for the **student** and **teacher** classes to be derived from a **person** class. In addition, other people may be connected with the university who are neither students nor teachers (administrators, alumni, consultants, and so on). I'll assume I don't want to bother creating specific classes for these miscellaneous categories, so I'll lump them all into the **person** class.

For simplicity, the only data in the **person** class is a name. One can imagine the other variables that might be appropriate to include as well, such as address, telephone number, and social security number. The **student** class includes the student's grade point average (GPA), and the **teacher** class includes the number of scholarly papers the teacher has published.

All the classes contain **getData()** and **putData()** functions for basic input and output. They also contain a function called **isOutstanding()**, which makes it easy for the school administrators to create a list of outstanding students and teachers for the venerable Awards Day ceremony. Listing 9-4 shows VIRTPERS.

Listing 9-4 VIRTPERS

```cpp
// virtpers.cpp
// virtual functions with person class
#include <iostream.h>

class person                    // person class
    {
    protected:
        char name[40];
    public:
        virtual void getData()
            { cout << "   Enter name: "; cin >> name; }
        virtual void putData()
            { cout << "\nName = " << name; }
        virtual void isOutstanding()
            { }                     // note: empty function body
    };
                                    // student class
class student : public person
```

```
   {
   private:
      float gpa;                // grade point average
   public:
      void getData()            // get student data from user
         {
         person::getData();
         cout << "   Enter student's GPA: ";
         cin >> gpa;
         }
      void putData()
         {
         person::putData();
         cout << "   GPA = " << gpa;
         }
      void isOutstanding()
         {
         if (gpa > 3.5)
            cout << " (This person is outstanding)";
         }
   };
                                // teacher class
class teacher : public person
   {
   private:
      int numPubs;              // number of papers published
   public:
      void getData()            // get teacher data from user
         {
         person::getData();
         cout << "   Enter number of teacher's publications: ";
         cin >> numPubs;
         }
      void putData()
         {
         person::putData();
         cout << "   Publications = " << numPubs;
         }
      void isOutstanding()
         {
         if(numPubs > 100)
            cout << " (This person is outstanding)";
         }
   };

void main(void)
   {
   person* persPtr[100];        // list of pointers to persons
   int n = 0;                   // number of persons on list
   char choice;                 // 'p', 's', etc.

   do
      {
```

continued on next page

continued from previous page

```
        cout << "Enter person, student or teacher (p/s/t): ";
        cin >> choice;
        if(choice=='s')                 // put new student
            persPtr[n] = new student;   //    in array
        else if(choice=='t')            // put new teacher
            persPtr[n] = new teacher;   //    in array
        else                            // put new person
            persPtr[n] = new person;    //    in array

        persPtr[n++]->getData();        // get data for person
        cout << "   Enter another (y/n)? ";  // do another person?
        cin >> choice;
        } while( choice=='y' );         // cycle until not 'y'

    for(int j=0; j<n; j++)
        {                               // print names of all
        persPtr[j]->putData();          // persons, and
        persPtr[j]->isOutstanding();    // say if outstanding
        }
    }   // end main()
```

The main() Program

In main(), the program first lets the user enter any number of person, student, and teacher names. For students, the program also asks for the GPA; for teachers, it asks for the number of publications. When the user is finished, the program prints out the names and other data for all persons, noting those students and teachers who are outstanding. Here's some sample interaction:

```
Enter person, student or teacher (p/s/t): p
    Enter name: Bob
    Enter another (y/n)? y
Enter person, student or teacher (p/s/t): s
    Enter name: Timmy
    Enter student's GPA: 1.2
    Enter another (y/n)? y
Enter person, student or teacher (p/s/t): s
    Enter name: Brenda
    Enter student's GPA: 3.9
    Enter another (y/n)? y
Enter person, student or teacher (p/s/t): s
    Enter name: Sandy
    Enter student's GPA: 2.4
    Enter another (y/n)? y
Enter person, student or teacher (p/s/t): t
    Enter name: Shipley
    Enter number of teacher's publications: 714
    Enter another (y/n)? y
Enter person, student or teacher (p/s/t): t
    Enter name: Wainright
    Enter number of teacher's publications: 13
    Enter another (y/n)? n
```

```
Name = Bob
Name = Timmy
    GPA = 1.2
Name = Brenda
   GPA = 3.9 (This person is outstanding)
Name = Sandy
   GPA = 2.4
Name = Shipley
   Publications = 714 (This person is outstanding)
Name = Wainright
   Publications = 13
```

The Classes

The person class contains a single data item, a string representing the person's name. The student and teacher classes add new data items to the person base class. The student class contains a variable gpa of type float, which represents the student's GPA. The teacher class contains a variable numPubs of type int, representing the number of papers the teacher has published. Students with a GPA over 3.5 and teachers who have published more than 100 papers are considered outstanding. (I'll refrain from comment on the desirability of these criteria for judging educational excellence.)

Virtual Functions

In the person class, all three functions, getData(), putData(), and isOutstanding(), are declared virtual. This is necessary because functions with these names exist in the derived classes as well, and objects of these derived classes will be accessed using pointers. The only way for the program to know what kind of object the pointer in persPtr[j] points to, in an expression such as

```
persPtr[j]->putData();
```

is if the putData() function is virtual. If it's declared virtual, the version of putData() appropriate to the class of object pointed to by persPtr[j] will be executed.

The isOutstanding() Function

In the student class, isOutstanding() displays the message This person is outstanding if the student's GPA is greater than 3.5, and in teacher class, it displays the same message if the teacher's numPubs variable is greater than 100. However, this function has an empty function body in the person class. The assumption is that there is no criterion for outstandingness in a mere person.

Because person::isOutstanding() doesn't do anything, could I remove it? No, it's required by the statement

```
persPtr[j]->isOutstanding();
```

in main(), because persPtr can hold pointers of type person*, even though it can also hold pointers of type student* or teacher*.

If I were sure I would never instantiate any person objects, I could insert an error message into the function body for person::isOutstanding(), as I'll do in the next example. An even better solution is to use a pure virtual function, which I'll discuss in Session 4.

Virtual Functions in Other Classes

Notice that a member function in a derived class can call a virtual member function of the base class using the scope resolution operator in the same way that overloaded functions can be accessed. For example, the `getData()` function in `student` calls the `getData()` function in `person`:

```
class student : public person
   {
   ...
   void getData()
      {
      person::getData();      // call base class virtual function
      cout << "    Enter student's GPA: ";
      cin >> gpa;
      }
   ...
   };
```

Virtual functions behave the same as nonvirtual functions, except when they are busy implementing polymorphism.

A Graphics Example

Let's explore another example of virtual functions, this one a graphics example derived from the SHAPES program from Chapter 7, Session 5. Classes representing a number of specific shapes (`cap`, `bowl`, and `square`) are derived from a general `shape` class.

One easy way to display a complex picture made out of such shape objects is to put pointers to the different shapes in an array and then draw all the shapes using a simple `for` loop:

```
for(int j=0; j<N; j++)
   sharray[j]->draw();
```

The VIRTSHAP (Listing 9-5) program makes this possible by declaring the `draw()` function to be virtual in the `shape` class.

Listing 9-5 VIRTSHAP

```
// virtshap.cpp
// draws shapes made from Xs on character-based display
// uses virtual draw() function
#include <iostream.h>
//////////////////////////////////////////////////////////////
class shape
   {
   private:
      int xCo, yCo;             // coordinates of shape
      int size;                 // size of shape
   protected:                   // read-only functions
      int getx() const { return xCo; }
      int gety() const { return yCo; }
      int getz() const { return size; }
      void down() const;        // declaration
   public:
```

```
                              // 3-arg constructor
      shape(int x, int y, int s) : xCo(x), yCo(y), size(s)
         {  }
      virtual void draw() const
         { cout << "Error: base virtual" << endl; }
   };

void shape::down() const       // move cursor down to top of shape
   {
   for(int y=0; y<yCo; y++)
      cout << endl;
   }
//////////////////////////////////////////////////////////////////
class square : public shape    // square shape
   {
   public:                     // 3-arg constructor
      square(int x, int y, int s) : shape(x, y, s)
         {  }
      void draw() const;       // declaration
   };

void square::draw() const      // draw a square
   {
   shape::down();              // position y at top of shape
   for(int y=0; y<getz(); y++) // move y down across shape
      {
      int x;
      for(x=1; x<getx(); x++)  // space over to shape
         cout << ' ';
      for(x=0; x<getz(); x++)  // draw line of Xs
         cout << 'X';
      cout << endl;
      }
   }
//////////////////////////////////////////////////////////////////
class cap : public shape       // cap (pyramid) shape
   {
   public:                     // 3-arg constructor
      cap(int x, int y, int s) : shape(x, y, s)
         {  }
      void draw() const;       // declaration
   };

void cap::draw() const         // draw a cap
   {
   shape::down();
   for(int y=0; y<getz(); y++)
      {
      int x;
      for(x=0; x < getx()-y+1; x++)
         cout << ' ';
      for(x=0; x<2*y+1; x++)
```

continued on next page

continued from previous page

```
          cout << 'X';
       cout << endl;
       }
   }
//////////////////////////////////////////////////////////////////
class bowl : public shape        // bowl (inverted pyramid) shape
   {
   public:                       // 3-arg constructor
      bowl(int x, int y, int s) : shape(x, y, s)
         {  }
      void draw() const;         // declaration
   };

void bowl::draw() const          // draw a bowl
   {
   shape::down();
   for(int y=0; y<getz(); y++)
      {
      int x;
      for(x=0; x < getx()-(getz()-y)+2; x++)
         cout << ' ';
      for(x=0; x < 2*(getz()-y)-1; x++)
         cout << 'X';
      cout << endl;
      }
   }
//////////////////////////////////////////////////////////////////
void main()
   {
   const int N = 3;              // number of shapes
   shape* sharray[N];            // array of pointers to shapes

   bowl bw(10, 0, 3);           // make a bowl
   square sq(20, 1, 5);         // make a square
   cap cp(30, 1, 7);            // make a cap

   sharray[0] = &bw;            // put their addresses in array
   sharray[1] = &sq;
   sharray[2] = &cp;

   cout << endl << endl;        // start two lines down

   for(int j=0; j<N; j++)       // display all three shapes
      sharray[j]->draw();
   }
```

The class specifiers in VIRTSHAP are similar to those in SHAPES, except that the **draw()** function in the **shape** class has been made into a virtual function.

In **main()**, the program sets up an array, **ptrarr**, of pointers to shapes. Next, it creates three objects, one each of the **bowl**, **square**, and **cap** classes, and places their addresses in the array. Now it's easy to draw all three shapes using the **for** loop. Figure 9-4 shows the output from VIRTSHAP (it's the same as that from SHAPES):

```
     XXXXX
      XXX
       X



              XXXXX
              XXXXX
              XXXXX
              XXXXX
              XXXXX



                       X
                      XXX
                     XXXXX
                    XXXXXXX
                   XXXXXXXXX
                  XXXXXXXXXXX
                 XXXXXXXXXXXXX
```

Figure 9-4
Output of the VIRTSHAP program

This is a powerful approach to combining graphics elements, especially when a large number of objects need to be grouped together and drawn as a unit.

No shape *Objects, Please*

In the VIRTSHAP program, the user should never try to create a **shape** object. The **shape** class serves only as a base class for the **square**, **cap**, and **bowl** classes. In case anybody ever does try to make a **shape** and draw it, I put an error message in the body of the **shape::draw()** function.

However, this is an inelegant way to find errors. It's always better to arrange things so the compiler will find the errors, rather than waiting for them to appear at runtime. Here I want the compiler to tell me if the class user has tried to instantiate a base class (**shape**) object. I'll show you how to do this using pure virtual functions in Session 4.

Initializing the Array

Incidentally, rather than using separate statements to create objects and place their addresses in the array, I could have simply initialized the array using object constructors:

```
shape* sharray[N] = { &bowl(10, 0, 3),    // initialize array
                      &square(20, 1, 5),
                      &cap(30, 1, 7) };
```

Virtual Functions and Constructors

The constructors in the classes in VIRTSHAP are not virtual. Are constructors ever virtual? No, they can't be, because an object's constructor sets up its virtual mechanism (the **vptr**) in the first place. (You don't see the code for this, of course, just as you don't see the code that allocates memory for an object.) Virtual functions can't even exist until the constructor has finished its job, so constructors can't be virtual.

Also, when you're creating an object, you usually already know what kind of object you're creating and can specify this to the compiler. Thus, there's not as much need for virtual constructors as there is for virtual functions that access pointers to already created objects.

Destructors, on the other hand, can and often should be virtual. I'll explore virtual destructors in Session 4.

1. The `getData()` function in the `person` class in VIRTPERS needs to be virtual because
   a. it is called from within member functions of derived classes.
   b. it will be invoked by base class objects.
   c. it will be invoked by pointers to derived class objects.
   d. it appears in both base and derived classes.
   e. it is used only in derived classes, not in the base class.

2. Which of the following are true statements about the VIRTPERS program?
   a. An array of pointers to `person` objects is more useful than an array of `person` objects.
   b. The `isOutstanding()` function would not need to be virtual if only `person` objects, not `student` or `teacher` objects, were outstanding.
   c. The `isOutstanding()` function cannot be accessed from `main()` without using pointers.
   d. Because `person` objects are never outstanding, you can remove the `isOutstanding()` function from the `person` class without altering the operation of the program.
   e. Because `person` objects are never outstanding, you can remove the `isOutstanding()` function from the `person` class without altering the operation of the program, provided that you make the function virtual in the `student` and `teacher` classes.

3. If the `main()` part of the VIRTPERS example did nothing but put `person`, `student`, and `teacher` objects in an array of type `person` and access them using statements such as

   `persArr[2].getData();`

   then
   a. everything would work just as it does in VIRTPERS.
   b. you could not access a student's GPA or a teacher's number of publications.
   c. there would be error messages from the compiler.
   d. there would be no need for virtual functions.
   e. none of the above.

4. The error message in the body of the `draw()` function in the `shape` class in VIRTSHAP
   a. will never be displayed if `shape` objects are always accessed using pointers.
   b. is not the most effective solution to keeping the user from using base class objects.
   c. is not necessary because it's impossible to create a `shape` object.

d. is not necessary because it's impossible to create a pointer to a **shape** object.

e. will be displayed at compile time, if at all.

5. The constructor in the **shapes** class in VIRTSHAP is not virtual because

a. constructors can never be virtual.

b. there are no constructors in the derived classes.

c. the constructors in the derived classes call the constructor in the base class.

d. you don't need to specify what kind of object you're creating when you create it.

e. constructors have no return type.

EXERCISE 1

Add an **erase()** member function to all the appropriate classes in the VIRTSHAP program. It should erase its shape by drawing over the shape with spaces (the " " character) wherever there were X characters before.

EXERCISE 2

Add a **move()** member function to all the appropriate classes in the VIRTSHAP program. It should be able to move a shape by erasing it with **erase()** (see Exercise 1), incrementing or decrementing one of the shape's coordinates and then redrawing it with **draw()**. Use this function to animate a shape; that is, to cause it to appear to move across the screen.

SESSION 3

DECOUPLING WITH POLYMORPHISM

In the last session you saw two examples in which polymorphism was exploited in an array of pointers to objects. However, this is not the only situation where polymorphism and virtual functions are important. Polymorphism can also be used to help isolate, or *decouple*, one part of a program from another.

As I noted earlier, OOP programs are divided into two parts, which are often written by different programmers at different times. First, classes are written by one set of programmers (the class creators); then, at some later time, code that uses these classes is written by another set of programmers (the class users). One benefit of reusability is realized when the same set of classes can be used over and over by different class users.

In most of the examples in this book, the class-user code is contained in a single function, **main()**. This makes the examples easier to understand, but it's not completely realistic. The user code in serious programs will normally be divided into many functions, which will be invoked from **main()** or from each other.

Where does polymorphism appear in this situation? The programming can often be simplified if the user code can work with a generic class, rather than trying to be aware of many different classes. This is because objects (or references or pointers to objects) will probably be passed and returned from one function to another, and if all these arguments and return values can be of a single class, coding is simplified. Another way of saying this is that it can be helpful to *decouple* the user code from specific classes.

The first example will show how polymorphism can be used when references are used as function arguments. Another example shows how polymorphism can be used with pointers as function arguments. Finally, I'll examine a larger program that demonstrates a more realistic programming situation.

Passing References

As a simple example of using polymorphism to decouple user code from classes, imagine a base class with many derived classes. Suppose that `main()` calls a global (nonmember) function, `func()`, that will do something to objects of all the derived classes. If `func()` needed to worry about handling many different kinds of objects in different ways, its code would become very complicated. However, using references and virtual functions, I can employ the same version of `func()` for many different classes.

When an object is passed to a function by reference, the syntax makes it appear that the object itself is being passed, but actually a pointer to the object is passed instead. As you've seen, pointers are always the same size no matter what they point to, so there's no loss of information if a reference to a derived class object is passed to a function that is expecting a reference to a base class object.

In the example, there is a base class `Base` and two derived classes, `Derv1` and `Derv2`. Statements in `main()` call `func()`, using reference arguments to pass `Derv1` and `Derv2` objects. Notice that the same `func()` handles both `Derv1` and `Derv2` objects. Listing 9-6 shows VIRTREF.

Listing 9-6 VIRTREF

```
// virtref.cpp
// tests virtual functions and passing objects by reference
#include <iostream.h>

class Base
    {
    public:
        virtual void speak()
            { cout << "\nBase speaks"; }
    };

class Derv1 : public Base
    {
    public:
        void speak()
            { cout << "\nDerv1 speaks"; }
    };
```

```
class Derv2 : public Base
   {
   public:
      void speak()
         { cout << "\nDerv2 speaks"; }
   };

void main()
   {
   void func(Base&);    // prototype
   Derv1 d1;            // create derived class object d1
   Derv2 d2;            // create derived class object d2

   func(d1);            // pass d1 by reference to func()
   func(d2);            // pass d2 by reference to func()
   }

void func(Base& obj)    // (note reference argument)
   {
   obj.speak();
   }
```

The `func()` function tells the object passed to it to call its `speak()` member function, which displays what class of object it is. Here's the output from VIRTREF:

```
Derv1 speaks
Derv2 speaks
```

Because the argument to `func()` is passed by reference, and because the `speak()` member function is virtual, `func()` doesn't need to know what kind of object it's sending the `speak()` message to. It knows the object is derived from `Base`, but that's all it needs to know. The object itself takes care of figuring out which version of `speak()` to call, as demonstrated by the output.

By contrast, suppose polymorphism could not be used and `func()` had to be aware of what kind of object it was working with. Either it would need something like a big `switch` statement to handle the different classes (and a way to figure out what class an object was) or `main()` would need to select one of many different versions of `func()`, depending on the class. Each of these solutions is unnecessarily complicated. By leaving an object's response to a message up to the object itself, you can make the user code independent of the actual class being used, with a resulting simplification in the code.

One advantage of this approach is that the same user code will work with classes that haven't even been invented. For example, in VIRTREF, if a `Derv3` class is added to the class hierarchy, `func()` will be happy to work with it, just as it does with `Derv1` and `Derv2`.

Of course, this decoupling effect works only if you use reference (or pointer) arguments. If you pass a derived class object itself to a function, it will be sliced down to the size of a base class object, just as it would be if you assigned it to a base class variable. Also, you must use virtual functions. If `speak()` were not virtual, the output of VIRTREF would be

```
Base speaks
Base speaks
```

In C++, polymorphism depends on virtual functions.

Although there's not much gain by using polymorphism in this short example, in a larger program, with many derived classes and many functions in the class-user code, it would be much more efficient for these functions to be written in terms of a single base class rather than a multiplicity of derived classes.

Passing Pointers

The same decoupling effect is achieved whether you pass references to objects or pointers to objects. I'll rewrite the VIRTREF program to use pointers instead of references. Listing 9-7 shows VIRTPTR.

Listing 9-7 VIRTPTR

```
// virtptr.cpp
// tests virtual functions and passing objects by pointer
#include <iostream.h>

class Base
    {
    public:
        virtual void speak()
            { cout << "\nBase speaks"; }
    };

class Derv1 : public Base
    {
    public:
        void speak()
            { cout << "\nDerv1 speaks"; }
    };

class Derv2 : public Base
    {
    public:
        void speak()
            { cout << "\nDerv2 speaks"; }
    };

void main()
    {
    void func(Base*);    // prototype (note reference argument)
    Derv1 d1;            // create derived class object d1
    Derv2 d2;            // create derived class object d2

    func(&d1);           // pass address of d1 to func()
    func(&d2);           // pass address of d2 to func()
    }

void func(Base* ptr)
    {
    ptr->speak();
    }
```

The classes are identical to those in VIRTREF, but `main()` passes addresses of objects, rather than references to them, to `func()` and uses the `->` operator to access `speak()`. Otherwise, the program works the same, and again the output is

```
Derv1
Derv2
```

Typically, references are appropriate when objects are created through definitions so their names are known, whereas pointers are used when objects are created with `new` and only pointers to them are available. References are safer than pointers. The value of a pointer can be changed by the programmer, possibly inadvertently, whereas a reference, once initialized, can't be changed.

A p e r s o n **Class Example**

Let's look at a larger example that gives more of the flavor of how polymorphism can make your code independent of specific classes. I'll rewrite the class-user part of the VIRTPERS example from Session 2. The goal is to give the end user more control over the program. The program will display a list of options, and the user can select whether to add a person to the database, to display all the persons on the database, or to exit the program. The user can add as many persons as seems desirable and display them all at any time.

To implement this increased capability, I'll divide the class-user part of the program into several functions. A `switch` statement in `main()` calls the appropriate function, depending on which key the user presses. There are two of these functions: `getPerson()` gets data from the user about a person to be added to the database and `displayPerson()` displays a person's data. The classes are the same as in VIRTPERS. Listing 9-8 shows PERSFUNC.

Listing 9-8 PERSFUNC

```
// persfunc.cpp
// passing pointers to objects that use virtual functions
#include <iostream.h>
#include <process.h>            // for exit()
/////////////////////////////////////////////////////////////
class person                    // person class
   {
   protected:
      char name[40];
   public:
      virtual void getData()
         { cout << "   Enter name: "; cin >> name; }
      virtual void putData()
         { cout << "\nName = " << name; }
      virtual void isOutstanding()
         { }                     // note: empty function body
   };
/////////////////////////////////////////////////////////////
class student : public person   // student class
   {
   private:
      float gpa;                 // grade point average
```

continued on next page

continued from previous page

```
   public:
       void getData()              // get student data from user
           {
           person::getData();
           cout << "    Enter student's GPA: ";
           cin >> gpa;
           }
       void putData()
           {
           person::putData();
           cout << "    GPA = " << gpa;
           }
       void isOutstanding()
           {
           if (gpa > 3.5)
               cout << " (This person is outstanding)";
           }
   };
///////////////////////////////////////////////////////////////
class teacher : public person   // teacher class
   {
   private:
       int numPubs;              // number of papers published
   public:
       void getData()            // get teacher data from user
           {
           person::getData();
           cout << "    Enter number of teacher's publications: ";
           cin >> numPubs;
           }
       void putData()
           {
           person::putData();
           cout << "    Publications = " << numPubs;
           }
       void isOutstanding()
           {
           if(numPubs > 100)
               cout << " (This person is outstanding)";
           }
   };
///////////////////////////////////////////////////////////////
void main(void)
   {
   person* persPtr[100];      // list of pointers to persons
   int n = 0;                 // number of persons on list
   char choice;
   int j;

   person* getPerson();       // prototypes
   void displayPerson(person*);

   while(1)                   // cycle until exit
```

```
      {
      cout << endl
            << "'a' to add new person" << endl
            << "'d' to display all persons" << endl
            << "'x' to exit program" << endl
            << "Enter selection: ";
      cin >> choice;
      switch(choice)
         {
         case 'a':
            persPtr[n++] = getPerson();
            break;
         case 'd':
            for(j=0; j<n; j++)
               displayPerson( persPtr[j] );
            break;
         case 'x':
            for(j=0; j<n; j++)
               delete persPtr[j];    // delete all person objects
            exit(0);
            break;
         default:
            cout << "\nNo such selection";
         }  // end switch
      }  // end while
   }  // end main()
/////////////////////////////////////////////////////////////
person* getPerson()              // function returns a person
   {
   person* tp;                   // pointer to person
   char choice;

   cout << "Enter person, student or teacher (p/s/t): ";
   cin >> choice;
   if(choice=='s')               // put new student
      tp = new student;         //    in array
   else if(choice=='t')          // put new teacher
      tp = new teacher;         //    in array
   else                          // put new person
      tp = new person;          //    in array

   tp->getData();                // get data for person
   return tp;                    // return pointer to person
   }  // end getPerson()'
/////////////////////////////////////////////////////////////
void displayPerson(person* pp) // function displays a person
   {
   pp->putData();                // display data, and
   pp->isOutstanding();          // say if outstanding
   }  // end displayPerson()
```

Here's some sample interaction with the program in which the user adds a person, two students, and a teacher to the database and then displays all four.

```
'a' to add new person,
'd' to display all persons
'x' to exit program
Enter selection: a
Enter person, student or teacher (p/s/t): p
   Enter name: Harriet

'a' to add new person,
'd' to display all persons
'x' to exit program
Enter selection: a
Enter person, student or teacher (p/s/t): s
   Enter name: Steve
   Enter student's GPA: 2.5

'a' to add new person,
'd' to display all persons
'x' to exit program
Enter selection: a
Enter person, student or teacher (p/s/t): s
   Enter name: Francine
   Enter student's GPA: 3.9

'a' to add new person,
'd' to display all persons
'x' to exit program
Enter selection: a
Enter person, student or teacher (p/s/t): t
   Enter name: Marshall
   Enter number of teacher's publications: 50

'a' to add new person,
'd' to display all persons
'x' to exit program
Enter selection: d

Name = Harriet
Name = Steve    GPA = 2.5
Name = Francine    GPA = 3.9 (This person is outstanding)
Name = Marshall    Publications = 50
```

You can continue to add persons and display the contents of the database as long as you like (at least until you exceed the size of the persPtr array). When you select x, the program terminates.

Note that there is no mention at all in main() and displayPerson() of any class other than person. The displayPerson() function takes a pointer to person as an argument, and the getPerson() function returns a pointer to a person. The only place student and teacher objects are explicitly mentioned in the user code is in getPerson(), where an object of the type requested by the user is created with new.

This isolation of the user code from specific classes makes these functions surprisingly immune to any changes in the class hierarchy. Even if the class creators issued a new revision of the classes, adding new derived classes to the program, say

```
class administrator : public person
    { };
```
and
```
class football_coach : public person
    { };
```

you would not need to make any changes at all to `main()` or `displayPerson()`, and you would need to add only a few lines to `getPerson()`.

1. In C++, polymorphism
   a. requires virtual functions.
   b. allows increased separation of classes and class-user code.
   c. requires inheritance.
   d. allows increased separation of code in one class and code in another class.
   e. requires pointers or references to objects.

2. To use polymorphism, when an object is passed to a function by reference,
   a. the object must be a base class object.
   b. the object must be a derived class object.
   c. the function's argument type must be a reference to the base class.
   d. the function's argument type must be a reference to the object's class.
   e. statements within the function will affect an object created within the function.

3. To use polymorphism to decouple specific classes from the class-user code,
   a. the classes to be decoupled must be base classes.
   b. the classes to be decoupled must be derived classes.
   c. requires a class hierarchy with virtual functions in the base class.
   d. can result in significantly simpler code for the class user.
   e. doesn't make sense.

4. If you derive a class called `gradStudent` from the `student` class in PERSFUNC, then
   a. `main()`, `getPerson()`, and `displayPerson()` will require extensive rewriting.
   b. the compiler will issue an error message because virtual functions can't be used with more than one level of inheritance.
   c. you'll need to add some lines to the `switch` statement in `main()`.
   d. you'll need to add some lines to the `getPerson()` function.
   e. no change is necessary to the user code.

5. You can't pass a pointer to a derived class object to a function whose argument type is a pointer to a base class object because
   a. the parts of the object specific to the derived class will be sliced off.
   b. the function will treat the object as a base class object.
   c. polymorphic functions must operate on base class pointers.
   d. the data in the object that's specific to the derived class will be inaccessible.
   e. none of the above.

EXERCISE 1

Add an **administrator** class to the PERSFUNC program. It should be derived from **person**. What distinguishes an **administrator** object from other **person** objects is a member variable called **salary**, which is a floating-point number with values from $75,000 on up. Administrators with a **salary** value greater than $200,000 are considered to be outstanding. Make the necessary changes to the user code so that **administrator** objects can be added to the database.

EXERCISE 2

Add an option to the PERSFUNC program that allows the user to search the database for a specific person. This option can be accessed with the letter **s**, for search. The user will be prompted to enter the name of the person to be found. An appropriate function, called **findPerson()**, will be called from **main()** with this name as an argument and will carry out the search, displaying any matching names. To the extent possible, use polymorphism for this function.

SESSION 4

ABSTRACT CLASSES AND VIRTUAL DESTRUCTORS

I'll cover two topics in this session, both related to virtual functions. The first is abstract classes, which are classes from which no objects will be instantiated, but serve as the base for derived classes. Abstract classes are enforced in C++ using *pure virtual functions*. The second topic is virtual destructors, which are often a good idea if you don't want pieces of old objects left lying around in memory.

Abstract Classes

In the VIRTPERS program in Session 2, I instantiated base class **person** objects as well as derived class **student** and **teacher** objects. In the VIRTSHAP program, on the other hand, I don't instantiate any base class **shape** objects, but only derived class **cap**, **bowl**, and **square** objects. In VIRTPERS, I assume that a generic **person** object will be useful in the program, whereas in VIRTSHAP, I assume that the **shape** class exists only as a starting point for deriving other classes and that it doesn't make sense to instantiate a generic **shape** object (which would not, after all, even *have* a specific shape).

I can call the **shape** class in VIRTSHAP an *abstract class*, which means that no actual objects will be derived from it. Abstract classes arise in many situations. A factory can make a sportscar or a truck or an ambulance, but it can't make a generic vehicle. The factory must know the details about what *kind* of vehicle to make before it can actually make one. Similarly, you'll see sparrows, wrens, and robins flying around, but you won't see any generic birds.

Some situations require an abstract base class, whereas others don't. More often than not, using abstract base classes is a good idea. There's a certain clarity about treating the base class as something special, something that doesn't need to worry about having its own objects. In the VIRTPERS program, for example, it might be better to make **person** an abstract class and derive a **miscellaneous** class from it for all the **person** objects that aren't teachers or students.

Actually, the **shape** class in VIRTSHAP is an abstract class only in the eyes of humans. The compiler is ignorant of our decision to make it an abstract class, and would not complain if we said

```
shape s3(5, 6, 7);    // legal but doesn't make sense
```

I have arranged for the **draw()** function in **shape** to display an error message:

```
class Base                       // base class
   {
   public:
       virtual void show()        // virtual function
           { cout << "\nError: base version of show()"; }
   };
```

This keeps me from trying to draw a **shape**, but it's not a complete solution. I can still create **shape** objects, even if I can't draw them; and, if I do try to draw a shape, I won't discover the error until the message is displayed at runtime.

Pure Virtual Functions

It would be nice if, having decided to create an abstract base class, I could instruct the compiler to actively *prevent* any class user from ever making an object of that class. This would give me more freedom in designing the base class because I wouldn't need to plan for actual objects of the class, but only for data and functions that would be used by derived classes. As you may have guessed, there is a way to tell the compiler that a class is abstract: You define at least one *pure virtual function* in the class.

A pure virtual function is a virtual function with no body (another OOP sentence that sounds as if it describes an esoteric religious concept). The body of the virtual function in the base class is removed, and the notation **=0** is added to the function declaration.

A Short Example

The first example of a pure virtual function is adapted from the VIRT program in Session 1. Listing 9-9 shows VIRTPURE.

Listing 9-9 VIRTPURE

```
// virtpure.cpp
// pure virtual function
#include <iostream.h>

class Base                       // base class
   {
   public:
       virtual void show() = 0;   // pure virtual function
   };

class Derv1 : public Base        // derived class 1
   {
   public:
       void show()
```

continued on next page

continued from previous page

```
              { cout << "\nDerv1"; }
   };

class Derv2 : public Base              // derived class 2
   {
   public:
      void show()
         { cout << "\nDerv2"; }
   };

void main()
   {
   Derv1 dv1;            // object of derived class 1
   Derv2 dv2;            // object of derived class 2

// Base ba;             // Error: cannot create instance of
                        // abstract base class
   }
```

Now the virtual function is declared as

```
virtual void show() = 0;  // pure virtual function
```

The equal sign here has nothing to do with assignment; the value 0 is not assigned to anything. The =0 syntax is simply how you tell the compiler that a function will be pure—that is, will have no body.

You might wonder, if you can remove the body of the virtual **show()** function in the base class, why you can't remove the function altogether. That would be even cleaner, but it doesn't work. Without a virtual function **show()** in the base class, statements such as

```
Base list[3];
list[0] = new Derv1;
list[0]->show();     // can't do this
```

would not be valid because the base class version of **show()** would always be executed.

The shape *Example*

If I rewrite the **shape** class from VIRTSHAP to use a pure virtual function for **show()**, I can prohibit the instantiation of any base class objects. Listing 9-10 shows PURESHAP.

Listing 9-10 PURESHAP

```
// pureshap.cpp
// draws shapes made from Xs on character-based display
// uses pure virtual draw() function in base class
#include <iostream.h>
/////////////////////////////////////////////////////////////
class shape
   {
   private:
      int xCo, yCo;          // coordinates of shape
      int size;              // size of shape
   protected:                // read-only functions
```

```
      int getx() const { return xCo; }
      int gety() const { return yCo; }
      int getz() const { return size; }
      void down() const;        // declaration
   public:
                                 // 3-arg constructor
      shape(int x, int y, int s) : xCo(x), yCo(y), size(s)
         { }
      virtual void draw() const = 0;  // pure virtual function
   };

void shape::down() const        // move cursor down to top of shape
   {
   for(int y=0; y<yCo; y++)
      cout << endl;
   }
//////////////////////////////////////////////////////////////
class square : public shape     // square shape
   {
   public:                      // 3-arg constructor
      square(int x, int y, int s) : shape(x, y, s)
         { }
      void draw() const;        // declaration
   };

void square::draw() const       // draw a square
   {
   shape::down();               // position y at top of shape
   for(int y=0; y<getz(); y++)  // move y down across shape
      {
      int x;
      for(x=1; x<getx(); x++)   // space over to shape
         cout << ' ';
      for(x=0; x<getz(); x++)   // draw line of Xs
         cout << 'X';
      cout << endl;
      }
   }
//////////////////////////////////////////////////////////////
class cap : public shape        // cap (pyramid) shape
   {
   public:                      // 3-arg constructor
      cap(int x, int y, int s) : shape(x, y, s)
         { }
      void draw() const;        // declaration
   };

void cap::draw() const          // draw a cap
   {
   shape::down();
   for(int y=0; y<getz(); y++)
      {
      int x;
```

continued on next page

continued from previous page

```
      for(x=0; x < getx()-y+1; x++)
         cout << ' ';
      for(x=0; x<2*y+1; x++)
         cout << 'X';
      cout << endl;
      }
   }
////////////////////////////////////////////////////////////////
class bowl : public shape       // bowl (inverted pyramid) shape
   {
   public:                      // 3-arg constructor
      bowl(int x, int y, int s) : shape(x, y, s)
         { }
      void draw() const;        // declaration
   };

void bowl::draw() const         // draw a bowl
   {
   shape::down();
   for(int y=0; y<getz(); y++)
      {
      int x;
      for(x=0; x < getx()-(getz()-y)+2; x++)
         cout << ' ';
      for(x=0; x < 2*(getz()-y)-1; x++)
         cout << 'X';
      cout << endl;
      }
   }
////////////////////////////////////////////////////////////////
void main()
   {
// shape x(1, 2, 3);   // error: can't instantiate abstract object

   const int N = 3;    // number of shapes
                       // array of pointers to shapes
   shape* sharray[N] = { &bowl(10, 0, 3),
                         &square(20, 1, 5),
                         &cap(30, 1, 7) };

   cout << endl << endl;       // start two lines down
   for(int j=0; j<N; j++)      // display all three shapes
      sharray[j]->draw();
   }
```

The Compiler on Watch

You can't create an object of a class that includes a pure virtual function and you can't write a function call that passes or returns an object of such a class by value. Thus, in `main()` in the PURESHAP program I couldn't declare functions such as

```
void func(shape);  // error
```

or

```
shape func();        // error
```

The compiler knows that passing and returning by value will create an object and it won't let this happen with an abstract class. Passing and returning objects of an abstract class by reference or pointer is OK because the pointers will actually point to derived class objects.

Abstract Classes and Pure Virtual Functions

It might seem arbitrary to use pure virtual functions as the signal to the compiler that a class will be abstract. However, pure virtual functions and abstract classes are two sides of a coin. If you will never instantiate any objects from the base class, then it does no harm to have functions in that class that can't be executed. Also, an abstract class will, by definition, have other classes derived from it. To make use of polymorphism, these derived classes will require virtual functions in the base class. Usually at least one such function doesn't do anything in the base class. We call such functions pure virtual functions and let the compiler know about them with the notation =0.

Pure Virtual Functions with Bodies

Sometimes you might want to make a base class into an abstract class, but this class needs member functions that don't need bodies. All the base class functions may be accessed by functions in derived classes, for example. Fortunately, you can make a function with a body into a pure virtual function just as you can a function without a body. Here's an example from the EMPINH program in Chapter 7, Session 2. To make the `employee` class into an abstract class (which is how it's used in this example), add the `=0` notation to the `getdata()` function in the `employee` class, but leave the function body intact:

```
virtual void getdata() = 0
    {
    employee::getdata();
    cout << "   Enter title: "; cin >> title;
    cout << "   Enter golf club dues: "; cin >> dues;
    }
```

Virtual Destructors

If you use any virtual functions in a class, pure or otherwise, you will probably want to make the destructor for that class virtual. Why? To understand the problem, examine Listing 9-11 which features a base class and a derived class, both with nonvirtual destructors. It's called NOVIDEST.

Listing 9-11 NOVIDEST
```
// novidest.cpp
// non-virtual function used as base class destructor
#include <iostream.h>

class Base
    {
    public:
        ~Base()
            { cout << "\nBase destructor"; }
    };
```

continued on next page

continued from previous page

```
class Derv : public Base
    {
    public:
        ~Derv()
            { cout << "\Derv destructor"; }
    };

void main()
    {
    Base* pb = new Derv;
    delete pb;      // output is "Base Destructor"
    cout << "\nProgram terminates";
    }
```

Is the Derived Class Destructor Executed?

Recall that a derived class object typically contains data from both the base class and the derived class (although that's not true in NOVIDEST, which doesn't have any data). To ensure that such data is properly disposed of, it may be essential that destructors for both base and derived classes are called. But the output of NOVIDEST is

```
Base Destructor
Program terminates
```

This is the same problem you saw before with ordinary (nondestructor) functions. If a function isn't virtual, only the base class version of the function will be called when it's invoked using a base class pointer, even if the contents of the pointer is the address of a derived class object. Thus in NOVIDEST, the `Derv` class destructor is never called. This could be a problem if this destructor did something important.

Not Unless It's Virtual

To fix this problem, I can make the base class destructor virtual, as shown in VIRTDEST (Listing 9-12).

Listing 9-12 VIRTDEST

```
// virtdest.cpp
// tests virtual destructors
#include <iostream.h>

class Base
    {
    public:
        virtual ~Base() = 0
            { cout << "\nBase destructor"; }
    };

class Derv : public Base
    {
    public:
        ~Derv()
            { cout << "\Derv destructor"; }
    };
```

```
void main()
   {
   Base* pb = new Derv;
   delete pb;     // output is "Derv Destructor, Base Destructor"
   cout << "\nProgram terminates";
   }
```

The output from VIRTDEST is

```
Derv Destructor
Base Destructor
Program terminates
```

Now both destructors are called. Of course in this simple example, it doesn't matter if the derived class constructor is called because there's nothing for it to do. Let's look at an example where there's more point to calling the derived class destructor.

A More Realistic Example

Derived class objects may use system resources that need to be released when the object is destroyed. Perhaps the derived class objects use **new** to allocate memory. It is essential to have a matching **delete** in the derived class destructor and that this destructor be called when the derived class object is destroyed. Otherwise, the memory allocated by the derived class object would become an orphan, inaccessible but still allocated, wasting system resources and potentially leading to catastrophic memory problems.

The next example, an extension of the PERSFUNC program, shows how this might look. It features a **person** class and a **gradStudent** class derived from it. I'll assume in this program that I want to use **new** to obtain memory for a grad student's name and thesis topic, rather than storing these strings in arrays.

The data item in **person** is a pointer to the name, and in **gradStudent** it's a pointer to the thesis topic. I'll use constructors to obtain memory for the name and topic, and destructors to delete this memory. Listing 9-13 shows DESTPERS.

Listing 9-13 DESTPERS
```
// destpers.cpp
// virtual destructors and the person class
#include <iostream.h>
#include <string.h>                    // for strlen(), strcpy()
/////////////////////////////////////////////////////////////////
class person                           // person class
   {
   protected:
      char* nameptr;
   public:
      person(char* np)                 // 1-arg constructor
         {
         int length = strlen(np);      // find length of name
         nameptr = new char[length+1]; // allocate memory
         strcpy(nameptr, np);          // put name in memory
         }
      virtual ~person() = 0            // destructor
         {
         cout << "\nperson Destructor";
```

continued on next page

continued from previous page

```
            if(nameptr != NULL)          // if it has it been used,
                delete[] nameptr;        // delete name
            }
        virtual void putData()
            { cout << "\nName = " << nameptr; }
    };   // end person class
//////////////////////////////////////////////////////////////////
class gradStudent : public person  // gradStudent class
    {
    private:
        char* topicptr;                  // ptr to thesis topic
    public:
        gradStudent(char* n, char* t) : // 2-arg constructor
                                   person(n), topicptr(NULL)
            {
            int length = strlen(t);      // find length of topic
            topicptr = new char[length+1]; // allocate memory
            strcpy(topicptr, t);         // put topic in memory
            }
        ~gradStudent()                   // destructor
            {
            cout << "\ngradStudent destructor";
            if(topicptr != NULL)         // if it has it been used,
                delete[] topicptr;       // delete thesis topic
            }
        virtual void putData()
            {
            person::putData();
            cout << "\n   Thesis topic = " << topicptr;
            }
    };   // end gradStudent class
//////////////////////////////////////////////////////////////////
void main(void)
    {
    int j;
    const int total = 3;
    person* persPtr[3];          // list of pointers to persons

    char name[40];               // temporary storage
    char topic[80];

    for(j=0; j<total; j++)       // get data, make gradStudents
        {
        cout << "\nEnter name: ";
        cin >> name;
        cout << "   Enter thesis topic: ";
        cin >> topic;
        persPtr[j] = new gradStudent(name, topic);
        }
    for(j=0; j<total; j++)       // display gradStudents
        persPtr[j]->putData();
    for(j=0; j<total; j++)       // delete gradStudents
        delete persPtr[j];
    }  // end main()
```

The constructors in `person` and `gradStudent` obtain memory with `new` for the grad student's name and thesis topic, respectively. Their destructors delete this memory. Both destructors are called for each object, as shown by the output, so all allocated memory is guaranteed to be freed. Here's some sample interaction with `destpers`. (I've used the unsophisticated stream operator `cin>>` for text input, so only one-word strings are acceptable.)

```
Enter name: Wiffington
    Enter thesis topic: SomeAspectsOfGastropodBehavior

Enter name: Brown
    Enter thesis topic: SocksWornByRevolutionaryGenerals

Enter name: Pennybrook
    Enter thesis topic: ColorsThatEnhanceMoodOfValleyGirls

Name = Wiffington
    Thesis topic = SomeAspectsOfGastropodBehavior
Name = Brown
    Thesis topic = SocksWornByRevolutionaryGenerals
Name = Pennybrook
    Thesis topic = ColorsThatEnhanceMoodOfValleyGirls

gradStudent destructor
person destructor
gradStudent destructor
person destructor
gradStudent destructor
person destructor
```

When Do You Use Virtual Functions?

I noted at the beginning of this section that it's a good policy to make a destructor virtual in any class that has virtual functions. This is actually essential only when the following conditions are true: First, classes will be derived from the class in question; second, objects of derived classes will be deleted using base class pointers; third, the destructors in any of these related classes do something important like deallocating resources. If a class has virtual functions, it's likely that all these conditions will be met, if not now then at some point during the development or use of the class. (Remember, you can't predict today how a class may be used tomorrow.)

Once one function in a class is virtual, there's no additional overhead to making other functions virtual because as soon as one function is virtual, a virtual table is added to every object. Thus it doesn't cost you much to follow the rule of making the destructor virtual in any class with virtual functions.

QUIZ 4

1. An abstract class
   a. may represent a generic category such as "geographical locations" or "trees".
   b. tells the compiler what it is by including a virtual function.
   c. tells the compiler what it is by including a pure virtual function.

    d. tells the compiler what it is with the keyword `abstract`.

    e. is one from which no objects will be instantiated.

2. Usually, a pure virtual function
    a. has no function body.
    b. will never be called.
    c. will be called only to delete an object.
    d. tells the compiler what it is, using the notation `=0`.
    e. is defined only in derived classes.

3. Which of the following statements are true?
    a. It's acceptable to use a pure virtual function in an abstract class because you will always invoke abstract objects using pointers.
    b. A pure virtual function guarantees that no object can be instantiated from the class in which it's defined.
    c. A pure virtual function is useful whether the class in which it's defined is used as a base class or not.
    d. It's all right to use a function with no body in an abstract class because you never execute any of the functions in an abstract class.
    e. If you have one or more pure virtual functions in a class, the class is abstract.

4. If a base class destructor is not virtual, then
    a. it can't be called.
    b. it can't be called when accessed through a pointer.
    c. destructors in derived classes can't be called.
    d. destructors in derived classes can't be called when accessed through a pointer to the base class.
    e. it cannot have a function body.

5. Which of the following make it more likely that you would use a virtual destructor in a particular class?
    a. The class is used as a base class.
    b. The class contains no virtual functions.
    c. Objects of derived classes will be deleted using a variable whose type is a pointer to the base class.
    d. Objects of the base class will be deleted using a variable whose type is a pointer to the derived class.
    e. Destructors in the base or derived classes are necessary to deallocate system resources.

Start with the program from Exercise 1 of Session 2 in this chapter which added an `erase()` function to the `shape` class in VIRTSHAP. Make this `erase()` function into a pure virtual function and make any necessary changes to the rest of the program to accommodate this change.

Consider the EMPINH program in Chapter 7, Session 2. Retrofit the classes in this program with virtual functions or pure virtual functions as appropriate. Fix things so it's impossible to instantiate an **employee** object. Write a **main()** that fills an array of type **employee*** with pointers to different kinds of employees whose data is supplied by the user and then displays all the employee data.

MIDCHAPTER DISCUSSION

George: What's all the fuss about virtual functions? It looks to me like they're useful only in this one particular situation, where you use base class pointers to refer to derived class objects. If I just avoid that situation, then I don't need to worry about virtual functions at all.

Estelle: I must admit that thought crossed my mind too. But aren't virtual functions one of the three pillars of OOP, or something? So they must be important.

Don: I think the point is that using base class pointers to derived class objects gives you so much power that you'll want to use them all the time.

Estelle: Or at least when you have derived classes.

Don: But that's probably most of the time. It looks like inheritance isn't just a way of organizing classes. It's also a stepping stone to polymorphism.

George: So what does polymorphism buy you? I mean, it sounds like something the vice squad should investigate.

Estelle: With polymorphism, one statement can draw any shape, one statement can display data for any kind of person, one global function can operate on many different kinds of objects.

Don: Polymorphism lets the class user stop worrying about *how* something will be done and concentrate on *what* will be done. To draw an object, all you do is send it a message saying "Draw yourself." You don't even need to know what kind of object it is.

Estelle: As long as it's stored in a base class array or something like that.

Don: Right. You do need to set things up a little.

George: Well, I've decided I don't need to understand virtual functions.

Don: Because you're never going to use them?

George: No, because I'm joining the foreign legion.

Estelle: Poor fellow, he's polymorphically impaired.

Session 5

RUNTIME TYPE IDENTIFICATION

Sometimes you need to find the class of an object. You may wonder how you could lose track of an object's class. However, imagine that you have an array of pointers to objects and these pointers may point to objects of several different derived classes, as in the VIRTPERS program Session 2 in this chapter. If you're a global function that has accessed one of these pointers, how can you find out what kind of object it points to?

I know I can use such a pointer to call a virtual function for the object and the appropriate function will be called depending on the type of object. The virtual function mechanism knows what kind of object the pointer points to. However, this information is not immediately available to the programmer.

A Simple Example

Fortunately, most recent C++ compilers include a special function, `typeid()`, that allows you to find the type (or class, which is the same thing) of an object. This is called Runtime Type Identification, or RTTI. Listing 9-14, TYPEID, shows how `typeid()` works.

Listing 9-14 TYPEID

```
// typeid.cpp
// demonstrates typeid() function
#include <iostream.h>
#include <typeinfo.h>         // for typeid()

class ClassA
    { };

class ClassB
    { };

void main()
    {
    ClassA ObjA;
    ClassB ObjB;

    if( typeid(ObjA) == typeid(ClassA) )
        cout << "\nObjA is an object of ClassA";
    else
        cout << "\nObjA is not a member of ClassA";

    if( typeid(ObjB) == typeid(ClassA) )
        cout << "\nObjB is an object of ClassA";
    else
        cout << "\nObjB is not an object of ClassA";
    }
```

Here's the output from the program:

```
ObjA is an object of ClassA
ObjB is not an object of ClassA
```

You need to include the TYPINFO.H header file. You can use either an object name or a class name as an operand for `typeid()`, so it's easy to see if an object is from a particular class. The return value from `typeid()` is a pointer that is useful for comparison purposes, as with the `==` and `!=` operators. The `typeid()` function also works with basic types such as `int` and `float`.

A More Realistic Example

You'll typically need RTTI when you have base class pointers that contain addresses of derived class objects. This is the situation described earlier in this chapter where virtual functions make a class polymorphic. It may occur when you have an array of pointers to objects or when functions take references or a pointers to a base class as arguments.

Suppose, for example, that I want to modify the VIRTPERS program from Session 2 in this chapter so it indicates what kind of `person` object (`student`, `teacher`, or `person`) is being displayed. Listing 9-15 shows RTTIPERS, which does exactly that.

Listing 9-15 RTTIPERS

```cpp
// rttipers.cpp
// runtime type identification with person class
#include <iostream.h>
#include <typeinfo.h>          // for typeid()

class person                   // person class
   {
   protected:
      char name[40];
   public:
      virtual void getData()
         { cout << "   Enter name: "; cin >> name; }
      virtual void putData()
         { cout << "Name=" << name; }
   };
                               // student class
class student : public person
   {
   private:
      float gpa;               // grade point average
   public:
      void getData()           // get student data from user
         {
         person::getData();
         cout << "   Enter student's GPA: ";
         cin >> gpa;
         }
      void putData()
         {
         person::putData();
         cout << "   GPA=" << gpa;
```

continued on next page

continued from previous page

```
            }
   };
                                    // teacher class
class teacher : public person
   {
   private:
       int numPubs;              // number of papers published
   public:
       void getData()            // get teacher data from user
          {
          person::getData();
          cout << "   Enter number of teacher's publications: ";
          cin >> numPubs;
          }
       void putData()
          {
          person::putData();
          cout << "   Publications=" << numPubs;
          }
   };

void main(void)
   {
   person* persPtr[100];      // list of pointers to persons
   int n = 0;                 // number of persons on list
   char choice;               // 'p', 's', etc.

   do
       {
       cout << "Enter person, student or teacher (p/s/t): ";
       cin >> choice;
       if(choice=='s')                  // put new student
           persPtr[n] = new student;    //    in array
       else if(choice=='t')             // put new teacher
           persPtr[n] = new teacher;    //    in array
       else                             // put new person
           persPtr[n] = new person;     //    in array

       persPtr[n++]->getData();         // get data for person
       cout << "   Enter another (y/n)? ";  // do another person?
       cin >> choice;
       } while( choice=='y' );          // cycle until not 'y'

   for(int j=0; j<n; j++)
       {                                // display class name
       if( typeid(*persPtr[j]) == typeid(student) )
           cout << "\nStudent, ";
       else if( typeid(*persPtr[j]) == typeid(teacher) )
           cout << "\nTeacher, ";
       else if( typeid(*persPtr[j]) == typeid(person) )
           cout << "\nPerson,  ";
       else
           cout << "\nError: unknown type";
```

```
    persPtr[j]->putData();          // display name
    }  // end for

  for(int j=0; j<n; j++)            // delete all objects
    delete persPtr[j];
  }  // end main()
```

Here's some typical interaction with the program. The user enters data for four persons, and the program then displays this data, including the class of the person.

```
Enter person, student or teacher (p/s/t): p
   Enter name: Smith
   Enter another (y/n)? y
Enter person, student or teacher (p/s/t): p
   Enter name: Johnson
   Enter another (y/n)? y
Enter person, student or teacher (p/s/t): s
   Enter name: Harrison
   Enter student's GPA: 3.3
   Enter another (y/n)? y
Enter person, student or teacher (p/s/t): t
   Enter name: McConnel
   Enter number of teacher's publications: 104
   Enter another (y/n)? n

Person,   Name=Smith
Person,   Name=Johnson
Student,  Name=Harrison   GPA=3.3
Teacher,  Name=McConnel   Publications=104
```

As you can see, RTTI can save you the trouble of storing, say, a string specifying the class of each object. Instead, you can find out from the object itself what it is (although you do need to know all the possibilities in advance).

1. RTTI
   a. takes place at compile time.
   b. is seldom useful because you always know what class something is.
   c. is applicable to base class objects.
   d. is applicable to derived class objects.
   e. is an acronym for Random True Type Identification.

2. In the TYPEID program,
   a. the type ID of objects is compared with the type ID of classes.
   b. comparison operators are required.
   c. the argument to typeid() is a pointer.
   d. the argument to typeid() is a string.
   e. the header file TYPEID.H must be included.

3. In the RTTIPERS program,
   a. the class creator arranges for type information to be stored in each object.
   b. the class user arranges for type information to be stored in each object.
   c. the compiler arranges for type information to be stored in each object.
   d. `typeid()` uses contextual analysis of the source code to determine the type of an object.
   e. `typeid()` and a comparison operator determine the type of an object.

4. Using RTTI in the RTTIPERS program
   a. gives extra information to the end user.
   b. could be avoided, but at the expense of object size.
   c. isn't necessary if you use virtual functions.
   d. isn't necessary if you instantiate only objects of the base class.
   e. makes all objects slightly larger.

5. The return value from `typeid()` is
   a. a pointer to the object used as an argument.
   b. for classes with virtual functions, possibly the address of the class `vtable`.
   c. useful for comparison with other `typeid()` calls.
   d. a pointer to a string representing the class name.
   e. useful only with abstract classes.

EXERCISE 1

Start with the EMPINH program from Chapter 7, Session 2. Change `main()` so that when members of the various derived classes are instantiated, pointers to them are placed in an array of type `employee*`. Assume you can't change the existing class hierarchy. Use RTTI in `main()` to display the type of each object whose pointer is stored in the array at the same time you invoke `putdata()` to display the object's data.

SESSION 6

FRIEND FUNCTIONS

A *friend function* is a function that is not a member of a class, but nevertheless has access to the private and protected members of the class.

Ordinarily, the policies of encapsulation and data hiding dictate that nonmember functions should not be able to access an object's private or protected data. The policy is, if you're not a member, you can't get in. However, there are situations where such rigid discrimination leads to considerable inconvenience. Friend functions are a way around this inconvenience.

One such situation arises when you want to use a nonobject on the left side of an overloaded operator. Another place where friend functions are helpful is when you want to use functional notation with an object as the argument. I'll examine these uses for friend functions in this session. In Session 7 I'll explore a related topic, friend classes.

The "Left-Side" Problem

In the ADDAIR example (Chapter 6, Session 1), I overloaded the + operator to add two **airtime** objects together. This worked fine as long as the objects being added together really were **airtime** objects:

```
at3 = at1 + at2;
```

No Problem on the Right

Suppose that, as a class creator, I want to make it possible for class users to write expressions that add an integer, representing hours, to an **airtime**:

```
at2 = at1 + 3;
```

For example, 2:33 + 5 would be 7:33. It's fairly easy to make this happen when the integer is on the right side of the operator, as shown here. If there's a one-argument constructor in the **airtime** class, the compiler will automatically use it to convert the integer to an **airtime** value and then add the two **airtimes**. Listing 9-16, AIRNOFRI, shows a possible scenario.

Listing 9-16 AIRNOFRI

```
// airnofri.cpp
// overloads the + operator for airtime class,
// integer cannot be used for on left of operator
#include <iostream.h>

class airtime
   {
   private:
      int hours;              // 0 to 23
      int minutes;            // 0 to 59
   public:
                              // 0, 1 or 2 arg constructor
      airtime(int h = 0, int m = 0) : hours(h), minutes(m)
         { }
      void display()          // output to screen
         { cout << hours << ':' << minutes; }

      void get()              // input from user
         {
         char dummy;
         cin >> hours >> dummy >> minutes;
         }
                              // overloaded + operator
      airtime operator + (airtime right)
         {
         airtime temp;        // make a temporary object
         temp.hours = hours + right.hours; // add data
         temp.minutes = minutes + right.minutes;
         if(temp.minutes >= 60)           // check for carry
            {
            temp.hours++;
            temp.minutes -= 60;
            }
```

continued on next page

continued from previous page

```
          return temp;          // return temporary object by value
          }
  };  // end class airtime

void main()
  {
  airtime at1, at2;

  cout << "Enter an airtime: ";
  at1.get();

  at2 = at1 + 3;               // add integer to airtime
  cout << "airtime + 3 = ";
  at2.display();               // display sum

// at2 = 3 + at1;              // error: illegal structure operation
  }
```

The constructor in this program handles three situations: no arguments, one argument, or two arguments. (I could also have used three separate constructors.) In its role as a one-argument constructor, the constructor is used by the compiler to convert the 3 in main() into an airtime(3, 0) value, which is then added to whatever airtime value the user entered for at1. Here's some sample interaction:

```
Enter an airtime: 6:45
airtime + 3 = 9:45
```

The operator+() function, with a little help from the constructor, has no problem when a nonobject (an integer) appears on the right side of the + operator.

Not So Easy on the Left

As you can see from the commented last line in the AIRNOFRI listing, however, the compiler will signal an error if you attempt to put an integer value on the left of the + operator:

```
at2 = 3 + at1;    // no good
```

Why doesn't this work? Overloading disguises what's actually happening. Remember that the overloaded + operator is really just a member function, called by the object on its left and taking the object on its right as an argument. If I write things out as the compiler sees it, the problem will be clearer. Here's what a call to operator+() really means, when the integer is on the right:

```
at2 = at1.operator+(3);   // ok
```

This looks all right. But here's the corresponding situation when the integer is on the left:

```
at2 = 3.operator+(at1);   // illegal; '3' isn't an object
```

Member functions must be invoked by an object of their class, and 3 is not an airtime object. So although you can add an integer to an airtime, you can't add an airtime to an integer. This is a serious inconsistency for class users.

Friends to the Rescue

In this situation, there's nothing like a friend function. A friend can be defined outside of any class or other function, as if it were a normal (nonmember) global function. Its connection to the class is that, within the class, it's declared to be a friend. Listing 9-17 shows AIRFRI.

Listing 9-17 AIRFRI

```cpp
// airfri.cpp
// overloads + operator for airtime class,
// uses friend function to permit integer on left of + operator
#include <iostream.h>
/////////////////////////////////////////////////////////////////
class airtime
    {
    private:
        int hours;              // 0 to 23
        int minutes;            // 0 to 59
    public:
                                // 0, 1, or 2 arg constructor
        airtime(int h = 0, int m = 0) : hours(h), minutes(m)
            {  }

        void display()          // output to screen
            { cout << hours << ':' << minutes; }

        void get()              // input from user
            {
            char dummy;
            cin >> hours >> dummy >> minutes;
            }

        friend airtime operator+(airtime, airtime); // declaration

    };  // end class airtime
/////////////////////////////////////////////////////////////////
                            // friend function: overloaded + operator
airtime operator + (airtime left, airtime right)
    {
    airtime temp;           // make a temporary object
    temp.hours = left.hours + right.hours; // add data
    temp.minutes = left.minutes + right.minutes;
    if(temp.minutes >= 60)                // check for carry
        {
        temp.hours++;
        temp.minutes -= 60;
        }
    return temp;            // return temporary object by value
    }
/////////////////////////////////////////////////////////////////
void main()
    {
    airtime at1, at2;
```

continued on next page

continued from previous page
```
cout << "Enter an airtime: ";
at1.get();

at2 = at1 + 3;              // add integer to airtime
cout << "airtime + 3 = ";
at2.display();              // display sum

at2 = 3 + at1;              // add airtime to integer
cout << "\n3 + airtime = ";
at2.display();              // display sum
}
```

A function declaration (the last statement in the `airtime` class) makes `operator+()` a friend:

```
friend airtime operator+(airtime, airtime);
```

This declaration can be placed anywhere in the class; it doesn't matter, at least to the compiler, if it goes in the `public` or the `private` section. However, it belongs conceptually in the public section because it's part of the public interface to the class. That is, any class user can invoke the friend function; it's not accessible only to class members. Therefore, friend function declarations are commonly placed in the public section.

As you can see, the `operator+()` function (which appears just after the `airtime` class in the listing) is not a member function of `airtime`; if it were, its declarator would be

```
airtime airtime::operator + (airtime left, airtime right)
```

Nevertheless, it can access `hours` and `minutes`, which are private data members of `airtime`. It can do this because it has declared a friend within the class.

The `operator+()` friend function takes two arguments, called `left` and `right`. Because it's a standalone function and not a class member, it's not invoked by an object; it's simply called from `main()` like any other global function. Both objects to be added are therefore available as arguments.

As a general rule, the friend version of a function always takes one more argument than the member version. Internally, the friend `operator+()` function in AIRFRI is similar to the member version in AIRNOFRI, except that it refers to the data in the `airtime` arguments as `left.hours` and `right.hours`, whereas the member version uses `hours` and `right.hours`. The function returns the sum as a third `airtime` value.

If either argument, whether on the left or right, is an integer, the compiler will use the one-argument constructor to convert the integer to an airtime and then add the two airtimes. Statements in `main()` show both situations, and the compiler has no problem with either one.

Breaching the Walls

I should note that, during the development of C++, friend functions were controversial. Conflict raged over the desirability of including this feature. On the one hand, it adds flexibility to the language; on the other, it is not in keeping with the philosophy that only member functions can access a class's private data.

How serious is the breach of data integrity when friend functions are used? A friend function must be declared as such within the class whose data it will access. Thus, a programmer who does not have access to the source code for the class cannot make a function into a friend. In this respect, the integrity of the class is still protected. Current thinking is that friends are not a serious threat to data integrity.

Even so, friend functions are conceptually messy and potentially can lead to a spaghetti-code situation if numerous friends muddy the clear boundaries between classes. For this reason, friend functions should be used sparingly. Always use a member function unless there's a compelling reason to use a friend. If you find yourself using a lot of friends, you might want to rethink the design of the program.

Friends for Functional Notation

Sometimes a friend function allows a more obvious syntax for calling a function than does a member function. For example, suppose I want a function that will square (multiply by itself) an object of the English class and return the result in square feet, as a type float. The MISQ example (Listing 9-18) shows how this might be done with a member function.

Listing 9-18 MISQ

```
// misq.cpp
// member square() function for Distance
#include <iostream.h>

class English                       // English class
   {
   private:
      int feet;
      float inches;
   public:
      English(int ft, float in)     // 2-arg constructor
         { feet = ft; inches = in; }
      void showdist()               // display
         { cout << feet << "\'-" << inches << '\"'; }

      float square();               // member function declaration
   };

float English::square()            // return square of
   {                               // this English object
   float fltfeet = feet + inches/12;   // convert to float
   float feetsqrd = fltfeet * fltfeet;  // find the square
   return feetsqrd;                // return square feet
   }

void main()
   {
   English dist(3, 6.0);           // 1-arg constructor (3'-6")

   float sqft = dist.square();     // return square of dist
                                   // display distance and square
   cout << "\nDistance = "; dist.showdist();
   cout << "\nSquare = " << sqft << " square feet";
   }
```

The `main()` part of the program creates an `English` distance value, squares it, and prints out the result. The output shows the original distance and the square:

```
Distance = 3'-6"
Square = 12.25 square feet
```

That is, if there's a table 3'-6" on each side, it has an area of 12.25 square feet. In `main()`, I use the statement

```
sqft = dist.square();
```

to find the square of `dist` and assign it to `sqft`. This works all right, but if you want to work with `English` objects using the same syntax that you use with ordinary numbers, you would probably prefer a functional notation:

```
sqft = square(dist);
```

You can achieve this effect by making `square()` a friend of the `English` class, as shown in FRISQ (Listing 9-19).

Listing 9-19 FRISQ

```cpp
// frisq.cpp
// friend square() function for English class
#include <iostream.h>

class English                    // English class
   {
   private:
      int feet;
      float inches;
   public:
      English(int ft, float in)  // 2-arg constructor
         { feet = ft; inches = in; }
      void showdist()            // display
         { cout << feet << "\'-" << inches << '\"'; }

      friend float square(English);  // friend function
   };

float square(English d)          // return square of
   {                             // the argument
   float fltfeet = d.feet + d.inches/12;  // convert to float
   float feetsqrd = fltfeet * fltfeet;    // find the square
   return feetsqrd;              // return square feet
   }

void main()
   {
   English dist(3, 6.0);         // two-arg constructor (3'-6")

   float sqft = square(dist);    // return square of dist
                                          // display distance and square
```

```
cout << "\nDistance = "; dist.showdist();
cout << "\nSquare = " << sqft << " square feet";
}
```

Now you can use the more intuitive

```
float sqft = square(dist);
```

Although, as a member function in MISQ, `square()` takes no arguments, it takes one as a friend function in FRISQ. Again, the friend version of a function always requires one more argument than the member version.

Friends as Bridges

Here's another situation in which friend functions might come in handy. Imagine that you want a function to operate on objects of two different classes. Perhaps the function will take objects of the two classes as arguments and operate on their private data. If the two classes are inherited from the same base class, then you may be able to put the function in the base class. But what if the classes are unrelated?

Listing 9-20 shows a simple example, BRIDGE, that shows how friend functions can act as a bridge between two classes.

Listing 9-20 BRIDGE
```
// bridge.cpp
// friend functions
#include <iostream.h>

class beta;                    // needed for frifunc declaration

class alpha
   {
   private:
      int data;
   public:
      alpha()  { data = 3; }              // no-arg constructor
      friend int frifunc(alpha, beta);    // friend function
   };

class beta
   {
   private:
      int data;
   public:
      beta()  { data = 7; }              // no-arg constructor
      friend int frifunc(alpha, beta);    // friend function
   };

int frifunc(alpha a, beta b)           // function definition
   {
   return( a.data + b.data );
   }
```

continued on next page

continued from previous page

```
void main()
    {
    alpha aa;
    beta bb;
    cout << frifunc(aa, bb);                // call the function
    }
```

In this program, the two classes are `alpha` and `beta`. The constructors in these classes initialize their single data items to fixed values (3 in `alpha` and 7 in `beta`).

I want the function `frifunc()` to have access to both these private data members, so I make it a friend function. It's declared with the `friend` keyword in both classes:

```
friend int frifunc(alpha, beta);
```

An object of each class is passed as an argument to the function `frifunc()` and accesses the private `data` member of both classes through these arguments. The function doesn't do much: It adds the data items and returns the sum. The `main()` program calls this function and prints the result.

A minor point: Remember that a class can't be referred to until it has been declared. Class `beta` is referred to in the declaration of the function `frifunc()` in class `alpha`, so `beta` must be declared before `alpha`. Hence the declaration

```
class beta;
```

at the beginning of the program.

QUIZ 6

1. A friend function
    a. must be a member function of the class that declares it a friend.
    b. must be invoked by the class that declares it a friend.
    c. must be invoked by an object of the class that declares it a friend.
    d. can access the private data of the class that declares it a friend.
    e. can access the nonpublic data of any class derived from the class that declares it a friend.

2. Typically, the private class data accessed by a friend function
    a. is in an object created by the friend function.
    b. is in the object that invoked the friend function.
    c. is in an object sent to the friend function as an argument.
    d. must be static class data.
    e. is in an object of a different class than that in which the function is declared to be a friend.

3. Friend functions are helpful in functional notation because they
    a. use parentheses following the function name.
    b. take no arguments.
    c. aren't related to a specific class.
    d. operate on an object passed as an argument.
    e. allow other functions to access their class data.

4. Which of the following statements are true?
   a. Any function can use a friend function to access the private data of the class with which the friend function is associated.
   b. For a function to be a friend, the keyword `friend` must appear in its definition.
   c. A friend function must be declared in the class whose friend it will be.
   d. A friend function is specified by its location in the listing.
   e. Friends are especially useful for overloaded operators.

5. Which of the following statements are true?
   a. A function can be a friend of more than one class.
   b. A class can be a friend of a function.
   c. More than one function can be a friend of a class.
   d. Member functions from different classes could use a friend function to exchange private data between the classes.
   e. A friend function can be called in a statement in `main()`.

EXERCISE 1

Write an `operator-()` function that subtracts two `airtime` values. Assume a larger `airtime` will never be subtracted from a smaller. Make it possible for an integer, representing hours, to be subtracted from an `airtime` and for an `airtime` to be subtracted from an integer.

EXERCISE 2

Create a function for the `English` class that returns the square of an `English` value, in square feet, type `float`. Write a `main()` that tests this function.

SESSION 7

FRIEND CLASSES

Classes, as well as functions, can be friends. The usual reason for using friend classes is to facilitate interclass communication. In this session I'll start with some skeleton examples of such communication and then show a more ambitious program that models a horse race, with `track` and `horse` classes that need to communicate with each other.

Interclass Communication

Suppose you have two classes, `alpha` and `beta`, that are closely associated with each other. In fact, they are so closely associated that one class needs to access the other's private data directly (without using public access functions). You don't want to make the data public because then anyone could alter it by mistake. Also, neither class is a "kind of" the other, so you don't want to relate them using inheritance. How do you arrange for one class to access another's private members? The answer is to use friend classes, but there's more to it than that.

In interclass communication, it makes a difference which class specification appears first in the listing. You can't refer to members of a class that hasn't been specified yet because the compiler won't know anything about them. If `alpha` is specified before `beta`, then it's easy for member functions of `beta` to refer to private members of `alpha`, but harder for functions in `alpha` to access private data in `beta`. I'll start with an easy case.

Accessing Private Members in a Previously Defined Class

Listing 9-21, INTERC1, shows how a member function of class `beta`, whose specification follows that of class `alpha`, can access the private data in `alpha`.

Listing 9-21 INTERC1

```
// interc1.cpp
// a class accesses data in a previously-defined class
#include <iostream.h>

class alpha
   {
   private:
      friend class beta;      // so beta can access alpha data
      int adata;              // alpha's private data
   };

class beta
   {
   public:
      void bfunc()
         {
         alpha objA;          // make an object to
         objA.adata = 3;      // access private alpha data
         }
   };
```

The key here is declaring class `beta` a friend of class `alpha`:

```
friend class beta;    // so beta can access alpha data
```

This gives any member function of class `beta` access to any private or protected data in class `alpha`. Both keywords `friend` and `class` are necessary. Notice that the declaration is placed in the private section of `alpha`. As with friend functions, the compiler doesn't care where the declaration is placed, but it's conceptually more accurate to place it in the private section because the friend connection between `alpha` and `beta` is used only within the two classes; it's not part of the public interface (accessed by the class user).

It's important to recognize that (unless they are related by inheritance) a class member cannot access data in another class in the abstract. That is, you can't say

```
alpha::adata = 3;   // Error: object is required
```

as you could if `beta` were derived from `alpha`. They are separate classes, and friendship is not the same as family. There must be an actual object (or a pointer to an actual object, as you'll see later) in which the data resides:

```
alpha objA;
objA.adata = 3;
```

Accessing Private Members in a Not Yet Defined Class

Now suppose a member function of alpha wants to access private data in beta. This is a problem because the specification for beta appears after that for alpha and the compiler needs to see a class specified before it can access its members. (Yes, you could reverse them, but suppose you want beta to access alpha's data as well?)

In this case, the trick is to move the afunc() member function definition out of alpha and place it after the specification for beta. Listing 9-22 shows INTERC2.

Listing 9-22 INTERC2
```
// interc2.cpp
// class accesses data in a not-yet-defined class

class alpha
   {
   public:
      void afunc();            // function declaration
   };                          // (definition must follow beta)

class beta
   {
   private:
      friend class alpha;      // so alpha can access beta data
      int bdata;               // beta's data
   };

void alpha::afunc()           // alpha's function
   {
   beta objB;                  // create beta object
   objB.bdata = 3;             // access its private data
   };
```

I *declare* afunc() in alpha, but *define* it later, following the beta specification. The compiler therefore knows what beta looks like when it compiles afunc() and, because alpha is a friend of beta, can handle statements that access beta's private data. Again, notice that this data must be in an actual object.

Pointers in Interclass Communication

In real programs, when one class accesses data in another, it's more common to refer to objects using pointers to them than it is to refer to them directly, as I did in INTERC1 and INTERC2. The next example not only shows how objects can be accessed with pointers, it also demonstrates two-way communication: alpha accessing beta's private data and beta accessing alpha's private data.

The idea in using pointers for interclass communication is that each class contains pointers to objects of the other class. In the kind of interclass communication I'm describing here, there are often different numbers of objects of the two classes. In the example, I'll assume that each alpha object is associated with two beta objects. It follows that class alpha has two pointers to beta (so alpha can access beta data) and class beta has one pointer to alpha (so beta can access alpha data).

In addition, each class is declared to be a friend of the other. Listing 9-23 shows INTERC3.

Listing 9-23 INTERC3

```
// interc3.cpp
// interclass communication using pointers and friend classes
#include <iostream.h>
/////////////////////////////////////////////////////////////////
class alpha                    // an alpha is associated with
   {                           // several betas
   private:
      friend class beta;       // for beta access to alpha data
      beta* bptr1;             // pointers to betas
      beta* bptr2;
      int adata;
   public:
      alpha();                 // constructor (defined after beta)
      void afunc();            // function (defined after beta)
   };
/////////////////////////////////////////////////////////////////
class beta                     // several betas are
   {                           // associated with an alpha
   private:
      friend class alpha;      // for alpha access to beta data
      alpha* aptr;             // pointer to "our" alpha
      int bdata;               // data
   // note: constructor is private
      beta(alpha* ap) : aptr(ap)  // 1-arg construtor
         { }                   // initializes pointer to alpha
   public:
      void bfunc()
         {
         aptr->adata = 3;      // access private alpha data
         }
   };
/////////////////////////////////////////////////////////////////
alpha::alpha()                 // alpha constructor
   {                           // (must be defined after beta)
   bptr1 = new beta(this);     // make betas
   bptr2 = new beta(this);
   }
void alpha::afunc()            // alpha function
   {                           // (must be defined after beta)
   bptr1->bdata = 4;           // accesses private beta data
   bptr2->bdata = 5;
   }
/////////////////////////////////////////////////////////////////
void main()
   {
   alpha objA;
   objA.afunc();
   }
```

I again use the trick of defining alpha's functions after the beta specification because both the alpha constructor and afunc() require access to beta data. You can see that alpha's function afunc() accesses the bdata in both beta objects and that beta's function bfunc() accesses the adata in the alpha object.

How are all these objects created? Let's assume that the class user creates only alpha objects. If the user could create beta objects, the two-beta-one-alpha arrangement could be violated. To ensure that the user can't create a beta, we make the beta constructor private, so only friends of beta can make betas.

When an alpha object is created, its constructor creates two beta objects. It does this by calling the beta constructor and passing it its own this pointer. Thus, every beta can locate the alpha that it's associated with. Because alpha's constructor uses new to create its two beta objects, it can access them by pointer as well. Everyone knows where everyone else is.

A Horse Race Example

Let's put what you've learned about friend classes and interclass communication together in a horse race game program. This is a simulation program in which a number of horses appear on the screen and, starting from the left, race to a finish line on the right. Each horse's speed is determined randomly so there is no way to figure out in advance which one will win. The spectators can (although we do not condone this) place bets on which horse will win. The program uses character graphics, so the horses are easily (although somewhat crudely) displayed.

This program has some peculiarities. First, in the version shown here, it works only with Borland compilers because it uses several library functions specific to Borland. These are delay(), gotoxy(), clrscr(), random(), and randomize(). Second, it's a DOS program because the delay() function doesn't work in Windows. That means you can't develop it as a Borland EasyWin target, you must develop it as a DOS program, as described in Appendix C. Other compilers have similar but not identical functions, so you may need to adapt the program appropriately.

Operation of FRIHORSE

When the program, FRIHORSE, is started, it asks the user to supply the race's distance and the number of horses that will run in it. The classic unit of distance for horse racing (at least in English-speaking countries) is the furlong, which is 1/8 of a mile. Typical races are 6, 8, 10, or 12 furlongs. You can specify from 1 to 10 horses. The program draws vertical start and finish lines and lines corresponding to furlongs. Each horse is represented by a rectangle with a number in the middle. Figure 9-5 shows the screen with a race in progress.

Designing the Horse Race

How do we approach an object-oriented design for the horse race? Your first question might be, is there a group of similar entities that you're trying to model? Yes, the horses. So it seems reasonable to make each horse an object. There will be a class called horse which will contain data specific to each horse, such as its number and the distance it has run so far (which is used to display the horse in the correct screen position).

However, there is also data that applies more to the track as a whole than to each horse, such as the track length, the elapsed time (starting from 0:00 at the start of the race), and the total number of horses. What do we do with this track-related (as opposed to horse-related) data? One possibil-

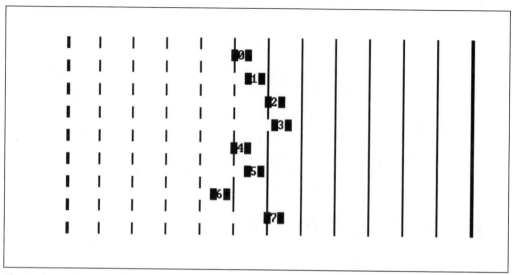

Figure 9-5   Output of the HORSE program

ity is to make a class called, say, **track**, and install this data in it. Then we'll have a single **track** object and many **horse** objects.

How should the track and the horses communicate? We could use inheritance to make the horses descendants of the track, but this doesn't make much sense because the horses aren't a "kind of" race track; they're a completely different thing.

The approach I use here is to make the **horse** class a friend of **track** so that the horses can access private track data. Also, I don't want the class user to be able to create or access horse objects, which (unlike their real-life counterparts) can't exist without a track. Therefore, I make the constructor and member functions of the **horse** class private. However, the track needs to access these horse member functions, so I make **track** a friend of **horse**.

The class user creates a single track object, and the track creates the horses. The track and the horses communicate with each other using pointers and the friend relationships, as demonstrated in the INTERC3 example. (You'll see other ways to organize the track and horses in Session 8.) Listing 9-24 shows FRIHORSE.

Listing 9-24 FRIHORSE

```
// frihorse.cpp
// models horse race, uses friends
// (Note: Borland specific. See text.)
#include <iostream.h>
#include <dos.h>                      // for delay()
#include <conio.h>                    // for gotoxy(), etc.
#include <stdlib.h>                   // for random()
#include <time.h>                     // for randomize()
const int CPF = 5;                    // screen columns/furlong
/////////////////////////////////////////////////////////////////
```

```
class track
   {
   private:
      friend class horse;        // let horses access data
      horse* hptr;               // pointer to horse memory
      int total;                 // total number of horses
      int count;                 // horses created so far
      int track_length;          // track length in furlongs
      float elapsed_time;        // time since start of race
   public:
      track(float, int);         // 2-arg constructor
      void track_tick();         // time tick; entire track
      ~track();                  // destructor
   };  // end track class
/////////////////////////////////////////////////////////
class horse
   {
   private:
      friend class track;        // let track access functions
      track* ptr_track;          // pointer to track
      int horse_number;          // this horse's number
      float finish_time;         // this horse's finish time
      float distance_run;        // distance since start
                                 // note: private member functions
      horse() : distance_run(0.0)  // construct a horse
         { }
      void horse_init(track* pt)    // initialize a horse
         {
         ptr_track = pt;
         horse_number = (ptr_track->count)++;
         }
      void horse_tick();         // time tick for one horse
   };  // end class horse
/////////////////////////////////////////////////////////
void horse::horse_tick()              // for each horse
   {                                  // display horse & number
   gotoxy( 1 + int(distance_run * CPF), 2 + horse_number*2 );
   cout << " \xDB" << horse_number << "\xDB";
   if(distance_run < ptr_track->track_length + 1.0/CPF)
      {
      if( random(3) % 3 )          // skip about 1 of 3 ticks
         distance_run += 0.2;      // advance 0.2 furlongs
      finish_time = ptr_track->elapsed_time;   // update finish time
      }
   else
      {                                  // display finish time
      int mins = int(finish_time)/60;
      int secs = int(finish_time) - mins*60;
      cout << " Time=" << mins << ":" << secs;
      }
   }
/////////////////////////////////////////////////////////
```

continued on next page

continued from previous page

```
                                             // two-arg constructor
track::track(float l, int t) : track_length(l), total(t),
                                    count(0), elapsed_time(0.0)
   {
   randomize();                          // initialize random numbers
   clrscr();                             // clear screen
                                         // display track
   for(int f=0; f<=track_length; f++)    // for each furlong
      for(int r=1; r<=total*2 + 1; r++)  // for each screen row
         {
         gotoxy(f*CPF + 5, r);
         if(f==0 || f==track_length)
            cout << '\xDE';              // draw start or finish line
         else
            cout << '\xB3';              // draw furlong marker
         }
                                         // create horses
   hptr = new horse[total];              // get memory for all horses
   for(int j=0; j<total; j++)            // initialize each horse
      (hptr+j)->horse_init(this);        // with track pointer
   }
void track::track_tick()
   {
   elapsed_time += 1.75;                 // update time

   for(int j=0; j<total; j++)            // for each horse,
      (hptr+j)->horse_tick();            // update horse
   }
track::~track()                          // destructor
   {
   delete hptr;                          // delete memory for horses
   }
//////////////////////////////////////////////////////////////////
void main()
   {
   float length;
   int nhorses;

   cout << "\nEnter track length (furlongs, 6 to 12): ";
   cin >> length;
   cout << "\nEnter number of horses (1 to 10): ";
   cin >> nhorses;

   track t(length, nhorses);   // create track and horses

   while( !kbhit() )           // exit on keypress
      {
      t.track_tick();          // move and display all horses
      delay(500);              // wait 1/2 second
      }
   t.~track();                 // destroy track and horses
   }
```

Creating the Horses

In `track::create_horses()`, I use `new` to obtain memory for all the `horse` objects at once. (I can't use an array because I don't know in advance how many horses the user will specify.) Member functions in `track` can then access each horse through the pointer returned from `new`, plus an index `j` to specify the particular horse.

As each horse is created, its constructor numbers it sequentially, using the track's count of how many horses have been created so far.

Keeping Time

Simulation programs usually involve an activity taking place over a period of time. To model the passage of time, such programs typically energize themselves at fixed intervals. In the FRIHORSE program, the `main()` program uses a `while` loop to call a `track` function, `tick_track()`, repeatedly; the time tick is sent to the track as a whole. The `tick_track()` function then makes a series of calls, one for each horse, to the horse function `horse_tick()` (which should not be confused with the insect that carries equine fever). This function then redraws each horse in its new position.

1. For all the members of a class **B** to be able to access the private data of a previously defined (and unrelated) class **A**,
   a. class **A** must be defined as a friend.
   b. member function definitions of **B** must follow the class specification for **A** in the listing.
   c. the member functions of class **B** must be defined outside the class.
   d. within **A**, **B** must be declared to be a friend of **A**.
   e. within **B**, **A** must be declared to be a friend of **B**.

2. For the members of a class **A** to be able to access the private data of a class **B**, whose specification follows **A** in the listing,
   a. class **B** must be defined as a friend.
   b. member function definitions of **A** must follow the class specification for **B**, in the listing.
   c. the member functions of class **A** must be defined outside the class.
   d. within **A**, **B** must be declared to be a friend of **A**.
   e. within **B**, **A** must be declared to be a friend of **B**.

3. Which of the following statements, describing the INTERC3 program, are true?
   a. An `alpha` object knows where related `beta` objects are because it created them with `new`.
   b. The pointer to an `alpha` object, defined within `beta`, is used by `alpha` to access private `beta` data.
   c. Member functions of `beta` must be defined following the specification for `alpha`.
   d. The friend relationship is unnecessary when each class contains pointers to objects of the other.
   e. The `beta` objects know where their related `alpha` object is because they are friends of `alpha`.

4. Which of the following statements, concerning the FRIHORSE program, are true?
   a. The track class does not need to know where the horse objects are stored in memory.
   b. The new operator is called once to create each horse object.
   c. The horse objects find out what time it is by accessing private data in track.
   d. The horse objects find out how far they've gone by accessing private data in track.
   e. The track class does not need to be a friend of the horse class.

5. In the FRIHORSE program,
   a. a single call to the horse_tick() function moves all the horses.
   b. the horse class creates the track.
   c. the track class contains data specific to each horse.
   d. the track class communicates with the horses using a pointer.
   e. the horse objects are stored contiguously in memory.

EXERCISE 1

Modify the INTERC3 program so that each alpha object is associated with 100 beta objects. Store pointers to the beta objects in an array in alpha. As before, each class should be able to access the other's private data.

EXERCISE 2

Add a third class gamma to the INTERC3 program. Arrange for each alpha object to be associated with one beta object and one gamma object. Organize things so that alpha and beta objects can access one another's private data, alpha and gamma can do the same, but there is no such communication between beta and gamma.

SESSION 8

NESTED CLASSES AND STATIC MEMBER DATA

Let's look at two variations of the FRIHORSE program from the last session. The first program uses a new idea: nested classes. The second uses a concept you encountered in Chapter 4, static data. These examples provide evidence that there is often more than one way to design an object-oriented program.

Nested Classes

You can place one class specification inside another:

```
class alpha
   {
```

```
private:
    class beta;
        {
        };
};
```

Here, **beta** is said to be nested inside **alpha**. What's the advantage of this? For one thing, it can help mirror the conceptual relationship of the classes. If **beta** is used only by **alpha** and will never be accessed or instantiated outside **alpha**, then it makes sense to place it completely within **alpha**.

There's another advantage to nested classes. Remember that normal class names and member names have global scope; that is, they are visible throughout the entire program. However, in this example, because **beta** (along with its members, if it had any) is hidden inside **alpha**, **beta**'s member names can be used for other purposes elsewhere in the program without fear of conflict. Such *name clashes* can be a problem in large programs with thousands of names. It's always good practice to minimize the number of names in the global name space. (Another solution to name clashes is a recently adopted C++ feature called *namespaces*, which I'll describe in Chapter 11, Session 7.)

Communication Between Nested Classes

How do nested classes communicate with each other? They don't have automatic access to each other's data just because they're nested. As with ordinary nonnested classes, special efforts must be made to allow communication. One approach is to use friend classes. Listing 9-25 shows an example, called NESTED.

Listing 9-25 NESTED

```
// nested.cpp
// one class nested inside another

class alpha
    {
    private:
        int adata;
        /////////////////////////
        class beta
            {
            private:
                int bdata;
                friend class alpha;      // alpha is a friend of beta
            public:
                void bfunc()
                    {
                    alpha objA;
                    objA.adata = 3;      // access private alpha data
                    }
            };  // end class beta
        /////////////////////////
        friend class alpha::beta;        // beta is a friend of alpha
                                         // (must follow beta)
    public:
        void afunc()
            {
            beta objB;
```

continued on next page

continued from previous page

```
            objB.bdata = 2;          // access private beta data
            objB.bfunc();
            }
   };   // end class alpha

void main()
   {
   alpha objA;
   objA.afunc();
   }
```

The member function `afunc()` in `alpha` can access the private `bdata` in `beta`, and `bfunc()` in `beta` can access the private `adata` in `alpha`. As in the examples in the last session, access must be to variables in actual objects. Notice too that the statement

```
friend class alpha::beta;
```

must follow the specification for `beta` within the `alpha` specification. It must also use the complete name of `beta`, which, because it is nested within `alpha`, is `alpha::beta`. Within `beta`, `alpha` is made a friend in the usual way.

Because `beta` is hidden in `alpha`, you can't write something like

```
void main()
   {
   alpha::beta objB;   // Error: can't make a beta object
   }
```

The `beta` class is unknown outside of `alpha`.

Horse Racing and Nested Classes

The larger-scale example of nested classes is similar to the FRIHORSE program, but the `horse` class specification has been placed inside the `track` specification. (See the warnings about FRIHORSE before attempting to compile NESHORSE.) Listing 9-26 shows NESHORSE.

Listing 9-26 NESHORSE

```
// neshorse.cpp
// models horse race, uses friends and nested classes
// (Note: Borland specific. See text.)
#include <iostream.h>
#include <dos.h>                 // for delay()
#include <conio.h>               // for kbhit()
#include <stdlib.h>              // for random()
#include <time.h>                // for randomize()
const int CPF = 5;               // screen columns/furlong
class horse;
/////////////////////////////////////////////////////////////
class track
   {
   private:
      /////////////////////////////////////////////////////////////
      class horse                    // nested class
         {
         private:
            track* ptr_track;         // pointer to track
```

```
          int horse_number;        // this horse's number
          float finish_time;       // this horse's finish time
          float distance_run;      // distance since start
      public:
          horse() : distance_run(0.0)      // construct a horse
             { }
          void horse_init(track* pt)       // initialize a horse
             {
             ptr_track = pt;
             horse_number = (ptr_track->count)++;
             }
          void horse_tick();               // time tick for one horse
       };  // end class horse
    //////////////////////////////////////////////////////////
    horse* hptr;                   // pointer to horse memory
                                   // (must follow horse class)

    int total;                     // total number of horses
    int count;                     // horses created so far
    int track_length;              // track length in furlongs
    float elapsed_time;            // time since start of race
    friend class track::horse;
  public:
    track(float, int);             // two-arg constructor
    void track_tick();             // time tick for entire track
    ~track()                       // destructor
       {
       delete hptr;                // delete horse memory
       }
  };  // end track class
//////////////////////////////////////////////////////////
                                   // 2-arg constructor
track::track(float l, int t) : track_length(l), total(t),
                                   count(0), elapsed_time(0.0)
   {
   randomize();                    // initialize random numbers
   clrscr();                       // clear screen
                                   // display track
   for(int f=0; f<=track_length; f++) // for each furlong
      for(int r=1; r<=total*2 + 1; r++)  // for each screen row
         {
         gotoxy(f*CPF + 5, r);
         if(f==0 || f==track_length)
            cout << '\xDE';        // draw start or finish line
         else
            cout << '\xB3';        // draw furlong marker
         }
                                   // create horses
   hptr = new horse[total];        // get memory for all horses
   for(int j=0; j<total; j++)      // initialize each horse
      (hptr+j)->horse_init(this);  // with track pointer
   }
void track::track_tick()
   {
   elapsed_time += 1.75;                // update time
```

continued on next page

continued from previous page

```
    for(int j=0; j<total; j++)        // for each horse,
        (hptr+j)->horse_tick();       // update horse
    }

void track::horse::horse_tick()       // for each horse
    {                                 // display horse & number
    gotoxy( 1 + int(distance_run * CPF), 2 + horse_number*2 );
    cout << " \xDB" << horse_number << "\xDB";
    if(distance_run < ptr_track->track_length + 1.0/CPF)
        {
        if( random(3) % 3 )           // skip about 1 of 3 ticks
            distance_run += 0.2;      // advance 0.2 furlongs
        finish_time = ptr_track->elapsed_time;   // update finish time
        }
    else
        {                             // display finish time
        int mins = int(finish_time)/60;
        int secs = int(finish_time) - mins*60;
        cout << " Time=" << mins << ":" << secs;
        }
    }
//////////////////////////////////////////////////////////////////
void main()
    {
    float length;
    int nhorses;

    cout << "\nEnter track length (furlongs): ";
    cin >> length;
    cout << "\nEnter number of horses (1 to 10): ";
    cin >> nhorses;

    track t(length, nhorses);   // create track and horses

    while( !kbhit() )           // exit on keypress
        {
        t.track_tick();         // move and display all horses
        delay(500);             // wait 1/2 second
        }
    t.~track();                 // delete horses
    }
```

Because `horse` is nested within `track`, the class user, represented by `main()`, can't make the potential mistake of instantiating a `horse` object:

```
void main()
    {
    horse h;    // Error: undefined class
    ...
    }
```

This is true even though the member functions of `horse`, including the constructor, are public.

Horse Racing and Static Data

For the final example in this chapter, I'll return to a topic touched on in Chapter 4: static member data. As you may recall, static data and functions are specific to a class, not to an object. Only static functions may manipulate static data. Can I use static data in the horse racing program?

I start off the design, as with other versions of the horse racing program, by creating a `horse` class. But when I start to think about things, I realize that I don't need to make the track-related data, (track length, elapsed time, and total number of horses) into a separate class. Because static members occur only once for an entire class, I can use them to represent data and functions common to all members of the `horse` class. The track is common to all the horses, so it can be represented by static data and functions.

To modify FRIHORSE to use static data, I can take all the members that were formerly in the `track` class and make them static members of the `horse` class.

The `horse` constructor operates on each horse individually, so it's convenient to have another function, which I call `init_track()`, to initialize the various static (track-oriented) data. This is a static function because it's called only once for the entire class, not in connection with a particular `horse` object. The nonstatic member functions, which operate on each horse individually, need not be accessed from outside the class, so they are made private. Only the track-related functions, `init_track()` and `track_tick()`, require public access. (Again, read the warnings for FRIHORSE before attempting to compile STAHORSE.) Listing 9-27 shows STAHORSE.

Listing 9-27 STAHORSE

```
// stahorse.cpp
// models a horse race, uses static data for track
// (Note: Borland specific. See text.)
#include <iostream.h>
#include <dos.h>                  // for delay()
#include <conio.h>                // for kbhit()
#include <stdlib.h>               // for random()
#include <time.h>                 // for randomize()
const int CPF = 5;               // screen columns per furlong

class horse
   {
   private:
      // track characteristics (declarations only)
      static horse* hptr;         // pointer to horse memory
      static int total;           // total number of horses
      static int count;           // horses created so far
      static int track_length;    // track length in furlongs
      static float elapsed_time;  // time since start of race

      // horse characteristics
      int horse_number;           // this horse's number
      float finish_time;          // this horse's finish time
      float distance_run;         // distance since start
      // note: private horse-related member functions
      horse()                     // constructor for each horse
         {
```

continued on next page

continued from previous page

```
            horse_number = count++;      // set our horse's number
            distance_run = 0.0;          // haven't moved yet
            }
        void horse_tick();               // time tick for one horse
    public:
        static void init_track(float l, int t); // initialize track
        static void track_tick();        // time tick for entire track
        static void kill_track()         // delete all the horses
            {
            delete hptr;
            }
    };

horse* horse::hptr;                      // define static (track) vars
int horse::total;
int horse::count = 0;
int horse::track_length;
float horse::elapsed_time = 0.0;

void horse::init_track(float l, int t) // static (track) function
    {
    total = t;                           // set number of horses
    track_length = l;                    // set track length
    randomize();                         // initialize random numbers
    clrscr();                            // clear screen
                                         // display track
    for(int f=0; f<=track_length; f++)   // for each furlong
        for(int r=1; r<=total*2 + 1; r++)  // for each screen row
            {
            gotoxy(f*CPF + 5, r);
            if(f==0 || f==track_length)
                cout << '\xDE';          // draw start or finish line
            else
                cout << '\xB3';          // draw furlong marker
            }
    hptr = new horse[total];             // get memory for all horses
    }

void horse::track_tick()                 // static (track) function
    {
    elapsed_time += 1.75;                // update time

    for(int j=0; j<total; j++)           // for each horse,
        (hptr+j)->horse_tick();          // update horse
    }

void horse::horse_tick()                 // for each horse
    {                                    // display horse & number
    gotoxy( 1 + int(distance_run * CPF), 2 + horse_number*2 );
    cout << " \xDB" << horse_number << "\xDB";
    if(distance_run < track_length + 1.0/CPF)  // until finish,
        {
        if( random(3) % 3 )              // skip about 1 of 3 ticks
```

```
            distance_run += 0.2;          // advance 0.2 furlongs
        finish_time = elapsed_time;       // update finish time
        }
    else
        {                                 // display finish time
        int mins = int(finish_time)/60;
        int secs = int(finish_time) - mins*60;
        cout << " Time=" << mins << ":" << secs;
        }
    }

void main()
    {
    float length;
    int nhorses;

    cout << "\nEnter track length (furlongs): ";
    cin >> length;
    cout << "\nEnter number of horses (1 to 10): ";
    cin >> nhorses;
                                // initialize track and horses
    horse::init_track(length, nhorses);

    while( !kbhit() )           // exit on keypress
        {
        horse::track_tick();    // move and display all horses
        delay(500);             // wait 1/2 second
        }
    horse::kill_track();        // delete horses from memory
    }
```

Of the three approaches to the horse race program, FRIHORSE in Session 7, and NESHORSE and STA-HORSE in this session, which is best? The track is an entity, so it may make more sense to represent it with a class rather than with static functions in the `horse` class. Also, `horse` objects should only be created by a `track` object, so nesting `horse` inside `track` is conceptually more appropriate. Thus, NESHORSE seems to be the winner. But a slightly different situation might profit from the static data approach. Look at each programming situation individually and maybe try different approaches to see which is best.

1. When a class B is nested within a class A,
    a. member functions of B can always access the private data in A.
    b. member functions of A can always access the private data in B.
    c. every object of class A automatically contains one object of class B.
    d. the names used for B and its members are not visible outside A.
    e. class A can access class B members only if B is in the public part of A.

2. Which of the following are true?
   a. If you nest the same specification for a class **c** within both **A** and **B**, which are otherwise unrelated classes, then every object of **c**, created in **A**, is automatically accessible to **B**.
   b. If you nest a class **c** within a class **B**, which is itself nested within a class **A**, then every object of **c**, created in **B**, is automatically accessible to **A**.
   c. If you nest a class **B** within a class **A**, then within **A** you must refer to **bdata**, a member of **B**, as **A::B::bdata**.
   d. If you nest a class **B** within the public part of a class **A**, then outside of **A** (e.g., in **main()**) you must refer to the **B** class as **A::B**.
   e. If you nest a class **B** within a class **A**, then to declare that **B** is a friend of **A**, you must use the name **B::A**.

3. In the NESHORSE program, statements in **main()** can't access **horse** objects. Which of the following prevents this?
   a. The **horse** class is nested within the track **class**.
   b. The **horse** class is nested within the private part of the track **class**.
   c. The **horse** constructor is private.
   d. All **horse** objects are created in the **track** class.
   e. All **horse** objects are created in the private part of the **track** class.

4. Static data
   a. is defined within a class but declared outside the class.
   b. can be modified only by static functions.
   c. represents data common to all objects of a class.
   d. is global data that is visible to any function, including **main()**.
   e. continues to exist even if all objects of a class are destroyed.

5. In the STAHORSE program,
   a. there are no **horse** objects, which are instead represented by static data and functions.
   b. static data and functions in the **horse** class play the same role as the **track** class in the FRIHORSE example.
   c. because it's a nested class, the function **init_track()** must be accessed from **main()** using the full name **horse::init_track()**.
   d. the constructor for the **horse** class is private so horses can't be instantiated from **main()**.
   e. the **track** class is a static friend of **horse**.

EXERCISE 1

Rewrite the NESTED program so that each **alpha** object is associated with two **beta** objects, which it creates. Have these **alpha** and **beta** objects access each other's private data using pointers. Make the access possible using friends. In **main()**, create an **alpha** object.

EXERCISE 2

Rewrite the NESTED program so that class **beta** is represented by static data and functions in **alpha**.

SUMMARY: CHAPTER 9

In this chapter I've focused on two major topics: virtual functions and friends. Virtual functions are the mechanism that C++ uses to implement polymorphism. In a general sense, polymorphism means that one thing takes different forms; in C++ it means that one function call causes different functions to be executed, depending on the class of the object that made the call.

Virtual functions are used in the context of addresses of derived class objects stored in base class pointers. These pointers may be array elements or function arguments. If a member function is declared virtual in a base class, then, when the function is invoked by a base class pointer, the compiler will examine the type of object whose address is stored in the pointer, rather than the type of the pointer, to determine which function to call. This allows a very simple and intuitive way to perform a series of function calls to related objects or to create a global function that can work with objects of many related classes.

Pure virtual functions are denoted with the =0 notation. They are associated with an abstract base class, that is, a class from which no objects will be instantiated and that serves only as a common ancestor of other classes. If a class has one or more pure virtual functions, it is defined as an abstract class because the compiler will not allow objects to be instantiated from it.

A friend function is a global function (or a member function of a class) that is granted access to the nonpublic data of a class. The class grants this access by declaring the function to be a friend. Friend functions are useful in overloaded operators when the variable on the left side of an operator is not a class member. They are also useful when functional notation, rather than member access syntax (the . or -> operators), is desired for objects.

If an entire class is declared to be a friend of a second class, it has access to all the member functions and data of the second class, whether they are public or private. This provides a method for closely related classes to communicate. Actually, only objects of such classes communicate with each other; classes can't access each other's data in the abstract (unless the data is static).

A class can be nested within another class. When this happens, the inside class is known to the outside class, but is hidden from the outside world. Communication between objects of nested classes requires the same use of friends as does communication between unrelated classes.

END-OF-CHAPTER DISCUSSION

Estelle: There don't seem to be any rules for how to design object-oriented programs. How are you supposed to know whether one class should be derived from another, or should be its friend, or should not be related at all?

George: Or maybe two classes should be merged into one class, or one of the classes should be made into static data inside the other. Or we should all go back to procedural programming!

Don: I guess you learn by experience. And trial and error. You've got to experiment to get the best program design.

Estelle: There's definitely more to getting comfortable with OOP than with procedural programming.

George: But there are shortcuts. I had this revelation. I don't need to use virtual functions because I can figure out the class of an object using RTTI and then use a `switch` statement, or maybe an `else if` ladder, to figure out what function to call.

Don: That's very clever, but I think you've just defeated the whole purpose of virtual functions. You've expanded a one-statement function call into all those decisions.

Estelle: And if someone adds a new derived class or something, you'll need to add new code to your `switch` statement.

George: Oops. I see what you mean. Maybe there's something in this virtual function business after all.

Don: There's hope for you yet, George.

CHAPTER 10

STREAMS AND FILES

This chapter focuses on the C++ stream classes. I'll start off with a look at the hierarchy in which these classes are arranged and I'll summarize their important features. I'll show how to use the error-handling capabilities built into these classes. A substantial part of this chapter is devoted to showing how to perform disk file activities using C++ streams. You'll learn how to read and write data to files in a variety of ways, and how files and OOP are related. Later in the chapter, I'll introduce several other features of C++ that are related to files, including in-memory text formatting and overloading the << and >> operators to work with files. I'll finish with some character-related file activities: command-line arguments, sending data to the printer, and redirection.

SESSION 1

STREAM CLASSES

A *stream* is a general name given to a flow of data in an input/output situation. For this reason, streams in C++ are often called *iostreams*. An iostream can be represented by an object of a particular class. For example, you've already seen numerous examples of the `cin` and `cout` stream objects used for input and output.

Up to this point, I've approached stream classes and objects on an ad hoc basis, introducing just what I needed to discuss other aspects of C++. In this session, I'll be a little more systematic, focusing on stream classes, their member functions, and how they all fit together.

Advantages of Streams

Old-fashioned C programmers may wonder what advantages there are to using the stream classes for I/O instead of traditional C functions such as `printf()` and `scanf()` and—for files—`fprintf()`, `fscanf()`, and so on.

One reason is that the stream classes are less prone to errors. If you've ever used a `%d` formatting character when you should have used a `%f` in `printf()`, you'll appreciate this. There are no such formatting characters in streams, because each object already knows how to display itself. This removes a major source of program bugs.

Second, you can overload existing operators and functions, such as the insertion (`<<`) and extraction (`>>`) operators, to work with classes you create. This makes your classes work in the same way as the built-in types, which again makes programming easier and more error free (not to mention more aesthetically satisfying).

You may wonder if C++ stream I/O is important if you plan to program in an environment with a Graphics User Interface (GUI) such as Windows, where direct text output to the screen is not used. Yes, iostreams are still important because they are the best way to write data to files and to format data in memory for later use in dialog boxes and other GUI elements.

The Stream Class Hierarchy

The stream classes are arranged in a rather complex hierarchy. You don't need to know everything about this hierarchy to perform I/O, but you may find an overview helpful. Figure 10-1 shows the arrangement of the most important of these classes.

I've already made extensive use of some stream classes. The extraction operator `>>` is a member of the `istream` class, and the insertion operator `<<` is a member of the `ostream` class. Both of these classes are derived from the `ios` class. The `cout` object, representing the standard output stream, which is usually directed to the video display, is a predefined object of the `ostream_withassign` class, which is derived from the `ostream` class. Similarly, `cin` is an object of the `istream_with-assign` class, which is derived from `istream`.

The classes used for input and output to the video display and keyboard are declared in the header file IOSTREAM.H, which I routinely included in my examples in previous chapters. The classes used specifically for disk file I/O are declared in the file FSTREAM.H. Figure 10-1 shows which classes are

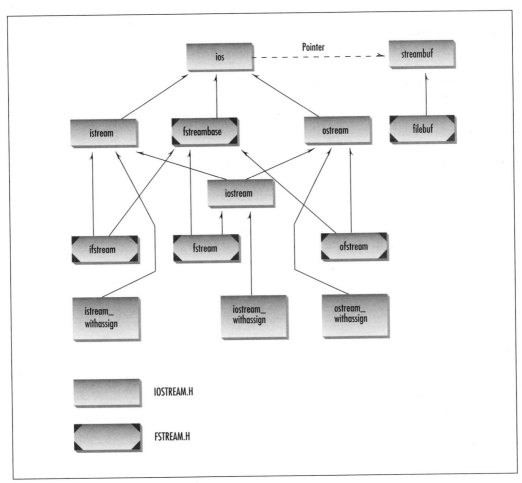

Figure 10-1   Stream class hierarchy

in each of these two header files. (Also, some manipulators are declared in IOMANIP.H and in-memory classes are declared in STRSTREA.H.) You may find it educational to print out the contents of these header files and trace the relationships among the various classes. Many questions about streams can be answered by studying their class and constant declarations. They're in your compiler's INCLUDE subdirectory.

As you can see in Figure 10-1, the `ios` class is the base class for the iostream hierarchy. It contains many constants and member functions common to input and output operations of all kinds. Some of these, such as the `showpoint` and `fixed` formatting flags, you've seen already. The `ios` class also contains a pointer to the `streambuf` class, which contains the actual memory buffer into which data is read or written and the low-level routines for handling this data. Ordinarily, you don't need to worry about the `streambuf` class, which is referenced automatically by other classes, but sometimes access to this buffer is helpful.

The `istream` and `ostream` classes are derived from `ios` and are dedicated to input and output, respectively. The `istream` class contains such member functions as `get()`, `getline()`, `read()`, and the extraction (`>>`) operators, whereas `ostream` contains `put()` and `write()` and the insertion (`<<`) operators.

The `iostream` class is derived from both `istream` and `ostream` by multiple inheritance. Classes derived from the `iostream` class can be used with devices, such as disk files, that may be opened for both input and output at the same time. Three classes—`istream_withassign`, `ostream_with-assign`, and `iostream_withassign`—are inherited from `istream`, `ostream`, and `iostream`, respectively. They add assignment operators to these classes so that `cin`, `cout`, and so on can be assigned to other streams. (You'll see what this means when I talk about redirection.)

The summary of stream classes in this session contains considerable information. You may want to skim this session now and return to it later when you need to know how to perform a particular stream-related activity.

The `ios` Class

The `ios` class is the granddaddy of all the stream classes and contains the majority of the features you need to operate C++ streams. The three most important features are the formatting flags, the error-status bits, and the file operation mode. I'll look at formatting flags and error-status bits now. I'll save the file operations mode for later, when I talk about disk files.

Formatting Flags

Formatting flags are a set of `enum` definitions in `ios`. They act as on/off switches that specify choices for various aspects of input and output format and operation. I won't provide a detailed discussion of each flag because you've already seen some of them in use and others are more or less self-explanatory. Some I'll discuss later in this chapter. Table 10-1 presents a complete list of the formatting flags.

TABLE 10-1

Flag	Meaning
skipws	Skip (ignore) whitespace on input.
left	Left adjust output [12.34].
right	Right adjust output [12.34].
internal	Use padding between sign or base indicator and number [+12.34].
dec	Convert to decimal.
oct	Convert to octal.
hex	Convert to hexadecimal.
showbase	Use base indicator on output (0 for octal, 0x for hex).
showpoint	Show decimal point on output.
uppercase	Use uppercase X, E, and hex output letters ABCDEF (the default is lowercase).
showpos	Display '+' before positive integers.

Flag	Meaning
scientific	Use exponential format on floating-point output [9.1234E2].
fixed	Use fixed format on floating-point output [912.34].
unitbuf	Flush all streams after insertion.
stdio	Flush stdout, stderror after insertion.

Table 10-1 ios *formatting flags*

There are several ways to set the formatting flags, and different flags can be set in different ways. Because they are members of the ios class, flags must usually be preceded by the name ios and the scope-resolution operator (e.g., ios::skipws). All the flags can be set using the setf() and unsetf() ios member functions. For example,

```
cout.setf(ios::left);     // left justify output text
cout >> "This text is left-justified";
cout.unsetf(ios::left);   // return to default (right justified)
```

Many formatting flags can be set using manipulators, so let's look at them now.

Manipulators

Manipulators are formatting instructions inserted directly into a stream. You've seen examples before, such as the manipulator endl, which sends a new line to the stream and flushes it:

```
cout << "To each his own." << endl;
```

I've also used the setiosflags() manipulator:

```
cout << setiosflags(ios::fixed)      // use fixed decimal point
     << setiosflags(ios::showpoint)  // always show decimal point
     << var;
```

As these examples demonstrate, manipulators come in two flavors: those that take an argument and those that don't. Table 10-2 summarizes the no-argument manipulators.

Manipulator	Purpose
ws	Turn on whitespace skipping on input.
dec	Convert to decimal.
oct	Convert to octal.
hex	Convert to hexadecimal.
endl	Insert new line and flush the output stream.
ends	Insert null character to terminate an output string.
flush	Flush the output stream.
lock	Lock file handle.
unlock	Unlock file handle.

Table 10-2 *No-argument* ios *manipulators*

You insert these manipulators directly into the stream. For example, to output `var` in hexadecimal format, you can say

```
cout << hex << var;
```

The states set by no-argument manipulators remain in effect until the stream is destroyed, so you can, for example, output many numbers in hex format with only one insertion of the `hex` manipulator.

Table 10-3 summarizes the manipulators that take arguments. You need the IOMANIP.H header file for these functions.

Manipulator	Argument	Purpose
`setw()`	field width (`int`)	Set field width for output.
`setfill()`	fill character (`int`)	Set fill character for output (default is a space).
`setprecision()`	precision (`int`)	Set precision (number of digits displayed).
`setiosflags()`	formatting flags (`long`)	Set specified flags.
`resetiosflags()`	formatting flags (`long`)	Clear specified flags.

Table 10-3 `ios` *manipulators with arguments*

Manipulators that take arguments affect only the next item in the stream. For example, if you use `setw` to set the width of the field in which one number is displayed, you'll need to use it again for the next number.

Functions

The `ios` class contains a number of functions that you can use to set the formatting flags and perform other tasks. Table 10-4 shows most of these functions, except those that deal with errors, which I'll examine in the next session.

Function	Purpose
`ch = fill();`	Return the fill character (fills unused part of field; default is space).
`fill(ch);`	Set the fill character.
`p = precision()`	Get the precision (number of digits displayed for floating point).
`precision(p);`	Set the precision.
`w = width();`	Get the current field width (in characters).
`width(w);`	Set the current field width.

Function	Purpose
`setf(flags);`	Set specified formatting flags (e.g., `ios::left`).
`unsetf(flags);`	Unset specified formatting flags.
`setf(flags, field);`	First clear field, then set flags.

Table 10-4 `ios` *functions*

These functions are called for specific stream objects using the normal dot operator. For example, to set the field width to 14, you can say

```
cout.width(14);
```

Similarly, the following statement sets the fill character to an asterisk (as for check printing):

```
cout.fill('*');
```

You can use several functions to manipulate the `ios` formatting flags directly. For example, to set left justification, use

```
cout.setf(ios::left);
```

To restore right justification, use

```
cout.unsetf(ios::left);
```

A two-argument version of `setf()` uses the second argument to reset all the flags of a particular type or *field*. Then the flag specified in the first argument is set. This makes it easier to reset the relevant flags before setting a new one. Table 10-5 shows the arrangement.

First argument: flags to set	Second argument; field to clear
`dec, oct, hex`	`basefield`
`left, right, internal`	`adjustfield`
`scientific, fixed`	`floatfield`

Table 10-5 *Two-argument version of* `setf()`

For example,

```
cout.setf(ios::left, ios::adjustfield);
```

clears all the flags dealing with text justification and then sets the `left` flag for left-justified output.

By using the techniques shown here with the formatting flags, you can usually figure out a way to format I/O not only for the keyboard and display, but, as you'll see later in this chapter, for files as well.

The `istream` **Class**

The `istream` class, which is derived from `ios`, performs input-specific activities, or *extraction*. It's easy to confuse extraction and the related output activity, *insertion*. Figure 10-2 emphasizes the difference.

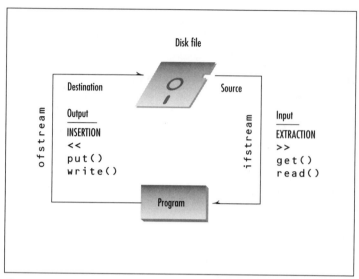

Figure 10-2   Input and output

Table 10-6 lists the functions you'll most commonly use from the `istream` class.

Function	Purpose
>>	Formatted extraction for all basic (and overloaded) types.
get(ch);	Extract one character into `ch`.
get(str)	Extract characters into array `str`, until `'\0'`.
get(str, MAX)	Extract up to `MAX` characters into array.
get(str, DELIM)	Extract characters into array `str` until specified delimiter (typically `'\n'`). Leave delimiting char in stream.
get(str, MAX, DELIM)	Extract characters into array `str` until `MAX` characters or the `DELIM` character. Leave delimiting char in stream.
getline(str, MAX, DELIM)	Extract characters into array `str` until `MAX` characters or the `DELIM` character. Extract delimiting character.
putback(ch)	Insert last character read back into input stream.
ignore(MAX, DELIM)	Extract and discard up to `MAX` characters until (and including) the specified delimiter (typically `'\n'`).
peek(ch)	Read one character, leave it in stream.

Function	Purpose
count = gcount()	Return number of characters read by a (immediately preceding) call to get(), getline(), or read().
read(str, MAX)	For files. Extract up to MAX characters into str until EOF.
seekg(position)	Sets distance (in bytes) of file pointer from start of file.
seekg(position, seek_dir)	Sets distance (in bytes) of file pointer from specified place in file: seek_dir can be ios::beg, ios::cur, ios::end.
position = tellg(pos)	Return position (in bytes) of file pointer from start of file.

Table 10-6 istream *functions*

You've seen some of these functions, such as get(), before. Most of them operate on the cin object, representing the keyboard as well as disk files. However, the last four deal specifically with disk files. You'll see how they work later in this chapter.

The ostream **Class**

The ostream class handles output or insertion activities. Table 10-7 shows the most commonly used member functions of this class.

Function	Purpose
<<	Formatted insertion for all basic (and overloaded) types.
put(ch)	Insert character ch into stream.
flush()	Flush buffer contents and insert new line.
write(str, SIZE)	Insert SIZE characters from array str into file.
seekp(position)	Sets distance in bytes of file pointer from start of file.
seekp(position, seek_dir)	Set distance in bytes of file pointer from specified place in file. seek_dir can be ios::beg, ios::cur, or ios::end.
position = tellp()	Return position of file pointer, in bytes.

Table 10-7 ostream *functions*

The last four functions deal specifically with disk files.

The `iostream` and the `_withassign` Classes

The `iostream` class, which is derived from both `istream` and `ostream`, acts only as a base class from which other classes, specifically `iostream_withassign`, can be derived. It has no functions of its own (except constructors and destructors). Classes derived from `iostream` can perform both input and output.

There are three `_withassign` classes:

`istream_withassign,` derived from `istream`
`ostream_withassign,`   derived from `ostream`
`iostream_withassign,` derived from `iostream`

These `_withassign` classes are much like those they're derived from except they include overloaded assignment operators so their objects can be copied.

Why do you need separate copyable and uncopyable stream classes? In general, it's not a good idea to copy stream class objects. Each such object is associated with a particular `streambuf` object, which includes an area in memory to hold the object's actual data. If you copy the stream object, it causes confusion if you also copy the `streambuf` object. However, in a few cases it's important to be able to copy a stream object, as in the case of redirection of the predefined objects `cout` and `cin`. (I'll discuss redirection later in this chapter.)

Accordingly, the `istream`, `ostream`, and `iostream` classes are made uncopyable (by making their overloaded copy constructors and assignment operators private), whereas the `_withassign` classes derived from them can be copied.

Predefined Stream Objects

I've already made extensive use of two predefined stream objects that are derived from the `_with-assign` classes: `cin` and `cout`. These are normally connected to the keyboard and display, respectively. The two other predefined objects are `cerr` and `clog`. Table 10-8 lists all four.

Name	Class	Used for
`cin`	`istream_withassign`	Keyboard input
`cout`	`ostream_withassign`	Normal screen output
`cerr`	`ostream_withassign`	Error output
`clog`	`ostream_withassign`	Log output

Table 10-8   *Predefined stream objects*

The `cerr` object is often used for error messages and program diagnostics. Output sent to `cerr` is displayed immediately, rather than being buffered, as output sent to `cout` is. Also, output to `cerr` cannot be redirected. For these reasons, you have a better chance of seeing a final output message from `cerr` if your program dies prematurely. Another object, `clog`, is similar to `cerr` in that it is not redirected, but its output is buffered, whereas `cerr`'s is not.

1. Which of the following are advantages of C++ iostreams over the old C language `printf()` and `scanf()` approach?
   a. Most people are already familiar with `printf()` and `scanf()`.
   b. Iostreams allow the same interface for user-created classes as for built-in types.
   c. With iostreams, you don't need to learn weird formatting codes such as `%d` and `%f`.
   d. With iostreams, errors are more likely to be caught at compile time rather than at runtime.
   e. You don't need to specify the type of data being input or output because the compiler can figure it out.

2. The iostream class hierarchy
   a. has no user-accessible member functions.
   b. has as a base class the `iostream` class.
   c. can handle the keyboard and display, but not files.
   d. relates various classes from which objects, representing data streams, can be instantiated.
   e. uses multiple inheritance.

3. `ios` formatting flags
   a. work only with output.
   b. can be set using manipulators.
   c. can be set using `ios` member functions.
   d. include `fill()`.
   e. include `fixed`.

4. Manipulators
   a. include `endl`.
   b. include `fill()`.
   c. are inserted directly into a stream.
   d. are called with the dot operator, like any member function.
   e. cannot take arguments.

5. The `ostream` class
   a. is used to instantiate the `cout` object.
   b. is used to instantiate the `cin` object.
   c. is used to derive the `ostream_withassign` class.
   d. contains a member function that inserts a character into a stream.
   e. is directly derived from the `iostream` class.

Due to its theoretical nature, this session contains no exercises.

STREAM ERRORS

So far, I've used a rather straightforward approach to input and output in this book, using statements of the form

```
cout << "Good morning";
```

and

```
cin >> var;
```

However, as you may have discovered, this approach assumes that nothing will go wrong during the I/O process. This isn't always the case, especially on input. What happens if a user enters the string "nine" instead of the integer 9, or pushes (ENTER) without entering anything? What happens if there's a hardware failure? I'll explore such problems in this session. Many of the techniques you'll see here are applicable to file I/O as well.

Error-Status Bits

The stream error-status bits are an `ios enum` member that report errors that occurred in an input or output operation. They're summarized in Table 10-9.

Name	Meaning
goodbit	No errors (no bits set, value = 0).
eofbit	Reached end of file.
failbit	Operation failed (user error, premature EOF).
badbit	Invalid operation (no associated `streambuf`).
hardfail	Unrecoverable error.

Table 10-9   *Error-status bits*

Figure 10-3 shows the position of these bits in the error-status byte.

Various `ios` functions can be used to read (and even set) these error bits, as summarized in Table 10-10.

Function	Purpose
int = eof();	Returns true if EOF bit set.
int = fail();	Returns true if fail bit or bad bit or hard-fail bit set.
int = bad();	Returns true if bad bit or hard-fail bit set.
int = good();	Returns true if everything OK; no bits set.
clear(int=0);	With no argument, clears all error bits; otherwise sets specified bits, as in `clear(ios::failbit)`.

Table 10-10   *Functions for error bits*

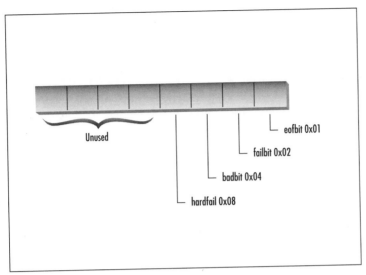

Figure 10-3   Error-status byte

Inputting Numbers

Let's see how to handle errors when inputting numbers. This approach applies to numbers read both from the keyboard and from disk, as you'll see later. The idea is to check the value of goodbit, signal an error if it's not true, and give the user another chance to enter the correct input.

```
while(1)                                     // cycle until input OK
   {
   cout << "\nEnter an integer: ";
   cin >> i;
   if( cin.good() )                          // if no errors
      {
      cin.ignore(10, '\n');                  // remove newline
      break;                                 // exit loop
      }
   cin.clear();                              // clear the error bits
   cout << "Incorrect input";
   cin.ignore(10, '\n');                     // remove newline
   }
cout << "integer is " << i;                  // error-free integer
```

The most common error this scheme detects when reading keyboard input is the user typing nondigits (such as "nine" instead of 9). This causes the failbit to be set. However, it also detects system-related failures that are more common with disk files.

Floating-point numbers (float, double, and long double) can be analyzed for errors in the same way as integers.

Too Many Characters

Too many characters sounds like a difficulty experienced by movie directors, but extra characters can also present a problem when reading from input streams. This is especially true when there are errors. Typically, extra characters are left in the input stream after the input is supposedly completed. They are then passed along to the next input operation even though they are not intended for it. Often a new line remains behind, but sometimes other characters are left over as well. To get rid of these extraneous characters, the `ignore(MAX, DELIM)` member function of `istream` is used. It reads and throws away up to `MAX` characters, including the specified delimiter character. In the example, the line

```
cin.ignore(10, '\n');
```

causes `cin` to read up to 10 characters, including the (`'\n'`), and removes them from the input.

No-Input Input

Whitespace characters, such as [TAB], [SPACE] and `'\n'`, are normally ignored (skipped) when inputting numbers. This can have some undesirable side effects. For example, users, prompted to enter a number, may simply press the [ENTER] key without typing any digits. (Perhaps they think that this will enter 0, or perhaps they are simply confused.) In the code shown above, as well as the simple statement

```
cin >> i;
```

pressing [ENTER] causes the cursor to drop down to the next line while the stream continues to wait for the number. What's wrong with the cursor dropping to the next line? First, inexperienced users, seeing no acknowledgment when they press [ENTER], may assume the computer is broken. Second, pressing [ENTER] repeatedly normally causes the cursor to drop lower and lower until the entire screen begins to scroll upward. This is all right in teletype-style interaction where the program and the user simply type at each other. In text-based graphics programs, however, scrolling the screen disarranges and eventually obliterates the display.

Thus it's important to be able to tell the input stream *not* to ignore whitespace. This is done by clearing the `skipws` flag:

```
cout << "\nEnter an integer: ";
cin.unsetf(ios::skipws);           // don't ignore whitespace
cin >> i;
if( cin.good() )
   {
   // no error
   }
// error
```

Now if the user types [ENTER] without any digits, `failbit` will be set and an error will be generated. The program can then tell the user what to do or reposition the cursor so the screen does not scroll.

Inputting Strings and Characters

The user can't really make any mistakes inputting strings and characters because all input, even numbers, can be interpreted as a string. However, if coming from a disk file, characters and strings should still be checked for errors in case an EOF or something worse is encountered. Unlike the situation with numbers, you often do want to ignore whitespace when inputting strings and characters.

Error-Free Distances

Let's look at a program in which user input to the English `Distance` class is checked for errors. This program accepts `Distance` values in feet and inches from the user and displays them. If the user commits an entry error, the program rejects the input with an appropriate explanation to the user and prompts for new input.

The program is very simple except that the member function `getdist()` has been expanded to handle errors. Parts of this new code follow the approach of the fragment shown previously. I've also added some statements to ensure that the user does not enter a floating-point number for feet. This is important because, whereas the feet value is an integer, the inches value is floating point, and the user could easily become confused.

Ordinarily, if it's expecting an integer, the extraction operator simply terminates without signaling an error when it sees a decimal point. The program wants to know about such an error, so it reads the feet value as a string instead of an `int`. It then examines the string with a homemade function `isint()`, which returns true if the string proves to be an `int`. To pass the `int` test, the string must contain only digits and they must evaluate to a number between -32,768 and 32,767 (the range of type `int`). If the string passes the `int` test, the program converts it to an actual `int` with the library function `atoi()`.

The inches value is an integer. The program checks its range, which should be 0 or greater and less than 12.0. The program also checks it for `ios` error bits. Most commonly, the fail bit will be set because the user typed nondigits instead of an integer. Listing 10-1 shows ENGLERR.

Listing 10-1 ENGLERR

```
// englerr.cpp
// input checking with English Distance class
#include <iostream.h>
#include <string.h>                 // for strchr()
#include <stdlib.h>                 // for atoi()

int isint(char*);                   // prototype
const int IGN = 10;                 // characters to ignore

class Distance                      // English Distance class
    {
    private:
        int feet;
        float inches;
    public:
```

continued on next page

continued from previous page

```
      Distance()                    // constructor (no args)
         { feet = 0; inches = 0.0; }
      Distance(int ft, float in)    // constructor (two args)
         { feet = ft; inches = in; }
      void showdist()               // display distance
         { cout << feet << "\'-" << inches << '\"'; }
      void getdist();               // get length from user
   };

void Distance::getdist()            // get length from user
   {
   char instr[80];                  // for input string

   while(1)                         // cycle until feet are right
      {
      cout << "\n\nEnter feet: ";
      cin.unsetf(ios::skipws);      // do not skip white space
      cin >> instr;                 // get feet as a string
      if( isint(instr) )            // is it an integer?
         {                          // yes
         cin.ignore(IGN, '\n');     // eat chars, including newline
         feet = atoi(instr);        // convert to integer
         break;                     // break out of 'while'
         }                          // no, not an integer
      cin.ignore(IGN, '\n');        // eat chars, including newline
      cout << "Feet must be an integer\n";  // start again
      }  // end while feet

   while(1)                         // cycle until inches are right
      {
      cout << "Enter inches: ";
      cin.unsetf(ios::skipws);      // do not skip white space
      cin >> inches;                // get inches (type float)
      if(inches>=12.0 || inches<0.0)
         {
         cout << "Inches must be between 0.0 and 11.99\n";
         cin.clear(ios::failbit);   // "artificially" set fail bit
         }
      if( cin.good() )              // check for cin failure
         {                          // (most commonly a non-digit)
         cin.ignore(IGN, '\n');     // eat the newline
         break;                     // input is OK, exit 'while'
         }
      cin.clear();                  // error; clear the error state
      cin.ignore(IGN, '\n');        // eat chars, including newline
      cout << "Incorrect inches input\n";  // start again
      }  // end while inches
   }
```

```
int isint(char* str)                 // return true if the string
   {                                  //   represents type int
   int slen = strlen(str);            // get length
   if( slen==0 || slen > 5)           // if no input, or too long
      return 0;                       // not an int
   for(int j=0; j<slen; j++)          // check each character
                                      // if not digit or minus
      if( (str[j] < '0' || str[j] > '9') && str[j] != '-' )
         return 0;                    // string is not an int
   long n = atol(str);                // convert to long int
   if( n< -32768L || n>32767L )       // is it out of int range?
      return 0;                       // if so, not an int
   return 1;                          // it is an int
   }

void main()
   {
   Distance d;                        // make a Distance object
   char ans;
   do
      {
      d.getdist();                    // get its value from user
      cout << "\nDistance = ";
      d.showdist();                   // display it
      cout << "\nDo another (y/n)? ";
      cin >> ans;
      cin.ignore(IGN, '\n');          // eat chars, including newline
      } while(ans != 'n');            // cycle until 'n'
   }
```

I've used another dodge here: setting an error-state flag manually. I do this because I want to ensure that the inches value is greater than 0 but less than 12.0. If it isn't, I turn on the **failbit** with the statement

```
cin.clear(ios::failbit);   // set failbit
```

When the program checks for errors with **cin.good()**, it will find the **failbit** set and signal that the input is incorrect.

All-Character Input

Another approach to error handling is to read all input, even numbers, as strings. Your code can then parse the string, character by character, to determine whether the user has typed something reasonable. If so, it can be converted to the appropriate kind of number. The details of this approach depend on the specific input you expect, so I won't show an example; if you're trying to write the most bullet-proof code possible, this is probably the best way to go.

Of course, even when reading characters, you should still check for errors using the error-status bits.

QUIZ 2

1. The error-status bits
   a. can be read but not altered by user code.
   b. can be used to determine if end-of-file has occurred.
   c. are part of the `iostream` class.
   d. can be checked using functions such as `fail()` and `bad()`.
   e. are all set if `good()` returns false.

2. The `ignore(MAX, DELIM)` member function of `istream`
   a. always reads exactly `MAX` characters.
   b. reads up to `MAX` characters or until a `DELIM` character is encountered, whichever comes first.
   c. is used to format output.
   d. causes the same effect as setting the `ios::skipws` flag.
   e. gets rid of unwanted input.

3. The `clear()` function
   a. is a friend of the `iostream` class.
   b. is a member of the `iostream` class.
   c. can be used to set the `goodbit`.
   d. can be used to clear all the error bits at once.
   e. can be used to clear the entire display screen.

4. In the ENGLERR program, the user cannot enter
   a. a floating-point value for feet.
   b. an integer value for inches.
   c. a value for feet that's greater than 32,767.
   d. an inches value greater than or equal to 11.99.
   e. letters in place of numbers.

5. The safest way to handle user input is
   a. to convert numbers to character strings after reading them.
   b. to not worry about the error-status bits.
   c. to handle things exactly as in the ENGLERR program.
   d. to read all input as strings of characters and then to analyze them.
   e. to read only integers.

EXERCISE 1

Rewrite `get()` the member function of the `airtime` class in the ADDAIR program (from Chapter 6, Session 1) so that it incorporates the same kind of input error checking that is found in ENGLERR. Notify the user if the `hours` value is not between 0 and 23 and the `minutes` value is not between 0 and 59.

EXERCISE 2

Rewrite the `get()` function referred to in Exercise 1 so user input is read as a string and then is parsed and converted into hours and minutes values.

SESSION 3

DISK FILE I/O WITH STREAMS

Disk files require a different set of classes than files used with the keyboard and screen. These are `ifstream` for input, `fstream` for input and output, and `ofstream` for output. Objects of these classes can be associated with disk files and you can use their member functions to read and write to the files.

Referring back to Figure 10-1, you can see that `ifstream` is derived from `istream`, `fstream` is derived from `iostream`, and `ofstream` is derived from `ostream`. These ancestor classes are in turn derived from `ios`. Thus the file-oriented classes derive many of their member functions from more general classes. The file-oriented classes are also derived, by multiple inheritance, from the `fstreambase` class. This class contains an object of class `filebuf`, which is a file-oriented buffer with associated member functions derived from the more general `streambuf` class. For many file-based operations, `streambuf` is accessed automatically, but you'll see cases where you can access it directly as well.

The `ifstream`, `ofstream`, and `fstream` classes are declared in the FSTREAM.H file. This file also includes the IOSTREAM.H header file, so there is no need to include it explicitly; FSTREAM.H takes care of all stream I/O.

C programmers will note that the approach to disk I/O used in C++ is quite different from that used in C. The old C functions, such as `fread()` and `fwrite()`, will work in C++, but they are not well suited to the object-oriented environment. As with `printf()` and `scanf()`, they aren't extensible, whereas you can extend the C++ iostream approach to work with your own classes. Incidentally, be careful about mixing the old C functions with C++ streams. They don't always work together gracefully (although there are ways to make them cooperate).

Formatted File I/O

There are two basic kinds of disk I/O in C++: formatted and binary. In formatted I/O, numbers are stored on disk as a series of characters. Thus 6.02, rather than being stored as a 4-byte type `float` or an 8-byte type `double`, is stored as the characters `'6'`, `'.'`, `'0'`, and `'2'`. This can be inefficient for numbers with many digits, but it's appropriate in many situations and easy to implement. Characters and strings are stored more or less normally.

Writing Data

The following program writes a character, an integer, a type double, and two strings to a disk file called FDATA.TXT. There is no output to the screen. Listing 10-2 shows FORMATO.

Listing 10-2 FORMATO

```
// formato.cpp
// writes formatted output to a file, using <<

#include <fstream.h>              // for file I/O

void main()
   {
   char ch = 'x';                 // character
   int j = 77;                    // integer
   double d = 6.02;               // floating point
   char str1[] = "Kafka";         // strings
   char str2[] = "Proust";        // (no embedded spaces)

   ofstream outfile("fdata.txt"); // create ofstream object

   outfile << ch                  // insert (write) data
           << j
           << ' '                 // needs space between numbers
           << d
           << str1
           << ' '                 // needs space between strings
           << str2;
   }
```

Here the program defines an object called outfile to be a member of the ofstream class. At the same time, it initializes the object to the file name FDATA.TXT. This initialization sets aside various resources for the file, and accesses or *opens* the file of that name on the disk. If the file doesn't exist, it is created. If it does exist, it is truncated and the new data replaces the old. The outfile object acts much as cout did in previous programs, so the insertion operator (<<) is used to output variables of any basic type to the file. This works because the insertion operator is appropriately overloaded in ostream, from which ofstream is derived.

When the program terminates, the outfile object goes out of scope. This calls its destructor, which closes the file, so you don't need to close the file explicitly.

There are several potential formatting glitches. First, you must separate numbers (such as 77 and 6.02) with nonnumeric characters. Because numbers are stored as a sequence of characters rather than as a fixed-length field, this is the only way the extraction operator will know, when the data is read back from the file, where one number stops and the next one begins. Second, strings must be separated with whitespace for the same reason. This implies that strings cannot contain imbedded blanks. In this example, I use the space character (" ") for both kinds of delimiters. Characters need no delimiters, because they have a fixed length.

You can verify that FORMATO has indeed written the data by examining the FDATA.TXT file with any text-based editor.

Reading Data

Any program can read the file generated by FORMATO by using an ifstream object that is initialized to the name of the file. The file is automatically opened when the object is created. The program can then read from it using the extraction (>>) operator.

Listing 10-3 shows the FORMATI program, which reads the data back in from the FDATA.TXT file.

Listing 10-3 FORMATI

```
// formati.cpp
// reads formatted output from a file, using >>

#include <fstream.h>
const int MAX = 80;

void main()
    {
    char ch;                        // empty variables
    int j;
    double d;
    char str1[MAX];
    char str2[MAX];

    ifstream infile("fdata.txt");   // create ifstream object
                                    // extract (read) data from it
    infile >> ch >> j >> d >> str1 >> str2;

    cout << ch << endl              // display the data
         << j << endl
         << d << endl
         << str1 << endl
         << str2 << endl;
    }
```

Here the ifstream object, which I name infile, acts much the way cin did in previous programs. Provided I have formatted the data correctly when inserting it into the file, there's no trouble extracting it, storing it in the appropriate variables, and displaying their contents. The program's output looks like this:

```
x
77
6.02
Kafka
Proust
```

Note that the numbers are converted back to their binary representations for storage in the program. That is, the 77 is stored in the variable j as a type int, not as two characters, and the 6.02 is stored as a double.

Strings with Embedded Blanks

The technique of the last examples won't work with strings containing embedded blanks. To handle such strings, you need to write a specific delimiter character after each one and use the getline() function, rather than the extraction operator, to read them in. The next program, OLINE (Listing 10-4), outputs some strings with blanks embedded in them.

Listing 10-4 OLINE

```
// oline.cpp
// file output with strings
#include <fstream.h>              // for file functions

void main()
    {
```

continued on next page

continued from previous page

```
   ofstream outfile("TEST.TXT");       // create file for output
                                       // send text to file
   outfile << "I fear thee, ancient Mariner!\n";
   outfile << "I fear thy skinny hand\n";
   outfile << "And thou art long, and lank, and brown,\n";
   outfile << "As is the ribbed sea sand.\n";
   }
```

When you run the program, the lines of text (from Samuel Taylor Coleridge's *The Rime of the Ancient Mariner*) are written to a file. Each one is specifically terminated with a newline ('\n') character.

To extract the strings from the file, the program creates an `ifstream` and reads from it one line at a time using the `getline()` function, which is a member of `istream`. This function reads characters, including whitespace, until it encounters the '\n' character and places the resulting string in the buffer supplied as an argument. The maximum size of the buffer is given as the second argument. The contents of the buffer are displayed after each line. Listing 10-5 shows ILINE.

Listing 10-5 ILINE

```
// iline.cpp
// file input with strings
#include <fstream.h>                   // for file functions

void main()
   {
   const int MAX = 80;                 // size of buffer
   char buffer[MAX];                   // character buffer
   ifstream infile("TEST.TXT");        // create file for input
   while( infile )                     // until end-of-file
      {
      infile.getline(buffer, MAX);     // read a line of text
      cout << buffer;                  // display it
      }
   }
```

The output of ILINE to the screen is the same as the data written to the TEST.TXT file by OLINE: the four-line Coleridge stanza. The program has no way of knowing in advance how many strings are in the file, so it continues to read one string at a time until it encounters an EOF. Incidentally, don't use this program to read random text files. It requires all the text lines to terminate with the '\n' character, and if you encounter a file in which this is not the case, the program may hang.

Detecting End-of-File

As you have seen, objects derived from `ios` contain error-status bits that can be checked to determine the results of operations. When you read a file little by little, as we do in OLINE, you will eventually encounter an end-of-file condition. The EOF is a signal sent to the program from the hardware when there is no more data to read. In ILINE, I could have used the following construction to check for this:

```
while( !infile.eof() )    // until eof encountered
```

However, checking specifically for an `eofbit` means that I won't detect the other error bits, such as the `failbit` and `badbit`, which may also occur, although more rarely. To do this, I could change the loop condition:

```
while( infile.good() )    // until any error encountered
```

But even more simply, I can test the stream directly, as I do in OLINE:

```
while( infile )              // until any error encountered
```

Any stream object, such as `infile`, has a value that can be tested for the usual error conditions, including EOF. If any such condition is true, the object returns a zero value. If everything is going well, the object returns a nonzero value. This value is actually a pointer, but the "address" returned has no significance except to be tested for a zero or nonzero value.

Character I/O

The `put()` and `get()` functions, which are members of `ostream` and `istream`, respectively, can be used to output and input single characters. Listing 10-6 shows, OCHAR, which outputs a string one character at a time.

Listing 10-6 OCHAR

```
// ochar.cpp
// file output with characters
#include <fstream.h>            // for file functions
#include <string.h>             // for strlen()

void main()
    {
    char str[] = "Time is a great teacher, but unfortunately "
             "it kills all its pupils.  Berlioz";

    ofstream outfile("TEST.TXT");    // create file for output
    for(int j=0; j<strlen(str); j++)  // for each character,
        outfile.put(str[j]);         // write it to file
    }
```

In this program, an `ofstream` object is created as it was in OLINE. The length of the string is found using the `strlen()` function and the characters are output using `put()` in a `for` loop. The aphorism by Hector Berlioz (a 19th-century composer of operas and program music) is written to the file TEST.TXT. I can read this file back in and display it using the ICHAR program (Listing 10-7).

Listing 10-7 ICHAR

```
// ichar.cpp
// file input with characters
#include <fstream.h>            // for file functions

void main()
    {
    char ch;                        // character to read
    ifstream infile("TEST.TXT");    // create file for input
    while( infile )                 // read until EOF
        {
        infile.get(ch);             // read character
```

continued on next page

continued from previous page

```
        cout << ch;                    // display it
        }
    }
```

This program uses the `get()` function and continues reading until the EOF is reached. Each character read from the file is displayed using `cout`, so the entire aphorism appears on the screen.

Direct Access to the streambuf Object

Another approach to reading characters from a file is the `rdbuf()` function, a member of the `ios` class. This function returns a pointer to the `streambuf` (or `filebuf`) object associated with the stream object. This object contains a buffer that holds the characters read from the stream so you can use the pointer to it as a data object in its own right. Listing 10-8 shows ICHAR2.

Listing 10-8 ICHAR2

```
// ichar2.cpp
// file input with characters
#include <fstream.h>                   // for file functions

void main()
    {
    ifstream infile("TEST.TXT");       // create file for input

    cout << infile.rdbuf();            // send its buffer to cout
    }
```

This program has the same effect as ICHAR. It also takes the prize for the shortest file-oriented program.

Binary I/O

You can write a few numbers to disk using formatted I/O, but if you're storing a large amount of numerical data, it's more efficient to use binary I/O in which numbers are stored as they are in the computer's RAM memory rather than as strings of characters. In binary I/O an integer is always stored in 2 bytes, whereas its text version might be 12345, requiring 5 bytes. Similarly, a `float` is always stored in 4 bytes, whereas its formatted version might be 6.02314e13, requiring 10 bytes.

The next example shows how an array of integers is written to disk and then read back into memory using binary format. I use two new functions: `write()`, a member of `ofstream`, and `read()`, a member of `ifstream`. These functions think about data in terms of bytes (type `char`). They don't care how the data is formatted, they simply transfer a buffer full of bytes from and to a disk file. The parameters to `write()` and `read()` are the address of the data buffer and its length. The address must be cast to type `char`, and the length is the length in bytes (characters), *not* the number of data items in the buffer. Listing 10-9 shows BINIO.

Listing 10-9 BINIO

```
// binio.cpp
// binary input and output with integers

#include <fstream.h>                   // for file streams

const int MAX = 100;                   // number of ints
```

```
int buff[MAX];                        // buffer for integers

void main()
   {
   int j;
   for(j=0; j<MAX; j++)               // fill buffer with data
      buff[j] = j;                    // (0, 1, 2, ...)
                                      // create output stream
   ofstream os("edata.dat", ios::binary);
                                      // write to it
   os.write( (char*)buff, MAX*sizeof(int) );
   os.close();                        // must close it

   for(j=0; j<MAX; j++)               // erase buffer
      buff[j] = 0;
                                      // create input stream
   ifstream is("edata.dat", ios::binary);
                                      // read from it
   is.read( (char*)buff, MAX*sizeof(int) );

   for(j=0; j<MAX; j++)               // check data
      if( buff[j] != j )
         { cerr << "\nData is incorrect"; return; }
   cout << "\nData is correct";
   }
```

You must use the `ios::binary` argument in the second paramter to `write()` and `read()` when working with binary data. This is because the default, text mode, takes some liberties with the data. For example, in text mode, the `'\n'` character is expanded into 2 bytes—a carriage return and a line-feed—before being stored to disk. This makes a formatted text file more readable for simple text editors, but causes confusion when applied to binary data because every byte that happens to have the ASCII value 10 is translated into 2 bytes.

So far in the examples, there has been no need to close streams explicitly because they are closed automatically when they go out of scope; this invokes their destructors and closes the associated file. However, in BINIO, because both the output stream `os` and the input stream `is` are associated with the same file, EDATA.DAT, the first stream must be closed before the second is opened. I use the `close()` member function for this.

Object I/O

Because C++ is an object-oriented language, it's reasonable to wonder how objects can be written to and read from disk. The next examples show the process. The `person` class, used in several previous examples (e.g., the VIRTPERS program in Chapter 9, Session 2) supplies the objects.

Writing an Object to Disk

When writing an object, you generally want to use binary mode. This writes the same bit configuration to disk that was stored in memory and ensures that numerical data contained in objects is handled properly. Listing 10-10 shows OPERS, which asks the user for information about an object of class `person` and then writes this object to the disk file PERSON.DAT.

Listing 10-10 OPERS

```
// opers.cpp
// saves person object to disk
#include <fstream.h>                      // for file streams

class person                             // class of persons
    {
    protected:
        char name[40];                   // person's name
        int age;                         // person's age
    public:
        void getData(void)               // get person's data
            {
            cout << "Enter name: "; cin >> name;
            cout << "Enter age: "; cin >> age;
            }
    };

void main(void)
    {
    person pers;                         // create a person
    pers.getData();                      // get data for person
                                         // create ofstream object
    ofstream outfile("PERSON.DAT", ios::binary);
    outfile.write( (char*)&pers, sizeof(pers) );   // write to it
    }
```

The getData() member function of person is called to prompt the user for information, which it places in the pers object. Here's some sample interaction:

```
Enter name: Coleridge
Enter age: 62
```

The contents of the pers object are then written to disk using the write() function. I use the sizeof operator to find the size of the pers object.

Reading an Object from Disk

Reading an object back from the PERSON.DAT file requires the read() member function. Listing 10-11 shows IPERS.

Listing 10-11 IPERS

```
// ipers.cpp
// reads person object from disk
#include <fstream.h>                      // for file streams

class person                             // class of persons
    {
    protected:
        char name[40];                   // person's name
        int age;                         // person's age
```

```
    public:
       void showData(void)              // display person's data
          {
          cout << "\n    Name: " << name;
          cout << "\n    Age: " << age;
          }
    };

void main(void)
    {
    person pers;                         // create person variable
    ifstream infile("PERSON.DAT", ios::binary); // create stream
    infile.read( (char*)&pers, sizeof(pers) );  // read stream
    pers.showData();                     // display person
    }
```

The output from IPERS reflects whatever data the OPERS program placed in the PERSON.DAT file:

```
Name: Coleridge
Age: 62
```

Compatible Data Structures

To work correctly, programs that read and write objects to files, as do OPERS and IPERS, must be talking about the same class of objects. Objects of class `person` in these programs are exactly 42 bytes long, with the first 40 occupied by a string representing the person's name and the last 2 containing an `int` representing the person's age. If two programs thought the name field was a different length, for example, neither could accurately read a file generated by the other.

Notice, however, that although the `person` classes in OPERS and IPERS have the same data, they may have different member functions. The first includes the single function `getData()`, whereas the second has only `showData()`. It doesn't matter what member functions you use, because members functions are not written to disk along with the object's data. The data must have the same format, but inconsistencies in the member functions have no effect. This is true only in simple classes that don't use virtual functions.

If you read and write objects of derived classes to a file, you must be even more careful. Objects of derived classes that use virtual functions include the `vptr` (discussed in Chapter 9, Session 1). This pointer holds the address of the table of virtual functions used in the class. When you write an object to disk, this number is written along with the object's other data. If you change a class's member functions, this number changes as well. If you write an object of one class to a file and then read it back into an object of a class that has identical data but different member functions, you'll encounter big trouble if you try to use virtual functions on the object. The moral: Make sure a class that reads an object is *identical* to the class that wrote it.

I/O with Multiple Objects

The OPERS and IPERS programs wrote and read only one object at a time. The next example opens a file and writes as many objects as the user wants. Then it reads and displays the entire contents of the file. Listing 10-12 shows DISKFUN.

Listing 10-12 DISKFUN

```cpp
// diskfun.cpp
// reads and writes several objects to disk
#include <fstream.h>                    // for file streams

class person                            // class of persons
    {
    protected:
        char name[40];                  // person's name
        int age;                        // person's age
    public:
        void getData(void)              // get person's data
            {
            cout << "\n   Enter name: "; cin >> name;
            cout << "   Enter age: "; cin >> age;
            }
        void showData(void)             // display person's data
            {
            cout << "\n   Name: " << name;
            cout << "\n   Age: " << age;
            }
    };

void main(void)
    {
    char ch;
    person pers;                        // create person object
    fstream file;                       // create input/output file
                                        // open for append
    file.open("PERSON.DAT", ios::app | ios::out
                                | ios::in | ios::binary );

    do                                  // data from user to file
        {
        cout << "\nEnter person's data:";
        pers.getData();                 // get one person's data
                                        // write to file
        file.write( (char*)&pers, sizeof(pers) );
        cout << "Enter another person (y/n)? ";
        cin >> ch;
        }
    while(ch=='y');                     // quit on 'n'

    file.seekg(0);                      // reset to start of file
                                        // read first person
    file.read( (char*)&pers, sizeof(pers) );
    while( !file.eof() )                // quit on EOF
        {
```

```
        cout << "\nPerson:";                // display person
        pers.showData();
        file.read( (char*)&pers, sizeof(pers) );  // read another
    }                                        // person
}
```

Here's some sample interaction with DISKFUN. The output shown assumes that the program has been run before and that two **person** objects have already been written to the file.

```
Enter person's data:
    Enter name: McKinley
    Enter age: 22
Enter another person (y/n)? n

Person:
    Name: Whitney
    Age: 20
Person:
    Name: Rainier
    Age 21
Person:
    Name: McKinley
    Age: 22
```

One additional object is added to the file and the entire contents, consisting of three objects, are then displayed.

The fstream *Class*

So far in this chapter, the file objects I created were for either input or output. In DISKFUN, I want to create a file that can be used for both input and output. This requires an object of the **fstream** class, which is derived from **iostream**, which is derived from both **istream** and **ostream**, so it can handle both input and output.

The open() *Function*

In previous examples, I created a file object and initialized it in the same statement:

```
ofstream outfile("TEST.TXT");
```

In DISKFUN, I use a different approach: I create the file in one statement and open it in another using the **open()** function, which is a member of the **fstream** class. This is a useful approach in situations where the open may fail. You can create a stream object once and then try repeatedly to open it without the overhead of creating a new stream object each time.

The Mode Bits

You've seen the mode bit **ios::binary** before. In the **open()** function, I include several new mode bits. The mode bits, defined in **ios**, specify various aspects of how a stream object will be opened. Table 10-11 shows the possibilities.

Mode Bit	Result
in	Open for reading (default for *ifstream*).
out	Open for writing (default for *ofstream*).
ate	Start reading or writing at end-of-file (*AT End*).
app	Start writing at end-of-file (*APPend*).
trunc	Truncate file to zero length if it exists (*TRUNCate*).
nocreate	Error when opening if file does not already exist.
noreplace	Error when opening for output if file already exists, unless ate or app is set.
binary	Open file in binary (not text) mode.

Table 10-11   *Mode bits for* open() *function*

In DISKFUN, I use app because I want to preserve whatever was in the file before; whatever I write to the file will be added at the end of the existing contents. I use in and out because I want to perform both input and output on the file, and I use binary because I'm writing binary objects. The vertical bars between the flags cause the bits representing these flags to be combined (ORed) together into a single integer so that several flags can apply simultaneously.

I write one person object at a time to the file using the write() function. When I've finished writing, I want to read the entire file. Before doing this, I must reset the file's current position. I do this with the seekg() function (which I'll examine in the next session, on file pointers). It ensures I'll start reading at the beginning of the file. Then, in a while loop, I repeatedly read a person object from the file and display it on the screen.

This continues until I've read all the person objects—a state that I discover using the eof() function, which returns the state of the ios::eofbit.

1. To perform stream I/O with disk files in C++, you should
   a. open and close files as in procedural languages.
   b. create objects that are associated with specific files.
   c. include the IOSTREAM.H header file.
   d. use classes derived from ios.
   e. use C language library functions to read and write data.

2. In formatted file I/O,
   a. you read data directly into individual variables.
   b. an integer requires the same number of bytes in the file as it does when converted to a string.
   c. an integer requires the same number of bytes in the file as it does in RAM.
   d. a carriage return is stored as 1 byte.
   e. you must explicitly write an EOF character at the end of every file.

3. In binary file I/O,
   a. you use the `iostream::binary` mode bit.
   b. writing each variable requires a separate call to `write()`.
   c. an integer requires the same number of bytes in the file as it does when converted to a string.
   d. an integer requires the same number of bytes in the file as it does in RAM.
   e. the stream objects think of the data as a buffer of bytes.

4. When using streams to write objects to a disk file,
   a. you must use the `iostream::out` flag.
   b. each object's data and member functions are stored on the disk.
   c. you should use formatted I/O.
   d. you can write to an object of the `fstream` class.
   e. objects should be read back into variables of the identical class from which they were written.

5. Which of the following statements, concerning stream I/O with disk files, are true?
   a. Objects cannot be stored on disk as objects; their data must be stored as individual variables.
   b. For an object of a user-defined class to be written to disk, the class must contain member functions for this purpose.
   c. You can write to a stream object, and then, without closing it, read from it.
   d. A mode bit can be used with `open()` to specify that an attempt to open a nonexistent file will fail.
   e. You cannot send output to a file without destroying any data already in the file.

EXERCISE 1

Start with the `airtime` class (as in the ADDAIR program from Chapter 6, Session 1) and write a `main()` that asks for an indefinite number of airtime values from the user and writes them all, with a single statement, to a disk file. Destroy whatever was in the file before.

EXERCISE 2

Add code to the above example to read the contents of the file and display it.

FILE ERRORS AND FILE POINTERS

This session comprises two short topics: how to handle errors in file I/O and how to specify the exact place in a file where data will be written or read.

Error Handling in File I/O

In the file-related examples presented so far, I have not concerned myself with error situations. In particular, I have assumed that the files I opened for reading already existed and that those opened for writing could be created or appended to. I've also assumed that there were no failures during reading or writing. In a real program, it is important to verify such assumptions and take appropriate action if they turn out to be incorrect. A file that you think exists may not, or a file name that you assume you can use for a new file may already apply to an existing file. Or there may be no more room on the disk or a diskette drive door may be open.

Reacting to Errors

The next program shows how such errors are most conveniently handled. All disk operations are checked after they are performed. If an error has occurred, a message is printed and the program terminates. I've used the technique, discussed earlier, of checking the return value from the object itself to determine its error status. The program opens an output stream object, writes an entire array of integers to it with a single call to **write()**, and closes the object. Then it opens an input stream object and reads the array of integers with a call to **read()**. Listing 10-13 shows REWERR.

Listing 10-13 REWERR

```
// rewerr.cpp
// handles errors during input and output

#include <fstream.h>     // for file streams
#include <process.h>     // for exit()

const int MAX = 1000;
int buff[MAX];

void main()
   {
   int j;
   for(j=0; j<MAX; j++)                     // fill buffer with data
      buff[j] = j;

   ofstream os;                             // create output stream
                                            // open it
   os.open("a:edata.dat", ios::trunc | ios::binary);
   if(!os)
      { cerr << "\nCould not open output file"; exit(1); }
```

```
cout << "\nWriting...";                      // write buffer to it
os.write( (char*)buff, MAX*sizeof(int) );
if(!os)
   { cerr << "\nCould not write to file"; exit(1); }
os.close();                                  // must close it

for(j=0; j<MAX; j++)                          // clear buffer
   buff[j] = 0;


ifstream is;                                  // create input stream
is.open("a:edata.dat", ios::binary);
if(!is)
   { cerr << "\nCould not open input file"; exit(1); }


cout << "\nReading...";                       // read file
is.read( (char*)buff, MAX*sizeof(int) );
if(!is)
   { cerr << "\nCould not read from file"; exit(1); }

for(j=0; j<MAX; j++)                          // check data
   if( buff[j] != j )
      { cerr << "\nData is incorrect"; exit(1); }
cout << "\nData is correct";
}
```

Analyzing Errors

In the REWERR example, I determined whether an error occurred in an I/O operation by examining the return value of the entire stream object.

```
if(!is)
   // error occurred
```

Here, is returns a pointer value if everything went well, but 0 if it didn't. This is the shotgun approach to errors: No matter what the error is, it's detected in the same way and the same action is taken. However, it's also possible, using the ios error-status bits, to find out more specific information about a file I/O error. You've already seen some of these status bits at work in screen and keyboard I/O. The next example, FERRORS (Listing 10-14), shows how they can be used in file I/O.

Listing 10-14 FERRORS

```
// ferrors.cpp
// checks for errors opening file
#include <fstream.h>             // for file functions

void main()
   {
   ifstream file;
   file.open("GROUP.DAT", ios::nocreate);

   if( !file )
      cout << "\nCan't open GROUP.DAT";
```

continued on next page

continued from previous page

```
   else
      cout << "\nFile opened successfully.";
   cout << "\nfile = " << file;
   cout << "\nError state = " << file.rdstate();
   cout << "\ngood() = " << file.good();
   cout << "\neof() = " << file.eof();
   cout << "\nfail() = " << file.fail();
   cout << "\nbad() = " << file.bad();
   file.close();
   }
```

This program first checks the value of the object **file**. If its value is zero, the file probably could not be opened because it didn't exist. Here's the output from FERRORS when that's the case:

```
Can't open GROUP.DAT
file = 0x1c730000
Error state = 4
good() = 0
eof() = 0
fail() = 4
bad() = 4
```

The error state returned by **rdstate()** is 4. This is the bit that indicates the file doesn't exist; it's set to 1. The other bits are all set to 0. The **good()** function returns 1 (true) only when no bits are set, so it returns 0 (false). I'm not at EOF, so **eof()** returns 0. The **fail()** and **bad()** functions return nonzero because an error occurred.

In a serious program, some or all of these functions should be used after every I/O operation to ensure that things have gone as expected.

File Pointers

Each file object has associated with it two integer values called the *get pointer* and the *put pointer*. These are also called the *current get position* and the *current put position*, or—if it's clear which one is meant— simply the *current position*. These values specify the byte number in the file where writing or reading will take place. (The term *pointer* in this context should not be confused with C++ pointers used as address variables.)

You'll often want to start reading an existing file at the beginning and continue until the end. When writing, you may want to start at the beginning, deleting any existing contents, or at the end, in which case you can open the file with the **ios::app** mode specifier. These are the default actions, so no manipulation of the file pointers is necessary. However, there are times when you must take control of the file pointers yourself so that you can read from or write to an arbitrary location in the file. The **seekg()** and **tellg()** functions allow you to set and examine the get pointer, and the **seekp()** and **tellp()** functions perform the same actions on the put pointer.

Specifying the Position

I showed an example of positioning the get pointer in the DISKFUN program, where the **seekg()** function set it to the beginning of the file so that reading would start there. This form of **seekg()** takes one argument, which represents the absolute byte position in the file. The start of the file is byte 0, so that's what I used in DISKFUN. Figure 10-4 shows how this looks.

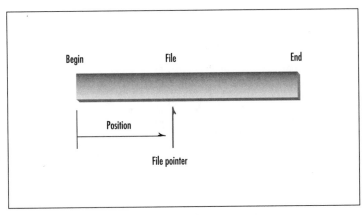

Figure 10-4 The seekg() function with one argument

Specifying the Offset

The **seekg()** function can be used in two ways. You've seen the first, where the single argument represents the position from the start of the file. You can also use it with two arguments, where the first argument represents an offset from a particular location in the file and the second specifies the location from which the offset is measured. There are three possibilities for the second argument: **beg** is the beginning of the file, **cur** is the current pointer position, and **end** is the end of the file. The statement

```
seekp(-10, ios::end);
```

for example, will set the put pointer to 10 bytes before the end of the file. Figure 10-5 shows this arrangement.

Listing 10-15 shows an example that uses the two-argument version of **seekg()** to find a particular **person** object in the PERSON.DAT file already created with DISKFUN and to display the data for that particular person.

Listing 10-15 SEEKG

```cpp
// seekg.cpp
// seeks particular person in file
#include <fstream.h>            // for file streams

class person                    // class of persons
   {
   protected:
      char name[40];            // person's name
      int age;                  // person's age
   public:
      void showData(void)       // display person's data
         {
         cout << "\n   Name: " << name;
         cout << "\n   Age: " << age;
         }
   };
```

continued on next page

continued from previous page

```
void main(void)
   {
   person pers;                          // create person object
   ifstream infile;                      // create input file
   infile.open("PERSON.DAT", ios::binary);  // open file

   infile.seekg(0, ios::end);           // go to 0 bytes from end
   int endposition = infile.tellg();       // find where we are
   int n = endposition / sizeof(person);   // number of persons
   cout << "\nThere are " << n << " persons in file";

   cout << "\nEnter person number: ";
   cin >> n;
   int position = (n-1) * sizeof(person);  // number times size
   infile.seekg(position);              // bytes from begin
                                        // read one person
   infile.read( (char*)&pers, sizeof(pers) );
   pers.showData();                      // display the person
   }
```

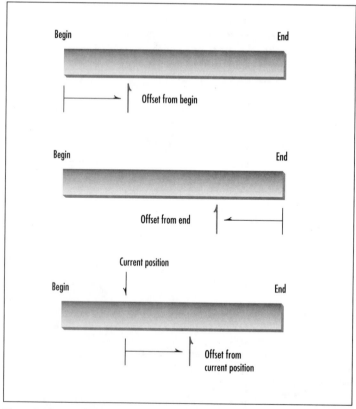

Figure 10-5   The seekg() function with two arguments

Here's the output from the program, assuming that the PERSON.DAT file is the same as that just accessed in the DISKFUN example:

```
There are 3 persons in file
Enter person number: 2

   Name: Rainier
   Age: 21
```

For the user, I number the items starting at 1, although the program starts numbering at 0, so person 2 is the second person of the three in the file.

The first thing the program does is figure out how many persons are in the file. The first step is to position the get pointer at the end of the file with the statement

```
infile.seekg(0, ios::end);
```

The tellg() Function

The `tellg()` function returns the current position of the get pointer. After positioning the pointer at the end of the file, the program uses `tellg()` to return the get pointer position; this is the length of the file in bytes. Next, the program calculates how many **person** objects are in the file by dividing the file size by the size of a **person**; it then displays the result.

In the output shown, the user specifies the second object in the file and the program calculates how many bytes into the file this is using **seekg()**. It then uses **read()** to read one **person**'s worth of data starting from that point. Finally, it displays the data with **showData()**.

QUIZ 4

1. If an error occurs when you use **open()** on an **ofstream** object called **ofile**, then
   a. it's just an EOF, so you can always go ahead and write to the file.
   b. the **ofile** object has not been created.
   c. the file associated with **ofile** has not been opened.
   d. **ofile** will be true.
   e. **ofile** will be false.

2. If an error occurs when you use **read()** on an **ifstream** object called **ifile**, then
   a. it could be an EOF.
   b. you can discover the type of error by examining the value of **ifile**.
   c. you must immediately destroy the **ifile** object.
   d. **ifile** will be true.
   e. **ifile** will be false.

3. Which of the following statements, concerning member functions of **ifstream**, are true?
   a. The **rdstate()** function returns the error-status byte.
   b. The **ferror()** function reports the error status.
   c. The **good()** function returns 0 if an error occurred.
   d. No function exists to tell if an EOF occurred.
   e. No function exists to tell if the diskette door is open.

4. Which of these statements are true?
   a. The file pointer value handled by `seekg()` and similar functions is an address.
   b. The `tellg()` function tells the disk drive where to position the file pointer.
   c. You need to know how your data is formatted in a file to make any use of `seekg()` and `tellg()`.
   d. The two-argument version of `seekg()` can use the `ios::beg` constant.
   e. You must always start reading at the beginning of a file.

5. The `seekg()` member function
   a. can be used with one argument to position the `get` pointer to a specified number of bytes from the end of the file.
   b. can be used to read the position of the `get` pointer.
   c. can position the `get` pointer relative to its previous location.
   d. works with binary files.
   e. works with formatted files.

EXERCISE 1

Rewrite the DISKFUN example from Session 3 so that every file operation is checked for errors.

EXERCISE 2

Write a variation of the SEEKG program in this session that allows the user to overwrite a specified record in the PERSON.DAT file with new data for a single person. You can use the `seekp()` member function.

MIDCHAPTER DISCUSSION

George: Well, I already know C, so I'm just going to go on using `printf()` and `scanf()` and all that stuff. It works and I don't want to waste my time learning all these new member functions and this weird class structure.

Estelle: What about the errors you get when you use the wrong formatting character, like `%f` with a integer? You can blow up the program. If you use iostreams, you can't make that mistake.

George: I don't make those mistakes any more.

Don: Of course not. But I've got a feeling you'll regret that approach, even aside from the errors. Wait until we hear about overloading the insertion and extraction operators.

George: I can wait.

SESSION 5

FILE I/O USING MEMBER FUNCTIONS

So far, I've let the `main()` function handle the details of file I/O. This is nice for demonstrations, but in real object-oriented programs, it's natural to include file I/O operations as member functions of the class. In this session I'll show two programs that do this. The first program uses ordinary member functions in which each object is responsible for reading and writing itself to a file. The second program shows how static member functions can read and write all the objects of a class at once.

Objects That Read and Write Themselves

More often than not, it makes sense to let each member of a class read and write itself to a file. This is a simple approach and works well if there aren't many objects to be read or written at one time. In this example, I add member functions—`diskOut()` and `diskIn()`—to the `person` class. These functions allow a `person` object to write itself to disk and read itself back in.

I've made some simplifying assumptions. First, all objects of the class will be stored in the same file, called PERSON.DAT. Second, new objects are always appended to the end of the file. An argument to the `diskIn()` function allows me to read the data for any person in the file. To prevent attempts to read data beyond the end of the file, I include a static member function, `diskCount()`, that returns the number of persons stored in the file. Listing 10-16 shows REWOBJ.

Listing 10-16 REWOBJ
```
// rewobj.cpp
// person objects do disk I/O
#include <fstream.h>                   // for file streams

class person                          // class of persons
   {
   protected:
      char name[40];                  // person's name
      int age;                        // person's age
   public:
      void getData(void)              // get person's data
         {
         cout << "\n   Enter name: "; cin >> name;
         cout << "   Enter age: "; cin >> age;
         }
      void showData(void)             // display person's data
         {
         cout << "\n   Name: " << name;
         cout << "\n   Age: " << age;
         }
      void diskIn(int);               // read from file
      void diskOut();                 // write to file
      static int diskCount();         // return number of
                                      //    persons in file
   };
```

continued on next page

continued from previous page

```
void person::diskIn(int pn)          // read person number pn
   {                                 // from file
   ifstream infile;                  // make stream
   infile.open("PERSON.DAT", ios::binary);   // open it
   infile.seekg( pn*sizeof(person) );        // move file ptr
   infile.read( (char*)this, sizeof(*this) ); // read one person
   }


void person::diskOut()               // write person to end of file
   {
   ofstream outfile;                 // make stream
                                     // open it
   outfile.open("PERSON.DAT", ios::app | ios::binary);
   outfile.write( (char*)this, sizeof(*this) ); // write to it
   }


int person::diskCount()              // return number of persons
   {                                 // in file
   ifstream infile;
   infile.open("PERSON.DAT", ios::binary);
   infile.seekg(0, ios::end);        // go to 0 bytes from end
                                     // calculate number of persons
   return infile.tellg() / sizeof(person);
   }


void main(void)
   {
   person p;                         // make an empty person
   char ch;

   do                                // save persons to disk
      {
      cout << "\nEnter data for person:";
      p.getData();                   // get data
      p.diskOut();                   // write to disk
      cout << "Do another (y/n)? ";
      cin >> ch;
      }
   while(ch=='y');                   // until user enters 'n'

   int n = person::diskCount();      // how many persons in file?
   cout << "\nThere are " << n << " persons in file";
   for(int j=0; j<n; j++)            // for each one,
      {
      cout << "\nPerson #" << (j+1);
      p.diskIn(j);                   // read person from disk
      p.showData();                  // display person
      }
   }
```

There shouldn't be too many surprises here: You've seen most of the elements of this program before. It operates in the same way as the DISKFUN program. Notice, however, that all the details of disk operation are invisible to `main()`, having been hidden away in the `person` class.

I don't know in advance where the data is that I'm going to read and write because each object is in a different place in memory. However, the `this` pointer always tells me where I am when I'm in a member function. In the `read()` and `write()` stream functions, the address of the object to be read or written is `this` and its size is `sizeof(*this)`.

Here's some output, assuming there were already two persons in the file when the program was started:

```
Enter data for person:
    Enter name: Acheson
    Enter age: 63
Enter another (y/n)? y

Enter data for person:
    Enter name: Dulles
    Enter age: 72
Enter another (y/n)? n

Person #1
    Name: Stimson
    Age: 45
Person #2
    Name: Hull
    Age: 58
Person #3
    Name: Acheson
    Age: 63
Person #4
    Name: Dulles
    Age: 72
```

If you want the user to be able to specify the file name used by the class, instead of hard-wiring it into the member functions as I do here, you could create a static member variable (say, `char fileName[]`) and a static function to set it. Or, you might want to associate each object with a different file using a nonstatic function.

Classes That Read and Write Themselves

Let's assume you have many objects in memory and you want to write them all to a file. It's not efficient to have a member function for each object open the file, write one object to it, and then close it, as in the REWOBJ example. It's much faster—and the more objects there are, the truer this is—to open the file once, write all the objects to it, and then close it.

Static Functions

One way to write many objects at once is to use a static member function, which applies to the class as a whole rather than to each object. This function can write all the objects at once. How will such a function know where all the objects are? It can access an array of pointers to the objects, which can be stored as static data. As each object is created, a pointer to it is stored in this array. A static data member also keeps track of how many objects have been created. The static write function can open the file; then, in a loop, it can go through the array, writing each object in turn; finally, it can close the file.

Size of Derived Objects

To make things really interesting, let's make a further assumption: The objects stored in memory are different sizes. Why would this be true? This situation typically arises when several classes are derived from a base class. For example, consider the EMPINH program from Chapter 7, Session 2. Here I have an employee class that acts as a base class for the manager, scientist, and laborer classes. Objects of these three derived classes are different sizes because they contain different amounts of data. Specifically, in addition to the name and employee number, which apply to all employees, there are title and golf club dues for the manager and a number of publications for the scientist. There is nothing additional for the laborer.

I would like to write the data from a list containing all three types of derived objects (manager, scientist, and laborer) using a simple loop and the write() member function of ofstream. But to use this function, I need to know how large the object is because that's the second argument to write().

Suppose I have an array of pointers (call it arrap[]) to objects of type employee. These pointers can point to objects of the three derived classes. (See the VIRTPERS program in Chapter 9, Session 2 for an example of an array of pointers to objects of derived classes.) I know that if I'm using virtual functions, I can make statements such as

```
arrap[j]->putdata();
```

The version of the putdata() function that matches the object pointed to by the pointer will be used rather than the function in the base class. But can I also use the sizeof() function to return the size of a pointer argument? That is, can I say

```
ouf.write( (char*)arrap[j], sizeof(*arrap[j]) );   // no good
```

No, because sizeof() isn't a virtual function. It doesn't know that it needs to consider the type of object pointed to rather than the type of the pointer. It will always return the size of a base class object.

Using the typeid() Function

How can I find the size of an object if all I have is a pointer to it? One answer is the typeid() function, introduced in Chapter 9, Session 5. I can use this function to find the class of an object, and then use this class name in sizeof(). The next example shows how this works. Once I know the size of the object, I can use it in the write() function to write the object to disk.

I've added a simple user interface to the EMPLOY program and made the member-specific functions virtual so I can use an array of pointers to objects. I've also incorporated some of the error-detection techniques discussed in the last session.

This is a rather ambitious program. It demonstrates many techniques that could be used in a full-scale database application. It also shows the real power of OOP. How else could you use a single statement to write objects of different sizes to a file? Listing 10-17 shows EMPL_IO.

Listing 10-17 EMPL_IO

```
// empl_io.cpp
// performs file I/O on employee objects
// handles different sized objects

#include <fstream.h>          // for file-stream functios
#include <conio.h>            // for getche()
```

```
#include <process.h>          // for exit()
#include <typeinfo.h>         // for typeid()

const int LEN = 32;           // maximum length of last names
const int MAXEM = 100;        // maximum number of employees

enum employee_type {tmanager, tscientist, tlaborer};

class employee                // employee class
   {
   private:
      char name[LEN];          // employee name
      unsigned long number;    // employee number
      static int n;            // current number of employees
      static employee* arrap[]; // array of ptrs to emps
   public:
      virtual void getdata()
         {
         cout << "\n   Enter last name: "; cin >> name;
         cout << "   Enter number: ";       cin >> number;
         }
      virtual void putdata()
         {
         cout << "\n   Name: " << name;
         cout << "\n   Number: " << number;
         }
      virtual employee_type get_type();  // get type
      static void add();        // add an employee
      static void display();    // display all employees
      static void read();       // read from disk file
      static void write();      // write to disk file
      static void destroy();    // delete objects from memory
   };

// static variables
int employee::n;                          // current number of employees
employee* employee::arrap[MAXEM];  // array of ptrs to emps

// manager class
class manager : public employee
   {
   private:
      char title[LEN];         // "vice-president" etc.
      double dues;             // golf club dues
   public:
      void getdata()
         {
         employee::getdata();
         cout << "   Enter title: ";           cin >> title;
         cout << "   Enter golf club dues: "; cin >> dues;
         }
      void putdata()
         {
         employee::putdata();
```

continued on next page

continued from previous page

```
                cout << "\n    Title: " << title;
                cout << "\n    Golf club dues: " << dues;
                }
        };

// scientist class
class scientist : public employee
    {
    private:
        int pubs;                        // number of publications
    public:
        void getdata()
            {
            employee::getdata();
            cout << "    Enter number of pubs: "; cin >> pubs;
            }
        void putdata()
            {
            employee::putdata();
            cout << "\n    Number of publications: " << pubs;
            }
        };

// laborer class
class laborer : public employee
    {
    };

// add employee to list in memory
void employee::add()
    {
    cout << "\n'm' to add a manager"
            "\n's' to add a scientist"
            "\n'l' to add a laborer"
            "\nType selection: ";
    switch( getche() )
        {                                // create specified employee type
        case 'm': arrap[n] = new manager;    break;
        case 's': arrap[n] = new scientist; break;
        case 'l': arrap[n] = new laborer;    break;
        default: cout << "\nUnknown employee type"; return;
        }
    arrap[n++]->getdata();        // get employee data from user
    }

// display all employees
void employee::display()
    {
    for(int j=0; j<n; j++)
        {
        cout << '\n' << (j+1);  // display number
        switch( arrap[j]->get_type() )    // display type
            {
            case tmanager:    cout << ". Type: Manager";    break;
            case tscientist:  cout << ". Type: Scientist"; break;
```

```
            case tlaborer:      cout << ". Type: Laborer";    break;
            default: cout << ". Unknown type"; return;
            }
         arrap[j]->putdata();       // display employee data
         }
    }

// return the type of this object
employee_type employee::get_type()
    {
    if( typeid(*this) == typeid(manager) )
       return tmanager;
    else if( typeid(*this)==typeid(scientist) )
       return tscientist;
    else if( typeid(*this)==typeid(laborer) )
       return tlaborer;
    else
       { cout << "\nBad employee type"; exit(1); }
    return tmanager;
    }

// write all current memory objects to file
void employee::write()
    {
    int size;
    cout << "\nWriting " << n << " employees.";
    ofstream ouf;                  // open ofstream in binary
    employee_type etype;           // type of each employee object

    ouf.open("EMPLOY.DAT", ios::trunc | ios::binary);
    if(!ouf)
       { cout << "\nCan't open file"; return; }
    for(int j=0; j<n; j++)         // for every employee object
       {                           // get it's type
       etype = arrap[j]->get_type();
                                   // write type to file
       ouf.write( (char*)&etype, sizeof(etype) );
       switch(etype)               // find its size
          {
          case tmanager:   size=sizeof(manager); break;
          case tscientist: size=sizeof(scientist); break;
          case tlaborer:   size=sizeof(laborer); break;
          }                        // write employee object to file
       ouf.write( (char*)(arrap[j]), size );
       if(!ouf)
          { cout << "\nCan't write to file"; return; }
       }
    }

// read data for all employees from file into memory
void employee::read()
    {
    int size;                      // size of employee object
    employee_type etype;           // type of employee
```

continued on next page

continued from previous page

```
   ifstream inf;                  // open ifstream in binary
   inf.open("EMPLOY.DAT", ios::binary);
   if(!inf)
      { cout << "\nCan't open file"; return; }
   n = 0;                         // no employees in memory yet
   while(1)
      {                           // read type of next employee
      inf.read( (char*)&etype, sizeof(etype) );
      if( inf.eof() )             // quit loop on eof
         break;
      if(!inf)                    // error reading type
         { cout << "\nCan't read type from file"; return; }
      switch(etype)
         {                        // make new employee
         case tmanager:      // of correct type
            arrap[n] = new manager;
            size=sizeof(manager);
            break;
         case tscientist:
            arrap[n] = new scientist;
            size=sizeof(scientist);
            break;
         case tlaborer:
            arrap[n] = new laborer;
            size=sizeof(laborer);
            break;
         default: cout << "\nUnknown type in file"; return;
         }                        // read data from file into it
      inf.read( (char*)arrap[n], size  );
      if(!inf)                    // error but not eof
         { cout << "\nCan't read data from file"; return; }
      n++;                        // count employee
      }  // end while
   cout << "\nReading " << n << " employees";
   }

// delete memory allocated for employees
void employee::destroy()
   {
   for(int j=0; j<n; j++)
      delete arrap[j];
   }

void main()
   {
   while(1)
      {
      cout <<  "\n'a' -- add data for an employee"
               "\n'd' -- display data for all employees"
               "\n'w' -- write all employee data to file"
               "\n'r' -- read all employee data from file"
               "\n'x' -- exit"
               "\nType selection: ";
      switch( getche() )
         {
```

```
   case 'a':              // add an employee to list
      employee::add();
      break;
   case 'd':              // display all employees
      employee::display();
      break;
   case 'w':              // write employees to file
      employee::write();
      break;
   case 'r':              // read all employees from file
      employee::read();
      break;
   case 'x':              // exit program
      employee::destroy();
      return;
   default: cout << "\nUnknown command";
   }
   }   // end while
}
```

Code Number for Object Type

You've learned how to find the class of an object that's in memory, but how do you know the class of the object whose data you're about to read from the disk? There's no magic function to help you with this one. When I write an object's data to disk, I need to write a code number (the **enum** variable **employee_type**) directly to the disk just before the object's data. Then when I am about to read an object back from the file to memory, I read this value and create a new object of the type indicated. Finally, I copy the data from the file into this new object.

No Homemade Objects, Please

Incidentally, you might be tempted to read an object's data into just any place, say into an array of type **char**, and then set a pointer to object to point to this area, perhaps with a cast to make it kosher:

```
char someArray[MAX];          // object's data is in this array
aClass* aPtr_to_Obj;          // create pointer
aPtr_to_Obj = (aClass*)someArray;  // don't do this
```

However, an array of type **char**, even if it contains an object's data, is not an object. Attempts to use the array, or a pointer to the array, as if it points to an object will lead to trouble. There are only two legitimate ways to create an object. You can define it explicitly at compile time:

```
aClass anObj;                 // ok
```

or you can create it with **new** at runtime, and assign its location to a pointer:

```
aPtr_to_Obj = new aClass;     // ok
```

When you create an object properly, its constructor is invoked. This is necessary even if you have not defined a constructor and are using the default constructor. An object is more than an area of memory with data in it; it is also a set of member functions, some of which, like a default constructor, you don't even see.

Interaction with *EMPL_IO*

Here's some sample interaction with the program in which the user creates a manager, a scientist, and a laborer in memory, writes them to disk, reads them back in, and displays them. (For simplicity, multiword names and titles are not allowed; say "VicePresident," not "Vice President")

```
'a' -- add data for an employee
'd' -- display data for all employees
'w' -- write all employee data to file
'r' -- read all employee data from file
'x' -- exit
Type selection: a
'm' to add a manager
's' to add a scientist
'l' to add a laborer
Type selection: m
    Enter last name: Johnson
    Enter number: 1111
    Enter title: President
    Enter golf club dues: 20000

'a' -- add data for an employee
'd' -- display data for all employees
'w' -- write all employee data to file
'r' -- read all employee data from file
'x' -- exit
Type selection: a
'm' to add a manager
's' to add a scientist
'l' to add a laborer
Type selection: s
    Enter last name: Faraday
    Enter number: 2222
    Enter number of pubs: 99

'a' -- add data for an employee
'd' -- display data for all employees
'w' -- write all employee data to file
'r' -- read all employee data from file
'x' -- exit
Type selection: a
'm' to add a manager
's' to add a scientist
'l' to add a laborer
Type selection: l
    Enter last name: Smith
    Enter number: 3333

'a' -- add data for an employee
'd' -- display data for all employees
'w' -- write all employee data to file
'r' -- read all employee data from file
'x' -- exit
```

```
Type selection: w
Writing 3 employees

'a' -- add data for an employee
'd' -- display data for all employees
'w' -- write all employee data to file
'r' -- read all employee data from file
'x' -- exit
Type selection: r
Reading 3 employees

'a' -- add data for an employee
'd' -- display data for all employees
'w' -- write all employee data to file
'r' -- read all employee data from file
'x' -- exit
Type selection: d
1. Type: Manager
   Name: Johnson
   Title: President
   Golf club dues: 20000
2. Type: Scientist
   Name: Faraday
   Number: 2222
   Number of publications: 99
3. Type: Laborer
   Name: Smith
   Number: 3333
```

Of course, you can also exit the program after writing the data to disk. When you start it up again, you can read the file back in and all the data will reappear.

It would be easy to add functions to this program to delete an employee, retrieve data for a single employee from the file, search the file for employees with particular characteristics, and so forth.

QUIZ 5

1. In the REWOBJ program, how does each **person** object identify itself so it can insert itself in the same place in memory when it is read back from the disk?
   a. There's a table of pointers to all **person** objects so each one knows where it came from and where it should go.
   b. The **diskIn()** and **diskOut()** functions operate on generic **person** objects so these objects don't need to identify themselves.
   c. The data for each **person** object, stored in the disk file, includes the **this** pointer value for the object so it can be restored to the same spot in memory.
   d. The data for each **person** object, stored in the disk file, includes an index number for the object so it can be restored to the same spot in memory.
   e. Objects don't need to go back into the same place in memory.

2. The `person` objects in REWOBJ are arranged in the PERSON.DAT file
   a. by employee name.
   b. by employee number.
   c. in the same order as in the table of `this` pointers.
   d. randomly.
   e. in the order they were entered by the user.

3. In the EMPL_IO program, how does the class `employee` know what objects of the class exist?
   a. The class doesn't need to know anything about its objects.
   b. Each object contains a code number that indicates if it exists.
   c. The associated `company` class contains a table of `employee` objects.
   d. The `employee` class contains, in static data, a table of pointers to all existing `employee` objects.
   e. It examines its own `this` pointer.

4. In the EMPL_IO program, the object type is discovered by _____ when writing to the disk file and by _____ when reading from the disk file.
   a. values of the `this` pointer; array index values
   b. `typeid()`; code numbers
   c. code numbers; array index values
   d. array index values; `typeid()`
   e. All objects are of the same type so there is no need for such determination.

5. If you read the data for an object of class `alpha` from a disk file into an array of type `char`,
   a. you can then identify the type of the object using the `typeid()` function on the array.
   b. the section of the array occupied by the data becomes an object of class `alpha`.
   c. all will be well if you know the type of the object before accessing the array.
   d. you should then create an empty object of class `alpha` and copy the data into it.
   e. the compiler will signal an error.

EXERCISE 1

Apply the technique of REWOBJ, where objects read and write themselves, to the `airtime` class, as seen in the ADDAIR example in Chapter 6, Session 1. That is, create `diskIn()` and `diskOut()` member functions for `airtime`. In `main()`, get data for many `airtime` values from the user, write them to disk, read them back in, and display them.

EXERCISE 2

Write a function for the EMPL_IO program that will search the file for an employee with a given employee number and display all the employee's information.

SESSION 6

OVERLOADING THE << AND >> OPERATORS

In this session I'll show how to overload the extraction and insertion operators. This is a powerful feature of C++. It lets you treat I/O for user-defined data types in the same way as for basic types such as `int` and `double`. For example, if you have an object of class `crawdad` called `cd1`, you can display it with the statement

```
cout << cd1;
```

just as if it were a basic data type.

You can overload the extraction and insertion operators so they work with the display and keyboard (`cout` and `cin`). With a little more care, you can also overload them so they work with disk files as well. In this session, I'll look at examples of both these approaches.

Overloading for `cout` and `cin`

Listing 10-18 shows an example, ENGLIO, that overloads the insertion and extraction operators for the `English` class so they work with `cout` and `cin`.

Listing 10-18 ENGLIO

```
// englio.cpp
// overloaded << and >> operators
#include <iostream.h>

class English                              // English class
   {
   private:
      int feet;
      float inches;
   public:
      English()                            // constructor (no args)
         { feet = 0; inches = 0.0; }
      English(int ft, float in)            // constructor (two args)
         { feet = ft; inches = in; }
      friend istream& operator >> (istream& s, English& d);
      friend ostream& operator << (ostream& s, const English& d);
   };

istream& operator >> (istream& s, English& d)  // get distance
   {                                           // from user
   cout << "\nEnter feet: ";  s >> d.feet;     // using
   cout << "Enter inches: ";  s >> d.inches;   // overloaded
   return s;                                   // >> operator
   }
```

continued on next page

continued from previous page

```
ostream& operator << (ostream& s, const English& d)   // display
   {                                                  // distance
   s << d.feet << "\'-" << d.inches << '\"';          // using
   return s;                                          // overloaded
   }                                                  // << operator

void main()
   {
   English dist1, dist2;             // define English objects
   cout << "\nEnter two English values:";
   cin >> dist1 >> dist2;            // get values from user

   English dist3(11, 6.25);          // define, initialize dist3

                                     // display distances
   cout << "\ndist1 = " << dist1 << "\ndist2 = " << dist2;
   cout << "\ndist3 = " << dist3;
   }
```

This program asks the user for two distance values and then displays these values and another value (11'-6.25") that was initialized in the program. Here's some sample interaction:

```
Enter feet: 10
Enter inches: 3.5

Enter feet: 12
Enter inches: 6

dist1 = 10'-3.5"
dist2 = 12'-6"
dist3 = 11'-6.25"
```

Notice in `main()` how convenient and natural it is to treat `English` objects like any other data type, using statements such as

```
cin >> dist1 >> dist2;
```

and

```
cout << "\ndist1=" << dist1 << "\ndist2=" << dist2;
```

The `operator<<()` and `operator>>()` functions must be friends of the `English` class, because the `istream` and `ostream` objects appear on the left side of the operator. (See the discussion of friend functions in Chapter 9, Session 6.) They return, by reference, an object of `istream` (for `>>`) or `ostream` (for `<<`). These return values permit chaining so that more than one value can be input or output in a single statement.

The operators take two arguments, both passed by reference. The first is an object of `istream` (for `>>`; often this is `cin`) or of `ostream` (for `<<`; often this is `cout`). The second argument is the object to be displayed, an object of class `English` in this example. The fact that the stream and the `English` object are passed by reference allows them to be modified by the function. The `>>` operator takes input from the stream specified in the first argument and copies it into the member data of the object specified by the second argument. The `<<` operator copies the data from the object specified by the second argument and sends it into the stream specified by the first argument. You can overload the insertion and extraction operators for other classes using this same approach.

Notice the `const` before the second argument of the overloaded `<<` operator. It guarantees that outputting an `English` value won't alter it.

Overloading for Files

The next example shows how you might overload the `<<` and `>>` operators in the `English` class so they work with both file I/O and `cout` and `cin`. Listing 10-19 shows ENGLIO2.

Listing 10-19 ENGLIO2

```
// englio2.cpp
// overloaded << and >> operators work with files
#include <fstream.h>

class English                        // English English class
    {
    private:
        int feet;
        float inches;
    public:
        English()                        // constructor (no args)
            { feet = 0; inches = 0.0; }
        English(int ft, float in)        // constructor (two args)
            { feet = ft; inches = in; }
        friend istream& operator >> (istream& s, English& d);
        friend ostream& operator << (ostream& s, const English& d);
    };

istream& operator >> (istream& s, English& d)  // get distance
    {                                          // from file or
    char dummy;   // for ('), (-), and (")     // keyboard
                                               // with
    s >> d.feet >> dummy >> dummy >> d.inches >> dummy;
    return s;                                  // overloaded
    }                                          // >> operator

ostream& operator << (ostream& s, const English& d)  // send
    {                                          // to file or
    s << d.feet << "\'-" << d.inches << '\"';  // screen with
    return s;                                  // overloaded
    }                                          // << operator

void main()
    {
    char ch;
    English dist1;
    ofstream ofile;                  // create and open
    ofile.open("DIST.DAT");          // output stream
```

continued on next page

continued from previous page

```
   do
      {
      cout << "\nEnter English: ";
      cin >> dist1;                    // get distance from user
      ofile << dist1;                  // write it to output str
      cout << "Do another (y/n)? ";
      cin >> ch;
      }
   while(ch != 'n');
   ofile.close();                      // close output stream

   ifstream ifile;                     // create and open
   ifile.open("DIST.DAT");             // input stream

   cout << "\nContents of disk file is:";
   while(1)
      {
      ifile >> dist1;                  // read dist from stream
      if( ifile.eof() )                // quit on EOF
         break;
      cout << "\nDistance = " << dist1;  // display distance
      }
   }
```

I've made minimal changes to the overloaded operators themselves. The **>>** operator no longer prompts for input because it doesn't make sense to prompt a file. When getting input from the keyboard, I assume the user knows exactly how to enter a feet and inches value, including the various punctuation marks. (Type an integer value for feet, a quote, a hyphen, a float value for inches, and a double quote: **19'-2.5".**) The **<<** operator is unchanged. The program asks for input from the user, writing each **English** value to the file as it's obtained. When the user is finished with input, the program reads and displays all the values from the file. Here's some sample interaction:

```
Enter Distance: 3'-4.5"
Do another (y/n)? y

Enter Distance: 7'-11.25"
Do another (y/n)? y

Enter Distance: 11'-6"
Do another (y/n)? n

Contents of disk file is:
Distance = 3'-4.5"
Distance = 7'-11.25"
Distance = 11'-6"
```

The distances are stored character by character to the file. In this example, the contents of the file would be

```
3'-4.5"7'-11.25"11'-6"
```

If the user fails to enter the distances with the correct punctuation, the distances won't be written to the file correctly and the file won't be readable for the **<<** operator. In a real program, error checking on input would be essential.

Overloading for Binary I/O

So far, you've seen examples of overloading `operator<<()` and `operator>>()` for formatted I/O. Can they be overloaded to perform binary I/O? Certainly, and, as I noted earlier, this may be a more efficient way to store information, especially if your object contains much numerical data.

As an example, I'll show how to store data for `person` objects to disk files in binary format (see the VIRTPERS example in Chapter 9, Session 2). Binary format means that the data on the disk will be in the same format as the object's data in memory. This data consists of a 40-character name field and a 1-integer age field. Member functions of `person` are used to acquire this data from the keyboard and display it. The operators **<<** and **>>** are overloaded to write the data to a disk file and read it back, using the `read()` and `write()` iostream functions. Listing 10-20 shows PERSIO.

Listing 10-20 PERSIO

```
// persio.cpp
// overloading << and >> for person objects
// storing binary data in file
#include <fstream.h>                    // for file streams

class person                           // class of persons
   {
   protected:
      enum {SIZE=40};                  // size of name buffer
      char name[SIZE];                 // person's name
      int age;                         // person's age
   public:
      void getData()                   // get data from keyboard
         {
         cout << "\n   Enter name: "; cin.getline(name, SIZE);
         cout << "   Enter age: ";  cin >> age;
         cin.ignore(10, '\n');
         }
      void putData()                   // display data on screen
         {
         cout << "\n   Name = " << name;
         cout << "\n   Age = " << age;
         }
      friend istream& operator >> (istream& s, person& d);
      friend ostream& operator << (ostream& s, person& d);

      void persin(istream& s)          // read file into ourself
         {
         s.read( (char*)this, sizeof(*this) );
         }
      void persout(ostream& s)         // write our data to file
```

continued on next page

continued from previous page

```
            {
            s.write( (char*)this, sizeof(*this) );
            }
    };
                                        // get data from disk
istream& operator >> (istream& s, person& d)
    {
    d.persin(s);
    return s;
    }
                                        // write data to disk
ostream& operator << (ostream& s, person& d)
    {
    d.persout(s);
    return s;
    }

void main(void)
    {                                   // create 4 persons
    person pers1, pers2, pers3, pers4;
    cout << "\nPerson 1";
    pers1.getData();                    // get data for pers1
    cout << "\nPerson 2";
    pers2.getData();                    // get data for pers2
                                        // create output stream
    ofstream outfile("PERSON.DAT", ios::binary);
    outfile << pers1 << pers2;          // write to file
    outfile.close();
                                        // create input stream
    ifstream infile("PERSON.DAT", ios::binary);
    infile >> pers3 >> pers4;           // read from file into
    cout << "\nPerson 3";              // pers3 and pers4
    pers3.putData();                    // display new objects
    cout << "\nPerson 4";
    pers4.putData();
    }
```

I had to overcome a slight glitch in the overloaded `<<` and `>>` operators. As you've seen, these operators must be friend functions because a stream object instead of a `person` is used as the left-hand argument. However, because I'm using binary format, it is most convenient to access the `person` object's data directly from its location in memory, which is handled with the `this` pointer. Unfortunately, the `this` pointer is not accessible in friend functions. So, from within the overloaded `<<` and `>>` operators, I call other functions that *are* `person` member functions: `persin()` and `persout()`, which do the actual writing and reading.

In `main()`, the program obtains data for two person objects from the user, writes to disk, reads it back into two different person objects, and displays their contents. Here's some sample interaction:

```
Person 1
   Enter name: George Harrison
   Enter age: 33
Person 2
   Enter name: Emily Dickinson
```

```
Enter age: 25

Person 3
    Name = George Harrison
    Age = 33
Person 4
    Name = Emily Dickenson
    Age = 25
```

As you've seen, chaining is possible with the overloaded operators so that a single statement in `main()` writes two `person` objects to the disk file:

```
outfile << pers1 << pers2;
```

and a single statement reads data from the file into two other `person` objects:

```
infile >> pers3 >> pers4;
```

1. Which of these statements are true?
   a. Overloading the `<<` and `>>` operators means authorizing the compiler to create new versions of these operators to work with a user-written class.
   b. You cannot overload the `<<` and `>>` operators to perform input and output with disk files.
   c. You could use functions to do most things overloaded operators do.
   d. If the user-written object was passed by value in the overloaded `>>` operator, no data could be placed in it.
   e. If the stream was passed by value in the overloaded `<<` operator, no data could be written to it.

2. To overload the `<<` and `>>` operators to work with `cout` and `cin`, you will probably
   a. redefine `cout` and `cin`.
   b. write statements within `operator<<()` and `operator>>()` to input and output basic variable types.
   c. make these operators member functions of a stream.
   d. make these operators member functions of the class whose objects you want to input and output.
   e. use friend functions.

3. Although the overloaded `>>` and `<<` operators are defined to work with `ostream` and `istream` objects, they can also work with `ofstream` and `ifstream` objects, as in the ENGLIO program, because
   a. `ofstream` and `ifstream` are different names for `istream` and `ostream`.
   b. `ofstream` and `ifstream` are derived from for `istream` and `ostream`.
   c. the overloaded `>>` and `<<` operators work with any stream class.
   d. the overloaded `>>` and `<<` operators are virtual functions.
   e. the overloaded `>>` and `<<` operators are friend functions.

4. To permit multiple uses of the << or >> operators in a single statement (chaining),
   a. these operators must return appropriate stream objects.
   b. only objects instantiated from streams can be input or output.
   c. only basic types can be input and output.
   d. these operators must return an object of their own class.
   e. these operators must return by reference.

5. When overloading the << and >> operators to work with binary files,
   a. there will be runtime errors.
   b. the compiler will report an error.
   c. the `read()` and `write()` functions of `istream` and `ostream` can be used.
   d. you must copy the object's data into a buffer before writing it to disk.
   e. the data on the disk is stored in the same format as the data in the object in memory.

EXERCISE 1

Write overloaded << and >> operators, for use with `cout` and `cin`, for the `airtime` class. Write a `main()` similar to that in ENGLIO to exercise these operators.

EXERCISE 2

Extend the `airtime` operators of Exercise 1 so they work in binary mode for files. Write a `main()` similar to that in PERSIO to exercise these operators.

SESSION 7

MEMORY AS A STREAM OBJECT

You can treat a section of memory as a stream object, inserting data into it just as you would into a file. This is called *in-memory formatting*; it's useful in many situations, for example, with functions in GUI environments (such as Windows) that write to a dialog box or a window that requires the data to be a string, even if numbers are being displayed. It's convenient to compose this string in a section of memory, using iostreams with formatted I/O, and then to call the GUI function with the string as an argument. (C programmers remember using the `sprintf()` function in similar situations.) There are, of course, many other situations where in-memory formatting is convenient.

Fixed Buffer Size

A family of stream classes implements such in-memory formatting. For output to memory, there is `ostrstream`, which is derived from (among other classes) `ostream`. For input from memory, there is `istrstream`, derived from `istream`; and for read/write memory objects, there is `strstream`, derived from `iostream`. To use memory stream objects, you need the STRSTREA.H header file. The next example shows how to use both the `ostrstream` and the `istrstream` objects. Listing 10-21 shows STRSTR.

Listing 10-21 STRSTR

```
// strstr.cpp
// strstream memory objects
#include <strstrea.h>              // for ostrstream class
const int SIZE = 80;              // size of memory buffer

void main()
   {
   char membuff[SIZE];           // buffer in memory
   ostrstream omem(membuff, SIZE);  // make output memory object

   int oj = 77;                  // data variables
   double od = 890.12;           // for output to memory
   char ostr1[] = "Kafka";
   char ostr2[] = "Freud";


   omem << "oj= " << oj << endl     // output data to
        << "od= " << od << endl     // memory object
        << "ostr1= " << ostr1 << endl
        << "ostr2= " << ostr2 << endl
        << ends;                    // end the buffer with '\0'

   cout << membuff;                 // display the memory buffer

   char dummy[20];                  // new variables for input
   int ij;
   double id;
   char istr1[20];
   char istr2[20];

   istrstream imem(membuff, SIZE);  // make input memory object
                                    // extract data
   imem >> dummy >> ij >> dummy >> id // into new variables
        >> dummy >> istr1>> dummy >> istr2;
                                    // display variables
   cout << "\nij=" << ij << "\nid=" << id
        << "\nistr1=" << istr1 << "\nistr2=" << istr2;
   }
```

The `ostrstream` *Object*

One way to use an `ostrstream` object is to start with a data buffer of type `char*`. You then create an `ostrstream` object, using the memory buffer and its size as arguments to the object's constructor. Now you can send formatted text to the `ostrstream` object, using the `<<` operator, just as if you were sending the text to `cout` or a disk file. That's what I do in the first part of STRSTR.

When you run the program, `membuff` will be filled with the formatted text:

```
j= 77\nd= 890.12\nstr1= Kafka\nstr2= Freud\n\0
```

You can format the text using manipulators, just as you do for `cout`. The manipulator `ends` inserts a `'\0'` character at the end of the string. (Don't forget this manipulator; the string must be zero terminated, and this doesn't happen automatically.) The program now displays the contents of the buffer as a string of type char:

```
cout << membuff;
```

Here's the resulting output:

```
oj= 77
od= 890.12
ostr1= Kafka
ostr2= Freud
```

In this example, the program displays the contents of the buffer only to show what the buffer looks like. Ordinarily, you would have a more sophisticated use for this formatted text, such as passing the address of the buffer to a GUI function for display in a dialog box.

Input Memory Streams

The most common use for in-memory formatting is to store text in memory, as I've shown, using an `ostrstream` object. However, you can also read formatted data out of memory and store it in variables. This allows you to convert many values at once from alphanumeric form into numerical variables, instead of using individual C language conversion functions such as `atof()` and `atoi()`.

The second part of STRSTR creates an `istrstr` object, `imem`, and associates it with the same memory buffer, `membuff`, that was used for the earlier `ostrstream` object. Then the program reads data out of `imem` into appropriate variables. This automatically converts the formatted `char*` data in `membuff` into variables of type `int`, `double`, and `char*`. Finally, STRSTR displays the value of these variables to show that the conversion process has produced correct results. Here's the second part of the program's output:

```
ij=77
id=890.12
istr1=Kafka
istr2=Freud
```

Note that, for this conversion process to work, individual variables in `membuff` must be delimited by whitespace. That's why I leave a space after the equal sign when writing the data into `omem` in the first part of the program.

Also note that when I read data out of `imem` into individual variables, I am not interested in the text (such as `oj=`) that introduces the variables. I read these short strings into a buffer called `dummy` and then forget about them.

Universality

To focus attention on the techniques of using in-memory formatting, I have shown standalone `main()` programs in the examples in this session. If you're writing an object-oriented program, you will probably want to place the routines that handle in-memory I/O in member functions so that objects can read and write themselves to memory (see the REWOBJ example in Session 5 in this chapter).

If you handle things correctly when you do this, you can use the same member functions to read and write objects to memory that you use to read and write them to disk files. Overload the << and

>> operators to work with disk files. Then let the name of the file object (whether **istream** or **istrstream**, or **ostream** or **ostrstream**) be passed as an argument to the function, rather than hard-wired into the function, as I show in REWOBJ.

File Pointers

Incidentally, you may be interested to know that you can use file pointers, such as those handled with **seekg()** and **tellp()**, with in-memory objects such as **istrstream** and **ostrstream**, just as you can with file objects.

Dynamic Buffer Size

There's a second kind of **ostrstream** object. Instead of associating the object with a user-defined buffer, as I showed in STRSTR, you can create an **ostrstream** object that allocates its own storage and adjusts its size dynamically to hold whatever you put in it. To do this, simply define the object with no arguments. Once it's defined, fill it with data and it will expand to hold what you put in. As you continue to add data, the object will continue to expand. Listing 10-22 shows AUTOSTR.

Listing 10-22 AUTOSTR

```
// autostr.cpp
// writes formatted data into memory; uses dynamic ostrstream
#include <strstrea.h>            // for ostrstream class

void main()
    {
    ostrstream omem;   // create dynamic stream object

    omem << "j=" << 111 << endl       // insert numbers
         << "k=" << 2.3456 << endl;   // into ostrstream object
    omem << ends;                     // terminate with '\0'

    char* p = omem.str();    // get address of buffer
    cout << p;               // display it
    }
```

I create a dynamic **ostrstream** object (note the lack of arguments) and put data in it: the integer 111 and the floating-point value 2.3456. To display its contents, I use the **str()** member function to return a pointer (type **char***) to the section of memory containing the data:

```
char* p = omem.str();
```

This pointer can then be sent on to another function to display the data or access it for other purposes. In the program, I insert the pointer in **cout**:

```
cout << p;
```

The output looks like this:

```
j=111
k=2.3456
```

Typically, the pointer value is sent to a GUI function to display the data.

This use of the dynamic `ostrstream` object works nicely, relieving you of the work of setting up a buffer of your own and worrying about how big to make it. If you use the approach shown—putting data into the object using a single statement, then getting the value of a pointer to the data, and never changing the contents or accessing the data again—then everything works as expected.

However, going much beyond this approach can lead you quickly into a realm akin to black magic. Why is this? Remember that dynamic `ostrstream` objects, rather than relying on a user-supplied buffer, must dynamically allocate memory to store their data. When you put data in them, they find memory for just that amount of data. If you then add more data, they may need to move the data to a different place in memory to accommodate the increased buffer size. But if you've already found out where the data is using `str()`, the object can no longer move the data. It therefore *freezes* itself. Once it's frozen, you can't add more data. Also, you are responsible for releasing its memory yourself, using `delete`. All things considered, it's probably not worth the hassle to go beyond the simple approach shown here.

1. In-memory formatting means
   a. rearranging your computer's physical memory.
   b. rearranging the data in memory to eliminate unused spaces.
   c. storing (or retrieving) numerical and other data as a string in memory.
   d. creating an object of type `ostream`.
   e. creating an object of type `strstream`.

2. A regular (nondynamic) `ostrstream` object
   a. is used to store data in a disk file.
   b. is told by the code that creates it how much data it can hold.
   c. can store `int` and `float` values in the same format as memory variables.
   d. must be associated with a data buffer located elsewhere in the program.
   e. creates its own data buffer.

3. An `istrstream` object
   a. allocates its own data buffer.
   b. writes data to either a disk file or the screen display.
   c. reads data from either a disk file or the keyboard.
   d. takes formatted data from memory and stores it in variables.
   e. takes data from variables and stores it as formatted data in memory.

4. A dynamic `ostrstream` object
   a. is called dynamic because it destroys its data automatically when it goes out of scope.
   b. uses the member function `str()` to store data.
   c. allocates its own memory buffer for the data stored in it.
   d. cannot be deleted.
   e. must be given a limit on buffer size.

5. Unless you really know what you're doing, you shouldn't use multiple data inputs and outputs with dynamic `ostrstream` objects because
   a. actually, this is OK.
   b. finding out where the data is stored freezes it.
   c. an object might move its data after you find out where it is.
   d. all pointers are relative.
   e. dynamic data is changing too fast to read.

EXERCISE 1

Adapt the REWOBJ example from Session 5 of this chapter so the `person` class works with in-memory formatting as well as with disk files. As noted earlier, this is conveniently done by overloading the `<<` and `>>` operators and specifying the type of object to be read or written to as an argument passed to the member functions.

EXERCISE 2

Start with Exercise 1 of Session 5 in this chapter, which added `diskIn()` and `diskOut()` member functions to the `airtime` class. Rewrite this example so it works with in-memory formatting as well as with disk files, using a technique similar to that in Exercise 1.

SESSION 8

PRINTER OUTPUT AND OTHER REFINEMENTS

In this last session I'll look at three short topics that are related to iostreams: command-line arguments, printer output, and redirection. These topics are all more or less specific to DOS (and UNIX) programs, so if you plan never to program in DOS or UNIX, you can probably skip this session.

Command-Line Arguments

If you use DOS programs, you are probably familiar with command-line arguments, used when invoking a program from the DOS C prompt. (Actually, you can also use command-line arguments when you invoke a program using the Windows Run command. However, they are not commonly used in Windows.) Command-line arguments are typically used to pass the name of a data file to an application at the same time you start the application. For example, you can invoke a word processor application and the document it will work on at the same time:

```
C>wordproc afile.doc
```

Here, `afile.doc` is a command-line argument. How can you get a C++ program to read command-line arguments? Listing 10-23 shows an example, COMLINE, that reads and displays as many command-line arguments as you care to type. Multiple arguments are separated by spaces.

Listing 10-23 COMLINE

```
// comline.cpp
// demonstrates command-line arguments
#include <iostream.h>

void main(int argc, char* argv[] )
    {
    cout << "\nargc = " << argc;

    for(int j=0; j<argc; j++)
        cout << "\nArgument " << j << " = " << argv[j];
    }
```

Here's some sample interaction with the program where the user types three command-line arguments:

```
C>comline uno dos tres

argc = 4
Argument 0 = C:\CPP\CHAP14\COMLINE.EXE
Argument 1 = uno
Argument 2 = dos
Argument 3 = tres
```

To read command-line arguments, the `main()` function (don't forget it's a function!) must itself be given two arguments. The first, `argc` (for *argument count*), represents the total number of command-line arguments. The first command-line argument is always the path name of the current program. The remaining command-line arguments are those typed by the user; they are delimited by the space character. In the example above, they are *uno, dos,* and *tres.*

The system stores the command-line arguments as strings in memory and creates an array of pointers to these strings. In the example, the array is called `argv` (for *argument values*). Individual strings are accessed through the appropriate pointer, so the first string (the path name) is `argv[0]`, the second (*uno* in this example) is `argv[1]`, and so on. COMLINE accesses the arguments in turn and prints them out in a `for` loop that uses `argc`, the number of command-line arguments, as its upper limit.

You don't actually need to use the particular names `argc` and `argv` as arguments to `main()`, but they are so common that any other names would cause consternation to everyone but the compiler.

Listing 10-24 shows a program that uses a command-line argument for something useful. It displays the contents of a text file whose name is supplied by the user on the command line. Thus it imitates the DOS command Type.

Listing 10-24 OTYPE

```
// otype.cpp
// imitates TYPE command
#include <fstream.h>            // for file functions
#include <process.h>           // for exit()

void main(int argc, char* argv[] )
    {
```

```
if( argc != 2 )
    {
    cerr << "\nFormat: otype filename";
    exit(-1);
    }
char ch;                          // character to read
ifstream infile;                  // create file for input
infile.open( argv[1] );           // open file
if( !infile )                     // check for errors
    {
    cerr << "\nCan't open " << argv[1];
    exit(-1);
    }
while( infile.get(ch) != 0 )      // read a character
    cout << ch;                   // display the character
}
```

This program first checks to see if the user has entered the correct number of command-line arguments. Remember that the path name of OTYPE.EXE itself is always the first command-line argument. The second argument is the name of the file to be displayed, which the user should have entered when invoking the program:

```
C>otype ichar.cpp
```

Thus, the total number of command-line arguments should equal two. If it doesn't, the user probably doesn't understand how to use the program, and the program sends an error message via `cerr` to clarify matters.

If the number of arguments is correct, the program tries to open the file whose name is the second command-line argument (`argv[1]`). If the file can't be opened, the program signals an error. Finally, in a `while` loop, the program reads the file character by character and writes it to the screen.

A value of 0 for the character signals an EOF. This is another way to check for EOF. You can also use the value of the file object itself, as I've done before:

```
while( infile )
    {
    infile.get(ch);
    cout << ch;
    }
```

You could also replace this entire `while` loop with the statement

```
cout << infile.rdbuf();
```

as you saw in the ICHAR2 program in Session 3 in this chapter.

Printer Output

In DOS, it's fairly easy to send data to the printer. DOS predefines a number of special file names for hardware devices. These make it possible to treat the devices as if they were files. Table 10-12 shows these names.

Name	Device
CON	Console (keyboard and screen)
AUX or COM1	First serial port
COM2	Second serial port
PRN or LPT1	First parallel printer
LPT2	Second parallel printer
LPT3	Third parallel printer
NUL	Dummy (nonexistent) device

Table 10-12   *Predefined hardware file names*

In most systems, the printer is connected to the first parallel port, so the file name for the printer is PRN or LPT1. (You can substitute the appropriate name if your system is configured differently.)

The following program, EZPRINT (Listing 10-25), sends a string and a number to the printer, using formatted output with the insertion operator.

Listing 10-25 EZPRINT

```
// ezprint.cpp
// demonstrates simple output to printer

#include <fstream.h>                   // for file streams

void main(void)
   {
   char* s1 = "\nToday's winning number is ";
   int   n1 = 17982;

   ofstream outfile;                   // make a file
   outfile.open("PRN");                // open it for the printer
   outfile << s1 << n1 << endl;        // send data to printer
   outfile << '\x0D';                  // formfeed for page eject
   }
```

You can send any amount of formatted output to the printer this way. The \x0D character causes the page to eject from most printers.

This technique works only for DOS programs, so you must use a DOS target when you create EZPRINT (not an EasyWin or similar Windows-related target). Sending output to the printer from a Windows program is beyond the scope of this book.

The next example, OPRINT (Listing 10-26), prints the contents of a disk file, specified on the command line, to the printer. It uses the character-by-character approach to this data transfer.

Listing 10-26 OPRINT

```
// oprint.cpp
// imitates print command
#include <fstream.h>                   // for file functions
```

```
#include <process.h>            // for exit()

void main(int argc, char* argv[] )
   {
   if( argc != 2 )
      {
      cerr << "\nFormat: oprint filename";
      exit(-1);
      }
   char ch;                     // character to read
   ifstream infile;             // create file for input
   infile.open( argv[1] );      // open file
   if( !infile )                // check for errors
      {
      cerr << "\nCan't open " << argv[1];
      exit(-1);
      }
   ofstream outfile;                    // make file
   outfile.open("PRN");                 // open it for printer
   while( infile.get(ch) != 0 )         // read a character
      outfile.put(ch);                  // write character to printer
   }
```

You can use this program to print any text file, such as any of your .CPP source files. It acts much the same as the DOS Print command. Like the OTYPE example, this program checks for the correct number of command-line arguments and for a successful opening of the specified file.

Redirection

Note: The programs in this section should be executed from a DOS box in Windows or from DOS itself. You need to see a DOS prompt when invoking the program so you can enter additional information besides the program name.

In DOS, it's possible to read and write to files using only the objects cout and cin. These predefined objects normally represent the display and the keyboard, but they can be redirected by the user to represent disk files. Redirection is a technique, originally imported from UNIX into DOS, that allows the user additional flexibility in the way programs are used. Redirection is supplied by DOS, not by C++, but C++ supports it, so it's interesting to see how to use it. As an example, consider the program redir (Listing 10-27).

Listing 10-27 REDIR
```
// redir.cpp
// demonstrates redirection
// syntax: redir <source >destination
#include <iostream.h>
#include <iomanip.h>                      // for resetiosflags()

void main()
   {
   char ch;
   while( !cin.eof() )                    // quit on EOF
```

continued on next page

continued from previous page

```
   {
   cin >> resetiosflags(ios::skipws)     // keep whitespace
           >> ch;                         // read from std input
   cout << ch;                            // send to std output
   }
}
```

Before exploring how this program can be used for redirection, I should note that you must reset the `skipws` flag when getting input from `cin`. This is necessary because `cin` normally skips over whitespace, which includes spaces, new lines, and EOFs. We want to read all these characters.

Using the REDIR Program

When invoked in the usual way at the command line, REDIR simply echoes whatever the user types each time (ENTER) is pressed. Here's some sample interaction (from a poem by the 16th-century poet Ben Jonson):

```
C>redir
Truth is the trial of itself,          <--entered by the user
Truth is the trial of itself,          <--echoed by the program
And needs no other touch;
And needs no other touch;
And purer than the purest gold,
And purer than the purest gold,
Refine it ne'er so much.
Refine it ne'er so much.
^Z
```

The user enters the (CTRL)-(Z) key combination (or the (F6) function key) to terminate the program. This character is interpreted by the program as an EOF.

Using redirection gives the program additional capabilities. It can take input from the keyboard and write it to a disk file, display text from a disk file on the screen, or copy one file to another.

Redirecting Output

To redirect a program's output from the screen to a file, use the **>** operator. This is a DOS operator; it has nothing to do with C++ comparison or overloading. Here's how to invoke REDIR to take keyboard input and redirect it to a file called SAMPLE.TXT:

```
C>redir >sample.txt
If you would avoid suspicion,                <--entered by user
don't lace your shoes in a melon field.      <--entered by user
^Z                                           <--entered by user
```

The text you type will be written to SAMPLE.TXT. You can check this file with the DOS command Type to be sure it contains this text.

Redirecting Input

To redirect a program's input so it comes from a file and not the keyboard, use the < operator. Here's how to invoke REDIR to take data from the file SAMPLE.TXT and use it as input to the program, which then displays it:

```
C>redir <sample.txt
If you would avoid suspicion,       <--displayed by program
don't lace your shoes in a melon field.   <--displayed by program
```

Redirecting Input and Output

Both input and output can be redirected at the same time. As an example, here's how to use REDIR to copy one file to another:

```
C>redir <src.txt >dest.txt
```

Nothing is displayed, but you will find that SRC.TXT has been copied to DEST.TXT. Note that this works only for text files, not for binary files.

If you want to display a particular message on the screen even when the output of your program has been redirected to a file, you can use the `cerr` object. Insert this line into the `while` loop in REDIR:

```
cerr << ch;
```

Now try copying one file to another. Each character `ch` will be sent to the screen by `cerr`, even though the output to `cout` is going to a file.

Redirection and the _withassign Classes

The need to support redirection explains the `_withassign` classes discussed earlier. Redirection is carried out by setting the `cout` or `cin` stream object equal to another stream object: namely, one associated with the file name provided on the command line. But to set `cin` and `cout` equal to other objects, `cin` and `cout` must be derived from a class that supports the assignment operation. Most stream classes don't, but the three `_withassign` classes, from which `cout`, `cin`, and `cerr` are derived, do.

1. Command-line arguments
   a. are separated by whitespace characters.
   b. are separated by the space character.
   c. cannot be accessed from an application.
   d. take place between generals and admirals.
   e. are stored as strings in memory.

2. For command-line arguments, `argc` is _____ and `argv` is _____.
   a. the number of arguments typed by the user; a pointer to an array of pointers
   b. 1 plus the number of arguments typed by the user; a pointer to an array
   c. what the user types; what the operating system supplies
   d. always 2; always a file name
   e. the name of the application; a list of arguments

3. In C++, in the DOS environment, a printer
   a. can be treated like a write-only file with a specific name.
   b. needs to be opened like any other file.
   c. can easily receive and print graphics images.
   d. is usually connected to COM or LPT1.
   e. cannot be told to eject a page.

4. Using DOS redirection
   a. you can redirect program output that would normally go to the printer to a disk file.
   b. you can redirect program output that would normally go to the screen to a disk file.
   c. you can redirect program output that would normally go to a program to a formatted memory buffer.
   d. you can redirect a file that would normally go to a program to the screen.
   e. seldom occurs in Windows.

5. For the program PROG to read data from FILE1.DOC and write it to FILE2.DOC, you would write
   a. `prog <file1.doc >file2.doc`
   b. `file1.doc >prog >file2.doc`
   c. `file1.doc <prog <file2.doc`
   d. `file2.doc >prog >file1.doc`
   e. `file2.doc <prog <file1.doc`

EXERCISE 1

Write a member function that performs printer output for the `airtime` class.

EXERCISE 2

Revise the PERSIO program in Session 6 so that the name of the file that `person` objects are written to or read from is supplied by the user on the command line when the program is first invoked, rather than always being PERSON.DAT.

SUMMARY: CHAPTER 10

In this chapter I've covered a variety of topics connected with input/output in C++. I started with an overview of the stream class hierarchy and then looked at how errors are handled in streams. You saw how disk file I/O is performed using the stream classes, how file pointers determine where data is accessed within a file, and how file errors are handled.

Next I showed how member functions can incorporate file-handling capabilities into user-written classes. I showed how to overload the `<<` and `>>` operators to simplify I/O for class objects and how a section of memory can be treated as a disk file to simplify formatting. Finally, I covered three DOS-related capabilities: Redirection allows program output to be redirected from the screen to a file or input to be redirected from the keyboard to a file; printer output can be handled easily in DOS by treating the printer as a file with a special name; and, command-line arguments allow the user to specify information, such as a file to be opened, when a program is invoked.

END-OF-CHAPTER DISCUSSION

Estelle: This whole chapter doesn't seem relevant to OOP. It's just about files in old-fashioned procedural situations.

George: Well, thank heavens! I don't mind a break from OOP.

Don: But it's pretty obvious how to apply all this file-related stuff to OOP.

Estelle: You mean just put file-handling routines in member functions?

Don: Exactly. If an object needs to write itself to a file or read its data from a file, you just create a member function to do it. Then you can call that function from `main()` or wherever.

George: Anyway, iostreams *are* C++ classes. That's already pretty OOP.

Estelle: Well, that's true, but I'm just using the iostream classes. I'm not writing them.

George: That's all right with me.

Estelle: It does show how little you need to know about OOP to be a class *user*, as opposed to a class *creator*. That's one of the strengths of OOP: Once a class is written, it's easy to use.

George: WOUMT.

Estelle: I beg your pardon?

George: It's an acronym. Write Once, Use Many Times. Isn't that how classes are supposed to work?

Don: That's good, George. I like it.

George: What bothers me is that I still don't know how to do I/O in Windows.

Don: They don't teach that in this book.

Estelle: It's complicated.

Don: The point here is just to learn the fundamentals of OOP, that's why we use such simple I/O. Good luck if you want to learn Windows and C++ at the same time.

George: You mean I don't know everything there is to know already? I'm going to drop this programming stuff and go to barber school.

Estelle: Come on, George. Nothing worth doing is ever easy.

CHAPTER 11

TEMPLATES, EXCEPTIONS, AND MORE

This is a portmanteau chapter. The major topics are templates and exceptions, but in addition I cover the `string` class from the C++ standard library, multifile programs, the new explicit cast format, the `typedef` specifier, and overloading the function operator.

Templates are probably the most important of these topics. Templates are the underlying mechanism for modern container classes, such as the Standard Template Library (STL), which I discuss in Chapter 12. To a lesser extent, the exception mechanism for handling errors is also becoming a common feature of C++ programs. The multifile approach is used for all but the simplest C++ programs, so this too is an essential subject. Many of the other topics are necessary for an understanding of the STL and other sophisticated C++ programs.

SESSION 1

FUNCTION TEMPLATES

Suppose you want to write a function that returns the absolute value of two numbers. (As you no doubt remember from high school algebra, the absolute value of a number is its value without regard to its sign: The absolute value of 3 is 3; the absolute value of -3 is also 3.) Ordinarily, this function would be written for a particular data type:

```
int abs(int n)              // absolute value of ints
   {
   return (n<0) ? -n : n;  // if n is negative, return -n
   }
```

Here the function is defined to take an argument of type int and to return a value of this same type. But now suppose you want to find the absolute value of a type long. You need to write a completely new function:

```
long abs(long n)            // absolute value of longs
   {
   return (n<0) ? -n : n;
   }
```

And again, for type float:

```
float abs(float n)          // absolute value of floats
   {
   return (n<0) ? -n : n;
   }
```

The body of the function is the same in each case, but they must be separate functions because they handle variables of different types. It's true that in C++ these functions can all be overloaded to have the same name, but you must nevertheless write a separate definition for each one. (In the C language, which does not support overloading, functions for different types can't even have the same name. In the C function library, this leads to families of similarly named functions, such as abs(), fabs(), fabsl(), labs(), cabs(), and so on.)

Rewriting the same function body over and over for different types wastes time as well as space in the listing. Also, if you find you've made an error in one such function, you'll need to remember to correct it in each function body. Failing to do this correctly is a good way to introduce inconsistencies into your program.

It would be nice if there were a way to write such a function just once and have it work for many different data types. This is exactly what function templates do for you. The idea is shown schematically in Figure 11-1.

A Simple Function Template

The first example shows how to write an absolute value function as a template so it will work with any basic numerical type. This program defines a template version of abs() and then, in main(),

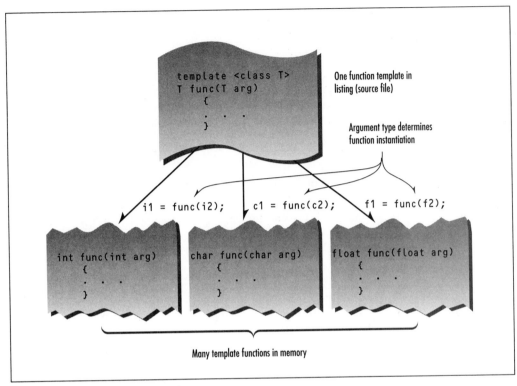

Figure 11-1 A function template

invokes this function a half-dozen times with different data types to prove that it works. Listing 11-1 shows TEMPABS.

Listing 11-1 TEMPABS

```
// tempabs.cpp
// template used for absolute value function

#include <iostream.h>

template <class T>                  // function template
T abs(T n)
        {
        return (n < 0) ? -n : n;
        }

void main()
        {
        int int1 = 5;
        int int2 = -6;
```

continued on next page

continued from previous page

```
      long lon1 = 70000L;
      long lon2 = -80000L;
      double dub1 = 9.95;
      double dub2 = -10.15;
                            // calls instantiate functions
      cout << "\nabs(" << int1 << ")=" << abs(int1);   // abs(int)
      cout << "\nabs(" << int2 << ")=" << abs(int2);   // abs(int)
      cout << "\nabs(" << lon1 << ")=" << abs(lon1);   // abs(long)
      cout << "\nabs(" << lon2 << ")=" << abs(lon2);   // abs(long)
      cout << "\nabs(" << dub1 << ")=" << abs(dub1);   // abs(double)
      cout << "\nabs(" << dub2 << ")=" << abs(dub2);   // abs(double)
      }
```

Here's the output of the program:

```
abs(5)=5
abs(-6)=6
abs(70000)=70000
abs(-80000)=80000
abs(9.95)=9.95
abs(-10.15)=10.15
```

As you can see, the `abs()` function now works with all three of the data types (`int`, `long`, and `double`) that I use as arguments. It will work on other basic types as well, and it will even work on user-defined data types, provided the less-than operator (`<`) and the unary minus (`-`) are appropriately overloaded.

Here's how to specify the `abs()` function so it works with multiple data types:

```
template <class T>            // function template
T abs(T n)
   {
   return (n<0) ? -n : n;
   }
```

This entire syntax, with a first line starting with the keyword `template` and the function definition following, is called a *function template*. How does this new way of writing `abs()` give it such amazing flexibility?

Function Template Syntax

The key innovation in function templates is to represent the data type used by the function not as a specific type such as `int`, but by a name that can stand for *any* type. In the function template above, this name is `T`. (There's nothing magic about this name; it can be anything you want, like `Type`, or `anyType`, or `FooBar`.) The `template` keyword signals the compiler that I'm about to define a function template. The keyword `class`, within the angle brackets, might just as well be called `type`. As you've seen, you can define your own data types using classes, so there's really no distinction between types and classes. The variable following the keyword `class` (`T` in this example) is called the *template argument*.

Throughout the definition of the function, whenever a specific data type such as `int` would ordinarily be written, I substitute the template argument, `T`. In the `abs()` function, this name appears only twice, both in the first line (the function declarator), as the argument type and return type. In more complex functions, it may appear numerous times throughout the function body as well.

What the Compiler Does

What does the compiler do when it sees the `template` keyword and the function definition that follows it? Well, nothing right away. The function template itself doesn't cause the compiler to generate any code. It can't generate code because it doesn't know yet what data type the function will be working with. It simply remembers the template for possible future use.

Code generation doesn't take place until the function is actually called (invoked) by a statement within the program. In TEMPABS, this happens in expressions such as `abs(int1)` in the statement

```
cout << "\nabs(" << int << ")=" << abs(int1);
```

When the compiler sees such a function call, it knows that the type to use is `int`, because that's the type of the argument `int1`. So it generates a specific version of the `abs()` function for type `int`, substituting `int` wherever it sees the name `T` in the function template. This is called *instantiating* the function template, and each instantiated version of the function is called a *template function*. (That is, a template function is a specific instance of a function template. Isn't terminology fun?)

The compiler also generates a call to the newly instantiated function and inserts it into the code where `abs(int1)` is. Similarly, the expression `abs(lon1)` causes the compiler to generate a version of `abs()` that operates on type `long`, as well as a call to this function, whereas the `abs(dub1)` call generates a function that works on type `double`. Of course, the compiler is smart enough to generate only one version of `abs()` for each data type. Thus, even though there are two calls to the `int` version of the function, the code for this version appears only once in the executable code.

Notice that the amount of RAM used by the program is the same whether I use the template approach or write three separate functions. What I've saved is having to type three separate functions into the source file. This makes the listing shorter and easier to understand. Also, if I want to change the way the function works, I need make the change in only one place in the listing instead of three.

The compiler decides how to compile the function based entirely on the data type used in the function call's argument (or arguments). The function's return type doesn't enter into this decision. This is similar to the way the compiler decides which of several overloaded functions to call.

A function template isn't really a function, because it does not actually cause program code to be placed in memory. Instead it is a pattern, or blueprint, for making many functions. This fits right into the philosophy of OOP. It's similar to the way a class isn't anything concrete (such as program code in memory), but a blueprint for making many similar objects.

Function Templates with Multiple Arguments

Let's look at another example of a function template. This one takes three arguments: two template arguments and one basic type. The purpose of this function is to search an array for a specific value. The function returns the array index for that value if it finds it, or -1 if it can't find it. The arguments are a pointer to the array, the value to search for, and the size of the array. In `main()`, the program defines four arrays of different types and four values to search for (treating type `char` as a number). Then it calls the template function once for each array. Listing 11-2 shows TEMPFIND.

Listing 11-2 TEMPFIND

```
// tempfind.cpp
// template used for function that finds number in array

#include <iostream.h>

// function returns index number of item, or -1 if not found
template <class atype>
int find(atype* array, atype value, int size)
        {
        for(int j=0; j<size; j++)
            if(array[j]==value)
                return j;
        return -1;
        }

char chrArr[] =    {1, 3, 5, 9, 11, 13};     // array
char ch = 5;                                 // value to find
int intArr[] =     {1, 3, 5, 9, 11, 13};
int in = 6;
long lonArr[] =    {1L, 3L, 5L, 9L, 11L, 13L};
long lo = 11L;
double dubArr[] = {1.0, 3.0, 5.0, 9.0, 11.0, 13.0};
double db = 4.0;

void main()
        {
        cout << "\n 5 in chrArray: index=" << find(chrArr, ch, 6);
        cout << "\n 6 in intArray: index=" << find(intArr, in, 6);
        cout << "\n11 in lonArray: index=" << find(lonArr, lo, 6);
        cout << "\n 4 in dubArray: index=" << find(dubArr, db, 6);
        }
```

Here I name the template argument `atype`. It appears in two of the function's arguments: as the type of a pointer to the array and as the type of the item to be matched. The third function argument, the array size, is always type `int`; it's not a template argument. Here's the output of the program:

```
 5 in chrArray: index=2
 6 in intArray: index=-1
11 in lonArray: index=4
 4 in dubArray: index=-1
```

The compiler generates four versions of the function, one for each type used to call it. It finds a 5 at index 2 in the character array it does not find a 6 in the integer array, and so on.

I should note that some programmers put the `template` keyword and the function declarator on the same line:

```
template<class atype> int find(atype* array, atype value, int size)
    {
    // function body
    }
```

Of course, the compiler is happy enough with this format, but I find it more forbidding and less clear than the multiline approach.

Template Arguments Must Match

When a template function is invoked, all instances of the same template argument must be of the same type. For example, in `find()`, if the array name is of type `int`, the value to search for must also be of type `int`. You can't say

```
int intarray[] = {1, 3, 5, 7};      // int array
float f1 = 5.0;                      // float value
int value = find(intarray, f1, 4);   // uh, oh
```

because the compiler expects all instances of `atype` to be the same type. It can generate a function

```
find(int*, int, int);
```

but it can't generate

```
find(int*, float, int);
```

because the first and second arguments must be the same type.

More Than One Template Argument

You can use more than one template argument in a function template. For example, suppose you like the idea of the `find()` function template, but you aren't sure how large an array it might be applied to. If the array is too large, then type `long` would be necessary for the array size instead of type `int`. On the other hand, you don't want to use type `long` if you don't need to. You want to select the type of the array size, as well as the type of data stored, when you call the function. To make this possible, you could make the array size into a template argument as well. I'll call it `btype`:

```
template <class atype, class btype>
btype find(atype* array, atype value, btype size)
   {
   for(btype j=0; j<size; j++)    // note use of btype
      if(array[j]==value)
          return j;
   return (btype)-1;
   }
```

Now you can use type `int` or type `long` (or even a user-defined type) for the size, whichever is appropriate. The compiler will generate different functions based not only on the type of the array and the value to be searched for, but also on the type of the array size.

Note that multiple template arguments can lead to many functions being instantiated from a single template. Two such arguments, if there were six basic types that could reasonably be used for each one, would allow the creation of up to 36 functions. This can take up a lot of memory if the functions are large. On the other hand, you don't instantiate a version of the function unless you actually call it.

Why Not Macros?

Old-time C programmers may wonder why I don't use macros to create different versions of a function for different data types. For example, the `abs()` function could be defined as

```
#define abs(n) ( (n<0) ? (-n) : (n) )
```

This has a similar effect to the class template in TEMPABS because it performs a simple text substitution and can thus work with any type. However, as I've noted before, macros aren't used much in C++. There are several problems with them. They don't perform any type checking. There may be several arguments to the macro that should be of the same type, but the compiler won't check whether or not they are. Also, the type of the value returned isn't specified, so the compiler can't tell if you're assigning it to an incompatible variable. In any case, macros are confined to functions that can be expressed in a single statement. There are also other, more subtle, problems with macros. On the whole, it's best to avoid them.

What Works?

How do you know whether you can instantiate a template function for a particular data type? For example, could you use the `find()` function from TEMPFIND to find a string (type `char*`) in an array of strings? To see if this is possible, check the operators used in the function. If they all work on the data type, then you can probably use it. The `find()` function, however, compares two variables using the equal-equal (`==`) operator. You can't use this operator with strings; you must use the `strcmp()` library function. Thus, `find()` won't work on `char*` strings. (However, it would work on a user-defined string class in which you overloaded the `==` operator.)

Start with a Normal Function

When you write a template function you're probably better off starting with a normal function that works on a fixed type: `int` or whatever. You can design and debug it without having to worry about template syntax and multiple types. Then, when everything works properly, you can turn the function definition into a template and check that it works for additional types.

 QUIZ 1

1. Template functions allow
   a. one function stored in memory to handle multiple data types.
   b. one function in the source file to handle multiple data types.
   c. user-defined types to be treated as ordinary types.
   d. user-defined types to be used as arguments to functions.
   e. one name to represent many data types within a function's definition in the source code.

2. Concerning this code:

```
template <class X>
X max(X n1, X n2)
        {
        return (n1 > n2) ? n1 : n2;
        }
```

which (if any) of the following statements are correct?

a. `n1` and `n2` are data types.

b. The keyword `class` means that you're defining a new class.

c. `X` represents a data type.

d. The keyword `template` means that you can use any numerical value for `X`.

e. The longest data type name will be returned.

3. If in your program you make the following four calls to the template function `abs()` (as it was declared in the TEMPABS example), how many instantiations of this function will be placed in memory?

```
abs(intvar1);
abs(intvar2);
abs(floatvar1);
abs(floatvar2);
```

a. 1

b. 2

c. 3

d. 4

e. none

4. A function template _____, whereas a template function _____ .

a. does not use a specific type, does use a specific type

b. does use a specific type, does not use a specific type

c. does not exist in memory, exists in memory

d. exists in memory, does not exist in memory

e. cannot be called, can be called

5. To instantiate a template function `tempfunc<>()` using a particular user-defined data type (class) `TYPE` as a template argument, `TYPE` must

a. overload the assignment operator (`=`).

b. overload the less-than operator (`<`).

c. contain the same data variables as those used in `tempfunc<>()`.

d. supply the same member functions as `tempfunc<>()`.

e. supply a member function to handle any operation used in `tempfunc<>()`.

EXERCISE 1

Write a template function that returns the largest of three numbers (of the same type) passed to it as arguments.

EXERCISE 2

Write a template function that searches through an array of any type, counting how many elements have a specific value.

CLASS TEMPLATES

The template concept can be applied to classes as well as to functions. Class templates are generally used for data storage (container) classes. Stacks and linked lists, which you encountered in previous chapters, are examples of data storage classes. However, the examples of these classes I presented could store data of only a single basic type. The `Stack` class in the STACKCON program from Chapter 5, Session 1, for example, could store data only of type `int`. Here's a condensed version of that class:

```
class Stack
   {
   private:
      int st[MAX];          // array of ints
      int top;              // index number of top of stack
   public:
      Stack();              // constructor
      void push(int var);   // takes int as argument
      int pop();            // returns int value
   };
```

If I wanted to store data of type `long` in a stack, I would need to define a completely new class:

```
class LongStack
   {
   private:
      long st[MAX];         // array of longs
      int top;              // index number of top of stack
   public:
      LongStack();          // constructor
      void push(long var);  // takes long as argument
      long pop();           // returns long value
   };
```

Similarly, I would need to create a new stack class for every data type I wanted to store. It would be nice to be able to write a single class specification that would work for variables of *all* types instead of a single basic type. As you may have guessed, class templates allow you to do this. I'll create a variation of STACKCON that uses a class template. Listing 11-3 shows TEMPSTAK.

Listing 11-3 TEMPSTAK
```
// tempstak.cpp
// implements stack class as a template

#include <iostream.h>
const int MAX = 100;          // size of array

template <class Type>
class Stack
   {
```

```
    private:
        Type st[MAX];          // stack: array of any type
        int top;               // number of top of stack
    public:
        Stack()                // constructor
            { top = -1; }
        void push(Type var)    // put number on stack
            { st[++top] = var; }
        Type pop()             // take number off stack
            { return st[top--]; }
    };

void main()
    {
    Stack<float> s1;           // s1 is object of class Stack<float>

    s1.push(1111.1);           // push 3 floats, pop 3 floats
    s1.push(2222.2);
    s1.push(3333.3);
    cout << "1: " << s1.pop() << endl;
    cout << "2: " << s1.pop() << endl;
    cout << "3: " << s1.pop() << endl;

    Stack<long> s2;            // s2 is object of class Stack<long>

    s2.push(123123123L);       // push 3 longs, pop 3 longs
    s2.push(234234234L);
    s2.push(345345345L);
    cout << "1: " << s2.pop() << endl;
    cout << "2: " << s2.pop() << endl;
    cout << "3: " << s2.pop() << endl;
    }
```

Here the the class **Stack** is presented as a template class. The approach is similar to that used in function templates. The **template** keyword signals that the entire class will be a template:

```
template <class Type>
class Stack
    {
    // data and member functions using template argument 'Type'
    };
```

A template argument, named **Type** in this example, is then used (instead of a fixed data type such as **int**) every place in the class specification where there is a reference to the type of the array **st**. There are three of these: the definition of **st**, the argument type of the **push()** function, and the return type of the **pop()** function.

Class templates differ from function templates in the way they are instantiated. To create an actual function from a function template, call it using arguments of a specific type. Classes, however, are instantiated by defining an object using the template argument:

```
Stack<float> s1;
```

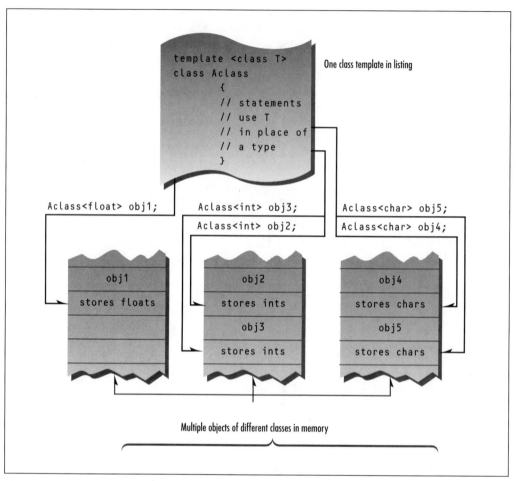

Figure 11-2   A class template

This creates an object, s1, that is a stack that stores numbers of type float. The compiler provides space in memory for this object's data, using type float wherever the template argument Type appears in the class specification. It also provides space for the member functions (if these have not already been placed in memory by another object of type Stack<float>). These member functions also operate exclusively on type float. Figure 11-2 shows how a class template and definitions of specific objects cause these objects to be placed in memory.

Creating a Stack object that stores objects of a different type, as in

```
Stack<long> s2;
```

creates not only a different space for data, but also a new set of member functions that operate on type long.

Note that the name of the type of **s1** consists of the class name **Stack** *plus the template argument*: **Stack<float>**. This distinguishes it from other classes that might be created from the same template, such as **Stack<int>** or **Stack<long>**.

The program exercises the **s1** and **s2** stacks by pushing and popping three values on each one and displaying each popped value. Here's the output of TEMPSTAK:

```
1: 3333.3       // float stack
2: 2222.2
3: 1111.1
1: 345345345    // long stack
2: 234234234
3: 123123123
```

In this example, the template approach gives me two classes for the price of one. I could instantiate class objects for other numerical types with just a single line of code.

Class Name Depends on Context

In the TEMSTAK example, the member functions of the class template were all defined within the class. If the member functions are defined externally (outside of the class specification), you need to use a new syntax. The next program shows how this works. Listing 11-4 shows TEMSTAK2.

Listing 11-4 TEMSTAK2

```
// temstak2.cpp
// implements stack class as a template
// member functions are defined outside the class

#include <iostream.h>
const int MAX = 100;

template <class Type>
class Stack
    {
    private:
        Type st[MAX];           // stack: array of any type
        int top;                // number of top of stack
    public:
        Stack();                // constructor
        void push(Type var);    // put number on stack
        Type pop();             // take number off stack
    };

template<class Type>
Stack<Type>::Stack()            // constructor
    {
    top = -1;
    }
```

continued on next page

continued from previous page
```
template<class Type>
void Stack<Type>::push(Type var) // put number on stack
    {
    st[++top] = var;
    }


template<class Type>
Type Stack<Type>::pop()                // take number off stack
    {
    return st[topñ];
    }



void main()
    {
    Stack<float> s1;         // s1 is object of class Stack<float>

    s1.push(1111.1);         // push 3 floats, pop 3 floats
    s1.push(2222.2);
    s1.push(3333.3);
    cout << "1: " << s1.pop() << endl;
    cout << "2: " << s1.pop() << endl;
    cout << "3: " << s1.pop() << endl;

    Stack<long> s2;          // s2 is object of class Stack<long>

    s2.push(123123123L);     // push 3 longs, pop 3 longs
    s2.push(234234234L);
    s2.push(345345345L);
    cout << "1: " << s2.pop() << endl;
    cout << "2: " << s2.pop() << endl;
    cout << "3: " << s2.pop() << endl;
    }
```

The expression `template<class Type>` must precede not only the class definition, but each externally defined member function as well. Here's how the `push()` function looks:

```
template<class Type>
void Stack<Type>::push(Type var)
    {
    st[++top] = var;
    }
```

The name `Stack<Type>` has been used to identify the class of which `push()` is a member. In a normal nontemplate member function, the name `Stack` alone would suffice:

```
void Stack::push(int var)  // Stack() as a non-template function
    {
    st[++top] = var;
    }
```

However, for a function template, you need the template argument as well: `Stack<Type>`.

Thus you see that the name of the template class is expressed differently in different contexts. Within the class specification, it's simply the name itself: `Stack`. For externally defined member functions, it's the class name plus the template argument name: `Stack<Type>`. When you define actual objects for storing a specific data type, it's the class name plus this specific type: `Stack<float>` (or whatever).

```
class Stack                        // Stack class specifier
   { };

void Stack<Type>::push(Type var)   // push() definition
   {    }

Stack<float> s1;                   // object of type Stack<float>
```

You must exercise considerable care to use the correct name in the correct context. It's easy to forget to add the `<Type>` or `<float>` to the `Stack`. The compiler hates it when you get this wrong.

Although it's not demonstrated in this example, the syntax when a member function returns a value of its own class can create some problems for you. Suppose you define a class `Int` that provides some augmentation for the `int` class, such as checking for overflow. Suppose further that you make this a template class so it can be instantiated using either type `int` or type `long`. If you use an external definition for a member function `xfunc()` of this class that returns type `Int`, you will need to use `Int<Type>` for the return type as well as preceding the scope resolution operator:

```
Int<Type> Int<Type>::xfunc(Int arg)
   {    }
```

The class name used as a type of a function argument, on the other hand, doesn't need to include the `<Type>` designation.

A Linked List Class Using Templates

Let's look at another example where templates are used for a data storage class. This is a modification of the LINKLIST program from Chapter 8, Session 7 (which I encourage you to reexamine). It requires not only that the `linklist` class itself be made into a template, but that the `link` structure, which actually stores each data item, be made into a template as well. Listing 11-5 shows TEMPLIST.

Listing 11-5 TEMPLIST
```
// templist.cpp
// implements linked list as a template

#include <iostream.h>

template<class TYPE>                // struct link<TYPE>
struct link                         // one element of list
// within this struct definition 'link' means link<TYPE>
   {
   TYPE data;                       // data item
   link* next;                      // pointer to next link
   };
```

continued on next page

continued from previous page

```
template<class TYPE>                 // class linklist<TYPE>
class linklist                       // a list of links
// within this class definition 'linklist' means linklist<TYPE>
    {
    private:
        link<TYPE>* first;           // pointer to first link
    public:
        linklist()                   // no-argument constructor
            { first = NULL; }        // no first link
        void additem(TYPE d);        // add data item (one link)
        void display();              // display all links
        ~linklist();                 // destructor
    };

template<class TYPE>
void linklist<TYPE>::additem(TYPE d)    // add data item
    {
    link<TYPE>* newlink = new link<TYPE>;   // make a new link
    newlink->data = d;               // give it data
    newlink->next = first;           // it points to next link
    first = newlink;                 // now first points to this
    }

template<class TYPE>
void linklist<TYPE>::display()       // display all links
    {
    link<TYPE>* current = first;     // set ptr to first link
    while( current != NULL )         // quit on last link
        {
        cout << endl << current->data;  // print data
        current = current->next;        // move to next link
        }
    }

template<class TYPE>                 // destructor
linklist<TYPE>::~linklist()          //      deletes all links
    {
    while( first != NULL )           // quit on last link
        {
        link<TYPE>* temp = first;    // 'temp' to current link
        first = temp->next;          // 'first' to next link
        delete temp;                 // delete current link
        }
    }

void main()
    {
    linklist<double> ld; // ld is object of class linklist<double>

    ld.additem(151.5);     // add three doubles to list ld
    ld.additem(262.6);
    ld.additem(373.7);
```

```
ld.display();          // display entire list ld

linklist<char> lch;  // lch is object of class linklist<char>

lch.additem('a');      // add three chars to list lch
lch.additem('b');
lch.additem('c');
lch.display();         // display entire list lch
}
```

In `main()`, the program defines two linked lists: one to hold numbers of type `double` and one to hold characters of type `char`. It then exercises the lists by placing three items on each one with the `additem()` member function, and displaying all the items with the `display()` member function. Here's the output of TEMPLIST:

```
373.7
262.6
151.5
c
b
a
```

Both the `linklist` class and the `link` structure make use of the template argument `TYPE` to stand for any type. (Well, not really *any* type; I'll discuss later what types can actually be stored.) Thus, not only `linklist` but also `link` must be templates, preceded by the line

```
template<class TYPE>
```

Notice that it's not just a class that's turned into a template. Any other programming constructs that use a variable data type must also be turned into templates, as the `link` structure is here.

As before, you must pay attention to how the class (and, in this program, a structure as well) is named in different parts of the program. Within its own specification, you can use the name of the class or structure alone: `linklist` and `link`. In external member functions, you must use the class or structure name and the template argument: `linklist<TYPE>`. When you actually define objects of type `linklist`, you must use the specific data type that the list is to store:

```
linklist<double> ld;   // defines object ld of class linklist<double>
```

Storing User-Defined Data Types

In the programs so far, I've used template classes to store basic data types. For example, the TEMPLIST program stored numbers of type `double` and type `char` in a linked list. Is it possible to store objects of user-defined types (classes) in these same template classes? The answer is yes, but with a caveat.

Employees in a Linked List

Examine the `employee` class in the EMPINH program in Chapter 7, Session 2. (Don't worry about the derived classes.) Could you store objects of type `employee` on the linked list of the TEMPLIST example? As with template functions, you can find out if a template class can operate on objects of a particular class by checking the operations the template class performs on those objects. The `linklist` class uses the overloaded insertion (`<<`) operator to display the objects it stores:

```
void linklist<TYPE>::display()
    {
    ...
    cout << endl << current->data;  // uses insertion operator (<<)
    ...
    };
```

This is not a problem with basic types, for which the insertion operator is already defined. Unfortunately, the `employee` class in the EMPINH program does not overload this operator, so I'll need to add this member function. Also, to simplify getting employee data from the user, I overload the extraction (>>) operator as well. Data from this operator is placed in a temporary object `emptemp` before being added to the linked list. Listing 11-6 shows TEMLIST2.

Listing 11-6 TEMLIST2

```
// temlist2.cpp
// implements linked list as a template
// demonstrates list used with employee class

#include <iostream.h>

//////////////////////////////////////////////////////////
// the employee class
//////////////////////////////////////////////////////////
const int LEN = 80;               // maximum length of names

class employee                         // employee class
    {
    private:
        char name[LEN];                // employee name
        unsigned long number;          // employee number
    public:
        friend istream& operator >> (istream& s, employee& e);
        friend ostream& operator << (ostream& s, employee& e);
    };

istream& operator >> (istream& s, employee& e)
    {
    cout << "\n   Enter last name: "; cin >> e.name;
    cout << "    Enter number: ";      cin >> e.number;
    return s;
    }
ostream& operator << (ostream& s, employee& e)
    {
    cout << "\n   Name: " << e.name;
    cout << "\n   Number: " << e.number;
    return s;
    }
```

```
//////////////////////////////////////////////////////////
// the linked list template
//////////////////////////////////////////////////////////
template<class TYPE>                        // struct "link<TYPE>"
struct link                                 // one element of list
   {
   TYPE data;                               // data item
   link* next;                              // pointer to next link
   };

template<class TYPE>                        // class "linklist<TYPE>"
class linklist                              // a list of links
   {
   private:
      link<TYPE>* first;                    // pointer to first link
   public:
      linklist()                            // no-argument constructor
         { first = NULL; }                  // no first link
      void additem(TYPE d);                 // add data item (one link)
      void display();                       // display all links
      ~linklist();                          // destructor
};

template<class TYPE>
void linklist<TYPE>::additem(TYPE d)        // add data item
   {
   link<TYPE>* newlink = new link<TYPE>;    // make a new link
   newlink->data = d;                       // give it data
   newlink->next = first;                   // it points to next link
   first = newlink;                         // now first points to this
   }

template<class TYPE>
void linklist<TYPE>::display()              // display all links
   {
   link<TYPE>* current = first;             // set ptr to first link
   while( current != NULL )                 // quit on last link
      {
      cout << endl << current->data;        // display data
      current = current->next;              // move to next link
      }
   }

template<class TYPE>                        // destructor
linklist<TYPE>::~linklist()                 //    deletes all links
   {
```

continued on next page

continued from previous page

```
    while( first != NULL )              // quit on last link
        {
        link<TYPE>* temp = first;       // 'temp' to current link
        first = temp->next;             // 'first' to next link
        delete temp;                    // delete current link
        }
    }
//////////////////////////////////////////////////////////////
// main() creates a linked list of employees
//////////////////////////////////////////////////////////////
void main()
    {                                   // lemp is object of
    linklist<employee> lemp;            // class "linklist<employee>"
    employee emptemp;                   // temporary employee storage
    char ans;                           // user's response ('y' or 'n')

    do
        {
        cin >> emptemp;         // get employee data from user
        lemp.additem(emptemp);  // add it to linked list 'lemp'
        cout << "\nAdd another (y/n)? ";
        cin >> ans;
        } while(ans != 'n');    // when user is done,
    lemp.display();             // display entire linked list
    }
```

In `main()`, the program instantiates a linked list called `lemp`. Then, in a loop, it asks the user to input data for an employee, and adds that employee object to the list. When the user terminates the loop, the program displays all the employee data. Here's some sample interaction:

```
Enter last name: Mendez
Enter number: 1233
Add another(y/n)? y

Enter last name: Smith
Enter number: 2344
Add another(y/n)? y

Enter last name: Chang
Enter number: 3455
Add another(y/n)? n

Name: Chang
Number: 3455

Name: Smith
Number: 2344

Name: Mendez
Number: 1233
```

Notice that the `linklist` class does not need to be modified in any way to store objects of type `employee`. This is the beauty of template classes: They will work not only with basic types, but with user-defined types as well.

What Can You Store?

You can tell whether you can store variables of a particular type in a data-storage template class by checking the operators in the member functions of that class. For example, is it possible to store a C string (type `char*`) in the `linklist` class in the TEMLIST2 program? Member functions in this class use the insertion (`<<`) and extraction (`>>`) operators on the stored objects. These operators work perfectly well with strings, so there's no reason you can't use this class to store strings, as you can verify for yourself. But if the member functions in a container class use any operators on stored objects that aren't defined for those objects, then you can't use the container class to store that type.

1. A template class `clatem` allows
   a. a member function of `clatem` to have a variable number of arguments.
   b. `clatem` to use data types that aren't known until compile time.
   c. `clatem` to use data types that aren't known until runtime.
   d. data types within `clatem` to be determined when objects of that class are specified.
   e. objects of `clatem` to act as if they were of several different data types.

2. Typically, an object instantiated from a templatized container class `temclass<T>`
   a. stores objects of a single type.
   b. stores objects of different types.
   c. stores objects (not pointers) that can be of different types, provided these types are all derived from a single type.
   d. shares in-memory member functions with all other objects of `temclass<T>`.
   e. shares in-memory member functions with all other objects of (say) `temclass<float>`.

3. Assuming a specification for a template class `temclass<T>`, memory space is allocated
   a. for member data and functions when any object of class `temclass<T>` is defined.
   b. for member data when any object of class `temclass<float>` is defined.
   c. for member data when the first object of class `temclass<float>` is defined.
   d. for member functions when any object of class `temclass<float>` is defined.
   e. for member functions when the first object of class `temclass<float>` is defined.

4. If the specification for a templatized container class has the form

```
template <class Type>
class ConClass
    {...};
```

then the type name of objects of this container class might be
   a. `ConClass` in the declarator of an externally defined member function of this class.
   b. `ConClass<Type>` in the declarator of an externally defined member function.
   c. `ConClass<float>` in an application that uses the container.
   d. `ConClass<float>` in the declarator of an inline member function.
   e. `ConClass<Type>` in the declarator of an inline member function.

5. When you use a templatized container class CON to store objects of a user-defined class UDC,
   a. there must be member functions in UDC to carry out any operation demanded by CON of the objects stored in it.
   b. class CON must overload the assignment (=) operator.
   c. class UDC must overload the assignment (=) operator.
   d. class CON must overload the << operator.
   e. class UDC must overload the << operator.

EXERCISE 1

Modify the TEMPSTAK program from this session so the Stack class stores objects of type employee.

EXERCISE 2

Write a program that stores airtime values in a container of type linklist<TYPE>, as seen in the TEMLIST2 example in this session.

SESSION 3

EXCEPTIONS

Exceptions provide a systematic, object-oriented approach to handling runtime errors generated by C++ classes. To qualify as an exception, such errors must occur as a result of some action taken within a program and they must be ones the program itself can discover. For example, a constructor in a user-written string class might generate an exception if the application tries to initialize an object with a string that's too long. Similarly, a program can check if a file was opened or written too successfully and generate an exception if it was not.

Not all runtime errors can be handled by the exception mechanism. For instance, some error situations are not detected by the program but by the operating system, which may then terminate the application. Examples are stack overflow, the user pressing the [CTRL]-[C] key combination, or a hardware divide-by-zero error.

Why Do We Need Exceptions?

Why do we need a new mechanism to handle errors? Let's look at how the process was handled in the past. In C language programs, an error is often signaled by returning a particular value from the function in which it occurred. For example, many math functions, such as sin() and cos(), return a special value to indicate an error, and disk file functions often return NULL or 0 to signal an error. Each time you call one of these functions, you check the return value:

```
if( somefunc() == ERROR_RETURN_VALUE )
    // handle the error or call error-handler function
else
    // proceed normally
```

```
if( anotherfunc() == NULL )
    // handle the error or call error-handler function
else
    // proceed normally
if( thirdfunc() == 0 )
    // handle the error or call error-handler function
else
    // proceed normally
```

The problem with this approach is that every single call to such a function must be examined by the program. Surrounding each function call with an `if...else` statement and inserting statements to handle the error (or to call an error-handler routine) makes the listing convoluted and hard to read. Also, it's not practical for some functions to return an error value. For example, imagine a `min()` function that returns the minimum of two values. All possible return values from this function represent valid outcomes. There's no value left to use as an error return.

The problem becomes more complex when classes are used because errors may take place without a function being explicitly called. For example, suppose an application defines objects of a class:

```
SomeClass obj1, obj2, obj3;
```

How will the application find out if an error occurred in the class constructor? The constructor is called implicitly, so there's no return value to be checked.

Things are complicated even further when an application uses class libraries. A class library and the application that makes use of it are often created by separate people: the class library by a vendor and the application by a programmer who buys the class library. This makes it even harder to arrange for error values to be communicated from a class member function to the program that's calling the function.

The exception mechanism was designed to minimize these difficulties and to provide a consistent, easy-to-implement approach to error handling, one that supports the concepts of OOP. All errors can be handled in one place and the normal code is not interlaced with error-handling statements.

Exception Syntax

Imagine an application that creates and interacts with objects of a certain class. Ordinarily, the application's calls to the class member functions cause no problems. Sometimes, however, the application makes a mistake, causing an error to be detected in a member function. This member function then informs the application that an error has occurred. When exceptions are used, this is called *throwing an exception*. In the application, a separate section of code is installed to handle the error. This code is called an *exception handler* or *catch block*: it *catches* the exceptions thrown by the member function. Any code in the application that uses objects of the class is enclosed in a *try block*. Errors generated in the try block will be caught in the catch block. Code that doesn't interact with the class need not be in a try block.. Figure 11-3 shows the arrangement.

The exception mechanism uses three new C++ keywords: `throw`, `catch`, and `try`. Also, the class creator will probably want to create a new kind of entity called an *exception class*. The next program, XSYNTAX (Listing 11-7), demonstrates these features of the exception mechanism. It is not a working program, only a skeleton to show the syntax.

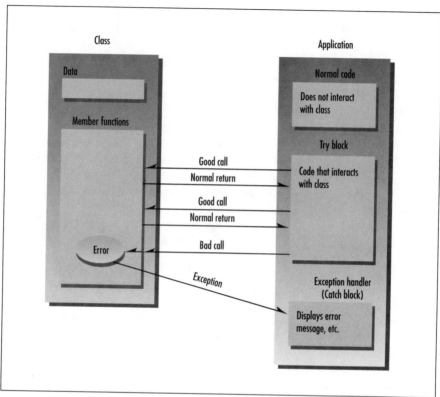

Figure 11-3   The exception mechanism

Listing 11-7 XSYNTAX

```
// xsyntax.cpp
// not a working program
class AClass                            // a class
   {
   public:
   class AnError                        // exception class
      {
      };
   void Func()                          // a member function
      {
      if( /* error condition */ )
         throw AnError();               // throw exception
      }
   };

void main()                            // application
   {
   try                                  // try block
```

```
    {
    AClass obj1;                // interact with AClass objects
    obj1.Func();               // may cause error
    }
catch(AClass::AnError)         // exception handler
    {                          // (catch block)
    // tell user about error, etc.
    }
}
```

This code starts with a class called `AClass`, which represents any class in which errors might occur. An exception class, `AnError`, is specified in the public part of `AClass`. The member functions of `AClass` check for errors. If they find one, they throw an exception, using the keyword `throw` followed by the constructor for the error class:

```
throw AnError();  // 'throw' followed by constructor for AnError class
```

In the `main()` part of the program, I enclose any statements that interact with `AClass` in a try block. If any of these statements causes an error to be detected in an `AClass` member function, an exception will be thrown and control will go to the catch block that immediately follows the try block.

A Simple Exception Example

Let's look at a working program example that uses exceptions. This example is derived from the STACK-CON program of Chapter 5, Session 1, which created a stack data structure in which integer data values could be stored. Unfortunately, this earlier example could not detect two common errors: the application program might attempt to push too many objects onto the stack, thus exceeding the capacity of the array, or it might try to pop too many objects off the stack, thus obtaining invalid data. In the XSTAK program (Listing 11-8), I use an exception to handle these two errors. I've made the stack small so it's easier to trigger an exception by pushing too many items.

Listing 11-8 XSTAK

```
// xstak.cpp
// demonstrates exceptions

#include <iostream.h>
const int MAX = 3;              // stack holds 3 ints

class Stack
    {
    private:
        int st[MAX];            // array of integers
        int top;                // index of top of stack
    public:
        class Range              // exception class for Stack
            {                    // note: empty class body
            };
```

continued on next page

continued from previous page

```
        Stack()                        // constructor
           { top = -1; }

        void push(int var)
           {
           if(top >= MAX-1)            // if stack full,
               throw Range();          // throw exception
           st[++top] = var;            // put number on stack
           }
        int pop()
           {
           if(top < 0)                 // if stack empty,
               throw Range();          // throw exception
           return st[topñ];            // take number off stack
           }
     };

void main()
   {
   Stack s1;

   try
      {
      s1.push(11);
      s1.push(22);
      s1.push(33);
//    s1.push(44);                              // oops: stack full
      cout << "1: " << s1.pop() << endl;
      cout << "2: " << s1.pop() << endl;
      cout << "3: " << s1.pop() << endl;
      cout << "4: " << s1.pop() << endl;        // oops: stack empty
      }
   catch(Stack::Range)                          // exception handler
      {
      cout << "Stack Full or Empty" << endl;
      }

   cout << "Arrive here after catch (or normal exit)" << endl;
   }
```

Let's examine four features of this program that deal with exceptions. In the class specification, there is an exception class. There are also statements that throw exceptions. In the application (the main() part of the program), there is a block of code that may cause exceptions (the try block) and a block of code to handle the exception (the catch block).

Specifying the Exception Class

The program first specifies an exception class within the `Stack` class:

```
class Range
   {    // note: empty class body
   };
```

Here the body of the class is empty, so objects of this class have no data and no member functions. All I really need in this simple example is the class name, `Range`. This name is used to connect a `throw` statement with a catch block. (The class body need not always be empty, as you'll see later.)

Throwing an Exception

An exception occurs in the `Stack` class if the application tries to pop a value when the stack is empty or tries to push a value when the stack is full. To let the application know that it has made such a mistake when manipulating a `Stack` object, the member functions of the `Stack` class check for these conditions using `if` statements and throw an exception if they occur. In XSTAK, the exception is thrown in two places, both using the statement

```
throw Range();
```

The `Range()` part of this statement invokes the (implicit) constructor for the `Range` class, which creates an object of this class. The `throw` part of the statement transfers program control to the exception handler (which I'll examine in a moment).

The try Block

All the statements in `main()` that might cause this exception—that is, statements that manipulate `Stack` objects—are enclosed in braces and preceded by the `try` keyword:

```
try
   {
   // code that operates on objects that might cause an exception
   }
```

This is simply part of the application's normal code; it's what you would need to write even if you weren't using exceptions. Not all the code in the program needs to be in a try block; just the code that interacts with the `Stack` class. Also, there can be many try blocks in your program, so you can access `Stack` objects from different places.

The Exception Handler (catch Block)

The code that handles the exception is enclosed in braces and preceded by the `catch` keyword, with the exception class name in parentheses. The exception class name must include the class in which it is located: `Stack::Range`:

```
catch(Stack::Range)
   {
   // code that handles the exception
   }
```

This construction is called the *exception handler*. It must immediately follow the try block. In XSTAK, the exception handler simply prints an error message to let the user know why the program failed.

Control "falls through" the bottom of the exception handler so you can continue processing at that point. Or the exception handler may transfer control elsewhere or terminate the program if there's no way to recover.

The Sequence of Events

Let's summarize the sequence of events when an exception occurs:

1. Code is executing normally outside a try block.

2. Control enters the try block.

3. A statement in the try block causes an error in a member function.

4. The member function throws an exception.

5. Control transfers to the exception handler (catch block) following the try block.

That's all there is to it. Notice how clean the resulting code is. Any of the statements in the try block could cause an exception, but I don't need to worry about checking a return value for each one because the try-throw-catch arrangement handles them all automatically. In the XSTAK example, I've deliberately created two statements that cause exceptions. The first,

```
s1.push(44);   // pushes too many items
```

causes an exception if you remove the comment symbol preceding it and the second,

```
cout << "4: " << s1.pop() << endl;   // pops item from empty stack
```

causes an exception if the first statement is commented out. Try it each way. In both cases, the same error message will be displayed:

```
Stack Full or Empty
```

This is the bare bones of the exception process. In the next session, I'll look at some enhancements.

1. Which of the following are C++ keywords?
   a. Range
   b. throw
   c. exception
   d. attempt
   e. catch

2. Exceptions
    a. provide a systematic way to handle errors detected in class member functions.
    b. were created to handle exceptionally large values.
    c. were created so a single class can handle different types of data.
    d. handle situations detected by the operating system.
    e. are not errors, only a different way to handle certain data values.

3. Which is the correct ordering of the following events?
    1. Control goes to catch block.
    2. Exception is thrown.
    3. Error occurs in try block.
    4. Error is detected by a member function.
    a. 2, 1, 3, 4
    b. 3, 4, 2, 1
    c. 2, 3, 4, 1
    d. 2, 3, 1, 4
    e. 3, 1, 4, 2

4. An object of an exception class
    a. is created when an error occurs.
    b. is created when an error is detected.
    c. is really an object of the class in which the error occurred.
    d. is said to be "thrown" when an exception occurs.
    e. is typically created within a member function.

5. Which of the following statements are true?
    a. Catch and try blocks have the same syntax as classes.
    b. The try block must *immediately* follow the catch block.
    c. An exception class is typically declared within the class whose objects will cause the exception.
    d. Try blocks are identified by the name of an exception class.
    e. Catch blocks are identified by the name of an exception class.

EXERCISE 1

Start with the ARROVER1 program from Chapter 6, Session 7. Modify the `safearay` class so that an exception is thrown if the user attempts to use an out-of-bounds index number. Revise `main()` so it uses try and catch blocks.

EXERCISE 2

Modify the `airtime` class from the ADDAIR program in Chapter 6, Session 1, so its `get()` member function throws an exception if the user enters a minutes value greater than 59. Revise `main()` to use try and catch blocks.

SESSION 4

EXCEPTIONS CONTINUED

In this session I'll pursue the exploration of exceptions. You'll learn about multiple exceptions, exceptions with arguments, and the built-in `xalloc` class, which handles memory errors.

Multiple Exceptions

You can design a class to throw as many exceptions as you want. To show how this works, I'll modify the XSTAK program from the last session to throw separate exceptions for attempting to push data on a full stack and attempting to pop data from an empty stack. Listing 11-9 shows XSTAK2.

Listing 11-9 XSTAK2

```
// xstak2.cpp
// demonstrates two exception handlers

#include <iostream.h>
const int MAX = 3;                      // stack holds 3 ints

class Stack
   {
   private:
      int st[MAX];                      // stack: array of integers
      int top;                          // index of top of stack
   public:
      class Full { };                   // exception class
      class Empty { };                  // exception class

      Stack()                           // constructor
            { top = -1; }

      void push(int var)                // put number on stack
            {
         if(top >= MAX-1)               // if stack full,
            throw Full();               // throw Full exception
         st[++top] = var;
         }
      int pop()                         // take number off stack
            {
         if(top < 0)                    // if stack empty,
            throw Empty();              // throw Empty exception
         return st[top--];
         }
   };

void main()
   {
   Stack s1;
```

```
    try
       {
       s1.push(11);
       s1.push(22);
       s1.push(33);
//     s1.push(44);                           // oops: stack full
       cout << "1: " << s1.pop() << endl;
       cout << "2: " << s1.pop() << endl;
       cout << "3: " << s1.pop() << endl;
       cout << "4: " << s1.pop() << endl;      // oops: stack empty
       }
    catch(Stack::Full)
       {
       cout << "Stack Full" << endl;
       }
    catch(Stack::Empty)
       {
       cout << "Stack Empty" << endl;
       }
    }
```

In XSTAK2, I specify two exception classes:

```
class Full  { };
class Empty { };
```

The statement

```
throw Full();
```

is executed if the application calls `push()` when the stack is already full, and

```
throw Empty();
```

is executed if `pop()` is called when the stack is empty. A separate catch block is used for each exception:

```
try
   {
   // code that operates on Stack objects
   }
catch(Stack::Full)
   {
   // code to handle Full exception
   }
catch(Stack::Empty)
   {
   // code to handle Empty exception
   }
```

All the catch blocks used with a particular try block must immediately follow the try block. In this case, each catch block simply prints a message: `Stack Full` or `Stack Empty`. Only one catch block is activated for a given exception. This group of catch blocks, or "catch ladder," operates a little like a `switch` statement, with only the appropriate section of code being executed. When an exception has been handled, control passes to the statement following all the catch blocks. (Unlike a `switch` statement, an exception doesn't require you to end each catch block with a `break`.)

Exceptions with the Distance Class

Let's look at another example of exceptions, this one applied to the infamous **Distance** class from previous chapters. A **Distance** object has an integer value of feet and a floating-point value for inches. The inches value should always be less than 12.0. A problem with this class in previous examples has been that it couldn't protect itself if the class user initialized an object with an inches value of 12.0 or greater. This could lead to trouble when the class tried to perform arithmetic because the arithmetic routines (such as **operator +**) assumed **inches** would be less than 12.0. Such erroneous values could also be displayed, thus confounding the user with impossible dimensions such as 7'-15".

Let's rewrite the **Distance** class to use an exception to handle this error, as shown in XDIST (Listing 11-10).

Listing 11-10 XDIST

```
// xdist.cpp
// exceptions with Distance class
#include <iostream.h>
#include <string.h>                    // for strcpy()

class Distance                         // English Distance class
   {
   private:
      int feet;
      float inches;
   public:
      class InchesEx { };              // exception class

      Distance()                       // constructor (no args)
         { feet = 0; inches = 0.0; }

      Distance(int ft, float in)       // constructor (two args)
         {
         if(in >= 12.0)                // if inches too big,
            throw InchesEx();          // throw exception
         feet = ft;
         inches = in;
         }

      void getdist()                   // get length from user
         {
         cout << "\nEnter feet: ";  cin >> feet;
         cout << "Enter inches: ";  cin >> inches;
         if(inches >= 12.0)            // if inches too big,
            throw InchesEx();          // throw exception
         }

      void showdist()                  // display distance
         { cout << feet << "\'-" << inches << '\"'; }
   };
```

```
void main()
   {
   try
      {
      Distance dist1(17, 3.5);       // 2-arg constructor
      Distance dist2;                // no-arg constructor
      dist2.getdist();               // get distance from user
                                     // display distances
      cout << "\ndist1 = ";  dist1.showdist();
      cout << "\ndist2 = ";  dist2.showdist();
      }
   catch(Distance::InchesEx)         // catch exceptions
      {
      cout << "\nInitialization error: "
              "inches value is too large.";
      }
   }
```

I install an exception class called `InchesEx` in the `Distance` class. Then, whenever the user attempts to initialize the inches data to a value greater than or equal to 12.0, I throw the exception. This happens in two places: in the two-argument constructor, where the programmer may make an error supplying initial values, and in the `getdist()` function, where the user may enter an incorrect value at the `Enter inches` prompt.

In `main()`, all interaction with `Distance` objects is enclosed in a try block, and the catch block displays an error message.

In a more sophisticated program, of course, you might want to handle a user error (as opposed to a programmer error) differently. It would be more user friendly to go back to the beginning of the try block and give the user a chance to enter another distance value.

Exceptions with Arguments

What happens if the application needs more information about what caused an exception? For instance, in the XDIST example, it might help the programmer to know what the bad inches value actually was. Also, if the same exception is thrown by different member functions, as it is in XDIST, it would be nice to know which of the functions was the culprit. Is there a way to pass such information from the member function, where the exception is thrown, to the application that catches it?

This question can be answered by remembering that throwing an exception involves not only transferring control to the handler, but also creating an object of the exception class by calling its constructor. In XDIST, for example, I create an object of type `InchesEx` when I throw the exception with the statement

```
throw InchesEx();
```

If I add data members to the exception class, I can initialize them when I create the object. The exception handler can then retrieve the data from the object when it catches the exception. It's like writing a message on a baseball and throwing it over the fence to your neighbor. I'll modify the XDIST program to do this. Listing 11-11 shows XDIST2.

Listing 11-11 XDIST2

```
// xdist2.cpp
// exceptions with arguments
#include <iostream.h>
#include <string.h>                      // for strcpy()

class Distance                          // English Distance class
   {
   private:
      int feet;
      float inches;
   public:
      class InchesEx                    // exception class
         {
         public:
            char origin[80];            // for name of routine
            float iValue;               // for faulty inches value

            InchesEx(char* or, float in)    // 2-arg constructor
               {
               strcpy(origin, or);          // store string
               iValue = in;                 // store inches
               }
         };                             // end of exception class

      Distance()                        // no-arg constructor
         { feet = 0; inches = 0.0; }

      Distance(int ft, float in)        // 2-arg constructor
         {
         if(in >= 12.0)
            throw InchesEx("2-arg constructor", in);
         feet = ft;
         inches = in;
         }

      void getdist()                    // get length from user
         {
         cout << "\nEnter feet: ";  cin >> feet;
         cout << "Enter inches: ";  cin >> inches;
         if(inches >= 12.0)
            throw InchesEx("getdist() function", inches);
         }

      void showdist()                   // display distance
         { cout << feet << "\'-" << inches << '\"'; }
   };

void main()
   {
   try
      {
      Distance dist1(17, 3.5);          // 2-arg constructor
```

```
   Distance dist2;                    // no-arg constructor
   dist2.getdist();                   // get value
                                      // display distances
   cout << "\ndist1 = ";  dist1.showdist();
   cout << "\ndist2 = ";  dist2.showdist();
   }
catch(Distance::InchesEx ix)          // exception handler
   {
   cout << "\nInitialization error in " << ix.origin
        << ".\n   Inches value of " << ix.iValue
        << " is too large.";
   }
}
```

There are three parts to the operation of passing data when throwing an exception: specifying the data members and a constructor for the exception class, initializing this constructor when I throw an exception, and accessing the object's data when I catch the exception. Let's look at these in turn.

Specifying Data in an Exception Class

It's convenient to make the data in an exception class public so it can be accessed directly by the exception handler. Here's the specification for the new InchesEx exception class in XDIST2:

```
class InchesEx                        // exception class
   {
   public:
      char origin[80];                // for name of routine
      float iValue;                   // for faulty inches value

      InchesEx(char* or, float in)    // 2-arg constructor
         {
         strcpy(origin, or);          // put string in object
         iValue = in;                 // put inches value in object
         }
   };
```

There are public variables for a string, which will hold the name of the member function being called, and a type float for the faulty inches value.

Initializing an Exception Object

How do I initialize the data when I throw an exception? In the two-argument constructor for the Stack class, I say

```
throw InchesEx("2-arg constructor", in);
```

and in the getdist() member function for Stack, it's

```
throw InchesEx("getdist() function", in);
```

When the exception is thrown, the handler will display the string and inches values. The string will tell you which member function is throwing the exception, and the value of in will report the faulty inches value detected by the member function. This additional data will make it easier for the programmer or user to figure out what caused the error.

Extracting Data from the Exception Object

How do I extract this data when I catch the exception? The simplest way is to make the data a public part of the exception class, as I've done here. Then in the catch block I can declare **ix** as the name of the exception object I'm catching. Using this name, I can refer to data in the usual way, using the dot operator:

```
catch(Distance::InchesEx ix)
   {
   // access 'ix.origin' and 'ix.iValue' directly
   }
```

I can then display the value of **ix.origin** and **ix.iValue**. Here's some interaction with XDIST2 if the user enters too large a value for inches:

```
Enter feet: 7
Enter inches: 13.5

Initialization error in getdist() function.
   Inches value of 13.5 is too large.
```

Similarly, if the programmer changes the definition of **dist1** in **main()** to

```
Distance dist1(17, 22.25);
```

the resulting exception will cause this error message:

```
Initialization error in 2-arg constructor.
   Inches value of 22.25 is too large.
```

Of course, I can make whatever use of the exception arguments I want, but they generally carry information that helps me diagnose the error that triggered the exception.

The xalloc Class

Some compilers contain built-in exception classes. The most commonly seen is probably **xalloc**, which is thrown if an error occurs when attempting to allocate memory with **new**. If you set up the appropriate try and catch blocks, you can make use of this class with very little effort. Listing 11-12, XALLOC, shows the approach used in Borland C++.

Listing 11-12 XALLOC

```
// xalloc.cpp
// demonstrates xalloc class (for Borland compilers)

#include <iostream.h>
#include <except.h>                    // for xalloc class

void main()
   {
   const unsigned int MAX = 60000;     // memory size (chars)
   char* ptr;                          // pointer to memory
   unsigned int j;                     // loop variable
```

```
try
   {
   ptr = new char[MAX];            // allocate memory
   // other statements that use 'new'
   }
catch(xalloc)                      // exception handler
   {
   cout << "\nxalloc exception: can't allocation memory.";
   exit(1);
   }
for(j=0; j<MAX; j++)               // fill memory with data
   *(ptr+j) = j%128;
for(j=0; j<MAX; j++)               // check data
   if(*(ptr+j) != j%128)
      {
      cout << "\nData error";
      exit(1);
      }
delete[] ptr;                      // release memory
cout << "\nMemory use is successful.";
}
```

I'll need to include the EXCEPT.H file, which contains the specification for the xalloc class (among others). Then I put all statements that use new in a try block. The catch block that follows handles the exception, usually by displaying an error message and terminating the program.

I can get this program to throw the xalloc exception by tinkering with the value of MAX. I can't allocate an entire data segment of 65,536 bytes, so as I increase MAX beyond 60,000 bytes, I'll eventually cause the xalloc exception to be thrown, which will print the error message and cause the program to terminate:

```
xalloc exception: can't allocate memory
```

The program includes for loops to fill the memory with data and verify that it's correct. Note that these statements don't need to be in the try block because they don't use new.

Exception Notes

I've shown only the simplest and most common approach to using exceptions. I won't go into further detail, but I will conclude with a few thoughts about exception usage.

Destructors Called Automatically

The exception mechanism is surprisingly sophisticated. When an exception is thrown, a destructor is called automatically for any object that was created by the code up to that point in the try block. This is necessary because the application won't know which statement caused the exception and, if it wants to recover from the error, it will (at the very least) need to start over at the top of the try block. The exception mechanism guarantees that the code in the try block will have been "reset," at least as far as the existence of objects is concerned.

Termination Oriented

After you catch an exception, you'll probably want to terminate your application. The exception mechanism gives you a chance to indicate the source of the error to the user and to perform any necessary clean-up chores before terminating. It also makes clean up easier by executing the destructors for objects created in the try block. This allows you to release system resources, such as memory, that such objects may be using. (DOS programs are supposed to release system resources automatically when they terminate, but Windows programs may not.)

However, in some cases you may not want to terminate your program. It is also possible to try to recover from the error. Perhaps your program can figure out what caused the error and correct it, or the user can be asked to input different data. When this is the case, the try and catch blocks are typically embedded in a loop, so control can be returned to the beginning of the try block (which the exception mechanism has attempted to restore to its initial state).

If there is no exception handler that matches the exception thrown, the program is unceremoniously terminated.

Function Nesting

The statement that causes an exception need not be located directly in the try block; it can also be in a function that is *called* by a statement in the try block (or in a function called by a function that is called by a statement in the try block, and so on). So you need to install a try block only on the program's upper level. Lower-level functions need not be so encumbered, provided they are called directly or indirectly by functions in the try block.

Can't Return to Throw Point

There's no way for an exception handler to return control to the location in the application that caused the exception. Exceptions act more like a `goto` than a function call (actually, more like the C-language `longjmp`, but I won't get into that). Control goes to the exception handler (catch block) and then (unless you do something else) falls through to the code following the catch block.

1. When you use multiple exceptions in a class,
   a. you must create several exception classes.
   b. there must be one try block for each exception.
   c. the exception class must take multiple arguments.
   d. the catch blocks must be contiguous.
   e. there can be no more than two exceptions.

2. Arguments in exceptions
   a. require member data in the exception class.
   b. are implemented using arguments to exception-object constructors.
   c. require the catch block to instantiate an object of the exception class.
   d. can provide additional information about an exception for the program's user.
   e. require a member function to catch exception objects with arguments.

3. In the **Distance** class in the XDIST2 program,
   a. multiple exceptions are used.
   b. an exception will be thrown if the value of feet is greater than 12.
   c. exceptions with multiple arguments are used.
   d. a member function prints an error message when an exception is detected.
   e. the class creator wrote code to detect the error.

4. Which of the following statements are correct?
   a. If there is no catch block corresponding to an exception that is thrown, then nothing happens.
   b. An exception will be handled normally even if it occurs in a function called from within the try block.
   c. If a class uses exceptions with arguments, then in the catch block the argument values can be obtained using the dot operator.
   d. Following an exception, you can arrange to return automatically to the statement in the try block following the one that caused the exception.
   e. If a class uses exceptions with arguments, then the values of these arguments must be specified in the try block.

5. The **xalloc** class
   a. lets you know exactly how much memory you obtained.
   b. handles exceptions caused by **new**.
   c. in a class that uses **new**, requires the class creator to write code that throws an exception.
   d. in a class that uses **new**, requires a class user to write code that throws an exception.
   e. requires statements that use **new** to appear only in class member functions.

EXERCISE 1

Modify the exception mechanism in the **airtime** class, as described in Exercise 2 of Session 3, so that its **get()** member function throws an exception not only if the user enters a minutes value greater than 59, but also if the user enters negative values for either hours or minutes. Use three separate exceptions. Revise **main()** to handle the additional exceptions.

EXERCISE 2

Modify the exception mechanism in the **airtime** class from Exercise 1 so that all exceptions supply the offending value of minutes or hours. Revise **main()** to display this data for the user.

MIDCHAPTER DISCUSSION

Estelle: The whole idea of template classes makes me uneasy.

George: Because you don't understand it?

Estelle: It's not that so much. They've taken this sort of very general idea of making a data type into a variable that you can plug specific types into, and all they use it for is container classes.

George: So?

Estelle: I don't know, I like to see more general purpose solutions to problems. It's like they put in a special keyword to add the number 27. Template classes just do one thing.

Don: I know what you mean. But after all, container classes are pretty important. They probably developed templates for container classes, but decided to make them as general as possible just in case something else turned up.

George: So there's something else you can do with template classes?

Don: Well, not that I know of, but people are coming up with new stuff all the time. I'll bet there are plenty of neat things you can do with templates.

George: What I want to know is, do people really use exceptions? It seems like a lot of baggage with all these try blocks and exception classes and everything. You'd think there'd be an easier way.

Estelle: It's not that bad.

Don: It makes more sense in larger programs, where a big chunk of code can throw all kinds of exceptions. It really simplifies things just to drop all that code into a try block instead of messing it up with lines and lines of error-handling code.

EXPLICIT CASTS, typedef, AND THE () OPERATOR

This session covers three unrelated topics: explicit casts, the typedef specifier, and overloading the function operator. None of these is vital to your understanding of C++. However, they all are used by the standard string class that is described in Session 6 in this chapter and in the Standard Template Library, the subject of Chapter 12. Thus it's probably a good idea to be familiar with them.

Explicit Casts

The ANSI/ISO C++ draft has introduced a new way to perform casts (explicitly changing a quantity from one type to another). One motivation for a new approach to casts is that old-style casts were hard to locate in a large listing during the debugging process. If you have statements that use the old C style cast, such as

```
intvar = (int)longvar;
```

or the newer C++ functional style cast, such as

```
intvar = int(longvar);
```

it's hard to find them in your listing because there's no specific keyword to search for. Casts are a frequent source of bugs because they "break" the C++ typing system, but if you can't find them, they're hard to fix.

Four new C++ keywords solve this problem: `static_cast`, `dynamic_cast`, `const_cast`, and `reinterpret_cast` allow explicit casts tailored for different situations. The format of these casts makes use of template notation to specify the target data type.

Casts are often a mistake and should be used with great restraint. However, sometimes they're the only efficient way to solve a problem.

Static Casts

The static cast is used in many situations where old-style casts were previously used. It allows you to change any basic type to any other basic type, even if information is potentially lost, as it might be going from a `long` to an `int`, for example. Here's how such a cast looks with the old C++ notation:

```
intvar = long(longvar);              // convert long to int
```

With an explicit cast, you would write it like this:

```
intvar = static_cast<int>(longvar);  // convert long to int
```

The destination type (the type to be converted to) is supplied as a template argument to `static_cast`. Of course, such casts are dangerous and should be used only when absolutely necessary and when you're sure no harmful effects will result from losing information.

The static cast also allows you to convert pointers-to-base-classes to pointers-to-derived-classes, and vice versa. The STA_CAST example (Listing 11-13) shows a variety of conversion situations.

Listing 11-13 STA_CAST

```
// sta_cast.cpp
// demonstrates static casts
#include <iostream.h>

class Base                           // base class
    { };

class Derv : public Base             // derived class
    { };

void main()
    {
    int intvar = 27;
    long longvar = 12341234L;

    longvar = intvar;                // ok
```

continued on next page

continued from previous page

```
    intvar = static_cast<int>(longvar); // ok, and more explicit

    intvar = longvar;                    // compiler warning
    intvar = int(longvar);               // ok (but dangerous)
    intvar = static_cast<int>(longvar); // ok (but dangerous)

    Base base;                           // base-class object
    Base* bptr;                          // base-class pointer

    Derv derv;                           // derived-class object
    Derv* dptr;                          // derived-class pointer

    bptr = &derv;                        // ok, upcast
    bptr = static_cast<Base*>(&derv);    // ok, and more explicit

//  dptr = &base;                        // compiler error, downcast
    dptr = (Derv*)&base;                 // ok (but dangerous)
    dptr = static_cast<Derv*>(&base);    // ok (but dangerous)
    }
```

It's normal to convert the addresses of derived class objects to base class pointers. The static cast makes this a more overt and easily identified activity. Going the other way is dangerous, but possible if you really want to. (There's no output from this example.)

Dynamic Casts

The dynamic cast is actually an alternative way of performing Runtime Type Identification (RTTI), described in Chapter 9, Session 5. It's useful if, for example, you're stepping through a base class array looking for objects of a specific derived class type (e.g., all the pointers to scientist objects in an array of type pointer to employee). This cast returns 0 if the object is not the desired type or a pointer to the object if it is the desired type.

Dynamic casts use the same format as static casts, but with the dynamic_cast keyword. They are normally used in the context of pointers to derived class types. Listing 11-14 shows DYN_CAST.

Listing 11-14 DYN_CAST

```
// dyn_cast.cpp
// demonstrates dynamic casts
#include <iostream.h>

class Base
    {
    public:                        // must be an abstract class
        void virtual dummy()
            {  }
    };

class Derv1 : public Base
    {  };

class Derv2 : public Base
    {  };
```

```
void main()
    {
    Base* bptrs[10];              // array of pointers to base objects

    Derv1 derv1;                  // objects of derived classes
    Derv2 derv2;

    bptrs[0] = &derv1;            // put addresses of objects in array
    bptrs[1] = &derv2;

    Derv1* d1ptr;                 // pointers to derived class objects
    Derv2* d2ptr;
                                  // these casts return valid addresses
    d1ptr = dynamic_cast<Derv1*>(bptrs[0]);   // there is a derv1
    cout << "\nd1ptr = " << d1ptr;            //     in bptrs[0]
    d2ptr = dynamic_cast<Derv2*>(bptrs[1]);   // there is a derv2
    cout << "\nd2ptr = " << d2ptr;            //     in bptrs[1]

                         // these casts return 0
    d1ptr = dynamic_cast<Derv1*>(bptrs[1]);   // no derv1
    cout << "\nd1ptr = " << d1ptr;            //     in bptrs[1]
    d2ptr = dynamic_cast<Derv2*>(bptrs[0]);   // no derv2
    cout << "\nd2ptr = " << d2ptr;            //     in bptrs[0]
    }
```

Notice that, for dynamic casts to work, the base class must be polymorphic; that is, it must contain at least one virtual function.

Element 0 of the `bptrs` array (an array of pointers to base class objects) contains a pointer to a `Derv1` object, and element 1 contains a pointer to a `Derv2` object. The first dynamic cast looks for a pointer to a `Derv1` object in element 0 and a pointer to a `Derv2` object in element 1. It finds both of them and returns their addresses. The second two dynamic casts look in the reversed locations and, not finding the requested types, return 0. Here's the output from DYN_CAST:

```
d1ptr = 0x3bcf2434
d2ptr = 0x3bcf2432
d1ptr = 0x00000000
d2ptr = 0x00000000
```

Normally, when you step through an array like this, you let the virtual function mechanism handle the selection of the correct function for the correct object. Sometimes, however, as when you can't modify the class (because someone else wrote it and you don't have the source code), you may need `dynamic_cast` (or the `typeid` approach to RTTI) to respond differently to different types of objects.

Dynamic casts, besides leading to potential program bugs, also impose additional overhead, another reason for avoiding them unless they're really necessary.

Const Casts

You've seen various examples of `const` variables, which, once initialized, cannot be modified. On rare occasions, it's useful to modify variables even though they are `const`. The const cast allows you to "cast away constness" (another C++ phrase with vaguely religious overtones).

You can't use `const_cast` directly on variables, only on pointers or references to variables. Probably it's most useful when a pointer or reference to a `const` variable is passed as an argument to function that needs to modify the variable. Listing 11-15, CON_CAST, shows how this cast is used.

Listing 11-15 CON_CAST

```
// con_cast.cpp
// demonstrates const casts
#include <iostream.h>

void main()
   {
   int var = 27;
   const int constvar = 33;

   var = constvar;                      // ok
// constvar = var;                      // error, modifies const

   int* ptr = &var;                     // ok
// int* ptr = &constvar;                // error, pointer not const
   const int* ptr_c = &constvar;        // ok, pointer to const

// ptr = ptr_c;                         // error, pointer not const
   ptr = const_cast<int*>(ptr_c);       // ok, casts away const
   }
```

Of course, you can always assign the value of a `const` variable to a non-`const` variable. However, you can't normally assign a value to a `const` variable.

```
constvar = var;              // no good
```

To overcome this limitation, first create a pointer to the object. This must be a pointer to `const`, as shown in the line

```
const int* ptr_c = &constvar;   // ok, pointer to const
```

Remember that a constant pointer to a nonconstant variable isn't the same as a pointer to a constant:

```
int* const c_ptr = &constvar;   // bad, const pointer to non-const
```

Normally, you can't take a pointer to a `const` variable and assign it to a pointer to a nonconstant variable because that would allow the constant variable to be modified:

```
ptr = ptr_c;                    // no good
```

However, using a `const_cast`, this becomes legitimate:

```
ptr = const_cast<int*>(ptr_c);
```

Such a cast should be used only in unusual situations as it violates the whole purpose of using `const` variables and thus removes a significant safety net from your program.

Reinterpret Casts

The reinterpret cast is the most powerful, and therefore the most dangerous, of the explicit casts. It can change pretty much anything into anything else: pointers into integers, floating-point numbers into bit patterns, and so on. It's useful in emergencies when nothing else works, but in general you probably shouldn't use this cast.

The typedef **Specifier**

Here's another C++ feature that deals with data types. The typedef specifier is used to give a different name to a type. For example, the declaration

```
typedef int error_number;
```

makes error_number equivalent to int. Now instead of declaring variables using int:

```
int en1, en2;
```

you can also say

```
error_number en1, en2;
```

The variables en1 and en2 will behave exactly the same as if they had been declared to be type int. What does this buy you? In this example, it may make your listing slightly clearer if you declare all variables that will hold error numbers to be of this type. It's a notational convenience.

Of course, even after using this typedef, you can continue to declare variables to be type int in the usual way. This typedef makes error_number equivalent to int, it doesn't make int equivalent to error_number.

Here's another example. If you're writing code that interfaces with hardware devices, you may need to think about bytes. You might then declare a new type byte:

```
typedef unsigned char byte;
```

Now you can declare variables of type byte:

```
byte high, low;
```

Notice that there's no problem using typedef even if the type to be renamed consists of multiple words, such as unsigned int.

Pointers and typedef

Don't confuse typedef with #define. The #define directive causes a simple substitution of one group of characters by another, such as a word processor's global search and replace. A typedef, on the other hand, creates a new name for a type. This becomes clearer in the case of pointers. The statement

```
typedef int* ptr_error_number;
```

makes ptr_error_number equivalent to pointer to int. The new type name has the pointer to (the asterisk) built in, so when you define variables you can say

```
ptr_error_number pen1, pen2, pen3;
```

without prefacing each variable with an asterisk. The #define directive could not handle this situation so gracefully.

Note that, unlike a class specification, typedef doesn't actually *create* a new type. It simply substitutes a new type name for an existing one.

Classes and typedef

You can apply the typedef specifier to classes just as easily as to basic types such as int. For example, suppose a class supplier is paranoid about *name clashes* (the supplier's class names being the same as some class user's existing class names). To avoid conflict, class suppliers may use very long class names that incorporate the company name:

```
class Universal_Amalgamated_Corporation_Employee_Class
    {
    . . .
    };
```

However, your listing will look excessively verbose with object declarations such as

```
Universal_Amalgamated_Corporation_Employee_Class emptemp;
```

You can simplify this code with a typedef:

```
typedef Universal_Amalgamated_Corporation_Employee_Class Uemployee;
```

Now you can declare the emptemp object using the considerably more comprehensible

```
Uemployee emptemp;
```

More Portable Code

Another reason to use typedef, besides simplifying long type names, is to make your code more easily adaptable to different environments.

For example, in 16-bit operating systems such as DOS and Windows 3.1, an int is 16 bits, whereas in 32-bit systems such as Windows 95, an int is 32 bits and a short is 16 bits. Suppose your program uses a quantity that must always be stored in a 16-bit variable. You can define such variables throughout your program using a made-up name:

```
int16 var1, var2;
```

Then, at the beginning of your program you can typedef this name to the appropriate type. In 16-bit systems, you would say

```
typedef int int16;
```

whereas in 32-bit systems you would say

```
typedef short int16;
```

Changing this single statement automatically changes the meaning of every declaration throughout your program.

Templates and typedef

When a template takes several arguments, its type name can grow large and unwieldy. For example, suppose you have a class declaration

```
template<class type1, class type2, class type3>
class myClass
    {
    ...
    };
```

Declaring an object of this class is a somewhat lengthy process:

```
myClass<float, double, char> george;
```

It can be even worse if the template arguments are classes:

```
template<payment_type, job_category, compensation_package, security_type>
class employee
    {
    ...
    };
```

Every time you define an object, you need to specify all the (potentially long) parameter names:

```
employee<part_time, skilled, health_only, intermediate> tempemp;
```

However, with a `typedef` such as

```
typedef employee<part_time, skilled, health_only, intermediate>
        part_time_machinist;
```

you can reduce object declarations to something more comprehensible:

```
part_time_machinist tempmach1;
```

Of course, the downside of `typedef` is that when you see a declaration such as this, you may need to go back to the top of the listing (or to a header file) to find out what `part_time_machinist` really means. Like many things in programming (and elsewhere), using `typedef` is a tradeoff.

Overloading the Function Operator

What is the function operator and why would you want to overload it? The function operator is simply the paired parentheses symbol: `()`. It's the symbol used to tell the compiler that a function is being declared or called. Like other operators, it can be overloaded. Overloading is useful in the special situation where you want a class object to behave like a function. The PARENS example (Listing 11-16) shows how this looks.

Listing 11-16 PARENS

```
// parens.cpp
// overloads the () operator
#include <iostream.h>
#include <iomanip.h>

class alpha            // class with overloaded function operator
    {
    public:
        long operator() (int j, int k)
            {
            return static_cast<long>(j) * static_cast<long>(k);
            }
    };

void main()
    {
```

continued on next page

continued from previous page

```
alpha multiply;     // object of that class

                    // use object like a function
double answer = multiply(20002, 30003);
cout << setprecision(10) << answer << endl;
}
```

Class `alpha` has nothing in it but a function consisting of the overloaded function operator. This operator takes two arguments, both type `int`, and multiplies them together, returning a type `double`. The output from the program is

600120006

Of course, you don't need a function for so simple an operation, but the example does demonstrate how arguments and return values are used with the overloaded function operator.

Once I've defined an object of class `alpha`, I can use this object as if it were a function. The compiler interprets a reference to `multiply()` as a call to the overloaded function operator in the `multiply` object.

The `multiply` object is called a *function object*. Function objects have several uses. One is that you can create a function that has a separate version for every process that calls it. (Every process using `multiply()` creates its own `alpha` object.) This is important in a multitasking environment if the function contains data that it should remember between calls (like a count of how many times it's been called or the last random number it generated). Problems can arise if several processes call the function and interfere with this data. However, if each process creates its own function object, it will have its own version of the data.

A function object is also useful when you need to specify a function as an argument to another function that specifies an object for the argument. You'll see examples of this in Chapter 12.

1. A static cast
   a. can be used to convert a `double` to a `float`.
   b. is necessary to convert a `float` to a `double`.
   c. can be used to convert a pointer to a derived class object to a pointer to a base class object.
   d. permits casts that can't be accomplished with the implicit-style casts (that use parentheses).
   e. makes it easier to find instances of casts in your source file.

2. Dynamic casts
   a. are usually applied to pointers of base class types.
   b. work only with polymorphic classes.
   c. perform tasks that can't be accomplished with old implicit-style casts.
   d. are another way to throw exceptions.
   e. are another way to provide runtime type identification.

3. A const cast
   a. may be used to cast away constness.
   b. can change a variable of type `const int` to type `int`.
   c. works only with pointers.
   d. works only with classes.
   e. works only with polymorphic classes.

4. The `typedef` specifier
   a. changes the meaning of basic type names such as `float` and `int`.
   b. can be used to shorten type names.
   c. could be used to give a name such as `George` to the type array of pointers to `int`.
   d. changes a variable of one type to a variable of another type.
   e. is a notational convenience.

5. Overloading the function operator
   a. requires a class with an overloaded constructor.
   b. requires a class with an overloaded `[]` operator.
   c. requires a class with an overloaded `{}` operator (braces).
   d. usually makes use of a constructor that takes arguments.
   e. allows you to create objects that act syntactically like functions.

EXERCISE 1

Revise the VIRTSHAP program from Chapter 9, Session 2, to use dynamic casts when storing the addresses of derived class objects in the base class array.

EXERCISE 2

Use a const cast to make it possible for the user to change the object `const noon` in the CONSTA2 program in Chapter 5, Session 7.

SESSION 6

THE STANDARD string CLASS

Part of the latest draft of the ANSI/ISO committee is a standard string class. This class allows arrays of characters to be treated as a new data type. The idea is similar to the `String` class in the STRIMEM program in Chapter 8, Session 6, but far more sophisticated.

The standard string class, called `basic_string`, is templatized and can be instantiated not only with type `char`, but also with the so-called "wide character" type used in foreign alphabets or even with user-defined types. I'll ignore these possibilities here and assume I'm working with strings of type `char`. When this is the case, the resulting class is `typedef`ed to the name of `string`.

The example programs in this section show some of the operations possible with the **string** class. I don't cover all the string class member functions, and many of these functions have additional formats, that is, different numbers and types of arguments, which I also don't cover. Consult the documentation for your particular library to see what's available.

Header Files

Vendors have implemented the standard string class in somewhat different ways. The examples I'll show in this section work with the Borland implementation of the string class and should work with other implementations as well. An exception to this is the name of the header file that contains the definitions of the various classes. This file might be called STRING (with no .H), BSTRING.H, CSTRING.H, or some other name, depending on the compiler vendor. In my listings, I'll use the Borland version, CSTRING.H, but you should substitute the appropriate variation if necessary. You may also need to specify a namespace (see Appendixes B and C).

Constructors and Operators

A variety of constructors allows you to create **string** objects in different ways. They can be initialized to zero length (the default constructor), to other **string** objects, to **char*** (ordinary C) strings, to sequences of characters anywhere in a **string** object or **char*** string, to individual characters, and to sequences of characters.

The first example program shows some of these possibilities. It also demonstrates the **length()** member function and the overloaded **<<**, **=**, and **+** operators. Listing 11-17 shows STRING1.

Listing 11-17 STRING1

```
// string1.cpp
#include <cstring.h>
#include <iostream.h>

void main()
   {
   string s1("IN HOC SIGNO VINCES");   // C string
   string s2('-', 19);                  // repeated character
   string s3(s1, 7);                    // start at position 7
   string s4(s1, 13, 6);                // 6 chars, from position 13

   cout << "s1 = " << s1 << endl;       // display strings
   cout << "s2 = " << s2 << endl;
   cout << "s3 = " << s3 << endl;
   cout << "s4 = " << s4 << endl << endl;

   string s5;                           // default constructor
   cout << "Before assignment, length of s5 = "
        << s5.length() << endl;
   s5 = s1;                             // assignment
   cout << "After assignment, length of s5 = "
        << s5.length() << endl << endl;

   string s6('-', 47);                  // fixed size string
   cout << "Length of s6 = "
        << s6.length() << endl;
```

```
    s6[0] = 'X';                         // array notation
    s6[46] = 'X';

    cout << "s6 = ";
    for(int j=0; j<47; j++)
        cout << s6[j];                   // array notation
    cout << endl;
                                         // concatenation
    string s7 = s1 + " (Motto of the Roman Empire)";
    cout << "s7 = " << s7 << endl << endl;

    cout << "s1[3]=" << s1[3] << endl;
    }
```

The << and >> operators are overloaded for input and output. The length() member function returns the number of characters in the current string object. ("Current" means the object for which the member function was called.) The overloaded [] operator allows you to access an individual character within a string if you know its position. The = operator works as you would expect, setting one string object equal to another, and the + operator concatenates two strings. Here's the output from STRING1:

```
s1 = IN HOC SIGNO VINCES
s2 = --------------------
s3 = SIGNO VINCES
s4 = VINCES

Before assignment, length of s5 = 0
After assignment, length of s5 = 19

Length of s6 = 47
s6 = X-----------------------------------------------X
s7 = IN HOC SIGNO VINCES (Motto of the Roman Empire)

s1[3]=H
```

In the last statement of the program, which generates the last line of output, I show that the [] operator is overloaded to allow access to individual characters in the string using the same syntax as with char* strings. Although I don't show it here, the [] operator can also be used on the left side of an equal sign to assign values to individual characters.

Member Functions

A variety of member functions allows sophisticated manipulation of string objects. In the next example, STRING2 (Listing 11-18), I'll demonstrate a half-dozen of these functions.

Listing 11-18 STRING2
```
// string2.cpp
// demonstrates insert(), remove(), find(), etc
#include <cstring.h>
#include <iostream.h>

void main()
    {
```

continued on next page

continued from previous page

```
string s1("Don told Estelle he would get the ring.");
cout << "s1 = " << s1 << endl;

s1.insert( 26, "not ");          // insert "not " before "get"
cout << "s1 = " << s1 << endl;

s1.remove(26, 4);                // remove "not "
s1.replace(9, 7, "Pam", 3);      // replace "Estelle" w/ "Pam"
cout << "s1 = " << s1 << endl;

int loc1 = s1.find("Pam");       // find "Pam"
cout << "Pam is at = " << loc1 << endl;

                                 // find first whitespace char
                                 //      following loc1
int loc2 = s1.find_first_of(" \t\n", loc1);
                                 // make substring "Pam"
string s2 = s1.substr(loc1, loc2-loc1);
cout << "Hi, " << s2 << endl;
}
```

Here's the output from STRING2:

```
s1 = Don told Estelle he would get the ring.
s1 = Don told Estelle he would not get the ring.
s1 = Don told Pam he would get the ring.
Pam is at 9
Hi, Pam
```

The insert(), remove(), and replace() Member Functions

The insert(pos, ptr) member function inserts the char* string ptr into its object, starting at position pos. The remove(pos, n) function removes n characters from its object, starting at position pos. The replace(pos, n, ptr) function removes n characters from its object, starting at pos, and replaces them with the char* string ptr.

The find() Member Function

The find(ptr, pos) member function looks for a pattern, formed from the char* string ptr, in its object, starting at location pos, and returns the location of the first such instance. (You can find multiple instances by changing pos and searching again.)

The find_first_of() Member Function

The find_first_of(ptr, pos) function is useful when you want to look for a character in a string object but you're not sure which character you want to find; that is, you're looking for any one of a number of characters. The ptr argument is a char* string consisting of all the possible characters, and pos is the location to start looking in the string object for the first one of these characters. In the example, I use this function to find the first whitespace character, whether a space, tab, or new line, following the beginning of a name ("Pam", which I found with the find() member function). This allows me to locate the end of the name, even if it falls at the end of a line or column.

The substr() *Member Function*

If you know the location of the beginning and the end of a sequence of characters in the middle of a string object, you can turn this sequence into another string object with the substr(pos, n) function, where pos is the beginning of the substring and n is its length. Here I use this function to make the substring "Pam", which is assigned to s2.

Passing string **Objects as Arguments**

One of the nice things about a string class is that you don't need to pass pointers as arguments to functions, as you do with ordinary char* strings. You simply pass the string object. The next example, STRING3 (Listing 11-19), shows how this looks and demonstrates some other important functions.

Listing 11-19 STRING3

```
// string3.cpp
// demonstrates passing and returning string arguments, etc.
#include <cstring.h>
#include <iostream.h>

void main()
   {
   string func(string);             // function prototype
   string s1("IN HOC SIGNO VINCES"); // string

   string s2 = func(s1);            // call the function
                                    // display return value
   cout << "main is displaying: " << s2 << endl;

   char char_arr[80];               // array of type char*
   int len = s1.length();           // length of string

   int n = s1.copy(char_arr, len, 0); // copy s1 to char_arr
   char_arr[len] = '\0';            // end the char* string
   cout << "characters copied = " << n << endl;
   cout << "char_arr = " << char_arr << endl;

   const char* ptr = s1.c_str();    // pointer to char*
   cout << "ptr = " << ptr << endl; // points to hidden array
   }

string func(string s)              // function
   {
   cout << "func is displaying argument: " << s << endl;
   return string("return value from func\n");
   }
```

The func() function is passed a string, which it displays. It then returns another string, which main() displays just to show that everything works as expected.

The `copy()` *Member Function*

The `copy()` function allows you to copy a `string` object (or part of it) to a `char*` string. More specifically, `copy(ptr, n, pos)` copies n characters from its object, starting at `pos`, to the `char*` string `ptr`.

The `c_str()` *Member Function*

The `c_str()` function converts a `string` object to a `char*` string. That is, it returns a pointer to a `char` array that contains the characters from the `string` object, plus a terminating `'\0'` character. The pointer returned from `c_str()` is `const`, so you can't modify anything in the `char` array; it's read-only. (Actually you can modify it if you cast away the constness of `ptr`, as I did in Session 5, but this is not usually a good idea.) Here's the output for STRING3:

```
func is displaying argument: IN HOC SIGNO VINCES
main is displaying: return value from func

characters copied = 19
char_arr = IN HOC SIGNO VINCES
ptr = IN HOC SIGNO VINCES
```

Arrays of `string` **Objects**

It's fun and easy to store string objects in arrays. With ordinary `char*` strings, you must set up either an array of arrays of type `char`, so that all the strings are the same length, or an array of pointers to strings. By contrast, `string` objects can be stored as easily as basic variables such as `int`, because they are all the same size; they take care of their own memory requirements behind the scenes.

In the example (Listing 11-20), I'll set up an array of `string` objects arranged in alphabetical order and then use the `compare()` member function to insert a new string, entered by the user, at the appropriate place in the array.

Listing 11-20 STRING4

```
// string4.cpp
// demonstrates arrays of strings, compare(), etc.
#include <cstring.h>
#include <iostream.h>

void main()
   {
   const int SZ = 10;                        // original number of names
   string new_name;
                                             // array of string objects
   string arr[SZ+1] = { "Adam", "Bob", "Clair", "Doug", "Emily",
                  "Frank", "Gail", "Harry", "Ian", "Joe" };

   cout << "Enter a name: ";                 // user supplies new string
   cin >> new_name;

   int j = 0;
   while(j < SZ+1)                           // check each name in array
```

```
    {
    int len = arr[j].length();
    int lex_comp = new_name.compare( arr[j], 0, len );
    if(lex_comp > 0)                     // if new one greater,
        j++;                             // go on to next name
    else                                 // otherwise,
        {
        for(int k=SZ-1; k>=j; k--)       // move all names that are
            arr[k+1] = arr[k];           //    above this one
        arr[j] = new_name;               // insert the new name
        break;                           // break out of while
        }  // end else
    }  // end while
if(j == SZ+1)                            // if new name follows
    arr[10] = new_name;                  // all the others

for(j=0; j<SZ+1; j++)                    // display all the names
    cout << arr[j] << endl;
}  // end main
```

The `compare()` *Member Function*

Most of the code in the program is concerned with figuring out where in the array to insert the new name. The function `compare(str, pos, n)` compares a sequence of n characters in its own object, starting at `pos`, with the `str` string object in its argument. The return value reveals how these two string objects are ordered alphabetically (or lexicographically, to use the 10 dollar word).

> Return value < 0: The current string follows the `str` argument alphabetically.

> Return value = 0: The current string is equal to `str`.

> Return value > 0: The current string precedes `str` alphabetically.

The program compares the new name with each of the array elements. If the new name is greater than the array element, the next element is examined. If not, the new name should be inserted at that point in the array and all the string objects from that point on up are moved to make this possible. Here's some interaction with STRING4 when the user enters `Dilbert` (the capital "D" is necessary):

```
Enter a name: Dilbert
Adam
Bob
Clair
Dilbert
Doug
Emily
Frank
Gail
Harry
Ian
Joe
```

The new name has been inserted into the array at the appropriate place.

Get Ready for the STL

Actually it's a lot easier than I show here to keep a group of string objects in order. In the next chapter you'll see that the Standard Template Library (STL) provides container classes to handle such tedious details for you.

1. When working with the `string` class from the standard C++ library,
   a. you treat pointers to `char` as a data type.
   b. you treat sequences of type `char` as a data type.
   c. you must define arrays to allocate memory for objects.
   d. the = and < operators are overloaded.
   e. you use C library functions such as `strlen()` and `strcmp()`.

2. Which of these statements are true?
   a. A constructor allows you to create a `string` object initialized to part of a `char*` string.
   b. You cannot create a `string` object with no characters.
   c. A member function of `string` allows you to replace part of a string object with a `char*` string.
   d. The `<<` and `>>` operators can be used the same way as they are with `char*` strings.
   e. The `find_first_of()` member function finds the first value in a specified range of values.

3. If you pass a string object as an argument to a function, the function's prototype might be
   a. `void func(char);`
   b. `void func(char*);`
   c. `void func(char[]);`
   d. `void func(string);`
   e. `void func(string*);`

4. To convert
   a. a `string` object to a `char*` string, you can use the `copy()` member function.
   b. a `string` object to a `char*` string, you can use the `c_str()` member function.
   c. a `char*` string to a `string` object, you can use the `copy()` member function.
   d. a `char*` string to a `string` object, you can use the `c_str()` member function.
   e. a `char*` string to a `string` object, you can use a constructor.

5. Which of these statements are true?
   a. You can initialize a `string` array with a list of `char*` strings, just as you can a `char*` array.
   b. The `compare()` member function compares the lengths of `string` objects.
   c. To assign one `string` object to another, you typically use the `strcpy()` function.
   d. The overloaded < operator compares the lengths of `string` objects.
   e. The expression `"George"` is a `string` object.

EXERCISE 1

Using appropriate **string** member functions, write a program that allows the user to enter a word and then displays all possible anagrams (arrangements of letters) of that word. For example, if the user enters **cat**, the program should display

```
cat
cta
atc
act
tca
tac
```

EXERCISE 2

Modify the LINKLIST program from Chapter 8, Session 7, so it stores **string** objects rather than **int**s.

SESSION 7

MULTIFILE PROGRAMS

In previous chapters I've shown how the various parts of a C++ program—such as class declarations, member functions, and a **main()** function—are combined. However, the programs in these chapters all consisted of a single file. Now let's look at program organization from a more global perspective, involving multiple files. In this session I'll discuss issues concerned with multifile programs. In the next session I'll show an example of a multifile program.

Reasons for Multifile Programs

There are several reasons for using multifile programs. These include the use of class libraries, the organization of programmers working on a project, and the conceptual design of a program. Let's reflect briefly on these issues.

Class Libraries

In traditional procedure-oriented languages, it has long been customary for software vendors to furnish libraries of functions. Other programmers then combine these libraries with their own custom-written routines to create an application for the end user.

Libraries provide ready-made functions for a wide variety of fields. For instance, a vendor might supply a library of functions for handling statistics calculations or for advanced memory management. Libraries that provide the functions necessary to create graphics user interface (GUI) programs are popular.

Because C++ is organized around classes rather than functions, it's not surprising that libraries for C++ programs consist of classes. What may be surprising is how superior a class library is to an old-fashioned function library. Because classes encapsulate both data and functions, and because they more closely model objects in real life, the interface between a class library and the application that makes use of it can be much cleaner than that provided by a function library.

For these reasons, class libraries assume a more important role in C++ programming than function libraries do in traditional programming. A class library can take over a greater portion of the programming burden. An applications programmer, if the right class library is available, may find that only a minimal amount of programming is necessary to create a final product. Also, as more and more class libraries are created, the chances of finding one that solves your particular programming problem continues to increase.

A class library often includes two components: public and private.

Public Components

To use a class library, the applications programmer needs to access various declarations, including class declarations. These declarations can be thought of as the public part of the library and are usually furnished in source code form as a header file with the .H extension. This file is typically combined with the client's source code using an `include` statement.

The declarations in such a header file need to be public for several reasons. First, it's a convenience to the client to see the actual definitions rather than to read a description of them. More important, the client's program will need to declare objects based on these classes and call on member functions from these objects. Only by declaring the classes in the source file is this possible.

Private Components

On the other hand, the inner workings of the member functions of the various classes don't need to be known by the client. The developers of the class library, like any other software developer, don't want to release source code if they can help it because the code might be illegally modified or pirated. Member functions—except for short inline functions—are therefore usually distributed in object form as .OBJ files or as library (.LIB) files. Figure 11-4 shows how the various files are related in a multifile system.

In the next session I'll show a program organized according to these principles. The program introduces a class of very large numbers. (By "very large," I mean integers with an almost unlimited number of digits.)

Organization and Conceptualization

Programs may be broken down into multiple files for reasons other than the accommodation of class libraries. As in other programming languages, such as C, a common situation involves a project with several programmers (or teams of programmers). Confining each programmer's responsibility to a separate file helps organize the project and define more cleanly the interface among different parts of the program.

A program is often divided into separate files according to functionality: One file can handle the code involved in a graphics display, for example, whereas another file handles mathematical analysis and a third handles disk I/O. In large programs, a single file may simply become too large to handle conveniently.

The techniques used for working with multifile programs are similar whatever the reasons for dividing the program. I'll discuss the steps you need to take to create a multifile program using a representative compiler: Borland C++. (Turbo C++ works the same way, and other compilers differ only in the details.)

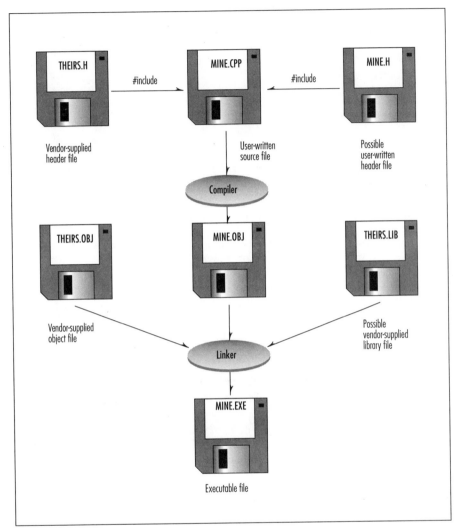

Figure 11-4   Files in a multifile application

How to Create a Multifile Program

Suppose you have purchased a commercial class file called THEIRS.OBJ. (A library file with the .LIB extension is dealt with in much the same way.) It probably comes with a header file, say THEIRS.H. You have also written your own program to use the classes in the library; your source file is called MINE.CPP. Now you want to combine these component files—THEIRS.OBJ, THEIRS.H, and MINE.CPP—into a single executable program.

Header Files

The header file THEIRS.H is easily incorporated into your own source file, MINE.CPP, with an `include` statement:

```
#include "THEIRS.H"
```

Quotes rather than angle brackets around the file name tell the compiler to look for the file first in the current directory rather than in the default include directory.

Directory

Make sure all the component files, THEIRS.OBJ, THEIRS.H, and MINE.CPP, are in the same directory. In fact, you will probably want to create a separate directory for the project to avoid confusion. This isn't necessary, but it's the simplest approach.

Multiple Files

For handling the details of development using multiple source files, see Appendix C for the Borland C++ compiler and Appendix D for Microsoft Visual C++.

Generally, you proceed in the same way as when developing a program with a single source file (MINE.CPP) and then add any additional files to the project (THEIRS.OBJ). Once you've done this, the compiler takes care of compiling any source files and linking the resulting .OBJ files together. You can run the resulting .EXE file (MINE.EXE) in the usual way.

Namespaces

The larger a program is, the greater the danger of *name clashes*, that is, a single name being used—inadvertently—to refer to several different things. This is a particular problem in multifile programs, where files may have been created by different programmers or different companies.

For example, suppose a class `alpha` is defined in a file A:

```
// file A
class alpha
   { };
```

In another file, which will eventually be linked with file A, there is also a specification for a class that—unbeknownst to the creators of file A—has been given the same name:

```
// file B
class alpha
   { };
```

The resulting name clash will cause linker errors. Programmers might then try to fix the problem by renaming one of the `alpha` classes. However, there's an easier way.

A recent revision to the draft ANSI C++ standard introduces a new solution to this problem: *namespaces*. A namespace is a section of a program specified by the keyword `namespace` and enclosed in brackets. A name used within a namespace does not have global visibility; instead, its scope is limited to the namespace.

Declaring Namespaces

In the A and B files shown on the previous page, the creators of the two files, George and Harry, could limit the visibility of the class alpha specifications by placing each one in its own namespace:

```
// file A
namespace NS_George
    {
    class alpha
        { };
    }
```

and

```
// file B
namespace NS_Harry
    {
    class alpha
        { };
    }
```

I show the namespaces in different files because they will frequently be used that way, but of course they could be in the same file as well. There's no necessary connection between files and namespaces.

Accessing Elements from Another Namespace

Within its own namespace, you would refer to alpha in the usual way. Outside its namespace, however, you must indicate which alpha class you're referring to. There are two approaches to this: You can use the scope resolution operator to specify a different namespace in a single statement or you can use the using directive to provide access throughout a different namespace to some or all the elements in that namespace.

To access an element in a different namespace in a way that affects only a single statement, precede the name of the element with the name of the namespace and the scope resolution operator (::). Here's how you might define two different kinds of alpha objects, for example:

```
// file C
namespace NS_Sally
    {
    ...
    NS_George::alpha   anAlpha1;   // create a George alpha object
    NS_Harry::alpha    anAlpha2;   // create a Harry alpha object
    ...
    }
```

To provide access to a specific element in one namespace throughout a second namespace, you can use the using declaration. In this code fragment, I make George's alpha class accessible throughout Sally's namespace:

```
// file C
namespace NS_Sally
    {
    using NS_George::alpha;
```

continued on next page

continued from previous page

```
...
alpha  anAlpha1;    // create a George alpha object
alpha  anAlpha2;    // create a George alpha object
...
}
```

To provide access to *all* the elements of one namespace throughout a second namespace, you can use the `using` keyword as a directive:

```
// file D
namespace NS_Estelle
   {
   using namespace NS_George;
   ...
   alpha  anAlpha1;    // create a George alpha object
   alpha  anAlpha2;    // create a George alpha object
   // also access any other elements in George's namespace
   ...
   }
```

With this scheme, Estelle can access any element in George's namespace (although in this example I've shown only one element: the `alpha` class).

Namespaces are sometimes used in class libraries so that to access classes from the library, you must specify the namespace using one of the access methods shown here.

Quiz 7

1. Which of the following are reasons for using multiple files?
   a. Member functions can be separated from member data.
   b. Each group of programmers may work on a separate file.
   c. Classes can be placed in different files than the code that uses the classes.
   d. Class specifications can be placed in a different file than member function code.
   e. The code in each file can have a different functionality.

2. In the highest level of program organization, private components of a class library
   a. take the form of .CPP or .H files.
   b. take the form of .LIB or .OBJ files.
   c. do not need to be accessed by the class user.
   d. do not need to be accessed by the application user.
   e. are differentiated from public components by the keywords `private` and `public`.

3. To combine a header file with your project, use
   a. an `#include` statement.
   b. the editor.
   c. the compiler.
   d. the linker.
   e. the .EXE file.

4. To combine several .OBJ files in your project, use
   a. an #include statement.
   b. the editor.
   c. the compiler.
   d. the linker.
   e. the .EXE file.

5. A namespace
   a. is created with the keyword namespace.
   b. ensures functions are visible throughout a program.
   c. limits the scope of global names.
   d. limits the scope of automatic variables.
   e. can be accessed with the keyword using.

Make the ARROVER1 program of Chapter 6, Session 7, into a multifile program. Put the class declarations into a file called SAFEARAY.H and the code for the member functions into a file called
SAFEARAY.CPP. Put the main() function in a file called SAFE_APP.CPP. Compile the SAFEARAY.CPP file into
an .OBJ file. Create a project in which the SAFE_APP.EXE file is dependent on the SAFEARAY.OBJ and SAFE_APP.CPP
files. Install the appropriate #include statements. Make sure the project compiles and runs correctly.

Apply the same approach as in the previous exercise to make the LINKLIST program of Chapter 8, Session
7, into a multifile program consisting of files LINKLIST.H, LINKLIST.CPP (which becomes LINKLIST.OBJ),
and LINK_APP.CPP. Make sure the project compiles and runs correctly.

A VERY-LONG-NUMBERS EXAMPLE

Here's an example that demonstrates how a program may be divided between files supplied by the
class creator and files written by the class user. The class provides a new data type: very long integer numbers. The class user can write programs employing this type.

   What can you do with very long numbers? Sometimes even the basic data type unsigned long
does not provide enough precision for certain integer arithmetic operations. unsigned long is the
largest integer type in 16-bit systems such as DOS and Windows 3.1, holding integers up to
4,294,967,295, or about 10 digits. This is about the same number of digits a pocket calculator can
handle. On 32-bit systems, type long may hold twice as many digits. If you need to work with numbers containing more significant digits than this, however, you have a problem.

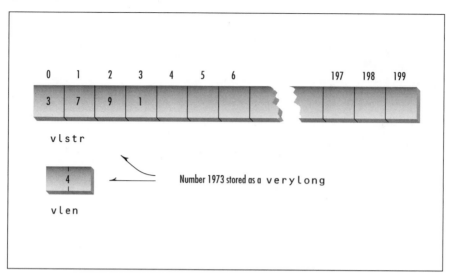

Figure 11-5   A `verylong` number

The example shows a way to solve this problem. It provides a class that holds numbers up to 200 digits long. If you want to make even longer numbers, you can change a single constant in the program. Need 1,000-digit numbers? No problem.

Note that the example program in this section, VERYLONG, in the VERYLONG.H file uses Borland's current version of the header file for the `string` class. This file is called CSTRING.H. If you're using a different compiler, you may need to make changes to the name of this header file (see Appendixes C and D).

Numbers as Strings

The `verylong` class stores numbers as objects of the standard `string` class described in Session 6 in this chapter. The `string` object contains the digits of the number stored as ASCII characters. By representing numbers as strings, I can make them as long as I want, although arithmetic operations will be slower.

There are two data members in the `verylong` class: a `string` object to hold the string of digits and an `int` to tell how long the string is. This length data isn't strictly necessary, but it saves using the `length()` member function to find the length of `string` objects over and over. The digits in the string are stored in reverse order, with the least significant digit stored first. This simplifies various operations on the string. Figure 11-5 shows a number stored as a string.

The Class Specifier

Here's the header file for the `verylong` class.

```
// verylong.h
// class specifier for very long integer type
```

```
#include <iostream.h>
#include <stdlib.h>          // for ltoa()
#include <cstring.h>         // for string class

const int SZ = 200;          // maximum digits in verylongs

class verylong
   {
   private:
      string vlstr;          // verylong number as a string
      int vlen;              // length of verylong string
      verylong multdigit(const int) const;   // prototypes for
      verylong mult10(const verylong) const; // private functions
   public:
      verylong() : vlen(0)             // no-arg constructor
         { }
      verylong(string& const s) :      // one-arg constructor
                  vlstr(s), vlen( s.length() )  // for string
         { }
      verylong(const unsigned long n)  // one-arg constructor
         {                                      // for long int
         char temp[SZ];      // utility char* string
         ltoa(n, temp, 10);  // convert n to char*
         strrev(temp);       // reverse char* string
         vlstr = temp;       // convert to string obj
         vlen = vlstr.length();  // find length
         }
      void putvl() const;              // display verylong
      void getvl();                    // get verylong from user
                                       // add verylongs
      verylong operator + (const verylong) const;
                                       // multiply verylongs
      verylong operator * (const verylong) const;
   };
```

The + and * operators are overloaded to provide addition and multiplication of verylong numbers. In addition to these public functions and the two data members, there are two private member functions. One multiplies a verylong number by a single decimal digit and one multiplies a verylong number by 10. These routines are used internally by the multiplication routine.

There are three constructors. One sets a verylong variable to 0 by setting its length, vlen, to 0. The second initializes a verylong to a string (which must already be in reverse order), and the third initializes it to a long int value.

The putvl() member function displays a verylong and the getvl gets a verylong value from the user. You can type as many digits as you like, up to 200. Note that there is no error checking in this routine; if you type a nondigit, the results are unpredictable.

You can perform addition and multiplication on verylongs using expressions such as

```
alpha = beta * gamma + delta;
```

just as you would with variables of basic types.

The Member Functions

Listing 11-21 shows `verylong.cpp`, the file that holds the member function definitions.

Listing 11-21 VERYLONG

```
// verylong.cpp
// implements very long integer type
#include "verylong.h"          // header file for verylong

void verylong::putvl() const            // display verylong
   {
   const char* cptr = vlstr.c_str();   // convert to char* string
   char* ptr = const_cast<char*>(cptr);  // cast away constness
   cout << strrev(ptr);                // reverse char* string
   }                                   //    and display it

void verylong::getvl()                  // get verylong from user
   {
   char temp[SZ];                      // utility char* string
   cin >> temp;                        // user enters digits
   strrev(temp);                       // reverse char* string
   vlstr = temp;                       // convert to string
   vlen = vlstr.length();              // find its length
   }
                                       // add verylongs
verylong verylong::operator + (const verylong v) const
   {
   int j;
   char temp[SZ];                      // utility char* string
                                       // find longest number
   int maxlen = (vlen > v.vlen) ? vlen : v.vlen;
   int carry = 0;                      // set to 1 if sum >= 10
   for(j = 0; j<maxlen; j++)           // for each position
      {
      int d1 = (j > vlen-1)    ? 0 : vlstr[j]-'0';   // get digit
      int d2 = (j > v.vlen-1) ? 0 : v.vlstr[j]-'0';  // get digit
      int digitsum = d1 + d2 + carry;                // add digits
      if( digitsum >= 10 )            // if there's a carry,
         { digitsum -= 10; carry=1; } // decrease sum by 10,
      else                            // set carry to 1
         carry = 0;                   // otherwise carry is 0
      temp[j] = digitsum + '0';       // insert char in string
      }
   if(carry==1)                       // if carry at end,
      temp[j++] = '1';                // last digit is 1
   temp[j] = '\0';                    // terminate string
   return verylong(temp);            // return temp verylong
   }
                                       // multiply verylongs
verylong verylong::operator * (const verylong v) const
   {
   verylong pprod;                     // product of one digit
```

```
   verylong tempsum;                   // running total
   for(int j=0; j<v.vlen; j++)         // for each digit in arg
      {
      int digit = v.vlstr[j] - '0';    // get the digit
      pprod = multdigit(digit);        // multiply this by digit
      for(int k=0; k<j; k++)           // multiply result by
         pprod = mult10(pprod);        //     power of 10
      tempsum = tempsum + pprod;       // add product to total
      }
   return tempsum;                     // return total of prods
   }
                                       // multiply argument by 10
verylong verylong::mult10(const verylong v) const
   {
   char temp[SZ];
   for(int j=v.vlen-1; j>=0; j--)      // move digits one
      temp[j+1] = v.vlstr[j];          //     position higher
   temp[0] = '0';                      // put zero on low end
   temp[v.vlen+1] = '\0';             // terminate string
   return verylong(temp);             // return result
   }
                                       // multiply this verylong
verylong verylong::multdigit(const int d2) const   // by digit
   {                                               // in argument
   int j;
   char temp[SZ];
   int carry = 0;
   for(j = 0; j<vlen; j++)             // for each position
      {                                // in this verylong
      int d1 = vlstr[j]-'0';           // get digit from this
      int digitprod = d1 * d2;         // multiply by that digit
      digitprod += carry;              // add old carry
      if( digitprod >= 10 )            // if there's a new carry,
         {
         carry = digitprod/10;         // carry is high digit
         digitprod -= carry*10;        // result is low digit
         }
      else
         carry = 0;                    // otherwise carry is 0
      temp[j] = digitprod+'0';         // insert char in string
      }
   if(carry != 0)                      // if carry at end,
      temp[j++] = carry+'0';           // it's last digit
   temp[j] = '\0';                    // terminate string
   return verylong(temp);             // return verylong
   }
```

The putvl() member function converts the vlstr object to a normal C++ char* string and dislays it. The getvl() member function reads a normal char* string from the keyboard, reverses it, and converts it to the string object vlstr. Both functions use the strrev() library function, which reverses a char* string, so the digits of the verylong are stored in reverse order but displayed normally.

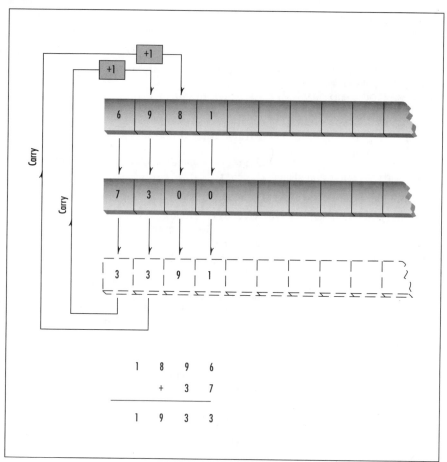

Figure 11-6   Adding `verylong` numbers

The `operator+()` function adds two `verylong`s and leaves the result in a third `verylong`. It does this by considering digits one at a time. It adds digit 0 from both numbers, storing a carry if necessary. Then it adds the digits in position 1, adding the carry if necessary. It continues until it has added all the digits in the larger of the two numbers. If the numbers are different lengths, the nonexistent digits in the shorter number are set to 0 before being added. Figure 11-6 shows the process.

Multiplication uses the `operator*()` function. This function performs multiplication by multiplying the multiplicand (the top number when you write it by hand) by each separate digit in the multiplier (the bottom number). It calls the `multdigit()` routine to do this. The results are then multiplied by 10 an appropriate number of times to shift the result to match the position of the digit, using the `mult10()` function. The results of these separate calculations are then added together using the `operator+()` function.

The Application Program

To test the `verylong` class, I wrote a program that calculates the factorial of an integer entered by the user. As you no doubt recall, the factorial of an integer is the result of multiplying the integer by all the integers smaller than itself (but greater than 0). That is, if the number is 5, its factorial is 5*4*3*2*1, which is 120. The factorials of large numbers are very large indeed. Listing 11-22 shows VL_APP.CPP.

Listing 11-22 VL_APP

```
// vl_app.cpp
// calculates factorials of larger numbers using verylong class
#include "verylong.h"              // verylong header file
void main()
    {
    unsigned long numb, j;
    verylong fact = 1;             // initialize verylong

    cout << "\n\nEnter number: ";
    cin >> numb;                   // input a long int

    for(j=numb; j>0; j--)          // factorial is numb *
        fact = fact * j;           //     numb-1 * numb-2 *
    cout << "Factoral is ";        //     numb-3 and so on
    fact.putvl();                  // display factorial
    }
```

In this program, `fact` is a `verylong` variable. The other variables, `numb` and `j`, don't need to be `verylong`s because they don't get so big. To calculate the factorial of 200, for example, `numb` and `j` require only three digits, whereas `fact` requires 158.

Notice how, in the expression

```
fact = fact * j;
```

the `long` variable `j` is automatically converted to `verylong`, using the one-argument constructor, before the multiplication is carried out.

Here's the output when I ask the program to find the factorial of 100:

```
Enter number: 100
Factoral is 9332621544394415268169923885626670049071596826438162
1468592963895217599993229915608941463976156518286253697920827223
758251185210916864000000000000000000000000
```

Try *that* using type `long` variables! Surprisingly, the routines are fairly fast; this program executes in a fraction of a second.

Subtraction and Division

I'll leave it as an exercise for you to create member functions to perform subtraction and division for the `verylong` class. These should overload the – and / operators. Warning: There's some work involved here. When you include subtraction, you will probably want to assume that any `verylong` number can be negative as well as positive. This complicates the addition and multiplication routines, which must do different things depending on the signs of the numbers.

After wading through almost this entire book, you deserve a break; there are no quiz questions for this session. You will automatically receive credit for a perfect score. Don't say I never did anything for you.

Figure out something you would like to make into a class library (A new data type to represent dollars-and-cents values? A new container class based on a queue? Airplanes in an air-traffic control simulator?). Implement this class library as separate .H and .OBJ files. Write a separate .CPP file that makes use of the class library. Use a template approach if appropriate. Install exceptions to catch any errors.

SUMMARY: CHAPTER 11

I've covered many disparate topics in this chapter. Template functions can operate on different kinds of data, with the data type supplied when the function is instantiated rather than when it's written. Template classes are usually used for container classes and allow containers (data structures) to store different types of data, with the type determined when an object of the class is instantiated.

Exceptions are a systematic approach to handling errors that occur in class member functions. An exception class is specified within the class in question, and exceptions are "thrown" using the **throw** keyword when errors are detected. In the application using the class, code that may generate errors is installed in a try block and code that handles an exception is installed in a catch block.

Explicit casts provide an alternative form of runtime type identification, allow **const** variables to be modified, and are more easily located with a source code editor than implicit casts. The **typedef** specifier gives a data type a new name. It can be used to give a potentially long and complicated type a shorter name, and for other purposes.

The **string** class that's now being made a part of the standard C++ library makes it far more convenient to work with text strings. Objects of the string class handle their own memory allocation, so users no longer need to set aside array space to hold strings. The **string** class also supplies many member functions to make string manipulation easier.

In the real world, C++ programs are divided into different files. This helps separate the work of different programmers, puts different kinds of functionality in different files, and allows the distribution of proprietary software without giving users access to the source code. I showed an example of a class library for a very long numbers data type in multifile form.

END-OF-CHAPTER DISCUSSION

George: What a hodgepodge! We covered everything but the kitchen sink in this chapter.

Estelle: You should be glad we didn't spend whole chapters on `typedef` and static casts and everything. That would have been really fun.

George: Are we really going to use this stuff? It seems pretty far out.

Don: Even if you don't use it, you should recognize it when you see it. Practically every listing I see uses `typedef`. Not so much the explicit casts; I think they're too new.

Estelle: The standard `string` class is pretty neat.

George: Well it's about time they did something with strings in C++. Imagine having to deal with arrays of characters instead of a real string type.

Don: Yes, no more worrying about always having enough memory for some string. Let the class handle it.

Estelle: The `string` class header files in my compiler aren't anything like what they talked about in Session 6, though.

Don: They said that would change. The `string` class is pretty new, and when they wrote this book, it wasn't clear what compiler vendors were really going to call them.

Estelle: I guess that's the trouble with being on the cutting edge.

George: Do you think anyone would really use that `verylong` number class?

Don: Maybe a mathematician.

George: There aren't even member functions to let you subtract and divide!

Don: But you'll have them written by next week, right?

George: Oh, no problem. I'll whip 'em off in no time 'cause I'm some kind of a genius programmer.

END OF CHAPTER EVALUATION

CHAPTER 12

THE STANDARD TEMPLATE LIBRARY

Most computer programs exist to process data. The data may represent a wide variety of real-world information: personnel records, inventories, text documents, the results of scientific experiments. Whatever it represents, data is stored in memory and manipulated in similar ways. University computer science programs typically include a course called Data Structures and Algorithms. Data structures refer to the ways data is stored in memory and algorithms refer to how data is processed.

C++ classes provide an excellent mechanism for creating a library of data structures. Since the development of C++, most compiler vendors and many third-party developers have offered libraries of *container classes* to handle the storage and processing of data. Recently, a new approach to a container class library has been added to the draft ANSI/ISO C++

standard. It's called the Standard Template Library (STL) and it was developed by Alexander Stepanov and Meng Lee of Hewlett Packard. STL is expected to become the standard approach to storing and processing data. Major compiler vendors are beginning to incorporate the STL into their products.

This chapter describes the STL and how to use it. The STL is large and complex, so I won't by any means describe everything about it; that would require a large book. (In fact, several are slated to be published by the time you read this.) I will introduce the STL and give examples of the more common algorithms and containers.

Be aware that the STL has not yet been officially adopted into the C++ standard. Before it is, it will probably undergo some changes, especially in such details as the names of header files. For details of its implementation, consult your vendor's documentation.

INTRODUCTION TO THE STL

The STL contains several kinds of entities. The three most important are containers, algorithms, and iterators.

A *container* is a way that stored data is organized in memory. In earlier chapters, I explored two kinds of containers: stacks and linked lists. Another container, the array, is so common that it's built into C++ (and most other computer languages). However, there are many other kinds of containers, and the STL includes the most useful. The STL containers are implemented by template classes so they can be easily customized to hold different kinds of data.

Algorithms are procedures that are applied to containers to process their data in various ways. For example, there are algorithms to sort, copy, search, and merge data. In the STL, algorithms are represented by template functions. These functions are not member functions of the container classes. Rather, they are standalone functions. Indeed, one of the striking characteristics of the STL is that its algorithms are so general. You can use them not only on STL containers, but also on ordinary C++ arrays and on containers you create yourself. (Containers also include member functions for more specific tasks.)

Iterators are a generalization of the concept of pointers: They point to elements in a container. You can increment an iterator, as you can a pointer, so it points in turn to each element in a container. Iterators are a key part of the STL because they connect algorithms with containers. Think of them as a software version of cables, like the cables that connect your computer to its peripherals. Iterators also connect different components together.

Figure 12-1 shows these three main components of the STL. In this session I'll discuss containers, algorithms, and iterators in slightly more detail. In subsequent sessions, I'll explore these concepts further with program examples.

Containers

A container is a way to store data, whether the data consists of built-in types such as `int` and `float` or of class objects. The STL makes available seven basic kinds of containers; three more are derived from the basic kinds. In addition, you can create your own containers based on the basic kinds. You

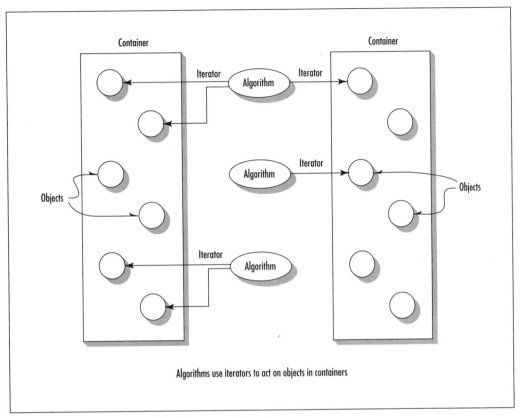

Algorithms use iterators to act on objects in containers

Figure 12-1   Containers, algorithms, and iterators

may wonder why you need so many kinds of containers. Why not use C++ arrays in all data storage situations? The answer is efficiency. An array is awkward or slow in many situations.

Containers in the STL fall into two categories: *sequence* and *associative*. The sequence containers are *vector*, *list*, and *deque*. The associative containers are *set*, *multiset*, *map*, and *multimap*. In addition, several containers are called *abstract data types*, which are specialized versions of other containers. These are *stack*, *queue*, and *priority_queue*. I'll look at these categories in turn.

Sequence Containers

A sequence container stores a set of elements that you can visualize as a line, like houses on a street. Each element is related to the other elements by its position along the line. Each element (except at the ends) is preceded by one specific element and followed by another. An ordinary C++ array is an example of a sequence container.

One problem with a C++ array is that you must specify its size at compile time, that is, in the source code. Unfortunately, you usually don't know when you write the program how much data will be stored in the array. So you must specify an array large enough to hold what you guess is the maximum amount of data. When the program runs, you will either waste space in memory by not filling the array or elicit an error message (or even blow up the program) by running out of space. The STL provides the vector container to avoid these difficulties.

Here's another problem with arrays. Say you're storing employee records and you've arranged them in alphabetical order by the employee's last name. If you now want to insert a new employee whose name starts with, say, L, then you must move all the employees from M to Z to make room. This can be very time-consuming. The STL provides the list container, which is based on the idea of a linked list, to solve this problem. Recall from the LINKLIST example in Chapter 8, Session 7, that a new item can easily be inserted in a linked list by rearranging several pointers.

The third sequence container is the deque, which can be thought of as a combination of a stack and a queue. A stack, as you may recall from previous examples, works on a last-in-first-out (LIFO) principle. Both input and output take place on the top of the stack. A queue, on the other hand, uses a first-in-first-out (FIFO) arrangement: Data goes in at the front and comes out at the back, like a line of customers in a bank. A deque combines these approaches so you can insert or delete data from either end. The word "deque" is derived from *Double-Ended QUEue*. It's a versatile mechanism that's not only useful in its own right, but can be used as the basis for stacks and queues, as you'll see later.

Table 12-1 summarizes the characteristics of the STL sequence containers. It includes the ordinary C++ array for comparison.

Container	Characteristic	Advantages and Disadvantages
Ordinary C++ array	Fixed size	Quick random access (by index number). Slow to insert or erase in the middle. Size cannot be changed at runtime.
Vector	Relocating, expandable array	Quick random access (by index number). Slow to insert or erase in the middle. Quick to insert or erase at end.
List	Doubly linked list	Quick to insert or delete at any location. Quick access to both ends. Slow random access.
Deque	Like vector, but can be accessed at either end	Quick random access (using index number). Slow to insert or erase in the middle. Quick to insert or erase (push and pop) at either the beginning or the end.

Table 12-1   *Basic sequence containers*

Instantiating an STL container object is easy. First, you must include an appropriate header file. Then you use the template format with the kind of objects to be stored as the parameter. Examples might be

```
vector<int> avect;  // create a vector of ints
```
or
```
list<airtime> departure_list;  // create a list of airtimes
```

Notice that there's no need to specify the size of STL containers. The containers themselves take care of all memory allocation.

Associative Containers

An associative container is not sequential; instead it uses *keys* to access data. The keys, typically numbers or stings, are used automatically by the container to arrange the stored elements in a specific order. It's like an ordinary English dictionary in which you access data by looking up words arranged in alphabetical order. You start with a key value (e.g., the word "aardvark," to use the dictionary example), and the container converts this key to the element's location in memory. If you know the key, it's quick to access the associated value.

There are two kinds of associative containers in the STL: maps and sets. A map associates a key (e.g., the word you're looking up) with a value (the definition of the word). The value can be any kind of object. A set is similar to a map, but it stores only the keys; there are no associated values. It's like a list of words without the definitions.

The map and set containers allow only one key of a given value to be stored. This makes sense in, say, a phone book where you can assume that multiple people don't have the same number. On the other hand, the multimap and multiset containers allow multiple keys. In an English dictionary, there might be several entries for the word "set," for example.

Table 12-2 summarizes the associative containers available in the STL.

Container	Characteristics	Advantages and Disadvantages
Map	Associates key with element Only one key of each value allowed	Quick random access (by key). Inefficient if keys not evenly distributed.
Multimap	Associates key with element Multiple key values allowed	Quick random access (by key). Inefficient if keys not evenly distributed.
Set	Stores only the keys themselves Only one key of each value allowed	Quick random access (by key). Inefficient if keys not evenly distributed.
Multiset	Stores only the keys themselves Multiple key values allowed	Quick random access (by key). Inefficient if keys not evenly distributed.

Table 12-2 *Basic associative containers*

Creating associative containers is just like creating sequential ones:

```
map<int> IntMap;   // create a map of ints
```

or

```
multiset<employee> machinists;   // create a multiset of employees
```

Member Functions

Algorithms are the heavy hitters of the STL, carrying out complex operations such as sorting and searching. However, containers also need member functions to perform simpler tasks that are specific to a particular type of container.

Table 12-3 shows some frequently used member functions whose name and purpose (not the actual implementation) are common to all the container classes.

Name	Purpose
`size()`	Returns the number of items in the container.
`empty()`	Returns true if container is empty.
`max_size()`	Returns size of the largest possible container.
`begin()`	Returns an iterator to the start of the container for iterating forward through the container.
`end()`	Returns an iterator to the past-the-end location in the container, used to end forward iteration.
`rbegin()`	Returns a reverse iterator to the end of the container for iterating backward through the container.
`rend()`	Returns a reverse iterator to the beginning of the container, used to end backward iteration.

Table 12-3 *Some member functions common to all containers*

Many other member functions appear only in certain containers or certain categories of containers. You'll learn more about these as I go along. Appendix B includes a table showing all the STL member functions and which ones exist for which containers.

Abstract Data Types

It's possible to use basic containers to create another kind of container called an *abstract data type,* or ADT. An ADT is a sort of simplified or conceptual container that emphasizes certain aspects of a more basic container; it provides a different *interface* to the programmer. The ADTs implemented in the STL are stacks, queues, and priority queues. As I noted, a stack restricts access to pushing and popping a data item on and off the top of the stack. In a queue, you push items at one end and pop them off the other end. In a priority queue, you push data in the front in random order, but when you pop the data off the other end, you always pop the largest item stored: The priority queue automatically sorts the data for you.

The mechanism the STL uses to create ADTs from the basic types is the *adaptor.* Adaptors are template classes that translate functions used in the ADT (such as push and pop) to functions used by the underlying container.

Stacks, queues, and priority queues can be created from different sequence containers, although the deque is often the most obvious choice. Table 12-4 shows the abstract data types and the sequence containers that can be used in their implementation.

Container	Implementation	Characteristics
Stack	Can be implemented as vector, list, or deque.	Insert (push) and remove (pop) at one end only.
Queue	Can be implemented as list or deque.	Insert (push) at one end, remove (pop) at other.
Priority queue	Can be implemented as vector or deque.	Insert (push) in random order at one end, remove (pop) in sorted order from other end.

Table 12-4 *Abstract data types*

You use a template within a template to instantiate an ADT. For example, here's a **stack** object that holds type **int**, instantiated from the **deque** class:

```
stack< deque<int> > astak;
```

A detail to note about this format is that you must insert a space between the two closing angle brackets. You can't write

```
stack<deque<int>> astak;   // syntax error
```

because the compiler will interpret the **>>** as an operator.

Algorithms

An algorithm is a function that does something to the items in a container (or containers). As I noted, algorithms in the STL are not member functions or even friends of container classes, as they are in most other container libraries, but standalone template functions. You can use them with built-in C++ arrays or with container classes you create yourself (provided the class includes certain basic functions).

Table 12-5 shows a few representative algorithms. I'll examine others as I go along. Appendix B contains a table listing all the currently available STL algorithms.

Algorithm	Purpose
find	Returns first element equivalent to a specified value.
count	Counts the number of elements that have a specified value.
equal	Compares the contents of two containers and returns true if all corresponding elements are equal.
search	Looks for a sequence of values in one container that correspond with the same sequence in another container.
copy	Copies a sequence of values from one container to another (or to a different location in the same container).

continued on next page

continued from previous page

Algorithm	Purpose
swap	Exchanges a value in one location with a value in another.
iter_swap	Exchanges a sequence of values in one location with a sequence of values in another location.
fill	Copies a value into a sequence of locations.
sort	Sorts the values in a container according to a specified ordering.
merge	Combines two sorted ranges of elements to make a larger sorted range.
accumulate	Returns the sum of the elements in a given range.
for_each	Executes a specified function for each element in a container.

Table 12-5 *Some typical STL algorithms*

Suppose you create an array of type `int`, with data in it:

```
int arr[8] = {42, 31, 7, 80, 2, 26, 19, 75};
```

You can then use the STL `sort()` algorithm to sort this array by saying

```
sort(arr, arr+8);
```

where `arr` is the address of the beginning of the array and `arr+8` is the past-the-end address (one item past the end of the array).

Iterators

Iterators are pointer-like entities used to access individual data items (which are usually called *elements*) in a container. Often they are used to move sequentially from element to element, a process called *iterating* through the container. You can increment an iterator with the ++ operator so it points to the next element, and you can dereference it with the * operator to obtain the value of the element it points to.

Like a pointer to an array element, some types of iterators can store (or "remember") the location of a specific container element. In the STL, an iterator is represented by an object of an iterator class.

Different classes of iterators must be used with different types of container. There are three major classes of iterators: forward, bidirectional, and random access. A *forward iterator* can move only forward through the container one item at a time. Its ++ operator accomplishes this. It can't move backward and it can't be set to an arbitrary location in the middle of the container. A *bidirectional iterator* can move backward as well as forward, so both its ++ and -- operators are defined. A *random-access iterator*, in addition to moving backward and forward, can jump to an arbitrary location. You can tell it to access location 27, for example.

There are also two specialized kinds of iterators. An *input iterator* can "point to" an input device (`cin` or a file) to read sequential data items into a container, and an *output iterator* can "point to" an output device (`cout` or a file) and write elements from a container to the device.

Although the values of forward, bidirectional, and random-access iterators can be stored (so they can be used later), the values of input and output iterators cannot be. This makes sense: The first three iterators point to memory locations, whereas input and output iterators point to I/O devices for which stored "pointer" values have no meaning. Table 12-6 shows the characteristics of these different kinds of iterators.

Iterator	Read/Write	Iterator Can Be Saved	Direction	Access
Random access	Read and write	Yes	Forward and back	Random
Bidirectional	Read and write	Yes	Forward and back	Linear
Forward	Read and write	Yes	Forward only	Linear
Output	Write only	No	Forward only	Linear
Input	Read only	No	Forward only	Linear

Table 12-6   *Iterator characteristics*

Potential Problems with the STL

The STL is still being refined and vendors are still bringing out new products to work with specific compilers, so the problems I mention here may have been solved by the time you read this. However, at present there are a few aspects of the STL that require some care. These problems result from the strain the STL's sophisticated template classes place on many compilers.

First, it's sometimes hard to find errors because the compiler reports them as being deep in a header file when they are really in the class user's code. You may need to resort to brute force methods such as commenting out one line of your code at a time to find the culprit.

Precompilation of header files, which speeds up compilation dramatically on compilers that offer it, may cause problems with the STL. If things don't seem to be working, try turning off precompiled headers.

The STL generates lots of compiler warnings from deep within the STL header files. `Conversion may lose significant digits` is a favorite. These appear to be harmless and can be ignored or turned off.

These minor complaints aside, the STL is a surprisingly robust and versatile system. Errors tend to be caught at compile time rather than at runtime. The different algorithms and containers present a very consistent interface; what works with one container or algorithm will usually work with another (assuming it's used appropriately).

This quick overview probably leaves you with more questions than answers. The following sessions should provide enough specific details of STL operation to make things clearer.

1. An STL container can be used to
   a. hold `int` values.
   b. hold objects of class `employee`.
   c. store elements in a way that makes them quickly accessible.
   d. compile C++ programs.
   e. organize the way objects are stored in memory.

2. Which of the following are STL sequence containers?
   a. multiset
   b. stack
   c. deque
   d. map
   e. list

3. Which of the following are STL associative containers?
   a. multiset
   b. stack
   c. deque
   d. map
   e. list

4. An algorithm is
   a. a standalone function that operates on containers.
   b. a link between member functions and containers.
   c. a friend function of a container class.
   d. a member function of a container class.
   e. a kind of pointer to objects in a container.

5. An iterator
   a. acts something like a function.
   b. cannot step backward through a container.
   c. always executes the same algorithm over and over.
   d. points to a specific object in a container.
   e. is the STL version of a `for` loop.

Because of its generality, this session contains no exercises.

SESSION 2
ALGORITHMS

The STL algorithms perform operations on collections of data. These algorithms were designed to work with STL containers, but one of the nice things about them is that you can apply them to ordinary C++ arrays. This may save you considerable work when programming arrays. It also offers an easy way to learn about algorithms, unencumbered with containers. In this session, I'll examine how some representative algorithms are actually used. (Remember that all the algorithms are listed in Appendix B.)

The find() Algorithm

The find() algorithm looks for the first element in a container that has a specified value. The FIND example program (Listing 12-1) shows how this looks when I'm trying to find a value in an array of ints.

Listing 12-1 FIND

```
// find.cpp
// finds the first element with a specified value
#include <iostream.h>
#include <algo.h>

int arr[] = { 11, 22, 33, 44, 55, 66, 77, 88 };

void main()
    {
    int* ptr;
    ptr = find(arr, arr+8, 33);   // find first 33
    cout << "First object with value 33 found at offset "
         << (ptr-arr) << endl;
    }
```

The output from this program is

```
First object with value 33 found at offset 2.
```

As usual, the first element in the array is number 0, so the 33 is found at offset 2.

Header Files

In this program, I've included the header file ALGO.H. In the version of the STL I'm using, this file contains the declarations of all the algorithms. Other header files are used for containers. If you're using a version of the STL from a different supplier, you may need to include a different header file. Some implementations use only one header file for all STL operations, whereas others use many different files but call them by slightly different names, such as ALGORTHM.H. or ALGORITHM (without the .H). You may also need to insert a `using namespace` directive in your code. See Appendixes C and D for more on this issue.

Ranges

The first two parameters to `find()` specify the range of elements to be examined. These values are specified by iterators. In this example, I use normal C++ pointer values, which are a special case of iterators.

The first parameter is the iterator of (or in this case, the pointer to) the first value to be examined. The second parameter is the iterator of the location one past the last element to be examined. Because there are 8 elements, this value is the first value plus 8. This is called a *past-the-end* value; it points to the element just past the end of the range to be examined.

This syntax is reminiscent of the normal C++ idiom in a `for` loop:

```
for(int j=0; j<8; j++)    // from 0 to 7
   {
   if(arr[j] == 33)
      {
      cout << "First object with value 33 found at offset "
         << j << endl;
      break;
      }
   }
```

In the FIND example, the `find()` algorithm saves you the trouble of writing this `for` loop. In more complicated situations, algorithms may save you from writing far more complicated code.

The `count()` Algorithm

Let's look at another algorithm, `count()`, which counts how many elements in a container have a specified value. This algorithm, instead of returning an iterator (pointer) value, as `find()` did, adds the count to an `int` variable supplied (by reference) as an argument to `count()`. The COUNT example (Listing 12-2) shows how this looks.

Listing 12-2 COUNT

```
// count.cpp
// counts the number of elements with a specified value
#include <iostream.h>
#include <algo.h>

int arr[] = { 33, 22, 33, 44, 33, 55, 66, 77 };

void main()
   {
   int n = 0;                  // must initialize
   count(arr, arr+8, 33, n);   // count number of 33's
                               //    add result to n
   cout << "There are " << n << " 33's in arr." << endl;
   }
```

The output is

```
There are 3 33's in arr.
```

You might expect `count()` to return the count, but adding the count to an existing number may be useful if you've already counted something and want to add the new count to the old one.

The `sort()` Algorithm

You can guess what the `sort()` algorithm does. Listing 12-3 shows an example, called SORT, of this algorithm applied to an array.

Listing 12-3 SORT

```
// sort.cpp
// sorts an array of integers
#include <iostream.h>
#include <algo.h>
                                // array of numbers
int arr[] = {45, 2, 22, -17, 0, -30, 25, 55};

void main()
   {
   sort(arr, arr+8);            // sort the numbers

   for(int j=0; j<8; j++)       // display sorted array
      cout << arr[j] << ' ';
   }
```

The output from the program is

```
-30, -17, 0, 2, 25, 45, 55
```

I'll look at some variations of this algorithm later.

The `search()` Algorithm

Some algorithms operate on two containers at once. For instance, whereas the `find()` algorithm looks for a specified value in a single container, the `search()` algorithm looks for a sequence of values specified by one container within another container. The SEARCH example (Listing 12-4) shows how this looks.

Listing 12-4 SEARCH

```
// search.cpp
// searches one container for a sequence in another container
#include <iostream.h>
#include <algo.h>

int source[] = { 11, 44, 33, 11, 22, 33, 11, 22, 44 };
int pattern[] = { 11, 22, 33 };

void main()
   {
   int* ptr;
   ptr = search(source, source+9, pattern, pattern+3);
```

continued on next page

continued from previous page

```
    if(ptr == source+9)                    // if past-the-end
        cout << "No match found";
    else
        cout << "Match at " << (ptr - source);
    }
```

The algorithm looks for the sequence 11, 22, 33, specified by the array `pattern`, within the array `source`. As you can see by inspection, this sequence is found in `source` starting at the fourth element (element 3). The output is

```
Match at 3
```

If the iterator value `ptr` ends up one past the end of the source, then no match has been found.

The arguments to algorithms such as `search()` don't need to be the same type of container. The source could be in an STL vector and the pattern could be in an array, for example. This kind of generality is a very powerful feature of the STL.

The `merge()` Algorithm

Listing 12-5 shows an algorithm that works with three containers, merging the elements from two source containers into a destination container.

Listing 12-5 MERGE

```
// merge.cpp
// merges two containers into a third
#include <iostream.h>
#include <algo.h>

int src1[] = { 2, 3, 4, 6, 8 };
int src2[] = { 1, 3, 5 };
int dest[8];

void main()
    {
    merge(src1, src1+5, src2, src2+3, dest);
    for(int j=0; j<8; j++)
        cout << dest[j] << ' ';
    }
```

The output, which displays the contents of the destination container, looks like this:

```
1 2 3 3 4 5 6 8
```

As you can see, merging preserves the ordering, interweaving the two sequences of source elements into the destination container.

Function Objects

Some algorithms can take something called a *function object* as an argument. A function object looks, to the user, much like a template function. However, it's actually an object of a template class that has a single member function: the overloaded `()` operator. This sounds mysterious, but it's easy to use.

Suppose you want to sort an array of numbers into descending instead of ascending order. The SORTEMP program (Listing 12-6) shows how to do this.

Listing 12-6 SORTEMP

```
// sortemp.cpp
// sorts array of floats in backwards order,
// uses greater<>()  function object
#include <iostream.h>
#include <algo.h>
                                        // array of floats
float fdata[] = { 19.2, 87.4, 33.6, 55.0, 11.5, 42.2 };

void main()
   {                                    // sort the floats
   sort( fdata, fdata+6, greater<float>() );

   for(int j=0; j<6; j++)               // display sorted floats
      cout << fdata[j] << endl;
   }
```

The array of **float** values is sorted using the **greater<>()** function object. Here's the output:

```
87.4
55
42.2
33.6
19.1
11.5
```

Besides comparisons, there are function objects for arithmetical and logical operations. I'll look at function objects more closely in Session 8.

User-Written Functions in Place of Function Objects

Function objects operate only on basic C++ types and on classes for which the appropriate operators (+, <, &&, and so on) are defined. If you're working with values for which this is not the case, you can substitute a user-written function for a function object. For example, the operator < is not defined for ordinary **char*** strings, but you can write a function to perform the comparison and use this function's address (its name) in place of the function object. The SORTCOM example (Listing 12-7) shows how to sort an array of **char*** strings.

Listing 12-7 SORTCOM

```
// sortcom.cpp
// sorts array of strings with user-written comparison function
#include <iostream.h>
#include <string.h>                     // for strcmp()
#include <algo.h>
                                        // array of strings
char* names[] = { "George", "Penny", "Estelle",
                  "Don", "Mike", "Bob" };

bool alpha_comp(char*, char*);          // prototype
```

continued on next page

continued from previous page

```
void main()
   {
   sort( names, names+6, alpha_comp );        // sort the strings

   for(int j=0; j<6; j++)                      // display sorted strings
      cout << names[j] << endl;
   }

bool alpha_comp(char* s1, char* s2)           // returns true if s1<s2
   {
   return ( strcmp(s1, s2)<0 ) ? true : false;
   }
```

The third argument to the `sort()` algorithm is the address of the `alpha_comp()` function, which compares two `char*` strings and returns true or false, depending on whether the first is lexicographically (i.e., alphabetically) less than the second. The output from this program is what you would expect:

```
Bob
Don
Estelle
George
Mike
Penny
```

Actually, you don't need to write your own function objects to handle text. If you use the `string` class from the standard library, you can use built-in function objects such as `less<>()` and `greater<>()` instead.

Boolean Type

The return value of the user-written function (`alpha_comp()` in this example) should be type `bool`. This type is specified in the BOOL.H header file (which is included in ALGO.H). On my system, type `bool` is #defined to be type `int`, `true` is 1, and `false` is 0; other systems vary but work the same way.

Adding _if to Algorithms

Some algorithms have versions that end in `_if`. These algorithms take an extra parameter called a *predicate*, which is a function object or a function. For example, the `find()` algorithm finds all elements equal to a specified value. However, it can do this only if the = operator is defined for the data type of the objects being searched. If = isn't defined, you can create an equality function that works with the `find_if()` algorithm to find elements with any arbitrary characteristic.

Listing 12-8 uses `char*` strings. The `find_if()` algorithm is supplied with a user-written `isDon()` function to find the first string in an array of strings that has the value "Don".

Listing 12-8 FIND_IF

```
// find_if.cpp
// searches array of strings for first name that matches "Don"
#include <iostream.h>
#include <string.h>              // for strcmp()
#include <algo.h>
                                 // array of strings
char* names[] = { "George", "Estelle", "Don", "Mike", "Bob" };
```

```
bool isDon(char*);              // prototype

void main()
  {
  char** ptr;
                                // find the first string "Don"
  ptr = find_if( names, names+5, isDon );

  if(ptr==names+5)              // display results
     cout << "Don is not on the list";
  else
     cout << "Don is element "
          << (ptr-names)
          << " on the list.";
  }

bool isDon(char* name)          // returns true if name=="Don"
  {
  return ( strcmp(name, "Don") ) ? false : true;
  }
```

Because "Don" is indeed one of the names in the array, the output from the program is

```
Don is element 2 on the list.
```

The address of the function `isDon()` is the third argument to `find_if()`, whereas the first and second arguments are, as usual, the first and the past-the-end addresses of the array.

The `find_if()` algorithm applies the `isDon()` function to every element in the range. If `isDon()` returns `true` for any element, then `find_if()` returns the value of that element's pointer (iterator). Otherwise, it returns a pointer to the past-the-end address of the array.

Various other algorithms, such as `count()`, `replace()`, and `remove()`, have `_if` versions.

The `for_each()` Algorithm

The `for_each()` algorithm allows you to do something to every item in a container. You write your own function to determine what that "something" is. Your function can't change the elements in the container, but it can use or display their values.

Here's an example in which `for_each()` is used to convert all the values of an array from inches to centimeters and display them. I write a function called `in_to_cm()` that multiplies a value by 2.54 and use this function's address as the third argument to `for_each()`. Listing 12-9 shows FOR_EACH.

Listing 12-9 FOR_EACH
```
// for_each.cpp
// uses for_each() to output inches array elements as centimeters
#include <iostream.h>
#include <algo.h>

void main()
  {                             // array of inches values
  float inches[] = { 3.5, 6.2, 1.0, 12.75, 4.33 };
  void in_to_cm(float);        // prototype
```

continued on next page

continued from previous page

```
                                        // output as centimeters
    for_each(inches, inches+5, in_to_cm);
    }

void in_to_cm(float in)        // convert and display as centimeters
    {
    cout << (in * 2.54) << ' ';
    }
```

The output looks like this:

8.89 15.748 2.54 32.385 10.9982

The transform() Algorithm

The transform() algorithm does something to every item in a container and places the resulting values in a different container (or the same one). Again, a user-written function determines what will be done to each item. The return type of this function must be the same as that of the destination container. The example is similar to FOR_EACH except that instead of displaying the converted values, the in_to_cm() function puts the centimeter values into a different array, centi[]. The main program then displays the contents of centi[]. Listing 12-10 shows TRANSFO.

Listing 12-10 TRANSFO

```
// transfo.cpp
// uses transform() to change array of inches values to cm
#include <iostream.h>
#include <algo.h>

void main()
    {                          // array of inches values
    float inches[] = { 3.5, 6.2, 1.0, 12.75, 4.33 };
    float centi[5];
    float in_to_cm(float);     // prototype
                               // transform into array centi[]
    transform(inches, inches+5, centi, in_to_cm);

    for(int j=0; j<5; j++)     // display array centi[]
        cout << centi[j] << ' ';
    }

float in_to_cm(float in)       // convert inches to centimeters
    {
    return (in * 2.54);        // return result
    }
```

The output is the same as that from the FOR_EACH program.

I've showed just a few of the algorithms in the STL. There are many others, but what I've shown here should give you an idea of the kinds of algorithms that are available and how to use them.

1. Algorithms can
   a. be used only on STL containers.
   b. obtain information about elements in a container.
   c. change the order of elements in a container.
   d. create and destroy containers.
   e. create and destroy the objects stored in containers.

2. The **find()** algorithm
   a. finds matching sequences of elements in two containers.
   b. finds a container that matches a specified container.
   c. takes two iterators as its first two arguments.
   d. takes two container elements as its first two arguments.
   e. finds an element in a container that matches a specified value.

3. A range is
   a. all the elements between two specified elements.
   b. all the elements in a container.
   c. a large, flat container dotted with buffalo.
   d. often supplied to an algorithm by two iterator values.
   e. all the values an element in a container can have.

4. Which of the following are true?
   a. Type **bool** is used as the return value of all algorithms to indicate success or failure.
   b. Type **bool** is appropriate for variables whose values are restricted to true and false.
   c. A user-written function can substitute for a function object, which is supplied to some algorithms.
   d. A function object can customize the behavior of an algorithm.
   e. The **sort()** algorithm can sort the elements in a container into an order based on the < operator overloaded for the class of the elements.

5. A user-written function whose address is supplied as the third argument to the **for_each()** algorithm
   a. must always return a **bool** value.
   b. copies the elements of one container into a different container.
   c. must be a member of the container class.
   d. will be applied to each element in a range.
   e. must take container elements as its first two arguments.

Write a program that applies the **sort()** algorithm to an array of floating-point values entered by the user and then displays the result.

EXERCISE 2

Write a program that applies the `sort()` algorithm to an array of names entered by the user and displays the result. Employ a user-written function to compare the names alphabetically.

SESSION 3

SEQUENTIAL CONTAINERS

As I noted earlier, there are two major categories of containers in the STL: sequence containers and associative containers. In this session, I'll introduce the three sequence containers: vectors, lists, and deques, focusing on how these containers work and on their member functions. You haven't learned about iterators yet, so there will be some operations that you can't perform on these containers. I'll examine iterators in the next session.

Each program example in the following sections introduces several member functions for the container being described. Remember, however, that different kinds of containers use member functions with the same names and characteristics, so what you learn about, say, `push_back()` for vectors will also be relevant to lists and queues.

Vectors

You can think of vectors as smart arrays. They manage storage allocation for you, expanding and contracting the size of the vector as you insert or erase data. You can use vectors much like arrays, accessing elements with the `[]` operator. Such random access is very fast with vectors. It's also fast to add (or *push*) a new data item onto the end (the *back*) of the vector. When this happens, the vector's size is automatically increased to hold the new item.

Member Functions `push_back()`, `size()`, *and Operator* `[]`

Listing 12-11, VECTOR, shows the most common vector operations.

Listing 12-11 VECTOR

```
// vector.cpp
// demonstrates push_back(), operator[], size()
#include <iostream.h>
#include <vector.h>

void main()
   {
   vector<int> v;                    // create a vector of ints

   v.push_back(10);                  // put values at end of array
   v.push_back(11);
```

```
    v.push_back(12);
    v.push_back(13);

    v[0] = 20;                      // replace with new values
    v[3] = 23;

    for(int j=0; j<v.size(); j++)   // display vector contents
        cout << v[j] << ' ';
}
```

I use the vector's default (no-argument) constructor to create a vector **v**. As with all STL containers, the template format is used to specify the type of variable the container will hold; in this case, type **int**. I don't specify the container's size, so it starts off at 0.

The **push_back()** member function inserts the value of its argument at the back of the vector. (The back is where the element with the highest index number is.) The front of a vector (where the element with index 0 is), unlike that of a list or queue, is not accessible. Here I push the values 10, 11, 12, and 13, so that **v[0]** contains 10, **v[1]** contains 11, **v[2]** contains 12, and **v[3]** contains 13.

Once a vector has some data in it, this data can be accessed—both read and written to—using the overloaded **[]** operator, just as if it were in an array. I use this operator to change the first element from 10 to 20 and the last element from 13 to 23. Here's the output from VECTOR:

20 11 12 23

Note that although I can access data that's already there, I can't user the **[]** operator in a way that would involve changing the size of the vector, as I can with **push_back()**. For example, trying to read or write to **v[27]** won't work because the vector has only four members.

The **size()** member function returns the number of elements currently in the container, which in VECTOR is 4. I use this value in the **for** loop to print out the values of the elements in the container.

Another member function, **max_size()** (which I don't demonstrate here), returns the maximum size to which a container can be expanded. This number depends on the type of data being stored in the container (the bigger the elements, the fewer of them you can store), the type of container, and the operating system. For example, on my system, **max_size()** returns 32,767 for a vector type **int**.

Member Functions swap(), empty(), back(), and pop_back()

Listing 12-12, VECTCON, shows some additional vector constructors and member functions.

Listing 12-12 VECTCON

```
// vectcon.cpp
// demonstrates constructors, swap(), empty(), back(), pop_back()
#include <iostream.h>
#include <vector.h>

void main()
    {                                // an array of floats
    float arr[] = { 1.1, 2.2, 3.3, 4.4 };

    vector<float> v1(arr, arr+4);    // initialize vector to array
```

continued on next page

continued from previous page

```
   vector<float> v2(4);          // empty vector of size 4

   v1.swap(v2);                  // swap contents of v1 and v2

   while( !v2.empty() )          // until vector is empty,
      {
      cout << v2.back() << ' ';  // display the last element
      v2.pop_back();             // remove the last element
      }                          // output: 4.4 3.3 2.2 1.1
   }
```

I've used two new vector constructors in this program. The first initializes the vector **v1** with the values of a normal C++ array passed to it as an argument. The arguments to this constructor are pointers to the start of the array and to the element one past the end. The second constructor sets **v2** to an initial size of 4, but does not supply any initial values. Both vectors hold type **float**.

The **swap()** member function exchanges all the data in one vector with all the data in another, keeping the elements in the same order. In this program, only garbage data is in v2, so it's swapped with the data in v1. I display v2 to show it now contains the data that was in v1. The output is

```
4.4, 3.3, 2.2, 1.1
```

The **back()** member function returns the value of the last element in the vector. I display this value with **cout**. The **pop_back()** member function removes the last element in the vector. Thus, each time through the loop there is a different last element. (It's a little surprising that **pop_back()** does not simultaneously return the value of the last element and remove it from the vector, as you've seen in previous examples with stacks, but it doesn't, so **back()** must be used as well.)

Some member functions, such as **swap()**, also exist as algorithms. When this is the case, the member function version is usually provided because it's more efficient for that particular container than the algorithm version. Sometimes you can use the algorithm as well, for example, to swap elements in two different kinds of containers.

Member Functions insert() *and* erase()

The **insert()** and **erase()** member functions insert or remove an element from an arbitrary location in a container. These functions aren't very efficient with vectors because all the elements above the insertion or erasure must be moved to make space for the new element or to close up the space where the erased item was. However, insertion and erasure may nevertheless be useful if they aren't used too often. Listing 12-13, VECTINS, shows how these member functions are used.

Listing 12-13 VECTINS
```cpp
// vectins.cpp
// demonstrates insert(), erase()
#include <iostream.h>
#include <vector.h>

void main()
   {
   int arr[] = { 100, 110, 120, 130 };    // an array of ints
   vector<int> v(arr, arr+4);             // initialize vector to array
   int j;
```

```
cout << "\nBefore insertion: ";
for(j=0; j<v.size(); j++)              // display all elements
    cout << v[j] << ' ';

v.insert( v.begin()+2, 115);          // insert 115 at element 2

cout << "\nAfter insertion:  ";
for(j=0; j<v.size(); j++)              // display all elements
    cout << v[j] << ' ';

v.erase( v.begin()+2 );               // erase element 2

cout << "\nAfter erasure:    ";
for(j=0; j<v.size(); j++)             // display all elements
    cout << v[j] << ' ';
}
```

The `insert()` member function (at least this version of it) takes two arguments: the place where an element will be inserted in a container and the value of the element. I add 2 to the `begin()` member function to specify element 2 (the third element) in the vector. The elements from the insertion point to the end of the container are moved upward to make room and the size of the container is increased by 1.

The `erase()` member function removes the element at the specified location. The elements above the deletion point are moved downward and the size of the container is decreased by 1. Here's the output from VECTINS:

```
Before insertion: 100 110 120 130
After insertion:  100 110 115 120 130
After erasure:    100 110 120 130
```

Lists

An STL list container is a doubly linked list in which each element contains a pointer not only to the next element but also to the preceding one. The container stores the address of both the front (first) and the back (last) elements, which makes for fast access to both ends of the list.

Member Functions `push_front()`, `front()`, *and* `pop_front`

Listing 12-14, LIST, shows how data can be pushed, read, and popped from both the front and the back.

Listing 12-14 LIST
```
// list.cpp
// demonstrates push_front(), front(), pop_front()
#include <iostream.h>
#include <list.h>

void main()
    {
    list<int> ilist;
```

continued on next page

continued from previous page

```
    ilist.push_back(30);            // push items on back
    ilist.push_back(40);
    ilist.push_front(20);           // push items on front
    ilist.push_front(10);

    int size = ilist.size();        // number of items

    for(int j=0; j<size; j++)
        {
        cout << ilist.front() << ' ';   // read item from front
        ilist.pop_front();              // pop item off front
        }
    }
```

The `push_front()`, `pop_front()`, and `front()` member functions are similar to `push_back()`, `pop_back()`, and `back()`, which you've already seen at work with vectors.

Note that you can't use random access for list elements because such access is too slow; that is, the `[]` operator is not defined for lists. If it were, this operator would need to traverse along the list, counting elements as it went, until it reached the correct one, a time-consuming operation. If you need random access, you should use a vector or a deque.

Lists are appropriate when you make frequent insertions and deletions in the middle of the list. Lists are not efficient for vectors and deques because all the elements above the insertion or deletion point must be moved. However, it's quick for lists because only a few pointers need to be changed to insert or delete a new item.

The `insert()` and `erase()` member functions are used for list insertion and deletion, but they require the use of iterators, so I'll postpone a discussion of these functions.

Member Functions `reverse()`, `merge()`, *and* `unique()`

Some member functions exist only for lists; no such member functions are defined for other containers. Listing 12-15, LISTPLUS, shows some of these functions. It begins by initializing two list-of-`int` objects using arrays.

Listing 12-15 LISTPLUS

```
// listplus.cpp
// demonstrates reverse(), merge(), and unique()
#include <iostream.h>
#include <list.h>

void main()
    {
    int arr1[] = { 40, 30, 20, 10 };
    int arr2[] = { 15, 20, 25, 30, 35 };

    list<int> list1(arr1, arr1+4);
    list<int> list2(arr2, arr2+5);

    list1.reverse();            // reverse list1: 10 20 30 40
    list1.merge(list2);         // merge list2 into list1
    list1.unique();             // remove duplicate 20 and 30
```

```
int size = list1.size();
for(int j=0; j<size; j++)          // for every item
   {
   cout << list1.front() << ' ';   // read item from front
   list1.pop_front();              // pop item off front
   }
}
```

The first list is in backward order, so I return it to normal sorted order using the `reverse()` member function. (It's quick to reverse a list container because both ends are accessible.) This is necessary because the second member function, `merge()`, operates on two lists and requires both of them to be in sorted order. Following the reversal, the two lists are

```
10, 20, 30, 40
15, 20, 25, 30, 35
```

Now the `merge()` function merges `list2` into `list1`, keeping everything sorted and expanding `list1` to hold the new items. The resulting content of `list1` is

```
10, 15, 20, 20, 25, 30, 30, 35, 40
```

Finally, I apply the `unique()` member function to `list1`. This function finds adjacent pairs of elements with the same value and removes all but the first. The contents of `list1` are then displayed. The output of LISTPLUS is

```
10, 15, 20, 25, 30, 35, 40
```

To display the contents of the list, I use the `front()` and `pop_front()` member functions in a `for` loop. Each element, from front to back, is displayed and then popped off the list. The process of displaying the list destroys it. This may not always be what you want, but at the moment it's the only way you have learned to access successive list elements. Iterators, described in the next session, will solve this problem.

Deques

A deque is a variation of a vector. Like a vector, it supports random access using the `[]` operator. However, unlike a vector (but like a list), a deque can be accessed at the front as well as the back. It's a sort of double-ended vector, supporting `push_front()`, `pop_front()`, and `front()`.

Memory is allocated differently for vectors and queues. A vector always occupies a contiguous region of memory. If a vector grows too large, it may need to be moved to a new location where it will fit. A deque, on the other hand, can be stored in several noncontiguous areas; it is segmented. A member function, `capacity()`, returns the largest number of elements a vector can store without being moved, but `capacity()` isn't defined for deques because deques don't need to be moved. Listing 12-16 shows DEQUE.

Listing 12-16 DEQUE

```
// deque.cpp
// demonstrates push_back(), push_front(), front()
#include <iostream.h>
#include <deque.h>
```

continued on next page

continued from previous page

```
void main()
  {
  deque<int> deq;

  deq.push_back(30);                 // push items on back
  deq.push_back(40);
  deq.push_back(50);
  deq.push_front(20);                // push items on front
  deq.push_front(10);

  deq[2] = 33;                       // change middle item

  for(int j=0; j<deq.size(); j++)
     cout << deq[j] << ' ';          // display items
  }
```

You've already seen examples of `push_back()`, `push_front()`, and operator `[]`. They work the same for deques as for other containers. The output of this program is

```
10 20 33 40 50
```

Figure 12-2 shows some important member functions for the three sequential containers.

1. A vector is an appropriate container if you
   a. want to insert lots of new elements at arbitrary locations in the vector.
   b. don't know at runtime how many elements the vector will hold.
   c. want to insert new elements, but always at the front of the container.
   d. are given an index number and you want to access the corresponding element quickly.
   e. are given an element value and you want to access the corresponding element quickly.

2. Which of the following statements are true?
   a. The `pop_back()` member function returns the value of the element at the back of the container.
   b. The `back()` member function returns the value of the element at the back of the container.
   c. The `pop_back()` member function removes the element at the back of the container.
   d. The `back()` member function removes the element at the back of the container.
   e. The `swap()` member function interchanges two adjacent elements in a container.

3. If you define a vector v with the default constructor, define another vector w with a one-argument constructor to a size of 11, and insert 3 elements into each of these vectors with `push_back()`, then
   a. `size()` will return 0 for v and 3 for w.
   b. `size()` will return 3 for v and 3 for w.
   c. `size()` will return 3 for v and 14 for w.
   d. `max_size()` will return two values that differ by 11.
   e. `max_size()` will return the same value for both vectors.

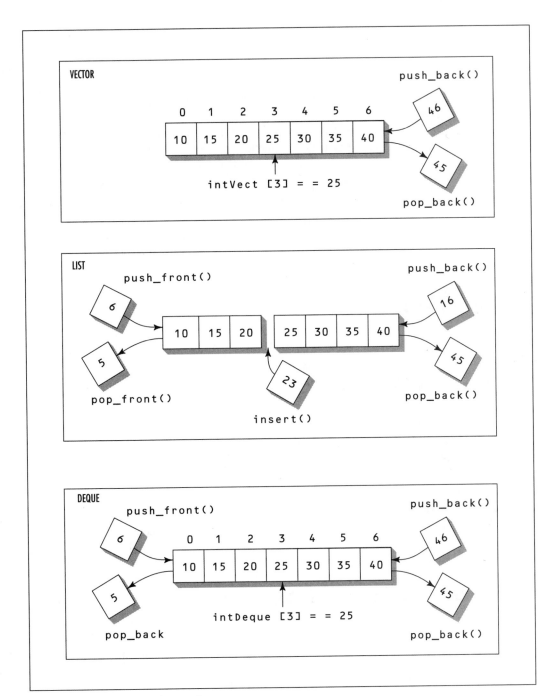

Figure 12-2 Sequential containers

4. Which of the following are true?
   a. The `reverse()` member function reverses pairs of adjacent elements.
   b. The `merge()` member function merges pairs of adjacent elements from one container into another container.
   c. The `unique()` member function returns the first of a sequence of elements that have the same value.
   d. The `push_front()` member function is not defined for lists.
   e. The `push_front()` member function is not defined for deques.

5. In a deque,
   a. data can be quickly inserted or deleted at any arbitrary location.
   b. data can be inserted or deleted at any arbitrary location, but the process is relatively slow.
   c. data can be quickly inserted or deleted at either end.
   d. data can be inserted or deleted at either end, but the process is relatively slow.
   e. elements always occupy contiguous locations in memory.

EXERCISE 1

Write a program that applies `reverse()`, `merge()`, and `unique()` to vectors.

EXERCISE 2

Write a program that uses `insert()`, `erase()`, and `swap()` on a deque.

SESSION 4

ITERATORS

Iterators may seem a bit mysterious, yet they are central to the operation of the STL. In this session, I'll first discuss the twin roles played by iterators: as smart pointers and as a connection between algorithms and containers. Then I'll show some examples of their use.

Iterators as Smart Pointers

It's often necessary to perform an operation on all the elements in the container (or perhaps a range of elements within the container). Displaying the value of each element in the container or adding its value to a total are examples. In an ordinary C++ array, such operations are carried out using a pointer (or the `[]` operator, which is the same underlying mechanism). For example, the following code iterates through a `float` array, displaying the value of each element:

```
float* ptr = start_address;
for(int j=0; j<SIZE; j++)
    cout << *ptr++;
```

I dereference the pointer **ptr** with the ***** operator to obtain the value of the item it points to, and increment it with the **++** operator so it points to the next item.

Ordinary Pointers Underpowered

However, with more sophisticated containers, plain C++ pointers have disadvantages. For one thing, if the items stored in the container are not placed contiguously in memory, handling the pointer becomes much more complicated; I can't simply increment it to point to the next value. For example, in moving to the next item in a linked list, I can't assume the item is adjacent to the previous one; I must follow the chain of pointers.

I may also want to store the address of some container element in a pointer variable so I can access the element at some future time. What happens to this stored pointer value if I insert or erase something from the middle of the container? It may not continue to be valid if the container's contents are rearranged. It would be nice if I didn't need to worry about revising all my stored pointer values when insertions and deletions take place.

One solution to these kinds of problems is to create a class of "smart pointers." An object of such a class basically wraps its member functions around an ordinary pointer. The **++** and ***** operators are overloaded so they know how to point to the elements in their container even if the elements are not contiguous in memory or change their locations. Here's how that might look in skeleton form:

```
class SmartPointer
   {
   private:
      float* p;    // an ordinary pointer
   public:
      float operator*()
         {  }
      float operator++()
         {  }
   };

void main()
   {
   ...
   SmartPointer sptr = start_address;
   for(int j=0; j<SIZE; j++)
      cout << *sptr++;
   }
```

Whose Responsibility?

Assuming I need a class of smart pointers, whose responsibility is it to create this class? As a class user, I certainly don't want the added complexity of writing the code myself.

On the other hand, there's a problem with making smart pointers members of the container class. I may need many pointers in a container, and it would be complicated for a container object itself to store these values. How many should be included? Should every container include, say, three pointers to its own elements? Or should it maintain a table of such pointers? The application should be able to create such a pointer whenever it needs one without such restrictions or complexity.

The approach chosen by the STL is to make smart pointers, called *iterators*, into a completely separate class (actually a family of templatized classes). The class user creates iterators by defining them to be objects of such classes.

Iterators as an Interface

Besides acting as smart pointers to items in containers, iterators serve another important purpose in the STL. They determine which algorithms can be used with which containers. Why is this necessary?

In some theoretical sense, you should be able to apply every algorithm to every container. In fact, many algorithms will work with all the STL containers. However, some algorithms are inefficient (i.e., slow) when used with some containers. The `sort()` algorithm, for example, needs random access to the container it's trying to sort; otherwise, it would need to iterate through the container to find each element before moving it, a time-consuming approach. Similarly, to be efficient, the `reverse()` algorithm needs to iterate backward as well as forward through a container.

Iterators provide a surprisingly elegant way to match appropriate algorithms with containers. As I noted, you can think of an iterator as a cable, like the cable used to connect your computer and printer. One end of the cable plugs into a container and the other plugs into an algorithm. However, not all cables plug into all containers, and not all cables plug into all algorithms. If you try to use an algorithm that's too powerful for a given container type, then you won't be able to find a cable (an iterator) to connect them. If you try it, you will receive a compiler error alerting you to the problem.

How many kinds of iterators (cables) do you need to make this scheme work? As it turns out, only five types are necessary. Figure 12-3 shows these five categories, arranged from bottom to top in order of increasing sophistication, except that input and output are equally unsophisticated. (This is *not* an inheritance diagram.)

If an algorithm needs only to step through a container in a forward direction, reading (but not writing to) one item after another, it can use an *input* iterator to connect itself to the container. If it steps through the container in a forward direction but writes to the container instead of reading from it, it can use an *output* iterator. If it steps along in the forward direction and both reads and writes, it must use a *forward* iterator. If it must be able to step both forward and back, it must use a *bidirectional* iterator. And if it must access any item in the container instantly, without stepping along to it, it must use a *random-access* iterator. Table 12-7 shows which operations each iterator supports.

Iterator	Step Forward	Read	Write	Step Back	Random Access
	++	value=*i	*i=value	--	[n]
Random-access iterator	x	x	x	x	x
Bidirectional iterator	x	x	x	x	
Forward iterator	x	x	x		
Output iterator	x		x		
Input iterator	x	x			

Table 12-7   *Capabilities of different iterator categories*

As you can see, all the iterators support the ++ operator for stepping forward through the container. The input iterator can also use the * operator on the right side of the equal sign (but not on the left):

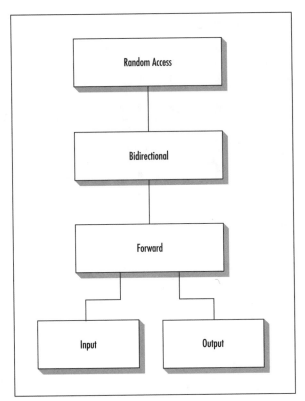

Figure 12-3   Iterator categories

```
value = *iter;
```

The output iterator can use the * operator only on the right:

```
*iter = value;
```

The forward iterator handles both input and output and the bidirectional iterator can be decremented as well as incremented. The random-access iterator can use the [ ] operator (as well as simple arithmetic operators such as + and –) to access any element quickly.

An algorithm can always use an iterator with *more* capability than it needs. If it needs a forward iterator, for example, it's all right to plug it into a bidirectional iterator or a random-access iterator.

Matching Algorithms with Containers

I've used a cable as an analogy to an iterator because an iterator connects an algorithm and a container. Let's focus on the two ends of this imaginary cable: the container end and the algorithm end.

Plugging the Cable into a Container

If you confine yourself to the basic STL containers, you will be using only two kinds of iterators. As shown in Table 12-8, the vector and deque require a random-access iterator, whereas the list, set, multiset, map, and multimap require only bidirectional iterators.

Iterator	Vector	List	Deque	Set	Multiset	Map	Multimap
Random Access	x		x				
Bidirectional	x	x	x	x	x	x	x
Forward	x	x	x	x	x	x	x
Input	x	x	x	x	x	x	x
Output	x	x	x	x	x	x	x

Table 12-8   *Iterator types accepted by containers*

How does the STL enforce the use of the correct iterator for a given container? When you define an iterator, you must specify what kind of container it will be used for. For example, if you've defined a list holding elements of type `int`,

```
list<int> iList;          // list of ints
```

then to define an iterator to this list you say

```
list<int>::iterator it;   // iterator to list-of-ints
```

When you do this, the STL automatically makes this iterator a bidirectional iterator because that's what a list requires. An iterator to a vector or a deque, on the other hand, is automatically created as a random-access iterator.

This automatic selection process is implemented, deep in ITERATOR.H and other header files, by having an iterator class for a specific container be derived (inherited) from a more general iterator class that's appropriate to a specific container. Thus, the iterators to vectors and deques are derived from the `random_access_iterator` class, whereas iterators to lists are derived from the `bidirectional_iterator` class.

You now see how containers are matched to their end of the fanciful iterator cables. A cable doesn't actually plug into a container; it is (figuratively speaking) hard-wired to it, like the cord on a toaster. Vectors and deques are always wired to random-access cables, whereas lists (and all the associative containers, which you'll encounter in Session 6) are always wired to bidirectional cables.

Plugging the Cables into the Algorithm

Now that you've seen how one end of an iterator cable is "wired" to the container, you're ready to look at the other end of the cable. How do iterators plug into algorithms? Every algorithm, depending on what it will do to the elements in a container, requires a certain kind of iterator. If the algorithm must access elements at arbitrary locations in the container, it requires a random-access iterator. If it will merely step forward through the iterator, it can use the less powerful forward iterator. Table 12-9 shows a sampling of algorithms and the iterators they require. (A complete version of this table is shown in Appendix B.)

Algorithm	Input	Output	Forward	Bidirectional	Random Access
for_each	x				
find	x				
count	x				
copy	x	x			
replace			x		
unique			x		
reverse				x	
sort					x
nth_element					x
merge	x	x			
accumulate	x				

Table 12-9 *Type of iterator required by representative algorithms*

Again, although each algorithm requires an iterator with a certain level of capability, a more powerful iterator will also work. The `replace()` algorithm requires a forward iterator, but it will work with a bidirectional or a random-access iterator as well.

Now imagine that algorithms have connectors with pins sticking out, as shown in Figure 12-4. Those requiring random-access iterators have five pins, those requiring bidirectional iterators have four pins, those requiring forward iterators have three pins, and so on.

The algorithm end of an iterator (a cable) has a connector with a certain number of holes. You can plug a five-hole iterator into a five-pin algorithm, and you can also plug it into an algorithm with four or fewer pins. However, you can't plug a four-hole (bidirectional) iterator into a five-pin (random-access) algorithm. So vectors and deques, with random-access iterators, can be plugged into any algorithm, whereas lists and associative containers, with only four-hole bidirectional iterators, can be plugged into less powerful algorithms.

The Tables Tell the Story

From Table 12-8 and 12-9, you can figure out whether an algorithm will work with a given container. Table 12-9 shows that the `sort()` algorithm, for example, requires a random-access iterator. Table 12-8 indicates that the only containers that can handle random-access iterators are vectors and deques. There's no use trying to apply the `sort()` algorithm to lists, sets, maps, and so on.

Any algorithm that does *not* require a random-access iterator will work with any kind of STL container because all these containers use bidirectional iterators, which is only one grade below random access. (If there were a singly linked list in the STL, it would use only a forward iterator, so it could not be used with the `reverse()` algorithm).

As you can see, comparatively few algorithms require random-access iterators. Therefore, most algorithms work with most containers.

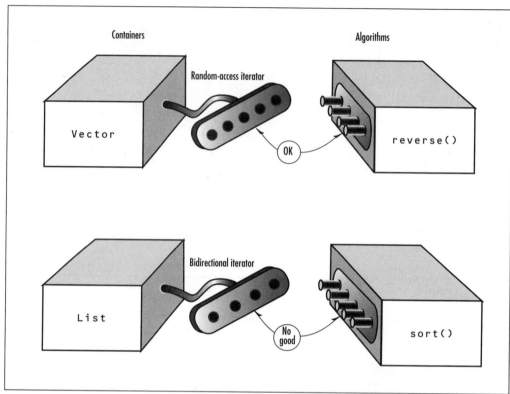

Figure 12-4   Iterators connecting containers and algorithms

Overlapping Member Functions and Algorithms

Sometimes you must decide between using a member function or an algorithm with the same name. The `find()` algorithm, for example, requires only an input iterator, so it can be used with any container. However, sets and maps have their own `find()` member function (unlike sequential containers). Which version of `find()` should you use? Generally, if a member-function version exists, it's because, for that container, the algorithm version is not as efficient as it could be; in these cases, you should probably use the member-function version.

Iterators at Work

Using iterators is considerably simpler than talking about them. You've already seen several examples of one of the more common uses where iterator values are returned by a container's `begin()` and `end()` member functions. I've disguised the fact that these functions return iterator values by treating them as if they were pointers. Now let's see how actual iterators are used with these and other functions.

Data Access

In containers that provide random-access iterators (vector and queue), it's easy to iterate through the container using the [ ] operator. Containers such as lists, which don't support random access, require a different approach. In previous examples, I've used a "destructive readout" to display the contents of a list by popping off the items one by one, as in the LIST and LISTPLUS examples in Session 3. A more practical approach is to define an iterator for the container. The LISTOUT program (Listing 12-17) shows how that might look.

Listing 12-17 LISTOUT

```
// listout.cpp
// iterator and for loop for output
#include <iostream.h>
#include <list.h>

void main()
   {
   int arr[] = { 2, 4, 6, 8 };       // array of ints
   list<int> iList(arr, arr+4);      // list initialized to array
   list<int>::iterator it;           // iterator to list-of-ints

   for(it = iList.begin(); it != iList.end(); it++)
      cout << *it << ' ';
   }
```

The program simply displays the contents of the iList container. The output is

```
2 4 6 8
```

I define an iterator of type list<int> to match the container type. As with a pointer variable, I must give an iterator a value before using it. In the for loop, I initialize it to iList.begin(), the start of the container. I can increment it with the ++ operator so it steps through the elements in a container, and I can dereference it with the * operator to obtain the value of each element it points to. I can also compare it for equality using the != operator so I can exit the loop when it reaches the end of the container at iList.end().

An equivalent approach, using a while loop instead of a for loop, might be

```
it = iList.begin();
while( it != iList.end() )
   cout << *it++ << ' ';
```

The *it++ syntax is the same as it would be for a pointer.

Data Insertion

I can use similar code to place data into existing elements in a container, as shown in LISTFILL (Listing 12-18).

Listing 12-18 LISTFILL

```
// listfill.cpp
// uses iterator to fill list with data
#include <iostream.h>
#include <list.h>

void main()
   {
   list<int> iList(5);        // empty list holds 5 ints
   list<int>::iterator it;    // iterator
   int data = 0;
                              // fill list with data
   for(it = iList.begin(); it != iList.end(); it++)
      *it = data += 2;
                              // display list
   for(it = iList.begin(); it != iList.end(); it++)
      cout << *it << ' ';
   }
```

The first loop fills the container with the int values 2, 4, 6, 8, 10, showing that the overloaded * operator works on the left side of the equal sign as well as on the right. The second loop displays these values.

Algorithms and Iterators

Algorithms, as I've discussed, use iterators as arguments (and sometimes as return values). The ITERFIND example (Listing 12-19) shows the find() algorithm applied to a list. (I know I can use the find() algorithm with lists because it requires only an input iterator.)

Listing 12-19 ITERFIND

```
// iterfind.cpp
// find() returns a list iterator
#include <iostream.h>
#include <algo.h>
#include <list.h>

void main()
   {
   list<int> iList(5);        // empty list holds 10 ints
   list<int>::iterator it;    // iterator
   int data = 0;
                              // fill list with data
   for(it = iList.begin(); it != iList.end(); it++)
      *it = data += 2;
                              // look for number 8
   it = find(iList.begin(), iList.end(), 8);
   if( it != iList.end() )
      cout << "\nFound 8";
   else
      cout << "\nDid not find 8.";
   }
```

2, 4, 6, 8, 10 values as in the last example. Then I use the `find()` algorithm to look for the number 8. If `find()` returns `iList.end()`, I know it's reached the end of the container without finding a match. Otherwise, it must have located an item with the value 8. Here the output is

```
Found 8
```

Can I use the value of the iterator to tell where in the container the 8 is located? You might think the offset of the matching item from the beginning of the container could be calculated from `(it - iList.begin())`. However, this is not a legal operation on the iterators used for lists. A list iterator is only a bidirectional iterator, so I can't perform arithmetic on it. I can do arithmetic on random-access iterators, such as those used with vectors and queues. Thus, if I were searching a vector `v` rather than a list `iList`, I could rewrite the last part of ITERFIND like this:

```
it = find(v.begin(), v.end(), 8);
if( it != v.end() )
    cout << "\nFound 8 at location " << (it-v.begin()) );
else
    cout << "\nDid not find 8.";
```

The output would be

```
Found 8 at location 3
```

Listing 12-20 shows another example in which an algorithm uses iterators as arguments. This one uses the `copy()` algorithm with a vector. The user specifies a range of locations to be copied from one vector to another, and the program copies them. Iterators specify this range.

Listing 12-20 ITERCOPY
```
// itercopy.cpp
// uses iterators for copy() algorithm
#include <iostream.h>
#include <vector.h>
#include <algo.h>

void main()
    {
    int beginRange, endRange;
    int arr[] = { 11, 13, 15, 17, 19, 21, 23, 25, 27, 29 };
    vector<int> v1(arr, arr+10);        // initialized vector
    vector<int> v2(10);                 // uninitialized vector

    cout << "Enter range to be copied (example: 2 5): ";
    cin >> beginRange >> endRange;

    vector<int>::iterator it1 = v1.begin() + beginRange;
    vector<int>::iterator it2 = v1.begin() + endRange;
    vector<int>::iterator it3;
                                        // copy range from v1 to v2
    it3 = copy( it1, it2, v2.begin() );
                                        // (it3 -> last item copied)
    it1 = v2.begin();                   // iterate through range
```

continued on next page

continued from previous page

```
   while(it1 != it3)                    // in v2, displaying values
      cout << *it1++ << ' ';
   }
```

Some interaction with this program is

```
Enter range to be copied (example: 2 5): 3 6
17 19 21
```

I don't want to display the entire contents of **v2**, only the range of items copied. Fortunately, **copy()** returns an iterator that points to the last item (actually one past the last item) that was copied to the destination container, **v2** in this case. The program uses this value in the **while** loop to display only the items copied.

1. Which of the following are true?
   a. An iterator is an object of an appropriate container class.
   b. An iterator indicating a specific container element is a class, not an object.
   c. An iterator class is derived from an appropriate container class.
   d. An iterator class for a specific container category (such as a list) is derived from a more general iterator class that is appropriate for that container (such as **bidirectional_iterator**).
   e. An iterator class is templatized.

2. An iterator
   a. knows how big the objects in its container are.
   b. can figure out where the objects in its container are located in memory.
   c. will usually point to an object in its container.
   d. can always move forward or backward through its container.
   e. requires the objects in its container to be located contiguously in memory.

3. Which of these statements are true?
   a. Iterators prevent the use of algorithms with containers that don't support that algorithm's task.
   b. An algorithm requiring random-access iterators will work with a list.
   c. An algorithm requiring bidirectional iterators will work with a vector.
   d. You can always use an iterator that's less powerful than a container requires.
   e. You can always use an iterator that's more powerful than an algorithm requires.

4. If **iter** is an iterator variable that is used in a **while** loop, then
   a. before entering the loop, **iter** should probably have been initialized to point to some element in a container.
   b. **iter** can point to ordinary C++ array elements.
   c. **iter** cannot be decremented.
   d. the expression ***iter++** will obtain the value of the element pointed to by **iter**.
   e. the expression ***iter++** will cause **iter** to point to the next element.

5. The `copy()` algorithm returns
   a. the number of elements copied.
   b. an iterator to an element in the range copied from.
   c. an iterator to an element in the range copied to.
   d. an iterator to the last item copied.
   e. `void`.

EXERCISE 1

Write a program that allows you to copy any range in a container to any other location in the same container where it will fit. Have the user specify the range and the location where it will be copied. Can you copy to a point inside the range? Try using `copy_backward()` instead of `copy()`.

EXERCISE 2

Write a program that will find not only the first element in a container that has a specified value, but all elements in the container that have that value.

MIDCHAPTER DISCUSSION

George: Just when I thought I was getting a grip on C++, along comes all this new stuff. It's like learning another language!

Estelle: Right, with all these containers and dozens and dozens of algorithms and member functions. It doesn't seem fair.

Don: But it's very powerful. If you ever need to store data in anything but an array, the STL will save you a huge amount of trouble.

Estelle: But have you looked in the STL header files? Some of that stuff is seriously complicated.

Don: Well, you don't really need to understand what's going on in those header files. I mean, it builds character to wade through them, but the beauty of OOP is that you can use classes without understanding them. All you need to understand is the user interface.

George: You mean the functions and stuff that go with a container.

Don: Exactly.

Estelle: The thing I don't understand is why we need iterators.

George: To be smart pointers and to keep you from using the wrong algorithm with the wrong container.

Estelle: I know, but isn't there a simpler way?

Don: Well, maybe you could just use pointers. But then you'd need to handle all the memory management stuff for a container by yourself, so you'd know where it was.

George: OK, I can see that. But where did they get the idea to use iterators to connect algorithms to containers?

Don: That way you can make the same algorithm work with many kinds of containers. I think the STL is the first set of container classes that uses iterators that way. Earlier container classes used member functions to do all the work, so there was a lot of duplication. If you had 10 containers and they each had 20 member functions, that was 200 member functions you had to worry about. In the STL, there's only one version of each algorithm.

Estelle: Pretty clever.

Don: I'll say.

SESSION 5
SPECIALIZED ITERATORS

In this session, I'll examine two specialized forms of iterators: iterator adapters, which can change the behavior of iterators in interesting ways, and stream iterators, which allow input and output streams to behave like iterators.

Iterator Adapters

The STL provides three variations on the normal iterator. These are the *reverse iterator*, the *insert iterator*, and the *raw storage iterator*. The reverse iterator allows you to iterate backward through a container. The insert iterator changes the behavior of various algorithms, such as `copy()` and `merge()`, so they insert data into a container rather than overwriting existing data. The raw storage iterator allows output iterators to store data in uninitialized memory, but it's used in specialized situations and I'll ignore it here.

Reverse Iterators

Suppose you want to iterate backward through a container from the end to the beginning. You might think you could say something like

```
list<int>::iterator it;             // normal iterator
it = iList.end();                   // start at end
while( it != iList.begin() )        // go to beginning
   cout << *it-- << ' ';            // decrement iterator
```

but unfortunately this doesn't work. For one thing, the range will be wrong (from n to 1, instead of from n-1 to 0).

To iterate backward, you must use a *reverse iterator*. The ITEREV program (Listing 12-21) shows an example where a reverse iterator is used to display the contents of a list in reverse order.

Listing 12-21 ITEREV

```
// iterev.cpp
// demonstrates reverse iterator
#include <iostream.h>
#include <list.h>

void main()
    {
    int arr[] = { 2, 4, 6, 8, 10 };  // array of ints
    list<int> iList(arr, arr+5);      // list initialized to array

    list<int>::reverse_iterator revit; // reverse iterator

    revit = iList.rbegin();            // iterate backwards
    while( revit != iList.rend() )     // through list,
        cout << *revit++ << ' ';       // displaying output
    }
```

The output of this program is

```
10 8 6 4 2
```

You must use the member functions `rbegin()` and `rend()` when you use a reverse iterator. (But don't try to use them with a normal forward iterator.) Confusingly, you're starting at the end of the container, but the member function is called `rbegin()`. Also, you must increment the iterator. Don't try to decrement a reverse iterator; `revit--` doesn't do what you want. With a `reverse_iterator`, always go from `rbegin()` to `rend()` using the increment operator.

Insert Iterators

Some algorithms, such as `copy()`, overwrite the existing contents (if any) of the destination container. The COPYDEQ program (Listing 12-22), which copies from one deque to another, provides an example.

Listing 12-22 COPYDEQ

```
// copydeq.cpp
// demonstrates normal copy with queues
#include <iostream.h>
#include <deque.h>
#include <algo.h>

void main()
    {
    int arr1[] = { 1, 3, 5, 7, 9 };    // initialize d1
    deque<int> d1(arr1, arr1+5);

    int arr2[] = { 2, 4, 6, 8, 10 };   // initialize d2
    deque<int> d2(arr2, arr2+5);
                                       // copy d1 to d2
    copy( d1.begin(), d1.end(), d2.begin() );

    for(int j=0; j<d2.size(); j++)     // display d2
        cout << d2[j] << ' ';
    }
```

The output of this program is

```
1 3 5 7 9
```

The contents of **d1** have been written over the contents of **d2**, so when I display **d2,** there's no trace of its former (even-numbered) contents. Usually this behavior is what you want. Sometimes, however, you'd rather have **copy()** insert new elements into a container along with the old ones than overwrite the old ones. You can cause this behavior by using an *insert iterator*. There are three flavors of this iterator:

 back_inserter inserts new items at the end

 front_inserter inserts new items at the beginning

 inserter inserts new items at a specified location

The DINSITER program (Listing 12-23) shows how to use a back inserter.

Listing 12-23 DINSITER

```cpp
// dinsiter.cpp
// demonstrates insert iterators with queues
#include <iostream.h>
#include <deque.h>
#include <algo.h>

void main()
    {
    int arr1[] = { 1, 3, 5, 7, 9 };    // initialize d1
    deque<int> d1(arr1, arr1+5);

    int arr2[] = {2, 4, 6};            // initialize d2
    deque<int> d2(arr2, arr2+3);

    copy( d1.begin(), d1.end(), back_inserter(d2) );

    cout << "\nd2: ";                  // display d2
    for(int j=0; j<d2.size(); j++)
        cout << d2[j] << ' ';
    }
```

The back inserter uses the container's **push_back()** member function to insert the new items at the end of the target container **d2**, following the existing items. The source container **d1** is unchanged. The output of the program, which displays the new contents of **d2**, is

```
2 4 6 1 3 5 7 9
```

If I specified a front inserter instead,

```cpp
copy( d1.begin(), d1.end(), front_inserter(d2) )
```

then the new items would be inserted into the front of the container. The underlying mechanism is the container's **push_front()** member function, which pushes the items one at a time, effectively reversing their order. The output would be

```
9 7 5 3 1 2 4 6
```

I can also insert the new items starting at any arbitrary element by using the **inserter** version of the insert iterator. For example, to insert the new items at the beginning of **d2**, I would say

```
copy( d1.begin(), d1.end(), inserter(d2, d2.begin() ) );
```
The first argument to `inserter` is the container to be copied into and the second is an iterator pointing to the location where copying should begin. Because `inserter` uses the container's `insert()` member function, the order of the elements is not reversed. The output resulting from this statement would be

```
1 3 5 7 9 2 4 6
```
By changing the second argument to `inserter`, I could cause the new data to be inserted anywhere in `d2`.

Note that a `front_inserter` can't be used with a vector, because vectors don't have a `push_front()` member function; they can be accessed only at the end.

Stream Iterators

Stream iterators allow you to treat files and I/O devices (such as `cin` and `cout`) as if they were iterators. This makes it easy to use files and I/O devices as arguments to algorithms. (This is another demonstration of the versatility of using iterators to link algorithms and containers.)

The major purpose of the input and output iterator categories is to support these stream iterator classes. Input and output iterators make it possible for appropriate algorithms to be used directly on input and output streams.

Stream iterators are actually objects of classes that are templatized for different types of input or output. There are two stream iterators: `ostream_iterator` and `istream_iterator`. Let's look at them in turn.

The `ostream_iterator` *Class*

An `ostream_iterator` object can be used as an argument to any algorithm that specifies an output iterator. In the OUTITER example (Listing 12-24), I use it as an argument to `copy()`.

Listing 12-24 OUTITER
```
// outiter.cpp
// demonstrates ostream_iterator
#include <iostream.h>
#include <algo.h>
#include <list.h>

void main()
    {
    int arr[] = { 10, 20, 30, 40, 50 };
    list<int> iList(arr, arr+5);              // initialized list

    ostream_iterator<int> ositer(cout, "--");  // ostream iterator

    cout << "\nContents of list: ";
    copy(iList.begin(), iList.end(), ositer);  // display the list
    }
```

I define an `ostream` iterator for reading type `int` values. The two arguments to this constructor are the stream to which the `int` values will be written and a string value that will be displayed following each value. The stream value is typically a file name or `cout`; here it's `cout`. When writing to `cout`, you can make the string consist of any characters you want; here I use two dashes.

The `copy()` algorithm copies the contents of the list to `cout`. The `ostream` iterator is used as the third argument to copy; it's the destination.

The output of OUTITER is

```
Contents of list: 10--20--30--40--50--
```

Listing 12-25, FOUTITER, shows how to use an `ostream` iterator to write to a file.

Listing 12-25 FOUTITER
```cpp
// foutiter.cpp
// demonstrates ostream_iterator with files
#include <fstream.h>
#include <algo.h>
#include <list.h>

void main()
    {
    int arr[] = { 11, 21, 31, 41, 51 };
    list<int> iList(arr, arr+5);        // initialized list

    ofstream outfile("ITER.DAT");       // create file object

    ostream_iterator<int> ositer(outfile, " ");   // iterator
                                        // write list to file
    copy(iList.begin(), iList.end(), ositer);
    }
```

I must define an `ofstream` file object and associate it with a file, here called ITER.DAT. This object is the first argument to the `ostream_itertor`. When writing to a file, use a whitespace character in the string argument, not characters such as `--`. This makes it easier to read the data back from the file. Here I use a space (" ") character.

There's no displayable output from FOUTITER, but you can examine the file ITER.DAT with an editor to see that it contains the data, which should be

```
11 21 31 41 51
```

The `istream_iterator` *Class*

An `istream_iterator` object can be used as an argument to any algorithm that specifies an input iterator. Listing 12-26, INITER, shows such objects used as the first two arguments to `copy()`. This program reads floating-point numbers entered into `cin` (the keyboard) by the user and stores them in a list.

Listing 12-26 INITER
```cpp
// initer.cpp
// demonstrates istream_iterator
#include <iostream.h>
#include <list.h>
#include <algo.h>

void main()
    {
    list<float> fList(5);               // uninitialized list
```

```
cout << "\nEnter 5 floating-point numbers";
cout << "\n(Type [Ctrl] [z] to terminate): ";
                              // istream iterators
istream_iterator<float, ptrdiff_t> cin_iter(cin);   // cin
istream_iterator<float, ptrdiff_t> end_of_stream;   // eos

                              // copy from cin to fList
copy( cin_iter, end_of_stream, fList.begin() );

cout << endl;                 // display fList
ostream_iterator<float> ositer(cout, "--");
copy(fList.begin(), fList.end(), ositer);
}
```

Some interaction with INITER is

```
Enter 5 floating-point numbers: 1.1   2.2   3.3   4.4   5.5
1.1--2.2--3.3--4.4--5.5--
```

Notice that for `copy()`, because the data coming from `cin` is the source and not the destination, I must specify both the beginning and the end of the range of data to be copied. The beginning is an `istream_iterator` connected to `cin`, which I define as `cin_iter` using the one-argument constructor. But what about the end of the range? The no-argument (default) constructor to `istream_iterator` plays a special role here. It always creates an `istream_iterator` object that represents the end of the stream.

How does the user generate this end-of-stream value when inputting data? By typing the CTRL-Z key combination, which transmits the end-of-file character normally used for streams. (Pressing ENTER won't end the file, although it will delimit the numbers.)

I use an `ostream_iterator` to display the contents of the list, although of course there are many other ways to do this.

At least on my compiler, I must perform any display output, such as the `Enter 5 floating-point numbers` prompt, not only before using the `istream` iterator, but even before defining it. As soon as this iterator is defined, it locks up the display waiting for input.

Listing 12-27, FINITER, uses a file instead of `cin` as input to the `copy()` algorithm.

Listing 12-27 FINITER

```
// finiter.cpp
// demonstrates istream_iterator with files
#include <fstream.h>
#include <list.h>
#include <algo.h>

void main()
   {
   list<int> iList;              // empty list
   ifstream infile("ITER.DAT");  // create input file object
                                 // (ITER.DAT must already exist)
                                 // istream iterators
   istream_iterator<int, ptrdiff_t> file_iter(infile);  // file
   istream_iterator<int, ptrdiff_t> end_of_stream;      // eos
```

continued on next page

continued from previous page

```
                                        // copy from infile to iList
copy( file_iter, end_of_stream, back_inserter(iList) );

cout << endl;                           // display iList
ostream_iterator<int> ositer(cout, "--");
copy(iList.begin(), iList.end(), ositer);
}
```

The output from FINITER is

`11--21--31--31--41--51--`

I define an `ifstream` object to represent the ITER.DAT file, which must already exist and contain data. (The FOUTITER program, if you ran it, will have generated this file.)

Instead of using `cout`, as in the `istream` iterator in the INITER example, I use the `ifstream` object named `infile`. The end-of-stream object is the same.

I've made another change in this program: It uses a `back_inserter` to insert data into `iList`. This makes it possible to define `iList` as an empty container instead of one with a specified size. This often makes sense when reading input because you may not know how many items will be entered.

1. To use a `reverse_iterator`, you should
   a. begin by initializing it to `end()`.
   b. begin by initializing it to `rend()`.
   c. begin by initializing it to `rbegin()`.
   d. increment it to move backward through the container.
   e. decrement it to move backward through the container.

2. Which of the following statements are true?
   a. The `back_inserter` iterator always causes the new elements to be inserted following the existing ones.
   b. The `inserter` iterator always causes the newly inserted elements to be placed before the existing ones.
   c. Insert iterators are normally used as arguments to the member functions `insert()`, `push_front()`, and `push_back()`.
   d. If you want to overwrite existing data, you should use the `front_inserter` iterator.
   e. Before using an insert iterator, you must write a statement to define it.

3. Stream iterators
   a. provide a handy way to perform I/O on container elements.
   b. are random-access iterators.
   c. allow you to treat the display and keyboard devices as if they were iterators.
   d. allow you to treat files as if they were iterators.
   e. cannot be used for algorithm arguments that require random-access iterators.

4. Which of the following statements are largely correct?
   a. The first argument to an `ostream_iterator` must be an `ostream` object.
   b. The first argument to an `ostream_iterator` represents an output device or file.

    c. An ostream_iterator is a forward_iterator.

    d. The second argument to an ostream_iterator specifies the EOL (end-of-line) character.

    e. The second argument to an ostream_iterator specifies the EOS (end-of-stream) character.

5. Which of the following are accurate statements?

    a. When using an istream_iterator with copy(), the end of the range to be copied from is indicated by the end() member function.

    b. When using an istream_iterator with copy(), the end of the range to be copied from is indicated by an istream_iterator object defined with the default constructor.

    c. An istream_iterator is an input_iterator.

    d. The second argument to an istream_iterator specifies the EOL (end-of-line) character.

    e. The second argument to an istream_iterator specifies the EOS (end-of-stream) character.

EXERCISE 1

Write a program that copies one file to another using the copy() algorithm and stream iterators. The user should supply both source and destination file names to the program.

EXERCISE 2

Write a program in which the merge() algorithm combines the contents of two containers and sends the results to cout using a stream iterator.

SESSION 6

ASSOCIATIVE CONTAINERS

The two main categories of associative containers in the STL are maps and sets. A map (sometimes called a *dictionary* or *symbol table*) stores *key* and *value* pairs. The keys are arranged in sorted order. You find an element using the key, and this gives you access to the value. A good analogy to a map is an ordinary dictionary. The alphabetized words correspond to the keys, and the definitions of the words are the values. Because the words in a dictionary are arranged in alphabetical order, you can quickly look up a particular word-definition combination. Similarly, your program, given a specified key, can quickly locate the key-value combination.

    A set is similar to a dictionary, but it stores only keys; there are no values. You can think of a set as a list of words without definitions.

    In both a set and a map, only one example of each key can be stored. It's like a dictionary that forbids more than one entry for each word. However, the STL has alternative versions of sets and maps.

There are actually four kinds of associative containers: set, multiset, map, and multimap. A *multi-set* and a *multimap* are similar to a set and a map, but can include multiple instances of the same key.

The advantages of associative containers are that, given a specific key, you can quickly access the information associated with this key; it is much faster than by searching item by item through a sequence container. On normal associative containers, you can also quickly iterate through the container in sorted order. (See also the note on the hash table versions of these containers at the end of this section).

Associative containers share many member functions with other containers. However, some algorithms, such as `lower_bound()` and `upper_bound()`, exist only for associative containers. Also, some member functions that do exist for other containers, such as the push and pop family (`push_back()` and so on), have no versions for associative containers. (It wouldn't make sense to use push and pop with associative containers because elements must always be inserted in their ordered locations, not at the beginning or the end of the container.)

I'll start the discussion of associative containers with sets, which are slightly simpler.

Sets and Multisets

Sets are often used to hold objects of user-defined classes such as employees in a database. (You'll see examples of this in Session 7.) However, sets can also hold simpler elements such as strings. Figure 12-5 shows how this looks. The objects are arranged in ordered form and are accessed using the key.

Listing 12-28, SET, shows a set that stores objects of class **string**. Again, I use the current Borland header file, CSTRING.H, to invoke the **string** class. Depending on your compiler, you may need to change this header file name to STRING, BSTRING.H, or some other name (see Appendixes C and D).

Listing 12-28 SET

```
// set.cpp
// set stores string objects
#include <iostream.h>
#include <set.h>
#include <cstring.h>

void main()
   {                              // array of string objects
   string names[] = {"Juanita", "Robert",
                     "Mary", "Amanda", "Marie"};
                              // initialize set to array
   set<string, less<string> > nameSet(names, names+5);
                              // iterator to set
   set<string, less<string> >::iterator iter;

   nameSet.insert("Yvette");   // insert some more names
   nameSet.insert("Larry");
   nameSet.insert("Robert");   // no effect; already in set
   nameSet.insert("Barry");
   nameSet.erase("Mary");      // erase a name
                              // display size of set
   cout << "\nSize=" << nameSet.size() << endl;
   iter = nameSet.begin();     // display members of set
```

```
while( iter != nameSet.end() )
   cout << *iter++ << '\n';

string searchName;            // get name from user
cout << "\nEnter name to search for: ";
cin >> searchName;
                              // find matching name in set
iter = nameSet.find(searchName);
if( iter == nameSet.end() )
   cout << "The name " << searchName << " is NOT in the set.";
else
   cout << "The name " << *iter << " IS in the set.";
}
```

To define a set, I specify the type of objects to be stored (in this case, class `string`) and the function object that will be used to order the members of the set. Here I use `less<>()` applied to `string` objects.

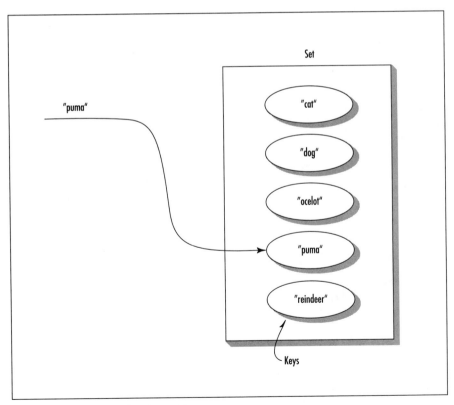

Figure 12-5   A set of string objects

As you can see, a set has an interface similar to other STL containers. I can initialize a set to an array and insert new members into a set with the `insert()` member function. To display the set, I can iterate through it.

To find a particular entry in the set, I use the `find()` member function. (Sequential containers use `find()` in its algorithm version.) Here's some sample interaction with SET, where the user enters "George" as the name to be searched for:

```
Size = 7
Amanda
Barry
Juanita
Larry
Marie
Robert
Yvette

Enter name to search for: George
The name George is NOT in the set.
```

Of course, the speed advantage of searching an associative container isn't apparent until you have many more entries than in this example.

Let's look at an important pair of member functions available only with associative containers. Listing 12-29, SETRANGE, shows the use of `lower_bound()` and `upper_bound()`.

Listing 12-29 SETRANGE

```cpp
// setrange.cpp
// tests ranges within a set
#include <iostream.h>
#include <set.h>
#include <cstring.h>

void main()
    {                           // set of string objects
    set<string, less<string> > organic;
                                // iterator to set
    set<string, less<string> >::iterator iter;

    organic.insert("Curine");   // insert organic compounds
    organic.insert("Xanthine");
    organic.insert("Curarine");
    organic.insert("Melamine");
    organic.insert("Cyanimide");
    organic.insert("Phenol");
    organic.insert("Aphrodine");
    organic.insert("Imidazole");
    organic.insert("Cinchonine");
    organic.insert("Palmitamide");
    organic.insert("Cyanimide");

    iter = organic.begin();     // display set
    while( iter != organic.end() )
```

```
    cout << *iter++ << '\n';

    string lower, upper;      // display entries in range
    cout << "\nEnter range (example C Czz): ";
    cin >> lower >> upper;
    iter = organic.lower_bound(lower);
    while( iter != organic.upper_bound(upper) )
        cout << *iter++ << '\n';
}
```

The program first displays an entire set of organic compounds. The user is then prompted to type in a pair of key values, and the program will display those keys that lie within this range. Here's some sample interaction:

```
Aphrodine
Cinchonine
Curarine
Curine
Cyanimide
Imidazole
Melamine
Palmitamide
Phenol
Xanthine

Enter range (example C Czz): Aaa Curb
Aphrodine
Cinchonine
Curarine
```

The `lower_bound()` member function takes an argument that is a value of the same type as the key. It returns an iterator to the first entry that is not less than this argument (where the meaning of "less" is determined by the function object used in the set's definition). The `upper_bound()` function returns an iterator to the first entry that is greater than its argument. Together, these functions allow you to access a specified range of values.

Maps and Multimaps

A map stores associations of keys and values. The keys can be strings or numbers. The values are often complicated objects, such as `employee` or `car_part` or `student_record` objects, although they can also be numbers or strings. For example, the key could be a word, and the value could be a number representing how many times that word appears in a document. Such a map could be used to construct a frequency table. Or the key could be an employee number, and the associated value could be the employee's personnel file. Figure 12-6 shows a map in which the keys are words and the values are phrases. This is similar to an ordinary dictionary.

Iterating Through Maps

Listing 12-30, MAP, demonstrates the same arrangement: a dictionary formed from word-phrase pairs stored in a map.

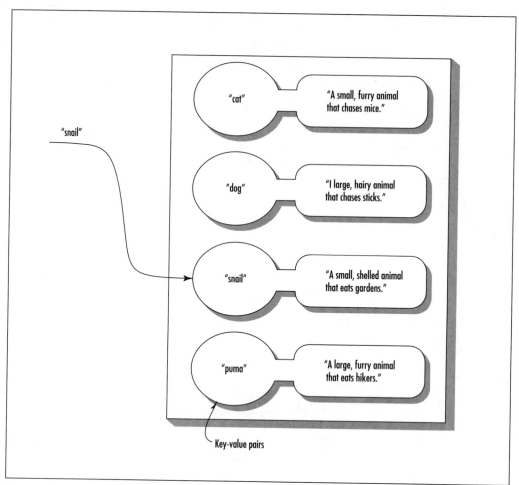

Figure 12-6 A map of word-phrase pairs

Listing 12-30 MAP

```
// map.cpp
// a map used as an English-language dictionary
#include <iostream.h>
#include <iomanip.h>
#include <map.h>
#include <cstring.h>

void main()
   {
   enum {SIZE = 80};
   char def[SIZE];            // definition (C string)
   string word = "";          // key (string object)
                              // shorten type name
```

```
typedef map< string, string, less<string> > map_type;

map_type diction;               // define a dictionary
                                // insert sample entries
diction.insert( map_type::value_type("cat",
                "A small furry animal that chases mice.") );
diction.insert( map_type::value_type("dog",
                "A large hairy animal that chases sticks.") );

while(true)                     // get entries from user
   {
   cout << "\nEnter word (or \"done\"): ";
   cin >> word;
   if(word == "done")
      break;
   cout << "Enter definition: ";
   cin.get(def, SIZE);          // (reads embedded blanks)
   diction.insert( map_type::value_type(word, def) );
   }
map_type::iterator iter;        // make an iterator
iter = diction.begin();         // set to beginning of dictionary
cout << endl << endl;
while( iter != diction.end() )
   {                            // display "word -- definition"
   cout << (*iter).first << " -- " << (*iter).second << endl;
   ++iter;
   }
}
```

The key values "cat" and "dog" and their definitions are already installed in the map by the program, but the user is encouraged to enter other word-definition pairs. Here's some sample interaction with the program when the user defines a snail:

```
Enter word (or "done"): snail
Enter definition: A small shelled animal that eats gardens.

Enter word (or "done"): done

cat -- A small furry animal that chases mice.
dog -- A large hairy animal that chases sticks.
snail -- A small shelled animal that eats gardens.
```

In the MAP program, the user can't insert definitions for `cat` or `dog` because these keys are already in the container and a map allows only one key with a given value. A multimap would allow the same key value to appear more than once.

The expression for the data type of the map container

```
map< string, string, less<string> >
```

is rather unwieldy to write. Because this expression appears several times in the listing, I use a `typedef` to condense it into the more manageable expression `map_type`:

```
typedef map< string, string, less<string> > map_type;
```

`typedefs` are typically used in this way when dealing with the templatized STL containers, especially maps and sets.

Pairs

The argument to the `insert()` function, `map_type::value_type(word, def)`, may look a little ponderous. It arises because maps and multimaps actually hold objects of type `pair`. The class `pair` is itself templatized so its objects can contain two objects of two other classes. You can make your own `pair` objects:

```
pair<string, string> dictopair = make_pair("cat", "A cat is a .....");
```

In the MAP.H header file, `value_type` is defined as a `pair` of values:

```
typedef pair<const Key, T> value_type;
```

This makes it convenient to supply values to `insert()`, as is done in this example and similar functions. Notice that the `char*` strings such as "cat" are converted automatically to `string` objects to match the type expected by `value_type`.

The names of the two members of `pair` are (appropriately) `first` and `second`. These members are used in the `while` loop to display the contents of the map:

```
cout << (*iter).first << " -- " << (*iter).second << endl;
```

Roughly speaking, when you combine values to put them into a map, you combine them with `value_type`, but to separate them when you take them out again, you use `first` and `second`.

The [ ] Operator

You can use the `find()` or `lower_bound()`/`upper_bound()` functions to search for a particular entry in a map, just as you can in sets. However, you can also use the `[]` operator. I'll demonstrate this with a map that holds pairs consisting of numbers and nautical expressions. In the 18th century, ships carried signal books listing hundreds of flag messages. To send a message, one ship would hoist flags indicating a certain number; another ship, perhaps several miles away, would read the flags with telescopes and then use the number to look up the message in its own flag book. The example program stores pairs consisting of flag numbers and their corresponding messages. If 18th-century ships had been equipped with computers, the program would have made looking up the message a much faster process. Listing 12-31 shows MAPBRACK.

Listing 12-31 MAPBRACK

```
// mapbrack.cpp
// demonstrates operator [] used for maps
#include <iostream.h>
#include <map.h>

void main()
    {
    typedef map< long, char*, less<int> > map_type;
```

```
map_type flaglist;                  // map holding flag messages
long code_number;

flaglist.insert( map_type::value_type(14072,
    "I are listing sharply and will soon founder.") );
flaglist.insert( map_type::value_type(12023,
    "The enemy is within sight and approaching rapidly.") );
flaglist.insert( map_type::value_type(16067,
    "I have dispatches. Prepare to receive our longboat.") );
flaglist.insert( map_type::value_type(13045,
    "Fall in line astern of me.") );
flaglist.insert( map_type::value_type(19092,
    "Stand off. This coast is rocky and uncharted.") );

while(true)                         // get code number from user
    {
    cout << "\n\nEnter flag code number (0 to terminate): ";
    cin >> code_number;
    if( !code_number )
       break;
    cout << "Message is:" << endl;
    cout << flaglist[code_number];  // access value with key
    }
}
```

Some sample interaction with the program might be

```
Enter flag code number (0 to terminate): 16067
Message is:
I have dispatches. Prepare to receive our longboat.

Enter flag code number (0 to terminate): 0
```

The expression

```
flaglist[code_number];
```

uses the key (the code number) in place of the index and returns the associated map value, in this case a `char*` string, which is then displayed. The overloaded `[]` operator provides an intuitively clear way to access entries in a map.

Hash Table Versions

There are alternative versions to all the sequence containers that can speed up access to individual items. These versions use a hash table as an underlying mechanism. Their disadvantage is that they do not allow rapid iteration through the container in sorted order. These containers are called *hash_set*, *hash_multiset*, *hash_map*, and *hash_multimap*. They are used in the same way as the normal versions, but are appropriate when searching speed is more critical than the ability to iterate through the container.

1. In an associative container,
    a. values are stored in sorted order.
    b. keys are stored in sorted order.
    c. sorting is always in alphabetical or numerical order.
    d. you must use the `sort()` algorithm to keep the contents sorted.
    e. you can't use iterators.

2. When defining a set, you must specify
    a. the underlying container that implements the set (vector, list, or deque).
    b. the data type of the keys.
    c. the data type of the values.
    d. a certain function object.
    e. the comparison that will be used to specify the order of the elements.

3. Which of the following statements are true?
    a. In a set, the `insert()` member function inserts a key in sorted order.
    b. In a multimap, the `insert()` member function does nothing if its argument is the same as an existing element in the container.
    c. If you initialize an associative container using an array, the order of the elements will necessarily be preserved.
    d. A map can have two or more elements with the same key value.
    e. The `erase()` member function won't remove an element from a set because if it did, the ordering would not be preserved.

4. A map
    a. is like a set, but can store multiple key values.
    b. can be thought of as a French dictionary.
    c. can use an iterator to access elements.
    d. stores pairs, each of which must hold an index number and an object.
    e. can use the `[]` operator to access elements.

5. In a map or multimap, the argument to the `insert()` member function
    a. requires that the data type of the container be specified.
    b. requires the typedef `value_type`.
    c. is an iterator to a key value.
    d. is a key-value pair.
    e. is either a key or a value.

Write a program that merges two maps into a single map.

EXERCISE 2

Write a program that creates a frequency table of the words in a text file. You can use a map where the words are the keys and the number of times the word appears in the file are the associated values. The program should obtain the name of the file from the user and display the frequency table.

SESSION 7
STORING USER-DEFINED OBJECTS

Of course, the big payoff with the STL is that you can use it to store and manipulate objects of classes that you write yourself (or that someone else has written). In this session, I'll show some examples.

A Set of `person` Objects

I'll start with a **person** class that includes a person's last name, first name, and telephone number. I'll create some members of this class and insert them in a set, thus creating a phone book database. The user interacts with the program by entering a person's name. The program then searches the list and displays the data for that person if it finds a match. I'll use a multiset so two or more person objects can have the same name. Listing 12-32 shows SETPERS.

Listing 12-32 SETPERS

```
// setpers.cpp
// uses a multiset to hold person objects
#include <iostream.h>
#include <multiset.h>
#include <cstring.h>

class person
   {
   private:
      string lastName;
      string firstName;
      long phoneNumber;
   public:                       // default constructor
      person() : lastName("blank"),
                 firstName("blank"), phoneNumber(0L)
         {  }
                              // 3-arg constructor
      person(string lana, string fina, long pho) :
             lastName(lana), firstName(fina), phoneNumber(pho)
         {  }
      friend bool operator<(const person&, const person&);
      friend bool operator==(const person&, const person&);

      void display() const     // display person's data
         {
```

continued on next page

continued from previous page

```
            cout << endl << lastName << ",\t" << firstName
                 << "\t\tPhone: " << phoneNumber;
        }
    };
                                // operator < for person class
bool operator<(const person& p1, const person& p2)
    {
    if(p1.lastName == p2.lastName)
        return (p1.firstName < p2.firstName) ? true : false;
    return (p1.lastName < p2.lastName) ? true : false;
    }
                                // operator == for person class
bool operator==(const person& p1, const person& p2)
    {
    return (p1.lastName == p2.lastName &&
            p1.firstName == p2.firstName ) ? true : false;
    }
////////////////////////////////////////////////////////////////
void main()
    {
                                // create person objects
    person pers1("Deauville", "William", 8435150);
    person pers2("McDonald", "Stacey", 3327563);
    person pers3("Bartoski", "Peter", 6946473);
    person pers4("KuangThu", "Bruce", 4157300);
    person pers5("Wellington", "John", 9207404);
    person pers6("McDonald", "Amanda", 8435150);
    person pers7("Fredericks", "Roger", 7049982);
    person pers8("McDonald", "Stacey", 7764987);
                                // multiset of persons
    multiset< person, less<person> > persSet;
                                // iterator to a multiset of persons
    multiset<person, less<person> >::iterator iter;

    persSet.insert(pers1);      // put persons in multiset
    persSet.insert(pers2);
    persSet.insert(pers3);
    persSet.insert(pers4);
    persSet.insert(pers5);
    persSet.insert(pers6);
    persSet.insert(pers7);
    persSet.insert(pers8);

    cout << "\nNumber of entries = " << persSet.size();

    iter = persSet.begin();     // display contents of multiset
    while( iter != persSet.end() )
        (*iter++).display();
                                // get last and first name
    string searchLastName, searchFirstName;
    cout << "\n\nEnter last name of person to search for: ";
    cin >> searchLastName;
    cout << "Enter first name: ";
    cin >> searchFirstName;
                                // create person with this name
```

```
person searchPerson(searchLastName, searchFirstName, 0);

                            // get count of such persons
int cntPersons = persSet.count(searchPerson);
cout << "Number of persons with this name = " << cntPersons;

                            // display all matches
iter = persSet.lower_bound(searchPerson);
while( iter != persSet.upper_bound(searchPerson) )
   (*iter++).display();
} // end main()
```

Necessary Member Functions

The `person` class is created pretty much in the usual way, but to work with STL containers, it must be provided with a few common member functions. These are a default (no-argument) constructor (which actually is not necessary in this example, but is usually essential), the overloaded < operator, and the overloaded == operator. These member functions are used by member functions of the `list` class and by various algorithms. You may need other member functions in other specific situations. (As in most classes, you should probably also provide overloaded assignment, copy constructors, and a destructor, but I'll ignore these here.)

The overloaded < and == operators should use `const` arguments. Generally, it's best to make them friends, but you can use member functions as well.

Ordering

The overloaded < operator specifies the way the elements in the set will be ordered. In SETPERS, I define this operator to order the last name of the person and, if the last names are the same, to order the first names. (I could have used the phone numbers to provide ordering or I could have ordered on any other data item included in the class.)

Here's some interaction with SETPERS. The program first displays the entire list (this would not be practical on a real database with a large number of elements). Because they are stored in a multiset, the elements are ordered automatically. Then, at the prompt, the user enters the name "McDonald, Stacey" (last name first). There are two persons on the list with this particular name, so they are both displayed.

```
Number of entries = 8
Bartoski,      Peter        phone: 6946473
Deauville,     William      phone: 8435150
Fredericks,    Roger        phone: 7049982
KuangThu,      Bruce        phone: 4157300
McDonald,      Amanda       phone: 8435150
McDonald,      Stacey       phone: 3327563
McDonald,      Stacey       phone: 7764987
Wellington,    John         phone: 9207404

Enter last name of person to search for: McDonald
Enter first name: Stacey
Number of persons with this name = 2
McDonald,      Stacey       phone: 3327563
McDonald,      Stacey       phone: 7764987
```

Just Like Basic Types

As you can see, once a class has been defined, objects of that class are handled by the container in the same way as variables of basic types.

I first use the `size()` member function to display the total number of entries. Then I iterate through the list, displaying all the entries.

Because I'm using a multiset, the `lower_bound()` and `upper_bound()` member functions are available to display all elements that fall within a range. Here both the lower and the upper bound are the same, so all persons with the same name are displayed. Notice that I must create a "fictitious" person with the same name as the person (or persons) I want to find. The `lower_bound()` and `upper_bound()` functions then match this person against those on the list.

A List of person Objects

You can quickly search a set or multiset for a person with a given name, as in the SETPERS example. If, however, I'm more concerned with being able to insert or delete a person object quickly, I might decide to use a list instead. The LISTPERS example (Listing 12-33) shows how this looks.

Listing 12-33 LISTPERS

```
// listpers.cpp
// uses a list to hold person objects
#include <iostream.h>
#include <list.h>
#include <algo.h>
#include <cstring.h>

class person
   {
   private:
      string lastName;
      string firstName;
      long phoneNumber;
   public:
      person() :                  // default constructor
          lastName("blank"), firstName("blank"), phoneNumber(0L)
         {  }
                                  // 3-arg constructor
      person(string lana, string fina, long pho) :
            lastName(lana), firstName(fina), phoneNumber(pho)
         {  }
      friend bool operator<(const person&, const person&);
      friend bool operator==(const person&, const person&);

      void display() const      // display all data
         {
         cout << endl << lastName << ",\t" << firstName
            << "\t\tPhone: " << phoneNumber;
         }
```

```
        long get_phone() const   // return phone number
            { return phoneNumber; }
    };
                                    // overloaded < for person class
bool operator<(const person& p1, const person& p2)
    {
    if(p1.lastName == p2.lastName)
        return (p1.firstName < p2.firstName) ? true : false;
    return (p1.lastName < p2.lastName) ? true : false;
    }
                                    // overloaded == for person class
bool operator==(const person& p1, const person& p2)
    {
    return (p1.lastName == p2.lastName &&
            p1.firstName == p2.firstName ) ? true : false;
    }
//////////////////////////////////////////////////////////
void main()
    {
    list<person> persList;        // list of persons
                                  // iterators to a list of persons
    list<person>::iterator iter1;
    list<person>::iterator iter2;
                                  // put persons in list
    persList.push_back( person("Deauville", "William", 8435150) );
    persList.push_back( person("McDonald", "Stacey", 3327563) );
    persList.push_back( person("Bartoski", "Peter", 6946473) );
    persList.push_back( person("KuangThu", "Bruce", 4157300) );
    persList.push_back( person("Wellington", "John", 9207404) );
    persList.push_back( person("McDonald", "Amanda", 8435150) );
    persList.push_back( person("Fredericks", "Roger", 7049982) );
    persList.push_back( person("McDonald", "Stacey", 7764987) );

    cout << "\nNumber of entries = " << persList.size();

    iter1 = persList.begin();    // display contents of list
    while( iter1 != persList.end() )
        (*iter1++).display();

// find person or persons with specified name (last and first)
    string searchLastName, searchFirstName;
    cout << "\n\nEnter last name of person to search for: ";
    cin >> searchLastName;
    cout << "Enter first name: ";
    cin >> searchFirstName;
                                  // make a person with that name
    person searchPerson(searchLastName, searchFirstName, 0L);
                                  // search for first match of names
    iter1 = find(persList.begin(), persList.end(), searchPerson);
    if( iter1 != persList.end() )
        {
```

continued on next page

continued from previous page

```
        cout << "Person(s) with that name is(are)";
        do
            {
            (*iter1).display();   // display matches
            iter2 = ++iter1;      // search for other matches
            iter1 = find(iter2, persList.end(), searchPerson);
            } while( iter1 != persList.end() );
        }
    else
        cout << "There is no person with that name.";

// find person or persons with specified phone number
    cout << "\n\nEnter phone number (format 1234567): ";
    long sNumber;                 // get search number
    cin >> sNumber;
                                  // iterate through list
    bool found_one = false;
    for(iter1=persList.begin(); iter1 != persList.end(); ++iter1)
        {
        if( sNumber == (*iter1).get_phone() )   // compare numbers
            {
            if( !found_one )
                {
                cout << "Person(s) with that phone number is(are)";
                found_one = true;
                }
            (*iter1).display();   // display the match
            }
        }  // end for
    if( !found_one )
        cout << "There is no person with that phone number";
    }  // end main()
```

Finding All persons *with a Specified Name*

I can't use the `lower_bound()`/`upper_bound()` member functions because I'm dealing with a list, not a set or map. Instead, I use the `find()` member function to find all the persons with a given name. If this function reports a hit, I must apply it again, starting one person past where the hit was, to see if there are other persons with the same name. This complicates the programming; I must use a loop and two iterators.

Finding All persons *with a Specified Phone Number*

Remember that in the person class, the overloaded < operator defines the ordering of the elements based on their names, both last and first. That makes it harder to search for a person with a specified phone number because the class member functions such as `find()` are intended to be used to find the primary search characteristic. In this example, I use the brute force approach to finding the phone number, iterating through the list, and making a "manual" comparison of the number I'm looking for and each member of the list:

```
if( sNumber == (*iter1).getphone() )
    ...
```

This won't be as fast as using `find()` or `lower_bound()`/`upper_bound()` to conduct the search. (In the next session, I'll show another approach, using function objects.)

The program first displays all the entries, then asks the user for a name and finds the matching `person` or `persons`. It then asks for a phone number and again finds any matching `persons`. Here's some interaction with LISTPERS:

```
Number of entries = 8
Deauville,      William        phone: 8435150
McDonald,       Stacey         phone: 3327563
Bartoski,       Peter          phone: 6946473
KuangThu,       Bruce          phone: 4157300
Wellington,     John           phone: 9207404
McDonald,       Amanda         phone: 8435150
Fredericks,     Roger          phone: 7049982
McDonald,       Stacey         phone: 7764987

Enter last name of person to search for: Wellington
Enter first name: John
Person(s) with that name is(are)
Wellington,     John           phone: 9207404

Enter phone number (format 1234567): 8435150
Person(s) with that number is(are)
Deauville,      William        phone: 8435150
McDonald,       Amanda         phone: 8435150
```

The program has found two people with the same phone number.

A List of `airtime` Objects

As the last example in this session, I'll show a list of `airtime` objects. (Remember that `airtime` object data comprises only hours and minutes, not seconds.) Listing 12-34, LISTAIR, shows how a number of `airtime` objects, stored on a list, can be added together. Airlines might use this to add the amount of time a pilot has spent in the air during a given week, for example. The addition is carried out by an overloaded + operator in the `airtime` class.

Listing 12-34 LISTAIR

```cpp
// listair.cpp
// adding airtime objects stored on a list
#include <iostream.h>
#include <list.h>

class airtime
   {
   private:
      int hours;                // 0 to 23
      int minutes;              // 0 to 59
   public:
                                // default constructor
      airtime() : hours(0), minutes(0)
         { }
```

continued on next page

continued from previous page

```
                                    // 2-arg constructor
        airtime(int h, int m) : hours(h), minutes(m)
            { }

        void display() const     // output to screen
            {
            cout << hours << ':' << minutes;
            }

        void get()               // input from user
            {
            char dummy;
            cout << "\nEnter airtime (format 12:59): ";
            cin >> hours >> dummy >> minutes;
            }
                                  // overloaded + operator
        airtime operator + (airtime right) const
            {                     // add members
            int temph = hours + right.hours;
            int tempm = minutes + right.minutes;
            if(tempm >= 60)       // check for carry
                {
                temph++;
                tempm -= 60;
                }                 // return sum
            return airtime(temph, tempm);
            }
                                  // overloaded < operator
        bool operator < (const airtime& at2) const
            {
            if(hours < at2.hours)
                return true;
            if(hours == at2.hours && minutes < at2.minutes)
                return true;
            return false;
            }
                                    // overloaded == operator
        bool operator == (const airtime& at2) const
            {
            if(hours == at2.hours && minutes == at2.minutes)
                return true;
            return false;
            }
    };  // end class airtime

void main()
    {
    char answer;
    airtime temp, sum;

    list<airtime> airlist;       // list and iterator
    list<airtime>::iterator iter;
    do
        {
```

```
    temp.get();                // get airtime from user
    airlist.push_back(temp);
    cout << "Enter another (y/n)? ";
    cin >> answer;
    } while (answer != 'n');

  iter = airlist.begin();      // iterate through list
  while( iter != airlist.end() )
      sum = sum + *iter++;     // add this airtime to sum
  cout << "\nsum = ";
  sum.display();               // display sum
  }
```

The `airtime` values are entered by the user. Once all these values have been obtained and stored on the list, the program iterates through the list, adding each value to an `airtime` object called `sum`. Finally, `sum` is displayed. (You'll see a more sophisticated way to do this in the next session.) Here's some interaction with LISTAIR:

```
Enter airtime (format 12:59): 1:22
Enter another (y/n)? y

Enter airtime (format 12:59): 0:19
Enter another (y/n)? y

Enter airtime (format 12:59): 2:13
Enter another (y/n)? y

Enter airtime (format 12:59): 1:45
Enter another (y/n)? n

sum = 5:39
```

In this session, I've concentrated on searching a container for specified elements using algorithms such as `find()`. However, you can apply any of the STL algorithms to objects of user-defined classes placed in STL arrays: You can sort them, merge them, copy them, and so on. As you can see, it's quite simple to store objects of almost any class in an STL container and manipulate these objects with STL algorithms.

1. Which of the following are differences between storing variables of basic types (such as `int`) in a container and storing objects of user-created classes?
    a. Certain container member functions don't work when containers hold objects of user-created classes.
    b. You must give values to basic variables before placing them in a container, but this isn't necessary for objects of user-created classes.
    c. Certain member functions must be supplied for the user-created classes.
    d. Random-access iterators don't work for user-created class objects.
    e. Objects of user-created classes must be defined after the class is created.

2. If you are going to store objects of a class T in an STL container, then T
   a. will probably require a default constructor.
   b. will definitely need a one-argument constructor.
   c. will not require an overloaded == operator unless it uses the equal function object.
   d. will definitely need an overloaded < operator.
   e. must include a pointer of type T* as a member to store its own location.

3. If you overload the < operator for a class T whose objects you are going to store in an STL container, then this operator
   a. will probably base the comparison on one or more member data items in T.
   b. will call on a function object to carry out the actual comparison.
   c. if the container is a list, will be used by find().
   d. if the container is a map, will be used to order the keys (not the values).
   e. if the container is a map, will be used to order the values (not the keys).

4. In which of the following containers might it make sense, under the appropriate circumstances, to store objects of the person class (as seen in the examples in this section)?
   a. A deque.
   b. A vector.
   c. A multiset.
   d. A map in which social security numbers are used as the key and person objects as the values.
   e. A map in which person objects are used both as the key and the value.

5. Which of these statements are reasonable?
   a. When you create a fictitious object to use as an argument to the find(), count(), or lower_bound() functions, this object must have valid data for all its members.
   b. Container member functions have direct access to the private data of objects stored in the container.
   c. If you overload an arithmetic operator (such as + or -) for a class whose objects you are going to store in an STL container, then you can use a dereferenced container iterator as the argument on the right of the operator, but not on the left.
   d. If iter is a container iterator and display() is a member function of the objects stored in the container, you can use iter->display() as a shorthand version of (*iter).display().
   e. The count() member function can return the number of elements in a container that have a specified value.

EXERCISE 1

Create a map of person objects (based on the person class in the LISTPERS example) using social security numbers (SSN) as keys. The user should be able to add or delete persons or search for a person with a given SSN. Provide the ability to search for persons with a particular name or telephone number as well.

EXERCISE 2

Create a `flight_information` class that holds the information necessary for displaying flight information on an airport "Departures" monitor. The information should include the airline and the destination city (`string` objects), the scheduled and current departure times (`airtime` values), and the gate number (an integer). Make a set to hold `flight_information` objects, sorted by destination and, for each destination, by scheduled departure time. The user should be able to add new information and display the sorted information.

SESSION 8

FUNCTION OBJECTS

Function objects are used extensively in the STL as arguments to certain algorithms. They allow you to customize the operation of these algorithms. I mentioned function objects in Session 2, where I showed an example of the predefined function object `greater` used to sort data in reverse order. In this session, I'll examine other predefined function objects and show you how to write your own so you have even greater control over what the STL algorithms do.

Recall that a function object is a function that has been wrapped in a class so it looks like an object. The class, however, has no data and only one member function, which is the overloaded `()` operator. The class is templatized so it can work with different types.

Predefined Function Objects

The predefined STL function objects, located in the FUNCTION.H file, are shown in Table 12-10. The letter `T` indicates any class, either user-written or a basic type. The variables `x` and `y` represent objects of class `T` passed to the function object as arguments.

Predefined Functions	Types	Return Value
plus	T = plus(T, T)	x+y
minus	T = minus(T, T)	x-y
times	T = times(T, T)	x*y
divide	T = divide(T, T)	x/y
modulus	T = modulus(T, T)	x%y
negate	T = negate(T)	-x
equal_to	bool = equal_to(T, T)	x == y
not_equal_to	bool = not_equal_to(T, T)	x != y
greater	bool = greater(T, T)	x > y
less	bool = less(T, T)	x < y

Table 12-10

continued on next page

continued from previous page

Predefined Functions	Types	Return Value
greater_equal	bool = greater_equal (T, T)	x >= y
less_equal	bool = less_equal (T, T)	x <= y
logical_and	bool = logical_and(T, T)	x && y
logical_or	bool = logical_or(T, T)	x || y
logical_not	bool = logical_not(T)	!x

Table 12-10 *Predefined function objects*

There are function objects for arithmetic operations, comparisons, and logical operations. The SORTEMP example in Session 2 showed how to use a comparison function object, `greater<>()`. Let's look at an example where an arithmetic function object might come in handy. The example (a variation of the LISTAIR example in Session 7) shows how the `plus<>()` function object can be used to add all the `airtime` values in a container. Listing 12-35 shows PLUSAIR.

Listing 12-35 PLUSAIR

```
// plusair.cpp
// uses accumulate() algorithm and plus() function object
#include <iostream.h>
#include <list.h>
#include <algo.h>

class airtime
   {
   private:
     int hours;            // 0 to 23
     int minutes;          // 0 to 59
   public:
                           // default constructor
     airtime() : hours(0), minutes(0)
        {  }
                           // 2-arg constructor
     airtime(int h, int m) : hours(h), minutes(m)
        {  }

     void display() const    // output to screen
        {
        cout << hours << ':' << minutes;
        }

     void get()              // input from user
        {
        char dummy;
        cout << "\nEnter airtime (format 12:59): ";
        cin >> hours >> dummy >> minutes;
        }
                           // overloaded + operator
     airtime operator + (const airtime right) const
        {                   // add members
        int temph = hours + right.hours;
```

```
        int tempm = minutes + right.minutes;
        if(tempm >= 60)        // check for carry
            { temph++; tempm -= 60; }
        return airtime(temph, tempm); // return sum
        }
                            // overloaded < operator
    bool operator < (const airtime& at2) const
        {
        if(hours < at2.hours)
            return true;
        if(hours == at2.hours && minutes < at2.minutes)
            return true;
        return false;
        }
                            // overloaded == operator
    bool operator == (const airtime& at2) const
        {
        if(hours == at2.hours && minutes == at2.minutes)
            return true;
        return false;
        }
    };  // end class airtime

void main()
    {
    char answer;
    airtime temp, sum;

    list<airtime> airlist;        // list and iterator
    list<airtime>::iterator iter;

    do
        {                          // get airtimes from user
        temp.get();
        airlist.push_back(temp);
        cout << "Enter another (y/n)? ";
        cin >> answer;
        } while (answer != 'n');
                            // sum all the airtimes
    sum = accumulate( airlist.begin(), airlist.end(),
                      airtime(0, 0), plus<airtime>() );

    cout << "\nsum = ";
    sum.display();              // display sum
    }
```

This program features the `accumulate()` algorithm, which returns the sum of all the elements in a range. The four arguments to `accumulate()` are the iterators of the first and last elements in the range, the initial value of the sum (usually 0 or its equivalent), and the operation to be applied to the elements. In this example I add them, but I could subtract them, multiply them, or perform other operations using different function objects. Here's some interaction with PLUSAIR:

```
Enter airtime (format 12:59) : 3:45
Enter another (y/n)? y

Enter airtime (format 12:59) : 5:10
Enter another (y/n)? y

Enter airtime (format 12:59) : 2:25
Enter another (y/n)? y

Enter airtime (format 12:59) : 0:55
Enter another (y/n)? n

sum = 12:15
```

The `accumulate()` algorithm is not only easier and clearer than iterating through the container myself to add the elements, it's also (unless I put a lot of work into my code) more efficient. (Another version of `accumulate()` can perform any operation I define, rather than summing the data.)

The `plus<>()` function object requires that the + operator be overloaded for the `airtime` class. (This operator should be a `const` function because that's what the `plus<>()` function object expects.)

The other arithmetic function objects work in a similar way. The logical function objects such as `logical_and<>()` can be used on objects of classes for which these operations make sense (e.g., type `bool` variables).

Writing Your Own Function Objects

If one of the standard function objects doesn't do what you want, you can write your own. The next example shows one reason why this might be necessary.

It's easy to sort a group of elements based on the relationship specified in the < operator. Simply inserting the elements into a set or multiset will achieve this kind of ordering, or, if the elements are in a sequential container, you can sort them using the normal version of `sort()` with two parameters.

Different Criteria for Sorting

Suppose, however, you want to sort the elements in a different order than that specified by the < operator. One solution is to specify the ordering criteria using a function object. The following example shows how a list of `person` objects can be sorted according to phone number using a function object, called `lessPhone()`, that I write myself. Listing 12-36 shows SORTPERS.

Listing 12-36 SORTPERS

```
// sortpers.cpp
// sorts person objects by name and phone number
#include <iostream.h>
#include <vector.h>
#include <multiset.h>
#include <algo.h>
#include <cstring.h>

class person
   {
   private:
```

```
      string lastName;
      string firstName;
      long phoneNumber;
   public:
      person() :                     // default constructor
          lastName("blank"), firstName("blank"), phoneNumber(0L)
        {  }
                                     // 3-arg constructor
      person(string lana, string fina, long pho) :
             lastName(lana), firstName(fina), phoneNumber(pho)
        {  }

      friend bool operator<(const person&, const person&);
      friend bool operator==(const person&, const person&);

      void display() const     // display person's data
         {
         cout << endl << lastName << ",\t" << firstName
              << "\t\tPhone: " << phoneNumber;
         }
      long get_phone() const   // return phone number
         { return phoneNumber; }
   };
                                     // overloaded < for person class
bool operator<(const person& p1, const person& p2)
   {
   if(p1.lastName == p2.lastName)
      return (p1.firstName < p2.firstName) ? true : false;
   return (p1.lastName < p2.lastName) ? true : false;
   }
                                     // overloaded == for person class
bool operator==(const person& p1, const person& p2)
   {
   return (p1.lastName == p2.lastName &&
           p1.firstName == p2.firstName ) ? true : false;
   }

// function object to compare person's phone number
class phoneLess : binary_function<person, person, bool>
   {
   public:
      bool operator() (const person& p1, const person& p2) const
         {
         return p1.get_phone() < p2.get_phone();
         }
   };

/////////////////////////////////////////////////////////////////
void main()
   {                             // a multiset of persons
   multiset< person, less<person> > persSet;
                                 // put persons in set
   persSet.insert( person("Deauville", "William", 8435150) );
```

continued on next page

continued from previous page

```
persSet.insert( person("McDonald", "Stacey", 3327563) );
persSet.insert( person("Bartoski", "Peter", 6946473) );
persSet.insert( person("KuangThu", "Bruce", 4157300) );
persSet.insert( person("Wellington", "John", 9207404) );
persSet.insert( person("McDonald", "Amanda", 8435150) );
persSet.insert( person("Fredericks", "Roger", 7049982) );
persSet.insert( person("McDonald", "Stacey", 7764987) );

                            // iterator to multiset
multiset< person, less<person> >::iterator iterset;
cout << "\nPersons sorted by name:";
iterset = persSet.begin(); // display contents of set
while( iterset != persSet.end() )
   (*iterset++).display();
                            // an empty vector of persons
vector<person> persVect( persSet.size() );
                            // copy from set to vector
copy( persSet.begin(), persSet.end(), persVect.begin() );
                            // sort vector by phone number
sort( persVect.begin(), persVect.end(), phoneLess() );

                            // iterator to a vector of persons
vector<person>::iterator itervect;
cout << "\n\nPersons sorted by phone number:";
itervect = persVect.begin();  // display contents of vector
while( itervect != persVect.end() )
   (*itervect++).display();
}  // end main()
```

The program starts out by putting the usual person objects in a set and displaying its contents to show ordering by name. Then the set is copied into a vector and the vector is sorted using the lessPhone() function object in the line

```
sort( persVect.begin(), persVect.end(), phoneLess() );
```

Here's the output of SORTPERS:

```
Persons sorted by name:
Bartoski,       Peter       phone: 6946473
Deauville,      William     phone: 8435150
Fredericks,     Roger       phone: 7049982
KuangThu,       Bruce       phone: 4157300
McDonald,       Amanda      phone: 8435150
McDonald,       Stacey      phone: 3327563
McDonald,       Stacey      phone: 7764987
Wellington,     John        phone: 9207404

Persons sorted by phone number:
McDonald,       Stacey      phone: 3327563
KuangThu,       Bruce       phone: 4157300
Bartoski,       Peter       phone: 6946473
Fredericks,     Roger       phone: 7049982
McDonald,       Stacey      phone: 7764987
Deauville,      William     phone: 8435150
```

```
McDonald,        Amanda        phone: 8435150
Wellington,      John          phone: 9207404
```

The `phoneLess` class is defined this way:

```
class phoneLess : binary_function<person, person, bool>
    {
    public:
        bool operator() (const person& p1, const person& p2) const
            {
            return p1.get_phone() < p2.get_phone();
            }
```

You could alternatively express this class as a `struct`, which makes it unnecessary to use the `public` designation (because everything in a `struct` is public by default). However, I prefer to use `class` to emphasize that I'm dealing with a class and not an old-fashioned C style `struct`.

Instead of comparing names, as the built-in `less<>()` function object would have, the overloaded `()` operator in the `phoneLess` class compares the phone numbers of the two `person` objects passed as arguments. It returns true if the first phone number is less than the second. The `sort()` algorithm uses this relationship to sort the vector.

The `phoneLess` class is derived from the `binary_function` class (actually a `struct`), which is defined in FUNCTION.H. The `binary_function` class specifies that two arguments must be supplied to the function object. This simplifies the syntax used to write the overloaded `operator()` function. (There's also a `unary_function` class, from which you can derive function objects taking one argument.)

Binding: Providing Values to Function Objects

The `find()` function uses the overloaded `==` operator to search in a container for objects of a user-defined class. Can you search for elements using different search criteria? One approach is to use the `find_if()` algorithm and an appropriate function object. However to do this, you need to learn about a new concept: *binding*, in which a value is bound to one function object to make another function object.

The FUNCPERS example (Listing 12-37) shows how a function object called `phoneEqual()` can find all entries with a given phone number.

Listing 12-37 FUNCPERS

```
// funcpers.cpp
// demonstrates function objects with person class
#include <iostream.h>
#include <list.h>
#include <algo.h>
#include <cstring.h>

class person
    {
    private:
        string lastName;
        string firstName;
        long phoneNumber;
```

continued on next page

continued from previous page

```cpp
   public:
      person() :                     // default constructor
         lastName("blank"), firstName("blank"), phoneNumber(0L)
         { }
                                     // 3-arg constructor
      person(string lana, string fina, long pho) :
            lastName(lana), firstName(fina), phoneNumber(pho)
         { }
      friend bool operator<(const person&, const person&);
      friend bool operator==(const person&, const person&);

      void display() const
         {
         cout << endl << lastName << ",\t" << firstName
              << "\t\tPhone: " << phoneNumber;
         }

      long get_phone() const  // return person's phone number
         { return phoneNumber; }
   };
                                     // overloaded < for person class
bool operator<(const person& p1, const person& p2)
   {
   if(p1.lastName == p2.lastName)
      return (p1.firstName < p2.firstName) ? true : false;
   return (p1.lastName < p2.lastName) ? true : false;
   }
                                     // overloaded == for person class
bool operator==(const person& p1, const person& p2)
   {
   return (p1.lastName == p2.lastName &&
           p1.firstName == p2.firstName ) ? true : false;
   }

// function object to compare person's phone number
class phoneEqual : binary_function<person, long, bool>
   {
   public:
      bool operator() (const person& p, const long& n) const
         {
         return (p.get_phone()==n) ? true : false;
         }
   };
/////////////////////////////////////////////////////////////////
void main()
   {

   list<person> persList;        // list of persons

   list<person>::iterator iter1;  // iterators to a
   list<person>::iterator iter2;  // list of persons
```

```
                            // put persons in list
persList.push_back( person("Deauville", "William", 8435150) );
persList.push_back( person("McDonald", "Stacey", 3327563) );
persList.push_back( person("Bartoski", "Peter", 6946473) );
persList.push_back( person("KuangThu", "Bruce", 4157300) );
persList.push_back( person("Wellington", "John", 9207404) );
persList.push_back( person("McDonald", "Amanda", 8435150) );
persList.push_back( person("Fredericks", "Roger", 7049982) );
persList.push_back( person("McDonald", "Stacey", 7764987) );

// find person or persons with specified phone number
cout << "\n\nEnter phone number (format 1234567): ";
long sNumber;                  // get search number
cin >> sNumber;
                            // search for first match
iter1 = find_if( persList.begin(),
                 persList.end(),
                 bind2nd(phoneEqual(), sNumber) ); // func obj
if( iter1 != persList.end() )
   {
   cout << "\nPerson(s) with that phone number is(are)";
   do
      {
      (*iter1).display();  // display match
      iter2 = ++iter1;       // search for another match
      iter1 = find_if( iter2,
                       persList.end(),
                       bind2nd(phoneEqual(), sNumber) );
      } while( iter1 != persList.end() );
   }
else
   cout << "There is no person with that phone number.";
}  // end main()
```

The `phoneEqual()` function object is similar to the `phoneLess()` function object in the SORT-PERS example. However, it is invoked somewhat differently by the `find_if()` algorithm.

The third argument to `find_if()` requires a function object. This function object, `phoneEqual()`, expects `find_if()` to supply two arguments to it: a `person` object and a `long` value representing the phone number. As `find_if()` iterates through the `persList` container checking each person object in turn, it repeatedly calls `phoneEqual()`. It knows which `person` object to pass to `phoneEqual()` because it knows where it is in the iteration process. But where does `find_if()` get the phone number to supply to `phoneEqual()`? I can't supply this number directly to the function object as an argument, like this

```
iter1 = find_if( persList.begin(),
                 persList.end(),
                 phoneEqual(sNumber) );  // can't do this
```

because `find_if()` must supply all the values to `phoneEqual` itself. Instead, I must *bind* the phone number and the function object together to make another function object. The `bind2nd` binder is used for this purpose:

```
iter1 = find_if( persList.begin(),
                 persList.end(),
                 bind2nd(phoneEqual(), sNumber) );
```

You can use either of two binders, **bind1st** or **bind2nd**, depending on whether the value you supply is the first or second argument to the function object. In **phoneEqual()**, it's the second; the **person** object is the first.

Here's some interaction with FUNCPERS:

```
Enter phone number (format 1234567): 9207474

Person(s) with that phone number is(are)
Wellington,      John            Phone: 9207404
```

If there are multiple instances of the same phone number, the program will find and display all of them.

1. Function objects can be used to
   a. customize the **find()** algorithm so it uses a different notion of equality than the normal overloaded == operator.
   b. sort the elements of a container using a different criteria than the normal overloaded **<** operator.
   c. customize the **copy()** algorithm so it sorts the objects it is copying.
   d. multiply all the elements of a container together, using the **accumulate()** algorithm.
   e. customize the **find_if()** algorithm to find all **person** objects with a specified first name.

2. You can use a predefined function object to
   a. provide a lexicographical comparison of two objects.
   b. negate two objects.
   c. find if one object is greater than or equal to another.
   d. subtract one object from another.
   e. set one object equal to another.

3. To use the **minus<>()** function object on objects of class **T**, you must
   a. overload the **accumulate()** algorithm to work with class **T**.
   b. provide objects of class **T** as arguments to this function object.
   c. write your own code for this function object.
   d. overload the (<) operator for class **T**.
   e. overload the (–) operator for class **T**.

4. To make a custom function object that is useful for objects of class **T** in a container of class **C**, you must
   a. create a class.
   b. overload **operator()** for class **T**.

    c. overload `operator()` for class `C`.

    d. derive a class from `T`.

    e. "wrap" a function in a class.

5. If you need to provide a value **v** to a custom function object that is used as an argument to an algorithm that will operate on objects of class `T` stored in a container of class `C`, then you must

    a. use **v** as the first argument to the function object.

    b. use **v** as the second argument to the function object.

    c. bind **v** to the function object.

    d. bind **v** to an object of class `T`.

    e. derive the function object from the `binary_function` class.

EXERCISE 1

Write a program that counts how many objects of type `person`, stored in an STL container, have the same first name. Use `count_if()` and a custom function object.

EXERCISE 2

The `remove()` algorithm removes all elements in a container that have a certain value or satisfy a condition specified by a function object. Write a program that allows the user to remove all the person objects from a container if they have a last name specified by the user. Use a function object to compare last names.

SUMMARY: CHAPTER 12

This chapter has presented a quick and dirty introduction to the STL. I've touched on the major topics, and you should have acquired enough information to begin using the STL in a useful way. For a fuller understanding of the STL, I strongly recommend that you avail yourself of a complete text on the topic.

You've learned that the STL consists of three main components: containers, algorithms, and iterators. Containers are divided into two groups: sequential and associative. Sequential containers are the vector, list, and deque. Associative containers are the set and map and the closely related multiset and multimap. Algorithms carry out operations on containers such as sorting, copying, and searching. Iterators act like pointers to container elements and provide connections between algorithms and containers.

Not all algorithms are appropriate for all containers. Iterators are used to ensure that algorithms and containers are appropriately matched. Iterators are defined for specific kinds of containers and used as arguments to algorithms. If the container's iterators don't match the algorithm, a compiler error results.

Input and output iterators connect directly to I/O streams, thus allowing data to be piped directly between I/O devices and containers. Specialized iterators allow backward iteration and can also change the behavior of some algorithms so they insert data rather than overwriting existing data.

Algorithms are standalone functions that can work on many different containers. In addition, each container has its own specific member functions. In some cases, the same function is available as both an algorithm and a member function.

STL containers and algorithms will work with objects of any class, provided certain member functions, such as the < operator, are overloaded for that class.

The behavior of certain algorithms such as `find_if()` can be customized using function objects. A function object is instantiated from a class containing only an `()` operator.

END-OF-CHAPTER DISCUSSION

George: OK, that's it. There's no way I'll ever understand function objects.

Estelle: How to use them? Or how they really work?

George: How they work. What's in all the header files.

Don: You don't need to understand how a class works to use it. That's the beauty of C++.

George: But I'd really like to feel...

Estelle: I know what you mean, George, but I agree with Don. As a user, I could really get to like the STL.

George: Well, you'll be surprised to know I'm with you on this one. It isn't that hard to use. But I've got to admit I was skeptical at first.

Estelle: You, George? That's hard to believe.

APPENDIX A

QUIZ ANSWERS

CHAPTER 1
Session 1
1. e
2. a, c, d
3. d
4. b
5. a

Session 2
1. c
2. b
3. e
4. a, c, e
5. a, b, c, e

Session 3

1. c

2. b, c, e

3. b

4. d

5. e

Session 4

1. a

2. b

3. a

4. b

5. b, c, e

Session 5

1. d

2. c, d

3. a, c, d

4. a, b, d

5. b

Session 6

1. d

2. a, e

3. b, c, d

4. b

5. b, d

Session 7

1. c, d, e
2. b, e
3. b
4. b, d
5. c

Session 8

1. a, b, e
2. b, c, d
3. a
4. d
5. c, d

CHAPTER 2

Session 1

1. a, d
2. c
3. c, d, e
4. b, c, d
5. a, d

Session 2

1. a, e
2. b
3. a, c
4. d, e
5. d

Session 3

1. b, c, e

2. a

3. b

4. c

5. c, d

Session 4

1. b, d

2. b, d

3. e

4. b, d

5. d

Session 5

1. e

2. b, c, d

3. c

4. a, b, d

5. c

Session 6

1. d, e

2. b, e

3. a, b, c

4. e

5. a, b

Session 7

1. a, b
2. c, d, e
3. b
4. b, e
5. a, d, e

Session 8

1. a, c
2. b, c, e
3. c, e
4. b
5. b

CHAPTER 3

Session 1

1. b
2. e
3. e
4. a
5. b

Session 2

1. c
2. c
3. a, d, e
4. c, e
5. c, d

Session 3

1. d

2. b

3. a

4. a, c, e

5. b

Session 4

1. a

2. b, e

3. b, c, d

4. c, e

5. a

Session 5

1. b, c, e

2. d

3. a, b

4. a, b, c

5. b, e

Session 6

1. e

2. b, c

3. b, c, e

4. b, c

5. a, c

Session 7

1. a, d
2. c, d
3. b, c, e
4. b, d
5. b, e

Session 8

1. b, c, e
2. c, d
3. d, e
4. a, b, c
5. a, d, e

CHAPTER 4
Session 1

1. c
2. a, d, e
3. d
4. d, e
5. b

Session 2

1. b, c
2. a, c
3. e
4. b
5. a, b

Session 3

1. b, d, e
2. b, c
3. a, d, e
4. c, d, e
5. c, d

Session 4

1. c
2. b
3. a, c, e
4. a, c
5. b, e

Session 5

1. d, e
2. b
3. c
4. b
5. c, e

Session 6

1. b, d
2. c, e
3. c, d
4. b, d, e
5. a, b, c

Session 7

1. a, d
2. b, c, d
3. e
4. c, d
5. a, e

Session 8

1. b
2. a
3. e
4. d
5. c

CHAPTER 5
Session 1

1. a, c
2. b, d
3. a, e
4. b, d
5. b

Session 2

1. c
2. a, b, e
3. b
4. d
5. a, c

Session 3

1. d

2. b

3. c, e

4. a

5. c, e

Session 4

1. c, d

2. a, b

3. b

4. d

5. b, d

Session 5

1. b, e

2. d

3. a, b

4. a, e

5. a, d

Session 6

1. e

2. d

3. c, d

4. c

5. a, b

Session 7

1. d

2. b

3. e

4. e

5. c

Session 8

1. b

2. d

3. a, e

4. c, e

5. c, d

CHAPTER 6

Session 1

1. a, b, c

2. d

3. b

4. a, d

5. b, e

Session 2

1. a, e

2. b, d

3. b, c, d, e

4. a

5. b

Session 3

1. b, d

2. e

3. a

4. a, c, e

5. b, e

Session 4

1. a

2. d

3. b

4. e

5. b, d

Session 5

1. c, d

2. b, e

3. c, d

4. c, e

5. a, c

Session 6

1. c

2. a, b, d, e

3. c, d

4. a

5. b, d

Session 7
1. c, d, e
2. c, e
3. a
4. a, c
5. b, c, d

Session 8
1. a, c
2. b, e
3. d
4. a, d, e
5. a, b

CHAPTER 7
Session 1
1. b, c
2. d
3. b
4. c
5. e

Session 2
1. a
2. b
3. a
4. c
5. b

Session 3

1. a, c, e
2. b, c
3. b
4. c
5.

Session 4

1. b, c
2. d
3. c
4. a, b
5. a, b, d, e

Session 5

1. a, b
2. c, e
3. c, e
4. a, b, e
5. b, c, d

Session 6

1. d, e
2. c
3. d
4. a, c
5. d, e

Session 7

1. b, e
2. a, c
3. a, e
4. c
5. b, d

Session 8

1. c, d
2. c, d, e
3. b
4. d
5. c

CHAPTER 8

Session 1

1. b
2. b, d, e
3. b
4. e
5. a, b

Session 2

1. e
2. c
3. b
4. b
5. a

Session 3

1. b, c

2. a

3. c, d, e

4. b, c

5. a, c

Session 4

1. b, d, e

2. b, c, d

3. a, b

4. d

5. e

Session 5

1. c, e

2. a, c

3. a, b, e

4. b

5. d, e

Session 6

1. a, e

2. c, d, e

3. d

4. d

5. b

Session 7

1. b, c
2. c
3. a, b, e
4. a, c, e
5. b, c

Session 8

1. b, d, e
2. c
3. a, b, d
4. c, e
5. b

CHAPTER 9

Session 1

1. d
2. b, d
3. a, b, e
4. c
5. b

Session 2

1. c
2. a, b
3. d, e
4. b
5. a

Session 3

1. a, b, c, e
2. b, c
3. b, c, d
4. d
5. e

Session 4

1. a, c, e
2. a, b, d
3. b, e
4. d
5. a, c, e

Session 5

1. c, d
2. a, b
3. e
4. a, b, d
5. c

Session 6

1. d
2. c
3. d
4. c, e
5. a, c, d, e

Session 7

1. d

2. b, c, e

3. a, c

4. c

5. d, e

Session 8

1. d

2. d, e

3. b

4. c, e

5. b, d

CHAPTER 10

Session 1

1. b, c, d, e

2. d, e

3. b, c, e

4. a, c

5. c, d

Session 2

1. b, d

2. b, e

3. c, d

4. a, c, e

5. d

Session 3

1. b, d
2. a, b, d
3. d, e
4. d, e
5. b, c, d

Session 4

1. c, e
2. a, e
3. c, e
4. c, d
5. d, e

Session 5

1. b, e
2. e
3. d
4. b
5. d

Session 6

1. c, d, e
2. b, e
3. b
4. a, e
5. c, e

Session 7

   1. c, e

   2. b, c, d

   3. d

   4. c

   5. b

Session 8

   1. b, e

   2. b

   3. a

   4. b, e

   5. a

CHAPTER 11

Session 1

   1. b, e

   2. c

   3. b

   4. a, c, e

   5. e

Session 2

   1. b, d

   2. a, e

   3. b, e

   4. b, c

   5. a

Session 3

1. b, e

2. a

3. b

4. b, d, e

5. c, e

Session 4

1. a, d

2. a, b, d

3. c, e

4. b, c

5. b

Session 5

1. a, c, e

2. b, c, e

3. a, c

4. b, c, e

5. e

Session 6

1. b, d

2. a, c, d

3. d

4. a, b, e

5. a

Session 7

1. b, c, d, e

2. b, c, d

3. a

4. d

5. a, c, e

Session 8

(There is no quiz for Session 8. Everyone receives a perfect score.)

CHAPTER 12

Session 1

1. a, b, c, e

2. c, e

3. a, c

4. a, b, e

5. d

Session 2

1. b, c

2. c, e

3. a, d

4. b, c, d, e

5. d

Session 3

1. b, d

2. b, c

3. c, e

4. e

5. b, c

Session 4

1. d, e

2. a, b, c

3. a, c, e

4. a, b, d, e

5. d

Session 5

1. c, d

2. a

3. a, c

4. a, b

5. b, c

Session 6

1. b

2. b, d, e

3. a

4. b, c

5. a, b, d

Session 7

1. c

2. a, d

3. a, d

4. a, b, c, d, e

5. e

Session 8

1. b, d, e

2. c, d

3. d, e

4. a, e

5. c, e

APPENDIX B

STL ALGORITHMS AND MEMBER FUNCTIONS

This appendix contains charts showing the algorithms and container member functions available in the Standard Template Library (STL). This information is based on The Standard Template Library by Alexander Stepanov and Ming Lee (1995), but we have extensively condensed and revised it, taking many liberties with their original formulation in the interest of quick understanding.

Algorithms

Table B-1 shows the algorithms available in the STL. The descriptions in this table offer a quick and condensed explanation of what the algorithms do; they are not intended to be serious mathematical definitions. For definitive explanations, with more information including the exact data types to use for arguments and return values, consult the Stepanov and Lee document.

The first column gives the function name, the second explains the purpose of the algorithm, and the third specifies the arguments. Return values are not systematically specified. Some are mentioned in the Purpose column and many are either obvious or not vital to using the algorithm.

In the Arguments column, the names `first`, `last`, `first1`, `last1`, `first2`, `last2`, `first3`, and `middle` represent iterators to specific places in a container. Names with numbers (like `first1`) are used to distinguish multiple containers. The name `first1`, `last1` delimits range 1, and `first2`, `last2` delimits range 2. The arguments `function`, `predicate`, `op`, and `comp` are function objects. The arguments `value`, `old`, `new`, `a`, `b`, and `init` are values of the objects stored in a container. These values are ordered or compared based on the `<` or `==` operator or the `comp` function object. The argument `n` is an integer.

In the Purpose column, movable iterators are indicated by `iter`, `iter1`, and `iter2`. When `iter1` and `iter2` are used together, they are assumed to move together step by step through their respective containers (or possibly two different ranges in the same container).

TABLE B-1

Name	Purpose	Arguments
Nonmutating Sequence Operations		
for_each	Applies `function` to each object.	first, last, function
find	Returns iterator to first object equal to `value`.	first, last, value
find_if	Returns iterator to first object for which `predicate` is true.	first, last, predicate
adjacent_find	Returns iterator to first adjacent pair of objects that are equal.	first, last
adjacent_find	Returns iterator to first adjacent pair of objects that satisfy `predicate`.	first, last, predicate
count	Adds to `n` the number of objects equal to `value`.	first, last, value, n
count_if	Adds to `n` the number of objects satisfying `predicate`.	first, last, predicate, n
mismatch	Returns first nonequal pair of corresponding objects in two ranges.	first1, last1, first2
mismatch	Returns first pair of corresponding objects in two ranges that don't satisfy `predicate`.	first1, last1, first2, predicate
equal	Returns true if corresponding objects in two ranges are all equal.	first1, last1, first2
equal	Returns true if corresponding objects in two ranges all satisfy `predicate`.	first1, last1, first2, predicate
search	Checks if second range is contained within the first. Returns start of match, or `last1` if no match.	first1, last1, first2, last2

Name	Purpose	Arguments
search	Checks if second range is contained within the first, where equality is determined by `predicate`. Returns start of match, or last1 if no match.	first1, last1, first2, last2, predicate

Mutating Sequence Operations

Name	Purpose	Arguments
copy	Copies objects from range 1 to range 2.	first1, last1, first2
copy_backward	Copies objects from range 1 to range 2, inserting them backwards, from last2 to first2.	first1, last1, first2
swap	Interchanges two objects.	a, b
iter_swap	Interchanges objects pointed to by two iterators.	iter1, iter2
swap_ranges	Interchanges corresponding elements in two ranges.	first1, last1, first2
transform	Transforms objects in range 1 into new objects in range 2 by applying `operator`.	first1, last1, first2, operator
transform	Combines objects in range 1 and range 2 into new objects in range 3 by applying `operator`.	first1, last1, first2, first3, operator
replace	Replaces all objects equal to `old` with objects equal to `new`.	first, last, old, new
replace_if	Replaces all objects that satisfy `predicate` with objects equal to `new`.	first, last, predicate, new
replace_copy	Copies from range 1 to range 2, replacing all objects equal to `old` with objects equal to `new`.	first1, last1, first2, old, new
replace_copy_if	Copies from range 1 to range 2, replacing all objects that satisfy `predicate` with objects equal to `new`.	first1, last1, first2, predicate, new
fill	Assigns `value` to all objects in range.	first, last, value
fill_n	Assigns `value` to all objects from `first` to `first+n`.	first, n, value
generate	Fills range with values generated by successive calls to function `gen`.	first, last, gen

continued on next page

continued from previous page

Name	Purpose	Arguments
`generate_n`	Fills from `first` to `first+n` with values generated by successive calls to function `gen`.	`first, n, gen`
`remove`	Removes from range any objects equal to `value`.	`first, last, value`
`remove_if`	Removes from range any objects that satisfy `predicate`.	`first, last, predicate`
`remove_copy`	Copies objects, except those equal to `value`, from range 1 to range 2.	`first1, last1, first2, value`
`remove_copy_if`	Copies objects, except those satisfying `pred`, from range 1 to range 2.	`first1, last1, first2, pred`
`unique`	Eliminates all but the first object from any consecutive sequence of equal objects.	`first, last`
`unique`	Eliminates all but the first object from any consecutive sequence of objects satisfying `predicate`.	`first, last, predicate`
`unique_copy`	Copies objects from range 1 to range 2, except only the first object from any consecutive sequence of equal objects is copied.	`first1, last1, first2`
`unique_copy`	Copies objects from range 1 to range 2, except only the first object from any consecutive sequence of objects satisfying `predicate` is copied.	`first1, last1, first2, predicate`
`reverse`	Reverses the sequence of objects in range.	`first, last`
`reverse_copy`	Copies range 1 to range 2, reversing the sequence of objects.	`first1, last1, first2`
`rotate`	Rotates sequence of objects around iterator `middle`.	`first, last, middle`
`rotate_copy`	Copies objects from range 1 to range 2, rotating the sequence around iterator `middle`.	`first1, middle1, last1, first2`
`random_shuffle`	Randomly shuffles objects in range.	`first, last`
`random_shuffle`	Randomly shuffles objects in range, using random-number function `rand`.	`first, last, rand`
`partition`	Moves all objects that satisfy `predicate` so they precede those that do not satisfy it.	`first, last, predicate`

Name	Purpose	Arguments
stable_partition	Moves all objects that satisfy predicate so they precede those that do not, and also preserves relative ordering in the two groups.	first, last, predicate

Sorting and Related Operations

Name	Purpose	Arguments
sort	Sorts objects in range.	first, last
sort	Sorts elements in range, using comp as comparison function.	first, last, comp
stable_sort	Sorts objects in range and maintains order of equal elements.	first, last
stable_sort	Sorts elements in range using comp as comparison function and maintains order of equal elements.	first, last, comp
partial_sort	Sorts all objects in range and places as many sorted values as will fit between first and middle. Order of objects between middle and last is undefined.	first, middle, last
partial_sort	Sorts all objects in range and places as many sorted values as will fit between first and middle. Order of objects between middle and last is undefined. Uses predicate to define ordering.	first, middle, last, predicate
partial_sort_copy	Same as partial_sort (first, middle, last), but places resulting sequence in range 2.	first1, last1, first2, last2
partial_sort_copy	Same as partial_sort (first, middle, last, predicate), but places resulting sequence in range 2.	first1, last1, first2, last2, comp
nth_element	Places the nth object in the position it would occupy if the whole range were sorted.	first, nth, last
nth_element	Places the nth object in the position it would occupy if the whole range were sorted using comp for comparisons.	first, nth, last, comp
lower_bound	Returns iterator to first position into which value could be inserted without violating the ordering.	first, last, value
lower_bound	Returns iterator to first position into which value could be inserted without violating an ordering based on comp.	first, last, value, comp

continued on next page

continued from previous page

Name	Purpose	Arguments
`upper_bound`	Returns iterator to last position into which `value` could be inserted without violating the ordering.	`first, last, value`
`upper_bound`	Returns iterator to last position into which `value` could be inserted without violating an ordering based on `comp`.	`first, last, value, comp`
`equal_range`	Returns a pair containing the lower bound and upper bound between which `value` could be inserted without violating the ordering.	`first, last, value`
`equal_range`	Returns a pair containing the lower bound and upper bound between which `value` could be inserted without violating an ordering based on `comp`.	`first, last, value, comp`
`binary_search`	Returns true if `value` is in the range.	`first, last, value`
`binary_search`	Returns true if `value` is in the range, where the ordering is determined by `comp`.	`first, last, value, comp`
`merge`	Merges sorted ranges 1 and 2 into sorted range 3.	`first1, last1, first2, last2, first3`
`merge`	Merges sorted ranges 1 and 2 into sorted range 3, where the ordering is determined by `comp`.	`first1, last1, first2, last2, first3, comp`
`inplace_merge`	Merges two consecutive sorted ranges— `first, middle` and `middle, last`—into `first, last`.	`first, middle, last`
`inplace_merge`	Merges two consecutive sorted ranges— `first, middle` and `middle, last`—into `first,last`, where the ordering is based on `comp`.	`first, middle, last, comp`
`includes`	Returns true if every object in the range `first2, last2` is also in the range `first1, last`. (Sets and multisets only.)	`first1, last1, first2, last2`
`includes`	Returns true if every object in the range `first2-last2` is also in the range `first1-last1`, where ordering is based on `comp`. (Sets and multisets only.)	`first1, last1, first2, last2, comp`

Name	Purpose	Arguments
set_union	Constructs sorted union of elements of ranges 1 and 2. (Sets and multisets only.)	first1, last1, first2, last2, first3
set_union	Constructs sorted union of elements of ranges 1 and 2, where the ordering is based on comp. (Sets and multisets only.)	first1, last1, first2, last2, first3, comp
set_intersection	Constructs sorted intersection of elements of ranges 1 and 2. (Sets and multisets only.)	first1, last1, first2, last2, first3
set_intersection	Constructs sorted intersection of elements of ranges 1 and 2, where the ordering is based on comp. (Sets and multisets only.)	first1, last1, first2, last2, first3, comp
set_difference	Constructs sorted difference of elements of ranges 1 and 2. (Sets and multisets only.)	first1, last1, first2, last2, first3
set_difference	Constructs sorted difference of elements of ranges 1 and 2, where the ordering is based on comp. (Sets and multisets only.)	first1, last1, first2, last2, first3, comp
set_symmetric_difference	Constructs sorted symmetric difference of elements of ranges 1 and 2. (Sets and multisets only.)	first1, last1, first2, last2, first3
set_symmetric_difference	Constructs sorted difference of elements of ranges 1 and 2, where the ordering is based on comp. (Sets and multisets only.)	first1, last1, first2, last2, first3, comp
push_heap	Places value from last1 into resulting heap in range first, last.	first, last
push_heap	Places value from last1 into resulting heap in range first, last, based on ordering determined by comp.	first, last, comp
pop_heap	Swaps the values in first and last1; makes range first, last1 into a heap.	first, last
pop_heap	Swaps the values in first and last1; makes range first, last1 into a heap, based on ordering determined by comp.	first, last, comp
make_heap	Constructs a heap out of the range first, last.	first, last
make_heap	Constructs a heap out of the range first, last, based on the ordering determined by comp.	first, last, comp

continued on next page

continued from previous page

Name	Purpose	Arguments
sort_heap	Sorts the elements in the heap `first, last`.	`first, last`
sort_heap	Sorts the elements in the heap `first, last`, based on the ordering determined by `comp`.	`first, last, comp`
min	Returns the smaller of two objects.	`a, b`
min	Returns the smaller of two objects, where the ordering is determined by `comp`.	`a, b, comp`
max	Returns the larger of two objects.	`a, b`
max	Returns the larger of two objects, where the ordering is determined by `comp`.	`a, b, comp`
max_element	Returns an iterator to the largest object in the range.	`first, last`
max_element	Returns an iterator to the largest object in the range, with an ordering determined by `comp`.	`first, last, comp`
min_element	Returns an iterator to the smallest object in the range.	`first, last`
min_element	Returns an iterator to the smallest object in the range, with an ordering determined by `comp`.	`first, last, comp`
lexico- graphical_ compare	Returns true if the sequence in range 1 comes before the sequence in range 2 alphabetically.	`first1, last1, first2, last2`
lexico- graphical_ compare	Returns true if the sequence in range 1 comes before the sequence in range 2 alphabetically, based on ordering determined by `comp`.	`first1, last1, first2, last2, comp`
next_ permutation	Performs one permutation on the sequence in the range.	`first, last`
next_ permutation	Performs one permutation on the sequence in the range, where the ordering is determined by `comp`.	`first, last, comp`
prev_ permutation	Performs one reverse permutation on the sequence in the range.	`first, last`
prev_ permutation	Performs one reverse permutation on the sequence in the range, where the ordering is determined by `comp`.	`first, last, comp`

Name	Purpose	Arguments
Generalized Numeric Operations		
`accumulate`	Sequentially applies `init = init + *iter` to each object in the range.	`first, last, init`
`accumulate`	Sequentially applies `init = op(init, *iter)` to each object in the range.	`first, last, init, op`
`inner_product`	Sequentially applies `init = init + (*iter1) * (*iter2)` to corresponding values from ranges 1 and 2.	`first1, last1, first2, init`
`inner_product`	Sequentially applies `init = op1( init, op2(*iter1, *iter2) )` to corresponding values from ranges 1 and 2.	`first1, last1, first2, init, op1, op2`
`partial_sum`	Adds values from start of range 1 to current iterator, and places the sums in corresponding iterator in range 2. `*iter2 = sum(*first1, *(first1+1), *(first1+2),...*iter1)`	`first1, last1, first2`
`partial_sum`	Sequentially applies `op` to objects between `first1` and current iterator in range 1, and places results in corresponding iterator in range 2. `answer = *first;` `for(iter=first+1; iter != iter1; iter++)` `op(answer, *iter)` `*iter2 = answer;`	`first1, last1, first2, op`
`adjacent_ difference`	Subtracts adjacent objects in range 1 and places differences in range 2. `*iter2 = *(iter1+1) - *iter1;`	`first1, last1, first2`
`adjacent_ difference`	Sequentially applies `op` to adjacent objects in range 1 and places results in range 2. `*iter2 = op(*(iter1+1), *iter1);`	`first1, last1, first2, op`

Table B-1 *Algorithms available in the STL*

MEMBER FUNCTIONS

The same names are used for member functions that have similar purposes in the different containers. However, no container class includes all the available member functions. Table B-2 is intended to show which member functions are available for each container. Explanations of the functions are not given, either because they are more or less self-evident, or because they are explained in the text.

	vector	list	deque	set	multi-set	map	multi-map	stack	queue	priority_queue	tree
operator ==	x	x	x	x	x	x	x	x	x		x
operator <	x	x	x	x	x	x	x	x	x		x
operator =	x	x	x	x	x	x	x				x
operator[]	x		x			x					
operator *		x	x								x
operator ()						x	x				
operator +			x								
operator -			x								
operator ++		x	x								x
operator --		x	x								x
operator +=			x								
operator -=			x								
begin	x	x	x	x	x	x	x				x
end	x	x	x	x	x	x	x				x
rbegin	x	x	x	x	x	x	x				x
rend	x	x	x	x	x	x	x				x
capacity	x										
empty	x	x	x	x	x	x	x	x	x	x	x
size	x	x	x	x	x	x	x	x	x	x	x
max_size	x	x	x	x	x	x	x				x
front	x	x	x						x		
back	x	x	x						x		
push_front		x	x								
push_back	x	x	x								
pop_front		x	x								
pop_back	x	x	x								
swap	x	x	x	x	x	x	x				x
insert	x	x	x	x	x	x	x				x
erase	x	x	x	x	x	x	x				x
key_comp				x	x	x	x				x
value_comp				x	x	x	x				
find				x	x	x	x				x
count				x	x	x	x				x
lower_bound				x	x	x	x				x
upper_bound				x	x	x	x				x
equal_range				x	x	x	x				x
top								x		x	
push								x	x	x	
pop								x	x	x	
reserve	x										
splice		x									
remove		x									
unique		x									
merge		x									
reverse		x									
sort		x									
rotate_left											x
rotate_right											x

Table B-2 *Member functions*

ITERATORS

Table B-3 lists the type of iterator required by each algorithm.

TABLE B-3

	Input	Output	Forward	Bidirectional	Random access
for_each	x				
find	x				
find_if	x				
adjacent_find	x				
count	x				
count_if	x				
mismatch	x				
equal	x				
search			x		
copy	x	x			
copy_backward	x	x			
iter_swap			x		
swap_ranges			x		
transform	x	x			
replace			x		
replace_if			x		
replace_copy	x	x			
fill			x		
fill_n		x			
generate			x		
generate_n		x			
remove			x		
remove_if			x		
remove_copy	x	x			
remove_copy_if	x	x			
unique			x		
unique_copy	x	x			
reverse				x	
reverse_copy		x		x	
rotate			x		
rotate_copy		x	x		
random_shuffle					x
partition				x	
stable_partition				x	
sort					x
stable_sort					x
partial_sort					x
partial_sort_copy	x				x
nth_element					x
lower_bound			x		
upper_bound			x		
equal_range			x		
binary_search			x		
merge	x	x			
inplace_merge				x	
includes	x				
set_union	x	x			
set_intersection	x	x			
set_difference	x	x			
set_symmetric_ difference	x	x			

continued on next page

continued from previous page

	Input	Output	Forward	Bidirectional	Random access
push_heap					x
pop_heap					x
make_heap					x
sort_heap					x
max_element	x				
min_element	x				
lexicographical_ comparison	x				
next_permutation				x	
prev_permutation				x	
accumulate	x				
inner_product	x				
partial_sum	x	x			
adjacent_ difference	x	x			

Table B-3 *Type of iterator required by algorithm*

APPENDIX C

BORLAND C++ AND TURBO C++ FOR WINDOWS

This appendix takes you through the steps of editing, compiling, linking, and running programs under Borland C++ and Turbo C++. We concentrate on Borland C++ 5.0, but most aspects of program development are the same for earlier versions of Borland C++ and for Turbo C++ for Windows. We assume you're running Windows 95 or later.

We'll also assume you're using the Integrated Development Environment (IDE), which is the easy way to develop programs. The IDE is the visual environment that lets you write your source file, compile and link it, run it, and debug it, all by making menu selections. You can also use command-line versions of the compiler and linker, but this approach is mostly applicable to advanced development situations.

COMPILER INSTALLATION

When the Borland compilers ask you what kind of installation you want, you can select Typical. This option is the simplest. However, if the only reason you're using the compiler is to experiment with the programs in this book, you will be loading many megabytes of unnecessary options. Most of these options are for creating various kinds of Windows programs that you don't need to worry about. For the character-based programs in this book you can dramatically reduce the amount of hard disk space required by the compiler if you select the Custom installation option and follow the guidelines described here.

The Borland installation program takes you through a series of windows, each with a number of check boxes or buttons for selecting various options. Details of these windows change from time to time, so without attempting to mention the exact sequence of windows and buttons, the options you want to select are described in general terms.

We'll assume that you accept all the directory names suggested by the installation program, such as C:\BC5\INCLUDE, C:\BC5\LIB, and so on.

EasyWin

The strategy is to compile all the example programs as EasyWin programs. This is a special form of Borland-specific program that you write as if it were a simple DOS character-based program, but that runs under Windows, in a window of its own. EasyWin programs can use simple teletype-style input/output operators and objects, like `cout` and `cin`, without worrying about the complexities of Windows' graphical user interface. This approach allows you to remain in Windows not only while you create a program, but also while you run it. This is more convenient than switching to DOS to run the program and then back to Windows to correct mistakes.

Target Platforms

The target platform (that is, the kind of executable program you want to make) for EasyWin programs is 16-bit Windows. You don't need 16-bit DOS, and you don't need 32-bit Windows.

Tools

The Tools window is a large window that leads you to a series of other windows.

Command-Line Tools

This appendix assumes you're going to use the IDE. If this is the case, you don't need command-line tools, so uncheck this option. You can develop programs using DOS-based command-line arguments, but usually programmers use this option only in special situations.

Visual Tools

The only visual tools you need are the Integrated Development Environment and the Turbo Debugger. You don't need Winsight, Control #D Look, Winspector, or Miscellaneous Tools.

The IDE includes the editor, compiler, and linker, and provides instant access to the debugger. This is the environment where you'll spend your development time.

Database Engine

You don't need the Borland Database Engine, so uncheck this box.

Libraries

You don't need Object Windows Libraries, Object Components Libraries, or Visual Database Tools libraries, so uncheck these options.

Under Run-Time libraries, you need Header Files and the Large Static library. You can uncheck Graphics, Dynamic Libraries, and the other sizes of Static Libraries.

Under Class Libraries you only need Static Class Libraries. You don't need the Obsolete Class Libraries, the Dynamic Class Libraries, or the Class Library Source.

Examples

These options offer example programs for various topics. You don't really need any of the example programs, but, if disk space is not too tight, the Standard Template libraries are helpful for this topic.

Help

The Help topics you select here will be available from the Help menu in the IDE. You'll probably want BCW and Library Reference (which tells how the IDE works), Borland Error Messages (which explains error messages from the compiler, linker, and so on), the Class Library Reference (which covers the stream classes), Documentation, and Borland C++ Tools.

You may want BC DOS and Library Reference, which covers a few DOS-only library functions.

When you've finished selecting options, the installation program will tell you how much hard disk space will be required. If it's too much, you can go back and delete some suggestions. Our typical installation might require between 35 and 45MB.

DEVELOPING YOUR PROGRAM

There are several steps to creating an executable C++ program: creating a project, writing the source code, compiling and linking, and running the resulting executable file. We'll look at these steps in turn.

Creating a Project

Select New from the File menu, and Project from the submenu. You'll get a New Target dialog box. Enter the project path and name. You should specify a separate directory, and your project name, with the extension IDE, like C:\MYPROGS\TEST1.IDE. Don't put anything in the compiler's \BIN\ directory (the default) because there's so much stuff there already it will be hard to find anything you add.

For the programs in this book you can copy the subdirectories for each chapter to a directory on your hard disk. There's no problem placing several projects in one directory.

For the HOTDOG1 program in Chapter 2, for example, your project path and name might be C:\INTERC\CHAP2\HOTDOG1.IDE.

The target type, as discussed above, is EasyWin. When you select this, the Platform is automatically changed to Windows 3.x (16). The Target Model (memory model) is set to Large. Uncheck the Class Library box; you won't need the Borland class libraries. Click the Advanced button and make sure that the .CPP Node button is selected in the Initial Nodes box, and that the .RC and .DEF boxes are not checked. You don't need either of these files for an EasyWin program.

Click OK in the New Target dialog box. It will go away and a Project window will appear. It will show two nodes (related files): hotdog1.exe, the target, and hotdog1.cpp, a dependent file.

If your source (.cpp) file already exists, you can now open it by selecting Open from the File menu. You may need to change the File Of Type box to C++ Source before selecting the correct directory and file name.

If you're writing a new program, select New from the File menu, and then Text Edit. A window will appear into which you can type the source file. Give this file the appropriate name (such as hotdog1.cpp) by selecting Save As from the File menu and filling in the name.

Directories

You will probably need to tell the IDE where various files will be placed. Select Project from the Options menu, and click on Directories in the Topics list. There are five fields for directory names. The Include and Library fields should be set automatically by the system. The INCLUDE directory holds header or include files, like IOSTREAM.H. The LIB file holds the binary code for the library routines. You should set the Source, Intermediate, and Final fields to the same directory in which you placed your .IDE (project) file, described earlier.

Compiling and Linking

There's a quick way and an educational way to compile and link your program. We'll look at the educational way first.

Select Compile from the Project menu. A box will appear that shows you the progress being made by the compiler, including the number of errors and warnings. If there are errors, the compile has failed and you'll need to modify the source file to correct the errors. Otherwise, click on the OK button. A new file, with an .OBJ extension (like HOTDOG1.OBJ), has been generated.

Select Build All from the Project menu. This will invoke the linker, which will transform the .OBJ file into the target .EXE executable file (like HOTDOG1.EXE).

Running Your Program

To execute your newly created program, select Run from the Debug menu. A window containing your program's output will appear on the screen.

When the program stops, the program's name in the window's titlebar will be preceded by the word *Inactive*.

Closing the Project

When you're done with a project, you should close it before exiting from the IDE. Click on the Project window to make sure it's the active window. Then select Close from the File menu.

Opening an Existing Project

Once you've created a project, you can open it again simply by selecting Open from the File menu, selecting the desired .IDE file from the list, and clicking the Open button. This will restore the IDE to the state the project was in when you closed it, with the source file in the edit window.

DOS Targets

Some of the example programs in this book, notably the horse racing programs FRIHORSE, NESHORSE, and STAHORSE in Chapter 9, must be developed as DOS programs. This requires a few changes to the procedure used for EasyWin programs.

In the NewTarget dialog box, select the Target Type as Application (instead of EasyWin). Then, in the Platform box, select DOS Standard. The Target Model box should automatically set itself to Large. The Class Library and Turbo Vision boxes should not be checked.

MULTIFILE PROGRAMS

In a multifile project there is more than one source file. (There can be multiple .OBJ files without multiple source files, but we won't explore that here.) A source file with the same name as the project, and located in the same directory, is automatically added to the project, you must tell the IDE explicitly about files with other names. Here's how to add additional source files to a project.

Open the project. If necessary, bring up the Project window by selecting it from the View menu. In the Project window, right-click on the node representing the .EXE file. For example, if you want to add the VL_APP.CPP file to the VERYLONG project (see Chapter 11, Session 8) click on the VERYLONG.EXE node. Select Add Node from the resulting menu. A dialog box called Add A Project To List appears. The desired source files should appear on the list in this box. Select the one you want, VL_APP.CPP in this example. Then click the Open button. The dialog box will disappear, and you'll see that a node representing the new file is now installed in the Project window. In VERYLONG, the VERYLONG.EXE file is now dependent on both VERYLONG.CPP and VL_APP.CPP.

THE STANDARD LIBRARY

Borland C++ 5.0 includes a version of the C++ Standard Library provided by Rogue Wave Software. We use the string class from this library in several programs in Chapter 11, and we use the Standard Template Library (STL) throughout Chapter 12.

As of this writing we are using a beta version of Borland C++ 5.0, and some of our example programs do not yet work correctly with the Standard Library in this version. These programs are therefore written to work with the earlier Borland C++ 4.5, and the third-party version of the STL from Modena Software in Santa Cruz, California (call 408-354-5616).

Using Third-Party Versions of the STL

Install the STL from a third-party vendor according to their instructions. When developing a program, you will need to tell the Borland compiler where to find the include files for the product. Select Project from the Options menu, and click on the Directories topic. In the Include field, enter the path to the third-party include directory before the path to the Borland include directory:

```
c:\modena\include;c:\bc5\include
```

You should also select Do Not Generate or Use from the Precompiled Headers Box, located under the Compiler topic in Options/Project.

Adapting Programs to Borland's STL

To use the Rogue Wave version of the STL that comes with Borland C++ 5.0, you'll need to change the header files shown in the example programs in this book. You'll also need to specify the namespace `std`. Here are some rules for doing this.

The .H extension is no longer used for header files. For example, you can say

```
#include <vector>
```

instead of

```
#include <vector.h>
```

Change CSTRING.H to STRING.

Change ALGO.H to ALGORITHM.

Change MULTISET.H to SET. The multiset classes are now in the same file as the set classes.

Change MULTMAP.H to MAP. The multimap classes are now in the same file as the map classes.

If a program uses certain algorithms like `allocate()`, use the file NUMERIC rather than ALGORITHM (or ALGO.H).

Precede your code with the directive

```
using namespace std;
```

This is critical to the operation of the STL, and error messages may not point out the source of the problem if you forget it.

As with third-party versions of the STL, you should select Do Not Generate or Use from the Precompiled Headers Box, located under the Compiler topic in Options/Project.

APPENDIX D

MICROSOFT VISUAL C++

This appendix discusses the installation of Microsoft Visual C++, and takes you through the steps of editing, compiling, linking, and running programs with this project. This description applies to Visual C++ version 4.0, but earlier and later versions should work in a similar way. We'll assume you're running Windows 95 or later.

We'll also assume you're using Microsoft Developer Studio, the visual development environment that runs in Windows. The MDS lets you write your source file, compile and link it, run it, and debug it, all by making menu selections. (A command-line version of the compiler can be run from the DOS prompt, but we'll ignore that possibility here.)

COMPILER INSTALLATION

Run the SETUP.EXE program in the MSDEV directory on the CD-ROM. You can select a "typical" installation if you have plenty of disk space, but if you want to install only the components necessary to develop the program in this book and similar "console applications" (which will be described in a moment), then you should select Custom installation. This cuts the hard disk space that you need for Visual C++ roughly in half, from almost 80MB to about 35MB.

We'll assume that you accept the directory name suggested by the installation program: C:\MSDEV\. Within this directory, the compiler and linker will be installed in a BIN subdirectory, header files will go in INCLUDE, library files will go in LIB, and so on.

Console Applications

The programs in this book will all compile to an application type that Microsoft calls a "Console Application". This is an MS-DOS character-based program in which a user and a program communicate with each other by displaying text, each line below the last. Of course such applications are not graphics-based, as full-scale Windows applications are. However, the text-only approach vastly simplifies the programming, and allows us to focus on the C++ language rather than the peculiarities of Windows programming. Our discussion of the installation procedure will assume you'll be developing only Console Applications.

Components

After you've selected Custom Installation, the SETUP program will present a dialog with a list of items, each with a check box. Here's how to handle each item on the list. In some cases the check boxes can't be altered directly; you need to click on the item to elicit a further list of check-boxed items.

Developer Studio

This must be checked. As we noted, it's the development environment you'll be using.

Visual C++ Build Tools

You should check this one too. It includes the compiler and linker you'll use to transform your source file into an executable file.

OLE Controls

Uncheck this one; we won't be worrying about Object Linking and Embedding in this book.

Runtime Libraries

Runtime libraries are files that contain all the functions your program will need to perform I/O, math, data conversion, string handling, and many other things that are not built into the C++ language. You'll need one such library to write C++ programs.

Click on this item and then on a button called Details to bring up a further series of four items: Static Library, Shared Library, Static Library Not Multithreaded, and Source Code. Check only one of these: Static Library Not Multithreaded. Uncheck the others. For the programs in this book you don't need multithreading, shared libraries, or source code.

Foundation Class Libraries

Click on this item to get to the next level of items, and then uncheck all of them. You don't need any of the foundation classes.

Database Options

Here, too, go to the next level of items, and uncheck all of them. You don't need any database options.

Tools

Go to the next level of items here as well, and uncheck all of them. You don't need any of these tools, which are for graphical Windows development.

Books Online

This choice lets you copy all the documentation from the CD to your hard disk. Uncheck it, unless you have lots of disk space. You'll find the documentation is readily accessible from the CD (as long as it's in the drive, of course).

DEVELOPING YOUR PROGRAM

There are several steps to creating an executable C++ program: creating a project workspace, writing the source code, compiling and linking, debugging (if necessary), and running the resulting executable file. We'll look at these steps in turn.

The Developer Studio Screen

Start the Microsoft Developer Studio. You'll see a complicated screen with many buttons and windows. You don't need to worry about all of this yet, but we'll point out a few main features. We'll also show you how to simplify the screen.

Toolbars

There are two toolbars at the top of the screen. You can increase the available screen space by making these go away. To do this, select Toolbars from the View menu (or right-click on either toolbar). A list of toolbars with check boxes appears. You can uncheck any you don't want.

Windows

The screen is initially divided into three windows. The first two aren't needed for development, but the third is.

The Project Workspace window is a tabbed window that initially has only one tab. This InfoView tab shows a hierarchy of icons containing Help information. You can explore what's available by clicking your way through the hierarchy. Once you've opened a project, this window develops two new tabs, one of which, ClassView, will show the classes in your program. The other, FileView, shows the files used by your program.

You can make the Project Workspace window go away by right-clicking on it and selecting Hide from the pop-up menu. It will reappear if you select Project Workspace from the View menu.

The InfoViewer Topic window displays the text of the Help topic selected in the Project Workspace window. It can be closed in the same way as normal windows.

You'll need the Output window at the bottom of the screen; it displays messages from the compiler and linker during the development process.

Creating a Project Workspace

Each program in Visual C++ has its own Project Workspace, which holds all the program's files and various other data. To write a program, you must first create a Project Workspace.

Select New from the File menu, and select Project Workspace from the list in the resulting dialog box. Click on OK.

You will now be given a choice of what kind of application you're going to create. As we noted, we'll be developing Console Applications. Select this icon from the list. Also, make sure the Win32 box in the Platforms list is checked.

You must also name your project. The project name should be the same as the that of the final executable program. If you want your program to be called HOTDOG1, for example, type this name into the Name field. In the Location field, you can use the default directory \MSDEV\PROJECTS\, or you can type in a different directory name. When you're done with this dialog, click the Create button.

The Developer Studio will automatically create a subdirectory with the same name as your project, so you might end up with a subdirectory called \MSDEV\PROJECTS\HOT-DOG1\. This subdirectory will hold all your project's files.

A file with the extension .MDP holds the information about the workspace. It's this file you'll need if you want to reopen your workspace at some future time.

Writing a Source File

Now you must write the source file for your program. Select New from the File menu, select Text File from the list, and click on OK. A window will appear on the right side of the screen. To name your text file, select Save As from the File menu, and (at least for one-file programs) enter the same file name as the project name, but with the .CPP extension, as in HOTDOG1.CPP. The complete path name for this example file would be \MSDEV\PROJECTS\HOTDOG1\HOTDOG1.CPP.

Now you can type your program into the window. When you're done, select Save from the File menu.

Inserting the Source File

Next you must associate the source file you've just written with the project. Select Insert Files Into Project from the Insert menu. Your source file should already be listed in the resulting dialog box; if not, type it in. Then click the Add button.

Building Your Program

There are basically two steps to building your program: compiling and linking. Compiling transforms your program from a human-readable source file with a .CPP extension to a machine-readable file with an .OBJ extension. Linking combines this .OBJ file with library files (extension .LIB) and possibly with other .OBJ files, and produces a final .EXE file that you can execute like any other program.

Compiling

Make sure the window that contains the .CPP file is active, then select Compile from the Build menu. Your program will compile, and the Output window at the bottom of the screen will show what's happening and report any errors or warnings.

Errors will prevent your program from running, and must be corrected before going on to the next step. Often the source of such errors is simply mistyping, but sometimes it's a conceptual error that requires some thought to unravel. Warnings won't prevent your program from running, but may signal potentially dangerous situations that should be corrected. When the program compiles successfully, an .OBJ file is created.

You can quickly find the line in your program that caused a syntax error by double-clicking on the error in the Output window.

Linking

To link your program, select Build from the Build menu. The .OBJ file will be combined with the appropriate .LIB file, and the .EXE file will be created.

Errors may arise from linking as well as from compiling, although they are not as frequent, especially when you have only one source file. To see a linker error, try misspelling the name **main** in your program. The linker expects to find this name, and if it doesn't, it lets you know. Linker errors are more common when you have multiple source files with inconsistent function or variable names. They also occur if the linker can't find a library file.

Running Your Program

You can run your program from within the Developer studio, or you can run it as a standalone program by invoking its .EXE file from either DOS or Windows.

Running from Within Developer Studio

To run your program from within the Developer Studio environment, select Execute from the Build menu. Your program's output will appear in a new MS-DOS window, and you can type in any information requested by the program. This window is a separate Windows program, with its own button on the Windows Task Bar, so you can switch back and forth between it and the Developer Studio as you can with any other program.

The Developer Studio adds the output line

`Press any key to continue`

after a console application has terminated. This gives you a chance to see any output before the program's window is destroyed. This text is not preceded by a carriage return and linefeed, so it may not look very aesthetic when appended to the program's output. You can add the statement

```
cout << endl;
```

at the end of your program to ensure that `Press any key to continue` goes on a separate line.

Running as a Standalone DOS Application

The executable version of your program is an .EXE file, which is located within a subdirectory called DEBUG, which is in the folder for your program's project. To run your program as a standalone DOS application, start up MS-DOS from the icon in your program list. Change directories to the DEBUG subdirectory within the directory for your project's workspace:

```
c:>cd \msdev\projects\myprog\debug
```

Then execute the program's .EXE file by entering its name:

```
c:>myprog
```

It's also possible to execute the program's .EXE file directly from Windows, although you may need to make a slight modification to some of the examples. To launch the application from Windows, simply double-click on the icon for its .EXE file.

The `Press any key to continue` prompt is not added to the end of programs when they are run as standalone applications from Windows, so many of the examples in this book will require you to add additional code at the end of the listing, such as

```
cout << "Enter any character to terminate: ";
char dummy;
cin >> dummy;   // wait for any character to be entered.
```

This will prevent the program from terminating before you have time to read the output.

Closing the Workspace

When you're done with a project, you should close the project workspace before exiting from the Developer Studio. To do this, select Close Workspace from the File menu.

Opening an Existing Project

Once you've created a project workspace, you can open it again by selecting Open Workspace from the File menu. A dialog box called Open Project Workspace appears. Navigate through the directories until you find the one that holds the project you want to open. Inside you'll find the .MDP file. Select it and click Open. This will restore the MDS to the state the project was in when you closed it, with the source file in the edit window.

Multifile Programs

Creating a program with multiple source (.CPP) files requires repeating the same steps described above for each file. Place all the source files in the folder created for the Project Workspace. Use Insert Files Into Project from the Insert menu to associate each source file with the project. Compile each source file separately. Then link them all together by selecting Build from the Build menu. Actually, the appropriate files will be compiled automatically if you simply select Build, although this makes it less clear what steps are involved in the built process.

To see what source files are used in a project, flip to the FileView tab in the Project Workspace window. You'll see not only the .CPP files, but the .H files, shown as a dependency.

THE STANDARD TEMPLATE LIBRARY

Microsoft Visual C++ includes the files for the Standard Template Library (STL) on the distribution CD, but (currently, at least) the setup program does not install them on your hard drive. To remedy this oversight, manually copy the entire contents of the \STL\ directory from the CD into the \MSDEV\INCLUDE\ directory on your hard drive. This will make files like ALGO.H and VECTOR.H accessible during normal program development.

You'll need to make a minor change to the examples shown in the book that use the `string` class: change CSTRING.H to BSTRING.H. This applies to several programs in Chapters 11 and 12.

DOS TARGETS

The FRIHORSE, NESHORSE, and STAHORSE programs in Chapter 9 were designed to work with the Borland C++ compiler. They contain calls to the Borland-specific library functions `clrscr()`, `delay()`, `gotoxy()`, `randomize()`, and `random()`. To work with other compilers, you'll need to find substitutes for these functions.

The file MSOFT.H, available in the APP_C directory on your CD-ROM, supplies such substitute functions. These functions have the same names as the Borland-specific functions, but internally they call functions that are supplied with Microsoft Visual C++ (versions 4.0 and later).

To make it possible to compile the horse programs with the Microsoft compiler, place MSOFT.H in the same directory as your source file, and insert the directive

```
#include "msoft.h"
```

at the beginning of your source file. (Use quotes, not angle brackets.) This will cause calls to the Borland functions to be translated into calls to appropriate Microsoft functions.

DEBUGGING

Even when your program compiles and links correctly, it still may not run the way you expected. The Developer Studio includes built-in debugging features that make it easy to track down errors. These are available from the Debug menu or using special keys.

Single-Stepping

The most fundamental debugging activity is single-stepping, or executing one program line at a time. There are two ways to do this. You can either step *into* functions called by program statements, executing all the statements within the function; or you can step *over* functions, treating a function call like a single statement. The F10 key single-steps over functions, while the F11 key single-steps into them.

Single-stepping is a useful way to see where your program is going. Sometimes you'll be surprised to see that it wanders off course; this may solve some problems all by itself.

You should probably avoid stepping into library functions, which are complicated and probably don't contain bugs anyway.

If your program requires input from the user, you'll need to switch to the program window from the Taskbar, and enter the necessary input.

The Watch Window

The usefulness of single-stepping is increased many-fold if you can watch what happens to the values of program variables as you move through the program. To do this you select Watch from the View menu to bring up a Watch window. Then you type the variable names that you want to watch into this window. The window displays the values, and the values change as you step through the program. Using watch windows on appropriate variables should catch most bugs.

Returning to Build Mode

When you're through debugging, select Stop Debugging from the Build menu. This will return you to the normal Build mode.

APPENDIX E

ASCII TABLE

DEC	HEX	Symbol	Key	DEC	HEX	Symbol	Key
0	00	(NULL)	CTRL 2	34	22	"	῀
1	01		CTRL A	35	23	#	#
2	02		CTRL B	36	24	$	$
3	03		CTRL C	37	25	%	%
4	04		CTRL D	38	26	&	&
5	05		CTRL E	39	27	∍	'
6	06		CTRL F	40	28	(	(
7	07		Beep	41	29	)	)
8	08		BACKSPACE	42	2A	*	*
9	09		TAB	43	2B	+	+
10	0A		Newline	44	2C	,	,
11	0B		Vertical Tab	45	2D	–	-
12	0C		Form Feed	46	2E	.	.
13	0D		ENTER	47	2F	/	/
14	0E		CTRL N	48	30	0	0
15	0F		CTRL O	49	31	1	1
16	10		CTRL P	50	32	2	2
17	11		CTRL Q	51	33	3	3
18	12		CTRL R	52	34	4	4
19	13		CTRL S	53	35	5	5
20	14		CTRL T	54	36	6	6
21	15		CTRL U	55	37	7	7
22	16		CTRL V	56	38	8	8
23	17		CTRL W	57	39	9	9
24	18		CTRL X	58	3A	:	:
25	19		CTRL Y	59	3B	;	;
26	1A		CTRL Z	60	3C	<	<
27	1B		ESC	61	3D	=	=
28	1C		CTRL \	62	3E	>	>
29	1D		CTRL]	63	3F	?	?
30	1E		CTRL 6	64	40	@	@
31	1F		CTRL -	65	41	A	A
32	20		SPACEBAR	66	42	B	B
33	21	!	!	67	43	C	C

DEC	HEX	Symbol	Key	DEC	HEX	Symbol	Key
68	44	D	(D)	109	6D	m	(m)
69	45	E	(E)	110	6E	n	(n)
70	46	F	(F)	111	6F	o	(o)
71	47	G	(G)	112	70	p	(p)
72	48	H	(H)	113	71	q	(q)
73	49	I	(I)	114	72	r	(r)
74	4A	J	(J)	115	73	s	(s)
75	4B	K	(K)	116	74	t	(t)
76	4C	L	(L)	117	75	u	(u)
77	4D	M	(M)	118	76	v	(v)
78	4E	N	(N)	119	77	w	(w)
79	4F	O	(O)	120	78	x	(x)
80	50	P	(P)	121	79	y	(y)
81	51	Q	(Q)	122	7A	z	(z)
82	52	R	(R)	123	7B	{	({)
83	53	S	(S)	124	7C			(|)
84	54	T	(T)	125	7D	}	(})
85	55	U	(U)	126	7E	~	(~)
86	56	V	(V)	127	7F	Δ	(CTRL) (←)
87	57	W	(W)	128	80	Ç	(ALT) 128
88	58	X	(X)	129	81	ü	(ALT) 129
89	59	Y	(Y)	130	82	é	(ALT) 130
90	5A	Z	(Z)	131	83	â	(ALT) 131
91	5B	[	([)	132	84	ä	(ALT) 132
92	5C	\	(\)	133	85	à	(ALT) 133
93	5D	]	(])	134	86	å	(ALT) 134
94	5E	^	(^)	135	87	ç	(ALT) 135
95	5F	_	(_)	136	88	ê	(ALT) 136
96	60	`	(`)	137	89	ë	(ALT) 137
97	61	a	(a)	138	8A	è	(ALT) 138
98	62	b	(b)	139	8B	ï	(ALT) 139
99	63	c	(c)	140	8C	î	(ALT) 140
100	64	d	(d)	141	8D	ì	(ALT) 141
101	65	e	(e)	142	8E	Ä	(ALT) 142
102	66	f	(f)	143	8F	Å	(ALT) 143
103	67	g	(g)	144	90	É	(ALT) 144
104	68	h	(h)	145	91	æ	(ALT) 145
105	69	i	(i)	146	92	Æ	(ALT) 146
106	6A	j	(j)	147	93	ô	(ALT) 147
107	6B	k	(k)	148	94	ö	(ALT) 148
108	6C	l	(l)	149	95	ò	(ALT) 149

DEC	HEX	Symbol	Key	DEC	HEX	Symbol	Key
150	96	û	ALT 150	191	BF		ALT 191
151	97	ù	ALT 151	192	C0		ALT 192
152	98	ÿ	ALT 152	193	C1		ALT 193
153	99	Ö	ALT 153	194	C2		ALT 194
154	9A	Ü	ALT 154	195	C3		ALT 195
155	9B	¢	ALT 155	196	C4		ALT 196
156	9C	£	ALT 156	197	C5		ALT 197
157	9D	¥	ALT 157	198	C6		ALT 198
158	9E	P_t	ALT 158	199	C7		ALT 199
159	9F	ƒ	ALT 159	200	C8		ALT 200
160	A0	á	ALT 160	201	C9		ALT 201
161	A1	í	ALT 161	202	CA		ALT 202
162	A2	ó	ALT 162	203	CB		ALT 203
163	A3	ú	ALT 163	204	CC		ALT 204
164	A4	ñ	ALT 164	205	CD		ALT 205
165	A5	Ñ	ALT 165	206	CE		ALT 206
166	A6	ª	ALT 166	207	CF		ALT 207
167	A7	º	ALT 167	208	D0		ALT 208
168	A8	¿	ALT 168	209	D1		ALT 209
169	A9		ALT 169	210	D2		ALT 210
170	AA		ALT 170	211	D3		ALT 211
171	AB		ALT 171	212	D4		ALT 212
172	AC		ALT 172	213	D5		ALT 213
173	AD		ALT 173	214	D6		ALT 214
174	AE		ALT 174	215	D7		ALT 215
175	AF		ALT 175	216	D8		ALT 216
176	B0		ALT 176	217	D9		ALT 217
177	B1		ALT 177	218	DA		ALT 218
178	B2		ALT 178	219	DB		ALT 219
179	B3		ALT 179	220	DC		ALT 220
180	B4		ALT 180	221	DD		ALT 221
181	B5		ALT 181	222	DE		ALT 222
182	B6		ALT 182	223	DF		ALT 223
183	B7		ALT 183	224	E0	α	ALT 224
184	B8		ALT 184	225	E1	β	ALT 225
185	B9		ALT 185	226	E2	Γ	ALT 226
186	BA		ALT 186	227	E3	π	ALT 227
187	BB		ALT 187	228	E4	Σ	ALT 228
188	BC		ALT 188	229	E5	σ	ALT 229
189	BD		ALT 189	230	E6	μ	ALT 230
190	BE		ALT 190	231	E7	τ	ALT 231

DEC	HEX	Symbol	Key		DEC	HEX	Symbol	Key
232	E8	Φ	(ALT) 232		244	F4	⌠	(ALT) 244
233	E9	Θ	(ALT) 233		245	F5	⌡	(ALT) 245
234	EA	Ω	(ALT) 234		246	F6	÷	(ALT) 246
235	EB	δ	(ALT) 235		247	F7	≈	(ALT) 247
236	EC	∞	(ALT) 236		248	F8	°	(ALT) 248
237	ED	φ	(ALT) 237		249	F9	•	(ALT) 249
238	EE	ε	(ALT) 238		250	FA	·	(ALT) 250
239	EF	∩	(ALT) 239		251	FB	√	(ALT) 251
240	F0	≡	(ALT) 240		252	FC	η	(ALT) 252
241	F1	±	(ALT) 241		253	FD	^{2}	(ALT) 253
242	F2	≥	(ALT) 242		254	FE	■	(ALT) 254
243	F3	≤	(ALT) 243		255	FF	(blank)	(ALT) 255

Note that IBM Extended ASCII characters can be displayed by holding down the (ALT) key and then typing the decimal code of the character on the keypad. Always type exactly three digits, using an initial 0 (or 00) if necessary.

APPENDIX F

PROGRAM LIST

CHAPTER 1: A FIRST LOOK AT OOP AND C++

Session 1 — Why Do We Need OOP?
    (No programs)

Session 2 — Features of Object-Oriented Languages
    (No programs)

Session 3 — Hot Dog Stands as Objects
    (No programs)

Session 4 — Basic C++ Data Types
    (No programs)

Session 5 — Introduction to Input/Output
    (No programs)

Session 6 — Member Functions
    (No programs)

Session 7 — Specifying a Class
    (No programs)

Session 8 — Creating and Interacting with Objects
    (No programs)

849

CHAPTER 2: WRITING COMPLETE OOP PROGRAMS

Session 1 — The Complete Hot Dog Stand Program
```
hotdog1
```

Session 2 — Loops
```
(No programs)
```

Session 3 — Simple Decisions
```
hotdog2
```

Session 4 — Advanced Decisions
```
hotdog3
```

Session 5 — A Class to Represent Time Values
```
time1
```

Session 6 — Function Arguments
```
houradd
time2
```

Session 7 — Arithmetic for User-Defined Types
```
timeadd
timecnv1
timemult
```

Session 8 — Function Return Values
```
timecnv2
timeret
```

CHAPTER 3: ARRAYS AND STRINGS

Session 1 — Array Fundamentals
```
(no programs)
```

Session 2 — Arrays as Instance Data
```
employ1
stack1
```

Session 3 — Arrays of Objects
```
arrayair
arrayemp
```

Session 4 — Strings
`stremp`

Session 5 — String Library Functions
`strclass`

Session 6 — Arrays of Strings
`weekdays`

Session 7 — Structures
`strustak`

Session 8 — `enum` **and** `bool`
`cardaray`

`bool`

CHAPTER 4: FUNCTIONS

Session 1 — Function Review and Function Declarations
(no programs)

Session 2 — Standalone Member Functions
`weekout`

Session 3 — Overloaded Functions
`overfun`

Session 4 — Default Arguments
`defargs`

Session 5 — Storage Classes
(no programs)

Session 6 — Static Members
`static`

Session 7 — Reference Arguments
`swapobj`

Session 8 — Returning by Reference
`retref`

Session 6 — Friend Functions

```
airnofri
airfri
misq
frisq
bridge
```

Session 7 — Friend Classes

```
interc1
interc2
interc3
frihorse (DOS)
```

Session 8 — Nested Classes and Static Member Data

```
nested (DOS)
neshorse (DOS)
stahorse (DOS)
```

CHAPTER 10: STREAMS AND FILES

Session 1 — Stream Classes

```
(no programs)
```

Session 2 — Stream Errors

```
englerr
```

Session 3 — Disk File I/O with Streams

```
formato
formati
oline
iline
ochar
ichar
ichar2
binio
opers
ipers
diskfun
```

Session 4 — File Errors and File Pointers

```
rewerr
ferrors
seekg
```

Session 5 — File I/O Using Member Functions

```
rewobj
empl_io
```

Session 6 — Overloading the << and >> Operators

```
englio
englio2
persio
```

Session 7 — Memory as a Stream Object

```
strstr
autostr
```

Session 8 — Printer Output and Other Refinements

```
comline (DOS)
otype (DOS)
ezprint (DOS)
oprint (DOS)
redir (DOS)
```

CHAPTER 11: TEMPLATES, EXCEPTIONS, AND MORE

Session 1 — Function Templates

```
tempabs
tempfind
```

Session 2 — Class Templates

```
tempstak
temstak2
templist
temlist2
```

Session 3 — Exceptions

```
xsyntax
xstak
```

Session 4 — Exceptions Continued
```
xstak2
xdist
xdist2
xalloc
```

Session 5 — Explicit Casts, `typedef`, and the ( ) Operator
```
sta_cast
dyn_cast
con_cast
parens
```

Session 6 — The Standard `string` Class
```
string1
string2
string3
string4
```

Session 7 — Multifile Programs
```
(no programs)
```

Session 8 — A Very-Long-Numbers Example
```
verylong
vl_app
```

CHAPTER 12: THE STANDARD TEMPLATE LIBRARY

Session 1 — Introduction to the STL
```
(no programs)
```

Session 2 — Algorithms
```
find
count
sort
search
merge
sortemp
sortcom
find_if
```

```
transfo
```

Session 3 — Sequential Containers

```
vector

vectcon

vectins

list

listplus

deque
```

Session 4 — Iterators

```
listout

listfill

iterfind

itercopy
```

Session 5 — Specialized Iterators

```
iterev

copydeq

dinsiter

outiter

foutiter

initer

finiter
```

Session 6 — Associative Containers

```
set

setrange

map

mapbrack
```

Session 7 — Storing User-Defined Objects

```
setpers

listpers

listair
```

Session 8 — Function Objects

```
plusair

sortpers

funcpers
```

INDEX

NOTES

NOTES

NOTES

NOTES

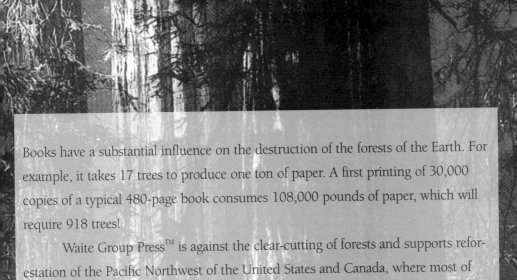

ENVIRONMENTAL AWARENESS

Books have a substantial influence on the destruction of the forests of the Earth. For example, it takes 17 trees to produce one ton of paper. A first printing of 30,000 copies of a typical 480-page book consumes 108,000 pounds of paper, which will require 918 trees!

Waite Group Press™ is against the clear-cutting of forests and supports reforestation of the Pacific Northwest of the United States and Canada, where most of this paper comes from. As a publisher with several hundred thousand books sold each year, we feel an obligation to give back to the planet. We will therefore support organizations that seek to preserve the forests of planet Earth.

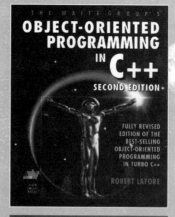

SOFTWARE LICENSE AGREEMENT

This is a legal agreement between you, the end user and purchaser, and The Waite Group®, Inc., and the authors of the programs contained in the disk. By opening the sealed disk package, you are agreeing to be bound by the terms of this Agreement. If you do not agree with the terms of this Agreement, promptly return the unopened disk package and the accompanying items (including the related book and other written material) to the place you obtained them for a refund.

SOFTWARE LICENSE

1.   The Waite Group, Inc. grants you the right to use one copy of the enclosed software pro-grams (the programs) on a single computer system (whether a single CPU, part of a licensed network, or a terminal connected to a single CPU). Each concurrent user of the program must have exclusive use of the related Waite Group, Inc. written materials.

2.   The program, including the copyrights in each program, is owned by the respective author and the copyright in the entire work is owned by The Waite Group, Inc. and they are therefore protected under the copyright laws of the United States and other nations, under interna-tional treaties. You may make only one copy of the disk containing the programs exclusive-ly for backup or archival purposes, or you may transfer the programs to one hard disk drive, using the original for backup or archival purposes. You may make no other copies of the pro-grams, and you may make no copies of all or any part of the related Waite Group, Inc. writ-ten materials.

3.   You may not rent or lease the programs, but you may transfer ownership of the programs and related written materials (including any and all updates and earlier versions) if you keep no copies of either, and if you make sure the transferee agrees to the terms of this license.

4.   You may not decompile, reverse engineer, disassemble, copy, create a derivative work, or otherwise use the programs except as stated in this Agreement.

GOVERNING LAW

This Agreement is governed by the laws of the State of California.

LIMITED WARRANTY

The following warranties shall be effective for 90 days from the date of purchase: (i) The Waite Group, Inc. warrants the enclosed disk to be free of defects in materials and workmanship under normal use; and (ii) The Waite Group, Inc. warrants that the programs, unless modified by the purchaser, will substantially perform the functions described in the documentation provided by The Waite Group, Inc. when operated on the designated hardware and operating system. The Waite Group, Inc. does not warrant that the programs will meet purchaser's requirements or that operation of a program will be uninterrupted or error-free. The program warranty does not cover any program that has been altered or changed in any way by anyone other than The Waite Group, Inc. The Waite Group, Inc. is not responsible for problems caused by changes in the operating characteristics of computer hardware or computer operating systems that are made after the release of the programs, nor for problems in the interaction of the programs with each other or other software.

THESE WARRANTIES ARE EXCLUSIVE AND IN LIEU OF ALL OTHER WARRANTIES OF MERCHANTABILITY OR FITNESS FOR A PARTICULAR PURPOSE OR OF ANY OTHER WARRANTY, WHETHER EXPRESS OR IMPLIED.

EXCLUSIVE REMEDY

The Waite Group, Inc. will replace any defective disk without charge if the defective disk is returned to The Waite Group, Inc. within 90 days from date of purchase.

This is Purchaser's sole and exclusive remedy for any breach of warranty or claim for contract, tort, or damages.

LIMITATION OF LIABILITY

THE WAITE GROUP, INC. AND THE AUTHORS OF THE PROGRAMS SHALL NOT IN ANY CASE BE LIABLE FOR SPECIAL, INCIDENTAL, CONSEQUENTIAL, INDIRECT, OR OTHER SIMILAR DAMAGES ARISING FROM ANY BREACH OF THESE WARRANTIES EVEN IF THE WAITE GROUP, INC. OR ITS AGENT HAS BEEN ADVISED OF THE POSSIBILITY OF SUCH DAMAGES.

THE LIABILITY FOR DAMAGES OF THE WAITE GROUP, INC. AND THE AUTHORS OF THE PROGRAMS UNDER THIS AGREEMENT SHALL IN NO EVENT EXCEED THE PURCHASE PRICE PAID.

COMPLETE AGREEMENT

This Agreement constitutes the complete agreement between The Waite Group, Inc. and the authors of the programs, and you, the purchaser.

Some states do not allow the exclusion or limitation of implied warranties or liability for incidental or consequential damages, so the above exclusions or limitations may not apply to you. This limited warranty gives you specific legal rights; you may have others, which vary from state to state.

MACMILLAN COMPUTER PUBLISHING USA

A VIACOM COMPANY

Technical Support:

If you cannot get the CD/Disk to install properly, or you need assistance with a particular situation in the book, please feel free to check out the Knowledge Base on our Web site at **http://www.superlibrary.com/general/support**. We have answers to our most Frequently Asked Questions listed there. If you do not find your specific question answered, please contact Macmillan Technical Support at **(317) 581-3833**. We can also be reached by email at **support@mcp.com**.

SATISFACTION REPORT CARD

Please fill out this card if you wish to know of future updates to *C++ Interactive Course*, or to receive our catalog.

First Name:

Last Name:

Street Address:

City: **State:**   **Zip:**

E-mail Address

Daytime Telephone: (   )

Date product was acquired: Month   Day   Year   Your Occupation:

Overall, how would you rate *C++ Interactive Course*?

☐ Excellent   ☐ Very Good   ☐ Good

☐ Fair   ☐ Below Average   ☐ Poor

What did you like MOST about this book?

What did you like LEAST about this book?

Please describe any problems you may have encountered with installing or using the disk:

How did you use this book (problem-solver, tutorial, reference...)?

What is your level of computer expertise?

☐ New   ☐ Dabbler   ☐ Hacker

☐ Power User   ☐ Programmer   ☐ Experienced Professional

What computer languages are you familiar with?

Please describe your computer hardware:

Computer _____ Hard disk _____

5.25" disk drives _____ 3.5" disk drives _____

Video card _____ Monitor _____

Printer _____ Peripherals _____

Sound Board _____ CD ROM _____

Where did you buy this book?

☐ Bookstore (name): _____

☐ Discount store (name): _____

☐ Computer store (name): _____

☐ Catalog (name): _____

☐ Direct from WGP   ☐ Other _____

What price did you pay for this book?

What influenced your purchase of this book?

☐ Recommendation   ☐ Advertisement

☐ Magazine review   ☐ Store display

☐ Mailing   ☐ Book's format

☐ Reputation of Waite Group Press   ☐ Other

How many computer books do you buy each year?

How many other Waite Group books do you own?

What is your favorite Waite Group book?

Is there any program or subject you would like to see Waite Group Press cover in a similar approach?

Additional comments?

Please send to: **Waite Group Press**
                         200 Tamal Plaza
                         Corte Madera, CA 94925

☐ **Check here for a free Waite Group catalog**

STOP!

BEFORE YOU OPEN THE DISK OR CD-ROM PACKAGE ON THE FACING PAGE, CAREFULLY READ THE LICENSE AGREEMENT.

Opening this package indicates that you agree to abide by the license agreement found in the back of this book. If you do not agree with it, promptly return the unopened disk package (including the related book) to the place you obtained them for a refund.